Public School Law
Teachers' and Students' Rights

Third Edition

MARTHA M. MCCARTHY
Indiana University

NELDA H. CAMBRON-MCCABE
Miami University (Ohio)

Allyn and Bacon
Boston   London   Toronto   Sydney   Tokyo   Singapore

Library of Congress Cataloging-in-Publication Data

McCarthy, Martha M.
    Public school law : teachers' and students' rights / Martha M.
McCarthy, Nelda H. Cambron-McCabe. — 3rd ed.
        p.   cm.
    Includes bibliographical references and index.
    ISBN 0-205-13500-5
    1. Teachers—Legal status, laws, etc.—United States.
    2. Students—Legal status, laws, etc.—United States.   I. Cambron-
McCabe, Nelda H.   II. Title.
KF4119.M38   1992
344.73′078—dc20
[347.30478]   91-39862
                                                         CIP

Printed in the United States of America

10 9 8 7 6 5 4 3 2 1   96 95 94 93 92

Contents

Preface

The third edition of *Public School Law: Teachers' and Students' Rights* provides a comprehensive treatment of the evolution and current status of the law governing public schools. The content of all chapters has been updated, and some sections have been added to reflect emerging issues of legal concern.

Since World War II, lawmakers have significantly reshaped educational policy. Most school personnel are aware of the burgeoning litigation and legislation, and some are familiar with the names of a few landmark Supreme Court decisions. Nonetheless, many teachers and administrators harbor misunderstandings regarding the basic legal concepts that are being applied to educational questions. As a result, they are uncertain about the legality of daily decisions they must make in the operation of schools. Information provided in this book should help alleviate concerns voiced by educators who feel that the scales of justice have been tipped against them.

Public School Law differs from other legal materials currently available to educators because it addresses legal principles applicable to practitioners in a succinct but comprehensive manner. Topics with a direct impact on educators and students are explored, and the tension between governmental controls and the exercise of individual rights is examined within the school context. The analysis of specific school situations relies on applicable constitutional and statutory law and judicial interpretations of these provisions. Implications of legal mandates are discussed, and guidelines are provided for school personnel.

We have attempted to present the material in a nontechnical manner, avoiding the extensive use of legal terms. However, the topics are thoroughly documented should the reader choose to explore specific cases or points of law in greater detail. Numerous explanatory notes are included at the end of each chapter to provide additional information on selected cases and to assist the reader in understanding specific concepts. Also, a glossary of basic terms and a table of cases are provided at the end of the book.

A few comments about the nature of the law might assist the reader in using this book. Laws are not created in a vacuum; they reflect the social and philosophical attitudes of society. Moreover, laws are made by individuals who have personal opinions and biases. Although we may prefer to think that the law is always objective, personal considerations and national political trends do have an impact on the development and interpretation of legal principles.

Also, the law is not static but rather is continually evolving as courts reinterpret constitutional and statutory provisions and legislatures enact new laws. In the 1960s and early 1970s, courts and legislative bodies tended to focus on the expansion of personal rights through civil rights laws and constitutional interpretations favoring the individual's right to be free from unwarranted governmental intrusions. Since 1975, however, judicial rulings have supported governmental authority to impose restraints on individual freedoms in the school context in the interest of the collective welfare. While the themes of educational equity and individual rights, which dominated litigation in the 1960s and early 1970s, remain important, efforts to attain educational excellence have generated a new genre of legal activity pertaining to teachers' qualifications and performance standards for students. Moreover, the educational agendas promoted by the religious and political right, such as prayer in public schools and curriculum censorship, have provoked substantial legal activity.

Throughout this book, much of the discussion of the law focuses on court cases, because the judiciary plays a vital role in interpreting constitutional and legislative provisions. Decisions are highlighted that illustrate points of law or legal trends, with particular emphasis on recent litigation. A few cases are pursued in depth to provide the reader with an understanding of the rationale behind the decisions. Reviewing the factual situations that have generated these controversies should make it easier for educators to identify potential legal problems in their own school situations.

As this book goes to press, judicial decisions are being rendered and statutes are being proposed that may alter the complexion of the law vis-à-vis teachers and students. Additionally, some questions confronting school personnel have not yet been addressed by the Supreme Court and have generated conflicting decisions among lower courts. It may be frustrating to a reader searching for concrete answers to learn that in a number of areas the law is far from clear.

In spite of unresolved issues, certain legal principles have been established and can provide direction in many school situations. It is important for educators to become familiar with these principles and to use them to guide their decisions. While the issues generating legal concern will change over time, knowledge of the logic underlying the law can make school personnel more confident in dealing with legal questions that have not been clarified by courts or legislatures.

We have attempted to arrange the chapters in a logical sequence for those reading the book in its entirety or using it as a text for school law courses. An introductory chapter establishes the legal context for the subsequent examination of students' and teachers' rights, and a concluding chapter provides a summary of the major legal principles. Subheadings appear within chapters to facilitate the use of this book for reference if a specific topic is of immediate interest. The reader is encouraged, however, to read the entire text, because some topics are addressed in several chapters from different perspectives, and many of the principles of law transcend chapter divisions. For example, litigation involving various aspects of teachers' rights has relied on precedents established in students' rights cases; the converse also has been true. Throughout the text, various sections are cross-referenced to alert the reader that a particular concept is also discussed elsewhere in the book. Taken together, the chapters provide an overall picture of the relationship among issues and the applicable legal principles.

Although the content is oriented toward practicing educators, the material should be of equal interest to educational policymakers because many of the legal generalizations pertain to all educational personnel. In addition, this book should serve as a useful guide for parents who are interested in the law governing their children in public schools. Given its comprehensive coverage of students' and teachers' rights, this book also is appropriate for use as a basic text for university courses or in-service sessions.

The material should assist school personnel in understanding the current application of the law, but it is not intended to serve as a substitute for legal counsel. Educators confronting legal problems should always seek the advice of an attorney. Also, there is no attempt here to predict the future course of courts and legislatures. Given the dynamic nature of the law, no single text can serve to keep school personnel abreast of current legal developments. If we can provide an awareness of rights and responsibilities, motivate educators to translate the basic concepts into actual practice, and generate an interest in further study of the law, our purposes in writing this book will have been achieved.

Acknowledgments

A number of individuals contributed to the completion of this book. Several colleagues provided thoughtful reviews of various chapters. For their insightful comments, we are indebted to Kevin Brown and Julia Lamber from the School of Law at Indiana University, Thomas Mulkeen from the Graduate School of Education at Fordham University, and Gail Sorenson from the School of Education at the State University of New York at Albany. In addition, Richard Hofmann, Miami University, provided invaluable technical assistance with the conversion to a new computer system.

We also are grateful to our students who reacted to various drafts of the chapters. Particular thanks go to John Dayton and Dan Bopp, who read all chapters and spent hours checking citations in the law library at Indiana University. Also, Barry Brumer, Shuba Krishnan, David Schanker, and Kent Zepick from Indiana University and Thomas Oldenski and Eileen Goode from Miami University assisted with cite checking and proofreading. Robert Baird, Assistant Editor with Pi Lambda Theta, provided helpful editorial suggestions for the entire text, and Carol Langdon, Research Analyst with the Indiana Education Policy Center, assisted in reading the page proofs. In addition, we are very appreciative of our secretaries, Jeanne Butler, Laura Rogers, and Jan Clegg, whose excellent word processing skills and cheerful attitudes facilitated production of the numerous drafts of this manuscript.

This book would not have been completed without the support of our families. Our parents offered constant encouragement as they do in all our professional endeavors. The contributions of our husbands, George Kuh and Harry McCabe, simply cannot be measured. They assumed far more than their share of family responsibilities during the writing of this book. Kari and Kristian Kuh were very understanding of their mother's preoccupation with this manuscript, and Kari even devoted part of her spring break to proofreading chapters. Although four-year-old Patrick McCabe did not quite understand the long hours his mother spent at the computer, he helped her discover that children's books are a wonderful antidote for having read too many court cases.

1
The Legal Foundation of Public Education

The authority for the establishment and control of American public education is grounded in law. State and federal constitutional and statutory provisions provide the framework within which school operational decisions are made. Policies and practices at any level of the educational enterprise must be consistent with legal mandates from higher authorities. The overlapping jurisdictions of federal and state constitutions, Congress and state legislatures, federal and state courts, and various governmental agencies (including local school boards) present a complex environment for educators attempting to comply with legal requirements. In an effort to untangle the various legal relationships, this chapter describes the major sources of law and how they interact to form the legal basis for public education. This overview establishes a context for subsequent chapters in which legal principles are discussed more fully as they apply to specific school situations.

STATE CONTROL OF EDUCATION

The tenth amendment to the United States Constitution stipulates that "the powers not delegated to the United States by the Constitution, nor prohibited by it to the states, are reserved to the states respectively, or to the people." The Supreme Court has recognized that this amendment was intended "to allay fears that the new national government might seek to exercise powers not granted, and that the states might not be able to exercise fully their reserved powers."[1] Since the Federal Constitution does not authorize Congress to provide for education, the legal control of public education resides with the state as one of its sovereign powers. The Supreme Court repeatedly has affirmed the comprehensive authority of the states and school officials "to prescribe and control conduct in the

1

schools'' as long as actions are consistent with fundamental federal constitutional safeguards.[2] The state's authority over education is considered comparable to its powers to tax and to provide for the general welfare of its citizens. While each state's educational system has unique features, many similarities are found across states.

LEGISLATIVE POWER

All state constitutions specifically address the legislative responsibility for establishing public schools. For example, the Arizona Constitution stipulates: "The legislature shall . . . provide for the establishment and maintenance of a general and uniform public school system. . . ."[3] The state legislature has plenary, or absolute, power to make laws governing education. In contrast to the federal government, which has only those powers specified in the United States Constitution, state legislatures retain all powers not expressly forbidden by state or federal constitutional provisions. In an early case, the Supreme Court of Virginia acknowledged the breadth of the state's plenary power regarding education:

> The legislature . . . has the power to enact any legislation in regard to the conduct, control, and regulation of the public free schools, which does not deny to the citizen the constitutional right to enjoy life and liberty, to pursue happiness and to acquire property.[4]

Courts have recognized the state legislature's authority to raise revenue and distribute educational funds, control teacher certification, prescribe curricular offerings, establish pupil performance standards, and regulate other specific aspects of public school operations. Legislatures are empowered to create, reorganize, consolidate, and abolish school districts, even over the objections of affected residents.[5] Moreover, states can mandate school attendance to ensure an educated citizenry. At present, all fifty states require that students between specified ages (usually six to sixteen) attend a public or private school or receive equivalent instruction.

In some instances, when state laws are subject to several interpretations, courts are called upon to clarify legislative intent. If the judiciary misinterprets the law's purpose, the legislature can amend the law in question to clarify its meaning. However, if a law is invalidated as abridging state or federal constitutional provisions or federal civil rights laws, the legislature must abide by the judicial directives. Also, a state's attorney general may be asked to interpret a law or to advise school boards on the legality of their actions. Unless overruled by the judiciary, the official opinion of an attorney general is binding.

Although the state legislature cannot relinquish its lawmaking powers, it can delegate to subordinate agencies the authority to make rules and regulations necessary to implement laws. These administrative functions must be carried out within the guidelines established by the legislature. Some states are quite liberal in delegating administrative authority, whereas other states prescribe detailed standards that must be followed by subordinate agencies. It is a widely held perception that local school boards control public education within this nation, but local boards have only those powers conferred by the state. Courts consistently have reiterated that the authority for public education is not a local one, but rather is a central power residing in the state legislature. School buildings are considered state property, local school board members are state officials, and teachers are state employees. Public school funds, regardless of where collected, are state funds.

STATE AGENCIES

Since it has been neither feasible nor desirable to include in statutes every minor detail governing public schools, all states have established some type of state board of education. This board typically supplies the structural details necessary to implement broad legislative mandates. In most states, members of the state board of education are elected by the citizenry or appointed by the governor, and the board usually functions immediately below the legislature in the hierarchy of educational governance.

Licensure is an important tool used by state boards to compel local school districts to abide by their directives. School districts often must satisfy state licensure or accreditation requirements as a condition of receiving state funds. Though licensure models vary among states, the most common approach involves the establishment of minimum standards in areas such as curriculum, teacher qualifications, instructional materials, and facilities. In some states, different grades of school accreditation exist, with financial incentives to encourage local schools to attain the highest licensure level. Since the mid-1980s, there has been some movement toward performance-based accreditation under which a school's performance is assessed against predicted outcomes calculated for the school in areas such as pupil achievement and absenteeism.[6]

Within legislative parameters, the state board of education can issue directives governing school operations. In some states, rules pertaining to such matters as competency testing for students and programs for children with disabilities are embodied in state board rules rather than state law. Courts generally have upheld decisions made by state boards of education, unless they have violated legislative or constitutional mandates. For example, the Kansas Supreme Court recognized that the state constitutional grant of general supervisory power to the state board of education meant that enabling legislation was unnecessary for the board to require local school districts to develop student and employee conduct regulations.[7] Also, the Sixth Circuit Court of Appeals upheld the Ohio State Board of Education's authority to compel a school district to be annexed to a neighboring district because it failed to meet minimum state standards.[8] The appeals court reasoned that the annexed district had no federal constitutional right to remain in existence.

The Supreme Court of Pennsylvania recognized the state board of education's authority to issue and enforce uniform student disciplinary regulations governing all schools in the state. Even though local school districts asserted that uniform guidelines were impractical and that local boards were entitled under state law to apply their own disciplinary codes, the court held that the "far reaching and unequivocal powers" granted by the legislature to the state board included the authority to enact statewide disciplinary policies.[9]

However, state boards of education cannot abrogate powers delegated by law to other agencies. In 1991 the North Carolina Supreme Court held that the state board's prohibition on local board contracts with Whittle Communications interfered with school districts' statutory authority to enter into contracts for supplementary materials.[10] The school board in question contracted to air daily classroom broadcasts of a television news program including advertisements (Channel One) in return for television equipment. The court reasoned that the contract was within the local board's statutory authority and could not be circumscribed by action of the state board of education.

In addition to the state board, generally considered a policymaking body, all states have designated a chief state school officer (often known as the superintendent of public instruction or commissioner of education) to function in an executive capacity. Traditionally, the duties of the chief state school officer (CSSO) have been regulatory in nature. However, other activities, such as research and long-range planning, have been added to this role. In some states, the CSSO is charged with adjudicating educational controversies, and citizens cannot invoke judicial remedies for a grievance pertaining to internal school operations until such administrative appeals have been exhausted. When considering an appeal of a CSSO's decision, courts will not judge the wisdom of the decision or overrule such a decision unless it is clearly arbitrary or against the preponderance of evidence.[11]

Each state also has established a state department of education, consisting of educational specialists who provide consultation to the state board, chief state school officer, and local school boards. State department personnel often collect data from school districts to ensure that legislative enactments and state board policies are properly implemented. Most state departments also engage in research and development activities to improve educational practices within the state.

LOCAL SCHOOL BOARDS

Although public education is state controlled in our nation, it is for the most part locally administered. All states except Hawaii have created local school boards in addition to state education agencies and have delegated certain administrative authority over schools to these local boards. Nationwide, there are approximately 15,700 school districts, ranging from a few students to several hundred thousand. Some states, particularly those with a large number of small school districts, have established intermediate or regional administrative units that perform regulatory or service functions for several local districts.

As with the delegation of authority to state agencies, delegation of powers to local school boards is handled very differently across states. Some states with a deeply rooted tradition of local control over education (e.g., Colorado) give local boards a great deal of latitude in making operational decisions about schools. In other states that tend toward centralized control of education (e.g., Florida), local boards must function within the framework of detailed legislative directives. State legislatures retain the legal responsibility for education and can restrict the discretion of local boards by enacting legislation to that effect.

Local school board members usually are elected by the citizenry within the school district.[12] The Supreme Court has recognized that the equal protection clause requires each qualified voter to be given an opportunity to participate in the election of board members, with each vote given the same weight as far as practicable.[13] When board members are elected from geographical districts, such districts must be established to protect voting rights under the "one person, one vote" principle. If "at-large" elections result in a dilution of the minority vote, an abridgment of the federal Voting Rights Act may be found.[14]

The state legislature can specify the qualifications, method of selection, and terms and conditions of local school board membership. Board members are considered public school officers with sovereign power, in contrast to school employees, who are hired to implement directives. Public officers cannot hold two offices if one is subordinate to the other, cannot have an interest in contracts made by their agencies, and in some states cannot occupy more than one office for which they receive pay. Generally, statutes stipulate procedures that must be followed in removing public officers from their positions. Typical causes for removal include neglect of duty, illegal performance of duty, breach of good faith, negligence, and incapacity.

A local board must act as a body; individual board members are not empowered to make policies or perform official acts on behalf of the board. School boards have some discretion in adopting operational procedures, but they are legally bound to adhere to such procedures once established.

While courts are reluctant to interfere with decisions made by boards of education and will not rule on the wisdom of such decisions, they will invalidate any board action that is arbitrary, capricious, or outside the board's legal authority (*ultra vires*).

School board meetings and records must be open to the public. Most states have enacted "sunshine" or "open meeting" laws, acknowledging that the public has a right to be fully informed regarding the actions of public agencies. What constitutes a meeting is sometimes defined by statute, and certain exceptions to open meeting requirements are usually specified. For example, in many states, school boards can meet in executive session to discuss matters that threaten public safety or pertain to pending or current litigation, personnel matters, collective bargaining, or the disposition of real property. While discussion of these matters may take place in closed meetings, statutes usually stipulate that formal action must take place in open meetings.[15]

Local school boards hold powers specified or implied in state law and other powers considered necessary to achieve the purposes of the express powers. These delegated powers generally encompass the authority to determine the specifics of the curriculum offered within the school district, raise revenue to build and maintain schools, select personnel, and enact other policies necessary to implement the educational program pursuant to law. Courts have recognized that without specific enabling legislation local boards have discretionary authority to establish and support secondary schools, kindergartens, nongraded schools, and various school-related programs; alter school attendance zones; and close schools.[16]

Some decisions have been challenged as beyond a local board's lawful scope of authority. The New York Court of Appeals held that, in the absence of any state regulations specifying a minimum length of instructional time for schools, the New York City Board of Education acted within its implied powers by shortening the instructional week by two forty-five-minute periods.[17] Where specifications are provided in state law, however, local boards must adhere to such mandates. The Wyoming Supreme Court held that the state law requiring the school year to be 175 days was violated by a school district's practice of compressing the school week into four days, even if the total amount of contact time was not substantially altered.[18]

Local school boards cannot delegate their decisionmaking authority to other agencies or associations. In an illustrative case, a New Jersey court ruled that a school board could not relinquish to the teachers' association responsibility for determining courses of study or settling classroom controversies.[19] Also, the Iowa Supreme Court held that a school board could not delegate its rule-making authority to a state high school athletic association.[20]

Local boards are authorized to perform discretionary duties (i.e., involving judgment), while school employees, such as superintendents, principals, and teachers, can perform only ministerial duties necessary to carry out policies. Hence, a superintendent can recommend personnel to be hired and propose a budget to the board, but the board must make the actual decisions. Although it might appear that educators at the building level retain little decisionmaking authority, administrators as well as classroom teachers can enact rules and regulations, consistent with board policy and law, to ensure the efficient operation of the school or class under their supervision.

Since the mid-1980s the notion of decentralizing many operational decisions to the school level (school-based management) has received considerable attention.[21] In 1990 the Illinois Supreme Court struck down a state law that established local school councils, empowered to hire personnel and approve budgets and programs, in the Chicago public schools.[22] The court reasoned that the plan, giving parents greater weight than other community residents in selecting council members, violated federal and state constitutional guarantees of equal voting rights for all citizens. However, the elimination of tenure for administrators was not found to impair the fourteenth amendment or contractual rights. Also, the court did not invalidate the practice of decentralizing operational decisions to the school level, noting that the law's constitutional defect could be remedied by altering the council selection process.[23]

FEDERAL ROLE IN EDUCATION

Unlike state constitutions, the Federal Constitution is silent regarding education; hence, individuals do not have an inherent federally protected right to an education.[24] The Federal Constitution does, however, confer basic rights on individuals, and these rights must be respected by school personnel. Furthermore, Congress exerts control over the use of federal education aid and regulates other aspects of schools through legislation enacted pursuant to its constitutionally granted powers.

UNITED STATES CONSTITUTION

A constitution, by definition, is a body of precepts providing the system of fundamental laws of a nation, state, or society. The United States Constitution establishes a separation of powers among the executive, judicial, and legislative branches of government. These three branches form a system of checks and balances to ensure that the intent of the Constitution is respected. The Federal Constitution also provides a systematic process for altering the document, if deemed necessary. Article V stipulates that amendments may be proposed by a two-thirds vote of each house of Congress, or by a special convention called by Congress upon the request of two-thirds of the state legislatures. Proposed amendments must then be ratified by three-fourths of the states in order to become part of the Constitution.

Since the Federal Constitution is the supreme law in this nation, state authority over education must be exercised in a manner consistent with its provisions. In 1958, the Supreme Court declared:

> It is, of course, quite true that the responsibility for public education is primarily the concern of the states, but it is equally true that such responsibilities, like all other state activity, must be exercised consistently with federal constitutional requirements as they apply to state action.[25]

The Supreme Court has interpreted various constitutional guarantees as they apply to educational matters. While all federal constitutional mandates affect public education to some degree, the following provisions have had the greatest impact on public school policies and practices.

General Welfare Clause. Under Article I, Section 8 of the Constitution, Congress has the power "to lay and collect taxes, duties, imposts and excises, to pay the debts and provide for the common defense and general welfare of the United States . . ." In 1937 the Supreme Court declared that the concept of general welfare is not static: "Needs that were narrow or parochial a century ago may be interwoven in our day with the well-being of the nation. What is critical or urgent changes with the times."[26] Although historically this clause has been the subject of much debate, the Supreme Court has interpreted the provision as allowing Congress to tax and spend public monies for a variety of purposes related to the general welfare.[27] The Court has stated that it will not interfere with the discretion of Congress in its domain, unless Congress exhibits a clear display of arbitrary power.[28]

Using the general welfare rationale, Congress has enacted legislation providing substantial federal support for research and instructional programs in areas such as science, mathematics, reading, special education, vocational education, career education, and bilingual education. Congress also has provided financial assistance for the school lunch program and for services to meet the special needs of various groups of students, such as the culturally disadvantaged. In addition, Congress has responded to national health and safety concerns with legislation such as the 1980 Asbestos School Hazard Detection and Control Act and the 1988 Indoor Radon Abatement Act, which require the inspection of school buildings and, if necessary, remedial action to assure the safety of students and employees.

Commerce Clause. Congress is empowered to "regulate commerce with foreign nations, among the several states, and with Indian tribes" under Article I, Section 8, Clause 3 of the Constitution. Safety, transportation, and labor regulations enacted pursuant to this clause have affected the operation of public schools. Traditionally, courts have favored a broad interpretation of "commerce" and an expanded federal role in regulating commercial activity to ensure national prosperity. Interpreting congressional powers to regulate commerce, in 1985 the Supreme Court held that a municipal mass transit system was subject to the minimum wage and overtime requirements of the federal Fair Labor Standards Act (FLSA).[29] This decision, *Garcia v. San Antonio Metropolitan Transit Authority,* overturned a precedent established in 1976 when the Court limited congressional authority to enforce federal minimum wage requirements in areas of "traditional" state governmental functions.[30] Concluding that attempts to identify such state functions that would be immune from federal requirements had been unworkable and inconsistent with established principles of federalism, the Court in *Garcia* found nothing in the FLSA destructive of state sovereignty. This decision eliminated the constitutional barrier to federal regulatory efforts governing other aspects of public employment, such as collective bargaining for public employees.[31]

Obligations of Contract Clause. Article I, Section 10 of the Constitution stipulates that states cannot enact any law impairing the obligation of contracts. Administrators, teachers, and noncertified personnel are protected from arbitrary dismissals by contractual agreements. School boards also enter into numerous contracts with individuals and companies in conducting school business. The judiciary often is called upon to evaluate the validity of a given contract or to assess whether a party has breached its contractual obligations.

First Amendment. The Bill of Rights, comprised of the first ten amendments to the Federal Constitution, safeguards individual liberties against governmental encroachment.[32] The most preciously guarded of these liberties are contained in the first amendment, which states:

> Congress shall make no law respecting an establishment of religion, or prohibiting the free exercise thereof; or abridging the freedom of speech, or of the press; or the right of the people peaceably to assemble, and to petition the government for a redress of grievances.

The religious freedoms contained in this amendment have evoked a number of lawsuits challenging governmental aid to and regulation of nonpublic schools and contesting public school policies and practices as advancing religion or impairing free exercise rights. Cases involving students' rights to express themselves and to distribute literature have been initiated under first amendment guarantees of freedom of speech and press. Also, teachers' rights to academic freedom and to speak out on matters of public concern have precipitated numerous lawsuits. The right of assembly has been the focus of litigation involving student clubs and employees' rights to organize and engage in collective bargaining.

Fourth Amendment. This amendment guarantees the right of citizens "to be secure in their persons, houses, papers, and effects against unreasonable searches and seizures." The Supreme Court has recognized that the basic purpose of the fourth amendment is "to safeguard the privacy and security of individuals against arbitrary invasions by governmental officials."[33] Since the late 1960s, this amendment has frequently appeared in educational cases involving drug-testing programs and searches of students' lockers, cars, and persons. A few cases also have involved alleged violations of teachers' fourth amendment rights by school officials.

Fifth Amendment. In part, this amendment provides that no person shall be "compelled in any criminal case to be a witness against himself, nor be deprived of life, liberty, or property without due process of law; nor shall private property be taken for public use, without just compensation." Several cases have addressed the application of the self-incrimination clause in instances where teachers have been questioned by superiors about their activities outside the classroom. The fifth amendment also has been used in educational litigation to protect citizens' rights to appropriate compensation for property acquired for school purposes. Due process litigation concerning schools usually has been initiated under the fourteenth amendment, which pertains directly to state action. However, many cases in the District of Columbia (involving topics such as desegregation and the rights of children with disabilities) have relied on the due process guarantees of the fifth amendment, because the fourteenth amendment does not apply in this jurisdiction.[34]

Ninth Amendment. The ninth amendment stipulates that "the enumeration in the Constitution, of certain rights, shall not be construed to deny or disparage others retained by the people." This amendment has appeared in educational litigation in which teachers have asserted that their right to personal privacy outside the classroom is protected as an unenumerated right. Also, grooming regulations applied to teachers and students have been challenged as impairing personal rights retained by the people under this amendment.

Fourteenth Amendment. The fourteenth amendment is the most widely invoked constitutional provision in school litigation since it specifically addresses state action. In part, the fourteenth amendment provides that no state shall "deny to any person within its jurisdiction, the equal protection of the laws.'' This clause has been significant in school cases involving alleged discrimination based on race, gender, ethnic background, and disabilities. In addition, school finance litigation often has been based on the equal protection clause.

The due process clause of the fourteenth amendment, which prohibits states from depriving citizens of life, liberty, or property without due process of law, also has played an important role in school litigation. Property rights are legitimate expectations of entitlement created through state laws, regulations, or contracts. Compulsory school attendance laws confer upon students a legitimate property right to attend school, and the granting of tenure gives teachers a property entitlement to continued employment. Liberty rights include interests in one's reputation and fundamental rights related to marriage, family matters, and personal privacy. In addition, the Supreme Court has interpreted fourteenth amendment liberties as *incorporating* the personal freedoms contained in the Bill of Rights.[35] Thus, the first ten amendments, originally directed toward the federal government, have been applied to state action as well. Although the principle of ''incorporation'' has been criticized,[36] Supreme Court precedent supports the notion that the fourteenth amendment restricts state interference with fundamental constitutional liberties. This principle is particularly important in school litigation since education is a state function; claims that public school policies or practices impair personal freedoms (e.g., first amendment free speech guarantees) are usually initiated through the fourteenth amendment.

The federal judiciary has identified both procedural and substantive components of due process guarantees. Procedural due process ensures fundamental fairness if the government threatens an individual's life, liberty, or property interests; minimum procedures required by the Federal Constitution are notice of the charges, an opportunity to refute the charges, and a hearing that is conducted fairly. Substantive due process requires that state action be based on a valid objective with means reasonably related to attaining the objective. In essence, substantive due process shields the individual against *arbitrary* governmental action that impairs life, liberty, or property interests.

Since the fourteenth amendment protects personal liberties against unwarranted *state* interference, private institutions, including private schools, may not be subject to these restrictions. For private school policies and practices to be challenged successfully under the fourteenth amendment, there must be sufficient governmental involvement in the private school to constitute ''state action.''[37] The Supreme Court has not articulated a precise standard by which to assess how much state involvement is necessary to trigger fourteenth amendment guarantees; rather, specific controversies are assessed on a case-by-case basis.

FEDERAL LEGISLATION

Congress is empowered to enact laws to translate the intent of the Federal Constitution into actual practices. Laws reflect the will of the legislative branch of government, which, theoretically in a democracy, represents the citizenry. Since the states have sovereign power regarding education, the federal government's involvement in public schools has been one of indirect support, not direct control.

Federal legislation affecting public education was enacted prior to ratification of the Federal Constitution. The Ordinances of 1785 and 1787, providing land grants to states for the maintenance of public schools, encouraged the establishment of public education in many states. However, it was not until the mid-twentieth century that Congress began to play a significant role in stimulating *targeted* educational reform through its spending powers under the general welfare clause. The most comprehensive law offering financial assistance to schools, the Elementary and Secondary Education Act of 1965 (ESEA), in part supplied funds for compensatory education programs for economically disadvantaged students. With passage of ESEA, federal aid to education doubled, and the federal government's contribution increased steadily until reaching its high point of over 9 percent of total public education revenue in 1981.

Congress and federal administrative agencies have exerted considerable influence in shaping public school policies and practices through categorical funding laws and their accompanying administrative regulations. Individual states or school districts have the option of accepting or rejecting such federal assistance, but if categorical aid is accepted, the federal government has the authority to prescribe guidelines for its use and to monitor state and local education agencies to ensure fiscal accountability.

Much of the federal categorical legislation enacted during the 1960s and 1970s provided funds to assist school districts in attaining equity goals and addressing other national priorities. For example, the Bilingual Education Act of 1968 and the Education for All Handicapped Children Act of 1975 (which became the Individuals with Disabilities Education Act of 1990) have provided federal funds to assist education agencies in offering services for students with special needs. Although in the 1980s Congress shifted away from its heavy reliance on categorical federal aid by consolidating some categorical programs into block grants with reduced funding and regulations, aid for economically disadvantaged, disabled, and English-deficient students has remained categorical in nature.

In addition to laws providing financial assistance to public schools, Congress has enacted legislation designed to clarify the scope of individuals' civil rights. Unlike the discretion enjoyed by state and local education agencies in deciding whether to participate in federal funding programs, educational institutions must comply with these civil rights laws.

Federal antidiscrimination laws are grounded in two distinct sources of federal authority. Some are enacted to enforce constitutional rights and have general application. Others are based on the federal government's authority to place restrictions on the expenditure of federal funds and apply only to recipients of federal financial assistance. Various federal agencies are charged with monitoring compliance with these laws and can bring suit against noncomplying institutions. Under most civil rights laws, individuals also can initiate private suits to compel compliance and, in some instances, to obtain personal remedies.

Several laws enacted in the latter part of the nineteenth century to protect the rights of African-American citizens were seldom the focus of litigation until the mid-twentieth century. These laws, particularly the Civil Rights Act of 1871, Section 1983, recently have been used by students and teachers to gain relief in instances where their federal rights have been violated by school policies and practices. Section 1983 provides a private right to bring suit for damages against any person who, acting under color of state law, impairs rights secured by the Federal Constitution and laws.[38] Although Section 1983 does not confer specific substantive rights, it has been significant in school cases because it allows individuals to obtain damages from school officials and school districts for abridgments of federally protected rights.

Subsequent civil rights laws enacted since the 1960s do confer substantive rights to protect citizens from discrimination. The vindication of employees' rights in school settings has generated substantial litigation under Title VII of the Civil Rights Act of 1964, which prohibits employment discrimination on the basis of race, color, gender, religion, or national origin. Modeled in part after Title VII, the Americans with Disabilities Act of 1990 provides specific protections in employment and public accommodations for individuals with disabilities. Also, the Age Discrimination in Employment Act of 1967 protects employees over forty against age-based employment discrimination. Other civil rights laws pertain only to institutions housing programs that receive federal funds, such as Title VI of the Civil Rights Act of 1964 (prohibiting discrimination on the basis of race, color, or national origin), Title IX of the Education Amendments of 1972 (barring gender discrimination against participants in education programs), and the Rehabilitation Act of 1973 (prohibiting discrimination against otherwise qualified handicapped persons).[39] Courts often have been called upon to interpret these acts and their regulations as they apply to educational practices.

Still other federal laws offer protections to individuals in educational settings and place responsibilities on school officials. For example, the Family Educational Rights and Privacy Act guarantees parental access to their children's school records and safeguards the confidentiality of such records. Also, federal laws protect human subjects in research projects and require parental consent before students participate in federally supported psychiatric or psychological examination, testing, or treatment designed to reveal information in specified sensitive areas. Courts have played an important role in interpreting the protections included in these laws and assuring compliance with the federal mandates.

FEDERAL ADMINISTRATIVE AGENCIES

Similar to state governments, much of the regulatory activity at the federal level is conducted by administrative agencies. The Office of Education was originally established in 1867, and it became part of the Department of Health, Education, and Welfare in 1953. In 1980 the Department of Education was created with a Secretary who serves as a member of the President's cabinet. The Secretary is appointed by the President with the advice and approval of the Senate.

The primary functions of the Department of Education are to coordinate federal involvement in education activities, to identify educational needs of national significance, to propose strategies to address these needs, and to provide technical and financial assistance to state and local education agencies. Approximately half of federal aid to education is administered by the Department of Education, and its regulations promulgated to implement funding laws have had a significant impact on many schools. The Department solicits public comments on proposed regulations, and Congress reviews the regulations to ensure their consistency with legislative intent. The Department of Education administers regulations for over 100 different programs ranging from services for Native American students to projects for school dropouts. The remaining educational programs are administered by the Departments of Agriculture, Labor, Defense, Justice, or Health and Human Services.

Through their regulatory activities, numerous federal agencies influence state and local educational policies. For example, the Office of Civil Rights and the Equal Employment Opportunity Commission have reviewed claims of discrimination in public schools and initiated suits against school districts that are not in compliance with civil rights laws. Also, the Environmental Protection Agency has placed obligations on schools in connection with asbestos removal and maintenance of safe school environments.[40] School districts can face the termination of federal assistance if they do not comply with such federal regulations.

FUNCTION AND STRUCTURE OF THE JUDICIAL SYSTEM

Judicial decisions are usually cited in conjunction with statutory and constitutional provisions as a major source of educational law. As early as 1835, Alexis de Tocqueville noted that "scarcely any political question arises in the United States that is not resolved, sooner or later, into a judicial question."[41] Courts, however, do not initiate laws as legislative bodies do; courts apply appropriate principles of law to settle disputes. The terms "common law" or "case law" refer to judicially created legal principles that are relied upon as precedent when similar factual situations arise.

Although many constitutional provisions and statutory enactments never become the subject of litigation, some provisions require judicial clarification. Since federal and state constitutions set forth broad policy statements rather than specific guides to action, courts serve an important function in interpreting such mandates and in determining the legality of various school policies and practices. It has been firmly established that the United States Supreme Court has the ultimate authority in interpreting federal constitutional guarantees.[42]

The Supreme Court has articulated specific guidelines for exercising the power of judicial review. The Court will not decide hypothetical cases and will not render an opinion on issues in nonadversarial proceedings. There must be a genuine controversy initiated by a party with standing to sue. To achieve such standing, the party must have a "real interest" in the outcome of the case, such as having been adversely affected by the challenged practice.

The Supreme Court also has declared that it will not anticipate a constitutional question or decide a case on constitutional grounds if there is some other basis for resolving the dispute. When an act of Congress is questioned, the Court attempts to "ascertain whether a construction of the statute is fairly possible by which the question may be avoided."[43] In applying appropriate principles of law to specific cases, the Court generally follows the doctrine of *stare decisis* (abide by decided cases), and thus relies on precedents established in previous decisions. On occasion, however, the Court does overrule a prior opinion.

When a suit is initiated, the trial court holds a hearing to make findings of fact based on the evidence presented, and then applies legal principles to those facts in rendering a judgment. If the ruling is appealed, the appellate court must accept the trial court's findings of fact unless they are clearly erroneous. The appeals court reviews the written record of the evidence but does not hold a hearing for witnesses to be questioned. The appellate court may accept the trial court's findings of fact but disagree with the conclusions of law. In such instances, the case is usually remanded to the trial court for reconsideration in light of the appropriate legal principles enunciated by the appeals court.

In addition to individual suits,[44] education cases often involve class-action suits brought on behalf of all similarly situated individuals. To be certified as a class action, the suit must satisfy rules of civil procedure that specify prerequisites to establish commonality of injury and circumstances among class members. If a suit is not properly certified as a class action, and the circumstances of the original plaintiff change (e.g., a student graduates from school before a judgment is rendered), the court may dismiss the suit as moot because the plaintiff is no longer being injured by the contested practice.

Various remedies are available through court action. In some suits, a court-ordered injunction is sought to compel school officials to cease a particular action or to remove restraints they have imposed on protected freedoms. For a court to issue an injunction, evidence must indicate that the complainant would likely prevail in a trial on the merits of the case. Judicial relief also can take the form of a declaration that specific rights must be respected. In addition, courts can order personal remedies such as reinstatement and removal of material from school records. Courts also can award damages to compensate individuals for the deprivation of their rights, and punitive damages can be assessed against state officials if such deprivations constitute a willful or reckless disregard of protected rights. Under certain circumstances, attorneys' fees also can be awarded.

In interpreting constitutional and statutory provisions, courts have developed various criteria to evaluate whether the law has been violated. These judicially created standards or "tests" are extremely important and in some instances appear to go beyond the original intent of the constitutional or statutory provision in question. Judicial standards for assessing claims under various constitutional and statutory provisions are continually evolving and being refined by courts. The judiciary thus occupies a powerful position in shaping the law through its interpretive powers.

Courts, however, will not intervene in a school-related controversy if the dispute can be settled in a legislative or administrative forum. In 1973, the Supreme Court emphasized that in situations involving "persistent and difficult questions of educational policies," the judiciary's "lack of specialized knowledge and experience counsels against premature interference with the informed judgments made at the state and local levels."[45] All state educational systems provide some type of administrative appeals procedure for aggrieved individuals to use in disputes involving internal school operations. Many school controversies never reach the courts because they are settled in these administrative forums. Under most circumstances, courts require such administrative appeals to be exhausted before court action is brought.

In evaluating the impact of case law, it is important to keep in mind that a judicial ruling applies as precedent within the geographical jurisdiction of the court delivering the opinion. It is possible for two state supreme courts or two federal courts to render conflicting decisions on an issue, and such decisions are binding in their respective jurisdictions until the United States Supreme Court rules on the issue. Only decisions of the Supreme Court have national application.

immediate

STATE COURTS

State courts are established pursuant to state constitutional provisions, and the structure of judicial systems varies among states. In contrast to federal courts, which have only those powers granted by the United States Constitution, state courts can review most types of controversies unless restricted by state law. State judicial systems usually include trial courts of general jurisdiction, courts of special jurisdiction, and appellate courts. All states have a court of last resort, and decisions rendered by state high courts can be appealed to the United States Supreme Court.

In most states, the court of last resort is called the supreme court or supreme judicial court. However, in New York and Maryland the highest court is the Court of Appeals, and in West Virginia it is the Supreme Court of Appeals. Courts occupying the next level in the state judiciary usually are referred to as appeals courts or superior courts. State trial courts of general jurisdiction often are called district or circuit courts, but in New York, trial courts are referred to as supreme courts of their respective counties. The most common special jurisdiction courts are juvenile, probate, domestic relations, and small claims courts. State judges are usually elected or appointed by the governor.

FEDERAL COURTS

Article III, Section I of the Federal Constitution establishes the Supreme Court and authorizes Congress to create other federal courts as necessary. The federal court system contains courts of special jurisdiction such as the Claims Court, Tax Court, and Court of International Trade. There are three levels of federal courts of general jurisdiction—district courts, circuit courts of appeal, and the Supreme Court. The number of federal district courts in a state is based on population. Each state has at least one federal district court; many states have two or three; and California, New York, and Texas each have four. Judgments at the district court level are usually presided over by one judge.

On the federal appeals level, the nation is divided into twelve geographic circuits, each with its own federal circuit court of appeals.[46] A thirteenth federal circuit court has national jurisdiction to hear appeals regarding specific claims (e.g., customs; copyrights, patents, and trademarks; international trade). Federal circuit courts have from three to fifteen judges, depending on the workload of the circuit. Although a federal circuit court decision is binding only in the states within that circuit, such decisions often influence other appellate courts when dealing with similar questions. The jurisdiction of the federal circuits is as follows:

- First Circuit: Maine, Massachusetts, New Hampshire, Rhode Island, and Puerto Rico

- Second Circuit: Connecticut, New York, and Vermont
- Third Circuit: Delaware, New Jersey, Pennsylvania, and the Virgin Islands
- Fourth Circuit: Maryland, North Carolina, South Carolina, Virginia, and West Virginia
- Fifth Circuit: Louisiana, Mississippi, Texas, and the Canal Zone
- Sixth Circuit: Kentucky, Michigan, Ohio, and Tennessee
- Seventh Circuit: Illinois, Indiana, and Wisconsin
- Eighth Circuit: Arkansas, Iowa, Minnesota, Missouri, Nebraska, North Dakota, and South Dakota
- Ninth Circuit: Alaska, Arizona, California, Idaho, Hawaii, Montana, Nevada, Oregon, Washington, and Guam
- Tenth Circuit: Colorado, Kansas, New Mexico, Oklahoma, Utah, and Wyoming
- Eleventh Circuit: Alabama, Florida, and Georgia
- D.C. Circuit: Washington, D.C.[47]
- Federal Circuit: National jurisdiction on specific claims

The United States Supreme Court is, of course, the highest court in the nation, beyond which there is no appeal. If the Supreme Court finds a specific practice unconstitutional (e.g., intentional school segregation), this judicial mandate applies nationwide. However, if the Court concludes that a given activity does not impair federal constitutional guarantees (e.g., corporal punishment), states and local school boards retain discretion in placing restrictions on the activity. In the latter instances, legal requirements will vary across jurisdictions. Congress can amend federal laws if the Supreme Court misinterprets congressional intent and has done so with a number of civil rights laws in response to Supreme Court rulings.[48] But Congress is not empowered to nullify the Court's interpretations of the Federal Constitution; the only recourse is to amend the Constitution.

The Supreme Court has original jurisdiction in cases in which a state is a party or involving federal ambassadors and other public ministers. The Court has appellate jurisdiction in other cases arising under the Constitution or federal laws or entailing disputes between states or parties residing in different states.[49] The Supreme Court disposes of approximately 5,000 cases a year, but renders a written opinion on the merits in less than 5 percent of these cases. The Court often concludes that the topic of a case is not appropriate or of sufficient significance to warrant Supreme Court review. Denial of review does not imply agreement with the lower court's decision. Since the Supreme Court has authority to determine which cases it will hear, many issues are left for resolution by lower courts. Accordingly, precedents regarding some school controversies must be gleaned from federal circuit courts or state supreme courts and may differ from one jurisdiction to another.

An individual need not exhaust state administrative appeals before initiating a federal suit if the abridgment of a federally protected right is involved, but some federal laws specify administrative procedures that must be pursued before commencing court action. Suits involving federal issues also may be heard by state courts, and the interpretation of federal rights by the state judiciary may be reviewed by the United States Supreme Court. Individuals have a choice as to whether to initiate a federal or state suit in these circumstances, but they cannot relitigate an issue in federal court if they have been denied relief by the state judiciary. In essence, a federal suit cannot be initiated if an issue has already been adjudicated by the state judiciary or could have been raised in the prior state litigation.

JUDICIAL TRENDS

Traditionally, the federal judiciary did not address educational concerns; fewer than 300 cases involving education had been initiated in federal courts prior to 1954.[50] However, starting with the landmark desegregation decision, *Brown v. Board of Education of Topeka* (1954),[51] federal courts assumed a significant role in resolving educational controversies. By 1970, litigation was clearly viewed as an important tool to influence social policies, and more legal challenges to school practices were initiated in the 1970s than in the preceding seven decades combined.[52] Much of this judicial intervention has involved the protection of individual rights and the attainment of equity for minority groups. Since the 1960s, courts have addressed nearly every facet of the educational enterprise, including students' rights to free expression, compulsory school attendance, curriculum censorship, school finance reform, employee dismissal practices, student discipline, educational malpractice, gender discrimination, collective bargaining, employees' privacy rights, desegregation, and the rights of students with disabilities and English language deficiencies.

The volume of federal cases pertaining to school issues reached its zenith in the 1970s, and since then has stabilized or declined in most areas (e.g., employment concerns, student discipline).[53] The notable exception to this trend has been cases dealing with the rights of children with disabilities, which have increased at a phenomenal rate during the past decade.[54]

Not only has there been a change in the volume of cases, but also there has been a shift in the posture of the federal judiciary. In the 1960s and early 1970s, federal courts expanded constitutional protections afforded to individuals in school settings, but since the 1980s the federal judiciary has exhibited more deference to the decisions of the legislative and executive branches and greater reluctance to extend the scope of civil rights. Kirp and Jensen have observed that "the heyday of educational policymaking by the courts seems to have run its course," and that "a reticent judiciary will not be so inclined as to further reshape decisionmaking in education as their pioneering predecessors."[55]

Judicial deference to policymakers nurtures diverse standards across states and local school districts. When the Supreme Court strikes down a practice under the Federal Constitution, standards become more uniform nationally, but when the Court defers to local boards, standards vary, reflecting local perspectives. As fewer constitutional suits are initiated, legislative enactments become more significant in specifying the scope of protected rights. If the federal judiciary continues to exhibit restraint, volatile political controversies will be assured because policymakers will have to grapple with issues that formerly were settled through judicial pronouncements.

Yet, implications of the federal judiciary's recent deference to legislative bodies should not be overstated. Although the debate will likely continue over whether courts have the competence to play a key role in shaping educational policies and whether it is legitimate for courts to play such a role, "no one today can defensibly argue that courts do not make policy for schools."[56] Despite the deceleration in federal litigation, the volume of federal school cases is still substantial, far outstripping any other nation. Moreover, the number of school cases at the state level has remained stable, and some state supreme courts have recently assumed an activist role in interpreting state constitutional mandates in school finance cases.[57] Rather than a diminished judicial role in influencing school policies, the locus of significant activity may simply shift from federal to state courts during the coming decade.[58]

CONCLUSION

American public schools are governed by a complex body of regulations that are grounded in constitutional provisions, statutory enactments, agency regulations, and court decisions. Since the mid-twentieth century, legislation relating to schools has increased significantly in both volume and complexity, and courts have played an important role in interpreting statutory and constitutional provisions. Although rules made at any level must be consistent with higher authority, administrators and teachers retain considerable latitude in establishing rules and procedures within their specific jurisdictions. As long as educators act reasonably and do not impair the protected rights of others, their actions will be upheld if challenged in court.

School personnel, however, cannot plead "ignorance of the law" as a valid defense for illegal actions.[59] Thus, educators should be aware of the constraints placed on their rule-making prerogatives by school board policies and federal and state constitutional and statutory provisions. Subsequent chapters of this book attempt to clarify the major legal principles affecting teachers and students in their daily school activities.

ENDNOTES

1. United States v. Darby, 312 U.S. 100, 124 (1941).
2. Tinker v. Des Moines Indep. School Dist., 393 U.S. 503, 507 (1969).
3. Arizona Const., Art. XI, § 1.
4. Flory v. Smith, 134 S.E. 360, 362 (Va. 1926).
5. *See, e.g.,* Kaupas v. Regional Bd. of School Trustees of Mason County, 361 N.E.2d 1157 (Ill. App. Ct. 1977); In re Township No. 143 North, Range 55 West, 183 N.W.2d 520 (N.D. 1971); DeJonge v. School Dist. of the Village of Bloomington, 139 N.W.2d 296 (Neb. 1966); Schwartzkopf v. State, 204 N.E.2d 342 (Ind. 1965); Alexander v. Randall, 133 N.W.2d 124 (Iowa 1965). However, state laws can place restrictions on making changes in school district boundaries. *See* State v. Board of Educ. of Anaconda School Dist., 741 S.W.2d 747 (Mo. Ct. App. 1987) (Missouri law requires voters in affected districts to approve boundary changes).
6. *See* Bruce C. Bowers, *State-Enforced Accountability of Local Districts*, ERIC Digest Series, No. EA 36 (Eugene, OR: ERIC Clearinghouse on Educational Management, 1989).
7. State *ex rel.* Miller v. Board of Educ. of Unified School Dist. No. 398, Marion County, 511 P.2d 705 (Kan. 1973). *See also* Matter of Tenure Hearing of Tyler, 566 A.2d 229 (N.J. Super. Ct. App. Div. 1989), *certification denied,* 583 A.2d 315 (N.J. 1990) (upheld state board of education's decision imposing penalty for conduct unbecoming a teacher of forfeiture of six months' salary and loss of salary increases for two school years).
8. Wilt v. Ohio State Bd. of Educ., 608 F.2d 1126 (6th Cir. 1979), *cert. denied,* 445 U.S. 964 (1980). *See also* Board of Educ. of Bratenahl Local School Dist. v. State Bd. of Educ., 373 N.E.2d 1238 (Ohio 1978), *cert. denied,* 439 U.S. 865 (1978).
9. Girard School Dist. v. Pittenger, 392 A.2d 261, 264 (Pa. 1978).
10. State of North Carolina v. Whittle Communications and the Thomasville City Bd. of Educ., 402 S.E.2d 556 (N.C. 1991).
11. *See, e.g.,* Botti v. Southwest Butler County School Dist., 529 A.2d 1206 (Pa. Commw. Ct. 1987); Eisbruck v. New York State Educ. Dep't, 520 N.Y.S.2d 138 (N.Y. Sup. Ct. 1987).
12. In some large cities, school board members are appointed by the mayor. Also, in a few states, such as Virginia, local board members are appointed by other agencies, such as the city council, the county board of supervisors, or a selection committee chosen by a local circuit court judge. *See* Irby v. Virginia State Bd. of Elections, 889 F.2d 1352 (4th Cir. 1989) (state's method of appointing members of local school boards is not intentionally discriminatory). *See also* Vereen v. Ben Hill County, Georgia, 743 F. Supp. 864 (M.D. Ga. 1990) (petitioners failed to establish that the Georgia statute authorizing grand juries to select members of county boards of education was enacted for racially discriminatory reasons). *But see* Searcy v. Williams, 656 F.2d 1003 (5th Cir. 1981) (a Georgia statute that established a former private school's board of trustees as the city's board of education and authorized the board's self-perpetuation was invalidated as unconstitutionally designed to exclude African Americans from the board).

13. Hadley v. Junior College Dist. of Metro. Kansas City, 397 U.S. 50 (1970). Whether a state can prohibit partisan endorsements in school board and other nonpartisan elections has been controversial. *See* Reene v. Geary, 911 F.2d 280 (9th Cir. 1990), *vacated and remanded,* 111 S. Ct. 2331 (1991), in which the federal appeals court struck down California's law prohibiting political parties from supporting or opposing candidates for nonpartisan offices, but the Supreme Court vacated the order because respondents did not establish a live controversy ripe for judicial resolution. *See also* Geary v. Renne, 914 F.2d 1249 (9th Cir. 1990) (upholding portions of the law allowing the state to remove "false, misleading, or inconsistent" material from candidate statements in voter information packets and to prohibit candidates from making reference to party affiliation or partisan activities when seeking nonpartisan offices).

14. 42 U.S.C. § 1971, *et seq.* (1988). Section 1973 states that "no practice or procedure shall be imposed or applied . . . in a manner which results in a denial or abridgment of the right . . . to vote on account of race . . ." *See* United States v. Marengo County Comm'n, 731 F.2d 1546 (11th Cir. 1984), *cert. denied,* 469 U.S. 976 (1984), *on remand,* 623 F. Supp. 33 (S.D. Ala. 1985); United States v. Uvalde Consol. Indep. School Dist., 625 F.2d 547 (5th Cir. 1980), *cert. denied,* 451 U.S. 1002 (1981).

15. *See* Connelly v. School Comm. of Hanover, 565 N.E.2d 449 (Mass. 1991) (under the Massachusetts open meeting law, selection of a principal by the school committee must be made in an open meeting, but the selection committee can hold private sessions to screen applicants). For a discussion of open meeting requirements, *see* James A. Rapp, ed., *Education Law,* vol. 1 (New York: Matthew Bender, 1984), Chapter 3, pp. 95–96; Supplement 1990, §3.06[3], p. 19.

16. *See, e.g.,* Espinal v. Salt Lake City Bd. of Educ., 797 P.2d 412 (Utah 1990); Nelson v. School Bd. of the Hill City School Dist. No. 51-2 of Pennington County, 459 N.W.2d 451 (S.D. 1990); Schwan v. Board of Educ. of Lansing School Dist., 183 N.W.2d 594 (Mich. Ct. App. 1970); Sinnott v. Colombet, 40 P. 329 (Cal. 1895); Stuart v. School Dist. No. 1 of the Village of Kalamazoo, 30 Mich. 69 (1874).

17. New York City School Bds. Ass'n v. Board of Educ., School Dist. of City of New York, 347 N.E.2d 568 (N.Y. 1976). *See also* Morgan v. Polk County Bd. of Educ., 328 S.E.2d 320 (N.C. Ct. App. 1985) (county school board was authorized to implement an experimental program lengthening the school day and term).

18. Johnston v. Board of Trustees, School Dist. No. 1, 661 P.2d 1045 (Wyo. 1983).

19. Board of Educ. of Rockaway Township v. Rockaway Township Educ. Ass'n, 295 A.2d 380 (N.J. Super. Ct. Ch. Div. 1972).

20. Bunger v. Iowa High School Athletic Ass'n, 197 N.W.2d 555 (Iowa 1972).

21. *See* James Guthrie, "School-Based Management: The Next Needed Education Reform," *Phi Delta Kappan,* vol. 68 (1986), pp. 305–309.

22. Fumarolo v. Chicago Bd. of Educ., 566 N.E.2d 1283 (Ill. 1990).

23. This law subsequently was amended to bring the selection process in line with the "one person, one vote" principle. *See* Peter Schmidt, "Illinois Legislature Revises Chicago School-Reform Law," *Education Week,* July 31, 1991, p. 12.

24. *See* San Antonio Indep. School Dist. v. Rodriguez, 411 U.S. 1 (1973).

25. Cooper v. Aaron, 358 U.S. 1, 19 (1958).

26. Helvering v. Davis, 301 U.S. 619, 641 (1937).

27. *See* United States v. Gettysburg Elec. Ry. Co., 160 U.S. 668 (1896); United States v. Butler, 297 U.S. 1 (1936); Helvering, *id.*
28. Helvering, *id.* at 644-645.
29. 469 U.S. 528 (1985). *See also* Equal Employment Opportunity Comm'n v. Wyoming, 460 U.S. 226 (1983).
30. National League of Cities v. Usery, 426 U.S. 833 (1976). The *Usery* decision halted proposals that were pending before Congress to establish a national collective bargaining law for public school teachers. *See* text with note 18, Chapter 11.
31. *See* Floyd Delon and Mark Van Zandt, "The Pendulum Continues to Swing: Garcia v. San Antonio Metropolitan Transit Authority," *Education Law Reporter,* vol. 26 (1985), pp. 1–11.
32. Several of the original states were reluctant to ratify the Federal Constitution without the promise of a statement of individual liberties. *See* Robert Rutland, *The Birth of the Bill of Rights, 1776–1791* (Chapel Hill, NC: University of North Carolina Press, 1955), Chapters 7, 8. For a discussion of the application of the Bill of Rights to state governmental action, *see* text with note 35, *infra.*
33. Camara v. Municipal Court of City and County of San Francisco, 387 U.S. 523, 528 (1967).
34. *See* note 47, *infra.*
35. *See* Cantwell v. Connecticut, 310 U.S. 296, 303 (1940); Gitlow v. New York, 268 U.S. 652, 666 (1925).
36. *See* James McClellan, *Joseph Story and the American Constitution* (Norman, OK: University of Oklahoma Press, 1971), pp. 144–145.
37. *See, e.g.,* Rendell-Baker v. Kohn, 457 U.S. 830 (1982); Burton v. Wilmington Parking Auth., 365 U.S. 715 (1961).
38. School boards as well as school officials are considered "persons" under 42 U.S.C. § 1983 (1988). *See* text with note 183, Chapter 8.
39. In 1988 the Civil Rights Restoration Act of 1987 was signed into law, 20 U.S.C. § 1681 (1988), clarifying that these three laws and the Age Discrimination Act of 1975 (barring age discrimination in federally assisted programs or activities) apply to entire *institutions* if any of their programs receive federal funds. This law was enacted in response to a contrary Supreme Court ruling, Grove City College v. Bell, 465 U.S. 555 (1984).
40. *See* "School Boards Urge More Money for Asbestos," *School Board News,* May 22, 1990, p. 7; Linda Brenza, "Asbestos in Schools and the Economic Loss Doctrine," *University of Chicago Law Review,* vol. 54 (1987), pp. 277–311; text with note 68, Chapter 12.
41. Alexis de Tocqueville, *Democracy in America,* rev. ed. (New York: Alfred A. Knopf, 1960), vol. 1, p. 280.
42. *See* Marbury v. Madison, 5 U.S. (1 Cranch) 137 (1803).
43. Crowell v. Benson, 285 U.S. 22, 62 (1932). *See also* Ashwander v. Tennessee Valley Auth., 297 U.S. 288, 348 (1936) (Brandeis, J., concurring).
44. Most educational litigation involves civil suits, initiated by individuals alleging injury by another private party. Civil suits often involve claims for damages or requests for specific conduct to cease because it impairs the individual's protected rights. In contrast, criminal suits are brought on behalf of society to punish an individual for committing a crime, such as violating compulsory school attendance laws.
45. San Antonio Indep. School Dist. v. Rodriguez, 411 U.S. 1, 42 (1973).

46. In 1981 the fifth federal circuit was divided into the fifth and eleventh circuits.

47. Washington, D.C., has its own federal district court and circuit court of appeals because only federal laws apply in this jurisdiction.

48. *See* text with notes 89, 103, Chapter 9, for a discussion of congressional reaction to the Supreme Court's misinterpretation of congressional intent.

49. *See* text with note 190, Chapter 8, for a discussion of eleventh amendment restrictions on federal lawsuits brought by citizens against the state.

50. John Hogan, *The Schools, the Courts, and the Public Interest* (Lexington, MA: D. C. Heath, 1985), p. 11.

51. 347 U.S. 483 (1954).

52. William Bennett, "Excessive Legalization in Education," *Chicago Daily Law Bulletin,* February 22, 1988, p. 2.

53. Perry Zirkel and Sharon Richardson, "The 'Explosion' in Educational Litigation," *Education Law Reporter,* vol. 53 (1989), pp. 767–768; Michael Imber and David Gayler, "A Statistical Analysis of Education-Related Litigation since 1900," *Educational Administration Quarterly,* vol. 24 (1988), pp. 55–78.

54. Zirkel and Richardson, *id.*

55. David Kirp and Donald Jensen, "The New Federalism Goes to Court," in *School Days, Rule Days,* Kirp and Jensen, eds. (Philadelphia: Falmer Press, 1986), pp. 368, 375.

56. Louis Fischer, "When Courts Play School Board," *Education Law Reporter,* vol. 51 (1989), p. 702. *See also* Perry Zirkel, "The Maturing Relationship of Courts and Schools," *Education Law Reporter,* vol. 35 (1987), p. 907.

57. *See* Abbott v. Burke, 575 A.2d 359 (N.J. 1990); Helena Elementary School Dist. No. 1 v. Montana, 784 P.2d 412 (Mont. 1990); Rose v. Council for Better Educ., 790 S.W.2d 186 (Ky. 1989); Edgewood Indep. School Dist. v. Kirby, 777 S.W.2d 391 (Tex. 1989).

58. *See* Martha McCarthy, "The Courts as Educational Policy Makers: Recent Trends and Future Prospects," *Educational Horizons,* vol. 69 (1990), pp. 4–9.

59. *See* Wood v. Strickland, 420 U.S. 308 (1975); text with note 175, Chapter 8.

2
Church–State Relations

Identifying the appropriate governmental relationship with religion has generated substantial controversy in our nation, and since the mid-twentieth century, schools have provided the battleground for some of the most volatile disputes. With the exception of school desegregation, church–state issues have elicited more active involvement of all three branches of government than any other school issue. This chapter provides an overview of the constitutional framework and legal developments pertaining to church–state relations involving education.

CONSTITUTIONAL FRAMEWORK

Fed. The first amendment to the United States Constitution stipulates in part that "Congress shall make no law respecting an establishment of religion or prohibiting the free exercise thereof." Although this amendment was directed solely toward the *federal* government, the fourteenth amend-*State* ment, adopted in 1868, specifically placed restrictions on *state* action impairing personal rights. In the twentieth century the Supreme Court has recognized that the fundamental concept of "liberty" embodied in the fourteenth amendment incorporates first amendment guarantees and safeguards them against state interference.[1] Since education is primarily a state function, most church–state controversies involving schools have been initiated through the fourteenth amendment.

Constitutional scholars have extensively debated whether the framers of the establishment and free exercise clauses intended to sever civil and sectarian affairs or merely to prohibit religious discrimination and governmental promotion of a particular sect.[2] While this debate seems likely to continue, the ultimate responsibility for interpreting the restrictions imposed by the first amendment on governmental action resides with the United States Supreme Court. The vast majority of constitutional law governing church–state relations has evolved since World War II, and the

25

Supreme Court has developed separate judicial tests for assessing claims under the establishment and free exercise clauses.

In the first major establishment clause decision involving education, *Everson v. Board of Education,* the Supreme Court in 1947 reviewed the history of the first amendment and concluded that the establishment clause (and its fourteenth amendment application to states) means:

> Neither a state nor the federal government can set up a church. Neither can pass laws which aid one religion, aid all religions, or prefer one religion over another. . . . Neither a state nor the federal government can, openly or secretly, participate in the affairs of any religious organizations or groups and vice versa. In the words of Jefferson, the clause against establishment of religion by law was intended to erect "a wall of separation between church and state."[3]

Since 1970 the Supreme Court has applied a *tripartite test* in assessing most establishment clause claims.[4] To withstand scrutiny under this test, governmental action must: (1) have a secular purpose, (2) have a primary effect that neither advances nor impedes religion, and (3) avoid excessive governmental entanglement with religion.[5] If governmental action fails any prong of the tripartite test, it will be struck down under the establishment clause. This three-part test is still applied in establishment clause cases involving school issues, but in recent decisions the Supreme Court has paid particular attention to whether the challenged governmental action has the purpose or effect of *endorsing* religion by conveying a message favoring a particular religious belief.[6] A majority of the current justices has voiced dissatisfaction with the tripartite test, so changes in establishment clause doctrine may be on the horizon.[7]

While the establishment clause primarily is used to challenge governmental *advancement* of religion, free exercise suits usually focus on *secular* (nonreligious) governmental regulations alleged to have a coercive effect on religious practices. In establishment clause cases, the legality of the governmental action itself is at issue, whereas in free exercise claims, individuals generally accept the legitimacy of the governmental regulation but assert a right to special treatment for religious reasons.

To evaluate free exercise claims, the judiciary traditionally has applied a balancing test that includes an assessment of whether practices dictated by a sincere and legitimate religious belief have been impeded by the governmental action, and if so, to what extent. If such an impairment is substantiated, the court then evaluates whether the state action serves a compelling interest that justifies the burden imposed on the exercise of religious beliefs. Even if such a compelling interest is shown, the government is expected to attain its objectives through means that are the least burdensome on free exercise rights.

In the most significant school case involving a free exercise claim, *Wisconsin v. Yoder,* the Supreme Court exempted Amish children from compulsory school attendance upon successful completion of eighth grade. Although noting that the assurance of an educated citizenry ranks at the "apex" of state functions, the Court nonetheless concluded that parental rights to practice their legitimate religious beliefs outweighed the state's interest in mandating two additional years of formal schooling for Amish youth. The Court declared that "a state's interest in universal education, however highly we rank it, is not totally free from a balancing process when it impinges on fundamental rights and interests."[8] The Court cautioned, however, that its ruling was limited to the Amish, who offer a structured vocational program to prepare their youth for a cloistered agrarian community rather than mainstream American society.

In a 1990 decision that did not involve a school controversy, the Supreme Court somewhat modified this balancing test, ruling that the "compelling governmental interest" justification is not required in cases involving free exercise challenges to criminal laws.[9] The case was initiated by two employees who had been fired for misconduct and subsequently denied unemployment benefits because they ingested peyote at a religious ceremony of the Native American Church. Distinguishing this case from *Yoder,* which involved a combination of free exercise rights and parental rights, the Court majority concluded that without such a "hybrid" situation, individuals cannot rely on the free exercise clause to be excused from complying with a valid criminal law prohibiting specific conduct.[10]

Not only do courts apply different criteria to assess free exercise in contrast to establishment clause claims, they also impose different remedies for violations of the two clauses. If an establishment clause violation is found, continuation of the unconstitutional governmental activity is prohibited. If governmental action is found to impair free exercise rights, accommodations to enable individuals to practice their beliefs may be required, but the governmental policy or program would not have to be eliminated.

The most troublesome church–state controversies involve competing free exercise and establishment clause claims because there is an inherent tension between the two clauses. Both "are cast in absolute terms, and either of which, if expanded to a logical extreme, would tend to clash with the other."[11] The principle that the first amendment demands wholesome governmental neutrality toward religion has been easier to assert than to apply. Accommodations to free exercise rights can be interpreted as advancing religion in violation of the establishment clause, but overzealous efforts to guard against state sponsorship of religion can impinge upon free exercise rights. This tension between the clauses has complicated the judiciary's task in assessing claims regarding governmental relations with sectarian schools and the role of religion in public schools. In the remainder of this chapter, applicable legal principles are identified and unresolved issues are highlighted in connection with various facets of church–state relations involving education.

RELIGIOUS INFLUENCES IN PUBLIC SCHOOLS

From colonial days until the mid-twentieth century, religious (primarily Protestant) materials and observances were prevalent in many public schools. In two precedent-setting decisions in the early 1960s, the Supreme Court prohibited public schools from sponsoring daily prayer and Bible reading, concluding that such activities advance religion in violation of the establishment clause.[12] The Court reasoned that the voluntary participation of students in the religious activities was irrelevant to the constitutional impairment. The fact that daily devotional activities were conducted under the auspices of the public school was sufficient to abridge the first amendment.

These decisions, however, left unresolved many issues pertaining to religious influences in public education. Is the constitutional violation lessened if students rather than teachers initiate the devotional activities? If religious observances are occasional rather than daily, is the threat of an establishment clause impairment reduced? Can religious speech be distinguished from other types of speech in applying restrictions? To date, only partial answers have been provided to these and related questions in the public school context, as illustrated by the following discussion.

School-Sanctioned Prayer

Students have a free exercise right to engage in *private* devotional activities in public schools if they do not interfere with regular school activities. Indeed, it would be difficult to monitor whether students were engaging in silent prayer. Individual students can even engage in audible prayer (e.g., before lunch), as long as the activity is private and nondisruptive. Controversies have focused on state laws or school board policies that condone student devotionals, thus placing the stamp of public school approval on such activities.

State laws calling for a period of silent meditation or prayer in public schools historically were assumed to be permissible under the first amendment,[13] but the judiciary has become more reluctant to accept the asserted secular purpose for such laws. In recent years, a West Virginia constitutional amendment and laws in several states calling for a period of silent meditation or prayer in public schools have been invalidated under the establishment clause.[14]

In 1985 the Supreme Court rendered its first decision on this issue in *Wallace v. Jaffree,* invalidating a 1981 Alabama silent prayer law under the establishment clause.[15] Based on an assessment of the law's legislative history, the Supreme Court concluded that it was intended to convey a clear preference for students to engage in prayer during the moment of silence. Since a 1978 Alabama law already authorized a period of silent meditation in public schools, the Court majority concluded that the only logical reason for adding the phrase "or voluntary prayer" in the 1981 amendment was to encourage students to pray. But the Court indicated that laws calling for silent meditation or prayer in public schools *without* a legislative intent to impose prayer might withstand scrutiny under the establishment clause.

The Court subsequently agreed to review a decision in which the Third Circuit Court of Appeals invalidated New Jersey's silent meditation statute as intended to promote religious observances in public schools even though it did not mention "prayer."[16] The Supreme Court, however, did not address the first amendment issue, dismissing the appeal on technical grounds. Therefore, the legality of meditation laws, which currently are on the books in almost half of the states, remains to be resolved on a case-by-case basis.

Some state legislatures and school boards have attempted to authorize voluntary *spoken* prayer during the school day, but these efforts have not withstood judicial scrutiny. Since 1980, the Supreme Court has affirmed without an opinion or declined to review decisions in which federal appellate courts struck down two state laws calling for voluntary spoken prayer in public schools, a school board's attempt to permit student-led prayers in school assemblies, and state-condoned devotional activities initiated by teachers.[17] The appeals courts reasoned that there was little constitutional distinction between such practices and the state-imposed devotional activities that the Supreme Court barred under the establishment clause in the early 1960s.

School personnel may be vulnerable to liability for impairing federally protected rights if they encourage or even permit violations of the establishment clause in public schools.[18] In 1988 the Eighth Circuit Court of Appeals awarded damages to a student who was subjected to prayers led by the band teacher at rehearsals and performances. The court concluded that the practice was condoned by the school board in violation of clearly established law.[19] In an earlier case the Tenth Circuit Court of Appeals recognized that plaintiffs can recover compensatory damages for the impairment of their rights under the establishment clause.[20] The court further held that punitive damages might be warranted if the conduct of school authorities is shown to represent reckless or callous indifference toward constitutional rights.

Traditionally, the judiciary appeared less inclined to find an establishment clause violation in baccalaureate services and prayers during graduation ceremonies than in routine devotional activities in public education. There has been no contention that baccalaureate programs and invocations are instructional rather than religious; instead, the activities have been defended primarily because of their transient, ceremonial nature.[21]

Since the mid-1980s, however, there have been conflicting rulings on this subject. Some courts have continued to endorse such practices,[22] but a number of courts have struck down religious observances in graduation ceremonies, finding that neither the extracurricular nature of the events nor the voluntary participation of students reduces the establishment clause impairment.[23] For example, in 1990 the First Circuit Court of Appeals affirmed that the use of clergy to offer nondenominational invocations or benedictions invoking a deity at public school graduation exercises unconstitutionally advances religion.[24] The lower court reasoned that the presence of prayer at this special occasion creates an identification of the school with religious practice. Courts also have struck down prayers and other devotional activities during extracurricular activities, such as athletic contests, sponsored by public schools.[25]

Because the Supreme Court has not condoned school-sponsored devotional activities during instructional time, attempts have been made to restrict the authority of federal courts to review school prayer cases[26] and to amend the Federal Constitution to authorize prayer in public education. Should such an amendment receive congressional endorsement and be ratified by the necessary thirty-eight states to become part of the Federal Constitution, the ramifications for the vitality of the first amendment's religion clauses would undoubtedly reach far beyond the issue of public school prayer.

STUDENT-INITIATED DEVOTIONAL MEETINGS

Particularly sensitive first amendment questions are raised in connection with student groups holding devotional meetings in public school facilities before or after school, because this issue pits free speech, free exercise, and association rights against establishment clause restrictions. Requests by students to hold devotional meetings in public educational facilities during noninstructional time created legal controversies throughout the 1980s.[27]

In 1981 the Supreme Court settled the issue for students attending state-supported institutions of higher education in *Widmar v. Vincent,* ruling that any infringement on student groups' access to a forum created for student expression on college campuses must be justified by a compelling governmental interest.[28] While recognizing that compliance with the establishment clause is such a compelling interest, the Court found no establishment clause violation in allowing all student groups equal access to campus facilities for their meetings. Applying the tripartite test, the Court determined that an equal access policy would have the secular purpose of making campus facilities available to all student organizations on a nondiscriminatory basis. Such a policy would not advance or impede religion since the school's endorsement of religious groups would not be implied any more than would its endorsement of student political groups. Furthermore, allowing equal campus access to all student groups would not excessively entangle the government with religion because minimal supervision of student gatherings is required on college campuses.

Distinguishing K–12 schools from college campuses, five federal appellate courts from 1980 to 1985 disallowed student-initiated devotional meetings held during noninstructional time in public schools.[29] These courts reasoned that public schools must guard against giving the impression that particular religious creeds are being advanced and concluded that the establishment clause requires some restrictions on high school students' rights to assemble and express religious views during noninstructional time.[30]

Voicing displeasure with the federal judiciary's reluctance to extend the *Widmar* rationale to the precollegiate level, Congress passed the Equal Access Act (EAA) in 1984. This Act stipulates that if a federally assisted public secondary school provides a limited open forum for noncurriculum student groups to meet during noninstructional time, "equal access" to that forum cannot be denied based on the "religious, political, philosophical or other content of the speech at such meetings."[31] If the meetings have a religious orientation, school employees can attend only in a "nonparticipatory capacity" to maintain discipline.[32] Under the EAA, public high schools can decline to establish a limited forum for student expression and thus confine school access during noninstructional time to curriculum-related student groups. Even if a limited open forum is created, school authorities still can curtail meetings that would disrupt educational activities.

Prior to 1990, lower courts offered conflicting opinions regarding the application and constitutionality of the EAA.[33] In 1990 the Supreme Court resolved some of the legal questions when it rendered a decision of first impression, *Board of Education of the Westside Community Schools v. Mergens*.[34] The controversy that eventually led to the Supreme Court's decision arose after a group of students at a Nebraska high school sought permission to form a club that would meet at the public school and engage in Bible discussions, prayer, and fellowship. The federal district court upheld school authorities' denial of the request, concluding that the EAA did not apply because all thirty student groups that met in the school were curriculum related and part of the student activities program designed to advance educational objectives. Thus, the high school had not created a limited open forum subject to the EAA.[35]

However, the Eighth Circuit Court of Appeals and ultimately the Supreme Court disagreed, ruling that the school could not bar the religious club from the limited forum it had created for noncurriculum student groups to hold meetings. The Supreme Court declared that "even if a public secondary school allows only one 'noncurriculum-related student group' to meet, the Act's obligations are triggered and the school may not deny other clubs, on the basis of the content of their speech, equal access to meet on school premises during noninstructional time.''[36] Acknowledging the law's ambiguity as to the definition of ''curriculum related,'' the majority concluded that student groups would be exempt from the Act's coverage only if they relate to subject matter that is currently, or soon would be, taught in the curriculum, if they relate to the body of courses as a whole, or if participation in the group is required as part of a course or awarded credit.[37]

Because the Court granted relief on statutory grounds, it was not necessary to address the students' claims that the denial of school access for religious meetings violated their free speech and free exercise rights. However, the Court did address the school district's contention that the EAA violates the establishment clause. Concluding that it does not, the justices were not of a single mind as to their reasoning. Only four justices concluded that the EAA satisfies the three-part test under the establishment clause since ''the logic of *Widmar* applies with equal force to the Equal Access Act.''[38] The plurality emphasized that ''there is a crucial difference between *government* speech endorsing religion, which the establishment clause forbids, and *private* speech endorsing religion, which the free speech and free exercise clauses protect.''[39]

[handwritten margin note: EAA was the response to Widmar v. US. v. Vincent]

The EAA was championed by the religious right, but homosexual groups, religious cults, and antinuclear protesters have attempted to use the Act to hold meetings in public school facilities. Fearing that controversial student groups at odds with school objectives will be granted school access under the EAA, some school boards have opted to eliminate any forum for student groups that are not an extension of the curriculum. But such efforts will not go unchallenged, as the definition of ''curriculum related'' remains open to multiple interpretations.

For more than two decades prior to the *Mergens* decision, the federal judiciary found no constitutional distinction between school authorities actually organizing religious activities and simply permitting students to do so; both practices under the auspices of the public school violated the establishment clause.[40] But the *Mergens* ruling represents a departure from the strict governmental neutrality toward religion that characterized earlier public school decisions. According to Justice Stevens, who wrote the sole dissenting opinion in *Mergens,* the majority came ''perilously close to an outright command to allow organized prayer . . . on school premises.''[41]

DISTRIBUTION OF RELIGIOUS LITERATURE

The Supreme Court has not addressed the distribution of religious literature in public schools, but a number of lower courts have prohibited religious sects from distributing materials to captive student audiences.

For example, several courts have struck down school board policies allowing the Gideon Society to visit schools and present Bibles to students who wish to accept them.[42] However, an Illinois federal district court held that school authorities could not prohibit the distribution of Gideon Bibles on the sidewalk in front of a high school. Even though the sidewalk was owned by the school, it was considered a public forum for use by the general public.[43]

More controversial are requests by *students* to distribute religious publications. Like meetings of student-initiated religious groups, these requests pit free speech protections against establishment clause restrictions. Some courts have applied the same legal principles to students' distribution of religious and nonreligious literature. A Colorado federal district court held that high school students had a free expression right to distribute a religious newsletter as long as the activity did not create a disturbance.[44] Also finding the distribution of religious literature to be protected speech, a Pennsylvania federal district court held that students were entitled to distribute religious material during noninstructional time.[45]

In contrast, a California appeals court held that a student religious club was not entitled to distribute its materials on the high school campus or advertise in the school's yearbook, and the United States Supreme Court declined to review this decision.[46] The state appeals court determined that the school did not maintain a limited forum for student clubs as only recognized school-related student groups were granted access to school facilities during noninstructional time. The court further concluded that even if the school had created a limited forum for noncurriculum student groups, the establishment clause would preclude using the prestige and authority of the school to advance religious causes.

RELIGIOUS DISPLAYS AND HOLIDAY OBSERVANCES

The display of religious documents and the observance of religious holidays in public schools remain controversial. In 1980 the Supreme Court declined to hear an appeal of a decision allowing religious holiday observances and the temporary display of religious symbols in public education,[47] but a week later, the divided Court struck down a Kentucky law calling for the posting of the Ten Commandments in public school classrooms.[48] In the first case, the historical and cultural significance of Christmas convinced the Eighth Circuit Court of Appeals that the prudent and objective observance of this holiday in public schools does not serve to advance religion, even though songs such as "Silent Night" are sung and the nativity scene is displayed.[49] The appeals court held that the school board's policy, allowing the observance of holidays with both a religious and a secular basis, had the nonreligious purpose of improving the overall instructional program. The court noted that much of the art, literature, and music associated with Christmas has acquired cultural importance that is no longer strictly religious.

In contrast, the five-member Supreme Court majority in the second case was not persuaded that the Ten Commandments' cultural significance justified posting this religious document in public schools.[50] Distinguishing the display of religious texts from the permissible use of religious literature in academic courses, the majority held that the purpose behind the Kentucky legislation was to advance a particular religious faith in violation of the establishment clause. The majority rejected the state judiciary's conclusion that the constitutional impairment was neutralized because the copies were purchased with private donations and carried the disclaimer that "[t]he secular application of the Ten Commandments is clearly seen in its adoption as the fundamental legal code of Western Civilization and the common law of the United States."[51]

In more recent decisions outside the school domain the Supreme Court has condoned the use of public funds or property for certain religious observances. For example, in 1984 the Court upheld the use of municipal funds to erect a Christmas display with the nativity scene in a private park, finding the creche to be a "traditional," rather than sectarian, holiday symbol.[52] The Court also divided evenly in a 1985 case, thus affirming the Second Circuit Appellate Court's decision, allowing two citizens' groups to display a creche in a public park during the Christmas season.[53] In 1989 the Supreme Court upheld the display in front of a government building of a menorah along with a Christmas tree and a sign declaring the city's salute to liberty, concluding that the display simply recognized Christmas and Chanukah as part of the winter holiday season.[54] Yet, in the same case the Court struck down a display of the nativity scene with a banner proclaiming "Gloria in Excelsis Deo" in the county courthouse as endorsing a patently Christian message. Although these decisions leave some ambiguity as to what distinguishes permissible from prohibited activities in the public school setting, school authorities would be well advised to ensure that holiday displays do not convey a religious message.

RELIGIOUS INSTRUCTION

Public school educators must adhere to establishment clause restrictions on governmental promotion of religious creeds. Because teachers have a captive audience in public schools, their actions have been scrutinized to ensure that classrooms are not used as a forum to indoctrinate sectarian beliefs. Choper has noted that the academic study of religion cannot "take the form of teaching 'that religion is sacred' nor present religious dogma as factual material."[55] The establishment clause clearly prohibits teachers from using their position of authority to influence students' religious beliefs.

As early as 1918 the Iowa Supreme Court concluded that Catholic nuns who were serving as public school teachers were unconstitutionally proselytizing students by teaching sectarian subjects.[56] More recently, the Supreme Court declined to review a decision in which the Eleventh Circuit Court of Appeals enjoined teacher-initiated devotional activities in an Alabama school district. The court reasoned that since public school teachers function as agents of the state, their actions—whether self-initiated or directed by the school board—are subject to establishment clause restrictions.[57] In 1990, the Tenth Circuit Court of Appeals also held that school officials could order the removal of religiously oriented books from a teacher's classroom library and require the teacher to keep his Bible out of sight and to refrain from silently reading it during school hours.[58] The same year the Seventh Circuit Court of Appeals rejected a junior high school teacher's claim that he had a constitutional right to teach the Biblical theory of creation in his social studies classes; the school board's prohibition on teaching nonevolutionary theory was considered appropriate because of establishment clause concerns.[59]

In several cases, teachers have been discharged for crossing the line from teaching *about* religion to proselytization. For example, a New York appeals court upheld the dismissal of a tenured teacher based on evidence that she had tried to recruit students to join her religious organization, conducted prayer sessions in her office, and used her classroom to promote her religious faith.[60] The South Dakota Supreme Court also upheld the nonrenewal of a biology teacher for devoting too much instructional time to the Biblical account of creation.[61] Recognizing that the teacher willfully disregarded repeated warnings to follow the school board's guidelines for teaching biology and to limit his discussion of the Genesis account, the court held that all procedural requirements were met prior to the personnel action. The judiciary has recognized that while an individual's freedom to *hold* religious beliefs is absolute, the establishment clause bars public school teachers' use of the "power, prestige, and influence" of their position to lead devotional activities.[62]

Teachers also can be discharged for disregarding selected aspects of the curriculum that conflict with their religious values. The Seventh Circuit Court of Appeals upheld a school board's dismissal of a kindergarten teacher who refused to teach patriotic topics for religious reasons, and the Supreme Court declined to review the case.[63] The teacher, who interpreted literally the Biblical prohibition against worshiping graven images, refused to teach about the American flag, the observance of patriotic holidays, and the importance of historical figures such as Abraham Lincoln. The appellate court noted that although the teacher enjoys the freedom to hold such beliefs, she has "no constitutional right to require others to submit to her views and to forego a portion of their education they would otherwise be entitled to enjoy."[64] The court further recognized that if all teachers were allowed to design their own curriculum based on their personal beliefs, students would receive a "distorted and unbalanced view of our country's history."[65]

The Constitution protects teachers' rights to exercise their religious beliefs, but their professional conduct is subject to regulation in the interest of maintaining an appropriate educational environment. Courts have rendered conflicting opinions, however, regarding whether teachers can be prohibited from wearing religious attire in public schools.[66]

Although proselytization of students by public school teachers violates the establishment clause, it is permissible to teach the Bible and other religious documents from a literary, cultural, or historical perspective. When daily Bible reading was barred from public schools in 1963, the Supreme Court emphasized that the academic study of religion is permissible and, indeed, desirable.[67]

Several studies in the latter 1980s indicated that the role of religion in the development of Western civilization is given insufficient and inaccurate treatment in textbooks and courses in part due to fear of violating first amendment restrictions.[68] Responding to these studies, in 1988 a coalition of national education and religious groups distributed a pamphlet describing proper, constitutional methods for public school instruction about the role of religion in society.[69] In conjunction with national efforts, a number of states have enacted or are considering policies to strengthen instruction about religion in the curriculum.[70]

However, the line is not always clear between teaching *about* religion and *instilling* religious tenets. Although comparative religion courses have seldom been controversial, numerous Bible study courses have been challenged as a ploy to advance sectarian beliefs. Courts have carefully evaluated curricular materials and even reviewed video tapes of lessons in determining whether such instruction fosters a particular creed. Courts consistently have struck down programs where private groups have controlled the hiring and supervision of personnel and the selection of curricular materials.[71] With evidence that religious tenets are being advanced in a course, the judiciary has required that the curriculum be redesigned to ensure that the subject matter is approached from an academic perspective.[72]

EXCUSAL FROM PUBLIC SCHOOL FOR RELIGIOUS INSTRUCTION AND OBSERVANCES

Although the Supreme Court has struck down the practice of using public school classrooms for clergy to provide religious training to public school students during the instructional day,[73] the Court has recognized that the school can accommodate religion by releasing students to receive such religious training *off* public school grounds. Noting that the state must not be hostile toward religion, the Court declared in 1952 that "when the state encourages religious instruction or cooperates with religious authorities by adjusting the schedule of public events to sectarian needs, it follows the best of our traditions.'[74] A release-time program was even upheld in a school district where students received an hour of religious instruction each week in a mobile unit parked at the edge of school property.[75] Courts have not been persuaded that academic instruction comes to a halt during the period when students are released for religious instruction, thus denying nonparticipating pupils their state created right to an education.[76] Confining students to a single choice of attending religious classes or remaining in the public school has not been found to advance religion.[77]

While upholding a release-time program in Utah, the Tenth Circuit Court of Appeals enjoined the school's practice of awarding course credit in the public high school for the secular aspects of daily instruction received at a Mormon seminary.[78] The court ruled that the award of credit for portions of the religious instruction would entangle school officials with the church because of the monitoring necessary to determine what parts of the courses were sectarian. However, the court reasoned that the time spent by students in the seminary program could be counted in satisfying compulsory school attendance and in calculating the school's eligibility for state aid.

Requests for students and teachers to be excused from public schools to observe religious holidays raise particularly delicate issues because such requests usually are made by members of minority sects; schools are closed when the majority of teachers and students are observing their religious holidays. Courts have been called on to determine how far public school authorities *must* go in accommodating religious holidays and how far they *can* go before such accommodations abridge the establishment clause.

Most litigation in this arena has involved claims by teachers that leave policies are discriminatory in their treatment of religious absences; such claims are addressed in Chapter 9. A few cases, however, have focused on students. In 1982 the Fifth Circuit Court of Appeals affirmed a federal district court's decision striking down a school's policy that allowed students only two excused absences for religious holidays.[79] The policy was challenged by student members of the Worldwide Church of God, a sect requiring observance of several holy days and a week-long religious convocation. The court found that the school's interests in promoting regular attendance and protecting teachers from extra work were not sufficiently compelling to justify requiring students to take unexcused absences to observe their religious holidays. Also rejected was the school's contention that allowing the absences would advance a particular faith in violation of the establishment clause.

The judiciary, however, has not condoned excessive student absences for religious reasons. For example, a Pennsylvania court rejected parents' request for their children to be absent every Friday, which is the sacred day of the Islamic religion.[80] Finding that the state could not assure an adequate education for children who miss one-fifth of instructional time, the court held that the state's interest in providing continuity in instruction prevailed over the parents' free exercise rights.

Also, courts have not been receptive to attempts to avoid school attendance altogether for religious reasons. The Virginia Supreme Court recognized that "no amount of religious fervor . . . in opposition to adequate instruction should be allowed to work a lifelong injury" to children.[81] Although parents can select private education for their children, courts have rejected parental claims that they have a first amendment right to *disregard* compulsory education laws in order to shield their children from the secular influences in public schools.[82] As discussed previously, the one judicially endorsed exception to attendance involves Amish children who have successfully completed eighth grade. In exempting the Amish from two additional years of compulsory education, the Supreme Court emphasized the uniqueness of the Amish lifestyle.[83]

RELIGIOUS EXEMPTIONS FROM PUBLIC SCHOOL ACTIVITIES

Teachers and other school employees have initiated a few requests for exemptions from public school activities that offend their religious beliefs, but most exemptions have been sought for students. Parents have asked that their children be excused from particular requirements that allegedly impair the practice of their religious tenets. In evaluating whether such requests must be honored by school authorities, courts have attempted to balance parents' interests in directing the religious upbringing of their children against the state's interest in ensuring an educated citizenry.

Courts have found free exercise rights overriding in striking down required student participation in certain public school activities and observances. In a landmark 1943 case, *West Virginia State Board of Education v. Barnette,* the Supreme Court ruled that students could not be required to salute the American flag in contravention of their religious beliefs.[84] This decision overturned a precedent established by the Court only three years earlier.[85] In *Barnette,* the Court held that refusal to participate in the flag-salute ceremony does not interfere with the rights of others to do so or threaten any type of disruption. Thus, state action to compel this observance unconstitutionally "invades the sphere of intellect and spirit" that the first amendment is designed "to reserve from all official control."[86] Based on *Barnette,* several courts subsequently have protected students' rights not only to decline to participate for religious or philosophical reasons in the flag-salute ceremony, but also to register a silent protest by remaining seated during the observance.[87] Of course, if students should carry the silent protest to an extreme, such as lying down during the observance, the threat of classroom disruption could justify curtailing such conduct.

Although the Supreme Court has not directly addressed teachers' free exercise rights in connection with patriotic observances in public schools, several lower courts have adopted the *Barnette* rationale in concluding that teachers, like students, have a first amendment right to refuse to pledge allegiance as a matter of personal conscience.[88] However, teachers cannot deny students the opportunity to engage in this observance.

Patriotic observances have not been the only source of controversy; religious exemptions also have been sought from components of the curriculum. Whereas teachers cannot assert a free exercise right to disregard aspects of the state-prescribed curriculum,[89] the judiciary has been more receptive to students' requests for exemptions from instructional requirements. Students, unlike teachers, are compelled to attend school, and for many this means a public school. Accordingly, the judiciary has been sensitive to the fact that certain public school policies may have a coercive effect on religious practices. In balancing the interests involved, courts consider the extent that the school requirement burdens the exercise of sincere religious beliefs, the governmental justification for the requirement, and alternative means available to meet the state's objectives. School authorities must have a compelling justification to deny students an exemption from a requirement that impairs the exercise of sincere religious beliefs.

Students have been successful in securing religious exemptions from various instructional activities, such as drug education, sex education, coeducational physical education, dancing instruction, officers' training programs, and specific course assignments where alternative assignments can satisfy the instructional objectives.[90] The relief ordered in these cases has entailed the excusal of specific children, but the secular activities themselves have not been disturbed.[91] Although students often have been excused on religious grounds from instruction in human sexuality, the judiciary has not yet clarified whether the state's interest in educating all students about the transmission of acquired immune deficiency syndrome (AIDS) justifies denying religious exemptions from mandatory AIDS instruction.[92]

Religious exemptions have not been honored where they have been found unnecessary to accommodate the practice of religious tenets or where exemptions would substantially disrupt the school or students' academic progress. In an illustrative case, parents were unsuccessful in obtaining an exemption for their children from health and music courses and from classes whenever instructional media were used. The New Hampshire federal district court declared that the requested exemption could lead to disruption of the public school's instructional program.[93]

Courts also have denied religious exemptions for student athletes if an excusal from specific regulations might pose a safety hazard or interfere with the management of athletic teams.[94]

In a widely publicized 1987 case, *Mozert v. Hawkins County Public Schools,* the Sixth Circuit Court of Appeals rejected fundamentalist parents' request that their children be excused from exposure to the basal reading series used in grades two through eight in a Tennessee school district.[95] The parents claimed that the readers conflicted with their religious beliefs, and the federal district court initially granted the exemption, ruling that the offended students had a first amendment right to "opt out" of reading instruction at school and study this subject at home with their parents, as long as they made satisfactory progress on standardized reading tests. The Sixth Circuit Court of Appeals, however, reversed the decision, reasoning that the readers did not burden the students' exercise of their fundamentalist religious beliefs. As the students were not required to profess a creed or perform religious exercises, the appeals court concluded that mere exposure to the content of the readers did not place an unconstitutional burden on the exercise of their religious tenets.

Requests for religious exemptions have increased recently because of efforts by conservative parents' organizations to secure legislation authorizing such exemptions. As discussed in Chapter 3, these groups have pressed for state pupil protection laws that require parental permission for children to participate in certain instructional activities that might offend religious, moral, or social values. They also have urged parents to rely on the 1978 amendment (Hatch Amendment) to the General Education Provisions Act, which entitles children to be excused from federally funded instruction involving psychiatric or psychological testing or treatment designed to reveal information in specified sensitive areas.[96] Thus, parents may be able to use statutory grounds to secure an exemption for their children from a specific instructional activity, even if they cannot substantiate that the activity impairs free exercise rights.

RELIGIOUS CHALLENGES TO THE SECULAR CURRICULUM

Some parents have not been content with securing religious exemptions for their own children and have pressed for elimination of various courses, activities, and instructional materials from public schools. Although courts often have been receptive to requests for individual exemptions from specific public school activities, the judiciary has not been inclined to allow the restriction of the secular curriculum to satisfy parents' religious preferences. In 1968, the Supreme Court recognized that "the state has no legitimate interest in protecting any or all religions from views distasteful to them."[97]

Recent challenges to the curriculum, however, raise complex questions involving what constitutes religious beliefs and practices that are subject to first amendment protections and restrictions. The Supreme Court has adopted an expansive view toward religion in some cases protecting the free exercise of beliefs,[98] but it has not yet found an establishment clause violation in connection with a nontheistic creed.[99] Only one federal appellate court has ruled that a public school curricular offering (instruction in transcendental meditation) unconstitutionally advances a nontraditional religious belief,[100] but several other courts have suggested that secular religions should be subjected to the same standards that are applied to theistic religions in determining whether the establishment clause has been breached.[101]

Allegations are increasing that aspects of the public school curriculum violate the establishment clause because they advance an antitheistic belief or "secular humanism," which disavows God and exalts humans as masters of their own destinies.[102] Evolution, sex education, and values clarification have been central targets, but few aspects of the curriculum have remained untouched by such claims. Those who have attacked humanistic aspects of the curriculum often have asked for the elimination of the offensive secular activities and their replacement with observances and instruction that promote the Christian faith. It has been asserted that because "secular humanism" is so pervasive in the public school curriculum, Christian doctrine also should be taught to give students a choice.[103] Courts, however, have not yet concluded that if, in fact, a secular religion is being unconstitutionally advanced, introduction of theistic instruction will remedy the constitutional infirmity.[104]

Even courts acknowledging that secular humanism may be a "religion" for first amendment purposes have not been persuaded that challenged public school courses and materials are advancing this creed. For example, in 1985 the Ninth Circuit Court of Appeals stated without explanation that secular humanism may be a religion, but rejected the assertion that the public school was promoting this antitheistic creed through a book used in the English curriculum.[105] The court found that Gordon Parks' *The Learning Tree,* detailing the struggles of a black youth, was religiously neutral and related to legitimate educational objectives.

In a 1987 case that attracted substantial media attention, the Eleventh Circuit Court of Appeals reversed an Alabama federal judge's conclusion that secular humanism was being unconstitutionally advanced in the Mobile County schools.[106] The judge had enjoined the school district's use of several dozen home economics, history, and social studies books found to advance secular humanism. The appellate court held that the books at issue did not promote an antitheistic creed but rather instilled "in Alabama public school children such values as independent thought, tolerance of diverse views, self-respect, maturity, self-reliance and logical decision-making."[107] In essence, the appeals court concluded that the materials challenged as advancing secular humanism were simply promoting sound education. The court further rejected the contention that the mere omission of religious facts in the curriculum represented unconstitutional hostility toward theistic beliefs.

Sex education classes have been particularly susceptible to charges that an antitheistic faith is being advanced, but courts have not endorsed these claims. In rejecting challenges to the inclusion of sex education in the curriculum, courts consistently have found that the courses in question present public health information that furthers legitimate educational objectives.[108] The judiciary also has ruled that the establishment clause precludes the state from barring such instruction simply to conform to the religious beliefs of some parents. In an illustrative case, the New Jersey Supreme Court unanimously endorsed the state's comprehensive sex education mandate, finding nothing in the curriculum guidelines suggesting antagonism toward Christianity.[109] However, the judiciary has acknowledged that students have a free exercise right to be excused from sex education classes if such instruction conflicts with their sectarian beliefs.[110]

Instruction pertaining to evolution also has been challenged as advancing a secular faith. Historically, some states by law barred evolution from the curriculum because it conflicted with the Biblical account of creation. In the famous Scopes "Monkey Trial" in 1927, the Tennessee Supreme Court upheld such a law, prohibiting the teaching of any theory that denies the Genesis version of creation or suggests "that man has descended from a lower order of animals."[111] In 1968, however, the United States Supreme Court struck down an Arkansas anti-evolution statute under the establishment clause, reasoning that evolution is science (not a secular religion) and a state cannot restrict student access to such information simply to satisfy religious preferences.[112]

Since creationists have been unable to convince the judiciary that evolution unconstitutionally advances a secular faith, recent efforts have focused on securing laws that require equal emphasis on the Biblical account of creation whenever evolution is taught in public schools. In 1987 the Supreme Court invalidated such a Louisiana statute; the law mandated "equal time" for creation science and evolution and required school boards to make available curriculum guides, teaching aids, and resource materials on creation science.[113] The Court concluded that the law was intended to discredit scientific information and advance religious beliefs in violation of the establishment clause. Rejecting the argument that the law promoted academic freedom, the Court reasoned that it actually inhibited teachers' discretion to incorporate scientific theories about the origin of humanity into the curriculum.

As discussed in Chapter 3, courts have not condoned parental attacks on various aspects of the public school curriculum that do not conform to their religious values, but more difficult legal questions are raised when *policymakers* support curriculum restrictions for religious reasons. Since courts show considerable deference to legislatures and school boards in educational matters, conservative parent organizations have pressed for state and federal legislation and school board policies barring instruction that allegedly conflicts with Christian doctrine.[114] There is some concern among educators that neutral, *nonreligious* instruction in public schools may be threatened by such efforts.

GOVERNMENTAL REGULATION OF PRIVATE SCHOOLS

Unquestionably parents have a legitimate interest in directing the upbringing of their children, including their education. In 1925 the Supreme Court afforded constitutional protection to private schools' rights to exist and to parents' rights to select private education as an alternative to public schooling. Yet, the Court also recognized that the state has a general welfare interest in mandating school attendance and regulating private education to ensure an educated citizenry, considered essential in a democracy.[115] Volatile disputes have resulted from conflicts between the state's exercise of its *parens patriae* authority to protect the welfare of children and parental interests in having their children educated in settings that reinforce their religious and philosophical beliefs. If the government interferes with parents' childrearing decisions, it must show that the intervention is necessary to protect the child or the state.[116] Since state regulation of home education programs is addressed in Chapter 3, the discussion here is confined to state regulation of private schools.

Currently, over 12 percent of all K–12 students attend private schools, about 85 percent of which are church-related.[117] Recent controversies over state regulation of religious schools have focused primarily on evangelical/fundamentalist academies and their refusal to comply with state standards, often resulting in the prosecution of parents for violating compulsory attendance mandates. The parents have asserted that the first amendment's prohibition against governmental action interfering with the free exercise of religion precludes the state from imposing regulations that threaten the sectarian mission of religious schools.

The Supreme Court has not clarified the scope of the state's authority and duty to regulate the *means* by which all children receive an education, and state courts have rendered conflicting opinions in this domain. For example, the Ohio Supreme Court invalidated comprehensive state regulations governing practically all aspects of the educational process in private schools as interfering with free exercise rights.[118] The Kentucky Supreme Court also struck down the application of certain state regulations to private schools, reasoning that the regulations interfered with the state constitutional guarantee that parents cannot be compelled to send their children to a school to which they may be conscientiously opposed.[119] The court suggested that the state should monitor the quality of secular education in private schools by requiring all students to take an examination; if students from a particular school consistently score poorly, grounds might be established for closing that school.

However, the supreme courts of Hawaii, Iowa, Michigan, Nebraska, North Dakota, and Vermont have upheld state minimum requirements (e.g., teacher certification standards, prescribed courses, maintenance of pupil records) for private schools, recognizing the state's obligation to ensure an educated citizenry.[120] In 1990 the United States Supreme Court declined to review a ruling in which the First Circuit Court of Appeals held that a religious academy must allow officials of the local school district to review its curricula and operations.[121] The review was pursuant to a Massachusetts law stipulating that religious schools must provide an education comparable to that offered in public schools, and the appeals court concluded that the law represented a reasonable exercise of the state's regulatory authority. Also, the Eighth Circuit Court of Appeals upheld an Iowa requirement that teachers in church schools must be certified by the state, and on remand, the federal district court also upheld regulations prescribing the curriculum in such schools.[122] Several of these decisions have been appealed to the Supreme Court, but the high court has declined to render an opinion on this subject.

Although most controversies over governmental regulation of private schools have involved state efforts to impose personnel and curriculum requirements, some disputes have focused on whether the first amendment entitles religious schools to special treatment under legislation governing other private employers. The Supreme Court has interpreted the Federal Unemployment Tax Act (a cooperative federal–state tax program providing benefits for unemployed workers) as exempting religious schools with no separate identity from the parent church.[123] The Court also has ruled that the National Labor Relations Board does not have jurisdiction over lay faculty in religious schools because Congress did not clearly specify such jurisdiction.[124] The Court resolved both of these cases based on its assessment of congressional intent, thus avoiding the issue of whether such exemptions would be *required* by the first amendment.

Several lower courts, however, have addressed church schools' assertions that the first amendment entitles them to special treatment under state or federal laws. The Second Circuit Court of Appeals concluded that the religion clauses do not preclude the New York Labor Relations Board from exerting jurisdiction over lay faculty in religious schools.[125] Some state high courts also have rejected first amendment claims that religious schools are exempt from tax assessments under state unemployment tax laws.[126] In addition, courts have held that religious schools' compliance with federal minimum wage and equal pay provisions of the Fair Labor Standards Act would not necessitate excessive governmental entanglement with religion or impair free exercise rights.[127] The judiciary also has ruled that private schools are subject to state and federal laws that protect employees against adverse employment consequences based on their race, gender, or age.[128]

An issue that has generated some controversy concerns whether the federal government can compel private schools to conform to national public policy as a condition of receiving federal tax-exempt status. In 1983, the Supreme Court held that private schools found to be practicing racial discrimination cannot receive recognition as tax-exempt entities, which would in effect confer a governmental benefit on such institutions. The Court concluded that the government's overriding, fundamental interest in eradicating racial discrimination outweighs any burden that the denial of tax-exempt status places on the schools' free exercise rights.[129] The Court declared that it would be "wholly incompatible with the concepts underlying tax exemption to grant the benefit of tax-exempt status to racially discriminatory private educational entities.[130]

This decision raised some concerns that sectarian schools might be required to conform to other national policies, such as prohibitions against sex discrimination, even if such mandates interfere with the religious mission of the schools. However, few schools actually have been denied tax-exempt status because of their discriminatory practices,[131] and considerable ambiguity still surrounds public policy considerations that must be satisfied by private schools as a condition of tax-exempt status.

GOVERNMENTAL AID TO PRIVATE SCHOOLS

There have been regular legislative attempts to provide public support for private schools, particularly in states with large private school populations, such as New York, Ohio, and Pennsylvania. Over three-fourths of the states provide public aid to private education, with the primary types being aid for transportation services, the loan of textbooks, state-required testing programs, special education for handicapped children, and guidance counseling.[132]

Although many private schools continue to seek various types of governmental financial support, some fundamentalist academies desire absolute autonomy from the government, fearing governmental control as an unavoidable condition of any type of financial assistance. Thus, there is a division among private school advocates in that some seek greater public support and adherence to government standards, while others eschew any type of aid and its accompanying regulations.[133]

Advocates of state aid to private education assert that parents should have educational choices, which are foreclosed to all but the wealthy without governmental assistance. It also is argued that private schools deserve public aid because they perform an important educational service in providing high-quality instruction and offering some relief to overburdened public schools. Critics of governmental aid to nonpublic schools have voiced concerns that such aid undermines public education and nurtures class and racial segregation in schools. However, the central argument against government support of private education is that the aid advances religion in violation of the establishment clause, since the vast majority of private schools are church-related.

The future prospects for governmental support of private education depend largely upon the Supreme Court's assessment of whether specific types of aid violate the first amendment. Some of the most significant Supreme Court decisions interpreting the establishment clause have pertained to the use of public funds for private—primarily sectarian—education. The following discussion focuses on the legality of two types of governmental assistance for nonpublic education: aid for student services in parochial schools and aid to encourage family educational choice.

AID FOR STUDENT SERVICES

Although the Supreme Court in the mid-twentieth century adopted Thomas Jefferson's metaphor that the establishment clause was intended to create a wall of separation between church and state,[134] several types of public assistance that primarily benefit *students* rather than religious *institutions* have received judicial endorsement. For example, the Supreme Court relied on the child-benefit doctrine in upholding the use of public funds to provide transportation services for nonpublic school students.[135] The Court equated the provision of school transportation with other public services such as police and fire protection. Some courts even have upheld special transportation accommodations for nonpublic school students, such as transporting these pupils when public schools are closed for vacation and providing private school transportation beyond public school district boundaries.[136]

However, the fact that courts have interpreted the establishment clause as allowing public aid to transport nonpublic school students does not mean that states *must* use public funds for this purpose. Courts in states such as Alaska, Missouri, Oklahoma, and Washington have ruled that transportation aid to private school students violates state constitutional provisions prohibiting the use of public funds for sectarian purposes.[137]

Similar to transportation aid, the Supreme Court has relied on the child-benefit doctrine in upholding the loan of textbooks, bought with public funds, to private school children. In 1968 the Court recognized that books are integral to a school's instructional program, but nonetheless the majority concluded that the loan of textbooks to private school students aids the child and not the religious enterprise.[138] Although this practice is permissible under the establishment clause, a number of state courts have invalidated this type of aid under their state constitutions.[139] In 1981 the California Supreme Court called the child-benefit doctrine "logically indefensible" in striking down a state law that provided for the loan of textbooks to nonpublic school students.[140]

In addition to finding that the establishment clause does not prohibit governmental assistance in providing transportation and textbooks for private school students, the Supreme Court has concluded that several other types of aid also are constitutionally permissible. For example, in 1977 the Court upheld a state law allowing the use of public funds to purchase reusable workbooks and manuals for loan to private schools and the provision of diagnostic services in nonpublic schools. The Court also endorsed the provision of therapeutic services for private school students, but concluded that such services must be performed in a public school or at a neutral site off private school premises. The Court reasoned that occasional diagnostic services performed in a sectarian school pose little threat of advancing religion, whereas regular therapeutic services might be used for religious purposes if offered in a "pervasively sectarian atmosphere."[141]

In 1980 the Court upheld New York's distribution of up to $20 million to private schools for the cost of record-keeping and testing services mandated by the state.[142] The Court distinguished this decision from its 1973 rejection of a New York law that provided state aid for teacher-developed tests as well as standardized tests.[143] The Court reasoned that teacher-developed tests would be extremely difficult to monitor and would necessitate excessive government entanglement to ensure that they were not used for sectarian purposes. In contrast, the subsequent law providing state aid *only* for standardized tests and record-keeping practices was found to pose little danger of advancing the religious mission of sectarian schools.

While the Supreme Court has upheld several types of state aid to private school students, aid that directly subsidizes religious schools or excessively entangles the state with sectarian affairs has not been allowed. Applying the tripartite test during the 1970s, the Court struck down measures allowing direct reimbursement for the costs of teachers' salaries, textbooks, and instructional materials in specified secular subjects; salary supplements for nonpublic school teachers of secular subjects; grants for the maintenance and repair of school facilities; tuition reimbursements to parents of nonpublic school pupils; the direct loan of instructional materials and audiovisual equipment to nonpublic schools; the provision of auxiliary programs, such as guidance counseling, speech and hearing services, and remedial instruction on private school premises; and state aid for field trip transportation.[144] In most of these cases, the Court majority concluded that the proposed aid would provide an impermissible subsidy to religious schools or would necessitate extensive governmental monitoring of parochial schools to ensure that the aid would support only secular activities.[145]

In 1985 the Supreme Court delivered two significant decisions, maintaining a commitment to the tripartite test and to church-state separation in connection with the use of public funds to provide parochial school services. In *School District of City of Grand Rapids v. Ball,* the Court affirmed a decision in which the Sixth Circuit Court of Appeals invalidated an extensive shared-time program in a Michigan school district.[146] Under the challenged program, the public school district rented space from forty parochial schools and one independent private school to offer a variety of enrichment and remedial courses to students who were enrolled in the private schools for the remainder of their instruction. The shared-time teachers were full-time public schools employees, and a "significant portion" previously taught in the nonpublic schools where they were assigned under the shared-time arrangement. Also at issue was a community education program offered at the close of the regular school day in classrooms leased from the private schools; virtually all the teachers were otherwise employed by the private schools where the community education classes were taught. Rejecting the argument that the challenged governmental aid flowed to the students rather than the religious institutions, the Court majority held that aid for instructional services in the parochial school building inescapably has the primary effect of providing a "direct and substantial advancement of the sectarian enterprise."[147] Although the Court invalidated shared-time programs under which public school districts in effect subsidize parochial schools, private school students can still participate in publicly supported auxiliary services provided at public schools or neutral sites.

In the second case, *Aguilar v. Felton,* the Supreme Court ended over a decade of litigation involving New York City's use of federal funds to provide services for private school students under Title I of the Elementary and Secondary Education Act of 1965.[148] Title I (which became Chapter 1 of the Education Consolidation and Improvement Act of 1981) provides funds for compensatory education programs in school districts with concentrations of low-income families.[149] To receive these funds, local education agencies must meet certain requirements, including the provision of comparable services for eligible students in private schools. The Court ruled that the use of publicly funded instructors to teach Title I classes composed exclusively of private school students in private school buildings advances religion and creates excessive governmental entanglement between church and state because of (1) the frequent contacts between public and private school personnel required to implement the program, and (2) the monitoring necessary to guarantee that only secular instruction is provided by public school teachers in religious schools. The Court declared that "the scope and duration of New York's Title I program would require a permanent and pervasive state presence in the sectarian schools receiving aid.''[150]

The Supreme Court did not invalidate the provision of comparable services for private school children under Title I/Chapter 1, but it did eliminate one option for providing such services. In light of this decision, remedial programs provided for parochial school students must be offered at public schools or neutral sites, or some other arrangement must be devised to meet the comparability requirement. In response to *Aguilar,* the United States Department of Education issued guidelines stipulating that federal funds can be used to purchase vans and mobile classrooms to provide services for private school students and that such expenses must be taken off the top of a state's Chapter 1 basic grants before allocating the remainder among public and private schools. These guidelines have generated conflicting lower court rulings, and in 1991 the Eighth Circuit Court of Appeals became the first federal appellate court to address the issue, upholding the guidelines' constitutionality.[151] The appeals court also ruled that the provision of remedial education services to private school students in mobile or portable classrooms located on *parochial* school property does not violate the establishment clause.

Also controversial have been federal allocations under Chapter 2 of the same law, which consolidates about forty former categorical programs into block grants to the states, 80 percent of which must flow to local education agencies for distribution to public and private schools. A federal district court struck down Louisiana's method of distributing Chapter 2 block grants as subsidizing religious schools in violation of the establishment clause.[152] The judge also invalidated a Louisiana program that provides materials, supplies, and equipment to parochial schools because the materials could be used for religious purposes. However, a California federal district court upheld the use of Chapter 2 funds at a group home for pregnant teens located on the premises of a religiously affiliated organization.[153]

Other federal aid programs that provide funds to students in parochial schools may also be vulnerable to first amendment attack. For example, a number of parochial school students have received instruction from public school teachers under the Individuals with Disabilities Education Act; given the *Aguilar* ruling, many of these services have been moved to neutral or public school sites. In 1988 the New York Court of Appeals held that children with disabilities attending a Satmar Hasidic school who were brought to the public school to receive remedial services were not entitled to be taught in settings segregated from non-Hasidic students.[154]

While the Supreme Court majority strictly applied the establishment clause in *Aguilar* and *Ball*, in a 1988 decision the Court appeared more receptive to governmental aid that flows to religious institutions. The Court in *Bowen v. Kendrick* upheld the facial validity of the Adolescent Family Life Act (AFLA), under which public and private agencies and organizations can receive federal grants to conduct research and provide educational and counseling services to reduce teenage sexual activity and pregnancy.[155] Rejecting the contention that the Act violates the establishment clause because some of the aid goes to religious organizations to provide the services, the Court majority concluded that the law had the secular purpose of reducing problems associated with teenage sexuality and pregnancy, did not advance religion despite the significant number of church-affiliated grantees, and did not require excessive governmental monitoring of sectarian affairs. The case was remanded for a determination of whether individual grants were administered in a constitutionally offensive manner.

Given the severely divided Supreme Court in decisions involving state aid to nonpublic schools since the 1970s, a discernible judicial trend in this area is difficult to identify. It appears that aid constituting a direct subsidy to religious schools violates the establishment clause, but criteria have not been provided to distinguish such impermissible aid from permissible aid that benefits the child. The Court's opinions in this domain have been criticized as "ad hoc," lacking theoretical consistency and firm constitutional grounding.[156] In 1985 Supreme Court Justice Rehnquist noted some of the anomalies:

> For example, a state may lend to parochial school children geography textbooks that contain maps of the United States, but the state may not lend maps of the United States for use in geography class. A state may lend textbooks on American colonial history, but it may not lend a film on George Washington, or a film projector to show it in history class. . . . Exceptional parochial school students may receive counseling, but it must take place outside of the parochial school, such as in a trailer parked down the street. A state may give cash to a parochial school to pay for the administration of state-written tests and state-ordered reporting services, but it may not provide funds for teacher-prepared tests on secular subjects (citations omitted).[157]

In recent cases the legality of given practices often has hinged on one vote. Without clear directives from the high court distinguishing permissible from prohibited types of governmental aid for private school services, continued legislative activity in this arena seems assured.

AID TO ENCOURAGE EDUCATIONAL CHOICE

Fearing that direct subsidies to private schools will be judicially struck down, private school advocates have pressed for indirect aid to make private schooling a viable choice for more families. Tax-relief measures for private school tuition and educational vouchers have received considerable attention in legislative forums.

Tax-Relief Measures. Tax benefits in the form of deductions or credits for private school expenses have been proposed at both state and federal levels. While Congress has not yet endorsed any proposals for federal income tax credits for private school tuition,[158] several states have enacted tax-relief measures for educational expenses. These state laws have generated two Supreme Court decisions and considerable activity in lower courts. The central constitutional question is whether such tax-relief measures advance religion in violation of the establishment clause because the primary beneficiaries are parents of parochial school children and ultimately religious institutions.

In 1973 the Supreme Court struck down a New York statute that allowed parents of private school students a state income tax benefit; they could subtract from their adjusted gross income a designated amount for each dependent for whom they had paid at least $50 in nonpublic school tuition.[159] Recognizing that over 85 percent of New York's private schools were sectarian, the Court concluded that the measure aided religion by rewarding parents who send their children to parochial schools.

A decade later, however, the Supreme Court upheld a Minnesota tax benefit program allowing parents of public or private school students to claim a limited state income tax deduction for educational expenses incurred for each elementary or secondary school dependent. The five-member Court majority in *Mueller v. Allen* found the Minnesota law "vitally different" from the earlier New York provision which bestowed benefits *only* on private school patrons.[160] The majority declared that "a state's decision to defray the cost of educational expenses incurred by parents—regardless of the type of schools their children attend—evidences a purpose that is both secular and understandable."[161] The majority opined that such state assistance to a "broad spectrum of citizens" does not have the primary effect of advancing religion, noting that most prior decisions invalidating state aid to parochial schools involved the direct transmission of public funds to such schools.

Seventeen states considered tax-deduction packages similar to the Minnesota program within a year after the *Mueller* decision, but none was enacted. Despite polls indicating considerable public support for tuition tax credits, where such measures have been subjected to a referendum, voters have not endorsed the concept.[162] For example, in 1990 Oregon voters soundly rejected a proposal that would have authorized a combination of tuition tax credits and the use of vouchers to facilitate students' attending private schools.[163] Nonetheless, continued debate over this issue at all levels of government seems assured.

Educational Vouchers. Proposals to fund education through vouchers have been introduced in Congress and several state legislatures, but to date no extensive voucher system has been implemented. Under a basic voucher plan, each elementary and secondary school student would be entitled to a voucher for a designated amount that could be redeemed at qualifying public or private schools.[164] Parents could supplement the voucher to provide a more expensive education for their children. Modifications of this basic proposal have been suggested that would vary the voucher amount based on family income, type of school selected, and/or educational needs of the student.[165] Whether such voucher proposals violate the establishment clause by advancing religious schools has not yet been litigated.

However, the likelihood that voucher systems could survive an establishment clause challenge was strengthened by the Supreme Court's 1986 decision in which all justices concurred that a visually handicapped individual could receive vocational rehabilitation aid to use for ministerial education. The Court in *Witters v. Washington Department of Services for the Blind* ruled that since the aid went directly to the student who then transmitted the funds to the educational institution of his choice, there was no advancement of sectarian education.[166] The aid was not considered a governmental subsidy to religious schools, and the student's *personal* choice to use rehabilitation aid to pursue religious education was not found to confer state endorsement on sectarian institutions.

This decision may simply be another illustration that the Supreme Court is not as likely to find an establishment clause violation in connection with governmental aid that flows to institutions of higher education than it is with aid to elementary and secondary schools.[167] However, possibly the Court will follow this precedent in upholding proposals for governmental aid to foster family choice in selecting private education below the college level.

Strategies to increase parental choice are receiving widespread attention in legislative forums, but only a few proposals to date include private schools.[168] One model being implemented in several states, "postsecondary options," provides high school students the opportunity to take courses at qualifying institutions of higher education, including religious colleges. In 1990, a federal court ruled that the Minnesota postsecondary options program was facially constitutional; the distribution of public funds to institutions that are not pervasively sectarian was found permissible under the establishment clause.[169]

Wisconsin enacted legislation in 1990 providing vouchers of $2,500 to enable up to 1,000 disadvantaged students in Milwaukee to attend nonsectarian private schools. The plan was challenged as violating the state constitutional requirement that public funds be used only for public purposes, and the circuit court judge upheld the program, reasoning that it served the legitimate public purpose of improving educational opportunities. However, the state appellate court reversed this decision on technical grounds, holding that the legislature was not authorized to attach local legislation to the state budget bill. Thus, the appeals court invalidated the choice plan without addressing the merits of the constitutional claims.[170]

Since the Supreme Court already has ruled that state tax deductions for educational expenses do not implicate the establishment clause[171] (even though the primary beneficiaries are religious school patrons), the Court might apply similar reasoning in reviewing voucher proposals. The Court may be more likely to endorse aid that flows to the individual family to encourage educational choice than aid that directly supports student services in private schools.

CONCLUSION

For the past forty years, church–state controversies have generated a steady stream of educational litigation, and there are no signs of diminishing legal activity in this domain. While some suits have involved claims under the free exercise clause, most school cases have focused on an interpretation of establishment clause prohibitions. Recent judicial action cannot easily be classified into "separation" or "accommodation" categories, but since the 1960s the federal judiciary has been more committed to enforcing establishment clause restrictions in elementary and secondary school settings than elsewhere. However, recent changes in the composition of the Court may signal a movement toward greater governmental accommodation of religion in establishment clause doctrine. The following generalizations characterize the current status of church–state relations involving schools.

1. State-imposed devotional activities in public schools, regardless of voluntary participation, violate the establishment clause.
2. Students have a free exercise right to engage in silent prayer in public schools; however, school officials cannot promote such silent devotionals.
3. Holidays with both secular and religious significance can be observed in an objective and prudent manner in public schools.
4. The Ten Commandments and other religious symbols cannot be posted permanently in public schools, and religious literature cannot be distributed under the auspices of the school.
5. Student devotional meetings held on state-supported college campuses do not abridge the establishment clause; content restrictions cannot be imposed on student-initiated meetings in a forum created for student expression.
6. If a high school that receives federal funds creates a limited open forum for student groups to meet during noninstructional time, religious clubs cannot be denied access to the forum.

7. The academic study of religion is permissible in public schools, but such instruction cannot be used as a ploy to instill religious beliefs.
8. Students can be released from public schools to receive religious instruction provided *off* public school grounds.
9. Students are entitled to excused absences to observe religious holidays as long as the absences do not place an undue hardship on the school.
10. Requests to evade compulsory school attendance mandates for religious reasons have been unsuccessful, but Amish children have been excused from mandatory schooling after successful completion of eighth grade.
11. Students can be excused from specific public school observances and activities that impede the practice of their religious beliefs if the management of the school or the students' academic progress is not disrupted.
12. Some courts have indicated that "secular humanism" may constitute a religion for first amendment purposes, but they have not ruled that challenged public school instruction (e.g., sex education, evolution) advances this faith.
13. Laws requiring equal emphasis on the Genesis account of creation when evolution is taught violate the establishment clause.
14. States have a general welfare interest in mandating school attendance to ensure an educated citizenry; however, parents have the right to select private schooling for their children.
15. States can regulate private education, but unduly restrictive regulations may impair free exercise rights.
16. Direct public subsidies to religious schools or aid that necessitates extensive governmental monitoring (e.g., auxiliary services provided in private schools, loan of audiovisual equipment, field trip transportation), violate the establishment clause.
17. Public aid for certain services that benefit the child and not the religious institution (e.g., transportation, loan of textbooks, standardized testing programs) does not violate the establishment clause.
18. Shared-time programs, under which parochial school students receive some instruction from public school teachers in facilities leased from a private school, unconstitutionally aid religious institutions.
19. Income tax deductions that reflect educational expenses associated with both private and public elementary and secondary schooling are permissible, but income tax credits for *only* private school tuition violate the establishment clause.
20. Governmental aid that encourages individual choice in education (e.g., vouchers that can be redeemed at public or private schools)

seems less vulnerable to first amendment attack than aid that
directly flows to sectarian institutions.

ENDNOTES

1. *See* Cantwell v. Connecticut, 310 U.S. 296, 303 (1940); Gitlow v. New York,
   268 U.S. 652, 666 (1925).
2. As noted in Chapter 1, the notion that the fourteenth amendment incorporates
   first amendment guarantees and applies them to state action has been
   criticized. *See* James McClellan, *Joseph Story and the American Constitution*
   (Norman, OK: University of Oklahoma Press, 1971), pp. 144–145.
3. 330 U.S. 1, 15–16 (1947). *See* text with note 135, *infra*.
4. *But see* Marsh v. Chambers, 463 U.S. 783 (1983) (the Court relied primarily on
   "tradition" rather than the tripartite test in rejecting an establishment clause
   challenge to the use of state funds to support a chaplain to open legislative
   sessions with a prayer).
5. Walz v. Tax Comm'n of the City of New York, 397 U.S. 664 (1970). The
   tripartite test was first used in an education case the following year in Lemon v.
   Kurtzman, 403 U.S. 602 (1971), and is often called the *Lemon* test.
6. *See, e.g.*, County of Allegheny v. American Civil Liberties Union, 109 S. Ct.
   3086, 3100 (1989).
7. *See* County of Allegheny, *id.* at 3134 (1989) (Kennedy, J., concurring in part,
   dissenting in part); Edwards v. Aguillard, 482 U.S. 578, 636–640 (1987) (Scalia,
   J., dissenting); Aguilar v. Felton, 473 U.S. 402, 426–430 (1985) (O'Connor, J.,
   dissenting); Wallace v. Jaffree, 472 U.S. 38, 108–113 (1985) (Rehnquist, J.,
   dissenting); Roemer v. Maryland Bd. of Public Works, 426 U.S. 736, 768–769
   (1976) (White, J., concurring in judgment). *See also* note 24, *infra*.
8. 406 U.S. 205, 214 (1972).
9. Employment Div., Dep't of Human Resources of Oregon v. Smith, 110 S. Ct.
   1595 (1990).
10. A bill has been introduced in Congress that would nullify this ruling and restore
    the "compelling governmental interest" requirement in *all* free exercise
    claims, Religious Freedom Restoration Act of 1990, H.R. 5377, 101st Cong., 2d
    Sess. (1990).
11. Walz v. Tax Comm'n of the City of New York, 397 U.S. 664, 668–669 (1970).
12. School Dist. of Abington Township v. Schempp, 374 U.S. 203 (1963); Engel v.
    Vitale, 370 U.S. 421 (1962).
13. *See* Gaines v. Anderson, 421 F. Supp. 337 (D. Mass 1976); Opinion of the
    Justices, 307 A.2d 558 (N.H. 1973).
14. May v. Cooperman, 780 F.2d 240 (3d Cir. 1985), *appeal dismissed sub nom.*
    Karcher v. May, 484 U.S. 72 (1987); Jaffree v. Wallace, 705 F.2d 1526, 1535–
    1536 (11th Cir. 1983), *aff'd*, 472 U.S. 38 (1985); Beck v. McElrath, 548 F.
    Supp. 1161 (M.D. Tenn. 1982), *appeal dismissed, vacated, and remanded*, 718
    F.2d 1098 (6th Cir. 1983); Walter v. West Virginia Bd. of Educ., 610 F. Supp.
    1169 (S.D. W. Va. 1985); Duffy v. Las Cruces Public Schools, 557 F. Supp.
    1013 (D.N.M. 1983).

15. 705 F.2d 1526 (11th Cir. 1983), *aff'd,* 472 U.S. 38 (1985). Although several state practices were contested in this case, the Supreme Court agreed to address only the silent prayer statute. *See* note 17, *infra,* for the disposition of the other issues.

16. Karcher v. May, 484 U.S. 72 (1987) (plaintiffs lacked standing to challenge the appellate court's ruling).

17. Jaffree v. Board of School Comm'rs of Mobile County, 705 F.2d 1526 (11th Cir. 1983), *cert. denied in part,* 466 U.S. 926 (1984) (teacher-initiated devotional activities); Jaffree v. Wallace, 705 F.2d 1526 (11th Cir. 1983), *aff'd mem. in part,* 466 U.S. 924 (1984) (Alabama voluntary prayer law); Karen B. v. Treen, 653 F.2d 897 (5th Cir. 1981), *aff'd mem.,* 455 U.S. 913 (1982) (Louisiana voluntary prayer law); Collins v. Chandler Unified School Dist., 644 F.2d 759 (9th Cir. 1981), *cert. denied,* 454 U.S. 863 (1981) (student-led prayers in school assemblies).

18. *See* 42 U.S.C. § 1983 (1988); Wood v. Strickland, 420 U.S. 308, 322 (1975) (public school officials cannot use ignorance of the law as a defense under Section 1983 for violating an individual's clearly established federal rights). For a discussion of liability under Section 1983, *see* text with note 166, Chapter 8.

19. Steele v. Van Buren Pub. School District, 845 F.2d 1492 (8th Cir. 1988).

20. Bell v. Little Axe Indep. School Dist. No. 70, 766 F.2d 1391, 1408–1413 (10th Cir. 1985). *But see* Memphis Community School Dist. v. Stachura, 477 U.S. 299 (1986) (compensatory damages must be based on actual injury suffered and cannot be based on the abstract value or importance of constitutional rights); text with note 199, Chapter 8.

21. Upholding invocations and benedictions during the graduation ceremony, *see* Grossberg v. Deusebio, 380 F. Supp. 285 (E.D. Va. 1974); Wiest v. Mt. Lebanon School Dist., 320 A.2d 362 (Pa. 1974), *cert. denied,* 419 U.S. 967 (1974). Upholding baccalaureate programs, *see* Chamberlin v. Dade County Bd. of Pub. Instruction, 160 So. 2d 97 (Fla. 1964), *rev'd,* 377 U.S. 402 (1964); Goodwin v. Cross County School Dist. No. 7, 394 F. Supp. 417 (E.D. Ark. 1973).

22. *See* Jones v. Clear Creek Indep. School Dist., 930 F.2d 416 (5th Cir. 1991) (student volunteers could present nonsectarian graduation prayers). *See also* Stein v. Plainwell Community Schools, 822 F.2d 1406 (6th Cir. 1987) (while voicing general approval of invocations and benedictions in graduation ceremonies, the appeals court held that the observances at issue endorsed one religious view, Christianity, in violation of the establishment clause).

23. *See* Lundberg v. West Monona Community School Dist., 731 F. Supp. 331 (N.D. Iowa 1989); Graham v. Central Community School Dist., 608 F. Supp. 531 (S.D. Iowa 1985); Sands v. Morongo Unified School Dist., 809 P.2d 809 (Cal. 1991); Kay v. David Douglas School Dist. No. 40, 719 P.2d 875 (Or. Ct. App. 1986), *vacated,* 738 P.2d 1389 (Or. 1987), *cert. denied,* 484 U.S. 1032 (1988); Bennett v. Livermore, 238 Cal. Rptr. 819 (Cal. Ct. App. 1987). *See also* Guidry v. Broussard, 897 F.2d 181 (5th Cir. 1990) (school authorities' rejection of a student's valedictory speech because it would have the primary effect of advancing religion did not violate the student's free speech rights); Smith v. Board of Educ., North Babylon Union Free School Dist., 844 F.2d 90 (2d Cir.

1988) (scheduling high school commencement exercises on a student's sabbath did not abridge the free exercise clause).

24. Weisman v. Lee, 908 F.2d 1090 (1st Cir. 1990), *cert. granted,* 111 S. Ct. 1305 (1991). The Justice Department submitted a brief asking the high court to use this case to "jettison the framework" of the tripartite test whenever "the practice under assault is a non-coercive, ceremonial acknowledgment of the heritage of a deeply religious people." Liz Armstrong, "High Court Asked to Uphold Prayer at Graduation," *Education Week,* March 6, 1991, p. 24.

25. *See* Jager v. Douglas County School Dist., 862 F.2d 824 (11th Cir. 1989), *cert. denied,* 490 U.S. 1090 (1989); Doe v. Aldine Indep. School Dist., 563 F. Supp. 883 (S.D. Tex. 1982).

26. *See* Lawrence Sager, "The Supreme Court 1980 Term, Forward: Constitutional Limitations on Congress' Authority to Regulate the Jurisdiction of the Federal Courts," *Harvard Law Review,* vol. 95 (1981), pp. 17–89. Senator Jesse Helms of North Carolina has been a central proponent of such "court-stripping" measures. *See* 135 Cong. Rec. S684 (daily ed. Jan. 25, 1989). From 1979 to 1988 there were 14 votes on court-stripping legislation, 134 Cong. Rec. S10785 (daily ed. Aug. 3, 1988).

27. Some recent controversies have also focused on requests by religious groups to use public school facilities, and a range of judicial opinions has been offered. Several courts have relied on the first amendment's free speech clause in enjoining public schools from barring religious meetings where a forum for community meetings has been established. *See* Gregoire v. Centennial School Dist., 907 F.2d 1366 (3d Cir. 1990), *cert. denied,* 111 S. Ct. 253 (1990); Deeper Life Christian Fellowship v. Board of Educ. of the City of New York, 852 F.2d 676 (2d. Cir. 1988). However, other courts have held that even though school districts allow community groups to use school faciltities, the refusal to grant access for religious services or programs advocating particular religious viewpoints serves the compelling state interest of complying with the establishment clause. *See* Lamb's Chapel v. Center Moriches Union Free School Dist., 736 F. Supp. 1247 (E.D.N.Y. 1990); Wallace v. Washoe County School Dist., 701 F. Supp. 187 (D. Nev. 1988).

28. 454 U.S. 263 (1981). For a discussion of the public forum doctrine, *see* text with note 29, Chapter 4.

29. Bender v. Williamsport Area School Dist., 741 F.2d 538 (3d Cir. 1984), *vacated,* 475 U.S. 534 (1986); Bell v. Little Axe Indep. School Dist. No. 70, 766 F.2d 1391 (10th Cir. 1985); Nartowicz v. Clayton County School Dist., 736 F.2d 646 (11th Cir. 1984); Lubbock Civil Liberties Union v. Lubbock Indep. School Dist., 669 F.2d 1038 (5th Cir. 1982), *cert. denied,* 459 U.S. 1155 (1983); Brandon v. Board of Educ. of Guilderland Cent. School Dist., 635 F.2d 971 (2d Cir. 1980), *cert. denied,* 454 U.S. 1123 (1981). The *Bell* case was unique in that the student devotional meetings at issue involved elementary school students; the other cases involved high school students.

30. These courts found significant differences between public high schools and residential college campuses in that younger students are more impressionable, schooling through part of high school is compulsory, faculty supervision is required for student groups at the high school level, and high school students have access to their homes for religious meetings before or after school.

31. 20 U.S.C. § 4071 (1988). The EAA was a compromise measure; critics of school prayer proposals viewed the EAA as a vehicle to defuse the congressional momentum to enact a law sanctioning some type of daily prayer during the school day.

32. 20 U.S.C. § 4071(c)(3) (1988).

33. *See* Garnett v. Renton School Dist. No. 403, 874 F.2d 608 (9th Cir. 1989), *cert. granted and judgment vacated,* 110 S. Ct. 2608 (1990); Student Coalition for Peace v. Lower Merion School Dist., 776 F.2d 431 (3d Cir. 1985), *on remand,* 633 F. Supp. 1040 (E.D. Pa. 1986); Clark v. Dallas Indep. School Dist., 671 F. Supp. 1119 (N.D. Tex. 1987), *modified,* 701 F. Supp. 594 (N.D. Tex. 1988); Thompson v. Waynesboro Area School Dist., 673 F. Supp. 1379 (M.D. Pa. 1987).

34. 110 S. Ct. 2356 (1990).

35. Mergens, *id.*, No. CV 85-0-426 (D. Neb. 1988). The student clubs were allowed access to the school's bulletin boards, newspaper, public address system, and club fair.

36. Mergens, *id.*, 110 S. Ct. at 2364.

37. *Id.* at 2366.

38. *Id.* at 2371 (O'Connor, J., joined by Rehnquist, White, and Blackmun, J.J.). For a discussion of the tripartite test, *see* text with note 5, *supra.*

39. *Id.* at 2372. It appears that different standards are applied in evaluating curriculum-related activities under the EAA versus the free speech clause of the first amendment. For a discussion of school authorities' broad discretion under the first amendment to censor student expression that carries the school's imprimatur, *see* text with note 34, Chapter 4.

40. *See, e.g.,* Collins v. Chandler Unified School Dist., 644 F.2d 759, 761 (9th Cir. 1981), *cert. denied,* 454 U.S. 863 (1981).

41. 110 S. Ct. at 2391 (Stevens, J., dissenting).

42. *See* Meltzer v. Board of Pub. Instruction of Orange County, Florida, 548 F.2d 559 (5th Cir. 1977), *rehearing,* 577 F.2d 311 (5th Cir. 1978), *cert. denied,* 439 U.S. 1089 (1979) (although the appeals court indicated that a policy allowing the distribution of Gideon Bibles in public schools would violate the establishment clause, the final order did not provide a declaration to this effect as the school board had tabled its policy authorizing such distribution); Hernandez v. Hanson, 430 F. Supp. 1154 (D. Neb. 1977); Goodwin v. Cross County School Dist., 394 F. Supp. 417 (E.D. Ark. 1973); Tudor v. Board of Educ., 100 A.2d 857 (N.J. 1953), *cert. denied,* 348 U.S. 816 (1954); Miller v. Cooper, 244 P.2d 520 (N.M. 1952). *See also* Martha McCarthy, *A Delicate Balance: Church, State, and the Schools* (Bloomington, IN: Phi Delta Kappa, 1983), p. 42.

43. Bacon v. Bradley-Bourbonnais High School Dist. No. 307, 707 F. Supp. 1005 (C.D. Ill. 1989). *See also* Berger v. Rensselaer Cent. School Corp., No. L 90-19 (N.D. Ind. 1991) (upholding school district's policy allowing the distribution of religious literature by organizations such as the Gideon Society).

44. Rivera v. East Otero School Dist. R-1, 721 F. Supp. 1189 (D. Colo. 1989). *But see* Hemry by Hemry v. School Bd. of Colorado Springs, 760 F. Supp. 856 (D. Colo. 1991), in which the same court upheld time, place, and manner restrictions prohibiting students from distributing literature in the high school hallways—a nonpublic forum. In contrast to the situation in *Rivera,* the court

concluded that the restriction in this case was not content based, even though religious materials were at issue; all student literature was subjected to the same regulation.

45. Thompson v. Waynesboro Area School Dist., 673 F. Supp. 1379 (M.D. Pa. 1987).

46. Perumal v. Saddleback Valley Unified School Dist., 243 Cal. Rptr. 545 (Cal. Ct. App. 1988), *cert. denied,* 488 U.S. 933 (1989).

47. Florey v. Sioux Falls School Dist. 49-5, 619 F.2d 1311 (8th Cir. 1980), *cert. denied,* 449 U.S. 987 (1980).

48. Stone v. Graham, 599 S.W.2d 157 (Ky. 1980), *rev'd,* 449 U.S. 39 (1980).

49. Florey v. Sioux Falls School Dist. 49-5, 619 F.2d 1311 (8th Cir. 1980).

50. Stone v. Graham, 449 U.S. 39 (1980).

51. *Id.* at 41. *See also* Nartowicz v. Clayton County School Dist., 736 F.2d 646 (11th Cir. 1984) (barring the use of public school bulletin boards and public address systems to announce church-sponsored activities); Joki v. Board of Educ. of the Schuylerville Cent. School Dist., 745 F. Supp. 823 (N.D.N.Y. 1990) (enjoining display of religious painting in high school auditorium as conveying governmental endorsement of religion).

52. Lynch v. Donnelly, 465 U.S. 668 (1984).

53. McCreary v. Stone, 739 F.2d 716 (2d Cir. 1984), *aff'd by equally divided court sub nom.* Board of Trustees of Village of Scarsdale v. McCreary, 471 U.S. 83 (1985). *See also* Doe v. City of Clawson, 915 F.2d 244 (6th Cir. 1990) (upholding display of nativity scene on front lawn of city hall); American Civil Liberties Union of Kentucky v. Wilkinson, 895 F.2d 1098 (6th Cir. 1990) (upholding construction of an empty creche on the state capitol's grounds for use by private organizations to reenact the nativity scene during the Christmas season).

54. County of Allegheny v. American Civil Liberties Union, 109 S. Ct. 3086 (1989). *But see* Kaplan v. Burlington, 891 F.2d 1024 (2d Cir. 1989), *cert. denied,* 110 S. Ct. 2619 (1990) (striking down the solitary display of a large menorah in City Hall Park).

55. Jesse Choper, "Religion in the Schools: A Proposed Constitutional Standard," *Minnesota Law Review,* vol. 47 (1963), p. 382.

56. Knowlton v. Baumhover, 166 N.W. 202, 206 (Iowa 1918). *See also* Zellers v. Huff, 236 P.2d 949 (N.M. 1951).

57. Jaffree v. Board of School Comm'rs of Mobile County, 705 F.2d 1526 (11th Cir. 1983), *cert. denied in part,* 466 U.S. 926 (1984) (the absence of a state law or school board policy authorizing the devotional activities did not negate the constitutional violation). *See also* May v. Evansville-Vanderburgh School Corp., 787 F.2d 1105 (7th Cir. 1986) (school authorities were upheld in barring teachers from using the public school building to hold staff prayer meetings before school); Breen v. Runkel, 614 F. Supp. 355 (W.D. Mich. 1985) (teachers violated the establishment clause by praying in their classrooms, reading from the Bible, and telling Bible stories).

58. However, the court enjoined the school board from removing the Bible from the school library, noting that the Bible has significant literary and historical significance. Roberts v. Madigan, 921 F.2d 1047 (10th Cir. 1990).

59. Webster v. New Lenox School Dist. No. 122, 917 F.2d 1004 (7th Cir. 1990). *See also* Bishop v. Aronov, 926 F.2d 1066 (11th Cir. 1991) (upholding univer-

sity memoranda instructing faculty to refrain from interjecting religious beliefs or preferences during instructional time).

60. La Rocca v. Board of Educ. of Rye City School Dist., 406 N.Y.S.2d 348 (N.Y. App. Div. 1978), *appeal dismissed,* 386 N.E.2d 266 (N.Y. 1978).

61. Dale v. Board of Educ., Lemmon Indep. School Dist. 52-2, 316 N.W.2d 108 (S.D. 1982).

62. Fink v. Board of Educ. of the Warren County School Dist., 442 A.2d 837, 842 (Pa. Commw. Ct. 1982), *appeal dismissed,* 460 U.S. 1048 (1983) (upheld teacher's dismissal for refusing to comply with superintendent's directives to cease opening classes with devotional activities).

63. Palmer v. Board of Educ. of the City of Chicago, 603 F.2d 1271 (7th Cir. 1979), *cert. denied,* 444 U.S. 1026 (1980).

64. *Id.* at 1274.

65. *Id.*

66. Some courts have concluded that wearing religious garb by public school teachers does not present a threat of state advancement of religion as long as the teachers do not proselytize students. *See, e.g.,* Mississippi Employment Security Comm'n v. McGlothin, 556 So. 2d 324 (Miss. 1990), *cert. denied,* 111 S. Ct. 211 (1990); Rawlings v. Butler, 290 S.W.2d 801 (Ky. 1956); Gerhardt v. Heid, 267 N.W. 127, 135 (N.D. 1936). Other courts have recognized the state's authority to enact legislation prohibiting public school teachers from wearing religious garb as a proper exercise of legislative power to guard against promoting a religious atmosphere in public schools. *See, e.g.,* United States v. Board of Educ. for the School Dist. of Philadelphia, 911 F.2d 882 (3d Cir. 1990); Cooper v. Eugene School Dist. No. 4J, 723 P.2d 298 (Or. 1986), *appeal dismissed,* 480 U.S. 942 (1987).

67. School Dist. of Abington Township v. Schempp, 374 U.S. 203, 225 (1963).

68. *See* Timothy Smith, "High School History Texts Adopted for Use in the State of Alabama," *Religion & Public Education,* vol. 15 (1988), pp. 170–190; Paul Vitz, *Censorship: Evidence of Bias in our Children's Textbooks* (Ann Arbor, MI: Servant Books, 1986).

69. *Religion in the Public Schools, Questions and Answers* (1988) is sponsored by 14 organizations including the American Association of School Administrators, the Association for Supervision and Curriculum Development, and the National School Boards Association. The Williamsburg Charter Foundation, a nonsectarian, nonprofit organization, has sponsored a project to develop a model curriculum on religious liberty for use in grades five, eight, and eleven. *See* "Religion Curriculum Addresses Liberty, Pluralism," *Education Monitor,* November 27, 1990, p. 4; "National Education Leaders Offer Religion Curriculum," *School Board News,* November 9, 1988, p. 1.

70. See Charles Kniker, "A Survey of State Laws and Regulations Regarding Religion and Moral Education," *Religion & Public Education,* vol. 16 (1989), pp. 433–457.

71. *See* Doe v. Human, 923 F.2d 857 (8th Cir. 1990), *cert. denied,* 111 S. Ct. 1315 (1991); Hall v. Board of School Comm'rs, 656 F.2d 999 (5th Cir. 1981), *appeal after remand,* 707 F.2d 464 (11th Cir. 1983); Crockett v. Sorenson, 568 F. Supp. 1422 (W.D. Va. 1983); Wiley v. Franklin, 497 F. Supp. 390 (E.D. Tenn. 1980).

72. Most courts have cautioned that Bible study courses, which can pass first

amendment scrutiny, should be offered on an elective rather than required basis because even the academic study of religion may interfere with the tenets of some faiths. *But see* Vaughn v. Reed, 313 F. Supp. 431 (W.D. Va. 1970) (the excusal provision for students desiring not to participate in the contested Bible study course supported the conclusion that the course entailed indoctrination rather than the academic study of religion).

73. McCollum v. Board of Educ., 333 U.S. 203 (1948).
74. Zorach v. Clauson, 343 U.S. 306, 313–314 (1952).
75. Smith v. Smith, 523 F.2d 121 (4th Cir. 1975), *cert. denied,* 423 U.S. 1073 (1976). *But see* Doe v. Shenandoah County School Bd., 737 F. Supp. 913 (W.D. Va. 1990) (granting a preliminary injunction against Weekday Religious Education classes being held in buses—almost identical to public school buses—parked in front of the school, with instructors going into the school to recruit students).
76. Holt v. Thompson, 225 N.W.2d 678 (Wis. 1975).
77. There is some sentiment that programs in which all students are released early from school one day a week would be easier to defend constitutionally because students would not be confined to a choice between remaining at the public school or attending sectarian classes. *See* McCarthy, *A Delicate Balance,* p. 112.
78. Lanner v. Wimmer, 662 F.2d 1349 (10th Cir. 1981). The court noted that release-time classes might be used to satisfy elective hours for graduation if, unlike the situation in this case, state supervision is not required to determine what portions of the courses are religious.
79. Church of God v. Amarillo Indep. School Dist., 511 F. Supp. 613 (N.D. Tex. 1981), *aff'd,* 670 F.2d 46 (5th Cir. 1982) (per curiam).
80. Commonwealth v. Bey, 70 A.2d 693 (Pa. Super. Ct. 1950).
81. Rice v. Commonwealth, 49 S.E.2d 342, 348 (Va. 1948).
82. *See, e.g.,* Johnson v. Charles City Community Schools Bd. of Educ., 368 N.W.2d 74 (Iowa 1985), *cert. denied,* 474 U.S. 1033 (1985); Jernigan v. State, 412 So. 2d 1242 (Ala. Crim. App. 1982). For a discussion of the legal status of home education programs, *see* text with note 6, Chapter 3.
83. Wisconsin v. Yoder, 406 U.S. 205 (1972).
84. 319 U.S. 624 (1943).
85. Minersville School Dist. v. Gobitis, 310 U.S. 586 (1940).
86. Barnette, 319 U.S. at 642.
87. *See, e.g.,* Lipp v. Morris, 579 F.2d 834 (3d Cir. 1978); Goetz v. Ansell, 477 F.2d 636 (2d Cir. 1973).
88. *See* Russo v. Central School Dist. No. 1, 469 F.2d 623, 634 (2d Cir. 1972), *cert. denied,* 411 U.S. 932 (1973). *See also* Opinion of the Justices to the Governor, 363 N.E.2d 251 (Mass. 1977).
89. *See* text with note 63, *supra.*
90. *See* Spence v. Bailey, 465 F.2d 797 (6th Cir. 1972); Moody v. Cronin, 484 F. Supp. 270 (C.D. Ill. 1979); S.T. v. Board of Educ. of City of Millville, 113 N.J. 659 (N.J. Super. Ct. App. Div. 1988), *certification denied,* 552 A.2d 179 (N.J. 1988), *cert. denied,* 109 S. Ct. 3181 (1989); Valent v. New Jersey State Bd. of Educ., 274 A.2d 832 (N.J. Super. Ct. Ch. Div. 1971); Hardwick v. Board of School Trustees, 205 P. 49 (Cal. Ct. App. 1921).
91. *See* Mitchell v. McCall, 143 So. 2d 629 (Ala. 1962) (school authorities do not

have to make special arrangements or to alter programs to protect students from the embarrassment associated with nonparticipation).

92. *See, e.g.,* Ware v. Valley Stream High School Dist., 551 N.Y.S.2d 167 (N.Y. 1989) (denial of religious exemption from mandatory AIDS education was upheld by the trial court, but the Court of Appeals remanded the case for further fact finding because of the significant public and private interests in conflict).

93. Davis v. Page, 385 F. Supp. 395 (D.N.H. 1974). While governmental interests prevailed over free exercise rights in denying the exemption from academic classes, the court recognized that the students could be excused when audio-visual equipment was used solely for entertainment purposes. *See also* Ouimette v. Babbie, 405 F. Supp. 525 (D. Vt. 1975); McCarthy, *A Delicate Balance,* pp. 59–64.

94. *See* Menora v. Illinois High School Ass'n, 683 F.2d 1030 (7th Cir. 1982), *cert. denied,* 459 U.S. 1156 (1983); Keller v. Gardner Community Consol. Grade School Dist. 72C, 552 F. Supp. 512 (N.D. Ill. 1982).

95. 827 F.2d 1058 (6th Cir. 1987), *cert. denied,* 484 U.S. 1066 (1988).

96. 20 U.S.C. § 1232h (1988); 34 C.F.R. §§ 75, 76, 98 (1990). For a discussion of the controversy surrounding the Hatch Amendment, *see* text with note 160, Chapter 3. The proposed federal legislation to prohibit governmental restrictions on the free exercise of religious beliefs without a compelling governmental interest, if enacted, would strengthen grounds for students to secure religious exemptions from public school activities. *See* note 10, *supra.*

97. Epperson v. Arkansas, 393 U.S. 97, 107 (1968), quoting Joseph Burstyn, Inc. v. Wilson, 343 U.S. 495, 505 (1952).

98. *See* Thomas v. Review Bd. of the Indiana Employment and Security Div., 450 U.S. 707, 714 (1981); United States v. Seeger, 380 U.S. 163, 175 (1965); United States v. Ballard, 322 U.S. 78, 87 (1944).

99. Several courts have explicitly rejected claims that instruction in evolution or sex education advances an antitheistic belief. *See* text with notes 108–113, *infra.*

100. Malnak v. Yogi, 592 F.2d 197 (3d Cir. 1979). The court reasoned that instruction in transcendental meditation unconstitutionally advances the Science of Creative Intelligence, which was found to possess many attributes of a religion

101. *See* Fink v. Board of Educ. of the Warren County School Dist., 442 A.2d 837, 843 (Pa. Commw. Ct. 1982), *appeal dismissed,* 460 U.S. 1048 (1983); Jaffree v. James, 544 F. Supp. 727, 732 (S.D. Ala. 1982); Reed v. Van Hoven, 237 F. Supp. 48, 53 (W.D. Mich. 1965). The Supreme Court also has noted that "the state may not establish a 'religion of secularism' in the sense of affirmatively opposing or showing hostility to religion, thus 'preferring those who believe in no religion . . .' " School Dist. of Abington Township v. Schempp, 374 U.S. 203, 225 (1963). *See also* Torcaso v. Watkins, 367 U.S. 488, 495 n.11 (1961).

102. For a discussion of allegations that public schools are promoting a secular creed, *see* Martha McCarthy, "Secular Humanism and Education," *Journal of Law & Education,* vol. 19 (1990), pp. 467–498. *See also* text with note 91, Chapter 3.

103. *See* Jaffree v. Board of School Comm'rs of Mobile County, 554 F. Supp. 1104, 1129–1130 n. 41 (S.D. Ala. 1983).

104. *See, e.g.,* McLean v. Arkansas Bd. of Educ., 529 F. Supp. 1255 (E.D. Ark. 1982).

105. Grove v. Mead School Dist. No. 354, 753 F.2d 1528 (9th Cir. 1985), *cert. denied,* 474 U.S. 826 (1985).

106. Smith v. School Comm'rs of Mobile County, 655 F. Supp. 939 (S.D. Ala. 1987), *rev'd,* 827 F.2d 684 (11th Cir. 1987).

107. *Id.,* 827 F.2d at 692.

108. *See* Parental Rights v. San Mateo County Bd. of Educ., 124 Cal. Rptr. 68 (Cal. Ct. App. 1975), *appeal dismissed,* 425 U.S. 908 (1976); Cornwell v. State Bd. of Educ., 314 F. Supp. 340 (D. Md. 1969), *cert. denied,* 400 U.S. 942 (1970); Citizens for Hobolth v. Greenway, 218 N.W.2d 98 (Mich. 1974); Medeiros v. Kiyosaki, 478 P.2d 314 (Haw. 1970); Valent v. New Jersey State Bd. of Educ., 274 A.2d 832 (N.J. Super. Ct. Ch. Div. 1971).

109. Smith v. Ricci, 446 A.2d 501 (N.J. 1982), *appeal dismissed sub nom.* Smith v. Brandt, 459 U.S. 962 (1982).

110. For a discussion of this issue, *see* Valent v. New Jersey State Bd. of Educ., 274 A.2d 832, 840–841 (N.J. Super. Ct. Ch. Div. 1971).

111. Scopes v. State, 289 S.W. 363, 364 (Tenn. 1927).

112. Epperson v. Arkansas, 393 U.S. 97 (1968). *See also* Wright v. Houston Indep. School Dist., 486 F.2d 137 (5th Cir. 1973), *cert. denied,* 417 U.S. 969 (1974).

113. Edwards v. Aguillard, 482 U.S. 578 (1987). *See also* Daniel v. Waters, 515 F.2d 485 (6th Cir. 1975); McLean v. Arkansas Bd. of Educ., 529 F. Supp. 1255 (E.D. Ark. 1982).

114. In 1984 Congress amended a federal law providing grants for magnet schools to prohibit the funds from being used for instruction in "secular humanism," Education for Economic Security Act, Title VII—Magnet Schools Assistance, 20 U.S.C. § 4059 (1984), repealed and recodified, 20 U.S.C. § 3029 (1988). Neither the law nor its regulations defined "secular humanism." The stipulation subsequently was deleted from the law after a group of prominent authors initiated a suit alleging that the prohibition against "secular humanism" was unconstitutional. Nonetheless, legislative bodies continue to consider similar provisions.

115. Pierce v. Society of Sisters, 268 U.S. 510 (1925).

116. *See* Wisconsin v. Yoder, 406 U.S. 205, 214 (1972); text with note 8, *supra.*

117. National Center for Education Statistics, *Private Schools in the United States: A Statistical Profile, With Comparisons to Public Schools* (Washington, DC: U.S. Department of Education, 1991), p. 9; Allan Ornstein, "The Growing Nonpublic School Movement," *Educational Horizons,* vol. 67 (1989), p. 71.

118. State v. Whisner, 351 N.E.2d 750 (Ohio 1976). *See also* State *ex rel.* Nagle v. Olin, 415 N.E.2d 279 (Ohio 1980).

119. Kentucky State Bd. for Elementary and Secondary Educ. v. Rudasill, 589 S.W.2d 877, 879 (Ky. 1979), *cert. denied,* 446 U.S. 938 (1980). *See also* Bangor Baptist Church v. Maine Dep't of Educ., 576 F. Supp. 1299 (D. Me. 1983) (state compulsory school attendance law does not bar the operation of "unapproved" private schools).

120. State v. DeLaBruere, 577 A.2d 254 (Vt. 1990); State v. Toman, 436 N.W.2d 10 (N.D. 1989); Sheridan Rd. Baptist Church v. Department of Educ., 396 N.W.2d 373 (Mich. 1986); Johnson v. Charles City Community School Bd. of Educ., 368 N.W.2d 74 (Iowa 1985), *cert. denied*, 474 U.S. 1033 (1985); State v. Rivinius, 328 N.W.2d 220 (N.D. 1982), *cert. denied*, 460 U.S. 1070 (1983); State by Minami v. Andrews, 651 P.2d 473 (Haw. 1982); State *ex rel.* Douglas v. Faith Baptist Church of Louisville, 301 N.W.2d 571 (Neb. 1981), *appeal dismissed*, 454 U.S. 803 (1981).

121. New Life Baptist Church Academy v. Town of East Longmeadow, 885 F.2d 940 (1st Cir. 1989), *cert. denied*, 110 S. Ct. 1782 (1990).

122. Fellowship Baptist Church v. Benton, 815 F.2d 485 (8th Cir. 1987), *on remand*, 678 F. Supp. 213 (S.D. Iowa 1988).

123. St. Martin Evangelical Lutheran Church v. South Dakota, 451 U.S. 772 (1981).

124. National Labor Relations Bd. v. Catholic Bishop of Chicago, 440 U.S. 490 (1979).

125. Catholic High School Ass'n of the Archdiocese of New York v. Culvert, 753 F.2d 1161 (2d Cir. 1985).

126. *See* Baltimore Lutheran High School Ass'n v. Employment Security Admin., 490 A.2d 701 (Md. 1985); Salem College & Academy v. Employment Div., 695 P.2d 25 (Or. 1985).

127. *See, e.g.,* DeArment v. Harvey, 932 F.2d 721 (8th Cir. 1991); Dole v. Shenandoah Baptist Church, 899 F.2d 1389 (4th Cir. 1990), *cert. denied*, 111 S. Ct. 131 (1990).

128. *See, e.g.,* Ohio Civil Rights Comm'n v. Dayton Christian Schools, 477 U.S. 619 (1986) (Commission was authorized to investigate an employee's claim of sex discrimination against a private religious school; however, the Commission could consider the school's religious justification for what would otherwise be considered illegal conduct); Equal Employment Opportunity Comm'n v. Mississippi College, 626 F.2d 477, 487–488 (5th Cir. 1980), *cert. denied*, 453 U.S. 912 (1981) (federal agency's investigation into college's hiring practices under Title VII of the Civil Rights Act of 1964 would not constitute "ongoing interference" with the institution's religious practices); Sacred Heart School Bd. v. Labor Industry Review Comm'n, 460 N.W.2d 430 (Wis. Ct. App. 1990) (Commission could investigate age discrimination claim in religious school).

129. Bob Jones Univ. v. United States, 461 U.S. 574, 592 (1983).

130. *Id.* at 595. *See also* Norwood v. Harrison, 413 U.S. 455 (1973) (state funds could not be used to provide textbooks for private school students attending racially discriminatory private schools); Virginia Educ. Fund v. Commissioner of Internal Revenue, 799 F.2d 903 (4th Cir. 1986) (fund created to solicit monies for segregated private schools was not entitled to a tax exemption as a charitable organization without evidence that the schools operated under nondiscriminatory admissions policies).

131. In 1984 the Supreme Court ended an eight-year-old federal suit brought by minority parents seeking to force the Internal Revenue Service to be more assertive in withdrawing tax exemptions from racially discriminatory private schools. The Court majority reasoned that the parents did not have standing

to sue the executive branch to induce more stringent regulatory activity, Allen v. Wright, 468 U.S. 737 (1984).

132. *See* "State Financial Support for Private Education," *Education Week,* April 22, 1987, pp. 18–19; Center for State Legislation and School Law, *Aid to Private Schools* (Alexandria, VA: National School Boards Association, 1985).

133. *See* Chester Finn, "The Politics of Public Aid to Private Education," in *The Changing Politics of School Finance,* Nelda Cambron-McCabe and Allan Odden, eds. (Cambridge, MA: Ballinger, 1982), pp. 183–210.

134. This statement was made in 1802 in a letter refusing a Baptist association's request for a day to be established for fasting and prayer in thanksgiving for the nation's welfare. *See* Robert Healey, *Jefferson on Religion in Public Education* (New Haven, CT: Yale University Press, 1962), pp. 128–140.

135. Everson v. Board of Educ., 330 U.S. 1 (1947).

136. *See, e.g.,* Members of Jamestown School Comm. v. Schmidt, 699 F.2d 1 (1st Cir. 1983), *cert. denied,* 464 U.S. 851 (1983); McKeesport Area School Dist. v. Pennsylvania Dep't of Educ., 392 A.2d 912 (Pa. 1978), *appeal dismissed,* 446 U.S. 970 (1980).

137. *See* Matthews v. Quinton, 362 P.2d 932 (Alaska 1961), *cert. denied,* 368 U.S. 517 (1962); McVey v. Hawkins, 258 S.W.2d 927 (Mo. 1953); Visser v. Nooksack Valley School Dist. No. 506, 207 P.2d 198 (Wash. 1949); Gurney v. Ferguson, 122 P.2d 1002 (Okla. 1941), *cert. denied,* 317 U.S. 588 (1942).

138. Board of Educ. v. Allen, 392 U.S. 236 (1968). *See also* Cunningham v. Lutjeharms, 437 N.W.2d 806 (Neb. 1989).

139. *See* Elbe v. Yankton Indep. School Dist. No. 63-3, 372 N.W.2d 113 (S.D. 1985); Fannin v. Williams, 655 S.W.2d 480 (Ky. 1983); Bloom v. School Comm. of Springfield, 379 N.E.2d 578 (Mass. 1978); In re Advisory Opinion, 228 N.W.2d 772 (Mich. 1975); Paster v. Tussey, 512 S.W.2d 97 (Mo. 1974), *cert. denied,* 419 U.S. 1111 (1975); Gaffney v. State Dep't, 220 N.W.2d 550 (Neb. 1974).

140. California Teachers' Ass'n v. Riles, 632 P.2d 953, 962 (Cal. 1981).

141. Wolman v. Walter, 433 U.S. 229, 247 (1977). *See also* Meek v. Pittenger, 421 U.S. 349 (1975).

142. Committee for Pub. Educ. and Religious Liberty v. Regan, 444 U.S. 646 (1980).

143. Levitt v. Committee for Pub. Educ. and Religious Liberty, 413 U.S. 472 (1973).

144. Wolman v. Walter, 433 U.S. 229 (1977); Meek v. Pittenger, 421 U.S. 349 (1975); Committee for Pub. Educ. and Religious Liberty v. Nyquist, 413 U.S. 756 (1973); Lemon v. Kurtzman, 403 U.S. 602 (1971).

145. It should be noted that the Supreme Court has been more receptive to governmental aid to institutions of higher education than to private elementary and secondary schools. *See* Roemer v. Board of Pub. Works of Maryland, 426 U.S. 736 (1976) (upholding noncategorical grants to private colleges and universities); Hunt v. McNair, 413 U.S. 734 (1973) (approving the use of state revenue bonds to finance private college and university construction); Tilton v. Richardson, 403 U.S. 672 (1971) (allowing federal grants for private college and university construction). *See also* text with note 167, *infra.*

146. 718 F.2d 1389 (6th Cir. 1983), *aff'd*, 473 U.S. 373 (1985).

147. *Id.*, 473 U.S. at 393, citing Wolman v. Walter, 433 U.S. at 250.

148. 473 U.S. 402 (1985). *See also* Wheeler v. Barrera, 417 U.S. 402 (1974), *judgment modified*, 422 U.S. 1004 (1975).

149. The law is now Chapter 1 of the 1988 Hawkins-Stafford Elementary and Secondary School Improvement Act, 20 U.S.C. § 2701, *et seq.* (1988).

150. Aguilar, 473 U.S. at 412–413. For a discussion of the Court's emphasis on the "locale" of the publicly supported services, *see* Martha McCarthy, "State Aid to Nonpublic Schools," *Journal of Education Finance*, vol. 11 (1986), pp. 278–293.

151. Pulido v. Cavazos, 728 F. Supp. 574 (W.D. Mo. 1989), *rev'd*, 934 F.2d 912 (8th Cir. 1991). The court also upheld the contested "bypass" provision, under which federal funds are not distributed to private schools through state and local education agencies because of state restrictions of the use of public funds for private purposes. The court concluded that taking the costs associated with administering the "bypass" provision off the top of Chapter 1 allocations did not violate the establishment clause. *See also* Walker v. San Francisco Unified School Dist., 761 F. Supp. 1463 (N.D. Cal. 1991). *But see* Barnes v. Cavazos, No. C-80-0501-L(A) (W.D. Ky. 1990).

152. Helms v. Cody, No. 85-5533 (E.D. La. 1990).

153. Walker v. San Francisco Unified School Dist., 741 F. Supp. 1386 (N.D. Cal. 1990).

154. Board of Educ. of the Monroe-Woodbury Cent. School Dist. v. Wieder, 531 N.Y.S.2d 889 (N.Y. 1988).

155. 484 U.S. 1002 (1988).

156. *See* Committee for Pub. Educ. and Religious Liberty v. Regan, 444 U.S. 646, 671 (1980) (Stevens, J., dissenting); Steve Gey, "Rebuilding the Wall: The Case for a Return to the Strict Interpretation of the Establishment Clause," *Columbia Law Review*, vol. 81 (1981), pp. 1463–1490.

157. Wallace v. Jaffree, 472 U.S. 38, 110-111 (1985) (Rehnquist, J., dissenting).

158. In 1982 President Reagan proposed federal income tax credits of up to 50 percent of each child's tuition costs to a maximum of $500 and with a limitation that only families earning $50,000 or less would be entitled to the full credit. Similar measures have regularly been introduced in Congress since 1977, but none has yet been enacted.

159. Committee for Public Educ. and Religious Liberty v. Nyquist, 413 U.S. 756 (1973). *See also* Rhode Island Fed'n of Teachers AFL/CIO v. Norberg, 630 F.2d 855 (1st Cir. 1980); Public Funds for Public Schools of New Jersey v. Byrne, 590 F.2d 514 (3d Cir. 1979), *aff'd*, 442 U.S. 907 (1979).

160. 463 U.S. 388, 398 (1983).

161. *Id.* at 395.

162. For a discussion of unsuccessful referenda in eleven states and the District of Columbia, *see* "Oregon Voters Reject School Choice Initiative," *Education Daily*, November 8, 1990, pp. 3–4; James Catterall, "Politics and Aid to Private Schools," *Educational Evaluation and Policy Analysis*, vol. 6 (1984), pp. 433–440. The soundest defeat was in Washington, D.C., where almost 90 percent of the voters rejected a 1981 tuition tax credit proposal.

163. "Voters Support Education in Most State Tax Measures," *Education Week*, November 20, 1990, p. 1.

164. Milton Friedman proposed vouchers to fund education in the latter 1950s. *See* Milton Friedman, *Capitalism and Freedom* (Chicago, IL: University of Chicago Press, 1962), Chapter 6.

165. For a discussion of various voucher models, *see* Nelda Cambron-McCabe, "Governmental Aid to Individuals: Parental Choice in Schooling," in *The Impacts of Litigation and Legislation on Public School Finance,* Julie Underwood and Deborah Verstegen, eds. (New York: Ballinger, 1990), pp. 103–121; L. D. Webb, Martha McCarthy, and Stephen Thomas, *Financing Elementary and Secondary Education* (Columbus, OH: Merrill, 1988), Chapters 8, 11.

166. 474 U.S. 481 (1986). However, on remand, the state supreme court held that the Washington Constitution prohibited such aid that flows to religious institutions, Witters v. State of Washington Comm'n for the Blind, 771 P.2d 1119 (Wash. 1989).

167. *See* Julie Underwood, "Public Funds for Private Schools: The Gap Between Higher and Lower Education Widens," *Education Law Reporter,* vol. 41 (1987), pp. 407–420; note 145, *supra.*

168. For a discussion of these strategies, *see* Education Commission of the States, *Public School Choice Activity in the States* (Denver: Author, 1989).

169. Minnesota Fed'n of Teachers v. Randall, 891 F.2d 1354 (8th Cir. 1989), *on remand,* 740 F. Supp. 694 (D. Minn. 1990).

170. Davis v. Grover, 464 N.W.2d 220 (Wis. Ct. App. 1990). The Wisconsin Constitution prohibits private or local legislation from being passed as part of a bill embracing more than one subject.

171. Mueller v. Allen, 676 F.2d 1195 (8th Cir. 1982), *aff'd,* 463 U.S. 388 (1983).

3
School Attendance and Instructional Issues

Although United States citizens have no federal constitutional right to a public education, each state constitution places a duty on its legislature to provide for free public schooling and thus creates an entitlement (property right) for all children to be educated at public expense. Substantial litigation has resulted from the collision of state interests in guaranteeing the general welfare and individual interests in exercising rights protected by constitutional and statutory law. This chapter focuses on legal mandates pertaining to various requirements and rights associated with school attendance and the instructional program. Other aspects of students' rights and responsibilities are explored in more detail in subsequent chapters.

COMPULSORY ATTENDANCE

All 50 states

At present, all fifty states compel children between specified ages to be educated and impose penalties on parents who do not comply with such mandates. The legal basis for compulsory education is grounded in the common law doctrine of *parens patriae,* which means that the state, in its guardian role, has the authority to enact reasonable laws for the welfare of its citizens. An educated citizenry is considered necessary to the state's well-being, and individuals are legally obligated to give up a measure of personal freedom in the interest of the state. Kentucky's compulsory attendance law is typical in requiring "each parent, guardian or other person residing in the state and having in custody or charge any child who has entered the primary school program or any child between the ages of six and sixteen" to send the child to school for the full school term.[1] Parents can be prosecuted in criminal or civil suits for failing to meet their legal obligations under compulsory school attendance laws; their children also can be expelled for excessive truancy or judicially ordered to return to school.[2] In some instances, truant children have been made wards of juvenile courts, with school attendance supervised by probation officers.[3]

Most states do not compel school attendance beyond age sixteen, but some states have enacted legislation designed to encourage high school graduation by conditioning a driver's license on school attendance for students under eighteen. In 1990 the West Virginia Supreme Court upheld such a state law as related to the legitimate goals of keeping teenagers in school and reducing automobile accidents by denying licenses to children who have not exhibited responsibility. However, the court held that before a license is revoked, school dropouts must be provided a hearing with appropriate school officials, rather than the Department of Motor Vehicles, to ascertain if the circumstances for dropping out are beyond the individual's control.[4]

Although states can require schooling, it was settled in 1925 that private school attendance can satisfy such mandates. In *Pierce v. Society of Sisters,* the Supreme Court invalidated an Oregon statute, requiring children between eight and sixteen years of age to attend *public* schools. The Court declared that "the fundamental theory of liberty upon which all governments in this union repose excludes any general power of the state to standardize its children by forcing them to accept instruction from public teachers only."[5] In essence, parents do not have the right to determine *whether* their children are educated, but they do have some control over *where* such education takes place. Legal developments pertaining to state regulation of private schools, 85 percent of which are church-related, are covered in Chapter 2.

In many states, compulsory attendance laws permit instruction outside of formal school settings as well as in public and private schools. In 1990 the Home School Legal Defense Association reported that thirty-three states had statutes or regulations authorizing home education.[6] Twenty-eight states require students educated at home to be tested to ensure that students are mastering basic skills. However, only two states, Iowa and Michigan, require home tutors to be certified, and two others, Arizona and Louisiana, require home tutors to pass an examination.[7]

In states that require attendance at a public or private school but do not specifically authorize home education, controversies have arisen over the definition of a "school." A few courts have interpreted such statutes as precluding home education as a means of satisfying compulsory attendance.[8] However, most courts have interpreted state laws requiring attendance at a public or nonpublic school as authorizing home education programs that meet state standards.[9] The supreme courts of Georgia and Wisconsin found compulsory attendance statutes to be unconstitutionally vague because they required parents to enroll their children in a public or private school but did not define what constitutes a private school.[10]

Where states authorize home education, courts have not spoken with a single voice regarding the constitutionality of requirements that such programs be "essentially equivalent" to public school offerings. For example, in 1989 the Second Circuit Court of Appeals rejected a vagueness challenge to the New York requirement that home instruction be provided by competent teachers and be substantially equivalent to public school offerings.[11] Similarly, the federal district court in Maine concluded that "equivalent instruction" is capable of objective measurement with a "core meaning that can reasonably be understood,"[12] and an Idaho appeals court held that the state law requiring home-schooled children to be "comparably instructed" to those educated in schools was not unconstitutionally vague.[13]

In contrast, the Minnesota Supreme Court ruled that the term "essentially equivalent" as used in the compulsory attendance statute (requiring home instructors' qualifications to be essentially equivalent to the minimum standard for public school teachers) was unconstitutionally vague for purposes of imposing criminal liability on parents for noncompliance.[14] Also, Pennsylvania legislation was considered vague and in violation of parents' due process rights because it did not prescribe standards for determining who would be considered a qualified tutor and what would be considered satisfactory curricula.[15]

Although the Arkansas Supreme Court in 1984 held that the state compulsory attendance law precluded home education,[16] the legislature subsequently enacted the Arkansas Home School Act, authorizing home instruction. In 1988 the Eighth Circuit Court of Appeals upheld the Act, which among other things requires students being taught at home to take annual standardized achievement tests and, when they reach age fourteen, to take minimum performance tests.[17] A child failing to score within eight months of grade level in specified subjects must be placed in a public, private, or parochial school. Rejecting parents' assertion that the law impairs privacy, free exercise, and equal protection rights (since home schooling is treated differently from private schools), the court held that the law served the state's compelling interest in educating its citizens. In a 1991 Kentucky case, the Sixth Circuit Court of Appeals also ruled that requiring a high school student to pass equivalency exams to gain public school credit for a religious home study program did not violate equal protection or free exercise rights.[18]

States have considerable latitude in establishing standards for alternatives to public education, and there is wide variance among states in requirements imposed. There seems to be a trend toward relaxing criteria that home school programs must satisfy and assuring adequacy by subjecting the students to standardized tests supervised by public school personnel.[19] It seems likely that parents will continue to assert a right to instruct their children at home, and the legal status of specific instructional programs will depend on judicial interpretations of applicable state statutes and administrative regulations.

EXCEPTIONS TO COMPULSORY ATTENDANCE

State laws generally recognize certain exceptions to compulsory attendance mandates. The most common exemption is for married students, who are emancipated from required school attendance because they have assumed adult responsibilities. Statutes often include other exceptions, such as students serving temporarily as pages for the state legislature and children who have reached age fourteen and have obtained lawful employment certificates.[20]

In addition to statutory exceptions, an exemption from compulsory attendance mandates has been granted on first amendment religious grounds to Amish children who have successfully completed the eighth grade.[21] However, most other attempts to keep children out of school for religious reasons have not been successful. In 1985, the Supreme Court declined to review a decision in which the Iowa high court refused to extend a statutory religious exemption from compulsory school attendance to fundamentalist Baptist children.[22] Under the state law in question, members of a recognized religious denomination, whose tenets conflict substantially with Iowa's stated educational goals and philosophy, can petition the state superintendent for an exemption from the law requiring children to be instructed by certified teachers. The Iowa Supreme Court reasoned that the exemption was intended only for the Amish, who lead isolated lives, and thus was not available to students whose religious tenets were not threatened by exposure to American culture. The court rejected the assertion that by limiting the exemption to the Amish, the state favored a particular religious sect in violation of the establishment clause.

Reasons other than religious convictions also have been unsuccessfully proffered as justification for noncompliance with compulsory attendance laws. For example, a North Carolina appeals court ruled that a "deep-rooted conviction for Indian heritage" was an insufficient basis for keeping children out of school.[23] The American Indian father testified that he refused to send his children to school because they were not taught about Indian history and culture. The court concluded that the children were "neglected" within the meaning of state law, because they were neither permitted to attend public school nor provided an alternative education. Also, the Tenth Circuit Court of Appeals rejected the assertion that the conflict between a school's grooming restrictions and Indian customs, traditions, and religious beliefs justified noncompliance with compulsory education mandates.[24]

Some parents have defended noncompliance with compulsory school attendance laws because of alleged unsafe conditions at the schools where their children have been assigned. Courts in general have rejected such claims,[25] though in a few situations courts have ruled that students' absences, based on a history of physical harassment by classmates, have warranted reassignment of the victimized children.[26]

HEALTH REQUIREMENTS

State agencies have the power not only to mandate school attendance, but also to require that students be in good health so as not to endanger the well-being of others.[27] In an early case the Supreme Court rejected a federal constitutional challenge to a Texas law authorizing local school officials to condition public and private school attendance on vaccination against communicable diseases.[28]

Numerous courts subsequently have upheld mandatory vaccination requirements, even when challenged on religious grounds, declaring that there need not be a pending epidemic to justify such requirements. Parents have been convicted for indirectly violating compulsory attendance laws by refusing to have their children vaccinated as a prerequisite to school admission. In a typical case, a New Jersey superior court rejected Christian Scientists' challenge to mandatory immunization against diphtheria as a condition of school attendance, noting that the school board had the authority to mandate immunization without waiting for an epidemic to occur.[29] Voicing similar reasoning in upholding a vaccination requirement, the Supreme Court of Arkansas declared that religious freedom does not mean that parents can "engage in religious practices inconsistent with the peace, safety, and health of inhabitants of [the] state."[30]

In some states, statutes provide for an exemption from required immunization for members of religious sects whose teachings oppose the practice as long as the welfare of others is not endangered by the exemption. These statutory religious exemptions have evoked a range of judicial interpretations. Some courts have invalidated restrictive exemptions because they discriminate against individuals who have sincere religious objections to vaccination but are not church members.[31] Other courts have upheld religious exemptions, interpreting them broadly as not requiring church membership or a prohibition against vaccination in official church doctrine.[32]

Several courts have rejected parental attempts to use statutory religious exemptions when their opposition to immunization was based on philosophical grounds. For example, in 1988 the Second Circuit Court of Appeals held that parents' sincere belief that immunization was contrary to the "genetic blueprint" was not a religious belief under the New York statutory religious exemption.[33] Also, a Kentucky federal district court ruled that a parent could not rely on the religious exemption merely because he was "philosophically opposed" to having his children immunized.[34] The court was not persuaded by the argument that the law was discriminatory because it granted an exemption to members of religious groups while denying the same privilege to those opposed to immunization on nonreligious grounds. An Ohio federal district court similarly held that parents' belief in "chiropractic ethics" did not entitle their children to a religious exemption from vaccination.[35]

The Supreme Court of Mississippi questioned the rationale for such religious exemptions from mandatory vaccination. The court concluded that a statutory exemption discriminated against parents who opposed immunization for nonreligious reasons, and further held that such an exemption defeated the purpose of an immunization requirement—to protect all students from exposure to communicable diseases. Accordingly, the court ruled that the state law requiring immunization as a prerequisite to school attendance must be applied to all students, regardless of the religious beliefs of parents.[36] Most other courts have reasoned that states are empowered to enact such statutory exemptions, but are not obligated to do so.

While it is well established that school attendance can be conditioned on vaccination against communicable diseases, states cannot abdicate their responsibility to educate children with such diseases. Children can be denied attendance in the regular school program if their presence poses a danger to others, but it is generally assumed that an alternative educational program (e.g., home instruction by computer) must be provided.

Substantial controversy has focused on school attendance by students with acquired immune deficiency syndrome (AIDS), a life-threatening disease that is transmitted through blood transfusions or the exchange of bodily fluids. Several states have adopted policies, modeled after guidelines issued by the National Centers for Disease Control (CDC), stipulating that students with AIDS should be allowed to attend public school unless they have open lesions, cannot control their bodily secretions, or display such behavior as biting. The CDC have suggested that determinations of whether individual students pose a health risk to others should be made on a case-by-case basis by a team of appropriate health and education personnel.

Despite considerable evidence that AIDS is not communicated through casual contact, some school boards have attempted to bar AIDS victims from public school classes. In such situations, infected students have sought judicial relief, asserting a right to attend school with their classmates. Courts have held that AIDS-infected children are protected by federal statutes barring discrimination against individuals with disabilities,[37] and consistently have ruled that public schools must enroll children with AIDS upon certification by health officials that they pose minimal risk of infecting others.[38]

In a widely publicized case, the Eleventh Circuit Court of Appeals reversed a lower court's decision that a separate cubicle must be constructed to segregate an AIDS victim from other children in a special education class. The court held that the trial court's finding of "a remote theoretical possibility" of transmission of AIDS from the child's tears, saliva, and urine did not support segregation of the child.[39] The case was remanded for additional findings concerning the child's risk of infecting classmates, and based on the evidence presented the lower court ordered the child admitted to school.

RESIDENCY REQUIREMENTS

In general courts have ruled that public schools are obligated to educate school-age children residing within the school district with intentions to remain. In an important 1982 decision, *Plyler v. Doe,* the Supreme Court held that school districts could not deny a free public education to resident children whose parents had entered the country illegally.[40] Recognizing the individual's significant interest in receiving an education, the Court ruled that classifications affecting access to education would have to be substantially related to an important governmental objective to satisfy the equal protection clause.[41] The Court found that Texas's asserted interest in deterring aliens from entering the country illegally was not important enough to deny students an opportunity to be educated.

Children who are wards of the state, living in orphanages or other state facilities, are usually considered residents of the school district where the facility is located, even though their parents live elsewhere in the state.[42] Also, courts have held that school districts cannot deny an education to homeless children being sheltered in their districts by asserting that such children are not residents.[43]

In contrast to the judiciary's position that school boards must provide free public schooling for resident students, courts in general have not required public schools to admit *nonresident* students tuition-free. In 1983 the Supreme Court upheld a Texas residency requirement allowing local school boards to deny tuition-free schooling to any minor who lives apart from a parent or legal guardian for the primary purpose of attending public school.[44] The court ruled that the requirement advanced the substantial state interest of assuring the high quality of public education enjoyed by residents (those living in a school district with the intent to remain).[45] Subsequently, a Texas appeals court upheld a school district's residency policy, even though it was more stringent than the state law in not making an exception for minors living apart from their parents or guardians for noneducational purposes.[46]

Other courts similarly have upheld residency requirements, reasoning that tuition must be paid when students' legal residence is outside the school district, even though they may live in the district with someone other than a legal guardian.[47] The Fifth Circuit Court of Appeals also recognized that students have no state-created right to attend public school tuition-free in the school district in which they formerly resided prior to changing their legal residence.[48] The Washington Supreme Court held that parents did not prove that their children's enrollment in their allegedly inadequate resident school district would be detrimental to their welfare; denial of the request for a transfer to another district did not abridge their state constitutional entitlement to an "ample education."[49]

As discussed in Chapter 4, several cases involving residency disputes have involved student athletes, and courts consistently have rejected efforts to establish limited guardianships to enable students to attend school tuition-free for athletic reasons. For example, an Indiana appeals court refused to recognize, for purposes of residency, a guardianship created to make a student eligible to participate in interscholastic sports in a school district where his parents did not reside.[50]

Departing from the prevailing judicial posture, the Eighth Circuit Court of Appeals in 1985 found that an Arkansas school district's residency requirement violated due process and equal protection guarantees.[51] The requirement denied tuition-free enrollment to minor students whose parents or guardians were not domiciled in the school district. Regarding the equal protection claim, the court held that the school district produced no evidence that a substantial state interest was advanced by the policy, which discriminated against the class of students who live apart from their parents and have no control over this situation. The court further concluded that the policy violated due process guarantees by creating an irrebuttable presumption that a student who does not reside with a parent or guardian is not living in the school district with the intent to remain.

Minnesota was the first state to enact an interdistrict open enrollment plan, and several other states have adopted similar "school choice" policies, allowing students to apply for transfers to any district within the state.[52] Transfer requests are subject to certain restrictions, such as space limitations and racial balance criteria, and participation by local districts is optional under some plans. In the absence of such statutory open enrollment plans, students do not have a right to attend school outside their resident district.

In some situations, however, courts have found that there are legitimate reasons for children to live apart from their parents. In an early case, the Colorado Supreme Court concluded that a child was placed in the home of another family to give him desirable influences and not primarily for educational reasons. Thus, the school district was instructed to consider the child a resident student.[53] The New Hampshire Supreme Court found that the major reason a child was living with his father during the school term, rather than with his mother, who had legal custody, was based on health rather than educational considerations. Accordingly, the school district of his father's residence was ordered to admit the student tuition-free.[54] Also, if school officials have erred in making a school district assignment, the affected student can assert a right to remain in the assigned school after the mistake is discovered.[55]

As a result of reductions in federal "impact aid" to compensate public school districts for pupils associated with tax-exempt federal property (e.g., military installations), there has been some controversy over the authority of school districts to charge tuition to these students who are temporary residents. The Fourth Circuit Court of Appeals in 1984 invalidated such a tuition policy, noting that the school district had a contract with the federal government to provide educational opportunities for federal dependents as a condition of receiving impact aid.[56]

From litigation to date, it appears that school districts have considerable latitude in establishing residency requirements for students as long as protected rights are respected. Although tuition can be charged to students who temporarily reside away from their parents for the sole purpose of attending school, students who are bona fide residents of the district— even those whose parents are temporarily assigned to federal installations or whose parents entered the country illegally—cannot be denied a free public education.

SCHOOL FEES

Public schools face mounting financial pressures from escalating costs of facilities, supplies, insurance, and services required by students with special needs. Also, intergovernmental competition for tax dollars is increasing, and citizens continue to press for tax relief. Thus, it comes as little surprise that school officials are considering options to transfer some of the fiscal burden for public school services and materials to students and their parents. Although the law is clear that public schools cannot charge tuition as a prerequisite to school attendance, various "user fees" for transportation, books, and course materials have been controversial.

TRANSPORTATION

Several courts have distinguished transportation charges from tuition charges, concluding that transportation is not an essential part of students' entitlement to a free public education.[57] Courts have upheld policies allowing school districts to differentiate between resident and nonresident students regarding transportation fees,[58] to provide one-way transportation only,[59] to impose geographic limitations on bus services,[60] and to charge for summer school transportation.[61]

In the only Supreme Court decision involving public school user fees, the Court in 1988 upheld a North Dakota statute permitting some school districts to charge a fee for bus transportation.[62] In 1979 North Dakota enacted the controversial law, authorizing nonreorganized school districts to charge a transportation fee, not to exceed the school district's estimated cost of providing the service.[63] When the school district in question implemented door-to-door bus service, it assessed a fee for approximately 11 percent of the costs, with the remainder supported by state and local tax revenues. Rejecting a parental challenge to the law, the Supreme Court concluded that the law served the legitimate purpose of encouraging school districts to provide bus services. Noting that the state is not obligated to provide school transportation services at all, the Court held that such services need not be provided free. The Court further concluded that the law's distinction between reorganized and nonreorganized school districts did not present an equal protection violation in the absence of proof that the statute was arbitrary and irrational.

In general, it appears that as long as school officials have a rational basis for their decisions, reasonable school transportation fees can be imposed. However, states do not have the same discretion regarding transportation for children with disabilities. Under federal and state laws, transportation is a related service that must be provided free if needed for a child with disabilities to participate in the educational program (see Chapter 5).

TEXTBOOKS, COURSES, AND MATERIALS

The legality of charging students for the use of public school textbooks has been contested with some regularity. In 1972, the Supreme Court sidestepped the federal constitutional issue in a New York case. The case focused on a school district's book rental system implemented under a state law that allowed school districts to decide by election whether to charge elementary school students a book rental fee. The Second Circuit Court of Appeals concluded that the law did not violate fourteenth amendment equal protection rights, even though it served to disadvantage children from poor families. The Supreme Court agreed to review the case, but before it had the opportunity to address the constitutional issue, voters in the district under litigation decided to assess a tax to purchase all textbooks in grades one through six. The Supreme Court, therefore, vacated the appellate court's judgment since no controversy remained for judicial resolution.[64]

Because the Supreme Court has not ruled on the validity of textbook fees under federal equal protection guarantees, resolution of this issue has been handled on the basis of each state's constitutional and statutory mandates. In several states, such as Arizona, Colorado, Indiana, and Wisconsin, constitutional provisions have been interpreted as permitting fees for public school textbooks.[65] While authorizing textbook fees, an Indiana federal district court ruled that students could not be suspended from school for their parents' failure to pay the fees. Such action was found to impair the state student disciplinary code and federal equal protection guarantees.[66] The Ninth Circuit Court of Appeals also recognized that students have a constitutional right not to be subjected to embarrassment, humiliation, or other penalties for failure to pay textbook fees.[67]

In other states, such as Idaho, Illinois, Michigan, and North Dakota, courts have interpreted state constitutional provisions as precluding the imposition of fees for textbooks.[68] Even in states where textbook fees have been judicially upheld, a waiver is usually provided for students who cannot afford to pay the assessed amount. The West Virginia high court interpreted the state constitution as requiring textbooks, workbooks, and other materials necessary for the state-prescribed curriculum to be provided free for students who cannot afford to purchase them.[69] However, the Arizona Supreme Court held that a school district's failure to supply indigent high school children with textbooks did not abridge equal protection or due process rights.[70]

In addition to fees for textbooks, fees for courses and supplies also have been challenged, generating a range of judicial opinions. The Supreme Court of Missouri ruled that the practice of charging course fees as a prerequisite to enrollment in academic classes impaired students' rights to free public schooling.[71] The Supreme Courts of Montana and New Mexico interpreted their state constitutions as prohibiting fees for required courses, but allowing reasonable fees for elective courses.[72] In contrast, the supreme courts of North Carolina and Illinois have concluded that their state constitutions permit public schools to charge supply fees for *any* courses.[73]

In some cases, the concept of charging parents for materials and other supplies has received judicial endorsement, but the manner of fee collection has been invalidated. A New York appeals court struck down a school district's annual supply fee for classroom materials, reasoning that while parents could be asked to furnish supplies for the children, imposition of a charge on parents who were unwilling to purchase the supplies through the school district violated state law.[74] The North Carolina Supreme Court ruled that parents who were financially able could be required to furnish supplies and materials for pupils' personal use or to pay "modest, reasonable" supply fees, but the court invalidated the school district's waiver policy for students who could not afford the fees.[75] The court reasoned that the policy was unconstitutional since it failed to provide a mechanism for notifying students or their parents of the availability of the waiver and the application process.

Currently, school districts in many states solicit fees from students for various consumable materials. The legality of such practices varies across states and depends primarily on the state judiciary's assessment of state constitutional provisions. An issue receiving increasing attention is the imposition of fees for participation in extracurricular activities; litigation pertaining to this topic is discussed in Chapter 4.

THE SCHOOL CURRICULUM

State legislation regarding the public school curriculum has become increasingly explicit, with some enactments challenged as violating individuals' protected rights. Also, curriculum policies of local school boards have been controversial. This section focuses on legal developments involving curriculum requirements/restrictions and instructional censorship.

REQUIREMENTS AND RESTRICTIONS

Courts repeatedly have recognized that the state retains the power to determine the public school curriculum as long as federal constitutional guarantees are respected. Although a few state constitutions include specific curriculum mandates, more typically the legislature is given responsibility to make such curricular determinations. States vary as to the specificity of legislative directives, but all states require instruction pertaining to the Federal Constitution. Most legislatures also mandate instruction in American history. Other subjects commonly required are English, mathematics, drug education, health, and physical education. Some state statutes specify what subjects will be taught in which grades, and many states have detailed legislation pertaining to vocational education, bilingual education, and special services for children with disabilities. State laws usually stipulate that local school boards must offer the state-mandated minimum curriculum and may supplement this, unless there is a statutory prohibition. In about half of the states, local school boards are empowered to adopt courses of study, but often they must secure approval from the state board of education.

In addition to authority over the public school curriculum, states also have the power to specify textbooks and to regulate the method by which such books are obtained and distributed. In most states, textbooks are prescribed by the state board of education or a textbook commission. A list of acceptable books typically is developed at the state level, and local school boards then adopt specific texts for course offerings within the district. However, in some states, such as Colorado, the local board is given almost complete authority in making textbook selections.

A Mississippi federal district court found evidence of racial bias on the part of a state textbook-rating committee that barred from the approved list a history textbook because of its controversial treatment of racial matters, particularly the reconstruction period and civil rights movement.[76] In addition to finding that the textbook committee's action violated civil rights statutes, the court held that the statutory scheme, authorizing the textbook approval committee to ensure that no unauthorized ideas were introduced in the classroom, deprived authors, educators, and students of their constitutionally protected rights to freedom of speech and press and due process of law. The scheme precluded further review of the committee's decisions and foreclosed any involvement of those affected by the decisions.

Parents often have challenged specific curricular offerings or prohibitions, asserting a right to control their children's course of study in public schools. As discussed in Chapter 2, courts have endorsed requests for specific children to be excused from selected course offerings (e.g., sex education) that offend their religious beliefs, as long as the exemption does not impede the student's academic progress or the management of the school.[77] Religious challenges to the courses themselves, however, have not found a receptive judicial forum. Courts consistently have held that the state and its agents (e.g., state and local boards of education) are empowered to determine the components of the public school curriculum within constitutional parameters.

Although states have considerable discretion in curricular matters, some legislative attempts to impose curriculum restrictions have run afoul of federal constitutional rights. The first curriculum case to reach the Supreme Court involved a 1923 challenge to a Nebraska law that prohibited instruction in a foreign language in any public or private school to children who had not successfully completed the eighth grade.[78] The state high court had upheld the dismissal of a private school teacher for teaching reading in German to elementary school students. In striking down the statute, the Supreme Court reasoned that the teacher's right to teach, the parents' right to engage him to instruct their children, and the children's right to acquire useful knowledge were protected liberties under the due process clause of the fourteenth amendment.

The Supreme Court in 1968 held that states are precluded by the first amendment from barring public school instruction, such as teaching about evolution, simply because it conflicts with certain religious views. The Court declared that "the first amendment does not permit the state to require that teaching and learning must be tailored to the principles or prohibitions of any religious sect or dogma."[79] More recently, the Supreme Court invalidated Louisiana's law requiring instruction in the Biblical account of creation whenever evolution was introduced in the curriculum, concluding that the law unconstitutionally advanced religion.[80]

If constitutional rights are not implicated, however, courts will uphold decisions of state and local education agencies in curricular matters. Courts have deferred to state authorities not only in determining courses of study but also in establishing standards for pupil performance[81] and imposing other instructional requirements.[82] For example, school districts can establish prerequisites and admission criteria for particular courses as long as such criteria are not arbitrary and do not serve to disadvantage certain groups of students. The Fifth Circuit Court of Appeals recognized that in the absence of an independent source, such as a state law entitling students to a particular course of study, students have no property right to be admitted to any class that is offered in the public school.[83] A New York court also rejected a student's assertion that he had a mandatory right to early graduation since he had accumulated sufficient credits. Noting that the program in question required completion of the twelfth grade, the court held that the judiciary does not have the power to review the competence of educational institutions in making academic judgments as to whether a student is entitled to a degree.[84]

Given the state's plenary power over education and the judiciary's relative lack of educational expertise, courts are generally reluctant to interfere with instructional decisions made by state and local education agencies. Courts will intervene only if such decisions are clearly arbitrary or impair constitutional rights.

CENSORSHIP OF INSTRUCTIONAL MATERIALS

Attempts to remove books from classrooms and libraries and to tailor curricular offerings and methodologies to particular religious and philosophical values have led to substantial litigation. Few aspects of the public school program remain totally untouched by recent censorship activities. With the multiple participants and interests involved in these disputes, the issues do not lend themselves to simple solutions. Although most persons agree that schools transmit values, there is little consensus regarding *which* values should be transmitted or *who* should make this determination. It has been estimated that approximately 200 organizations are involved in efforts to eliminate specific materials from public schools. Some challenges emanate from civil rights and consumer groups, contesting materials that promote racism, sexism, or bad health habits for students. However, most of the challenges come from conservative parent groups, alleging that particular instructional activities and materials are immoral and anti-Christian.[85] People for the American Way documented a steady increase in censorship attempts by these conservative groups during the 1980s, with 244 reported incidents in thirty-nine states during the 1989–1990 school year.[86] Efforts to restrict *course offerings* for religious reasons are addressed in Chapter 2, so the discussion here focuses primarily on censorship of *instructional materials*.

One of the first widely publicized censorship cases involved Kanawha County, West Virginia. In 1974, parents protested the school board's adoption of a series of English materials that they considered godless, communistic, profane, and otherwise inappropriate for use in the schools. National attention was aroused as the protests evolved into school boycotts, a coal miners' strike, shootings, a courthouse bombing, and even public prayer calling for the death of school board members. Although the federal district court upheld the board's authority to determine curricular materials and rejected the parents' contention that the books represented an infringement of constitutionally protected rights, book burnings and other public demonstrations continued.[87]

To date, courts have not allowed mere parental displeasure over instructional materials to dictate the public school curriculum, noting that parents' "sensibilities are not the full measure of what is proper education.''[88] In rejecting a parental objection to the use of Kurt Vonnegut's *Slaughterhouse Five* in the public school curriculum, a Michigan appeals court declared: ''Our Constitution does not command ignorance; on the contrary, it assures the people that the state may not relegate them to such a status and guarantees to all the precious and unfettered freedom of pursuing one's own intellectual pleasures in one's own personal way.''[89] More recently, federal appellate courts have rejected parental challenges to school boards' use of books that allegedly promote a religious creed placing reliance on science and human nature rather than God.[90] The courts have found the contested books to be religiously neutral and related to legitimate educational objectives.

While courts have not been receptive to challenges to school boards' curricular decisions simply because some materials or course content offend the sensibilities of specific students or parents, more difficult legal issues are raised when policymakers themselves (e.g., legislators, school board members) support the censorship activity. Bills calling for instructional censorship have been introduced in Congress and numerous state legislatures, with the central targets being materials and activities that allegedly advance ''secular humanism'' or ''new age'' philosophy.[91] In addition, conservative parent groups have sought school board policies to eliminate ''objectionable'' materials from public school classrooms and libraries.

The Supreme Court has recognized the broad discretionary authority of school boards to make decisions that reflect the ''legitimate and substantial community interest in promoting respect for authority and traditional values, be they social, moral, or political.''[92] Thus, the judiciary has been reluctant to interfere with school boards' prerogatives in selecting and eliminating instructional materials. The Second Circuit Court of Appeals on two occasions upheld a school board's right to remove particular books from public school libraries, noting that a book does not acquire tenure and therefore can be removed by the same authority that made the initial selection.[93] The court reasoned that a school board's decision to remove ''vulgar'' and ''obscene'' books and to screen future library acquisitions does not threaten the suppression of ideas.[94]

Similarly, in 1980 the Seventh Circuit Court of Appeals endorsed an Indiana federal district court's conclusion that ''it is legitimate for school officials to develop an opinion about what type of citizens are good citizens, to determine what curriculum and materials will best develop good citizens, and to prohibit the use of texts, remove library books, and delete courses from the curriculum as a part of the effort to shape students into good citizens.''[95] Recognizing that challenges by secondary school students to educational decisions made by local authorities can sometimes be valid, the court emphasized that such complaints must ''cross a relatively high threshold'' before implicating constitutional rights to justify federal court intervention. According to the appellate court, the judiciary should not interfere with a school board's broad discretion in making curricular determinations unless there is a "flagrant abuse" of that discretion.[96]

Although the judiciary has attempted to uphold school boards' authority to apply social and moral values in determining curricular materials and offerings, some courts have found that specific censorship activities have impaired students' protected rights to have access to information. For example, in 1976, the Sixth Circuit Court of Appeals ruled that a school board acted beyond its authority in removing books from the school library.[97] While upholding the board's right to override faculty judgments regarding the selection of books for academic courses and the school library, the court concluded that the board failed to demonstrate any compelling reason for removing books that had already been placed in the library. The court stated that the board was not forced to establish a library, but having done so, it could not place restrictions on the use of the library simply to conform to preferences of school board members.

Other courts have intervened if specific censorship activity has clearly been motivated by a desire to suppress particular viewpoints or controversial ideas. The New Hampshire federal district court held that the removal of *Ms.* magazine from the school library violated students' first amendment rights; board members' disapproval of the political orientation of *Ms.* was not a sufficient justification for their censorship action.[98] Also, the Eighth Circuit Court of Appeals afforded constitutional protection to students' rights to be exposed to controversial ideas when it struck down a Minnesota school board's attempt to ban certain films from school because of their ideological content.[99]

While there has been substantial activity in lower courts, the Supreme Court has rendered only one decision involving censorship efforts in public schools. This case, *Board of Education, Island Trees Union Free School District v. Pico*,[100] unfortunately, did not provide significant clarification regarding the scope of school boards' authority to restrict student access to particular materials. In fact, seven of the nine Supreme Court justices wrote separate opinions, conveying a range of viewpoints as to the governing legal principles.

At issue in *Pico* was the school board's removal of certain books from junior high and high school libraries and the literature curriculum, despite the contrary recommendation of a committee appointed to review the books.[101] The federal district court ruled in favor of the school board without a trial, holding that the board had acted within its authority in removing the controversial books. Reversing the lower court's decision, the Second Circuit Court of Appeals remanded the case for a trial to determine whether the school board's action impaired students' first amendment rights. The United States Supreme Court narrowly affirmed the appellate court's remand of the case because of irregularities in the removal procedures and unresolved factual questions regarding the school board's motivation. However, only three of the Supreme Court justices endorsed the notion that students have a protected right to receive information.[102] And even those justices recognized the broad authority of school boards to remove materials that are "pervasively vulgar" or educationally unsuitable and indicated that a trial might have been unnecessary if the school board had employed regular and unbiased procedures in reviewing the controversial materials.[103] The *Pico* plurality also emphasized that the controversy involved *library* books, which are not required reading for students, noting that school boards "might well defend their claim of absolute discretion in matters of *curriculum* by reliance upon their duty to inculcate community values."[104]

Further strengthening the broad discretion of school authorities in *curriculum-related* censorship was a 1988 Supreme Court decision involving students' free speech rights, *Hazelwood School District v. Kuhlmeier*.[105] The Court declared that public school authorities can censor student expression in school-related activities to ensure that the expression is consistent with educational objectives. The Court's conclusion that expression appearing to represent the school can be restricted for educational reasons has been cited by courts upholding school boards' censorship decisions. For example, the Eleventh Circuit Court of Appeals upheld a Florida school board's action, barring use of a humanities book because it included Aristophanes' *Lysistrata* and Chaucer's *The Miller's Tale,* which board members considered vulgar and immoral. Although voicing disapproval of the board basing its decision on fundamentalist religious views, the court nonetheless relied on *Hazelwood* in deferring to the board's broad discretion in curricular matters.[106] Also relying on *Hazelwood,* a California appeals court acknowledged that school boards can censor instructional materials for educational reasons. However, the court noted that this authority does have limits; motives of board members must be assessed to ensure that they are not barring materials for religious reasons.[107]

Though specific issues may change, controversy surrounding the selection of materials for the library and curriculum will likely persist in public schools. Judge Rosenn of the Third Circuit Court of Appeals noted the "inherent tension" between the school board's two essential functions of "exposing young minds to the clash of ideologies in the free marketplace of ideas" and instilling basic community values in our youth.[108] School boards would be wise to establish procedures for reviewing objections to course content and library materials,[109] and such procedures should be established before a controversy arises. Criteria for the acquisition and elimination of instructional materials should be clearly articulated and educationally defensible. Once a process is in place to evaluate complaints relating to the instructional program, school boards should follow it carefully, as courts will show little sympathy when a school board ignores its own established procedures.

STUDENT PROFICIENCY TESTING

Acknowledging the state's authority to establish academic standards, including mandatory examinations, the judiciary traditionally has been reluctant to interfere with assessments of pupil performance. In 1978 the Supreme Court distinguished an academic determination from a disciplinary action, noting that the former "judgment is by its nature more subjective and evaluative than the typical factual questions presented in the average disciplinary decision."[110] The Court emphasized that academic performance is properly assessed by professional educators who have expertise in this area.

Courts have recognized that assurance of an educated citizenry is an appropriate state goal and that the establishment of minimum performance standards to give value to a high school diploma is a rational means to attain that goal.[111] Courts also have endorsed local school boards' authority to go beyond state minimum standards in establishing testing requirements for promotion and/or high school graduation, as long as the additional requirements are not prohibited by state law. In 1982 an Illinois federal district court noted that "local boards of education and their staffs have the right, if not a positive duty, to develop reasonable means to determine the effectiveness of their educational programs with respect to all individual students to whom they issue diplomas."[112]

The concept of proficiency examinations is not new, but the use of performance tests as a condition of grade promotion or the receipt of a high school diploma has a relatively brief history. In 1976 only four states had enacted student proficiency testing legislation. By 1987, however, thirty states had enacted laws or administrative regulations pertaining to statewide performance testing programs, and one-third of the states were conditioning receipt of a high school diploma on passage of a test.[113] Without question, student proficiency testing has become a pervasive and controversial national phenomenon.

Although the state's authority to assess student performance has not been questioned, the implementation of specific testing programs has been legally challenged as impairing students' rights to fair and nondiscriminatory treatment. Litigation has focused primarily on tests used as a prerequisite to receipt of a high school diploma, but principles established in these cases have implications for testing programs used for grade promotion as well.

In the leading case, *Debra P. v. Turlington,* the Fifth Circuit Court of Appeals addressed a fourteenth amendment challenge to Florida's statewide proficiency testing program in 1981.[114] Regarding the due process claim, the appeals court affirmed the trial court's conclusion that thirteen months' notice of the test requirement was insufficient for students to prepare for the test used as a diploma sanction.[115] The court recognized that by making schooling mandatory, the state created a property interest—a valid expectation that students would receive diplomas if they passed required courses. Given this property interest, the due process clause entitles students to sufficient notice of conditions attached to high school graduation and an opportunity to satisfy the standards before a diploma can be withheld. Further implicating due process guarantees, the record suggested that the state may have administered a fundamentally unfair test covering material that had not been taught in Florida schools. To satisfy the fourteenth amendment on remand, the state would have to prove that students were being *adequately prepared* for the examination.

Regarding the claim that the higher failure rate of African-American students presented an equal protection clause violation, the appeals court noted that some students subjected to the test had started elementary school under segregated conditions and the state did not adequately refute that the disparate failure rate was the result of prior racial discrimination. The state was enjoined from using the test as a diploma sanction until it could produce evidence that the testing program was fundamentally fair and nondiscriminatory. However, the continued use of the test to determine remediation needs was found constitutionally permissible. The court noted that the disproportionate placement of minority students in remedial programs *per se* does not abridge the equal protection clause without evidence of intentional discrimination.

After a lengthy trial on remand, the district court ruled that the injunction should be lifted, and the appeals court affirmed this decision in 1984.[116] The state convinced the judiciary that the test was instructionally valid in that it covered material taught to Florida students; the state provided data from a survey of all teachers and a sample of students, interviews with teachers and administrators, and an analysis of curriculum guides and other documents. Also, the state substantiated that racial differences in pass rates were not caused by lingering effects of past school segregation. Indeed, data showing significant improvement among African-American students during the six years the test had been administered convinced the court that the testing program could help remedy the effects of past discrimination.

Other courts have reiterated the principles established in the *Debra P.* litigation.[117] Courts have not clarified, however, the due process standards that apply to tests used to determine grade promotion or remedial needs. In 1984 the Eleventh Circuit Court of Appeals upheld a school board's policy requiring students to exhibit reading proficiency at grade level for promotion, reasoning that students do not have a property right to expect promotion based on substandard scholastic achievement.[118] However, if a test is used as the *sole* basis for denying grade promotion, the judiciary possibly would view such action as implicating a property right, requiring adequate notice and preparation for the test. It is generally agreed that students who fail proficiency examinations are entitled to remediation and the opportunity to retake the test. Indeed, if a student's deficiencies are identified and appropriate remediation is not provided, grounds for a successful instructional negligence suit may be strengthened.[119]

An area of potential legal vulnerability concerns application of competency tests to children with disabilities. Courts in general have ruled that the state does not have to alter its academic standards for students with disabilities; they can be denied grade promotion or a diploma if they do not meet the specified standards.[120] Such children, however, cannot be denied the *opportunity* to satisfy requirements (including tests) for promotion or a diploma. Whether children with disabilities who are removed from the regular instructional program to receive special services could successfully assert that they are not being prepared to pass a proficiency examination has not been addressed by the judiciary.

In some situations, children with mental disabilities are given the option of not taking a proficiency examination if the teams charged with planning their individualized education programs (IEPs) conclude that there is little likelihood of mastering the material covered on the test. Children excused from the test requirement are usually awarded certificates of school attendance or other alternative diplomas. If children with disabilities were awarded regular diplomas based on successful completion of their IEPs, while other students who failed the test were denied diplomas, equal protection rights might be implicated.[121]

The Seventh Circuit Court of Appeals has suggested that children with disabilities may need lengthier notice of a proficiency test requirement than other students to ensure an adequate opportunity for the material on the test to be incorporated into their IEPs.[122] Students with disabilities also are entitled to special accommodations in the administration of examinations to ensure that their knowledge, rather than their disability, is being assessed. Since most performance tests have been validated with nonhandicapped children, the examinations may be vulnerable to legal challenge under the Individuals with Disabilities Education Act, which stipulates that tests must be validated for the specific purpose for which they are used and must be selected and administered to reflect accurately students' aptitude or achievement.[123]

Specific proficiency testing programs will likely generate additional litigation on constitutional and statutory grounds. Educators can take steps to avert successful legal challenges by ensuring that: (1) students are adequately prepared for the tests; (2) students are advised upon entrance into high school of test requirements as a prerequisite to graduation; (3) tests are not intentionally discriminatory and do not perpetuate the effects of past school segregation; (4) students who fail are provided remedial opportunities and the chance to retake the examinations; and (5) appropriate accommodations are made for children with disabilities.

EDUCATIONAL MALPRACTICE

A topic prompting litigation since the mid-1970s is instructional negligence, commonly referred to as educational malpractice.[124] Initial suits focused on whether students have a right to attain a predetermined level of achievement in return for state-mandated school attendance; parents asserted a right to expect their children to be functionally literate upon high school graduation. More recent cases have involved allegations that school authorities have breached their duty to diagnose students' deficiencies and place them in appropriate instructional programs. This section includes an overview of these claims in which plaintiffs have sought damages from school districts for instructional negligence.

In the first educational malpractice suit to receive substantial attention, *Peter W. v. San Francisco Unified School District,* a student asserted that the school district was negligent in teaching, promoting, and graduating him from high school with the ability to read only at the fifth-grade level.[125] He also claimed that his performance and progress had been misrepresented to his parents, who testified that they were unaware of his deficiencies until he was tested by a private agency after high school graduation. Concluding that the school district did not have a duty to guarantee that the student mastered basic academic skills, the California appeals court reasoned that the complexities of the teaching/learning process made it impossible to place the entire burden on the school to assure student literacy. The court found no legitimate connection between the school district's conduct and the alleged injury, declaring that to hold the school district liable would expose all educational agencies to countless "real or imagined" tort claims of "disaffected students and parents."[126]

Subsequently, the New York Court of Appeals dismissed a $5 million educational malpractice suit brought by a learning-disabled high school graduate who claimed that he was unable to complete job applications and cope with the problems of everyday life.[127] As in the California case, the New York high court concluded that the school could not be held accountable for ensuring that all students, with their varying abilities to learn, attain a specified reading level before high school graduation. The court reasoned that disputes over proper educational placements should not be resolved by the judiciary.

In 1979, the same court dismissed what had appeared to be the only successful educational malpractice suit. A state appellate court had awarded a former public school student $500,000 in damages after concluding that the New York City Board of Education had negligently diagnosed his needs and erroneously instructed him in a program for the mentally retarded for twelve years.[128] The thrust of the negligence claim was that the school psychologist's report, recommending reassessment of the child within two years of the original evaluation, was ignored for over a decade—even though he scored in the ninetieth percentile on reading readiness tests at ages eight and nine. Upon high school graduation, he was required to have his intelligence tested to continue receiving social security payments after his eighteenth birthday. At that time he scored in the normal range and thus became ineligible to remain in the occupational training program for individuals with disabilities. According to a psychologist and psychiatrist who testified at the trial, the plaintiff suffered lengthy depression caused by his awareness that he was essentially uneducated and could not earn a living.

Distinguishing this case from previous educational malpractice suits, the lower court noted that school personnel committed affirmative acts of negligence (i.e., ignoring the psychologist's report) that placed crippling burdens on the student. Nonetheless, the New York Court of Appeals by a narrow margin reversed the lower court's ruling and held that it was not the role of the judiciary to make such educational policy determinations. The New York high court emphasized that instructional negligence claims should not be entertained by the judiciary, but should be handled instead through the state educational system's administrative appeals.

Other courts also have indicated a reluctance to intervene in such educational policy decisions.[129] For example, in 1984 a California appellate court dismissed a negligence suit in which parents sought damages for the school district's alleged breach of its duty under state and federal statutes to evaluate and develop an individualized education plan for their child with emotional and mental disabilities.[130] Rejecting the contention that there was an implied duty that had been breached, the court observed that the societal interest in providing special education to students with disabilities is not advanced by transforming special education laws "into springboards for private damages suits."[131] Similarly, the Supreme Court of Alaska refused to allow damages against a school district for the alleged misclassification of a student with dyslexia,[132] and a New Jersey superior court ruled that a school district's failure to provide remedial instruction for a student was not actionable in a tort suit for damages.[133]

Although no educational malpractice claim has yet been successful, some courts have recognized circumstances under which plaintiffs possibly could recover damages in an instructional tort action. In a Maryland case plaintiffs did not prevail in establishing instructional malpractice for *unintentional* negligent acts in evaluating a child's learning disabilities and inappropriately instructing the child, but the state high court held that parents could maintain an action to prove that the defendants *intentionally* engaged in acts that injured a child placed in their educational care. Although recognizing that the parents' burden of proof would be substantial, the court indicated that they had a right to attempt to prove such an allegation. Distinguishing intentional from unintentional acts, the court noted the availability of administrative remedies to settle the latter.[134]

The Supreme Court of Montana went further, ruling that *unintentional* acts might result in liability where school authorities have violated mandatory statutes pertaining to special education placements.[135] Declaring that school districts have a duty to exercise reasonable care in testing and placing exceptional students in appropriate programs, the court concluded that damages could be assessed for injuries resulting from a breach of that duty. On remand, however, the trial court held that the plaintiff failed to present evidence substantiating that the child was erroneously placed in a segregated special education class, and the state high court subsequently affirmed this ruling.

In 1984 the New York high court unanimously allowed damages in a medical malpractice suit, even though the consequences were educational, but it barred damages in an instructional negligence suit by a one-vote margin. In the latter case, which the Supreme Court declined to review, the New York high court ruled that a student who was incorrectly diagnosed at age ten, after having been tested in English although he understood only Spanish, was not entitled to damages from the child-care agency for its alleged failure to obtain suitable instruction to enable him to learn to read.[136] The plaintiff attempted to distinguish his claim from prior malpractice suits against schools in that his charges were against the child-care agency responsible for his upbringing after his mother abandoned him at age seven. Rejecting this contention, the court determined that the issue involved educational policy matters regarding which instructional programs might have been preferable and was not actionable in a negligence suit.

In the other case, the same court awarded damages to an individual who was admitted to a state school at age two, diagnosed as retarded when he was actually deaf, and instructed in classes for the retarded for the next nine years.[137] The failure to reassess the student upon learning that he was deaf was considered a "discernible act of medical malpractice on the part of the state" rather than a mere mistake in judgment pertaining to the student's educational program.[138] Concluding that the state school resembled a hospital and the student's records resembled medical records, the court held that damages for medical malpractice were appropriate.

The New York high court distinguished the two cases based on the age of the students when institutionalized, the nature of the institutions, and the kinds of care administered. These distinctions have been questioned by legal commentators, however, and there is some sentiment that prospects for a successful educational malpractice suit involving *placement negligence* may be more promising than they appeared in the 1970s.[139] The increasing legislative specificity pertaining to student proficiency standards and special education placements may strengthen the grounds for such suits. Even though it seems unlikely that public schools in the near future will be held responsible for a specified quantum of student achievement, it is conceivable that schools will be held legally accountable for diagnosing pupils' needs, placing them in appropriate instructional programs, and reporting their progress to parents.[140]

INSTRUCTIONAL PRIVACY RIGHTS

The protection of students' privacy rights has become an increasingly volatile issue in political forums. State and federal laws have been enacted to ensure the confidentiality of students' records. In addition, laws have been enacted to protect students from mandatory participation in research projects or instructional activities designed to reveal personal information in sensitive areas. This section provides an overview of legal developments pertaining to students' privacy rights in instructional matters.

STUDENT RECORDS

The Supreme Court has recognized that constitutional protection is afforded to a zone of personal privacy;[141] thus, there must be a compelling justification for governmental action that impairs privacy rights, including the right to have personal information about oneself kept confidential. As a result of this acknowledged right, questions about who has access to public school students' permanent files and the contents of such files have been the source of controversy.

Legal challenges to school record-keeping procedures have resulted in court orders that school officials expunge irrelevant information from students' permanent folders. In an early case, the Supreme Court of Oklahoma ordered the removal from the school register of a notation that a pupil had been "ruined by tobacco and whiskey."[142] Finding no evidence to support the statement's veracity, the court concluded that the student was unjustly defamed. In some situations, students have brought successful libel suits for damages against school authorities who allegedly have recorded and communicated false defamatory information about them.[143]

Because of widespread dissatisfaction with educators' efforts to ameliorate abuses associated with student record keeping practices, Congress enacted the Family Educational Rights and Privacy Act (FERPA) in 1974.[144] This law stipulates that federal funds may be withdrawn from any educational agency or institution that: (1) fails to provide parents access to their child's educational records; or (2) disseminates such information (with some exceptions) to third parties without parental permission. Upon reaching age eighteen, students may exercise the rights guaranteed to parents under this law.

Education officials may assume that a parent is entitled to exercise rights under FERPA unless state law or a court order bars a parent's access to his or her child's records under specific circumstances and the education agency has been instructed accordingly.[145] In 1981 a New York court ruled that the noncustodial father of a fifth-grade child was still a "psychological guardian" and was entitled to inspect the education records of his child despite the contrary wishes of the child's mother.[146]

After reviewing a student's permanent file, the parent or eligible student can request that the information be amended if it is believed to be inaccurate, misleading, or in violation of the student's protected rights. If school authorities decide that an amendment is not warranted, the parent or eligible student must be advised of the right to a hearing. The hearing officer may be an employee of the school district, but may not be an individual with a direct interest in the outcome of the hearing. Either party may be represented by counsel at the hearing, and the hearing officer must issue a written decision summarizing the evidence presented and the rationale for the ruling. If the hearing officer concludes that the records should not be amended, the parent or eligible student has the right to place in the file a personal statement specifying objections. Individuals can file a complaint with the U.S. Department of Education if they believe a school district is not complying with the provisions of FERPA.[147]

Other federal laws include additional protections regarding the confidentiality and accessibility of student records. For example, the Individuals with Disabilities Education Act stipulates that records of children with disabilities must be accessible to their parents or guardians.[148] Furthermore, interpreters must be hired, if necessary, to translate the contents of students' files for parents, and parental consent is required before such records can be disclosed to third parties.

Many states also have enacted legislation addressing the privacy of student records. Indiana law is typical in stipulating that school boards must maintain a list of all persons or agencies having access to personal files, furnish prior notice before such information is disclosed to a third party, and inform individuals of their rights to access and to contest the accuracy or appropriateness of the material in such files.[149]

Both state and federal privacy laws recognize certain exceptions to disclosure provisions. For example, a teacher's daily records pertaining to pupil progress are exempt as long as the records are kept in the sole possession of the faculty member. However, private notes become education records and are subject to legal specifications if they are shared, even among educators who have a legitimate need for access to such information.

Under FERPA, certain public directory information, such as students' names, addresses, dates and places of birth, major fields of study, and degrees and awards received, can be released without parental consent. However, any educational agency releasing such data must give public notice of the specific categories it has designated as "directory" and must allow a reasonable period of time for parents to inform the agency that any or all of this information should not be released on their child without their prior consent.[150]

A student's records also can be released to officials of a school where the student is transferring if the parents or eligible student are notified, or the sending institution has given prior notice that it routinely transfers such records. A Maryland appeals court rejected a claim that a school's release of a student's records, including psychological reports, to the school where the student was transferring represented an invasion of privacy actionable in a suit for damages. There was no evidence that any unauthorized individuals had access to the information in the records or that any unwarranted publicity resulted from the release of the records.[151]

Similarly, students' privacy rights do not preclude federal and state authorities from having access to data needed to audit and evaluate federally supported education programs. These data, however, are to be collected in a way that prevents the disclosure of personally identifiable information. Also, composite information on pupil achievement can be released to the public as long as individual students are not personally identified. Courts have ruled that names must be deleted as well as gender and race if students could be identified by such information; names also must be scrambled if an alphabetical list would reveal the identity of individual students.[152] In an illustrative case, a Louisiana appeals court rejected a claim that the release of composite achievement data by school officials violated students' privacy rights, declaring that the public had the right to examine the rankings of schools participating in a school effectiveness study conducted by the state department of education.[153]

Students' records must be disclosed if subpoenaed by a court. In compelling a school district to reveal records of individual pupils, a New York federal district court held that FERPA does not preclude the disclosure of student records where a genuine need for the information outweighs the students' privacy interests. In this case, data on the performance of individual students were needed to substantiate charges that inadequate instructional programs were being provided for children with English language deficiencies.[154] Also, a New York appeals court ruled that the records of students in a teacher's class would have to be disclosed (obliterating identifying data) for use by the teacher in defending charges pertaining to his competence. The court reasoned that "any degree of confidentiality accorded to the students' records must yield to the [teacher's] right to prepare his defense to the charges made against his reputation and his competence in his profession."[155]

Since Congress, state legislatures, and the judiciary have indicated a continuing interest in safeguarding the privacy rights of students in connection with school records, school boards would be wise to reassess their policies to ensure that they are adhering to the mandates included in federal and state laws. School personnel, however, should use some restraint before purging information from student files. Pertinent material that is necessary to provide continuity in a student's instructional program *should* be included in a permanent record and available for use by authorized personnel. It is unfortunate that fear of federal sanctions under FERPA has resulted in deletion of useful information—along with material that should be removed—from student records.

The mere fact that information in a student's file is negative does not imply that the material is inappropriate. Courts have held that school authorities have an obligation to record relevant data pertaining to students' activities as long as such information is accurate. In an illustrative Pennsylvania case, students sought to enjoin school officials from noting in their permanent records and communicating to institutions of higher education that they had participated in a demonstration at graduation ceremonies. The federal district court denied the injunction, reasoning that the objective account of what occurred at the graduation exercises, with no reference as to the propriety of the demonstration, did not result in any "immediate, irreparable harm" to the students.[156] Furthermore, the court held that school officials have a *duty* to record and communicate true factual information about students to institutions of higher learning in order to present an accurate picture of applicants for admission.

PUPIL PROTECTION LAWS

Increasing attention has focused on the protection of public school students involved in research projects and experimental treatment programs. Parents have voiced concern over what they perceive to be non-academic programs that invade family privacy. In 1973 a Pennsylvania federal district court enjoined implementation of a project in which potential drug abusers were to be identified (through a questionnaire) and subjected to peer and faculty counseling. The court determined that such an invasion of privacy without informed consent violated protected rights of subjects and their parents.[157]

State legislatures as well as Congress have enacted laws to protect students' privacy in connection with research activities in public schools. Under federal law, human subjects are protected in research projects supported by federal grants and contracts in any private or public institution or agency.[158] Informed consent must be obtained before placing subjects at risk of being exposed to physical, psychological, or social injury as a result of participating in research, development, or related activities. All education agencies are required to establish review committees to ensure that the rights and welfare of all subjects are adequately protected.

In 1974 two amendments to the General Education Provisions Act required among other things that all instructional materials in federally assisted research or experimentation projects (designed to explore new or unproven teaching methods or techniques) be made available for inspection by parents of participating students. The amendments also stipulated that children could not be required to participate in such research or experimentation projects if their parents objected in writing. In 1978 Congress enacted an additional amendment, referred to as the Hatch Amendment after its sponsor, Orrin Hatch. The Hatch Amendment retained the protection of parents' rights to examine instructional materials in experimental programs and further required parental consent before students participate in federally supported programs involving psychiatric or psychological examination, testing, or treatment designed to reveal information in specified sensitive areas pertaining to personal beliefs, behaviors, and family relationships.[159] The Department of Education's regulations broadly define psychiatric or psychological examination or treatment as including activities that are not directly related to academic instruction and are designed to obtain personal information or affect behaviors or attitudes. The Department is charged with reviewing complaints under this law; if an educational institution is found in violation and does not comply within a reasonable period, federal funds can be withheld.

After the Hatch Amendment's regulations became effective in 1984, this previously obscure provision became extremely controversial, pitting conservative parents' groups against professional education associations. The dispute did not focus on the protection of students' rights in research and experimental programs, but rather on ambiguities in the regulations regarding the scope and intent of the amendment and the federal government's role in resolving curriculum complaints. A coalition of more than thirty education and civil rights organizations faulted the regulations for being so vague that they provide "inroads" for conservative groups to interpret "psychological treatment" as covering any subject matter that is controversial or may require a value response from students.[160] The coalition developed guidelines in an attempt to clarify the limited scope of the Hatch Amendment.[161]

The coalition has voiced concerns that the Hatch Amendment and similar pupil protection provisions being enacted or considered by many state legislatures will negate local school boards' prerogatives in curriculum matters. Although these pupil protection measures are couched in terms of protecting students' privacy rights by granting them *exemptions* from particular instructional activities, if a substantial number of exemptions are requested, a given instructional activity itself may be eliminated from the curriculum. Professional education associations, while supporting students' privacy rights in experimental programs, are opposed to the conservative groups' reliance on pupil protection provisions to force *alterations* in the public school program.[162]

CONCLUSION

The state and its agents enjoy considerable latitude in regulating various aspects of public education, but any requirements that restrict students' activities must be reasonable and necessary to carry out legitimate educational objectives. Whenever students' or parents' protected rights are impaired, school authorities must be able to substantiate that there is an overriding public interest to be served. From an analysis of court cases and legislation pertaining to general requirements and rights associated with school attendance and the instructional program, the following generalizations seem warranted.

1. The state can compel children between specified ages to attend school.[163]
2. Students can satisfy compulsory attendance mandates by attending private schools and, in most states, by receiving equivalent instruction (e.g., home tutoring) that is comparable to the public school program.
3. School officials can require immunization against diseases as a condition of school attendance.
4. Students cannot be excluded from public school because of particular health conditions, unless school attendance would endanger the health of others.
5. Public school districts must provide an education for bona fide resident children (even those who have entered the country illegally), but children who live apart from their parents for educational purposes are not entitled to tuition-free schooling.
6. Fees can be charged for public school transportation as long as the fees are rationally related to legitimate state objectives.
7. Fees can be charged for the use of public school textbooks and for supplies associated with courses unless such fees are prohibited by state constitutional or statutory provisions.
8. The state and its agencies have the authority to determine public school course offerings and instructional materials, and such curricular determinations will be upheld by courts unless clearly arbitrary or in violation of constitutional or statutory rights.
9. School boards can eliminate instructional materials considered educationally unsuitable if objective procedures are followed in making such determinations.
10. Courts defer to school authorities in assessing student performance, in the absence of evidence of arbitrary or discriminatory academic decisions.
11. Proficiency examinations can be used to determine pupil remedial needs and as a prerequisite to high school graduation if students are given sufficient notice prior to implementation of the test requirements and are provided adequate preparation for the examinations.
12. Public schools do not owe students a duty to ensure that a specified level of achievement is attained.
13. Parents and eighteen-year-old students must be granted access to

the student's school records and an opportunity to contest the contents.

14. School personnel must ensure the accuracy of information contained in student records and maintain the confidentiality of such records.
15. Parents have the right to inspect materials used in federally funded experimental projects, and students have a right to be excused from participation in such programs involving psychiatric or psychological testing or treatment designed to reveal information in specified sensitive areas pertaining to personal beliefs, behaviors, and family relationships.

ENDNOTES

1. Ky. Rev. Stat. § 159.010 (Supp. 1990). For an analysis of compulsory education laws across states, *see* Patricia Lines, *Compulsory Education Laws and Their Impact on Public and Private Education* (Denver, CO: Education Commission of the States, 1985).
2. *See, e.g.,* Trower v. Maple, 774 F.2d 673 (5th Cir. 1985); *In re* C.S., 382 N.W.2d 381 (N.D. 1986); New Mexico v. Edgington, 663 P.2d 374 (N.M. Ct. App. 1983), *cert. denied,* 464 U.S. 940 (1983); Williams v. Board of Educ., Marianna School Dist., 626 S.W.2d 361 (Ark. 1982).
3. *See In re* Michael G., 243 Cal Rptr. 224 (Cal. 1988); *In re* K.M.B., 452 N.E.2d 876 (Ill. App. Ct. 1983), *certification denied,* 483 N.E.2d 666 (Ill. 1985).
4. Means v. Sidiropolis, 401 S.E.2d 447 (W. Va. 1990).
5. 268 U.S. 510, 535 (1925).
6. Christopher Klicka, *Home Schooling in the United States: A Statutory Analysis* (Paeonian Springs, CA: Home School Legal Defense Association, 1990), p. i.
7. Upholding required certification of home tutors, *see* Fellowship Baptist Church v. Benton, 815 F.2d 485 (8th Cir. 1987); People v. DeJonge, 449 N.W.2d 899 (Mich. Ct. App. 1989), *remanded,* 461 N.W.2d 365 (Mich. 1990). In 1991 a South Carolina judge upheld the state's test requirement for home tutors, Lawrence v. South Carolina State Bd. of Educ., No. 98-CP-40-4040 (Anderson County Ct., 1991). *See* "Update," *Education Week,* March 6, 1991, p. 3.
8. Burrow v. Arkansas, 669 S.W.2d 441 (Ark. 1984); New Mexico v. Edgington, 663 P.2d 374 (N.M. Ct. App. 1983), *cert. denied,* 464 U.S. 940 (1983); State v. Garber, 419 P.2d 896 (Kan. 1966), *cert. denied and appeal dismissed,* 389 U.S. 51 (1967). The Arkansas and New Mexico laws subsequently were amended to authorize home education.
9. *See, e.g., In re* D. B., 767 P.2d 801 (Colo. Ct. App. 1988); Delconte v. State, 329 S.E.2d 636 (N.C. 1985). *See also* Duro v. District Attorney, 712 F.2d 96, 99 (4th Cir. 1983), *cert. denied,* 465 U.S. 1006 (1984) (interpreting the North Carolina compulsory attendance law as placing the burden on parents choosing

to educate their children at home to prove that the instruction would prepare the children ''to be self-sufficient participants in our modern society or enable them to participate intelligently in our political system''); Ralph Mawdsley and Steven Permuth, "Home Instruction for Religious Reasons: Parental Right or State Option?" *Education Law Reporter,* vol. 4 (1984), pp. 941–952.

10. Wisconsin v. Popanz, 332 N.W.2d 750 (Wis. 1983); Roemhild v. Georgia, 308 S.E.2d 154 (Ga. 1983).

11. Blackwelder v. Safnauer, 866 F.2d 548 (2d Cir. 1989). While this case was pending, the New York Board of Regents adopted new regulations clarifying that home school programs will be subject to home visits *only* when placed on probation because their individualized instructional plans have not been approved by local school authorities.

12. Bangor Baptist Church v. Maine Dep't of Educ. and Cultural Services, 549 F. Supp. 1208 (D. Me. 1982). *See also* Bangor Baptist Church v. Maine Dep't of Educ. and Cultural Services, 576 F. Supp. 1299 (D. Me. 1983).

13. Bayes v. Idaho, 785 P.2d 660 (Idaho Ct. App. 1989). *See also* Mazanec v. North Judson–San Pierre School Corp., 614 F. Supp. 1152 (N.D. Ind. 1985), *aff'd,* 798 F.2d 230 (7th Cir. 1986) (constitutional challenge to Indiana's compulsory attendance law was rejected where parents were prosecuted for thwarting efforts to verify compliance; the district court's finding that the home education program was essentially equivalent to public school instruction did not entitle the parents to injunctive or monetary relief).

14. Minnesota v. Newstrom, 371 N.W.2d 525 (Minn. 1985).

15. Jeffery v. O'Donnell, 702 F. Supp. 516 (M.D. Pa. 1988).

16. Burrow v. Arkansas, 669 S.W.2d 441 (Ark. 1984).

17. Murphy v. Arkansas, 852 F.2d 1039 (8th Cir. 1988).

18. Vandiver v. Hardin County Bd. of Educ., 925 F.2d 927 (6th Cir. 1991).

19. Klicka, *Home Schooling in the United States: A Statutory Analysis.*

20. *See, e.g.,* Ind. Code Ann. § 20-8.1-3-18; § 20-8.1-4-3 (Supp. 1990).

21. Wisconsin v. Yoder, 406 U.S. 205 (1972).

22. Johnson v. Charles City Community Schools Bd. of Educ., 368 N.W.2d 74 (Iowa 1985), *cert. denied,* 474 U.S. 1033 (1985). *See also* Johnson v. Prince William County School Bd., 404 S.E.2d 209 (Va. 1991) (upholding school board's denial of parents' application for a religious exemption from the compulsory school attendance law because they failed to establish that bona fide religious beliefs were the basis for their request).

23. *In re* McMillan, 226 S.E.2d 693, 695 (N.C. Ct. App. 1976). *See also In re* Baum, 401 N.Y.S.2d 514 (N.Y. App. Div. 1978).

24. Hatch v. Goerke, 502 F.2d 1189 (10th Cir. 1974) (however, expulsion of the student without a hearing for refusing to cut his hair was found to impair due process rights).

25. *See In re* Gregory B., 387 N.Y.S.2d 380 (N.Y. Fam. Ct. 1976); Commonwealth v. Ross, 330 A.2d 290 (Pa. Commw. Ct. 1975).

26. *See* People v. Y.D.M., 593 P.2d 1356 (Colo. 1979); *In re* Foster, 330 N.Y.S.2d 8 (N.Y. Fam. Ct. 1972).

27. Student health concerns have caused some school boards, particularly in urban areas, to establish school-based clinics, offering services ranging from immunization to disease diagnosis and treatment. The number of these clinics increased from 1 in 1970 to 138 in 1988. The most controversial aspect of the

clinics has been their involvement in prescribing and dispensing forms of birth control. *See* Dan Gardner and Mark Buechler, *School-Based Health Clinics* (Bloomington, IN: Consortium on Educational Policy Studies, 1989).

28. Zucht v. King, 260 U.S. 174 (1922). *See also* Jacobson v. Massachusetts, 197 U.S. 11 (1905).

29. Board of Educ. of Mountain Lakes v. Maas, 152 A.2d 394 (N.J. Super. Ct. App. Div. 1959), *aff'd,* 158 A.2d 330 (N.J. 1960) (per curiam), *cert. denied,* 363 U.S. 843 (1960). *See also* Maricopa County Health Dep't v. Harmon, 750 P.2d 1364 (Ariz. Ct. App. 1987); Calandra v. State College Area School Dist., 512 A.2d 809 (Pa. Commw. Ct. 1986).

30. Cude v. Arkansas, 377 S.W.2d 816, 818–819 (Ark. 1964). *See also* Mannis v. Arkansas *ex rel.* Dewitt School Dist., 398 S.W.2d 206 (Ark. 1966), *cert. denied,* 384 U.S. 972 (1966) (parents could not evade mandatory vaccination requirement by withdrawing their child from public school and starting a parochial school that the parents asserted was not subject to the state health requirement).

31. *See, e.g.,* Sherr v. Northport–East Northport Union Free School Dist., 672 F. Supp. 81 (E.D.N.Y. 1987); Davis v. State, 451 A.2d 107 (Md. 1982); Dalli v. Board of Educ., 267 N.E.2d 219 (Mass. 1971) (the court noted that the legislature could remedy the defect in the Massachusetts law by expanding the exemption to cover sincere religious objections to immunization regardless of church membership). *See also* Avard v. Dupuis, 376 F. Supp. 479 (D.N.H. 1974) (statutory religious exemption was unconstitutionally vague because it vested complete discretion in local school boards to determine whether an exemption would be granted).

32. *See, e.g.,* Maier v. Besser, 341 N.Y.S.2d 411 (N.Y. Sup. Ct. 1972); State v. Miday, 140 S.E.2d 325 (N.C. 1965).

33. Mason v. General Brown Cent. School Dist., 851 F.2d 47 (2d Cir. 1988).

34. Kleid v. Board of Educ. of Fulton, Kentucky Indep. School Dist., 406 F. Supp. 902 (W.D. Ky. 1976).

35. Hanzel v. Arter, 625 F. Supp. 1259 (S.D. Ohio 1985) (claims that the immunization requirement impaired constitutional privacy and due process rights also were rejected. *See also* Heard v. Payne, 665 S.W.2d 865 (Ark. 1984) (statement from chiropractor could not satisfy medical exemption from immunization).

36. Brown v. Stone, 378 So. 2d 218 (Miss. 1979), *cert. denied,* 449 U.S. 887 (1980).

37. *See* Thomas v. Atascadero Unified School Dist., 662 F. Supp. 376 (C.D. Cal. 1987); District 27 Community School Bd. v. Board of Educ. of the City of New York, 502 N.Y.S.2d 325 (N.Y. Sup. Ct. 1986).

38. *See, e.g.,* Doe v. Dolton Elementary School Dist. No. 148, 694 F. Supp. 440 (N.D. Ill. 1988); Parents of Child, Code No. 870901W v. Coker, 676 F. Supp. 1072 (E.D. Okla. 1987); Phipps v. Saddleback Valley Unified School Dist., 251 Cal. Rptr. 720 (Cal. Ct. App. 1988); In re Ryan White, No. 86-144 (Ind. Cir. Ct., Clinton County, 1986). *See also* New York Ass'n for Retarded Children v. Carey, 612 F.2d 644 (2d Cir. 1979) (handicapped children with hepatitis B cannot be excluded from or segregated in public schools).

39. Martinez v. School Bd. of Hillsborough County, Florida, 861 F.2d 1502, 1506 (11th Cir. 1988), *on remand,* 711 F. Supp. 1066 (M.D. Fla. 1989).

40. 457 U.S. 202 (1982). *See* text with note 9, Chapter 5.

41. For a discussion of standards of judicial review under the equal protection clause, *see* text with note 1, Chapter 5; note 2, Chapter 9.

42. *See, e.g.*, Steven M. v. Gilhool, 700 F. Supp. 261 (E.D. Pa. 1988); State *ex rel.* Doe v. Kingery, 203 S.E.2d 358 (W. Va. 1974); University Center, Inc. v. Ann Arbor Pub. Schools, 191 N.W.2d 302 (Mich. 1971). However, a state facility can charge tuition for children who are legal wards of another state. *See, e.g.*, Steven M, *id.*; East Texas Guidance and Achievement Center v. Brockette, 431 F. Supp. 231 (E.D. Tex. 1977). *See also* Catlin v. Sobel, 569 N.Y.S.2d 353 (N.Y. 1991) (parents must prove that they have surrendered parental control of their severely disabled child for the child to be considered a resident of the school district where cared for since infancy by a family for a fee).

43. *See, e.g.*, Orozco by Arroyo v. Sobol, 703 F. Supp. 1113 (S.D.N.Y. 1989); Harrison v. Sobol, 705 F. Supp. 870 (S.D.N.Y. 1988).

44. Martinez v. Bynum, 461 U.S. 321 (1983).

45. *Id.* at 328. Justice Marshall faulted the majority for not drawing a distinction between "residence" (having a well-settled connection in a locale) and "domicile" (one's true, fixed, permanent home), arguing that an individual may have more than one residence and that states should not be allowed to deny free schooling to all but domiciliary students. He asserted that the Court's use of a domicile requirement to establish residence for school purposes is not supported by prior Supreme Court decisions, *id.* at 338–342 (Marshall, J. dissenting).

46. Rodriguez v. Ysleta Indep. School Dist., 663 S.W.2d 547 (Tex. Ct. App. 1983). *See also* Jackson v. Waco Indep. School Dist., 629 S.W.2d 201 (Tex. Ct. App. 1982).

47. *See, e.g.*, Harris v. Hall, 572 F. Supp. 1054 (E.D.N.C. 1983); State *ex rel.* Henry v. Board of Educ., Madison Plains Local Schools, 485 N.E.2d 732 (Ohio Ct. App. 1984); Connelly v. Gibbs, 445 N.E.2d 477 (Ill. App. Ct. 1983); Delta Special School Dist. v. McGehee Special School Dist., 659 S.W.2d 508 (Ark. 1983); *In re* Proios, 443 N.Y.S.2d 828 (N.Y. Surrogate Ct. 1981).

48. Daniels v. Morris, 746 F.2d 271 (5th Cir. 1984).

49. Ramsdell v. North River School Dist. No. 200, 704 P.2d 606, 609 (Wash. 1985). *See also* Camer v. Seattle School Dist. No. 1, 762 P.2d 356 (Wash. Ct. App. 1988), *review denied*, 112 Wash. 2d 1006 (Wash. 1989), *cert. denied*, 110 S. Ct. 204 (1989); note 133, *infra*.

50. Kriss v. Brown, 390 N.E.2d 193 (Ind. Ct. App. 1979). *See also In re* United States *ex rel.* Missouri State High School Activities Ass'n, 682 F.2d 147 (8th Cir. 1982); text with note 140, Chapter 4.

51. Horton v. Marshall Pub. Schools, 769 F.2d 1323 (8th Cir. 1985). *But see* Clayton v. White Hall School Dist., 875 F.2d 676 (8th Cir. 1989) (rejecting an equal protection challenge to an Arkansas school district's policy allowing nonresident children of certified and administrative employees, but not other employees, to attend school in the district; the policy was considered rationally related to the objective of recruiting high-quality teachers and administrators).

52. *See* Education Comm'n of the States, *Public School Choice Activity in the States* (Denver: Author, 1989).

53. Fangman v. Moyers, 8 P.2d 762 (Colo. 1932). *See also* Pat v. Stanwood School Dist., 705 P.2d 1236 (Wash. Ct. App. 1985); *In re* Curry, 318 N.W.2d 567 (Mich. Ct. App. 1982).

54. Luoma v. Union School Dist. of Keene, 214 A.2d 120 (N.H. 1965). *See also* Takeall by Rubenstein v. Ambach, 609 F. Supp. 81 (S.D.N.Y. 1985) (an eighteen-year-old student was entitled to notice of the basis for the school board's decision to deny him tuition-free admission as an emancipated student and to notice of the availability of administrative appeals).
55. *See* Burdick v. Independent School Dist. No. 52 of Oklahoma County, 702 P.2d 48 (Okla. 1985).
56. United States v. Onslow County Bd. of Educ., 728 F.2d 628 (4th Cir. 1984).
57. *See* Kadrmas v. Dickinson Pub. Schools, 487 U.S. 450 (1988); Sutton v. Cadillac Area Pub. Schools, 323 N.W.2d 582 (Mich. Ct. App. 1982).
58. *See* Fenster v. Schneider, 636 F.2d 765 (D.C. Cir. 1980).
59. *See* Shaffer v. Board of School Directors, 730 F.2d 910 (3d Cir. 1984).
60. *See* State *ex rel.* Rosenberg v. Grand Coulee Dam School Dist. No. 301, 536 P.2d 614 (Wash. 1975).
61. *See* Crim v. McWhorter, 252 S.E.2d 421 (Ga. 1979).
62. Kadrmas v. Dickinson Pub. Schools, 487 U.S. 450 (1988).
63. Under the law, a school board could waive any fee for families financially unable to pay, but school districts were not obligated to implement such waivers. However, benefits such as diplomas and grades were not to be affected by nonpayment of fees.
64. Johnson v. New York State Educ. Dep't, 449 F.2d 871 (2d Cir. 1971), *vacated and remanded,* 409 U.S. 75 (1972) (per curiam).
65. Marshall v. School Dist. RE No. 3, Morgan County, 553 P.2d 784 (Colo. 1976); Carpio v. Tucson High School Dist. No. 1 of Pima County, 524 P.2d 948 (Ariz. 1974), *cert. denied,* 420 U.S. 982 (1975); Chandler v. South Bend Community School Corp., 312 N.E.2d 915 (Ind. 1974); Board of Educ. v. Sinclair, 222 N.W.2d 143 (Wis. 1974).
66. Carder v. Michigan City School Corp., 552 F. Supp. 869 (N.D. Ind. 1982).
67. Canton v. Spokane School Dist. No. 81, 498 F.2d 840 (9th Cir. 1974).
68. Cardiff v. Bismarck Pub. School Dist., 263 N.W.2d 105 (N.D. 1978); Beck v. Board of Educ. of Harlem Consol. School Dist., 344 N.E.2d 440 (Ill. 1976); Bond v. Ann Arbor School Dist., 178 N.W.2d 484 (Mich. 1970); Paulson v. Minidoka County School Dist. No. 331, 463 P.2d 935 (Idaho 1970).
69. Vandevender v. Cassell, 208 S.E.2d 436 (W. Va. 1974).
70. Carpio v. Tucson High School Dist. No. 1 of Pima County, 524 P.2d 948 (Ariz. 1974).
71. Concerned Parents v. Caruthersville School Dist., 548 S.W.2d 554 (Mo. 1977).
72. Norton v. Board of Educ. of School Dist. No. 16, Hobbs Mun. Schools, 553 P.2d 1277 (N.M. 1976); Granger v. Cascade County School Dist., 499 P.2d 780 (Mont. 1972). Courts also have upheld reasonable fees for drivers' education because it is not a mandatory course for high school graduation. *See* Messina v. Sobol, 553 N.Y.S.2d 529 (N.Y. App. Div. 1990), *appeal dismissed mem.,* 560 N.Y.S.2d 129 (N.Y. 1990); Parsippany–Troy Hills Educ. Ass'n v. Board of Educ., Township of Parsippany–Troy Hills, 457 A.2d 15 (N.J. Super. Ct. App. Div. 1983), *petition for certification denied,* 468 A.2d 182 (N.J. 1983). *See also* Ambroiggio v. Board of Educ., 427 N.E.2d 1027 (Ill. App. Ct. 1981) (upholding a lunchroom supervision fee for students who were not provided bus transportation, lived within 0.7 mile from school, and ate at school).
73. Sneed v. Greensboro City Bd. of Educ., 264 S.E.2d 106, 114 (N.C. 1980); Beck

v. Board of Educ. of Harlem Consol. School Dist., 344 N.E.2d 440, 442 (Ill. 1976). *See also* Association for Defense of Washington Local School Dist. v. Kiger, 537 N.E.2d 1292 (Ohio 1989) (upholding state law authorizing school districts to withhold grades or credit if students failed to pay fees for materials used in courses; however, school boards could not collect fees for materials used for administrative rather than instructional purposes).

74. Sodus Cent. School v. Rhine, 406 N.Y.S.2d 175 (N.Y. App. Div. 1978).
75. Sneed v. Greensboro City Bd. of Educ., 264 S.E.2d 106, 114 (N.C. 1980) (reasonable user fees for musical instruments, gym uniforms, etc. also were upheld). *See also* Lorenc v. Call, 789 P.2d 46 (Utah App. Ct. 1990), *certification denied*, 795 P.2d 1138 (Utah 1990) (waiver policy limiting eligibility to families receiving public assistance was invalidated as too restrictive).
76. Loewen v. Turnipseed, 488 F. Supp. 1138 (N.D. Miss. 1980).
77. *See* text with note 90, Chapter 2.
78. Meyer v. Nebraska, 262 U.S. 390 (1923).
79. Epperson v. Arkansas, 393 U.S. 97, 106 (1968).
80. Edwards v. Aguillard, 482 U.S. 578 (1987). *See* text with note 113, Chapter 2.
81. *See* text with note 110, *infra,* for a discussion of the judicial reluctance to interfere with academic assessments of student performance.
82. In two early cases, courts upheld disciplinary action against students who refused, on their parents' orders, to participate in instructional activities. State v. Webber, 108 Ind. 31 (Ind. 1886); Lander v. Seaver, 32 Vt. 114 (Vt. 1859).
83. Arundar v. Dekalb County School Dist., 620 F.2d 493 (5th Cir. 1980).
84. Fiacco v. Santee, 421 N.Y.S.2d 431 (N.Y. App. Div. 1979). *See also* Bennett v. City School Dist. of New Rochelle, 497 N.Y.S.2d 72 (N.Y. App. Div. 1985) (students have no protected right to be admitted to a full-time program for the gifted); text with note 83, Chapter 5.
85. Some of the most well known conservative groups are Jerry Falwell's Liberty Federation (formerly Moral Majority), Phyllis Schlafly's Eagle Forum, Pat Robertson's National Legal Foundation, Tim LaHaye's American Coalition for Traditional Values, Beverly LaHaye's Concerned Women for America, and Mel and Norma Gabler's Educational Research Analysts. *See* Martha McCarthy, "Secular Humanism and Education," *Journal of Law & Education,* vol. 19 (1990), pp. 467–498.
86. People for the American Way, *Attacks on the Freedom to Learn* (Washington, DC: Author, 1990).
87. Williams v. Board of Educ. of County of Kanawha, 530 F.2d 972 (4th Cir. 1975).
88. Right to Read Defense Comm. of Chelsea v. School Comm. of Chelsea, 454 F. Supp. 703, 713 (D. Mass. 1978), citing Keefe v. Geanakos, 418 F.2d 359, 361-362 (1st Cir. 1969).
89. Todd v. Rochester Community Schools, 200 N.W.2d 90, 93–94 (Mich. Ct. App. 1972).
90. *See* Smith v. School Comm'rs of Mobile County, 827 F.2d 684 (11th Cir. 1987); Grove v. Mead School Dist., 753 F.2d 1528 (9th Cir. 1985), *cert. denied,* 474 U.S. 826 (1985); text with notes 105–107, Chapter 2.
91. As discussed in Chapter 2, "secular humanism" is alleged to be a "religion" that disavows God. "New age" philosophy, like secular humanism, has become a catchall phrase used by critics to refer to any activities or materials that

allegedly promote a one-world government and one-world religion. *See* Mc-Carthy, "Secular Humanism and Education;" Edward Jenkinson, "The New Age of Schoolbook Protest," *Phi Delta Kappan,* vol. 70 (1988), pp. 66–69. For a discussion of federal legislation backed by conservative parent groups, *see* text with note 159, *infra;* note 96, Chapter 2.

92. Board of Educ., Island Trees Union Free School Dist. No. 26 v. Pico, 457 U.S. 853, 864 (1982). *See also* Bethel School Dist. No. 403 v. Fraser, 478 U.S. 675, 684 (1986); text with note 21, Chapter 4; Zykan v. Warsaw Community School Corp., 631 F.2d 1300, 1306–1307 (7th Cir. 1980).

93. Bicknell v. Vergennes Union High School Bd. of Directors, 638 F.2d 438 (2d Cir. 1980); Presidents Council, Dist. 25 v. Community School Bd. No. 25, 457 F.2d 289 (2d Cir. 1972), *cert. denied,* 409 U.S. 998 (1972). *See* Chapter 8 for a discussion of teachers' rights to academic freedom.

94. Bicknell, *id.* at 441.

95. Zykan v. Warsaw Community School Corp., 631 F.2d 1300, 1303 (7th Cir. 1980). The students also alleged that the contracts of two teachers were not renewed for improper motives. Finding the allegations "creative," the appellate court concluded that such claims are properly initiated by employees who have suffered the harm and not by students. *See also* Cary v. Board of Educ. of Adams-Arapahoe School Dist., 598 F.2d 535 (10th Cir. 1979).

96. Zykan, *id.* at 1306. *See also* Seyfried v. Walton, 668 F.2d 214 (3d Cir. 1981) (performances by the high school drama club were a part of the school program and, therefore, the school board could prohibit performance of the musical *Pippin* because of its explicit sexual scenes).

97. Minarcini v. Strongsville City School Dist., 541 F.2d 577 (6th Cir. 1976). *See also* Right to Read Defense Comm. of Chelsea v. School Comm. of Chelsea, 454 F. Supp. 703 (D. Mass. 1978) (removal of an anthology from the high school library violated first amendment rights of students and faculty).

98. Salvail v. Nashua Bd. of Educ., 469 F. Supp. 1269 (D.N.H. 1979). *See also* Wexner v. Anderson Union High School Dist. Bd. of Trustees, 258 Cal. Rptr. 26 (Cal. Ct. App. 1989), *review denied,* No. S010543 (Cal. 1989) (rejecting a school board's attempt to remove selected books from the public school library because of their "offensive" content).

99. Pratt v. Independent School Dist., 670 F.2d 771, 777 (8th Cir. 1982).

100. 474 F. Supp. 387 (E.D.N.Y. 1979), *rev'd and remanded,* 638 F.2d 404 (2d Cir. 1980), *aff'd,* 457 U.S. 853 (1982).

101. Several board members received a list of "objectionable" books from a conservative parents' organization. Subsequently, the board ordered eleven books removed from the library despite the superintendent's objection to the directive. The superintendent urged the board to follow its policy for handling such problems and thus appoint a committee to study the materials and make recommendations. The board eventually did appoint a review committee, but disregarded the committee's recommendations by ordering the removal of nine books from the school libraries.

102. Justices Brennan, Marshall, and Stevens supported this contention. Justices Blackmun and White also agreed that the case warranted a trial, but they did not endorse the plurality opinion's treatment of the first amendment issue. *See* David Schimmel, "The Limits on School Board Discretion: Board of Education v. Pico," *Education Law Reporter,* vol. 6 (1983), pp. 296–298.

103. After the Supreme Court's *Pico* decision, the Island Trees School Board voted to return the controversial books to the school libraries, thus averting the need for a trial regarding the board's motivation for the original censorship.
104. 457 U.S. at 869 (1982).
105. 484 U.S. 260 (1988). For a discussion of this case, *see* text with note 34, Chapter 4.
106. Virgil v. School Bd. of Columbia County, Florida, 862 F.2d 1517 (11th Cir. 1989).
107. McCarthy v. Fletcher, 254 Cal. Rptr. 714 (Cal. Ct. App. 1989).
108. Seyfried v. Walton, 668 F.2d 214, 219 (3d Cir. 1981) (Rosenn, J., concurring).
109. *See* Daniel Callison and Cynthia Kittleson, "Due Process Principles Applied to the Development of Reconsideration Policies," *Collection Building,* vol. 6, no. 4 (1985), pp. 3–9.
110. Board of Curators of Univ. of Missouri v. Horowitz, 435 U.S. 78, 89–90 (1978). *See also* Regents of Univ. of Michigan v. Ewing, 474 U.S. 214 (1985); Mauriello v. University of Medicine and Dentistry of New Jersey, 781 F.2d 46 (3d Cir. 1986), *cert. denied,* 479 U.S. 818 (1986); Greenhill v. Bailey, 519 F.2d 5 (8th Cir. 1975).
111. Debra P. v. Turlington, 644 F.2d 397, 402 (5th Cir. 1981).
112. Brookhart v. Illinois State Bd. of Educ., 534 F. Supp. 725, 728 (C.D. Ill. 1982).
113. Most competency tests assess proficiency in communication and computation skills, and the educational efficacy of student competency testing has generated substantial debate. *See* Jon Marshall, *State Initiatives in Minimum Competency Testing for Students* (Policy Issue Series, No. 3) (Bloomington, IN: Consortium on Educational Policy Studies, 1987).
114. 644 F.2d 397 (5th Cir. 1981).
115. The trial court had enjoined use of the test as a graduation requirement for a period of four years, 474 F. Supp. 244, 269 (M.D. Fla. 1979). Other courts have upheld tests used as a diploma sanction with between two and four years' notice. *See* cases in note 117, *infra.*
116. Debra P. v. Turlington, 564 F. Supp. 177 (M.D. Fla. 1983), *aff'd,* 730 F.2d 1405 (11th Cir. 1984). It should be noted that the fifth federal circuit was divided into the fifth and eleventh circuits while this case was in progress.
117. *See* Anderson v. Banks, 540 F. Supp. 761 (S.D. Ga. 1982), *appeal dismissed sub nom.* Johnson v. Sikes, 730 F.2d 644 (11th Cir. 1984); Board of Educ., Northport–East Northport Union Free School Dist. v. Ambach, 457 N.E.2d 775 (N.Y. 1983), *cert. denied,* 465 U.S. 1101 (1984).
118. Bester v. Tuscaloosa City Bd. of Educ., 722 F.2d 1514 (11th Cir. 1984). *See also* Sandlin v. Johnson, 643 F.2d 1027 (4th Cir. 1981) (upholding the public school's authority to condition promotion to third grade on successful completion of the requisite level of the Ginn reading series); Doe v. Pennsylvania, 593 F. Supp. 54 (E.D. Pa. 1984) (equal protection and due process rights were not implicated in the use of a standardized test as a criterion for admission to a special communications class for the gifted); text with note 65, Chapter 5, for a discussion of challenges to ability-grouping schemes.
119. Litigation involving claims of instructional negligence is addressed in the next section of this chapter.

120. *See* Brookhart v. Illinois State Bd. of Educ., 697 F.2d 179 (7th Cir. 1983); Board of Educ., Northport–East Northport Union Free School Dist. v. Ambach, 457 N.E.2d 775 (N.Y. 1983), *cert. denied,* 465 U.S. 1101 (1984); Anderson v. Banks, 540 F. Supp. 761 (S.D. Ga. 1982).

121. *See* Martha McCarthy, "The Application of Competency Testing Mandates to Handicapped Children," *Harvard Educational Review,* vol. 53 (1983), pp. 148–150.

122. Brookhart v. Illinois State Bd. of Educ., 697 F.2d 179, 187 (7th Cir. 1983).

123. 34 C.F.R. §§ 104.35(b)(3) and 300.532(c) (1990). *See* Chapter 5 for a discussion of this law, which was formerly the Education for All Handicapped Children Act.

124. *See* Chapter 12 for an overview of tort law pertaining to negligence suits.

125. 131 Cal. Rptr. 854 (Cal. Ct. App. 1976).

126. *Id.* at 861.

127. Donohue v. Copiague Union Free Schools, 391 N.E.2d 1352 (N.Y. 1979).

128. Hoffman v. Board of Educ., 410 N.Y.S.2d 99 (N.Y. App. Div. 1978), *rev'd,* 424 N.Y.S.2d 376 (N.Y. 1979).

129. *See* Poe v. Hamilton, 565 N.E.2d 887 (Ohio Ct. App. 1990) (rejecting a student's claim for damages in the absence of evidence that the teacher's disregard of school board guidelines was reckless and the proximate cause of the student's failure in the teacher's course); Aubrey v. School Dist. of Philadelphia, 437 A.2d 1306 (Pa. Commw. Ct. 1981) (rejecting a claim of educational negligence initiated by a student who failed a health education class containing material dealing with human sexuality; disputes over the inclusion of sex education in the curriculum or over a student's grades in a specific course are not matters that should be settled in judicial forums).

130. Keech v. Berkeley Unified School Dist., 210 Cal. Rptr. 7 (Cal. Ct. App. 1984).

131. *Id.* at 11. *See also* Smith v. Alameda County Social Services Agency, 153 Cal. Rptr. 712 (Cal. Ct. App. 1979) (rejecting a damages claim for alleged inappropriate placement in a class for the mentally retarded).

132. D.S.W. v. Fairbanks North Star Borough School Dist., 628 P.2d 554 (Alaska 1981). *See also* Doe v. Board of Educ. of Montgomery County, 453 A.2d 814 (Md. 1982); Johnson v. Clark, 418 N.W.2d 466 (Mich. Ct. App. 1987); Tubell v. Dade County Pub. Schools, 419 So. 2d 388 (Fla. Dist. Ct. App. 1982).

133. Myers v. Medford Lakes Bd. of Educ., 489 A.2d 1240 (N.J. Super. Ct. App. Div. 1985). *See also* Camer v. Seattle School Dist. No. 1, 762 P.2d 356 (Wash. Ct. App. 1988), *review denied,* 112 Wash. 2d 1006 (Wash. 1989), *cert. denied,* 110 S. Ct. 204 (1989) (found frivolous was a suit alleging that the Seattle School District was not respecting state laws as to student discipline, course content, and student assessment practices, thus denying children their entitlement to a basic education guaranteed by the state constitution); Bishop v. Indiana Technical Vocational College, 742 F. Supp. 524, 525 (N.D. Ind. 1990) (suit alleging that college's provision of inferior educational experience interfered with the federal right to "pursuit of happiness" was frivolous; "educational malpractice is a matter of state law that does not, by itself, deprive its victims of their constitutional rights").

134. Hunter v. Board of Educ. of Montgomery County, 439 A.2d 582 (Md. 1982).

135. B.M. v. State, 649 P.2d 425 (Mont. 1982), *after remand,* 698 P.2d 399 (Mont. 1985).

136. Torres v. Little Flower Children's Services, 485 N.Y.S.2d 15 (N.Y. 1984), *cert. denied,* 474 U.S. 864 (1985).
137. Snow v. State, 469 N.Y.S.2d 959 (N.Y. App. Div. 1983), *aff'd,* 485 N.Y.S.2d 987 (N.Y. 1984).
138. *Id.,* 469 N.Y.S.2d at 964. The dissenting justices in *Torres* asserted that both cases involved "custodial malpractice" for failure to provide appropriate care for children placed in the institutions' custody, 485 N.Y.S.2d at 22–23 (Meyer, J., dissenting, joined by Cooke, C. J., and Wachtler, J.).
139. *See* Perry A. Zirkel, "Educational Malpractice: Cracks in the Door?" *Education Law Reporter,* vol. 23 (1985), pp. 453–460.
140. *See* Julie O'Hara, "The Fate of Educational Malpractice," *Education Law Reporter,* vol. 14 (1984), pp. 887–895.
141. *See* Griswold v. Connecticut, 381 U.S. 479 (1965); text with note 135, Chapter 8.
142. Dawkins v. Billingsley, 172 P. 69 (Okla. 1918).
143. *See, e.g.,* Elder v. Anderson, 23 Cal. Rptr. 48 (Cal. Ct. App. 1962). *See also* Chapter 12 for a discussion of tort law.
144. 20 U.S.C. § 1232g (1988); 34 C.F.R. § 99 *et seq.* (1990). Students cannot rely on FERPA to challenge teachers' grading procedures. *See* Tarka v. Cunningham, 917 F.2d 890 (5th Cir. 1990).
145. 34 C.F.R. § 99.5 (1990).
146. Page v. Rotterdam-Mohonasen Cent. School Dist., 441 N.Y.S.2d 323 (N.Y. Sup. Ct. 1981).
147. Most courts have ruled that since the Department of Education has enforcement authority, individuals are not authorized to bring a private suit to compel compliance with FERPA. *See, e.g.,* Girardier v. Webster College, 563 F.2d 1267, 1276–1277 (8th Cir. 1977). However, the Second Circuit Court of Appeals ruled that FERPA regulations do not preclude an individual suit for damages under 42 U.S.C. § 1983 (1988) to remedy FERPA violations, Fay v. South Colonie Cent. School Dist., 802 F.2d 21 (2d Cir. 1986). For a discussion of Section 1983 liability, *see* text with note 166, Chapter 8.
148. *See* text with note 90, Chapter 5 for a more detailed discussion of this law.
149. Ind. Code Ann. §§ 4-1-6-2 to 4-1-6-5 (1984).
150. 20 U.S.C. § 1232g(a)(5)(B) (1988). *See* Brent v. Paquette, 567 A.2d 976 (N.H. 1989) (students' names and addresses and names of their parents were exempt from disclosure under the New Hampshire "right to know" law). *See also* Bauer v. Kincaid, 759 F. Supp. 575 (W.D. Mo. 1991) (under Missouri law, institutions of higher education must release campus crime reports; such reports are not considered educational records protected from disclosure by FERPA).
151. Klipa v. Board of Educ. of Anne Arundel County, 460 A.2d 601 (Md. Ct. Spec. App. 1983).
152. *See, e.g.,* Bowie v. Evanston Community Consol. Dist. 65, 538 N.E.2d 557 (Ill. 1989); Human Rights Auth. of State Guardianship Comm'n v. Miller, 464 N.E.2d 833 (Ill. App. Ct. 1984); Kryston v. Board of Educ., East Ramapo Cent. School Dist., 430 N.Y.S.2d 688 (N.Y. App. Div. 1980).
153. La Plante v. Stewart, 470 So. 2d 1018 (La. Ct. App. 1985), *certification denied,* 476 So. 2d 352 (La. 1985). The court reasoned that the study was intended to identify factors that affect learning and not to determine the

proficiency of individual students or to evaluate the performance of specific teachers or administrators. Thus, the results of the study were considered public records and were not included within the scope of exclusions from the state's public records law. *But see* Western Services, Inc. v. Sargent School Dist. No. RE-33J, 719 P.2d 355 (Colo. Ct. App. 1986), *rev'd en banc,* 751 P.2d 56 (Colo. 1988) (requested student scholastic data were exempt from disclosure under state open records law).

154. Rios v. Read, 480 F. Supp. 14 (E.D.N.Y. 1977).

155. Board of Educ., Island Trees Union Free School Dist. v. Butcher, 402 N.Y.S.2d 626, 627 (N.Y. App. Div. 1978).

156. Einhorn v. Maus, 300 F. Supp. 1169, 1171 (E.D. Pa. 1969). *See also* Price v. Young, 580 F. Supp. 1 (E.D. Ark. 1983) (a parent could not use FERPA to challenge his son's rejection for the National Honor Society based on anonymous faculty recommendations).

157. Merriken v. Cressman, 364 F. Supp. 913 (E.D. Pa. 1973). For a discussion of legal issues associated with drug testing among students, *see* text with note 154, Chapter 6.

158. 42 U.S.C. § 201 *et seq.* (1988); 45 C.F.R. § 46 (1990).

159. 20 U.S.C. § 1232h (1988); 34 C.F.R. §§ 75, 76, and 98 (1990). The sensitive areas specified in the law are political affiliations; potentially embarassing mental or psychological problems; sexual behavior and attitudes; illegal, antisocial, self-incriminating, and demeaning behavior; critical appraisals of family members; legally recognized, privileged relationships; or income (other than that required to determine eligibility for financial assistance programs).

160. "Hatch Shuns Conservatives and Educational Groups; Clarifies Privacy Rule," *Education Daily,* February 20, 1985, p. 3.

161. Hatch Amendment Coalition and American Educational Research Association, *The Hatch Amendment Regulations: A Guidelines Document* (Washington, DC: AERA, 1985).

162. *See* Anne Lewis, "Little-Used Amendment Becomes Divisive, Disruptive Issue," *Phi Delta Kappan,* vol. 66 (1985), p. 668.

163. The notable exception to compulsory attendance pertains to Amish children who have successfully completed eighth grade. *See* Wisconsin v. Yoder, 406 U.S. 205 (1972); text with note 8, Chapter 2.

4

Students' Rights in
Noninstructional Matters

This chapter addresses students' rights in connection with selected noninstructional issues. The first two sections focus on first amendment freedoms of speech and press and closely related association rights. In the final two sections, the law governing student appearance and participation in extracurricular activities is examined.

FREEDOM OF SPEECH AND PRESS

Traditionally, it was accepted that public school authorities could restrict student expression for almost any reason. Since the mid-twentieth century, however, the Supreme Court has recognized that students do not shed their constitutional rights as a condition of public school attendance and that the public school is an appropriate setting in which to instill a respect for these rights, especially first amendment freedoms. The Court has noted that first amendment rights must receive "scrupulous protection" in schools "if we are not to strangle the free mind at its source and teach youth to discount important principles of our government as mere platitudes."[1] The Court also has recognized that schools function as "a marketplace of ideas" and that the "robust exchange of ideas" is "a special concern of the first amendment."[2]

The first amendment through its fourteenth amendment application to the states restricts governmental—in contrast to private—interference with citizens' free expression rights. The government, including public school boards, must have a compelling justification to curtail protected expression. Also shielded by the first amendment is the individual's right to remain silent when confronted with an illegitimate governmental demand for expression, such as mandatory participation in the salute to the American flag in public schools.[3] In short, the first amendment protects

109

decisions regarding what to say and what not to say; "the difference between compelled speech and compelled silence is without constitutional significance."[4]

Free expression rights are perhaps the most preciously guarded of individual liberties. In 1989 the Supreme Court recognized the broad reach of first amendment protection of expressive activities when it upheld a political protester's first amendment right to burn the American flag.[5] Despite their fundamental significance, however, free expression rights can be restricted. As Justice Oliver Holmes noted, freedom of speech does not allow an individual to yell "fire" in a crowded theater when there is no fire.[6] Although public school students enjoy free speech rights, the Supreme Court has recognized that "the constitutional rights of students in public school are not automatically coextensive with the rights of adults in other settings."[7] Free expression rights may be restricted by policies that are reasonably designed to take into account the special circumstances of the educational environment.

UNPROTECTED CONDUCT AND EXPRESSION   *spoken Slander*
written Liable

Before assessing whether specific expression enjoys first amendment protection, a threshold determination is whether the conduct constitutes expression *at all*. Only where conduct is intended to communicate an idea is it considered expression for first amendment purposes.[8] In discussing the limits of protected speech, an Oregon appellate court held that while college students had a first amendment right to distribute leaflets and collect petitions, erecting a tentlike structure on the school lawn was not protected expression and could be the basis for the students' conviction for criminal trespass.[9] More recently, the Eighth Circuit Court of Appeals reasoned that social and recreational dancing in public schools was not a form of expression enjoying first amendment protection.[10] Accordingly, the court rejected parents' first amendment challenge to the school board's denial of their request to rent the high school gymnasium for student dances.

A determination that specific conduct communicates an idea does not assure constitutional protection; the judiciary has recognized that certain types of expression are outside the protective arm of the first amendment. The following categories of student expression are not protected in the public school context.

Defamatory Expression. Defamation includes spoken (slander) and written (libel) statements that are false, expose another to public shame or ridicule, and are communicated to someone other than the person defamed.[11] Courts have upheld school authorities in banning libelous content from publications distributed at school and imposing sanctions on students responsible for such material, but regulations have been voided as vague and overbroad if they give school officials complete discretion to halt distribution of material they consider *potentially* libelous.[12]

Fair comment on the actions of public figures, unlike defamatory expression, is constitutionally protected. Public officials can establish that they have been defamed only with evidence that the comment was false and the speaker acted recklessly and with actual malice.[13] To be considered a public official, one must have substantial responsibility for or control over the conduct of governmental affairs; the mere fact that a matter attracts public attention does not transform a private individual into a public figure. School board members and superintendents are generally considered public officials for defamation purposes,[14] but courts have rendered conflicting opinions regarding whether teachers and coaches have assumed the risk of nonmalicious defamation.[15]

In several decisions prior to 1990, courts indicated that opinions, in contrast to assertions of fact, were constitutionally protected.[16] However, in 1990 the Supreme Court ruled that the first amendment does not necessitate a separate privilege for opinions in defamation suits. The Court held that statements appearing to be factual, even though couched as opinions, can be the basis for a successful defamation claim.[17]

Obscene, Vulgar, or Inflammatory Expression. The judiciary has held that individuals cannot claim a first amendment right to voice obscenities, but there is no precise definition of what constitutes obscene expression. In *Miller v. California,* which did not involve a school situation, the Supreme Court attempted to distinguish obscene material from material that would receive first amendment protection, using the following test:

> (a) whether "the average person, applying contemporary community standards" would find that the work, taken as a whole, appeals to the prurient interests; . . . (b) whether the work depicts or describes, in a patently offensive way, sexual conduct specifically defined by the applicable state law; and (c) whether the work, taken as a whole, lacks serious literary, artistic, political or scientific value (citations omitted).[18]

The *Miller* standard, however, has not clarified the concept of obscenity as applied to student expression in public schools. On several occasions, the Supreme Court has recognized the government's authority to adjust the definition of obscenity as applied to minors because the state's power to control children's conduct reaches beyond its authority to regulate adult behavior. For example, the Court upheld a state law prohibiting the sale to minors of magazines depicting female nudity. Acknowledging that the material was not obscene for adults, the Court ruled that the statute did not impair minors' free expression rights. The Court declared that because of the state's significant "interest in preventing distribution to children of objectionable material,'' it can accord minors ''a more restricted right than that assured to adults to judge and determine for themselves what sex material they may read or see.''[19] Literature distributed by students to classmates presumably should be subject to more stringent standards than applied to literature distributed to adults; yet, in several decisions rendered in the 1970s, the use of ''earthy words,'' profanity, and vulgarisms in student publications was *not* considered obscene.[20]

In a significant 1986 decision, *Bethel School District No. 403 v. Fraser,* the Supreme Court cast some doubt on the continued validity of these earlier rulings, at least where expression might be viewed as *representing the school*. Overturning the lower courts, the Supreme Court upheld disciplinary action against a student for using a sexual metaphor in a nominating speech during a student government assembly.[21] Concluding that the sexual innuendos were offensive to both teachers and students, the majority held that the school's legitimate interest in protecting the captive student audience from exposure to lewd, vulgar, and offensive speech justified the disciplinary action. The Court reiterated that speech protected by the first amendment for adults is not necessarily protected for children, reasoning that in the public school context the sensibilities of fellow students must be considered. The majority recognized that the inculcation of fundamental values of civility is an important objective of public schools and that the school board has the authority to determine what manner of speech is inappropriate in classes or assemblies.[22] The majority further rejected the contention that the student had no way of knowing that his expression would evoke disciplinary action, concluding that the school rule barring obscene and disruptive expression and teachers' admonitions that his planned speech was inappropriate provided adequate warning of the consequences of the expression.

The judiciary also has sanctioned regulations banning the use of ''fighting words'' or other types of inflammatory expression. Courts have differentiated expression that agitates and exhorts from speech that ''is a mere doctrinal justification of a thought or idea,'' leaving an opportunity for calm and reasonable discussion.[23] To illustrate, the Sixth Circuit Court of Appeals upheld a student's suspension for persisting to wear a Confederate flag sleeve patch in a racially tense, newly integrated Tennessee school.[24] Also, where high school students conspired and threatened to assault a teacher, a Louisiana appeals court ruled that the first amendment did not shield the students from expulsion.[25]

Courts have rendered conflicting decisions as to whether lewd or inflammatory student expression off school grounds can be the basis for disciplinary action. A Pennsylvania court upheld disciplinary action against a student for using indecent language toward a teacher at a shopping center, reasoning that the remark affected school discipline because other students witnessed the incident.[26] However, a federal district court in Maine disallowed the suspension of a high school student who made a vulgar gesture at a teacher in a restaurant parking lot after school. Concluding that the student's expression was protected by the first amendment in that it was not connected with any school activity, the court declared: "The first amendment protection of freedom of expression may not be made a casualty of the effort to force-feed good manners to the ruffians among us."[27]

SCHOOL-SPONSORED VERSUS PERSONAL EXPRESSION

In contrast to defamatory, obscene, lewd, or inflammatory expression, students' expression of political or ideological views is protected by the first amendment. Prior to 1986 federal courts broadly interpreted the constitutional protection afforded to such student expression in public schools.[28] However, the Supreme Court more recently has emphasized the distinction between *governmental* expression that appears to represent the school and *personal* expression of ideological views that merely occurs at school. The latter commands substantial constitutional protection, but student expression appearing to bear the school's imprimatur can be restricted to ensure its consistency with educational objectives. The Court's expansive interpretation of what constitutes school-sponsored expression has narrowed the circumstances under which a student can prevail in free expression claims.

School-Sponsored (Governmental) Expression. In recent first amendment litigation, an assessment of the type of forum the government has created for expressive activities has been important in determining the constitutionality of restrictions placed on expression rights. The Supreme Court has recognized that public places, such as streets or parks, are traditional public forums for assembly and communication where content-based restrictions cannot be imposed unless justified by a compelling governmental interest.[29] At the other end of the continuum is a nonpublic forum, such as a state-supported school, where expression can be confined to the express governmental purpose of the property. Content restrictions are permissible in a nonpublic forum to assure that expression is compatible with the intended governmental purpose, provided that regulations are reasonable and do not entail viewpoint discrimination.[30]

The government, however, can create a limited public forum for expression on public property that would otherwise be considered a nonpublic forum reserved for its governmental function. For example, a student activities program held after school might be established as a limited forum for student expression. Such limited public forums are subject to the same standards as applied to traditional public forums, but the government is not required to retain indefinitely the open character of the limited forum. Also, a limited forum can be restricted to a certain class of speakers (e.g., students) and/or to specific categories of expression (e.g., noncommercial speech).[31] The public forum doctrine has been controversial in several school cases, particularly the characteristics of a limited public forum.

During the 1970s and early 1980s a number of courts expansively interpreted the circumstances under which a limited forum for student expression was created in public schools. School-sponsored newspapers often were considered such forums, and accordingly, courts held that articles on controversial subjects such as abortion, the Vietnam War, and birth control could not be barred from these publications.[32] Courts scrutinized policies requiring prior administrative review of the content of school-sponsored as well as nonsponsored literature and placed the burden on school authorities to justify such prior review schemes. To withstand a first amendment challenge, prior review policies had to contain narrow, objective, and unambiguous criteria for determining what material was prohibited and procedures that allowed a speedy determination of whether materials met those criteria.[33]

In 1988, however, the Supreme Court delivered a decision of first impression, *Hazelwood School District v. Kuhlmeier,* holding that school authorities can censor student expression in school publications and other school-related activities as long as the censorship decisions are based on legitimate pedagogical concerns.[34] Rejecting the assertion that the school newspaper had been established as a public forum for student expression, the Court declared that only with school authorities' clear *intent* do school activities become a public forum.[35] At issue in *Hazelwood* was a high school principal's deletion of two pages from the newspaper because of the content of articles on divorce and teenage pregnancy and fears that individuals could be identified in the articles. The Court drew a clear distinction between the public school's *toleration* of personal student expression, which is constitutionally required under some circumstances, and its *promotion* of student speech that represents the school. Reasoning that student expression appearing to bear the school's imprimatur can be censored, the Court acknowledged school authorities' broad discretion to ensure that such expression is consistent with educational objectives. The Court expansively interpreted the category of student expression subject to censorship as that occurring in school publications and all school-sponsored activities (including extracurricular).

In the 1986 *Fraser* case discussed previously, the Supreme Court also broadly interpreted the scope of the public school's control over student expression. The Court held that a student government assembly, at which participation is voluntary, is not a public forum for student expression; school authorities are empowered to ensure that expression in such school-sponsored activities is not indecent.[36] In both *Hazelwood* and *Fraser,* the Court indicated that school boards could determine for themselves what expression is consistent with pedagogical objectives.[37]

Relying on *Hazelwood,* in 1989 the Sixth Circuit Court of Appeals reiterated that school authorities can exercise editorial control over the style and content of student speech in school-sponsored activities. Noting that civility is a legitimate pedagogical concern, the court held that a student could be disqualified from running for student council president because his candidacy speech was discourteous and rude. The court emphasized that "limitations on speech that would be unconstitutional outside the schoolhouse are not necessarily unconstitutional within it."[38] Acknowledging that whether specific expression is rude represents a judgment call with which the court might disagree, it nonetheless concluded that such decisions are "best left to the locally elected school board, not to a distant, life-tenured judiciary."[39]

Also echoing the *Hazelwood* rationale, the Ninth Circuit Court of Appeals in 1989 rejected Planned Parenthood's claim that the school's denial of its request to advertise in the school district's newspapers, yearbooks, and programs for athletic events violated free speech rights. The court concluded that the district could reject advertisements that were inconsistent with its educational mission or might interfere with the "proper function of education."[40] Planned Parenthood argued that it was the only group whose ads had been rejected, but the court held that selective access does not create a public forum for expression; such a forum must be created by express intent.

Similarly reflecting the broad discretion granted to school authorities, the Fourth Circuit Court of Appeals upheld a high school principal who barred the school's use of the Johnny Reb symbol following complaints that it offended black students.[41] Students protested the elimination of the symbol, and in one instance the principal delayed for a day a student's use of school bulletin boards to post notices urging students to attend the upcoming school board meeting. The court reasoned that the school can disassociate itself from controversial expression at odds with its objectives (i.e., the Johnny Reb symbol) and that the one-day delay in posting the notices constituted a minimal impairment of expression rights.

There are limits, however, on school authorities' wide latitude to censor student expression that bears the public school's imprimatur. Blatant viewpoint discrimination violates the first amendment. For example, the Ninth Circuit Court of Appeals held that a school board violated students' first amendment rights because it failed to produce a compelling justification for excluding an antidraft organization's advertisement from the school newspaper, while allowing military recruitment advertisements.[42] The board argued that it permitted nonstudents to engage only in nonpolitical, commercial expression in the paper and that military service advertisements fell within this category, whereas the antidraft material did not. Disagreeing, the appeals court noted the substantial political controversy surrounding military service and distinguished such advertisements from commercial speech intended primarily to advance economic interests. The court emphasized that even in a nonpublic forum, viewpoint discrimination is not permissible.

Similarly, the Eleventh Circuit Court of Appeals placed the burden on school authorities to justify viewpoint discrimination. The court affirmed with some modifications the federal district court's conclusion that the school board had unconstitutionally excluded a peace activist group from participating in the public school's career day and placing its literature on school bulletin boards and in offices of school guidance counselors when military recruiters were allowed such access.[43] The court found no compelling justification for discrimination against specific views that the board found distasteful. However, students cannot claim viewpoint discrimination where their expression is curtailed because it is derogatory toward racial or ethnic groups.[44]

Personal Expression. Student expression that does *not* bear the school's imprimatur is governed by the landmark Supreme Court decision, *Tinker v. Des Moines Independent School District,* rendered in 1969. In *Tinker,* three students were suspended from school for wearing armbands to protest the Vietnam War. School officials did not attempt to prohibit the wearing of all symbols, but instead prohibited the expression of one particular opinion. Concluding that school authorities punished the students for expression that was not accompanied by any disorder or disturbance, the Supreme Court ruled that "undifferentiated fear or apprehension of disturbance is not enough to overcome the right to freedom of expression."[45] Furthermore, the Court declared that school officials must have "more than a mere desire to avoid discomfort and unpleasantness that always accompany an unpopular viewpoint" in order to justify curtailment of student expression.[46] The Court emphasized that "students in school as well as out of school are 'persons' under our Constitution. They are possessed of fundamental rights which the state must respect."[47]

In *Tinker,* the Supreme Court echoed statements made in an earlier federal appellate ruling: a student may express opinions on controversial issues in the classroom, cafeteria, playing field, or any other place, as long as the exercise of such rights does "not materially and substantially interfere with the requirements of appropriate discipline in the operation of the school" or collide with the rights of others.[48] In both cases, the courts emphasized that educators have the authority and duty to maintain discipline in schools. School officials simply must consider students' constitutional rights as they exert control.[49]

As discussed previously, recent Supreme Court decisions have limited the application of the *Tinker* principle. The Court has broadly interpreted student expression that carries the imprimatur of the school, and such expression can be censored by school authorities for educational reasons.[50] *Tinker* now applies *only* to expression that clearly does not give the appearance of representing the school.

When determined that such protected personal expression is at issue, courts are then faced with the difficult task of assessing whether restrictions are justified in particular circumstances. Under the *Tinker* principle, personal expression can be curtailed if it is likely to result in a disruption of the educational process. The law is clear in allowing students to be punished after the fact if they cause a disruption, but the issuance of prior restraints on personal expression places a greater burden of justification on school authorities. The expectation of disruption must be based on "fact, not intuition" to justify restrictions.[51] The imposition of a prior restraint on speech must bear a substantial relationship to a "weighty" governmental interest,[52] "lest students' imaginations, intellects, and wills be unduly stifled or chilled."[53] In addition, any regulation must be drawn with narrow specificity so students know what activities are prohibited.

Courts, however, have endorsed restrictions on personal student expression if it is sufficiently linked to a disruption of the educational process. The Sixth Circuit Court of Appeals concluded that a rule banning the wearing of freedom buttons was lawful in a situation where the learning environment would be disrupted if pupils were allowed to wear the "badges of their respective disagreements."[54] Also, where student button-wearers have created disturbances within the school by harassing students not participating in the form of expression, restrictions on such conduct have been upheld.[55]

The burden is on school authorities to justify policies requiring administrative approval *before* students distribute unofficial (underground) publications, but such prior review is not unconstitutional *per se*. In 1987 the Eighth Circuit Court of Appeals rejected a vagueness challenge to a school board's policy requiring administrative review of unofficial student papers distributed at school and barring the distribution of material that is obscene, libelous, or pervasively indecent; advertises unlawful products or services; or would likely cause a substantial disruption of the educational process.[56] However, the court invalidated the part of the policy proscribing material that invades the privacy or endangers the health of others, reasoning that such expression would have to subject the school to a libel suit under state law in order to be curtailed. While upholding school authorities in reviewing underground student publications before distribution, the court emphasized that this policy could not be used to ban material simply because it was critical of school practices.

Several other courts have approved the *concept* of prior review of nonschool publications, but have found challenged policies constitutionally defective.[57] In post-*Hazelwood* decisions courts have continued to scrutinize prior review regulations applied to unofficial student publications, recognizing that the Constitution requires a high degree of specificity when imposing restraints on personal expression.[58] For example, the Ninth Circuit Court of Appeals held that school authorities in a Washington school district could not bar distribution of a student paper produced off campus and could not subject the paper's content to prior review. Noting that "prior restraints are permissible in only the rarest of circumstances," the court found overbroad the policy subjecting *all* nonschool publications to prior review for purposes of censoring the content.[59] Suspension of students for distributing the unauthorized paper at a school function was found to impair first amendment rights. Similarly, a New York federal district court held that the first amendment precludes school authorities from exercising editorial control over a student newspaper that is not part of the curriculum.[60]

Although prior restraints on personal expression may be legally vulnerable, courts are more inclined to support disciplinary action *after* the expression has occurred. Students can be punished and materials confiscated if the expression fosters a disruption of the educational process, is libelous or obscene, or encourages others to engage in dangerous or unlawful activity. For example, the Fourth Circuit Court of Appeals ruled that school administrators acted within their authority in banning further distribution on school property of a student publication that contained an advertisement for drug paraphernalia.[61] The court emphasized that the literature was not subjected to predistribution approval; copies were impounded only after distribution began. The school regulation authorizing the principal to halt the distribution of any publication encouraging actions that endanger the health or safety of students was not found to be unconstitutionally vague. Noting that commercial speech is not entitled to the same protection as other types of speech, the court held that school officials were not required to demonstrate that the harmful activity would lead to a substantial disruption. The court further ruled that the school district's appeals procedures for students to contest the confiscation of literature were adequate and not unduly lengthy.

In addition, courts have condoned disciplinary action against students who have engaged in walkouts or boycotts[62] and sit-ins[63] that have disrupted the school environment. School authorities have been upheld in punishing students for protests involving conduct such as blocking hallways, damaging property, causing students to miss class, or in other ways interfering with essential school activities.[64] To illustrate, the Eighth Circuit Court of Appeals held that students who disrupted a school assembly by walking out were properly suspended.[65] An Indiana federal district court also upheld disciplinary action against several students who attempted to incite a student walkout by distributing leaflets.[66] Recognizing that the students' action fell within the protective arm of the first amendment, the court nonetheless held that sanctions were justified because the school officials could reasonably forecast a serious disruption of the school environment. The fact that no disruption actually occurred did not negate the legitimate threat.

The Ninth Circuit Court of Appeals reasoned that school authorities were justified in confiscating signs (protesting the nonrenewal of a teacher's contract) that were brought to school by students who intended to distribute them.[67] While concluding that the signs posed a threat of disruption and thus could be confiscated, the court held that school authorities were not justified in suspending a student who initially refused to turn over his signs. The court declared that "the balancing necessary to enable school officials to maintain discipline and order allows curtailment but not necessarily punishment."[68] However, the court recognized that if the suspension had been based on the fact that the student violated a school rule by going to the parking lot to get the signs, rather than on the exercise of pure speech, the disciplinary action would have been condoned.

Courts have ruled that students cannot be disciplined for *nondisruptive* expression that is merely critical of school personnel or policies. In an illustrative case, the Seventh Circuit Court of Appeals upheld students' rights to criticize school personnel in a mimeographed paper containing editorials, poetry, and reviews pertaining to the school administration and urging students to reject "propaganda."[69] The paper included charges against the principal and an attack on the school's attendance requirements. Relying on *Tinker,* the court held that disciplinary action against the students responsible for the material unconstitutionally impaired protected rights because there was no evidence that the publication would create a disruption. Also, an Arkansas federal district court ruled that two football players could not be disciplined for their symbolic protest against the coach who they alleged had manipulated the homecoming queen election to preclude a black student from winning.[70]

Personal expression enjoys greater constitutional protection than does school-sponsored expression, but the judiciary consistently has endorsed the imposition of reasonable policies regulating the time, place, and manner of personal expression.[71] Voicing political and ideological views and distributing literature can be prohibited during instructional time. Also, courts have upheld bans on literature distribution near the doors of classrooms while class is in session, near building exits during fire drills, and on stairways when classes are changing.[72] Courts have concluded that such restrictions are justified to ensure that student expression and the distribution of student publications do not impinge upon other school activities.

Time, place, and manner regulations, however, must be reasonable, content-neutral, and uniformly applied to expressive activities. School officials must inform students specifically as to when and where they can express their ideas and distribute materials. Moreover, literature distribution cannot be relegated to remote times or places either inside or outside the school building, and regulations must not inhibit any person's right to accept or reject literature that is distributed in accordance with the rules.[73] Policies governing demonstrations should convey to students that they have the right to gather, distribute petitions, and express their ideas under nondisruptive circumstances.[74] Vague wording of a regulation pertaining to demonstrations may result in the judiciary concluding that the conduct cannot be punished because the demonstrators did not know in advance precisely what behavior was prohibited.[75]

Although the time, place, and manner of literature distribution can be reasonably regulated at school, restrictions cannot be placed on the distribution of such literature off school grounds unless such off-campus activity threatens the educational process. The Second Circuit Court of Appeals found that school officials overstepped their authority by disciplining high school students who published a satirical magazine in their homes and sold it at a local store.[76] While not addressing the question of whether distribution of the "vulgar" publication at school was permissible, the court enjoined school officials from punishing the student publishers for off-campus distribution of their magazine in the absence of evidence that the activity had an adverse impact on the school. The court concluded that to rule otherwise could subject students to school-imposed punishments for such behavior as watching X-rated movies on cable television in their own homes.

In general, commercial speech, where the speaker has economic motives, has not been afforded the same protection under the first amendment as speech intended to convey a particular point of view.[77] However, unlike obscene, lewd, inflammatory, or defamatory expression, commercial speech does enjoy some measure of constitutional protection. In 1989 the Supreme Court recognized that governmental restrictions on commercial speech need not be the least restrictive means to achieve the desired end; rather, there must be a reasonable "fit" between the restrictions and the governmental goal.[78]

Regulations prohibiting sales and fund-raising activities in public schools have generally been upheld as justified to preserve schools for their educational function and to prevent commercial exploitation of students. For example, the Second Circuit Court of Appeals declined to enjoin the implementation of a public school rule prohibiting students from soliciting funds from their classmates.[79] The students sought the injunction so they could distribute leaflets to solicit funds for the legal defense of persons on trial for antiwar demonstrations. In denying the injunction, the court asserted that it was unlikely that a court would find the school's rule overbroad.

Future Directions. It appears likely that courts will continue to be called upon to balance the interests involved when students' rights to express views and receive information collide with educators' duty to maintain an appropriate educational environment. Although the *Tinker* principle still applies to personal student expression, recent Supreme Court decisions have granted school authorities broad discretion to restrict student expression that appears to represent the school. Given that the federal judiciary seems less willing to use constitutional grounds to limit the prerogatives of school authorities, legislation may become more important in specifying the scope of students' free expression rights. In response to *Hazelwood,* several state legislatures have enacted laws granting student editors of school-sponsored papers specific rights in determining the content of those publications.[80] These laws may shift some of the litigation to the state level as students continue to assert their rights to free expression in public schools.

STUDENT-INITIATED CLUBS

Free expression and related association rights have been at issue in connection with the formation and recognition of student clubs. Freedom of association is not specifically included among first amendment protections, but the Supreme Court has recognized that associational rights are "implicit in the freedoms of speech, assembly, and petition."[81] The term "association" refers to the medium through which individuals seek to join with others to make the expression of their own views more effective.[82] This section focuses specifically on legal principles governing secret societies and student-initiated clubs with open membership.

Secret Societies. Public school pupils have unsuccessfully asserted that free expression and association rights shield student-initiated social organizations or secret societies with exclusive membership.[83] Courts have upheld school officials in denying recognition of secret societies and prohibiting student membership in such clubs. Some states, by statute, forbid student participation in a club that sustains itself by selecting new members "on the basis of the decision of its membership rather than upon the free choice of any pupil in the school who is qualified by the rules of the school to fill the special aims of the organization."[84] The judiciary has endorsed the notion that secret societies "tend to engender an undemocratic spirit of caste, to promote cliques, and to foster a contempt for school authority."[85] Although there are limitations on the discretion of public school officials to restrict students' out-of-class behavior,[86] public schools can prohibit students from participating in exclusive clubs that have a detrimental impact on the school environment. Various punishments, ranging from suspension to denial of participation in extracurricular activities, have been upheld as permissible penalties for membership in secret societies.[87]

In an illustrative case, a student challenged a California school district's regulation prohibiting student membership in any fraternity, sorority, or nonschool club perpetuating its membership by the decision of its own members.[88] The student claimed that a specific club was created to meet the objectives of "literature, charity, and scholarship," but the appeals court concluded that the club, despite its stated objectives, was a secret society in that new members were "rushed" each semester and then chosen through a secret voting process. Thus, the board's prohibition was considered reasonable to advance the school's educational mission.

Student Organizations with Open Membership. In contrast to bans on secret societies, prohibitions against student-initiated organizations with open membership may be more vulnerable to first amendment challenges. In 1972 the Supreme Court ruled that college authorities abridged the first amendment by denying recognition to a student political organization merely because they disagreed with the group's philosophy.[89] In several cases, courts also have held that student gay rights groups must be afforded similar recognition as available to other student organizations on college campuses.[90] The Supreme Court has acknowledged that where state-supported institutions of higher education have created a public forum for student groups to use campus facilities for expressive purposes, content restrictions imposed on such meetings must be justified by a compelling governmental interest.[91]

At the precollegiate level, even before Congress enacted the Equal Access Act (EAA), several courts had recognized that if a public high school allows student groups to meet during noninstructional time, a school access policy must be content-neutral.[92] The EAA enacted in 1984 codified these rulings by stipulating that if federally assisted secondary schools provide a limited open forum for noncurriculum student groups to meet during noninstructional time, access cannot be denied to specific groups based on the religious, political, philosophical, or other content of the groups' meetings.[93]

The EAA was championed by the religious right, but its protection of student expression is far broader than religious expression. Under the EAA, school authorities are not obligated to create such a forum for student groups to meet; public school access can be confined to student organizations that are an extension of the curriculum, such as drama groups, language clubs, and athletic teams. Also, even if a limited forum is established, school authorities can prohibit meetings that threaten a disruption.

Following enactment of the EAA, the Third Circuit Court of Appeals held that students have a private right to bring suit to compel compliance with the Act and remanded a case to give students an opportunity to prove that the school board had violated the EAA by denying their request to hold a peace exposition on school grounds. On remand, the federal district court concluded that the school board had created a limited open forum for student expression in the high school gymnasium and thus the Student Coalition for Peace was entitled to use the gym during noninstructional time to hold its peace exposition.[94]

As discussed in Chapter 2, the Supreme Court in 1990 rejected an establishment clause challenge to the EAA in *Board of Education of the Westside Community Schools v. Mergens*.[95] The Court reasoned that religious expression initiated by students during noninstructional time does not give the impression that the school endorses religion. The Court further held that if a federally assisted high school allows even one noncurriculum group to use school facilities during noninstructional time, the EAA guarantees equal access for other noncurriculum student groups.

It appears that there is one definition of a limited forum under the EAA and another more restrictive definition under the first amendment. The Supreme Court emphasized in 1988 that a public school activity becomes a limited forum for first amendment purposes only through *express intent* of school authorities,[96] but such intent is not necessary to trigger the EAA. Thus, constitutional challenges to limitations on student expression do not seem as promising as suits initiated under the EAA.

Of course, school authorities still retain a choice under the EAA; they can restrict school access to groups that are an extension of the curriculum, thus declining to establish a limited forum for any noncurriculum student-initiated meetings. As noted in Chapter 2, the definition of a "curriculum-related" group remains somewhat ambiguous and will likely generate additional litigation.

STUDENT APPEARANCE

Fads and fashions in hairstyles and clothing regularly have evoked litigation as educators have attempted to exert some control over pupil appearance. Courts have been called upon to weigh students' interests in selecting their attire and hair length against school authorities' interests in preventing disruptions to the school environment.

HAIRSTYLE

Substantial judicial activity, peaking in the 1970s, has focused on school regulations governing the length of male students' hair. The Supreme Court, however, has refused to hear appeals of these cases, and federal circuit courts of appeal have reached different conclusions in determining the legality of policies governing student hairstyle.

In the first, fourth, seventh, and eighth circuits, appellate courts have declared that hairstyle regulations impair students' first amendment freedom of symbolic expression, the fourteenth amendment right to personal liberty, or the right to privacy included in the ninth amendment's unenumerated rights.[97] For example, in 1969 the Seventh Circuit Court of Appeals ruled that school personnel failed to produce evidence of an overriding interest that would justify impairing students' rights to select their hairstyle, which "is an ingredient of personal freedom protected by the United States Constitution."[98] It was not established that any distraction occurred as a result of male students wearing long hair, or that academic performance of male students with long hair was inferior to that of their short-haired peers. The following year, the First Circuit Court of Appeals held that a male student's right to wear shoulder-length hair was a protected liberty under the fourteenth amendment.[99]

In contrast, appeals courts in the third, fifth, sixth, ninth, and tenth circuits have upheld grooming policies pertaining to pupil hairstyle.[100] In sanctioning a hair length restriction as reasonable, the Fifth Circuit Court of Appeals concluded from testimony that male students' wearing of long hair created some disturbances during school hours.[101] In a subsequent case, the same court noted that grooming restrictions constitute a "reasonable means of furthering the school board's undeniable interest in teaching hygiene, instilling discipline, asserting authority, and compelling uniformity."[102]

If school officials have offered health or safety reasons for grooming regulations, their policies typically have been upheld. For instance, the Third Circuit Court of Appeals held that a school board acted properly in requiring a student to cut his hair because the student's long, unclean hair was a health hazard in the school cafeteria.[103] Similarly, regulations requiring hair nets, shower caps, and other hair restraints intended to protect students from injury or to promote sanitation have been upheld, as long as such regulations have been narrowly drawn.[104] In a Maine case, the federal district court upheld a vocational school's regulation prohibiting students from wearing beards or long hair as necessary to create a positive image for potential employers visiting the school for recruitment purposes.[105] A Massachusetts federal district court similarly upheld a hair length code at a vocational school based on the rationale that neat appearance among the students enhances their employment prospects.[106]

Special grooming regulations as conditions of participation in extracurricular activities usually have been upheld if based on legitimate health or safety considerations. In an Illinois case, Jewish basketball players unsuccessfully challenged the state high school association rule forbidding basketball players from wearing hats or other headgear while playing. The Seventh Circuit Court of Appeals held that the players had no first amendment right to wear yarmulkes fastened by bobby pins and that the association's safety concerns, while not great, were not trivial either. The appeals court instructed the federal district court to retain jurisdiction in the case to give the students an opportunity to propose to the association a form of secure head covering appropriate for their faith that also would satisfy the association's safety concerns.[107]

Courts have not ruled in unison regarding whether grooming restrictions can be tied to extracurricular participation for school "image" reasons. The Eleventh Circuit Court of Appeals held that a school board's endorsement of a coach's cleanshaven requirement for student athletes was within the school board's power to regulate grooming and was not arbitrary or unreasonable.[108] Similarly, a California federal district court upheld the legality of a hair length regulation for student athletes, noting that the regulation had been devised by a committee of students, coaches, community members, and administrators.[109] Other courts, however, have ruled that students have a right to govern their appearance in all school activities, not merely academic programs. For example, the Fourth Circuit Court of Appeals held that it was unconstitutional for a public school to force compliance with a "hair code" by withholding extracurricular awards.[110]

Whether different hair length restrictions can be applied to male and female students has not been judicially clarified. A federal court in Ohio reasoned that long-haired male students could not be denied band participation if long-haired female students were not excluded.[111] However, a Mississippi federal district court ruled that a hair length restriction applied only to male students did not violate antidiscrimination provisions in connection with the receipt of federal aid under the Emergency School Aid Act.[112] In 1990 a Texas judge concluded that the state constitution's protection against gender discrimination did not apply to student hair length and thus declined to enjoin portions of a school district's dress code that prohibit boys from wearing earrings or hair that falls below the collar.[113]

ATTIRE

Although public school students' hair length has subsided as a major subject of litigation, other appearance fads have become controversial. For example, sweatshirts depicting Bart Simpson (e.g., "underachiever and proud of it") have recently been banned by some school boards, and these actions are likely to generate litigation.[114]

A few courts have concluded that attire decisions, like hairstyle decisions, are constitutionally protected. Courts have invalidated school rules prohibiting female students from wearing slacks, barring tie-dyed clothing and blue jeans, and requiring male students to wear socks.[115]

Other courts have upheld dress codes, and some have distinguished attire restrictions from hair regulations because clothes, unlike hair length, can be changed after school.[116] Even in situations where students' rights to govern their appearance have been upheld, the judiciary has noted that attire can be regulated if immodest and/or disruptive.[117] The New Hampshire Federal District Court elaborated on the school's authority to exclude students who are unsanitary or scantily clad:

> Good hygiene and the health of the other pupils require that dirty clothes of any nature, whether they be dress clothes or dungarees, should be prohibited. Nor does the court see anything unconstitutional in a school board prohibiting scantily clad students because it is obvious that the lack of proper covering, particularly with female students, might tend to distract other pupils and be disruptive of the educational process and school discipline.[118]

In 1987 an Illinois federal district court upheld a school district's policy prohibiting male students from wearing earrings. Rejecting a student's claim that the ban impaired his free expression rights, the court held that the policy was rationally related to the school's legitimate objective of inhibiting the influence of gangs, as earrings were used to convey gang-related messages.[119] An Idaho federal district court similarly reasoned that a school could prevent a student from wearing a T-shirt that depicted three high school administrators drunk on school grounds. In finding the shirt intolerable, the court noted that the student had no free expression right to portray administrators in a fashion undermining their authority and compromising the school's efforts to educate students about the harmful effects of alcohol.[120] Also, an Ohio federal court upheld the removal from the high school prom of two students dressed in clothing of the opposite sex. The court reasoned that the school board's dress regulations were "reasonably related to the valid educational purposes of teaching community values and maintaining school discipline."[121]

Although circuit appellate courts have differed in their interpretations of constitutional protections regarding grooming regulations, school officials would be wise to ensure that there is a legitimate educational justification for any grooming or dress code. If specific hairstyles or attire are vulgar or threaten a disruption of the educational process, restrictions will be upheld by courts. In addition, policies designed to protect the health and safety of students usually will be endorsed.

EXTRACURRICULAR ACTIVITIES

There has been considerable litigation pertaining to requirements and rights associated with extracurricular activities. Extracurricular activities are usually defined as those that are school-sponsored but are not part of regular class activities or the basis for academic credit. It is clear that once a state provides public education, students cannot be denied attendance without due process of law,[122] but there is less agreement regarding students' rights to participate in school-related activities.

Historically, school officials successfully asserted that extracurricular activities were benefits bestowed at the will of the school board, and courts endorsed the notion that the right to attend school did not include participation in school-related activities.[123] A few courts in the early 1970s ruled that extracurricular activities were an integral part of the total school program, and thus the right to attend school encompassed the right to participate in such activities.[124] However, the prevailing current view is that conditions can be attached to extracurricular participation that cannot be attached to school attendance.

Courts have not agreed regarding procedural protections that must be provided when students face suspension or expulsion from extracurricular activities. In 1976 the Tenth Circuit Court of Appeals recognized that school attendance could not be denied without procedural safeguards, but concluded that similar constitutional protections did not extend to extracurricular components of the school program.[125] More recently, the Fifth Circuit Court of Appeals held that a student's interest in participating in interscholastic athletics is not protected by the due process clause of the fourteenth amendment.[126] The Third Circuit Court of Appeals also upheld a student's sixty-day suspension from extracurricular activities for smoking marijuana and drinking beer on school property, ruling that the notice of charges did not have to specify the proposed punishment. The court concluded that there was no constitutionally protected property interest in participating in extracurricular activities and further noted that the punishment was reasonably related to the legitimate objective of discouraging student drug use.[127] In contrast, the New Hampshire Supreme Court ruled that extracurricular participation is more than a privilege and is entitled to due process protection as a property right.[128] An Arkansas federal district court also held that students could not be suspended from the high school football team without due process because of their property interest in participating on the team.[129]

While school authorities may not be constitutionally required to provide due process under all circumstances involving the denial of extracurricular participation, a hearing for the affected students to explain their version of the situation is always advisable. If school boards have established their own rules for suspending or expelling students from extracurricular activities, courts will require compliance.

The remainder of this section focuses on various aspects of extracurricular activities that have generated legal activity. Allegations of discrimination based on gender and marital status in connection with such activities are discussed in Chapter 5.

ATTENDANCE AND TRAINING REGULATIONS

It is common for extracurricular participation to be conditioned on required attendance at practice sessions and games or performances. An Illinois federal district court upheld a coach's rule prohibiting elementary school basketball players who miss practice (except for illness or death in the family) from participating in the next scheduled game.[130] The plaintiff student had been denied an excused absence from practice to attend a weekly catechism class at a Catholic church. Noting that the student could have made arrangements to attend catechism classes that would not conflict with basketball practice, the court concluded that the school had a legitimate interest in ensuring participation in practice sessions prior to games and could not be expected to arrange practices to accommodate the religious education classes of all team members. The Fourth Circuit Court of Appeals also rejected a parent's challenge to her son's removal from the high school band for missing a required band trip. The student had not been allowed to play in the band at a school game for disciplinary reasons, and as a result, his mother refused to let him participate in the mandatory trip. Finding the band director's conduct reasonable, the court held that the lawsuit was frivolous and awarded attorneys' fees to the defendant school district.[131]

However, in a case discussed previously, Arkansas students prevailed in challenging their suspension from the high school football team for walking out of a pep rally and refusing to participate in a scheduled game in protest of the coach's alleged manipulation of the homecoming queen election.[132] The coach defended his action as based on a policy under which any player is automatically suspended for missing a practice or game "without good cause," but the court held that the students were entitled to due process prior to suspensions that were predicated on their exercise of first amendment rights.

In addition to attendance requirements, courts have endorsed reasonable training and conduct rules as conditions of participation on public school athletic teams. Courts have held that school officials should be given latitude in establishing training standards for high school athletes to foster discipline on competitive teams.[133] The judiciary has upheld the suspension of students from interscholastic athletic competition for violating training regulations prohibiting smoking and drinking among athletes, reasoning that such regulations clearly serve the legitimate interest of deterring substance abuse by student athletes.[134] A New York trial court upheld the denial of a high school football letter to a student who violated such a training regulation even after the football season was over.[135]

An Illinois appeals court upheld a student's suspension from playing on the high school softball team because she violated the athletic code proscribing antisocial behavior considered detrimental to the team and to school spirit. The student was suspended for attending a party where minors were drinking beer; there was no allegation that the student herself was drinking. The court recognized that the coach had only advised students to avoid such parties and had not clearly defined what types of conduct were considered "antisocial behavior" under the policy. Nonetheless, the court reasoned that the disciplinary action was not "sufficiently egregious to come within the narrow concept of arbitrary or capricious official conduct which justifies the extraordinary intervention by the court in the operation of the public schools of the state."[136] In general, courts will not interfere with attendance requirements or training regulations simply because they appear harsh.[137] The judiciary also is reluctant to invalidate disciplinary action for rule violations unless clearly arbitrary or excessive.

RESTRICTIONS ON ELIGIBILITY

Courts generally have allowed school authorities great flexibility in formulating eligibility rules for extracurricular activities. Conditions such as skill prerequisites for athletic teams, academic and leadership criteria for honor societies, and musical proficiency for band and choral groups can be imposed. Members of athletic teams and other extracurricular groups often are selected through a competitive process, and students have no inherent right to be chosen. Selection can be based on subjective judgments, and as long as fair procedures are uniformly applied, courts will not disturb such decisions.[138] Conditions based on residence, age and length of eligibility, and academic performance are discussed below.

Residence. Courts have usually approved residency requirements as conditions of participation on athletic teams. High school athletic association rules that prohibit involvement in interscholastic competition for one year after a change in a student's school without a change in the parents' address are intended to prevent high schools, including private schools,[139] from recruiting student athletes. Several federal appellate courts have ruled that such residency requirements are rationally related to legitimate governmental interests and do not place an impermissible burden on students' rights to travel or their freedom of family association.[140]

Some courts, however, have ordered exceptions where a student's physical or mental welfare has necessitated the move. For example, a Texas student with severe psychiatric difficulties was taken out of his family home and placed with his maternal grandparents in another school district on his therapist's recommendation.[141] The therapist felt that the student's participation on the football team would be therapeutic, but the request was denied because of the interscholastic league's transfer policy. The federal district court granted an injunction concluding that athletic considerations did not prompt the student's move and that there were compelling medical and psychiatric reasons necessitating the change of residence and supporting the student's need to play on the football team. A few courts have even questioned whether such residency requirements for transfer students serve their intended purpose (i.e., deterring the recruitment of high school athletes), since students whose moves are not athletically motivated can be disadvantaged.[142] But in general, residency requirements continue to receive judicial endorsement.

Age and Length of Eligibility. Several courts have endorsed age restrictions on extracurricular participation in order to equalize competitive conditions. In a typical case, the Supreme Court of Oklahoma upheld as fair and reasonably related to legitimate state interests a rule, barring students who reach their nineteenth birthday by September 1 from participating in interscholastic athletics. The court agreed with the state defendants that older and more mature athletes could pose a threat to the health and safety of younger students and that the rule eliminated the possibility of "red shirting" athletes.[143]

A number of courts also have endorsed rules limiting athletic eligibility to eight consecutive semesters or four years after completion of eighth grade.[144] However, some exceptions to such rules have been judicially ordered. A Pennsylvania commonwealth court issued a preliminary injunction barring the state athletic association from enforcing an eight-semester rule where the students in question had been required to repeat courses because of extensive illnesses.[145] The Supreme Court of New Hampshire also held that a student, who had withdrawn from school during his sophomore year because of his health, was entitled to procedural due process before being denied team membership for violating the state athletic association's rule limiting eligibility to a specified length of time after completion of eighth grade.[146]

Academic Conditions. A nationwide trend among school districts is to condition extracurricular participation on satisfactory academic performance. Also, several states through legislation or administrative rules have adopted statewide "no pass, no play" provisions.[147]

Some of these academic conditions have generated litigation. In 1986 the Supreme Court dismissed an appeal of a decision in which the Texas Supreme Court upheld a state law that requires students, with some exceptions, to maintain a 70 average in all classes to be eligible for extracurricular participation.[148] The Texas high court reasoned that the law was rationally related to the state's legitimate interest in providing quality education to all students. Despite the law's exemption for students with disabilities and those enrolled in honors or advanced courses, the court found no equal protection violation. Rejecting the due process claim as well, the court held that the regulation does not violate the principles of fundamental fairness.

In 1985, the West Virginia Supreme Court also endorsed academic standards for extracurricular participation, holding that the state board of education's rule, requiring students to maintain a 2.0 grade point average (GPA) to participate, was a legitimate exercise of its supervisory power and furthered the goal of educational excellence. The court also upheld a county school board's regulation that went beyond the state policy by requiring students to maintain a passing grade in all classes as a prerequisite to extracurricular participation.[149] More recently, a Kentucky appeals court upheld a school board's policy requiring students to maintain a 2.0 GPA in five of six subjects as a condition of participating in extracurricular activities.[150] Also, a Louisiana student was unsuccessful in challenging a school rule requiring at least a 1.6 GPA to try out for the cheerleader squad. The Louisiana appeals court determined that the rule was rationally related to furthering the school's goal of academic excellence.[151]

In view of the current nationwide concern for educational excellence, school boards and state legislatures are apt to place additional academic conditions on extracurricular participation. Unless such policies are applied in a discriminatory manner, they will likely survive judicial challenges.

FEES FOR PARTICIPATION

An increasingly controversial issue is whether extracurricular participation can be conditioned on the payment of fees. In the early 1970s, several courts upheld practices whereby students were charged fees to participate in extracurricular activities. For example, in 1970 the Supreme Court of Idaho rejected a state constitutional challenge to a school district's policy requiring students to pay fees for extracurricular participation, concluding that such activities "are not necessary elements of a high school career."[152] The Wisconsin and Montana Supreme Courts reached similar conclusions regarding the legality of charging fees for activities that are optional or elective.[153]

In more recent cases, however, courts have rendered conflicting opinions on this issue. In 1984 the California Supreme Court struck down a school district's decision to adapt to its reduced budget by charging students fees for participation in dramatic productions, musical performances, and athletic competition. The court reasoned that extracurricular activities are an "integral fundamental part" of the educational program and thus encompassed within the state constitution's guarantee of a free public education.[154] The court was not persuaded that the school district's fiscal crisis justified the fees or that the constitutional defect was mitigated by school district waivers for indigent students. The court further held that the fee violated the state administrative code stipulating that students shall not be required to pay "any fee, deposit, or other charge officially authorized by law." Finding this regulation a valid exercise of the general regulatory authority of the state board of education, the court concluded that it precluded the imposition of fees for extracurricular activities.

In contrast, a Michigan appeals court upheld fees for participation on interscholastic athletic teams, noting the confidential waiver process available for students who could not afford the fees. The court recognized that no student had been denied participation because of inability to pay and further declared that interscholastic athletics are not considered an integral, fundamental part of the educational program that would necessitate providing them at no cost to students.[155] Given the fiscal constraints on school district budgets, fees for extracurricular activities are likely to be considered by an increasing number of school districts. The legality of such programs will depend on judicial interpretations of state law.

OTHER CONDITIONS

A number of other conditions have been attached to extracurricular participation. Some courts, for example, have upheld limitations on student participation in out-of-school athletic competition as a condition of varsity participation to protect students from overtaxing themselves and to make interscholastic athletics more competitive and fair.[156] Restrictions on the number of team members allowed to participate in championship games also have been upheld as rationally related to legitimate state objectives of reducing costs of play-off contests, promoting fair play in championship games, and preventing violence during such games.[157]

Students can be required to have physical examinations and to be in good physical health to participate on athletic teams. As discussed in Chapter 6, whether participation can be conditioned on students submitting to random drug testing (urinalysis) has not been clarified. The Seventh Circuit Court of Appeals has upheld such a drug-testing policy, reasoning that the policy was designed to promote the important governmental interest of ensuring the health and safety of student athletes.[158] However, a Texas federal district court reached an opposite conclusion, finding unconstitutional the school district's practice of subjecting participants in extracurricular activities to urinalysis without individualized suspicion of drug use.[159]

Restrictions imposed on the participation of students with disabilities on athletic teams also have been controversial. Although in 1977 the Second Circuit Court of Appeals rejected a federal challenge to a school board policy barring students with defective vision from participating in contact sports,[160] a partially sighted student subsequently brought suit under state law and was granted relief.[161] The New York appeals court enjoined the school district from excluding the student from contact sports, noting the availability of protective eyewear to minimize the risk of injury. Also, a student with one kidney secured a court order enjoining the school district from barring him from the high school football team. The Pennsylvania federal district court reasoned that the student was likely to prevail in establishing that his exclusion from the team based on his disability violated federal civil rights provisions that prohibit discrimination against otherwise qualified individuals with disabilities.[162] Given recent rulings, school authorities would be wise to have evidence of legitimate risks to health or safety before excluding specific children with disabilities from athletic teams.

Although extracurricular activities remain a heavily contested aspect of public school offerings, courts generally have allowed school authorities discretion in attaching conditions (e.g., academic standards, skill criteria, residency rules, and attendance and training regulations) to student participation. Educators should ensure, however, that all policies pertaining to extracurricular activities are reasonable, related to an educational purpose, clearly stated, publicized to parents and students, and applied without discrimination.

CONCLUSION

Noninstructional issues have generated a substantial amount of school litigation. Many of the cases have focused on students' first amendment freedoms of speech and press, but other constitutional rights, such as due process and equal protection guarantees, also have been asserted in challenging restrictions on students' noninstructional activities. In the latter 1960s and early 1970s, the federal judiciary expanded constitutional protections afforded to students in noninstructional matters. More recently, however, courts have emphasized that school officials can restrict student conduct and expression in school-related activities for educational reasons. Although judicial criteria applied in weighing the competing interests of students and school authorities continue to be refined, the following generalizations accurately characterize the current posture of the courts.

1. Students cannot assert a first amendment right to engage in defamatory, obscene, lewd, or inflammatory expression in public schools.
2. Student expression that represents the school is subject to restrictions; school authorities have broad discretion to censor such expression, provided the decisions are based on pedagogical concerns and do not entail viewpoint discrimination.
3. Student-initiated expression of ideological views that merely happens to take place at school (in contrast to representing the school) cannot be curtailed unless a material interference with or substantial disruption of the educational process can reasonably be forecast from the expression.
4. School authorities can restrict commercial solicitation on public school premises.
5. School authorities cannot bar controversial or critical content from nonschool student literature; policies requiring prior administrative review of such publications must clearly specify the

procedures for review and the types of material that are prohibited.

6. School authorities cannot punish students for the content of literature that is published and distributed off school grounds unless such distribution substantially interferes with the operation of the school.

7. Any regulation prohibiting a certain form of student expression or imposing time, place, and manner restrictions on expression must be specific, publicized to students and parents, and applied without discrimination.

8. School authorities can forbid student membership in secret societies and discipline students for joining such clubs.

9. Public school authorities are not required to provide school access to student clubs that are not an extension of the curriculum; however, if the school provides a limited open forum for student-initiated clubs to meet during noninstructional time, the access policy must be content-neutral.

10. Grooming standards for students can be imposed for health and safety reasons and to prevent a disruption of the educational process.

11. Students do not have an inherent right to participate in extracurricular activities.

12. School authorities have considerable latitude in attaching reasonable conditions to extracurricular participation (e.g., attendance and training regulations, residency requirements, academic standards, requirements pertaining to age and length of eligibility, etc.).

13. Restrictions can be imposed on student participation in extracurricular activities based on legitimate health and safety considerations.

14. Whether fees can be charged for extracurricular participation depends upon an interpretation of an individual state's constitutional and statutory provisions.

ENDNOTES

1. West Virginia Bd. of Educ. v. Barnette, 319 U.S. 624, 637 (1943). *See also* Shelton v. Tucker, 364 U.S. 479, 487 (1960); Sweezy v. New Hampshire, 354 U.S. 234, 250 (1957).
2. Keyishian v. Board of Regents, 385 U.S. 589, 603 (1967), quoting in part, United States v. Associated Press, 52 F. Supp. 362, 372 (S.D.N.Y. 1943), *aff'd,* 326 U.S. 1 (1945).
3. *See* West Virginia State Bd. of Educ. v. Barnette, 319 U.S. 624 (1943); text with note 84, Chapter 2.
4. Parate v. Isibor, 868 F.2d 821, 828 (6th Cir. 1989).

5. Texas v. Johnson, 491 U.S. 397 (1989). Congress responded to this decision with a law providing criminal penalties for any person who "knowingly mutilates, defaces, physically defiles, burns, maintains on the floor or ground, or tramples upon any flag of the United States," 18 U.S.C.A. § 700(a)(1) (1990). However, the Supreme Court found this law unconstitutional, United States v. Eichman, 110 S. Ct. 2404 (1990).
6. Schenck v. United States, 249 U.S. 47, 52 (1919).
7. Bethel School Dist. No. 403 v. Fraser, 478 U.S. 675, 682 (1986). *See also* Tinker v. Des Moines Indep. School Dist., 393 U.S. 503, 506–507 (1969).
8. *See* Jarman v. Williams, 753 F.2d 76 (8th Cir. 1985); Justice v. National Collegiate Athletic Ass'n, 577 F. Supp. 356 (D. Ariz. 1983).
9. State v. Ybarra, 550 P.2d 763 (Or. Ct. App. 1976).
10. Jarman v. Williams, 753 F.2d 76 (8th Cir. 1985). *See also* Clayton v. Place, 884 F.2d 376 (8th Cir. 1989), *cert. denied,* 110 S. Ct. 1811 (1990) (school district's policy prohibiting dances did not violate the establishment clause even though the policy supported the religious beliefs of a vocal segment of the community).
11. *See* Chapter 12 for a discussion of the principles of tort law governing personal damages suits for defamation.
12. *See* Bright v. Los Angeles Unified School Dist., 134 Cal. Rptr. 639, 648 (Cal. 1976).
13. *See* Hustler Magazine v. Falwell, 485 U.S. 46 (1988).
14. *See* Garcia v. Board of Educ. of Socorro Consol. School Dist., 777 F.2d 1403 (10th Cir. 1985), *cert. denied,* 479 U.S. 814 (1986) (school board member); Scott v. News-Herald, 496 N.E.2d 699 (Ohio 1986) (school superintendent). For a discussion of defamation charges against public officials, *see* Gertz v. Robert Welch, 418 U.S. 323 (1974); Curtis Publishing Co. v. Butts, 388 U.S. 130 (1967); Rosenblatt v. Baer, 383 U.S. 75 (1966); New York Times Co. v. Sullivan, 376 U.S. 254 (1964).
15. Finding that public school teachers and coaches are not public figures, *see* Warford v. Lexington Herald-Leader Co., 789 S.W.2d 758 (Ky. 1990), *cert. denied,* 111 S. Ct. 754 (1991); True v. Ladner, 513 A.2d 257 (Me. 1986); Franklin v. Lodge 1108, 159 Cal. Rptr. 131 (Cal. Ct. App. 1979). Finding such individuals to be public figures, *see* Scott v. News-Herald, 496 N.E.2d 699 (Ohio 1986); Johnston v. Corinthian Television Corp., 583 P.2d 1101 (Okla. 1978); Basarich v. Rodeghero, 321 N.E.2d 739 (Ill. App. Ct. 1974).
16. *See* Gertz v. Robert Welch, Inc., 418 U.S. 323 (1974); Ollman v. Evans, 750 F.2d 970 (D.C. Cir. 1984), *cert. denied,* 471 U.S. 1127 (1985); Dow v. New Haven Indep., Inc., 549 A.2d 683 (Conn. Super. Ct. 1987).
17. Milkovich v. Lorain Journal Co., 110 S. Ct. 2695 (1990).
18. 413 U.S. 15, 24 (1973).
19. Ginsberg v. New York, 390 U.S. 629, 636-637 (1968). *See also* New York v. Ferber, 458 U.S. 747 (1982), *on remand,* 441 N.E.2d 1100 (N.Y. 1982); Bookcase, Inc. v. Broderick, 218 N.E.2d 668, 671 (N.Y. 1966), *dismissed,* 385 U.S. 12 (1966) ("the concept of obscenity or of unprotected matter may vary according to the group to whom the questionable material is directed").
20. *See* Jacobs v. Board of School Comm'rs, 490 F.2d 601 (7th Cir. 1973), *vacated as moot,* 420 U.S. 128 (1975); Papish v. Board of Curators, 410 U.S. 667 (1973); Vail v. Board of Educ. of Portsmouth School Dist., 354 F. Supp. 592, 599 (D.N.H. 1973), *vacated and remanded,* 502 F.2d 1159 (1973).
21. 755 F.2d 1356 (9th Cir. 1985), *rev'd,* 478 U.S. 675 (1986). The student had been

suspended for two days and disqualified as a candidate for commencement speaker. However, he did eventually deliver a commencement speech, so his claim that the disqualification violated due process rights was not reviewed by the appellate court. On remand from the Supreme Court's reversal of the appellate decision, the student's request for partial attorneys' fees regarding his success on the due process claim at the district court level was denied, 807 F.2d 1507 (9th Cir. 1987).

22. *Id.,* 478 U.S. at 683. *See also* Hinze v. Superior Court of Marin County, 174 Cal. Rptr. 403 (Cal. Ct. App. 1981) (badge stating, "Fuck the Draft," was vulgar and not protected expression; a student who persistently refused to remove the button could be disciplined).

23. Stacy v. Williams, 306 F. Supp. 963, 972 (N.D. Miss. 1969), *aff'd,* 446 F.2d 1366 (5th Cir. 1971).

24. Melton v. Young, 465 F.2d 1332 (6th Cir. 1972), *cert. denied,* 411 U.S. 951 (1973).

25. Williams v. Turner, 382 So. 2d 1040 (La. Ct. App. 1980).

26. Fenton v. Stear, 423 F. Supp. 767, 771 (W.D. Pa. 1976).

27. Klein v. Smith, 635 F. Supp. 1440, 1442 (D. Me. 1986).

28. *See* William Valente, "Student Freedom of Speech in Public Schools— Another Turn," *Education Law Reporter,* vol. 46 (1988), pp. 889–895.

29. *See* Cornelius v. NAACP Legal Defense and Educ. Fund, 473 U.S. 788 (1985); Perry Educ. Ass'n v. Perry Local Educators' Ass'n, 460 U.S. 37 (1983).

30. Perry Educ. Ass'n, *id.*

31. Courts have used different terms to refer to this category (e.g., limited public forum, designated public forum, designated open forum), and some legal analysts have questioned whether a distinction actually exists between limited and nonpublic forums. *See* Gail Sorenson, "Public Forum Doctrine: Use and Abuse in Schools and Colleges," *NOLPE Notes,* February, 1990, pp. 1–3.

32. *See, e.g.,* Gambino v. Fairfax County School Bd., 564 F.2d 157 (4th Cir. 1977); Shanley v. Northeast Indep. School Dist., 462 F.2d 960 (5th Cir. 1972); Koppell v. Levine, 347 F. Supp. 456 (E.D.N.Y. 1972). *See also* Stanton v. Brunswick School Dep't, 577 F. Supp. 1560 (D. Me. 1984) (school officials could not reject a student's choice of a quotation to appear with her picture in the yearbook that was designed to convey an ideological position).

33. *See, e.g.,* Trachtman v. Anker, 563 F.2d 512 (2d Cir. 1977), *cert. denied,* 435 U.S. 925 (1978); Jacobs v. Board of School Comm'rs, 490 F.2d 601 (7th Cir. 1973), *vacated as moot,* 420 U.S. 128 (1975); Nitzberg v. Parks, 525 F.2d 378 (4th Cir. 1975); Sullivan v. Houston Indep. School Dist., 475 F.2d 1071 (5th Cir. 1973), *cert. denied,* 414 U.S. 1032 (1973).

34. 484 U.S. 260 (1988), *on remand,* 840 F.2d 596 (8th Cir. 1988). *See also* Leeb v. DeLong, 243 Cal. Rptr. 494 (Cal. Ct. App. 1988). Prior to *Hazelwood,* some courts had upheld censorship of school-sponsored publications, even those considered a forum for student expression, because of the libelous nature of the material at issue or the sensitive nature of the content (e.g., students' feelings about sex, contraception, homosexuality). *See* Nicholson v. Board of Educ., 682 F.2d 858 (9th Cir. 1982); Trachtman v. Anker, 563 F.2d 512 (2d Cir. 1977), *cert. denied,* 435 U.S. 925 (1978); Frasca v. Andrews, 463 F. Supp. 1043 (E.D.N.Y. 1979).

35. *Id.,* 484 U.S. at 267.

36. Bethel School Dist. No. 403 v. Fraser, 478 U.S. 675 (1986). *See also* Rust v. Sullivan, 111 S. Ct. 1759 (1991) (upholding prohibitions on the use of federal funds earmarked for family-planning services to support abortion counseling, referral, and activities advocating abortions). There is some sentiment that this decision may stimulate funding restrictions to curtail expression in public schools that the government does not endorse. *See* "High Court Abortion Ruling Raises Concerns for Educators," *Education Daily,* May 30, 1991, pp. 1–2.

37. As discussed in Chapter 3, some lower courts have relied on *Hazelwood* in granting school authorities broad discretion to censor the school curriculum as long as the decisions are based on pedagogical concerns. *See* Virgil v. School Bd. of Columbia County, 862 F.2d 1517 (11th Cir. 1989); text with note 106, Chapter 3.

38. Poling v. Murphy, 872 F.2d 757, 762 (6th Cir. 1989), *cert. denied,* 110 S. Ct. 723 (1990).

39. *Id.,* 872 F.2d at 761. *See also* Guidry v. Broussard, 897 F.2d 181 (5th Cir. 1990) (censorship of student's valedictory speech for the graduation ceremony was upheld); Bull v. Dardanelle Public School Dist. No. 15, 745 F. Supp. 1455 (E.D. Ark. 1990) (teachers' failure to approve high school student's candidacy for student council president was related to legitimate pedagogical concerns and was not in retaliation for his exercise of protected expression).

40. Planned Parenthood v. Clark County School Dist., 887 F.2d 935, 942 (9th Cir. 1989), quoting Burch v. Barker, 861 F.2d 1149, 1158 (9th Cir. 1988).

41. Crosby v. Holsinger, 852 F.2d 801 (4th Cir. 1988).

42. San Diego Comm. Against Registration and the Draft v. Governing Bd. of Grossmont Union High School Dist., 790 F.2d 1471 (9th Cir. 1986). *See also* Clergy and Laity Concerned v. Chicago Bd. of Educ., 586 F. Supp. 1408 (N.D. Ill. 1984).

43. Searcey v. Harris, 888 F.2d 1314 (11th Cir. 1989).

44. The conflict between free expression rights and antidiscrimination policies has recently been controversial on several university campuses. *See* The Dartmouth Review v. Dartmouth College, 889 F.2d 13 (1st Cir. 1989) (suspension of students following their confrontation with an African-American professor and publication of an article criticizing the professor did not impair students' constitutional rights); Doe v. University of Michigan, 721 F. Supp. 852 (Mich. 1989) (university's policy banning discriminatory harassment was found to be unconstitutionally vague and overbroad); Dennis Matthies, "Freedom from Harassment Remains a Basic Right, Doesn't It?" Stanford University *Campus Report,* February 15, 1989, p. 17.

45. 393 U.S. 503, 508 (1969).

46. *Id.* at 509.

47. *Id.* at 511.

48. *Id.* at 513, quoting Burnside v. Byars, 363 F.2d 744, 749 (5th Cir. 1966). *Compare with* Blackwell v. Issaquena County Bd. of Educ., 363 F.2d 749 (5th Cir. 1966); text with note 55, *infra.*

49. Relying on *Tinker,* a federal district court ruled that a homosexual student had a free expression right to select another male as his escort to the senior prom, as this action conveyed an ideological message, Fricke v. Lynch, 491 F. Supp. 381 (D.R.I. 1980).

50. *See* Hazelwood School Dist. v. Kuhlmeier, 484 U.S. 260 (1988), text with note

34, *supra*; Bethel School Dist. No. 403 v. Fraser, 478 U.S. 675 (1986), text with note 21, *supra*.

51. Butts v. Dallas Indep. School Dist., 436 F.2d 728, 731 (5th Cir. 1971).

52. Anderson v. Central Point School Dist. No. 6, 554 F. Supp. 600, 608 (D. Or. 1982), *aff'd,* 746 F.2d 505 (9th Cir. 1984).

53. Scoville v. Board of Educ. of Joliet, 425 F.2d 10, 14 (7th Cir. 1970), *cert. denied,* 400 U.S. 826 (1970).

54. Guzick v. Drebus, 431 F.2d 594, 600 (6th Cir. 1970), *cert. denied,* 401 U.S. 948 (1971).

55. *See* Blackwell v. Issaquena County Bd. of Educ., 363 F.2d 749 (5th Cir. 1966).

56. Bystrom v. Fridley High School, 822 F.2d 747 (8th Cir. 1987). Subsequently, the students who initially challenged the policy distributed another edition of their underground paper without securing administrative approval. Suspension of the students was upheld; school authorities could constitutionally punish students for expression that caused a disruption, was vulgar, and advocated violence against a teacher. Bystrom v. Fridley High School, 686 F. Supp. 1387 (D. Minn. 1987), *aff'd mem.,* 855 F.2d 855 (8th Cir. 1988).

57. *See, e.g.,* Quarterman v. Byrd, 453 F.2d 54 (4th Cir. 1971); Eisner v. Stamford Bd. of Educ., 440 F.2d 803 (2d Cir. 1971); Liebner v. Sharbaugh, 429 F. Supp. 744 (E.D. Va. 1977).

58. *See, e.g.,* Rivera v. East Otero School Dist. R-1, 721 F. Supp. 1189 (D. Colo. 1989); Claiborne v. Beebe School Dist., 687 F. Supp. 1358 (E.D. Ark. 1988).

59. Burch v. Barker, 861 F.2d 1149, 1155 (9th Cir. 1988).

60. Romano v. Harrington, 725 F. Supp. 687 (E.D.N.Y. 1989).

61. Williams v. Spencer, 622 F.2d 1200 (4th Cir. 1980). The newspaper also contained a potentially libelous cartoon, but the appeals court focused only on the health and safety issue, leaving open the question of libel.

62. *See* Tate v. Board of Educ., 453 F.2d 975 (8th Cir. 1972).

63. *See* Herman v. University of South Carolina, 457 F.2d 902 (4th Cir. 1972); Farrell v. Joel, 437 F.2d 160 (2d Cir. 1971); Gebert v. Hoffman, 336 F. Supp. 694 (E.D. Pa. 1972).

64. *See* Gebert, *id.;* Buttny v. Smiley, 281 F. Supp. 280 (D. Colo. 1968). In 1991 public schools nationwide experienced a wave of sit-ins, walkouts, and other demonstrations in response to the war in the Persian Gulf. *See* Mark Walsh, "Student Activism Forces Schools to Revisit Free Speech Policies," *Education Week,* February 6, 1991, pp. 12–13.

65. Tate v. Board of Educ., 453 F.2d 975 (8th Cir. 1972). *But see* Boyd v. Board of Directors of McGehee School Dist. No. 17, 612 F. Supp. 86 (E.D. Ark. 1985); text with note 70, *infra.*

66. Dodd v. Rambis, 535 F. Supp. 23 (S.D. Ind. 1981).

67. Karp v. Becken, 477 F.2d 171 (9th Cir. 1973).

68. *Id.* at 176.

69. Scoville v. Board of Educ. of Joliet, 425 F.2d 10, 12 (7th Cir. 1970), *cert. denied,* 400 U.S. 826 (1970). *See also* Baughman v. Freienmuth, 478 F.2d 1345 (4th Cir. 1973).

70. Boyd v. Board of Directors of McGehee School Dist. No. 17, 612 F. Supp. 86 (E.D. Ark. 1985) (punitive damages were assessed against the coach for imposing disciplinary action predicated on the students' exercise of protected expression).

71. *See, e.g.,* Shanley v. Northeast Indep. School Dist., 462 F.2d 960 (5th Cir.

1972); Riseman v. School Comm. of Quincy, 439 F.2d 148 (1st Cir. 1971). *See also* Heffron v. International Society for Krishna Consciousness, 452 U.S. 640 (1981) (upholding a restriction on literature distribution at a fairgrounds to maintain orderly movement of the fair crowd and protect citizens from fraudulent solicitation).

72. *See* Fujishima v. Board of Educ., 460 F.2d 1355 (7th Cir. 1972); Hemry by Hemry v. School Bd. of Colorado Springs, 760 F. Supp. 856 (D. Colo. 1991).

73. *See* Nicholson v. Board of Educ., Torrance Unified School Dist., 682 F.2d 858 (9th Cir. 1982); Vail v. Board of Educ. of Portsmouth School Dist., 354 F. Supp. 592 (D.N.H. 1973), *vacated and remanded,* 502 F.2d 1159 (1st Cir. 1973).

74. *See* Godwin v. East Baton Rouge Parish School Bd., 408 So. 2d 1214 (La. 1981), *appeal dismissed,* 459 U.S. 807 (1982).

75. *See* Boyd v. Board of Directors of McGehee School Dist. No. 17, 612 F. Supp. 86 (E.D. Ark. 1985) (students had not been adequately warned regarding what constituted "good cause" in connection with their suspension from the high school football team for engaging in a protest); text with note 70, *supra.*

76. Thomas v. Board of Educ., Granville Cent. School Dist., 607 F.2d 1043 (2d Cir. 1979), *cert. denied,* 444 U.S. 1081 (1980). The publication's only connection with the public school was that some copies were temporarily stored in a closet in a classroom. *But see* Baker v. Downey City Bd. of Educ., 307 F. Supp. 517 (C.D. Cal. 1969) (upholding suspension of students for using profane and vulgar language in a publication distributed immediately outside the school's entrance).

77. *See* Bolger v. Youngs Drug Products Corp., 463 U.S. 60, 64–75 (1983); Central Hudson Gas & Elec. Corp. v. Public Serv. Comm'n of New York, 447 U.S. 557, 562–563 (1980); Ohralik v. Ohio State Bar Ass'n, 436 U.S. 447, 455–456 (1978). Some recent controversies have focused on public school boards' signing contracts agreeing to air daily classroom broadcasts of a television news program for students that contains advertising (Channel One). In 1991 the North Carolina Supreme Court held that school boards have the legal authority to enter into such contracts for supplementary instructional materials, overturning a state board prohibition on local board contracts with Channel One, State v. Whittle Commmunications and the Thomasville City Bd. of Educ., 402 S.E.2d 556 (N.C. 1991). *See* text with note 10, Chapter 1.

78. Board of Trustees of the State Univ. of New York v. Fox, 492 U.S. 469 (1989). *See also* American Future Sys., Inc. v. Pennsylvania State Univ., 752 F.2d 854 (3d Cir. 1984), *cert. denied,* 473 U.S. 911 (1985); Glover v. Cole, 762 F.2d 1197 (4th Cir. 1985); Chapman v. Thomas, 743 F.2d 1056 (4th Cir. 1984), *cert. denied,* 471 U.S. 1004 (1985).

79. Katz v. McAulay, 438 F.2d 1058 (2d Cir. 1971), *cert. denied,* 405 U.S. 933 (1972). It should be noted, however, that some courts have distinguished expression with political and commercial elements from expression primarily intended to advance economic interests.

80. *See* Dianne Brockett, "Indiana Bill Would Protect Student Press Freedom," *School Board News,* March 6, 1991, p. 4; Robert Shoop, "States Talk Back to the Supreme Court: Students Should Be Heard as Well as Seen," *Education Law Reporter,* vol. 59 (1990), pp. 579–586. *See also* the discussion of the federal Equal Access Act at note 93, *infra.*

81. Healy v. James, 408 U.S. 169, 181 (1972).

82. *See* State Bd. for Community Colleges and Occupational Educ. v. Olson, 687 P.2d 429, 439 (Colo. 1984), *appeal after remand,* 759 P.2d 829 (Colo. Ct. App. 1988).

83. *See* notes 85, 87, 88, *infra. But see* Wright v. Board of Educ., 246 S.W. 43 (Mo. Ct. App. 1922) (school board regulation forbidding student membership in secret organizations was not authorized by the state legislature, and student conduct during out-of-school hours could not be regulated unless it was substantiated that it would clearly interfere with school discipline).

84. Ill. Rev. Stat., ch. 122, § 31–3 (1989).

85. Bradford v. Board of Educ., 121 P. 929, 931 (Cal. Ct. App. 1912). *See also* Burkitt v. School Dist. No. 1, Multnomah County, 246 P.2d 566 (Or. 1952).

86. *See* Thomas v. Board of Educ., Granville Cent. School Dist., 607 F.2d 1043 (2d Cir. 1979), *cert. denied,* 444 U.S. 1081 (1980); text with note 76, *supra.*

87. *See* Passel v. Fort Worth Indep. School Dist., 453 S.W.2d 888 (Tex. Civ. App. 1970), *appeal dismissed and cert. denied,* 402 U.S. 968 (1971); Holroyd v. Eibling, 188 N.E.2d 797 (Ohio Ct. App. 1962).

88. Robinson v. Sacramento Unified School Dist., 53 Cal. Rptr. 781 (Cal. Ct. App. 1966). A Texas court found no interference with parental childrearing rights in a school board's policy requiring parents to certify that their children attending secondary schools would not join or participate in the activities of fraternities, sororities, or secret societies, Passel v. Fort Worth Indep. School Dist., 453 S.W.2d 888 (Tex. Civ. App. 1970), *appeal dismissed and cert. denied,* 402 U.S. 968 (1971).

89. Healy v. James, 408 U.S. 169 (1972).

90. *See, e.g.,* Gay Students Services v. Texas A & M Univ., 737 F.2d 1317 (5th Cir. 1984), *cert. denied,* 471 U.S. 1001 (1985); Gay Students Org. of the Univ. of New Hampshire v. Bonner, 509 F.2d 652 (1st Cir. 1974). It should be noted that students cannot be forced to support, through their activity fee, organizations that espouse political and ideological philosophies the students oppose. *See* Galda v. Rutgers, 772 F.2d 1060 (3d Cir. 1985), *cert. denied,* 475 U.S. 1065 (1986) (first amendment precludes the university from compelling students to pay a fee to support a state public interest research group).

91. Widmar v. Vincent, 454 U.S. 263 (1981).

92. *See, e.g.,* Dixon v. Beresh, 361 F. Supp. 253 (E.D. Mich. 1973) (school authorities would have to present clear evidence that particular clubs would produce a disruption of the educational process in order to deny recognition to *selected* student organizations).

93. 20 U.S.C. § 4071 (1988). *See* text with note 31, Chapter 2.

94. Student Coalition for Peace v. Lower Merion School Dist., 776 F.2d 431 (3d Cir. 1985), *on remand,* 633 F. Supp. 1040 (E.D. Pa. 1986).

95. 110 S. Ct. 2356 (1990). The court rejected the contention that only noncurriculum, *advocacy* groups are protected under the EAA. For a discussion of the criteria applied in determining whether groups are curriculum related, *see* text with note 37, Chapter 2.

96. Hazelwood School Dist. v. Kuhlmeier, 484 U.S. 260, 267 (1988). The *Mergens* majority emphasized that the EAA's limited *open* forum is not the same as a limited *public* forum under the first amendment, 110 S. Ct. at 2367–2368, but Justice Stevens, dissenting, questioned this distinction, *id.* at 2383–2387.

97. *See* Massie v. Henry, 455 F.2d 779 (4th Cir. 1972); Bishop v. Colaw, 450 F.2d

1069 (8th Cir. 1971); Richards v. Thurston, 424 F.2d 1281 (1st Cir. 1970); Breen v. Kahl, 419 F.2d 1034 (7th Cir. 1969), *cert. denied*, 398 U.S. 937 (1970).

98. Breen, *id*. at 1036.

99. Richards v. Thurston, 424 F.2d 1281, 1286 (1st Cir. 1970).

100. *See* Zeller v. Donegal School Dist., 517 F.2d 600 (3d Cir. 1975), *overruling* Stull v. School Bd. of Western Beaver Jr.-Sr. High School, 459 F.2d 339 (3d Cir. 1972); King v. Saddleback Jr. College Dist., 445 F.2d 932 (9th Cir. 1971), *cert. denied*, 404 U.S. 979 (1971); Freeman v. Flake, 448 F.2d 258 (10th Cir. 1971), *cert. denied*, 405 U.S. 1032 (1972); Jackson v. Dorrier, 424 F.2d 213 (6th Cir. 1970), *cert. denied*, 400 U.S. 850 (1970); Ferrell v. Dallas Indep. School Dist., 392 F.2d 697 (5th Cir. 1968), *cert. denied*, 393 U.S. 856 (1968).

101. Ferrell, *id*. at 703. *See also* Karr v. Schmidt, 460 F.2d 609 (5th Cir. 1972), *cert. denied*, 409 U.S. 989 (1972).

102. Domico v. Rapides Parish School Bd., 675 F.2d 100, 102 (5th Cir. 1982). *See also* Ferrara v. Hendry County School Bd., 362 So. 2d 371 (Fla. Dist. Ct. App. 1978), *cert. denied*, 444 U.S. 856 (1979); Stevenson v. Board of Educ. of Wheeler County, Georgia, 426 F.2d 1154 (5th Cir. 1970), *cert. denied*, 400 U.S. 957 (1970) (upholding school policies requiring students to be cleanshaven).

103. Gere v. Stanley, 453 F.2d 205 (3d Cir. 1971).

104. *See* text with note 118, *infra*.

105. Farrell v. Smith, 310 F. Supp. 732 (D. Me. 1970).

106. Bishop v. Cermenaro, 355 F. Supp. 1269 (D. Mass. 1973).

107. Menora v. Illinois High School Ass'n, 683 F.2d 1030 (7th Cir. 1982), *cert. denied*, 459 U.S. 1156 (1983).

108. Davenport v. Randolph County Bd. of Educ., 730 F.2d 1395 (11th Cir. 1984). *See also* Zeller v. Donegal School Dist., 517 F.2d 600 (3d Cir. 1975); Humphries v. Lincoln Parish School Bd., 467 So. 2d 870 (La. Ct. App. 1985). Courts have rendered conflicting opinions regarding whether participation in the high school band can be conditioned on adherence to a hair length code. *Compare* Dostert v. Berthold Pub. School Dist. No. 54, 391 F. Supp. 876 (D.N.D. 1975) (school's interest in requiring uniformity in hair length to secure high marks in band competition was not a sufficiently compelling reason to interfere with students' constitutionally protected interest in determining their hair length) *with* Corley v. Daunhauer, 312 F. Supp. 811 (E.D. Ark. 1970) (public school band members can be required to conform to reasonable hair length regulations).

109. Neuhaus v. Torrey, 310 F. Supp. 192 (N.D. Cal. 1970). *See also* Christmas v. El Reno Bd. of Educ., Indep. School Dist. No. 34, 449 F.2d 153 (10th Cir. 1971) (student could be barred from an optional postgraduation diploma ceremony because of violating hair length regulation).

110. Long v. Zopp, 476 F.2d 180 (4th Cir. 1973) (recognizing that legitimate health and safety concerns might justify a hair restriction during football season, the court found no justification for denying a letter to a student who violated a hair restriction after football season ended). *See also* Dunham v. Pulsifer, 312 F. Supp. 411 (D. Vt. 1970) (a hair length regulation for student athletes had no legitimate relationship to team performance, discipline, or conformity or to the school's educational mission).

111. Cordova v. Chonko, 315 F. Supp. 953 (N.D. Ohio 1970). *See also* Sims v. Colfax Community School Dist., 307 F. Supp. 485 (S.D. La. 1970) (female student successfully challenged school rule prohibiting both males and females from wearing their hair longer than one finger width above the eyebrow).
112. Trent v. Perritt, 391 F. Supp. 171 (S.D. Miss. 1975).
113. Buckberry v. Board of Trustees, Lubbock Indep. School Dist., No. 90-531, 518 (Tex. Dist. Ct. 1990). *See also* Toungate v. Board of Trustees, Bastrop Indep. School Dist., No. 19904 (Tex. Dist. Ct. 1990); Mercer v. Board of Trustees, North Forest Indep. School Dist., 538 S.W.2d 201 (Tex. Civ. App. 1976).
114. *See* George Vlahakis, "Bart Mania Not Worth Having a Cow Over," *Indiana University Newspaper,* December 14, 1990, p. 12.
115. *See* Wallace v. Ford, 346 F. Supp. 156 (E.D. Ark. 1972); Press v. Pasadena Indep. School Dist., 326 F. Supp. 550 (S.D. Tex. 1971); Bannister v. Paradis, 316 F. Supp. 185 (D.N.H. 1970); Johnson v. Joint School Dist. No. 60, Bingham County, 508 P.2d 547 (Idaho 1973); Scott v. Board of Educ., Union Free School Dist. No. 17, 305 N.Y.S.2d 601 (N.Y. Sup. Ct. 1969).
116. *See, e.g.,* Fowler v. Williamson, 448 F. Supp. 497 (W.D.N.C. 1978) (upholding prohibition on wearing jeans to graduation ceremony); Dunkerson v. Russell, 502 S.W.2d 64 (Ky. 1973) (upholding a dress code provision forbidding female students from wearing jeans).
117. *See, e.g.,* Richards v. Thurston, 424 F.2d 1281 (1st Cir. 1970); Wallace v. Ford, 346 F. Supp. 156 (E.D. Ark. 1972); Bannister v. Paradis, 316 F. Supp. 185 (D.N.H. 1970); Westley v. Rossi, 305 F. Supp. 706 (D. Minn. 1969).
118. Bannister, *id.* at 189.
119. Olesen v. Board of Educ. of School Dist. No. 228, 676 F. Supp. 820 (N.D. Ill. 1987).
120. Gano v. School Dist. 411 of Twin Falls County, 674 F. Supp. 796 (D. Idaho 1987).
121. Harper v. Edgewood Bd. of Educ., 655 F. Supp. 1353, 1355 (S.D. Ohio 1987).
122. *See* Goss v. Lopez, 419 U.S. 565 (1975); text with note 37, Chapter 6.
123. *See, e.g.,* State *ex rel.* Indiana High School Athletic Ass'n v. Lawrence Circuit Court, 162 N.E.2d 250 (Ind. 1959).
124. *See* Davis v. Meek, 344 F. Supp. 298 (N.D. Ohio 1972); Moran v. School Dist. No. 7, 350 F. Supp. 1180 (D. Mont. 1972); Kelley v. Metropolitan County Bd. of Educ. of Nashville, 293 F. Supp. 485 (M.D. Tenn. 1968).
125. Albach v. Odle, 531 F.2d 983 (10th Cir. 1976). *See also* Pegram v. Nelson, 469 F. Supp. 1134 (M.D.N.C. 1979).
126. Niles v. University Interscholastic League, 715 F.2d 1027 (5th Cir. 1983), *cert. denied,* 465 U.S. 1028 (1984). *See also* Hardy v. University Interscholastic League, 759 F.2d 1233 (5th Cir. 1985).
127. Palmer v. Merluzzi, 868 F.2d 90 (3d Cir. 1989) (the student also was suspended from school for ten days). *See also* Haverkamp v. Unified School Dist. No. 380, 689 F. Supp. 1055 (D. Kan. 1986) (school authorities were upheld in removing a cheerleader from the squad after she was absent from school for personal reasons).
128. Duffley v. New Hampshire Interscholastic Athletic Ass'n, 446 A.2d 462 (N.H. 1982).

129. Boyd v. Board of Directors of the McGehee School Dist. No. 17, 612 F. Supp. 86 (E.D. Ark. 1985).
130. Keller v. Gardner Community Consol. Grade School Dist. 72C, 552 F. Supp. 512 (N.D. Ill. 1982).
131. Bernstein v. Menard, 728 F.2d 252 (4th Cir. 1984).
132. Boyd v. Board of Directors of the McGehee School Dist. No. 17, 612 F. Supp. 86 (E.D. Ark. 1985).
133. *See, e.g.,* Stevenson v. Wheeler County Bd. of Educ., 426 F.2d 1154 (5th Cir. 1970), *cert. denied,* 400 U.S. 957 (1970); Hasson v. Boothby, 318 F. Supp. 1183 (D. Mass. 1970).
134. *See, e.g.,* French v. Cornwell, 276 N.W.2d 216 (Neb. 1979); Braesch v. DePasquale, 265 N.W.2d 842, 846 (Neb. 1978), *cert. denied,* 439 U.S. 1068 (1979).
135. O'Connor v. Board of Educ., 316 N.Y.S.2d 799 (N.Y. Sup. Ct. 1970).
136. Clements v. Board of Educ. of Decatur Public School Dist. No. 61, 478 N.E.2d 1209, 1213 (Ill. App. Ct. 1985).
137. However, the Iowa Supreme Court invalidated a student's suspension from interscholastic competition for violating the association's rule prohibiting the use of alcoholic beverages among student athletes, reasoning that the school board unlawfully delegated its rule-making authority regarding student discipline to the athletic association, Bunger v. Iowa High School Athletic Ass'n, 197 N.W.2d 555 (Iowa 1972).
138. *See, e.g.,* Pfeiffer v. Marion Center Area School Dist., 917 F.2d 779 (3d Cir. 1990) (pregnant student could be dismissed from National Honor Society for engaging in premarital sexual activity in violation of the Society's standards; the case was remanded for consideration of the gender discrimination claim under Title IX of the Education Amendments of 1972); Bull v. Dardanelle Pub. School Dist. No. 15, 745 F. Supp. 1455 (E.D. Ark. 1990) (students have no constitutional right to run for student council; requirement that teachers approve council candidates was not void for vagueness); Karnstein v. Pewaukee School Bd., 557 F. Supp. 565 (E.D. Wis. 1983); Price v. Young, 580 F. Supp. 1 (E.D. Ark. 1983) (students do not have a property right at stake in connection with selection to the National Honor Society).
139. *See, e.g.,* Steffes v. California Interscholastic Fed'n, 222 Cal. Rptr. 355 (Cal. Ct. App. 1986). Most residency disputes have focused on transfers between schools, but some controversies have involved high school athletic association rules that bar nonresident students from participating in interscholastic sports. *See* Zeiler v. Ohio High School Athletic Ass'n, 755 F.2d 934 (6th Cir. 1985), *cert. denied,* 474 U.S. 818 (1985) (upholding the association's rule barring from interscholastic competition those students whose parents live in another state; the rule did not infringe upon protected rights of Michigan residents who attended private high schools in the Toledo area).
140. *See, e.g.,* Niles v. University Interscholastic League, 715 F.2d 1027 (5th Cir. 1983), *cert. denied,* 465 U.S. 1028 (1984); In re United States *ex rel.* Missouri State High School Activities Ass'n, 682 F.2d 147 (8th Cir. 1982); Walsh v. Louisiana High School Athletic Ass'n, 616 F.2d 152 (5th Cir. 1980), *cert. denied,* 449 U.S. 1124 (1981); Albach v. Odle, 531 F.2d 983 (10th Cir. 1976). *See also* Alabama High School Athletic Ass'n v. Scaffidi, 564 So. 2d 910 (Ala. 1990).

141. Doe v. Marshall, 459 F. Supp. 1190 (S.D. Tex. 1978), *vacated,* 622 F.2d 118 (5th Cir. 1980), *cert. denied,* 451 U.S. 993 (1981) (appeals court ruled that the case was moot because the student, who had continued to play football throughout high school, had graduated; however, attorneys' fees were awarded to the student). *See also* Doe v. Marshall, 694 F.2d 1038 (5th Cir. 1983), *cert. denied,* 462 U.S. 1119 (1983).

142. *See* Anderson v. Indiana High School Athletic Ass'n, 699 F. Supp. 719 (S.D. Ind. 1988); Sullivan v. University Interscholastic League, 616 S.W.2d 170 (Tex. 1981).

143. Mahan v. Agee, 652 P.2d 765 (Okla. 1982). *See also* Cavallaro v. Ambach, 575 F. Supp. 171 (W.D.N.Y. 1983) (exceptions are not required for athletes with disabilities); Blue v. University Interscholastic League, 503 F. Supp. 1030 (N.D. Tex. 1980); Arkansas Activities Ass'n v. Meyer, 805 S.W.2d 58 (Ark. 1991); Missouri State High School Activities Ass'n v. Schoenlaub, 507 S.W.2d 354 (Mo. 1974).

144. *See, e.g.,* Alabama High School Athletic Ass'n v. Medders, 456 So. 2d 284 (Ala. 1984); DeKalb County School System v. White, 260 S.E.2d 853 (Ga. 1979); California Interscholastic Fed'n v. Jones, 243 Cal. Rptr. 271 (Cal. Ct. App. 1988).

145. Pennsylvania Interscholastic Athletic Ass'n v. Geisinger, 474 A.2d 62 (Pa. Commw. Ct. 1984).

146. Duffley v. New Hampshire Interscholastic Athletic Ass'n, 446 A.2d 462 (N.H. 1982).

147. *See* Anne Koester, "No Pass, No Play Rules: An Incentive or an Infringement?" *Toledo Law Review,* vol. 19 (1987), pp. 87–111.

148. Spring Branch Indep. School Dist. v. Stamos, 695 S.W.2d 556 (Tex. 1985), *appeal dismissed,* 475 U.S. 1001 (1986).

149. Truby v. Broadwater, 332 S.E.2d 284 (W. Va. 1985).

150. Thompson v. Fayette County Pub. Schools, 786 S.W.2d 879 (Ky. Ct. App. 1990).

151. Rousselle v. Plaquemines Parish School Bd., 527 So. 2d 376 (La. Ct. App. 1988).

152. Paulson v. Minidoka County School Dist. No. 331, 463 P.2d 935, 938 (Idaho 1970).

153. Board of Educ. v. Sinclair, 222 N.W.2d 143 (Wis. 1974); Granger v. Cascade County School Dist., 499 P.2d 780 (Mont. 1972).

154. Hartzell v. Connell, 679 P.2d 35, 44 (Cal. 1984).

155. Attorney General v. East Jackson Pub. Schools, 372 N.W.2d 638 (Mich. Ct. App. 1985).

156. *See* Burrows v. Ohio High School Athletic Ass'n, 891 F.2d 122 (6th Cir. 1989) (association rule prohibiting soccer squad members from participating in spring independent soccer if they play fall interscholastic soccer was rationally related to the legitimate interest of promoting fairness in competition). *See also* Kite v. Marshall, 661 F.2d 1027 (5th Cir. 1981), *cert. denied,* 457 U.S. 1120 (1982); Eastern New York Youth Soccer Ass'n v. New York State Pub. High School Athletic Ass'n, 490 N.E.2d 538 (N.Y. 1986).

157. *See* The Florida High School Activities Ass'n v. Thomas, 434 So. 2d 306 (Fla. 1983).

158. Schaill v. Tippecanoe County School Corp., 864 F.2d 1309 (7th Cir. 1988). *See* text with note 155, Chapter 6.
159. Brooks v. East Chambers Consol. Indep. School Dist., 730 F. Supp. 759 (S.D. Tex. 1989).
160. Kampmeier v. Nyquist, 553 F.2d 296 (2d Cir. 1977). *See also* Rettig v. Kent City School Dist., 788 F.2d 328 (6th Cir. 1986), *cert. denied,* 478 U.S. 1005 (1986) (student with disabilities does not have a federal statutory right to be provided with an hour of extracurricular activities each week).
161. Kampmeier v. Harris, 411 N.Y.S.2d 744 (N.Y. App. Div. 1978). *See also* Wright v. Columbia Univ., 520 F. Supp. 789 (E.D. Pa. 1981); Swiderski v. Board of Educ., City School Dist. of Albany, 408 N.Y.S.2d 744 (N.Y. Sup. Ct. 1978).
162. Grube v. Bethlehem Area School Dist., 550 F. Supp. 418 (E.D. Pa. 1982).

5
Student Classification Practices

"Equal opportunity" is an exalted principle in our democratic heritage, but one that has not been easily translated into concrete school policies and practices. Although twentieth-century educators have asserted that all children should have an equal chance to develop their capabilities, only recently have judicial and legislative bodies addressed the scope of the public school's obligation to realize this goal. Various classification practices have been scrutinized to determine if they have impeded students' access to appropriate instructional programs. After a brief discussion of the legal context, this chapter focuses on student classifications based on gender, marriage and pregnancy, age, ability or achievement, disabilities, and native language. Racial classifications in connection with school desegregation are discussed in Chapter 13.

EQUAL PROTECTION GUARANTEES

The fourteenth amendment to the United States Constitution provides in part that "no state shall . . . deny to any person within its jurisdiction, the equal protection of the laws."[1] Historically, courts have allowed differential treatment of individuals, as long as the bases for the distinctions were reasonably related to legitimate governmental goals. Since challenged state action usually prevailed under this *rational basis* test, the Supreme Court in the 1960s developed a second equal protection standard to afford greater protection to individuals. If the classification of individuals for differential treatment is considered "suspect" or affects a fundamental interest, evidence of a compelling governmental objective is required to justify the state action. As legislation rarely has withstood analysis under this *strict scrutiny* standard of review, the decision as to which test to apply often has determined the outcome of equal protection cases. In essence, the identification of either a suspect classification or fundamental interest has been the critical factor in shifting the burden of proof to the state to justify its policies.

The Supreme Court has defined fundamental interests as those specifically mentioned in the Constitution, such as freedom of speech, as well as rights that are closely related to constitutional guarantees (i.e., "fundamental" by implication), such as the rights to vote, procreate, and travel.[2] Although many lower courts assumed that education was a fundamental interest by implication, in 1973 the Supreme Court delivered a landmark decision, *San Antonio Independent School District v. Rodriguez,* declining to hold that education is among the implied fundamental rights under the Federal Constitution.[3] In this case, plaintiffs alleged that resource inequities across Texas school districts impaired the fundamental right to an education, but the Court majority disagreed. The majority reasoned that challenged state action involving *relative* deprivations in education would trigger only the rational basis equal protection test, unless a suspect classification (e.g., race, alienage, or national origin[4]) was implicated. Finding that the state's scheme for funding education did not create a suspect classification, the Court held that as long as a minimally adequate education was provided for all children, the equal protection clause was satisfied.[5]

In identifying suspect classifications, the Supreme Court has considered factors such as whether the classification is based on an immutable characteristic, whether members of the class are stigmatized, whether there has been a history of discrimination against the class, and whether the class is politically powerless. To date, the judiciary has not declared that classifications based on gender, disabilities, or wealth are "suspect"; thus, state action based on such distinctions has not been subject to the strict scrutiny standard of review.[6]

Because of dissatisfaction with having to choose between the rational basis and the strict scrutiny standards, an intermediate test for evaluating equal protection claims emerged during the 1970s. While declining to expand the category of suspect classes and fundamental interests, the Court has invalidated some state action that traditionally would have withstood analysis under the rational basis test. The Court has required classifications affecting important individual interests to be substantially related to advancing significant governmental objectives.[7] Under this intermediate standard, state-imposed classifications must be necessary, not merely convenient, to achieve important governmental goals, and the Court has invalidated classification schemes if there have been reasonable, less restrictive means of reaching the same goal.[8]

In 1982 the Supreme Court in *Plyler v. Doe* invoked the intermediate standard in reviewing a Texas law that allowed school systems to deny undocumented alien children public schooling.[9] Unlike the *Rodriguez* case, which involved relative deprivations of education, *Plyler* involved the total exclusion of a class of students. Because of the importance of education to individuals and to the maintenance of society, the Court ruled that such a discriminatory classification could be upheld only if it furthered a substantial goal of the state. The state advanced several objectives for denying schooling to illegal alien children, such as preserving the state's financial resources, protecting the state from an influx of unlawful immigrants, maintaining high-quality education for resident children, and excluding children unlikely to remain in the state and contribute to its productivity. The Court found no evidence that the contested law would be an effective method to advance these objectives. Furthermore, any monetary savings that might be realized by denying free schooling to children of illegal aliens were insignificant compared to the costs to these children, the state, and the nation. Accordingly, the Court concluded that the state was unable to meet its burden of demonstrating that the classification advanced a substantial public interest.

In addition to constitutional protections, equal educational opportunities are guaranteed through various federal and state laws. These laws focus on classifications based on race, gender, national origin, age, religion, disabilities, and alienage. In many instances the laws create new substantive rights that are more extensive than constitutional guarantees. Among the significant federal laws discussed in this chapter are Title VI of the Civil Rights Act of 1964 (barring discrimination on the basis of race, color, or national origin in institutions with federally assisted programs), the Equal Educational Opportunities Act of 1974 (guaranteeing all children equal educational opportunity without regard to race, color, gender, or national origin), Title IX of the Education Amendments of 1972 (prohibiting gender discrimination in institutions with federally assisted educational programs), Section 504 of the Vocational Rehabilitation Act of 1973 (prohibiting discrimination against otherwise qualified handicapped individuals in programs receiving federal financial assistance), and the Individuals with Disabilities Education Act of 1990 (ensuring a free appropriate public education for children with disabilities).

How are these equal protection guarantees applied to public education? It might appear from a literal translation of "equality" that once a state establishes an educational system, all students must be treated in the same manner. Courts, however, have recognized that individuals are different and that equal treatment of unequals can have negative consequences. Accordingly, valid classification practices, designed to enhance the educational experiences of children by recognizing their unique needs, generally have been accepted as a legitimate prerogative of educators. Indeed, all schools classify students in some fashion, and state laws often specifically authorize or even require school boards to group students by academic levels, social maturity, athletic ability, gender, age, and many other distinguishing traits. It has been asserted that without these various classifications, the business of public education could not proceed.

While educators' authority to classify students has not been contested, the bases for certain classifications and the procedures used to make distinctions among students recently have been the focus of substantial litigation. To the extent that school classifications determine a student's access to various types of educational resources, courts and legislatures have looked closely at the practices, particularly if they have an adverse impact on vulnerable minority groups. In some instances, courts have interpreted "equal educational opportunity" as requiring more than neutral treatment of students and have ordered school officials to take affirmative steps to overcome the deficiencies of certain groups of students.[10]

CLASSIFICATIONS BASED ON GENDER

The judiciary has been called upon to review a growing number of claims of gender discrimination in public schools, but the applicable principles of law in this area are less settled than are those pertaining to racial discrimination.[11] Gender, like race, is "an immutable characteristic determined solely by the accident of birth,"[12] but the Supreme Court has been reluctant to apply the rigorous strict judicial scrutiny test to gender classifications. Hence, the arguments that have been so persuasive in desegregation litigation have been less effective when applied to claims of gender discrimination. Courts, nonetheless, have invalidated gender classifications that have not been sufficiently related to the achievement of a valid governmental objective.[13] This section focuses on legal developments pertaining to allegations of gender discrimination in high school athletics and academic programs.

HIGH SCHOOL ATHLETICS

In the school context, the most publicized gender discrimination litigation has centered around the denial of sports opportunities to women and gender segregation on interscholastic teams in noncontact and contact sports. Courts generally have ordered school districts to allow female athletes to compete with males in *noncontact* sports if no comparable programs have been available for women. In one of the first notable cases, the Eighth Circuit Court of Appeals invalidated a policy restricting participation on the interscholastic tennis, track, and cross-country ski teams to male students.[14] Concluding that the lack of alternative competitive programs for females raised a valid equal protection claim, the court rejected the nigh school athletic league's contention that relief was inappropriate because participation in interscholastic sports was a privilege and not a right. The court reasoned that whether or not there was an absolute right to engage in interscholastic athletics, female students were denied equal protection because benefits provided by the state to male students were denied to females. Most courts have echoed the Eighth Circuit Appellate Court's rationale in mandating that qualified female students be allowed to participate on interscholastic tennis, track, and other noncontact teams that have traditionally been reserved for male students.[15]

Without question, the most controversial issue involving high school athletics is the participation of males and females together in *contact* sports. Public schools traditionally have not provided teams for each gender in contact sports and thus have denied females the opportunity to participate on various interscholastic teams in sports such as football and basketball. In recent years, however, plaintiffs have challenged (1) the exclusion of females from varsity contact teams and (2) the provision of gender-segregated teams in certain contact sports.

Several courts have applied the intermediate equal protection test in determining whether the denial of interscholastic participation on the basis of gender violates the Federal Constitution and have ruled that female students must be provided the opportunity to participate in contact sports either through gender-segregated or coeducational teams. In a New York case, a federal district court reviewed a female student's request to try out for the junior varsity football squad.[16] The school district was unable to show that its policy of prohibiting mixed competition served an "important governmental objective." In rejecting the school district's assertion that its policy was necessary to ensure the health and safety of female students, the court noted that no female student was given the opportunity to show that she was as fit, or more fit, than the weakest male member of the team. Such a regulation was found to have no reasonable relation to the achievement of the school's objective of protecting the health of students. A Missouri federal district court also found the objective of ensuring safety to be inadequate to justify exclusion of all female students from the school's football team, especially when all males were eligible regardless of safety considerations.[17] The court further rejected the school district's claim that the goal of maximizing equal athletic opportunities for all students supported denying female students the right to participate in selected sports. Facts of the case did not substantiate the board's concern that coeducational teams would result in male domination of all sports.

A Wisconsin federal district court similarly ruled that female students have the right to compete for positions on traditionally male contact teams, declaring that once a state provides interscholastic competition, such opportunities must be provided to all students on equal terms.[18] The court reasoned that the objective of preventing injury to female athletes was not sufficient to justify the prohibition of coeducational teams in contact sports. In preventing the school district from denying female students the opportunity to participate in varsity interscholastic competition in certain contact sports, the court noted that school officials had options available other than establishing coeducational teams: Interscholastic competition in these sports could be eliminated for all students, or separate teams for females could be established. The court also recognized that if comparable gender-segregated programs were provided, female athletes could not assert the right to try out for the male team simply because of its higher level of competition arising from the abilities of team members.

Although policies excluding female students from varsity competition in certain sports have been struck down, the provision of gender-segregated contact teams has usually received judicial endorsement. An Illinois federal district court upheld a school district's policy of maintaining separate teams for male and female students in order to maximize the participation of all students in interscholastic sports.[19] A female student challenged the policy because it did not permit her to engage in the level of competition she needed to fully develop her athletic potential. Based on the fact that most males are better athletes than females, the court found that the maintenance of separate teams was a legitimate means of ensuring female students the opportunity to participate in interscholastic sports. All parties agreed that the male and female teams were equal in most respects (i.e., funding, facilities, personnel, time, etc.). The West Virginia high court, however, found unconstitutional a state athletic commission policy prohibiting females from participating on male teams when separate teams in the same or related sports were established for females.[20] For a highly skilled female baseball player, the court noted that baseball and softball were not substantially equivalent in terms of equipment used, playing field, and skill level required.

Title IX regulations require schools to allow coeducational *noncontact* teams if gender-segregated teams are not provided, but contact sports are excluded from this mandate.[21] Under the regulations, contact sports include "boxing, wrestling, rugby, ice hockey, football, basketball and other sports the purpose or major activity of which involves bodily contact."[22] There is general agreement that the regulation's exclusion of contact sports does not proscribe female participation but merely allows each school the flexibility of determining whether to meet the goal of equal athletic opportunity through single-gender or coeducational teams. In several instances, athletic association rules have limited the options available to school districts by prohibiting coeducational teams. The Sixth Circuit Court of Appeals reviewed an Ohio High School Athletic Association rule that prohibited coeducational participation in all contact sports in grades seven through twelve.[23] In this case, a school system that desired to establish coeducational interscholastic basketball teams at the middle school level challenged the association's rule. The appeals court, noting that compliance with Title IX rests with individual schools and not with athletic associations, concluded that the rule impermissibly restricted the discretion of school systems to provide equal athletic opportunities for female students. The court, however, emphasized that its ruling did not mean that all teams must be coeducational or that Title IX's regulations were unconstitutional because they permitted separate teams.[24]

Most courts have determined that school districts can satisfy their legal obligations by providing comparable, gender-segregated contact teams, but a few courts have ruled that *all* teams must be open to both males and females. The Supreme Court of Pennsylvania relied on the state's equal rights amendment in ruling that females must be allowed to compete with males in all contact sports, including football and wrestling.[25] The court noted that even if women's teams are available, female athletes are denied the opportunity to reach their full potential when they are limited to playing on such teams, which usually offer a lower level of competition.

In addition to challenging their exclusion from varsity contact teams, female athletes have contested the use of gender-based modifications in sports. The Sixth Circuit Court of Appeals addressed the legality of split-court rules for women's basketball, finding that the different rules were legitimate because of the differences between males and females in physical characteristics and capabilities.[26] The court found that there was no equal protection violation simply because basketball rules were tailored to accommodate differences between male and female athletes. An Oklahoma federal court followed the Sixth Circuit Appellate Court's reasoning,[27] but an Arkansas federal district court invalidated the use of separate basketball rules for males and females as lacking a rational basis.[28] According to a policy statement issued by the Department of Health, Education, and Welfare (now the Department of Education), Title IX allows split-court rules for women's basketball. The law requires schools to offer *comparable* athletic opportunities, but *not identical versions* of a single sport. It follows that the provision of a softball team for females and a baseball team for males would be legally permissible under Title IX.

Separate playing seasons for women's and men's teams have been challenged as a violation of the equal protection clause. The Supreme Court of Minnesota found the scheduling decision permissible based on the fact that the school districts lacked adequate tennis and swimming facilities to accommodate both teams at once and that one season was not substantially preferable to the other. While upholding the separation of playing seasons, the court emphasized that treatment of both teams must be "as nearly equal as possible"; a practice that benefited males at the expense of females would not be condoned.[29] In a decree establishing the framework for maintaining gender equity in Montana high school athletics, a federal district court held that the alignment of playing seasons for women's volleyball and basketball was not required to achieve equity.[30]

The majority of suits alleging gender discrimination in high school athletics has been initiated by women, but a few male students have asserted their right to compete for positions on all-female teams. While conflicting opinions have been rendered on this issue, it appears that males may be barred from these teams if their participation impedes athletic opportunities of females. The Ninth Circuit Court of Appeals upheld an

Arizona interscholastic association policy prohibiting males from playing on women's teams even though females were permitted to play on men's teams.[31] The court concluded that the policy was related to the important governmental objectives of achieving equal athletic opportunities for women and redressing past discrimination against them. According to the court, permitting males to participate on women's teams would thwart the realization of these legitimate goals; males would dominate women's teams because of their physiological advantage.

ACADEMIC PROGRAMS

Allegations of gender bias in public schools have not been confined to athletic programs. Differential treatment of males and females in academic courses and schools also has generated litigation. While the "separate but equal" principle has been applied in this area, as it has in athletics, rulings indicate that public school officials must bear the burden of showing exceedingly persuasive justification for classifications based on gender in academic programs. In a significant 1976 case, *Vorchheimer v. School District of Philadelphia*, the Third Circuit Court of Appeals held that the operation of gender-segregated public high schools, in which enrollment is voluntary and educational offerings are essentially equal, is permissible under the equal protection clause of the fourteenth amendment and the Equal Educational Opportunities Act of 1974.[32] The court distinguished *Vorchheimer* from prior decisions in which gender-based classifications had been invalidated because of the absence of a rational basis for differential treatment disadvantaging one gender. Noting that Philadelphia's gender-segregated college preparatory schools offered functionally equivalent programs, the court concluded that the separation of males and females was justified because adolescents might study more effectively in gender-segregated high schools. The appellate court reiterated that "gender has never been rejected as an impermissible classification in all instances."[33] The court also emphasized that the female plaintiff was not compelled to attend the gender-segregated academic school; she had the option of enrolling in a coeducational school within her attendance zone. Furthermore, the court stated that her petition to attend the male academic high school was based on personal preference rather than on an objective evaluation of the offerings available in the two schools.[34] Subsequently, the United States Supreme Court, equally divided, affirmed this decision without delivering an opinion.

In 1982, however, the Supreme Court struck down a nursing school's admission policy that restricted admission in degree programs to women.[35] In this situation, there were not comparable gender-segregated programs, but rather the denial of opportunities to members of one gender. Although the Court acknowledged that gender-based classifications may be justified in limited circumstances when a particular gender has been disproportionately burdened, it rejected the university's contention that its admission policy was necessary to compensate for past discrimination against women. The Court found no evidence that women had ever been denied opportunities in the field of nursing that would justify remedial action by the state.

Like gender-segregated programs and schools, gender-based *criteria for admission* have been challenged, and courts have relied on constitutional grounds in voiding standards that blatantly disadvantage either gender.[36] For example, the admission practices of the Boston Latin Schools were invalidated because they discriminated against female applicants.[37] Because of the different seating capacities of the two schools, the Latin School for males required a lower score on the entrance examination than did the school for females. While sanctioning the operation of gender-segregated schools, the federal district court was unsympathetic to the physical plant problems and ruled that the same entrance requirements had to be applied to both males and females. Similarly, the Ninth Circuit Court of Appeals concluded that a school district's plan to admit an equal number of male and female students to a high school with an advanced college preparatory curriculum violated equal protection guarantees because it resulted in stricter admission criteria for female applicants.[38] The court found that the school district's admission policy was an illegitimate means of reaching its admittedly desirable goal of balancing the number of male and female students enrolled in the school.

In 1989 Title IX and constitutional grounds were used to enjoin the New York State Education Department from awarding merit scholarships solely on the basis of the Scholastic Aptitude Test (SAT).[39] The court found that the scholarships, recognizing high school students for past academic achievement, were disproportionately awarded to male students based on their performance on the SAT (a test designed to predict college academic performance). Each year women scored approximately 60 points lower than men; the probability of this occurring by chance consistently over time is nearly zero. Based on this disparate impact and the court's conclusion that the practice would not "survive even the most minimal scrutiny" under the equal protection clause, the state was ordered to discontinue using the SAT as the sole criterion for recognizing student achievement.

Courts also have not sanctioned unequal educational opportunities for males and females. Female students have been successful in gaining admission to specific courses traditionally offered only to males. For example, the exclusion of female students from auto mechanics, wood shop, and metal shop has been invalidated as a denial of equal protection guarantees.[40] Also, courts have required industrial arts and home economics classes to be made available to male and female students on equal terms.[41]

Although most cases challenging the exclusion of one gender from specific curricular offerings have been settled on constitutional grounds,

Title IX regulations prohibit gender-segregated health, industrial arts, business, vocational-technical, home economics, and music classes in educational programs that receive federal funds. These regulations also prohibit gender discrimination in counseling and bar gender-based course requirements for graduation (e.g., home economics for females and industrial arts for males). Separate physical education classes also are prohibited under Title IX, although students may be grouped by skill levels.[42]

Gender-segregated student clubs also may be subject to challenge. The Fifth Circuit Court of Appeals found that a prestigious all-male university honor society violated Title IX because it had a pervasive discriminatory effect upon women.[43] Since the honor society represented the "best" in achievement and commanded respect campus-wide, the university's recognition of the club perpetuated gender bias. Accordingly, the appellate court held that the society's continued association with the university was impermissible. Although gender-segregated honoraries have not been prevalent at the high school level, some schools have maintained gender-segregated extracurricular clubs, and the legality of this practice seems doubtful.

UNRESOLVED QUESTIONS

Many diverse issues have been raised in these gender-bias suits, and claims of gender discrimination in academic as well as athletic programs seem destined to generate additional litigation. While the doctrine of "separate but equal" remains viable in a number of areas, courts are not in agreement as to the *type* of equality required under constitutional or statutory provisions. Difficult questions persist: Are gender-segregated varsity teams in noncontact and contact sports comparable if they have different levels of competition? What criteria should be used to gauge the equality between gender-segregated academic programs and/or schools? Under what circumstances is gender segregation unjustified, even if comparable opportunities are provided for both females and males? In the absence of a federal equal rights amendment, it appears that the Supreme Court will eventually have to address these questions and clarify the nature of gender equality required in public education.

CLASSIFICATIONS BASED ON MARRIAGE AND PREGNANCY

Legal principles governing the rights of married and pregnant students have changed dramatically since 1960. The evolution of the law in this area is indicative of the increasing judicial commitment to protect students from unjustified classifications that limit educational opportunities.

MARRIED STUDENTS

Historically, courts sanctioned differential treatment of married students in public education. In 1957 the Supreme Court of Tennessee upheld a school regulation requiring students to withdraw from school for the remainder of the term following their marriage.[44] In the early 1960s, an Ohio common pleas court upheld a school district regulation barring married students from participation in extracurricular activities, because school officials demonstrated that married athletes were often in a position to be idolized and copied by other students; the school's legitimate interest in curtailing underage marriages justified the policy.[45]

The Supreme Court has held that the right to marry is "one of the vital personal rights," thereby requiring classifications affecting this right to be justified by a compelling state interest.[46] Accordingly, most courts in recent decades have rejected the traditional view that students can be denied school attendance or participation in extracurricular activities because of their marital status. In an illustrative case, an Ohio federal court held that married students were entitled to equal treatment in all aspects of public education, including school-related activities. The court recognized extracurricular functions as "an integral part" of the total school program and declared that the Federal Constitution prohibited discrimination against married students in any school offerings.[47] Other courts also have invalidated the exclusion of married students from extracurricular activities, reasoning that once a state establishes such programs, it cannot exclude a certain class of students without showing a compelling state interest.[48]

PREGNANT STUDENTS

& Title IX – Civil Rights Act

School regulations that deny pregnant students an education or otherwise discriminate against them have been questioned under the fourteenth amendment, Title IX, and state laws.[49] Since the late 1960s, courts have generally placed the burden on school officials to demonstrate that any differential treatment of pregnant students is absolutely necessary for health reasons. In an illustrative Massachusetts case, a federal district court held that school authorities could not exclude a pregnant, unmarried student from regular high school classes.[50] School officials had proposed that the pregnant student be allowed to use all school facilities, attend school functions, participate in senior activities, and receive assistance from teachers in continuing her studies. However, she was not to attend school during regular school hours. Since there was no evidence of any educational or medical reason for this special treatment, the court held that the pregnant student had a constitutional right to attend classes with other pupils. Similarly, a Texas civil appeals court invalidated a public school rule that prohibited mothers from attending regular classes.[51] The only alternative available to the excluded students was to attend adult education classes, which required them to be at least twenty-one years of age. The appeals court ruled that such a policy violated pregnant students' entitlement to free public schooling.

Most litigation has involved constitutional claims, but the Supreme Court has held that classifications based on pregnancy do not constitute gender discrimination under the equal protection clause.[52] Accordingly, Title IX may afford greater protection to pregnant students than the Constitution in curricular as well as extracurricular activities.[53] Title IX's regulations specifically provide that recipients of federal funds cannot condition program admission or participation on parental status.

It would appear that any denial of equal opportunities to married and pregnant students must be justified by an overriding educational or health objective. School districts may offer special courses designed to address pregnant students' unique needs (e.g., instruction in child care), but such students should not be forced to enroll in special classes that segregate them from other pupils. Additionally, pregnant students should not be relegated to evening programs that offer limited instruction or require fees for academic courses. Restrictions placed on pregnant, unwed students for reasons (e.g., alleged lack of moral character) that are not grounded in valid health or safety considerations will no longer be tolerated by courts.[54]

CLASSIFICATIONS BASED ON AGE

Age is one of the factors most commonly used to classify individuals, not only in schools but also in society in general. A specified age is used as a prerequisite to obtaining a driver's license, buying alcoholic beverages, and voting in state and national elections. Age also is used to classify individuals for employment eligibility (e.g., child labor laws) and for mandatory retirement. Discrimination based on age has generated more litigation in connection with employees[55] than with elementary and secondary pupils, but a few public school situations have evoked legal challenges.

It is generally accepted that a specified age can be used as a school entrance requirement, as a criterion for compulsory education, and as a condition for participation in certain extracurricular activities. Students below or above state-established age limits for school enrollment do not have a constitutional right to attend school. For example, under Pennsylvania law, students between the ages of six and twenty-one must be provided a free public education, and school systems may provide kindergarten programs for children between the ages of four and six. A Pennsylvania commonwealth court held that since education is not mandated for children below the age of six, no constitutionally protected property interest exists, and a child under six can thus be excluded from kindergarten without a formal hearing.[56] In an earlier Pennsylvania case, a school district refused to admit a potential kindergarten student who did not meet the school district's minimum-age requirement.[57] The student's birthday was in October, and the policy stipulated that all students had to be five years old by September 1 to enroll in kindergarten. The state court upheld the board's age classification as rationally related to a legitimate educational purpose.

In a Maine case, focusing on a state law rather than a school board policy, parents contested a statute that required all children entering first grade to be six years old by October 15.[58] They asserted that their child, whose birthday fell short of the deadline by over two months, was academically ready for first grade and that he would lose interest in school if denied admission. Nonetheless, the federal court upheld the school board in enforcing the state's minimum-age law. The court relied on evidence substantiating a correlation between chronological age and school readiness in concluding that the law had a reasonable educational basis and, therefore, was constitutionally sound. Furthermore, the court noted the prohibitive costs that would be involved in making such a determination of readiness for each individual child.

Not all controversies over age restrictions have involved policies pertaining to school entrance. In New York City, parents challenged the refusal of school authorities to admit their son to a two-year accelerated progress class at his junior high school.[59] The accelerated program covered the regular three-year junior high school curriculum in two years. The student had completed elementary school and was academically qualified for the program, but was denied admission because he was six months younger than the required age. The board asserted that the age requirement for admission was justified because younger students needed an additional year at the junior high school level in order to develop emotionally, socially, and physiologically. The New York court upheld the requirement, concluding that "to thrust a youngster into an environment where all his classmates are older may result in the consequent impairment of the necessary social integration of the child with his classmates."[60] The court further emphasized that actions of school officials, taken in the best interests of students, should not be disturbed by the judiciary as long as such administrative determinations are reasonable.

Age also is one of the criteria used to determine entitlement to special services and programs under the Individuals with Disabilities Education Act. This federal law mandates that services must be available for all children with disabilities between the ages of three and twenty-one, but does not require a school district to provide programs for children with disabilities under the state's minimum school age unless programs are being provided for other children in this age group.[61] Concomitantly, if services are provided for other students beyond eighteen years of age,

students with disabilities are entitled to similar opportunities. The Tenth
Circuit Court of Appeals held that services for children with disabilities
could not be limited to twelve years when other children routinely were
allowed to repeat grades.[62] Generally, students with disabilities cannot
demand tuition-free services beyond the statutory limit of twenty-one
years of age.[63]

Courts have not concluded that the Federal Constitution requires
governmental action to reflect an "age blind" society. The judiciary has
recognized the unique characteristics of childhood in sanctioning reasonable age restrictions on students' activities, as long as age-based classifications are related to valid educational objectives.

CLASSIFICATIONS BASED ON ABILITY OR ACHIEVEMENT

Courts have upheld decisions related to grade placement, denial of promotion, and assignment to instructional groups as rationally related to
providing students instruction that is most appropriate to their abilities and
needs.[64] It is claimed that ability grouping permits more effective and
efficient teaching by allowing teachers to concentrate their efforts on
students with similar needs. Ability grouping is clearly permissible, but
some legal challenges have concerned the use of standardized intelligence
and achievement tests for determining pupil placements in regular classes
and special education programs. These suits have alleged that such tests
are racially and culturally biased and that their use to classify pupils often
results in erroneous placements that stigmatize the children involved.
Other challenges have arisen regarding the rights of gifted and talented
students to an appropriate education.

TRACKING SCHEMES

In the most widely publicized case pertaining to ability grouping, *Hobson
v. Hansen,* the use of standardized intelligence test scores to place
students in various ability tracks in Washington, D.C., was attacked as
unconstitutional.[65] Plaintiffs contended that some children were erroneously assigned to lower tracks and had very little chance of advancing to
higher tracks because of the limited curriculum and lack of remedial
instruction. The federal district court closely examined the test scores
used to assign students to the various tracks, analyzed the accuracy of the
test measurements, and concluded that mistakes often resulted from placing pupils on this basis. For the first time, a federal court evaluated testing
methods and concluded that they discriminated against minority children.
In prohibiting the continued use of ability-grouping schemes that resulted
in segregation, the court emphasized that it was *not* abolishing the use of

tracking systems *per se*: "What is at issue here is not whether defendants are entitled to provide different kinds of students with different kinds of education."[66] The court noted that classifications reasonably related to educational purposes are constitutionally permissible unless they result in discrimination against identifiable groups of children.

Ability grouping also has been invalidated in school systems with a history of purposeful segregation. Two years after *Hobson,* the Fifth Circuit Court of Appeals reviewed the legality of a tracking scheme in Jackson, Mississippi.[67] The court struck down the plan, holding that students could not be placed in classes on the basis of standardized test scores until a desegregated school district had been established to the court's satisfaction. In a later case, the court emphasized that ability grouping in a school system that has not fully erased its history of segregation may perpetuate the effects of past discrimination. The court noted, however, that "as a general rule, school systems are free to employ ability grouping, even when such a policy has a segregative effect, so long, of course, as such a practice is genuinely motivated by educational concerns and not discriminatory motives."[68]

Based on evidence indicating that ability grouping provided better educational opportunities for African-American students, the Eleventh Circuit Appellate Court in 1985 upheld grouping practices in several Georgia school districts even though they had not achieved desegregated status.[69] Ability grouping allowed resources to be targeted toward low-achieving students, and its effectiveness was demonstrated by gains on statewide tests and students being reassigned to higher level achievement groups. The court did note, however, that, unlike students in earlier cases, these students had not attended inferior segregated schools. School systems undergoing desegregation may be subjected to closer judicial review when implementing ability grouping, but such plans will be prohibited only if found to be a ploy to resegregate students.[70]

Although ability grouping is permissible, the assessment procedures used in placing students in instructional programs may be vulnerable to legal challenge if racial or cultural bias is shown. Courts have paid particular attention to the use of test scores in assigning students to special education programs because of the adverse effects that an incorrect placement can have on a child's future. Two cases provide the background for the debate on the use of standardized intelligence tests for determining placement of students. In both cases, plaintiffs alleged that standardized intelligence tests used for placement purposes were culturally biased against African-American children. In a California case, the Ninth Circuit Court of Appeals upheld a federal district court's decision enjoining school authorities from using the results of intelligence tests to place minority students in classes for the mentally retarded.[71] The federal district court had concluded that the testimony overwhelmingly demonstrated that the intelligence tests, which were the central element in the placement decisions, were biased against African-American students and contributed to the disproportionate placement of these students in special classes. Since the tests had been standardized for white, middle-class students, school officials were unable to show that they were valid for the placement of African-American students.[72]

In contrast, an Illinois federal district court, hearing many of the same expert witnesses, found little evidence of cultural bias in standardized intelligence tests.[73] Instead of reacting to the general issue of cultural bias, the Illinois federal judge reviewed each question on the tests to determine whether bias existed. The judge concluded that the few instances of cultural bias found in the test items would not significantly affect an individual's score and that the use of these test results in conjunction with other criteria for determining appropriate placements did not discriminate against African-American students.

The conclusions reached in these cases were quite different, but both courts emphasized that nonbiased assessment procedures must be used. The Ninth Circuit Court of Appeals prohibited intelligence tests as the single criterion for placement in special education programs; the Illinois court upheld the use of intelligence tests but as only one factor in the assessment. State and federal laws addressing the rights of children with disabilities reinforce that screening procedures for special education placements must be culturally and racially nondiscriminatory.[74] These laws stipulate that tests must be administered in the child's native language, validated for the specific purpose for which they are used, administered by trained personnel, and used only in conjunction with other criteria.

In addition to tests used for instructional placement purposes, other testing programs have generated claims that the instruments are culturally and racially biased, or that they have not been properly validated. As discussed in Chapter 3, proficiency tests have been challenged as violating students' due process and equal protection rights. The state's authority to assess student proficiency has been upheld, but in some situations the implementation of testing programs has been enjoined because the effects of prior racial discrimination have not been eliminated or students have not been provided adequate notice or preparation for the tests.

As noted, tracking is an acceptable instructional arrangement if it is based on sound educational reasons. However, the high incidence of placement of minority students in low-ability or special education classes has raised significant concerns. According to a 1991 study by the General Accounting Office (GAO), a disproportionate number of minority students are in these classes in over half the school districts nationally.[75] Although the data do not necessarily indicate that impermissible tracking is occurring, another study by the GAO raises inferences of discriminatory practices. The concern about appropriate placement has led the Office of Civil Rights (OCR) to renew its investigative efforts.[76] The OCR's new policy on ability grouping is being shared with districts where the data suggest that problems may exist with current practices.

GIFTED AND TALENTED STUDENTS

Often overlooked in assessing the appropriateness of educational programs are students labeled as "gifted and talented." Congress has defined such students as those "who give evidence of high performance capability in areas such as intellectual, creative, artistic, or leadership capacity, or in specific academic fields, and who require services or activities not ordinarily provided by the school in order to fully develop such capabilities."[77] Advocates for gifted students assert that these children require special attention similar to other groups such as children with disabilities, but few state or local education agencies have mandated the identification of gifted students or the establishment of special education programs for them.

Most of the legal activity in this area has taken place in legislative forums and has been directed primarily toward the need to provide services. Through the Gifted and Talented Children's Education Act of 1978, the federal government provided limited financial assistance to states attempting to serve these students, but this law was repealed in 1982.[78] In 1988, however, the federal government appropriated $20 million for fiscal year 1989 for research, training, and demonstration projects for gifted education. The Act also created the National Center for Research and Development in the Education of Gifted and Talented Children and Youth. At the state level, most legislatures have allocated some categorical funds for the gifted and talented, but in the early 1980s, less than 6 percent of the student population was receiving special services designed for the gifted.[79] This is modest considering estimates indicating that 10 to 15 percent of the school-age population may qualify for special programs for the gifted.[80]

Although the federal government provides some aid for gifted education, there is no federal law specifying substantive rights for the gifted as there is for children with disabilities. Thus, specific rights of gifted and talented students and the adequacy of programs provided must be interpreted under state laws. Pennsylvania, one of the leading states in mandating programs for the gifted, includes gifted and talented students under its designation of "exceptional children" who "deviate from the average in physical, mental, emotional or social characteristics to such an extent that they require special educational facilities or services."[81] The Pennsylvania Supreme Court interpreted this law as placing a mandatory obligation on school districts to establish individualized programs for gifted students beyond the general "enrichment" program.[82] The court, however, specified that the legislation did not require "exclusive individual programs outside or beyond the district's existing, regular and special education curricular offerings"; there was no duty to maximize a child's potential.[83]

Similar to Pennsylvania's law, gifted students in Connecticut also are covered by statutory protections pertaining to other categories of exceptional children. Under this law, students are entitled to private placements at public expense if appropriate programs are not available in the public education system.[84] New York law stipulates that school districts *should* develop programs to assist gifted students in achieving their full potential. An appellate court, however, found that the use of the word "should" indicated that the development of gifted programs was optional, not mandatory.[85] Consequently, the court held that a school district was permitted to serve only a portion of the students identified as gifted and to select those students through a lottery system.

Although litigation primarily has addressed the adequacy of programs under state mandates, students who have not qualified for gifted programs have challenged their exclusion as a violation of the equal protection clause of the fourteenth amendment. For a classification scheme to pass equal protection review, school officials need only show that selection procedures for gifted programs have a rational relationship to their objective of identifying gifted students since a suspect classification or a fundamental right is not affected. In two cases, a Pennsylvania federal district court held that the use of standardized tests or high IQ scores to identify gifted students did not impair students' constitutional rights.[86] While weaknesses could be noted in the two methods, the court found both procedures rationally related to the school district's objective of providing special opportunities to develop the abilities of gifted students.

CLASSIFICATIONS BASED ON DISABILITIES

Since children with disabilities represent a vulnerable minority group, their treatment has aroused much judicial and legislative concern. Courts have addressed the constitutional rights of such children to attend school and to be classified accurately and instructed appropriately. Federal and state laws have further delineated the rights of students with disabilities and have provided funds to assist school districts in meeting their special needs.

LEGAL FRAMEWORK

Though no firm precedent has been established by the United States Supreme Court regarding whether children with disabilities have a constitutional right to a public education, several lower courts have addressed the question. Two decisions rendered in the early 1970s identified the basic contours of the constitutional protections afforded children with disabilities. The first case challenged the constitutionality of a Pennsylvania state law that allowed school systems to exclude children with disabilities from school.[87] The case resulted in a consent agreement stating that these children could not be denied admission to public school programs or have their educational status changed without procedural due process. The agreement further stipulated that each mentally retarded child must be placed in a free public program of education and training appropriate to the child's capacity. *Mills v. D.C*

A District of Columbia case followed the principle established in the Pennsylvania agreement and expanded the right to an appropriate public education beyond the mentally retarded to all children alleged to be suffering from mental, behavioral, emotional, or physical deficiencies.[88] Moreover, the court held that fiscal concerns could not justify the denial of an education to a certain class of students. The court also ordered school officials to adhere to stringent due process procedures in pupil assignments, stating that any change affecting a student's instructional program for as much as two days had to be accompanied by some type of hearing to give parents an opportunity to contest the placement.

Litigation similar to the Pennsylvania and District of Columbia cases was initiated in many states during the 1970s, and the basic right of all children with disabilities to receive a public education was consistently upheld by courts. The Supreme Court's 1973 *Rodriguez* decision lent support to the contention that the total exclusion of selected children, such as those with disabilities, from public schools would not withstand constitutional scrutiny. Although stating that the right to an education is not an inherent fundamental right, the Court conceded that "some identifiable quantum of education" may be constitutionally protected.[89] Subsequently, in the *Plyler* decision, the Court refused to elevate education to a fundamental right but did conclude that a class of students (undocumented alien children) could not be excluded from public schools.[90] The judiciary to date, however, has not found that children with disabilities are a "suspect class" or that they have any "fundamental right" to a particular level of education. The basic legal principle that has evolved from constitutional challenges is that children with disabilities must have access to a public education; school systems cannot exclude them.

As often happens, legislation has paralleled court decisions regarding the rights of children with disabilities. While constitutional suits have been instrumental in directing attention to the plight of these children, state and federal laws have defined the specific rights of children with disabilities and the responsibilities of public schools. Two pieces of federal legislation, in particular, have altered the role of public school personnel. Section 504 of the Vocational Rehabilitation Act of 1973 prohibits the recipients of any federal financial assistance from discriminating against an otherwise qualified handicapped person solely because of the handicap.[91] The Individuals with Disabilities Education Act (IDEA), formerly the Education for All Handicapped Children Act (EHA), provides federal funds to assist state and local education agencies in offering appropriate educational programs for children with disabilities.[92] In essence, Section 504 is a civil rights law that stipulates what *cannot* be done in the treatment of individuals with disabilities, while the IDEA contains a blueprint of what *can* be done to upgrade educational opportunities for these children with special needs.

Under Section 504, a handicapped individual is one "who has a physical or mental impairment which substantially limits one or more of such person's major life activities."[93] The Supreme Court held that an individual suffering from the contagious disease of tuberculosis was a "handicapped individual" because she had a physical impairment (physiological condition affecting her respiratory system) and the impairment limited a major life activity (work).[94] Students suffering from chronic diseases such as acquired immune deficiency syndrome (AIDS) and hepatitis B also have been found to be protected against discriminatory treatment by Section 504.[95] The IDEA, however, applies to AIDS victims only if their physical condition adversely affects their educational performance, thereby requiring the provision of special education and related services.[96]

Section 504 is more global than the IDEA and applies to educational and noneducational agencies receiving any type of federal assistance. It prohibits discrimination against persons with disabilities in employment (see Chapter 9) and postsecondary education and requires public schools to provide appropriate educational services for all children with disabilities. Where rights are guaranteed by both Section 504 and the IDEA, an individual initiating a claim under Section 504 must exhaust the administrative procedures required under the IDEA prior to bringing court action.[97]

States have the option of declining to participate in the IDEA funding program, but they still must comply with Section 504's antidiscrimination mandate, which has been interpreted as requiring school districts to provide appropriate educational programs for children with disabilities.[98] Consequently, all states currently participate in the IDEA assistance program and must adhere to the law's regulations as a condition of receiving aid. Among the Act's major provisions are the following:

- States must institute a comprehensive program to identify all children with disabilities within the state. Under the Act, disabled children include those who are mentally retarded, hard of hearing, deaf, speech impaired, visually impaired, seriously emotionally disturbed, orthopedically impaired, other health impaired or learning disabled, or suffering from autism or traumatic brain injury.[99]
- No child with disabilities is to be excluded from an appropriate public education (zero reject).
- Individualized education programs must be developed for all children with disabilities.
- Policies and procedures must be established to safeguard due process rights of parents and children.

- Children with disabilities must be placed in the least restrictive educational setting, which means educating children with disabilities with other children to the maximum extent appropriate.
- Nondiscriminatory tests and other materials must be used in evaluating a child's level of achievement for placement purposes.
- Parents must have access to their child's records, and the confidentiality of such information must be respected.
- Comprehensive personnel development programs, which include in-service training for regular and special education teachers and ancillary personnel, must be established.
- One state agency must be accountable for ensuring that all provisions of the law are properly implemented by other agencies in the state serving children with disabilities.

The Act has generated substantial litigation, and the rights guaranteed by this law continue to be clarified. Throughout the following discussion, the law is referred to as the IDEA to maintain consistency, even though most of the cases were rendered when it was called the EHA.

FREE APPROPRIATE PUBLIC EDUCATION

Under the IDEA, states must assure that all children with disabilities have the right to a free appropriate public education (FAPE). An appropriate education is one that is designed to meet the unique needs of each child and includes special education and related services. "Special education" refers to "specially designed instruction, at no cost to parents or guardians, to meet the unique needs of a handicapped child, including classroom instruction, instruction in physical education, home instruction, and instruction in hospitals and institutions."[100] These services must be provided for children with disabilities between the ages of three and twenty-one, unless services are not provided for other children under or over regular school age.[101]

The central element of a free appropriate public education is the development of a written individualized education program (IEP) identifying the child's needs, annual instructional goals and objectives, specific educational services to be provided, and evaluation procedures. This program must be jointly prepared by school officials and the child's parents and must be reviewed at least annually. Lack of agreement between school officials and parents in the development or revision of the program is resolved through impartial due process hearings.

A continuing issue before the judiciary has been what level of educational services meets the FAPE requirement. Must it be an optimum program to maximize a child's learning potential or a minimum program to assure equal educational opportunity? The United States Supreme Court's interpretation of this provision in 1982 has been significant in shaping rights of students with disabilities.

In *Board of Education of the Hendrick Hudson Central School District v. Rowley,* the parents of Amy Rowley, a deaf student with minimal residual hearing, had requested that the school district provide a sign-language interpreter for Amy in her academic classes.[102] Amy's IEP specified a regular first-grade placement with special instruction from a tutor for the deaf one hour per day and a speech therapist three hours per week. Based on the advice of the IEP committee and others familiar with Amy's program, school officials concluded that an interpreter was unnecessary since her achievement was above average. Upon judicial review, the lower federal courts concluded that Amy had been denied a free appropriate public education because of the disparity between her academic potential and her achievement level. According to the district court, an appropriate educational program is one that maximizes the potential of children with disabilities "commensurate with the opportunity provided to other children."[103]

In rejecting this definition of "appropriate," the Supreme Court did not provide a specific substantive standard but rather noted that educational access should be meaningful. The Court reasoned that "the intent of the Act was more to open the door of public education to children with disabilities on appropriate terms than to guarantee any particular level of education once inside."[104] The Court concluded that the Act guarantees a "basic floor of opportunity," consisting of "access to specialized instruction and related services which are individually designed to provide educational benefit to the handicapped child."[105] Applying these principles, the Court held that Amy was receiving an appropriate education. She was receiving educational benefit from personalized instruction and related services, as evidenced by her better-than-average performance in class.

The standard of judicial review established in *Rowley* has been controlling in subsequent litigation. According to the Supreme Court, the role of courts in reviewing the appropriateness of educational programs under the Act is not to define what is an appropriate education. Rather, the review is limited to a twofold inquiry: Has the state complied with procedures identified in the Act, and is the IEP developed through these procedures "reasonably calculated to enable the child to receive educational benefits."[106] Lower courts have interpreted this to require educational programs that provide more than "trivial advancement."[107]

Following *Rowley,* courts have been reluctant to respond to parental demands for optimum programs where school systems are providing individualized programs that confer educational benefits. For example, New York parents were unsuccessful in demanding that their severely disabled child be taught in a class with a teacher/pupil ratio of six-to-one or less to assure maximum achievement.[108] The Second Circuit Appellate Court held that the central issue was whether educational benefits would be received in a placement with a ratio of twelve-to-one, not whether a ratio of six-to-one provided a better education. The Fourth Circuit Appellate Court ruled that in-home habilitative services were not required for an autistic student who had made educational progress in a day program.[109]

The Rhode Island Federal District Court concluded that while a residential placement might be the most effective placement for a specific child, the day program proposed by the school district met the IDEA's FAPE requirement.[110] Similarly, Maryland parents were unsuccessful in asserting that a private placement was more appropriate than the proposed public school placement because it involved less commuting time and greater opportunity to associate with nonhandicapped children.[111] Relying on *Rowley*, the appellate court concluded that parents must specifically allege that the proposed program is inadequate. The court noted that because the requested program is *more* appropriate, it does not follow that the recommended program is inappropriate.[112]

Although most litigation has concerned the types of educational programs and services that must be provided, a troubling question is whether students with severe disabilities are entitled to public school services at all. Courts have recognized that educational services for these children are costly and have noted that cost may be a consideration in selecting among placement options. For example, educating children with disabilities in the least restrictive environment is preferred under the IDEA, but the high cost of maintaining specialized services and resources may mean that a segregated facility is the least restrictive appropriate placement.[113]

Until recently, however, no federal court had denied a child with severe disabilities access to an educational program. In 1988 the New Hampshire Federal District Court held that a multiply disabled and profoundly retarded child was not entitled to special education services because he did not have the ability to benefit from them.[114] The child suffered from severe spasticity, cerebral palsy, brain damage, joint contractures, and cortical blindness; he was not ambulatory and was quadriplegic. Interpreting the language of the IDEA and its legislative history, the First Circuit Court of Appeals overturned the ruling, concluding that Congress intended for *all* children with disabilities to be educated.[115] Specifically, the court noted the word *all* permeates the statute, clearly implying a "zero-reject" policy. Furthermore, the law is explicit in granting priority to providing services for the most severely disabled. The appellate court noted that the Supreme Court in *Rowley* addressed the level and quality of services that must be provided, not criteria for access to those programs. The provision of services for severely disabled children is placing significant fiscal strains on some school districts and will likely remain controversial as districts are forced to consider the reallocation of limited financial resources among competing educational programs.[116]

In addition to federal laws, all states have statutes or administrative regulations granting children with disabilities specific rights. While most state mandates parallel federal requirements, some place additional obligations on school districts in ensuring a free appropriate public education. These higher state standards have been enforced in state and federal courts.[117]

The right of children with disabilities to receive a free appropriate public education also has been controversial in connection with state-mandated proficiency testing programs. As discussed in Chapter 3, several courts have rejected the assertion that conditioning the receipt of a high school diploma on passage of a competency test denies children with disabilities their right to a FAPE.[118] Relying on *Rowley,* courts have concluded that the intent of the Act is to guarantee access to specialized educational services, not to require "specific results." Courts have not been persuaded that students with disabilities are entitled to a high school diploma based on completion of their IEP objectives if other students must satisfy additional requirements, such as passage of an examination.

PROCEDURAL SAFEGUARDS

Extensive procedural safeguards are identified in the IDEA to ensure appropriate identification, evaluation, and placement of children with disabilities. The Fourth Circuit Court of Appeals has noted that "failures to meet the Act's procedural requirements are adequate grounds by themselves for holding that a school board failed to provide a FAPE."[119] Prior to the evaluation of a child, parents must be informed of their procedural rights, including a description of the process and the procedural safeguards. This includes the opportunity to examine the child's records and to obtain an independent educational evaluation of the child. The intent of the procedural safeguards is to ensure full parental participation at every stage of the administrative process.[120]

Prior to placement of a child with disabilities in a special education program, the IDEA requires a full evaluation. Federal regulations specify that no single criterion can be used to determine a child's placement. Pupil assignments must be based on a composite analysis of such data as teacher recommendations, the child's cultural background and adaptive behavior, and test scores. Issues often arise regarding the validity of tests used to evaluate and place students.[121] The Act requires that tests must be validated for the purposes for which they are used and administered in a child's native language by trained personnel; they also must accommodate physical limitations posed by the child's disability.

A school district's proposed program for a given child can be rejected solely on the ground that the district failed to comply with mandated evaluation procedures. For example, a New Jersey federal court invalidated a district's proposed IEP for a hearing-impaired child because of serious procedural violations related to the methodology used for assessment.[122] The recommendation was based upon simple observations;

no validated instrument was used to test the child's aptitude; tests focused only on a narrow range of behaviors; procedures used tended to be biased against deaf children; and no member of the evaluation team was an expert in the education of hearing-impaired children.

Under the IDEA, school districts must ensure that parents have full opportunity to participate in an IEP meeting at which a child's program is jointly developed by parents and educators. The Fourth Circuit Court of Appeals held that a Virginia school district violated the Act's procedures by unilaterally determining a child's placement and then developing an IEP to support the decision.[123] If parents are dissatisfied with the proposed classification of their child or the proposed IEP, they have the right to an impartial due process hearing to present complaints at the local and state levels. Parents, however, may seek judicial review of an administrative decision only after exhausting administrative procedures. Unless exceptional circumstances indicate that administrative remedies would be unproductive, courts will dismiss legal proceedings filed prior to exhaustion of administrative review.[124]

Extensive procedural safeguards surround any change in a child's placement. Before changing a substantive aspect of a student's program, written notice must be given to the parents of their right to review the proposed alteration. The Ninth Circuit Court of Appeals found that the reduction of a student's full-day program schedule to a part-day schedule without an IEP conference violated the student's rights under the Act.[125] While the guardians were aware that the student's program had been reduced because of several incidents of misbehavior, they were not notified of their right to object or to seek review of the decision.

The "stay-put" or "status quo" provision of the IDEA provides that unless school officials and parents agree otherwise, the child shall remain in the current educational placement.[126] The purpose of maintaining the current placement is to provide stability and continuity in the child's educational program. While school authorities are prohibited from changing a child's placement for educational reasons during review proceedings, they can impose short-term suspensions of not more than ten days if the child poses a danger to others or threatens disruption of the educational environment. A longer exclusion without parental consent would require judicial approval.[127]

PLACEMENT

After agreement has been reached on an individual education program, an appropriate placement must be made at public expense. Alternative placements may include a regular classroom with various support services, a regular classroom supplemented with resource room instruction, self-contained special classes, home instruction, and hospital or institutional instruction. Within this continuum of placements, the IDEA requires that the child must be educated in the least restrictive environment (LRE), which may be in a public or private school depending on the special needs of the child.

Least Restrictive Environment. The IDEA requires that "to the maximum extent appropriate, handicapped children, including children in public or private institutions or other care facilities, are to be educated with children who are not handicapped and the . . . removal of handicapped children from the regular educational environment [should occur] only when the nature or severity of the handicap is such that education in regular classes with use of supplementary aids and services cannot be achieved satisfactorily."[128] While this provision does not require that every child be educated in a regular classroom, the judiciary has noted that the term "to the maximum extent appropriate" does indicate a strong congressional preference for mainstreaming.

Courts, however, have consistently emphasized that mainstreaming must be balanced against the primary objective of providing an appropriate education for children with disabilities; the least restrictive requirement is not an absolute duty. The Fifth Circuit Court of Appeals, in noting the tension between the Act's mandate to mainstream and to design an education program to meet each child's special needs, concluded that the requirement to provide an appropriate education "qualifies and limits" the duty to place children in a regular classroom.[129] Adopting a similar position, the Ninth Circuit Court of Appeals supported school officials' decision that a neighborhood school was not appropriate because the severity of a child's disability required instruction by a specially certified teacher.[130] The Fourth Circuit Court of Appeals also held that the appropriate placement for an autistic child was a specialized vocational center rather than the high school nearest his home; even with special support services the mainstreamed program could not accommodate his special needs.[131] When a child's needs can be met in a regular classroom, however, courts have found other placements inappropriate. The Ninth Circuit Court of Appeals held that a proposed homebound program for a child suffering from cystic fibrosis and tracheomalacia did not satisfy the LRE requirement because the child's previous participation and progress in a regular classroom at a private school demonstrated that similar services could be provided in the public school.[132]

Several courts have developed standards for evaluating school systems' attempts to meet the mainstreaming requirement. The Sixth Circuit Court of Appeals advanced guidelines for determining when and to what extent mainstreaming must be provided for children with disabilities. In this case, parents of a severely mentally retarded child rejected school officials' recommended placement of their son in a school exclusively for mentally retarded children because it would not allow for contact with other children. In strongly supporting mainstreaming for all children, the appellate court stated:

> Where the segregated facility is considered superior, the court should deter-
> mine whether the services which make that placement superior could be
> feasibly provided in a non-segregated setting. If they can, the placement in the
> segregated school would be inappropriate under the Act.[133]

Finding this test too intrusive on local educational policy choices, the Fifth Circuit Court of Appeals posited an alternative two-part test for assessing compliance with the LRE requirement. First, the judiciary must determine whether education in the regular classroom, with the use of supplemental aids and services, can be achieved satisfactorily for a given child. Second, if a more restrictive placement is found to be appropriate, a determination must then be made as to whether the child is mainstreamed to the maximum extent appropriate.[134] This analysis necessitates a close examination of the nature and severity of the child's disability, the child's needs and abilities, and the school system's actions to address the child's needs.[135]

Private Placement. In addition to specifying that placement must be in the least restrictive environment, the IDEA requires public school districts to place children with disabilities in private facilities if appropriate public placements are unavailable. Conflicting rulings have been rendered as to whether the federal mandate requires school systems to incur all *noneducational* costs, such as medical and custodial expenses, associated with a private residential placement. Although the fiscal obligation placed on school systems can be substantial, courts have generally held that where educational needs necessitate residential placement, a school district or state must cover all costs.[136] The First Circuit Court of Appeals ordered a Massachusetts school district to pay residential costs because twenty-four-hour care, training, and reinforcement were essential for the child to make any educational progress.[137] The Act's provision for residential care, however, is not intended to compensate for a poor home environment or to serve as a means of delivering other social services; a residential placement is required only when the minimal educational benefits to which a child is entitled cannot be delivered through a day program.

In some situations where parents and school authorities have disagreed as to what is an appropriate placement, parents have unilaterally placed their children in private schools prior to exhaustion of the review process. School systems have maintained that such unilateral action forecloses later reimbursement to parents for tuition costs.[138] In 1985 the Supreme Court addressed parental rights in connection with unilateral placements in *School Committee of Town of Burlington, Massachusetts v.*

Department of Education of Massachusetts.[139] A parent disagreed with the school district's proposed educational placement of his learning-disabled child and, after seeking an independent evaluation from medical experts, enrolled the child in a private school. The Court rejected the school district's argument that a change in placement without the district's consent waived all rights to reimbursement. In the Court's opinion, denying relief would defeat the law's major objective of providing a free appropriate education. Where the school district's proposed placement is ultimately found to be inappropriate, reimbursement is considered necessary relief since the review process can be quite lengthy (eight years in this case). The Court reasoned that children should not be educationally disadvantaged by an inappropriate placement, nor should parents be economically penalized by removing their children.

One caveat, however, was issued by the Court: Parents who unilaterally seek private placement do so at their own financial risk. If the public school placement is found to be proper, reimbursement would be barred.[140] Parents cannot demand the "best" program; the Act requires only that a program be appropriate. Further, several federal appellate courts have held that the private school selected by the parents must meet state educational standards; reimbursement has been denied for placements in schools lacking state approval.[141]

In the wake of *Burlington,* lower courts have addressed the appropriateness of public school placements and whether reimbursements for private placements are justified. Tuition costs have been awarded when school officials have failed to comply with the Act's procedural requirements or to consider carefully the student's unique needs.[142] Parents, however, have been denied relief if school systems have followed all procedures set forth in the law and have designed a program to enable the child to receive educational benefits.[143] The Tenth Circuit Court of Appeals recognized that a private placement selected by parents was superior but relied on *Rowley* in reiterating that the Act does not require an education that maximizes a child's potential.[144] Accordingly, the court upheld the child's placement in the individualized multihandicapped program proposed by the school since it was designed to enable the child to receive educational benefits.

Although private placements may not necessarily be required under the IDEA, several courts have held that they may be mandated under state laws that exceed federal standards. The Third Circuit Court of Appeals held that continuation of a residential placement was required to provide a student with the "best" opportunity for educational success as required by New Jersey legislation.[145] Substantial evidence supported the private placement: The student regressed when he returned home for more than a week; he was unable to adjust to a less structured school environment; and his communication skills were enhanced where peers used sign language. Similarly, the First Circuit Court of Appeals interpreted a Massachusetts law as requiring a private placement "to assure the maximum possible development of a child with special needs."[146]

RELATED SERVICES

As noted previously, a free appropriate education includes both "special education and related services." Related services are defined as transportation and such developmental, corrective, and other supportive services (including speech pathology and audiology, psychological services, physical and occupational therapy, recreation, rehabilitation counseling, and social work services) that are necessary for a child with disabilities to benefit from special education.[147] Few controversies have arisen in these areas specifically identified in the law.[148] Transportation must be provided, even to medically fragile students,[149] and as the First Circuit Appellate Court noted, this may mean door-to-door transportation.[150] In addition, extracurricular and summer enrichment activities may be required for a child to obtain an appropriate education.[151] Reasonable modifications also must be made in school facilities; in one instance this required that a classroom be air-conditioned.[152]

The most difficult question in connection with related services is the distinction between medical and school health services. The Act excludes medical services except for diagnostic and evaluative purposes.[153] Parents, however, have asserted that certain "medical" needs must be addressed to enable children with disabilities to benefit from special education. In 1984 the Supreme Court in *Irving Independent School District v. Tatro* provided some clarification regarding the state's obligation to provide related services to meet medical needs.[154] This case involved an eight-year-old child with spina bifida and a neurogenic bladder, requiring clean intermittent catheterization (CIC) every three to four hours. The federal district court supported the school officials' decision to exclude CIC from the child's IEP because life-support services are not required; only services that arise from the effort to educate a child are mandatory. The Fifth Circuit Court of Appeals and the Supreme Court, however, disagreed, finding that CIC was required to enable the child to attend school and to benefit from the education she was guaranteed. The Supreme Court reasoned that "a service that enables a handicapped child to remain at school during the day is an important means of providing the child with the meaningful access to education that Congress envisioned."[155] Distinguishing CIC from medical services, the Court relied upon the definition of medical and school health services in the Act's regulations. Under the regulations, medical services are defined as "services provided by a licensed physician," while health services are categorized as "services provided by a qualified school nurse or other qualified person."[156] Since CIC is a procedure that can be performed by a nurse or a trained layperson, the Court concluded that it was not a medical service qualifying for exclusion under the Act.[157]

From decisions of lower federal courts, however, it appears that not all health services administered by nurses must be provided by school districts. The Second Circuit Court of Appeals found that *constant in-school* nursing care that must be performed by a skilled, trained health professional was not a school district's responsibility.[158] The nature of the child's disability necessitated extensive, specialized care that had to be administered by a licensed practical nurse or registered nurse; constant monitoring was needed to protect the child's life. The court distinguished intermittent care from constant care. A Pennsylvania federal district court adopted a similar distinction, noting that constant care was too intensive and costly and more closely related to medical services.[159] The court, however, cautioned that related services are not limited simply to services that can be provided at a low cost.

The Court in *Tatro* recognized specific limitations on the school district's responsibility to provide related services. In addition to specifying that school districts are not required to provide services that must be performed by a physician, the Court implied that services requiring specialized equipment would not be required under the Act. The Court also stated that students must be classified as "handicapped" to be entitled to related services, and only services necessary for a child to benefit from special education must be provided.[160] The Sixth Circuit Court of Appeals more recently noted that the related service must be designed to meet the child's unique needs caused by the disability.[161] Applying this test, the appellate court held that special transportation was not required for a deaf child since she could use the same transportation system as other children.

The *Tatro* decision provides significant guidance in identifying related services required under the IDEA, but psychotherapy is not easily classified. Generally, psychotherapy is provided only by licensed physicians. Yet, the Act specifically includes psychological and counseling services that could be considered part of psychotherapy. Several courts have concluded that psychotherapy is a related service when it is shown to be an integral part of the child's educational program.[162] For example, the Third Circuit Court of Appeals found that therapeutic services provided to a child in a specialized treatment program could not be separated from his educational program and thus were "an essential service" to enable the child to benefit from the educational program.[163] In contrast, an Illinois federal court classified psychiatric services as medical treatment and refused to require placement of a child in a psychiatric hospital.[164] In a later decision, however, the same court held that if psychotherapy and similar psychological services *can* be provided by professionals other than physicians, the mere fact that such services are performed by a psychiatrist does not render them nonreimbursable.[165]

In assessing what medically related services must be provided by public schools, it appears that one of the crucial questions is who provides the service. Those that *must* be performed by licensed physicians are excluded from the IDEA mandate, and others requiring intensive nursing care may not be required. In view of the range of medically related services that can be provided by nurses and other paraprofessionals, however, the scope of related services that school districts must provide remains extensive.

EXTENDED SCHOOL YEAR

Although the Supreme Court has not ruled on parental requests for extended school year programs, most federal appellate courts have held that states cannot restrict available services to the number of days provided other students.[166] These courts have not required year-round services for all children with disabilities but merely flexibility in state and local policies to permit consideration of a longer school program if needed for a child to attain reasonable education goals.[167] In the first case involving this issue, the Third Circuit Court of Appeals examined a Pennsylvania state education agency policy that limited publicly supported education for all students to 180 days.[168] The court found that this rigid restriction violated the Act because, regardless of a student's unique needs, a longer educational program could not be considered. The Eleventh Circuit Court of Appeals applied similar reasoning, holding that a Georgia statewide policy of limiting instruction to 180 days for children with disabilities did not allow for adequate consideration of an individual student's needs.[169] The court stated that its ruling required "no more than that the state *consider* the need for continuous education, along with a range of other concerns, when developing a plan of education . . ."[170]

Factors considered in determining whether a student is entitled to an extended program include evidence that the student would experience substantial regression; time required for the student to recoup lost benefits; severity of the child's impairment and the parents' ability to provide the educational structure at home; and relationship of the needed program to the child's disability. Of these factors, the regression-recoupment analysis has been the most dominant measure in determining the necessity for summer programs.[171] For example, the Sixth Circuit Court of Appeals held that a school district was not required to pay for a summer program for an autistic teenager because the summer break in his program would not substantially impede his progress.[172] The court noted, however, that a public school must provide summer services if expert testimony indicates that the child would significantly regress otherwise.

DISCIPLINE PRACTICES

Discipline practices may impair the rights guaranteed to children with disabilities under the IDEA. Most courts have found expulsions to constitute a change in placement requiring the full change-of-placement proceedings under the Act.[173] In 1988 the Supreme Court in *Honig v. Doe* agreed.[174] The case involved two California students who, after engaging in dangerous behavior, were suspended indefinitely pending the outcome of expulsion proceedings. A California federal district court and the Ninth Circuit Court of Appeals entered summary judgment for the students, finding that the indefinite suspension was a prohibited change in placement and violated the stay-put provision of the Act.

On appeal, the state superintendent of public instruction urged the Supreme Court to recognize a "dangerousness" exception to the stay-put requirement. The superintendent contended that Congress could not have intended that school officials return violent or dangerous students to the classroom during the lengthy administrative proceedings. Disagreeing, the Supreme Court stated that Congress deliberately stripped schools of the unilateral authority to exclude students with disabilities. The history of exclusion of such students prior to the enactment of the Act and the early litigation that guided the development of the law convinced the Court that the conspicuous absence of an emergency exception was intentional.

The Supreme Court, however, emphasized that school officials are not without options when confronted with a dangerous student. They can use a range of normal procedures, including detention, time outs, and restriction of privileges. A student who is an immediate threat can be suspended for up to ten days, which, according to the Court, does not constitute a change in placement. If the child continues to pose a threat and the parents refuse to agree to a change in placement, school officials can seek injunctive relief from the judiciary, but they bear the burden of showing that a child is truly dangerous.

It is well established that a student cannot be expelled from school if misconduct is related to the student's disability.[175] Some ambiguity remains as to whether expulsion is an acceptable disciplinary alternative where school officials find that the misbehavior is not a manifestation of the child's disability. Although the Supreme Court did not address this issue in *Honig,* other courts have considered the student's right to a free appropriate education when faced with such an expulsion. The Ninth Circuit Appellate Court held that expulsions (i.e., termination of all services) can be imposed if the misbehavior is unrelated to the disability and if proper procedures are followed.[176] The Fifth and Sixth Circuit Courts of Appeal agreed that students with disabilities can be expelled, but defined expulsion as removal from the current placement; they declined to permit complete cessation of educational services during the expulsion period.[177] An examination of the IDEA, its regulations, and policy statements from the Office of Special Education and Rehabilitative Services (U.S. Department of Education)[178] lends support to the assertion that all services cannot be terminated.[179] It appears that the appropriate action would not be expulsion, but removal of the student to a more restrictive placement on the continuum of alternative placements. Current practice indicates that few children are expelled; they are simply moved from a less restrictive environment to a more restrictive one.[180]

From judicial decisions interpreting students' rights under IDEA, Section 504, and the Federal Constitution, it is clear that students with disabilities are not exempt from reasonable disciplinary measures. Courts have approved a range of discipline procedures, such as time out, detention, assignment to study carrels, or the restriction of privileges.[181] For example, an Indiana federal district court rejected a hyperactive and emotionally disturbed student's due process and equal protection challenge to paddling, isolation seating, and taping of the mouth.[182] The paddling was not excessive and was preceded by a discussion with the child's father and warnings to the student. Isolation was characterized as a "relatively innocuous" discipline technique and was warranted because of the child's behavior. The taping of the student's mouth (performed by the student) was viewed as symbolic, rather than punitive, to remind the student to be silent. The Eighth Circuit Court of Appeals also held that an in-school suspension of three days in a special assignments class did not violate a student's substantive due process rights.[183] While the child did not have access to his special education teacher and other resources, he was given all class assignments, which he completed. Similarly, another federal court held that isolating a student with educational and emotional disabilities in a "time-out box" did not violate his substantive due process rights.[184] In an action dismissing a complaint because parents had not exhausted administrative remedies, the Tenth Circuit Court of Appeals noted that the use of a time-out room did not constitute a change of placement under federal law.[185]

It appears that courts will continue to mandate extensive procedural safeguards in the discipline of students with disabilities. At a minimum, a school system's discipline policy should contain procedures to ensure that a student is not expelled for misbehavior resulting from the disability. This entails a special assessment and review by individuals who are knowledgeable of the student's disability and program. If the school's policies authorize expulsion as an option for students with disabilities, provision for continuation of educational services should be addressed since it is unlikely that complete termination of the educational program is legally permissible. Although the Supreme Court recognized that short-term suspensions up to ten days can be employed, serial short suspensions also may result in a change in placement if cumulative days are significant. The frequent suspension of a student should alert school officials to the need to examine the appropriateness of the student's placement. As the IEP is developed, parents should be informed of the range of disciplinary measures that will be used to address behavioral problems.

Remedies for the Denial of an
Appropriate Education

In the absence of exceptional circumstances, damages are unavailable under the IDEA. The Supreme Court in *Burlington* drew a sharp distinction between awarding damages and requiring tuition reimbursement; the latter is simply recovery of justified costs which initially should have been incurred by the school district.[186] Compensatory education also may be available. In several instances involving gross procedural violations of the IDEA's regulations, courts have awarded compensatory education to students with disabilities who had reached the age of twenty-one.[187] The Eighth Circuit Court of Appeals found an award of compensatory educational services to be analogous to the granting of retroactive tuition reimbursement upheld by the Supreme Court in *Burlington*.[188]

Originally, the federal law did not provide courts the discretion to award attorneys' fees, but the law was amended with the enactment of the Handicapped Children's Protection Act (HCPA) in 1986 to permit awards of "reasonable attorneys' fees" to parents who prevail in any action or proceeding.[189] Impetus for the amendment came from the Supreme Court's 1984 decision, *Smith v. Robinson,* interpreting the IDEA as the exclusive means for enforcing the rights of children with disabilities to a free appropriate education.[190] In this case, the Court concluded that where rights were guaranteed by the IDEA, parents could not allege violations under either Section 1983 of the Civil Rights Act of 1871 or Section 504 of the Rehabilitation Act of 1973 to enlarge available remedies, such as attorneys' fees. Although the HCPA authorizes awards of attorneys' fees in IDEA cases, controversy has arisen over whether administrative hearings are covered under the "any action or proceeding" designation in the Act. A number of federal courts, including five circuit courts of appeal, have held that the legislative history of HCPA reflects an unequivocal intent that attorneys' fees are available for administrative hearings,[191] but the Supreme Court has not addressed this issue.

CLASSIFICATIONS BASED ON
NATIVE LANGUAGE

As indicated in the preceding section, courts and legislatures have directed attention to the *absence* of needed student classifications as well as to the existence of discriminatory classifications. In other words, the lack of special instruction for certain groups of children who cannot benefit from the mainstream educational program has been critically reviewed. Some of the legal activity dealing with such "functional exclusion" has focused on the rights of linguistic minority students, who allegedly have been denied an adequate education because of the absence of remedial English instruction. Title VI of the Civil Rights Act of 1964, the Equal Educational Opportunities Act of 1974, and the Bilingual Education Act of 1968 have been invoked to ensure the provision of special services for these students.

In the only United States Supreme Court decision involving English-deficient students, *Lau v. Nichols,* Chinese students asserted that the San Francisco public school program failed to provide for the needs of non-English-speaking students in violation of the equal protection clause of the fourteenth amendment and Title VI.[192] Both the federal district court and the Ninth Circuit Court of Appeals rejected the pupils' claim. The appellate court acknowledged that each student brought to school different advantages and disadvantages "caused in part by social, economic and cultural backgrounds," and that some of these disadvantages could be overcome by special instructional programs.[193] Nonetheless, the court reasoned that the provision of such special services, although desirable, was not constitutionally required.

The Supreme Court, however, reversed the appellate court's ruling and held that the lack of sufficient remedial English instruction violated Section 601 of Title VI. The Court concluded that quality of treatment was not realized merely by providing students with the same facilities, textbooks, teachers, and curriculum, and that requiring children to acquire English skills on their own before they could hope to make any progress in school made "a mockery of public education."[194] The Court emphasized that "basic English skills are at the very core of what these public schools teach," and, therefore, "students who do not understand English are effectively foreclosed from any meaningful education."[195]

Although the Supreme Court declined to address the constitutional issue in *Lau,* several lower courts have relied on equal protection guarantees in ordering bilingual-bicultural education programs in school districts where discrimination against linguistic minority students has been uncovered. For example, in 1972 the Fifth Circuit Court of Appeals affirmed the lower court's conclusion that the segregation of Mexican-American students in a Texas school district was unconstitutional.[196] As part of the remedial decree, the federal court ordered a comprehensive bilingual program. In another Texas case, a federal district court similarly mandated the expansion of bilingual programs in order to provide equal educational opportunities for Mexican-American students.[197] It is noteworthy that in the latter case the court did not find the existence of unconstitutional segregation, but still declared that the absence of an appropriate curriculum for bilingual students created an "inherently unequal" situation that placed a constitutional duty on school officials to provide for the unique needs of students with language deficiencies. Other federal courts have ordered school districts to provide special services for limited-English proficiency (LEP) students, even if only a few students within the district have needed such assistance,[198] and have required school officials to upgrade bilingual programs considered to be insufficient.[199] In 1975 the

Fifth Circuit Court of Appeals stated that "it is now an unlawful education practice to fail to take appropriate action to overcome language barriers."[200]

The Ninth Circuit Court of Appeals concluded, however, that school districts do not have a duty under the Federal Constitution or civil rights laws to ensure that all courses, instructors, testing procedures, and instructional materials for LEP students are bicultural and bilingual.[201] The appellate court reasoned that the provision of compensatory programs to cure students' language deficiencies satisfies the mandate in *Lau v. Nichols*. Courts have agreed that LEP students are entitled to special assistance, but consensus has not been reached as to whether they are entitled only to remedial English instruction or instruction in their native language as well.

Plaintiffs have a heavy burden of proof in establishing intentional discrimination under the equal protection clause and Title VI; however, such suits are not the only means to ensure that the language needs of linguistic minorities are met. The federal Equal Educational Opportunities Act (EEOA) of 1974 requires school systems to develop appropriate programs for LEP students. The act provides in part:

> No state shall deny equal educational opportunity to an individual on account of his or her race, color, sex, or national origin, by . . . the failure by an educational agency to take appropriate action to overcome language barriers that impede equal participation by its students in its instructional program.[202]

The EEOA does not impose a specific program of bilingual education on state and local education agencies, but rather requires "appropriate action." The Fifth Circuit Court of Appeals noted that Congress left state and local educational agencies "a substantial amount of latitude" in developing programs to meet their obligations under the EEOA.[203] The court found, however, that the legislative history of the EEOA provided almost no guidance in interpreting when a district's efforts are "appropriate." To assess the appropriateness of remediation programs and at the same time avoid prescribing educational standards, the court posed three questions:

1. Is the district's program based upon recognized, sound educational theory or principles?
2. Is the school system's program or practice designed to implement the adopted theory?
3. Has the program produced satisfactory results?[204]

Implicit in the first question is the recognition that several legitimate, competing strategies exist for meeting language deficiencies. Courts simply determine if a selected strategy is one recognized by education experts. Under the remaining questions, courts examine the level of resources committed to programs, the language competency of bilingual teachers, and efforts to assess such competency, methods of classifying students for instruction, and procedures for evaluating student progress.[205]

In the few legal challenges that have been raised against school systems' language remediation programs, the Fifth Circuit Appellate Court approach has been used to assess compliance with the EEOA. The Colorado Federal District Court, in assessing compliance of the Denver Public Schools, concluded that the law does not require a full bilingual education program for every single LEP student, but that the district has a duty to take action to eliminate barriers that prevent LEP children from participating in the system's educational program. According to the court, "good faith effort" is inadequate: "What is required is an effort which will be reasonably effective in producing intended results. . . ."[206] The Seventh Circuit Court of Appeals in examining Illinois's compliance with EEOA noted that "appropriate action" under the law certainly means more than "no action."[207]

Under the Bilingual Education Act of 1968, Congress provided supplemental funding for school districts to establish programs to meet the special educational needs of low-income students with limited-English proficiency.[208] The Bilingual Education Act of 1974 removed the criterion that children receiving such assistance had to be from low-income families and provided a more explicit definition of bilingual education as instruction in English and the child's native language to the extent necessary for the child to make effective progress.[209] Subsequently, in response to the *Lau* decision, the former Department of Health, Education, and Welfare issued advisory guidelines, known as the *Lau Remedies,* to assist school districts in designing programs to meet the needs of LEP students. In 1980, the Department of Education proposed formal regulations under Title VI of the Civil Rights Act of 1964 to prevent discrimination based on national origin in elementary and secondary education. The rules were withdrawn in 1981 because school districts and professional organizations objected to the proposed constraints on local prerogatives to design bilingual programs. Many states, however, have enacted legislation and/or administrative regulations pertaining to bilingual education. For example, Indiana law specifies that non-English-dominant students must be provided with bilingual-bicultural instruction designed to meet their language skill needs.[210]

The debate continues as to the "best" method for meeting the needs of LEP students. Unless mandated by state law, school districts are not required to offer bilingual-bicultural programs in which students are instructed in both their native language and English throughout their school years. Widely adopted alternatives to this approach include programs where students are placed in regular classrooms with special English instruction several hours a week (English as a second language programs) and transitional bilingual education, where students are provided special instruction in English but taught the basic curriculum in their native language until they have gained English proficiency. The latter alternatives have sparked considerable political discussion; the U.S. Secretary of Education and the director of the Office of Bilingual Education and Minority Language Affairs in 1989 urged support for native-language instruction for students.

The legal mandates pertaining to English-deficient students, in conjunction with directives on behalf of children with disabilities, raise several crucial issues regarding individual rights and the corresponding state duty to provide appropriate educational opportunities for all pupils. The mandates go beyond the mere right of every child to attend school. They address the suitability of the programs to the unique characteristics of pupils. Possibly, other classes of children who cannot benefit from the mainstream instructional program, such as the culturally disadvantaged or the gifted, may attempt to capitalize on the protections afforded to children with disabilities and limited-English proficiency in asserting their rights to a public school program designed to meet their unique needs.[211]

CONCLUSION

A basic purpose of public education is to enhance adult opportunities for all students, regardless of their innate characteristics. Accordingly, courts and legislatures have become increasingly assertive in guaranteeing that pupils have the chance to realize their capabilities while in school. Arbitrary classification practices that disadvantage certain groups of children no longer will be tolerated. On the other hand, valid classifications, applied in the best interests of students, are not being questioned. Indeed, legal mandates *require* the classification of certain pupils to ensure that they receive instruction appropriate to their needs. In exercising professional judgment pertaining to the classification of pupils, educators should be cognizant of the following generalizations drawn from recent judicial and legislative mandates.

1. Students cannot be segregated by gender in academic programs or schools unless there is a legitimate educational reason for maintaining gender segregation, and then only if comparable courses/schools are available to both males and females.
2. Criteria for admission to programs or schools cannot be gender-based.
3. If a school district establishes an interscholastic athletic program, such opportunities must be made available to male and female athletes on an equal basis (i.e., either mixed-gender teams or comparable gender-segregated teams).
4. Students cannot be disadvantaged based on their marital status.

5. Any differential treatment of pregnant students must be justified by valid health or safety considerations.
6. Students can be classified by age, but such classifications must be substantiated as necessary to advance legitimate educational objectives.
7. Ability-tracking schemes are permissible; however, any such schemes that result in the segregation of minority children will be carefully scrutinized by courts to ensure that they are not a ploy to perpetuate discrimination.
8. If ability grouping is used, pupil assignments should be based on multiple criteria such as tests, teacher recommendations, and the socioeconomic background and adaptive behavior of the child.
9. Children with disabilities are entitled to a free appropriate education in the least restrictive environment.
10. A free appropriate public education for a child with disabilities is one that provides meaningful access to an education program that confers some educational benefit; the best program or one that maximizes the child's potential is not required.
11. An individualized education program (including goals and objectives, specification of the services to be provided, and an education plan) must be developed for each child with disabilities.
12. Due process procedures must be followed in identifying, evaluating, or changing the educational placement of children with disabilities.
13. A parent may recover tuition costs for a unilateral private placement of a child with disabilities if the placement is later determined to be appropriate and the placement proposed by the public school is found to be inappropriate.
14. Related services necessary to support the specially designed instruction for children with disabilities are required; school districts are not obligated to provide medical services.
15. Disciplinary expulsion of children with disabilities is a change in placement and triggers the procedural safeguards of the IDEA; misconduct related to a disability cannot be the basis for expulsion.
16. Attorneys' fees are available for violations of the IDEA.
17. English-deficient children are entitled to compensatory instruction designed to overcome English language barriers.

ENDNOTES

1. Most states have similar antidiscrimination provisions. Connecticut law, for example, stipulates that "public schools shall be open to all children over five years of age without discrimination on account of race, color, sex, religion, or national origin . . . ," Conn. Gen. Stat. § 10–15 (1991).

2. *See* Dunn v. Blumstein, 405 U.S. 330 (1972) (right to vote in state elections); Shapiro v. Thompson, 394 U.S. 618 (1969) (right to interstate travel); Skinner v. Oklahoma, 316 U.S. 535, 541 (1942) (right to procreation).

3. 411 U.S. 1 (1973).

4. *See* Graham v. Richardson, 403 U.S. 365 (1971) (alienage); Brown v. Board of Educ. of Topeka, 347 U.S. 483 (1954) (race); Oyama v. California, 332 U.S. 633 (1948) (national origin).

5. The Supreme Court, however, later recognized that *Rodriguez* does not foreclose the possibility of an equal protection violation where a state has decided to divide resources unequally among school districts, Papasan v. Allain, 478 U.S. 265 (1986).

6. *See* San Antonio Indep. School Dist. v. Rodriguez, 411 U.S. 1 (1973) (wealth); Frontiero v. Richardson, 411 U.S. 677 (1973) (gender); Gurmankin v. Costanzo, 556 F.2d 184 (3d Cir. 1977), *cert. denied,* 450 U.S. 923 (1981) (disabilities).

7. *See* Dunn v. Blumstein, 405 U.S. 330 (1972).

8. *See* Bullock v. Carter, 405 U.S. 134 (1972); Eisenstadt v. Baird, 405 U.S. 438 (1972).

9. 457 U.S. 202 (1982).

10. *See* text with note 190, *infra.;* text with note 88, *infra.*

11. *See* Chapters 9 and 13 for a discussion of legal principles pertaining to race discrimination.

12. Frontiero v. Richardson, 411 U.S. 677, 686 (1973).

13. *See* Chapter 9 for further discussion of gender-based classifications.

14. Brenden v. Independent School Dist., 477 F.2d 1292 (8th Cir. 1973).

15. *See, e.g.,* Morris v. Michigan State Bd. of Educ., 472 F.2d 1207 (6th Cir. 1973); Gilpin v. Kansas State High School Activities Ass'n, 377 F. Supp. 1233 (D. Kan. 1973); Reed v. Nebraska School Activities Ass'n, 341 F. Supp. 258 (D. Neb. 1972). *See also* Croteau v. Fair, 686 F. Supp. 552 (E.D. Va. 1988) (females have the right to a fair tryout for a position on a team, but selection depends on demonstrated skills).

16. Lantz v. Ambach, 620 F. Supp. 663 (S.D.N.Y. 1985). *See also* Saint v. Nebraska Activities Ass'n, 684 F. Supp. 626 (D. Neb. 1988) (female permitted to participate in wrestling).

17. Force v. Pierce City R-VI School Dist., 570 F. Supp. 1020 (W.D. Mo. 1983).

18. Leffel v. Wisconsin Interscholastic Athletic Ass'n, 444 F. Supp. 1117 (E.D. Wis. 1978).

19. O'Connor v. Board of Educ. of School Dist. 23, 545 F. Supp. 376 (N.D. Ill.1982), *application to vacate stay denied,* 449 U.S. 1301 (1980).

20. Israel v. West Virginia Secondary Schools Activities Comm'n, 388 S.E.2d 480 (W. Va. 1989).

21. 34 C.F.R. § 106.41(b) (1990). Under Title IX, the Department of Education is empowered to terminate federal funds to institutions if charges of sex bias are substantiated.

22. *Id.*

23. Yellow Springs Exempted Village School Dist. Bd. of Educ. v. Ohio High School Athletic Ass'n, 647 F.2d 651 (6th Cir. 1981).

24. *See* Force v. Pierce City R-VI School Dist., 570 F. Supp. 1020 (W.D. Mo. 1983) (a similar prohibition against female participation was found unconstitutional under the equal protection clause of the fourteenth amendment).

25. Pennsylvania v. Pennsylvania Interscholastic Athletic Ass'n, 334 A.2d 839 (Pa. 1975). The Pennsylvania Equal Rights Amendment states: "Equality of rights under the law shall not be denied or abridged in the Commonwealth of Pennsylvania because of the sex of the individual," Pa. Const., art. I, § 28 (1990).

26. Cape v. Tennessee Secondary School Athletic Ass'n, 563 F.2d 793 (6th Cir. 1977).

27. Jones v. Oklahoma Secondary School Activities Ass'n, 453 F. Supp. 150 (W.D. Okla. 1977).

28. Dodson v. Arkansas Activities Ass'n, 468 F. Supp. 394 (E.D. Ark. 1979).

29. Striebel v. Minnesota State High School League, 321 N.W.2d 400, 402 (Minn. 1982).

30. Ridgeway v. Montana High School Ass'n, 749 F. Supp. 1544 (D. Mont. 1990).

31. Clark v. Arizona Interscholastic Ass'n, 695 F.2d 1126 (9th Cir. 1982), *cert. denied,* 464 U.S. 818 (1983). *See also* Clark v. Arizona Interscholastic Ass'n, 886 F.2d 1191 (9th Cir. 1989) (reaffirmed decision in Clark I in a case brought by the brother of the original plaintiff); Rowley v. Members of the Bd. of Educ. of St. Vrain Valley School Dist. RE-IJ, 863 F.2d 39 (10th Cir. 1988) (applied intermediate scrutiny test in denying preliminary injunctive relief to male student); B.C. v. Board of Educ., Cumberland Regional School Dist., 531 A.2d 1059 (N.J. Super. Ct. App. Div. 1987); Muladelis v. Haldane Cent. School Bd., 427 N.Y.S.2d 458 (N.Y. App. Div. 1980). *But see* Attorney General v. Massachusetts Interscholastic Athletic Ass'n, 393 N.E.2d 284 (Mass. 1979) (sex-based discrimination against males could not be justified by health or safety considerations or by the assertion that the rule was necessary to shield the emergent women's sports program from inundation by male athletes).

32. 532 F.2d 880 (3d Cir. 1976), *aff'd by an equally divided court,* 430 U.S. 703 (1977). *See also* United States v. Commonwealth of Virginia, 766 F. Supp. 1407 (W.D. Va. 1991) (single-gender military college upheld).

33. *Id.,* 532 F.2d at 886, quoting Kahn v. Shevin, 416 U.S. 351, 356 (1974).

34. In a later state case, a trial court declared that the two Philadelphia gender-segregated schools in *Vorchheimer* violated the fourteenth amendment and Pennsylvania's Equal Rights Amendment, concluding from a complete evidentiary record that the opportunities provided were *not equal.* Newberg v. Board of Pub. Educ., 478 A.2d 1352 (Pa. Super. Ct. 1984). *See* William D. Valente, *Education Law: Public and Private,* vol. 2 (St. Paul, MN: West Publishing Company, 1985), p. 73.

35. Mississippi Univ. for Women v. Hogan, 458 U.S. 718 (1982). *See also* "Detroit Board Agrees to Let Girls Attend Male-Only Academies," *School Law News,* August 29, 1991, p. 5.

36. Title IX regulations also stipulate that differential admission criteria cannot be applied to male and female students. 45 C.F.R. § 86.35(b) (1990).

37. Bray v. Lee, 337 F. Supp. 934 (D. Mass. 1972).

38. Berkelman v. San Francisco Unified School Dist., 501 F.2d 1264 (9th Cir. 1974).

39. Sharif by Salahuddin v. New York State Educ. Dep't, 709 F. Supp. 345 (S.D.N.Y. 1989).

40. *See, e.g.,* Della Casa v. Gaffney, No. 171673 (Cal. App. Dep't Super. Ct. 1973); Seward v. Della, No. 134173 (Cal. App. Dep't Super. Ct. 1973); Sanchez v. Baron, No. 69-C-1615 (E.D.N.Y. 1971).

41. *See* Hickey v. Black River Bd. of Educ., No. 73-889 (N.D. Ohio 1973).
42. *See* 45 C.F.R. § 86.34-36 (1990).
43. Iron Arrow Honor Society v. Heckler, 702 F.2d 549 (5th Cir. 1983), *vacated as moot,* 464 U.S. 67 (1983). *See also* Olesen v. Board of Educ. of School Dist. No. 228, 676 F. Supp. 820 (N.D. Ill. 1987) (prohibiting males from wearing earrings under an antigang policy did not violate equal protection rights of males because they were treated differently from females; earrings did not signify gang membership for females).
44. State *ex rel.* Thompson v. Marion County Bd. of Educ., 302 S.W.2d 57 (Tenn. 1957).
45. State *ex rel.* Baker v. Stevenson, 189 N.E.2d 181 (Ohio C.P. 1962). *See also* Board of Directors of Indep. School Dist. of Waterloo v. Green, 147 N.W.2d 854 (Iowa 1967).
46. Loving v. Virginia, 388 U.S. 1, 12 (1967).
47. Davis v. Meek, 344 F. Supp. 298, 301 (N.D. Ohio 1972). *See also* Holt v. Shelton, 341 F. Supp. 821 (M.D. Tenn. 1972); Moran v. School Dist. No. 7, Yellowstone County, 350 F. Supp. 1180 (D. Mont. 1972).
48. *See, e.g.,* Beeson v. Kiowa County School Dist. RE-I, 567 P.2d 801 (Colo. Ct. App. 1977); Bell v. Lone Oak Indep. School Dist., 507 S.W.2d 636, 641-642 (Tex. Civ. App. 1974).
49. *See* Grace Belsches-Simmons, "Teenage Pregnancy and Schooling: Legal Considerations," *Education Law Reporter,* vol. 24 (1985), pp. 1–11.
50. Ordway v. Hargraves, 323 F. Supp. 1155 (D. Mass. 1971).
51. Alvin Indep. School Dist. v. Cooper, 404 S.W.2d 76 (Tex. Civ. App. 1966). *See also* Perry v. Grenada Mun. Separate School Dist., 300 F. Supp. 748 (N.D. Miss. 1969).
52. *See* Geduldig v. Aiello, 417 U.S. 484 (1974). *See also* discussion of gender discrimination in Chapter 9.
53. 20 U.S.C. § 1681(a) (1988); 45 C.F.R. § 86.21(c)(2) (1990).
54. *See, e.g.,* Wort v. Vierling, 778 F.2d 1233 (7th Cir. 1985) (school officials could not expel student from the National Honor Society based on her pregnant, unwed status). *But see* Pfeiffer v. Marion Center Area School Dist., 917 F.2d 779 (3d Cir. 1990) (dismissal from National Honor Society for premarital sex, rather than pregnant, unwed status, does not violate Title IX).
55. *See* Chapter 9 for discussion of employment discrimination.
56. Goldsmith v. Lower Moreland School Dist., 461 A.2d 1341 (Pa. Commw. Ct. 1983).
57. O'Leary v. Wisecup, 364 A.2d 770 (Pa. Commw. Ct. 1976). *See also* Zweifel v. Joint Dist. No. 1, Belleville, 251 N.W.2d 822 (Wis. 1977).
58. Hammond v. Marx, 406 F. Supp. 853 (D. Me. 1975). *See also* Morrison v. Chicago Bd. of Educ., 544 N.E.2d 1099 (Ill. App. Ct. 1989).
59. Ackerman v. Rubin, 231 N.Y.S.2d 112 (N.Y. Sup. Ct. 1962).
60. *Id.* at 114.
61. *See* Stewart v. Salem School Dist. 24J, 670 P.2d 1048 (Or. Ct. App. 1983). *See also* Education of the Handicapped Amendments Act of 1986. The Act included strong incentives for states to serve three- to five-year-old children with disabilities by 1991 and to create programs for infants with disabilities. If states do not serve these children, they will lose funds appropriated for the preschool programs and will not be allowed to count three- to five-year-old children with

disabilities under the basic grant. 20 U.S.C. §§ 1408, 1461, 1462, & 1471–1485 (1986) (amended 1988 and 1990).

62. Helms v. Independent School Dist. No. 3 of Broken Arrow, Tulsa County, 750 F.2d 820 (10th Cir. 1984), *cert. denied,* 471 U.S. 1018 (1985).

63. *See, e.g.,* Adams Cent. School Dist. No. 090 v. Deist, 334 N.W.2d 775 (Neb. 1983) (no authority under federal or state law to order educational services beyond twenty-one years of age). *But see* Burr v. Sobol, 888 F.2d 258 (2d Cir. 1989), *cert. denied,* 110 S. Ct. 1298 (1990) (services required beyond twenty-one years of age where procedural violations of federal law occurred).

64. *See, e.g.,* Sandlin v. Johnson, 643 F.2d 1027 (4th Cir. 1981) (upheld denial of promotion for twenty-one second-grade students in a class of twenty-two for failure to pass Ginn Reading Series test).

65. 269 F. Supp. 401 (D.D.C. 1967), *aff'd sub nom.* Smuck v. Hobson, 408 F.2d 175 (D.C. Cir. 1969).

66. *Id.,* 269 F. Supp. at 511.

67. Singleton v. Jackson Mun. Separate School Dist., 419 F.2d 1211 (5th Cir. 1969). *See also* United States v. Gadsden County School Dist., 572 F.2d 1049 (5th Cir. 1978); Moore v. Tangipahoa Parish School Bd., 304 F. Supp. 244 (E.D. La. 1969).

68. Castaneda v. Pickard, 648 F.2d 989, 996 (5th Cir. 1981). On remand, the court affirmed the district court's finding that ability grouping did not discriminate on the basis of race, 781 F.2d 456 (5th Cir. 1986).

69. Georgia State Conference of Branches of NAACP v. State of Georgia, 775 F.2d 1403 (11th Cir. 1985). *See also* Bond v. Keck, 616 F. Supp. 565 (E.D. Mo. 1985) (African-American student's reassignment from highest ability math group to second highest group was appropriate based on her short attention span and poor time on task); Bond v. Keck, 629 F. Supp. 225 (E.D. Mo. 1986), *aff'd,* 802 F.2d 463 (8th Cir. 1986) (defendants were awarded attorneys' fees because suit was found to be frivolous and without foundation).

70. *See, e.g.,* Bester v. Tuscaloosa City Bd. of Educ., 722 F.2d 1514 (11th Cir. 1984).

71. Larry P. v. Riles, 495 F. Supp. 926 (N.D. Cal. 1979), *aff'd,* 793 F.2d 969 (9th Cir. 1984) (violations of Title VI, the Rehabilitation Act, and the Education for All Handicapped Children Act were found).

72. Although the initial ruling prohibited the use of intelligence tests only for the identification of students as mentally retarded, the trial court judge subsequently extended the prohibition to include the testing of all African-American students who are referred for special education. In 1991, however, these restrictions were eased to permit the use of standardized intelligence tests in assessing whether students qualify for special help or whether their special education placements are appropriate, Wilson v. Honig (N.D. Cal. 1991), cited in Debra Viadero, "Judge Lifts Curb on Tests for Special Education Services," *Education Week,* July 31, 1991, p. 18.

73. Parents in Action on Special Educ. v. Hannon, 506 F. Supp. 831 (N.D. Ill. 1980).

74. *See* discussion of Individuals with Disabilities Education Act at note 92, *infra.*

75. " 'GAO' Criticizes OCR Efforts to Limit Biased School Tracking," *School Law News,* May 9, 1991, p. 3.

76. "OCR to Warn Districts about Illegal Tracking of Students, *School Law News*, June 20, 1991, p. 5.
77. Gifted and Talented Students Education Act of 1988, 20 U.S.C. § 3061 *et seq.* (1988).
78. 20 U.S.C. § 3311 (1978) (repealed 1982).
79. 1990 State of the States Gifted and Talented Report, Council of the State Directors of Programs for the Gifted (Augusta, Maine, 1991).
80. *The Condition of Education*, Valena W. Plisko, ed. (Washington, DC: National Center for Education Statistics, 1983).
81. Pa. Stat. Ann. tit. 24 § 13-1371(1) (Purdon, West Supp. 1990).
82. Centennial School Dist. v. Commonwealth Dep't of Educ., 539 A.2d 785 (Pa. 1988). *See also* Lisa H. v. State Bd. of Educ., 447 A.2d 669 (Pa. Commw. Ct. 1982) (all students are not entitled to special individualized education, only those who deviate from the norm).
83. *Id.*, Centennial School Dist., 539 A.2d at 791.
84. Conn. Gen. Stat. §§ 10-76a, 10-76d(d) (1986).
85. Bennett v. City School Dist. of New Rochelle, 497 N.Y.S.2d 72 (N.Y. App. Div. 1985).
86. Student Roe v. Commonwealth of Pennsylvania, 638 F. Supp. 929 (E.D. Pa. 1986), *aff'd*, 813 F.2d 398 (3d Cir. 1987), *cert. denied*, 483 U.S. 1021 (1987); Student Doe v. Commonwealth of Pennsylvania, 593 F. Supp. 54 (E.D. Pa. 1984). In an unsuccessful Illinois suit, parents asked for injunctive relief and $1 million in damages because of the school district's alleged failure to meet the needs of their son, who had a measured intelligence of 170. Irwin v. Board of Educ., Community Consol. School Dist. No. 15, No. 79L49 (Ill. Cir. Ct., McKindry County, dismissed, June 1980).
87. Pennsylvania Ass'n for Retarded Children v. Commonwealth, 343 F. Supp. 279 (E.D. Pa. 1972).
88. Mills v. Board of Educ. of District of Columbia, 348 F. Supp. 866 (D.D.C. 1972).
89. San Antonio Indep. School Dist. v. Rodriguez, 411 U.S. 1, 36 (1973).
90. Plyler v. Doe, 457 U.S. 202 (1982).
91. 29 U.S.C. § 794 (1988).
92. 20 U.S.C. § 1401 (1991). *See, generally,* Laura F. Rothstein, *Special Education Law* (New York: Longman, 1990); Stephen B. Thomas, *Legal Issues in Special Education* (Topeka, KS: National Organization on Legal Problems of Education, 1985).
93. 29 U.S.C. § 706(7)(B) (1988).
94. School Bd. of Nassau County, Florida v. Arline, 480 U.S. 273 (1987).
95. *See, e.g.*, Doe v. Dolton Elementary School Dist. No. 148, 694 F. Supp. 440 (N.D. Ill. 1988); Ray v. School Dist. of Desoto County, 666 F. Supp. 1524 (M.D. Fla. 1987); Thomas v. Atascadero Unified School Dist., 662 F. Supp. 376 (C.D. Cal. 1987); In re Ryan White, No. 86-144 (Ind. Cir. Ct., Clinton County, 1986); District 27 Community School Bd. v. Board of Educ. of City of New York, 502 N.Y.S.2d 325 (N.Y. Sup. Ct. 1986).
96. *See, e.g.*, Martinez v. School Bd. of Hillsborough County, Florida, 861 F.2d 1502 (11th Cir. 1988), *on remand*, 711 F. Supp. 1066 (M.D. Fla. 1989); Doe v. Belleville Pub. School Dist. No. 118, 672 F. Supp. 342 (S.D. Ill. 1987).
97. 20 U.S.C.A. § 1415(e)(4) (1991). In reaction to the Supreme Court's holding in

Smith v. Robinson, 468 U.S. 992 (1984), that the IDEA was the exclusive remedy for enforcing the rights of children with disabilities, Congress specified in the Handicapped Children's Protection Act that the IDEA could not be construed to limit rights also available under the Constitution, Section 504, and other federal laws.

98. For several years New Mexico did not participate in the Act's funding, but after the Tenth Circuit Court of Appeals ruled that the state was obligated under Section 504 to provide appropriate educational programs for children with disabilities, the state decided to participate in the assistance program. *See* New Mexico Ass'n for Retarded Citizens v. State of New Mexico, 678 F.2d 847 (10th Cir. 1982).

99. 20 U.S.C.A. § 1401 (1991). The first attempt since enactment of the Act to expand the definition of disabilities occurred in 1990 with parent groups lobbying Congress to include children diagnosed as having "attention deficit disorder" (ADD). The bill to reauthorize discretionary programs under the IDEA defined ADD as a condition characterized by a developmentally inappropriate degree of inattention and often, but not always, associated with a developmentally inappropriate degree of impulsivity and/or overactivity. While the Act's definition of disability was not amended to include ADD, Congress requested that the Department of Education conduct a study of ADD.

100. 20 U.S.C.A. §1401(16) (1991). Despite the IDEA's revolutionary impact on programs and services for children with disabilities, significant concern exists that the implementation of the law has interfered with achieving the "spirit of the law." What has emerged is a group of proposals known as the Regular Education Initiative (REI). In general, these proposals advocate the restructuring of general and special education in order to create a new system in which most students who need assistance are provided that assistance in the regular classroom. Under the REI proposals, the present classification system and pull-out approach for mainstreaming would be eliminated. *See, generally,* Thomas M. Skrtic, "The Special Education Paradox: Equity as the Way to Excellence," *Harvard Educational Review,* vol. 61, no. 2 (May 1991), pp. 148–206.

101. *See* text with note 61, *supra.*

102. 458 U.S. 176 (1982).

103. 483 F. Supp. 528, 534 (S.D.N.Y. 1980).

104. Rowley, 458 U.S. at 192.

105. *Id.* at 200. The Supreme Court in *Rowley* held that the IDEA created substantive rights; however, a year earlier the Court declared that the Developmental Disabled Act did not. That Act was designed to *encourage,* but not to *mandate,* better services for the developmentally disabled. *See* Pennhurst State School and Hosp. v. Halderman, 451 U.S. 1 (1981).

106. Rowley, 458 U.S. at 207.

107. *See, e.g.,* Polk v. Central Susquehanna Intermediate Unit 16, 853 F.2d 171 (3d Cir. 1988); Board of Educ. of East Windsor School Dist. v. Diamond, 808 F.2d 987 (3d Cir. 1986); Abrahamson v. Hershman, 701 F.2d 223 (1st Cir. 1983).

108. Karl v. Board of Educ. of Geneseo Cent. School Dist., 736 F.2d 873 (2d Cir. 1984).

109. Burke County Bd. of Educ. v. Denton, 895 F.2d 973 (4th Cir. 1990).

110. Scituate School Comm. v. Robert B., 620 F. Supp. 1224 (D.R.I. 1985). *See also* Leonard v. McKenzie, 869 F.2d 1558 (D.C. Cir. 1989).
111. Hessler v. State Bd. of Educ. of Maryland, 700 F.2d 134 (4th Cir. 1983).
112. The District of Columbia Court of Appeals noted that "proof that loving parents can craft a better program than a state offers does not, alone, entitle them to prevail under the Act," Kerkam v. McKenzie, 862 F.2d 884, 886 (D.C. 1988).
113. *See, e.g.,* A.W. v. Northwest R-1 School Dist., 813 F.2d 158 (8th Cir. 1987), *cert. denied,* 484 U.S. 847 (1987); Roncker v. Walter, 700 F.2d 1058 (6th Cir.1983).
114. Timothy W. v. Rochester, New Hampshire, School Dist., No. C-84-733-L (D.N.H. 1988), *rev'd,* 875 F.2d 954 (1st Cir. 1989), *cert. denied,* 110 S. Ct. 519 (1989).
115. *Id.,* 875 F.2d 954 (1st Cir. 1989).
116. The Sixth Circuit Court of Appeals held that the Cincinnati Board of Education could provide home instruction for a child with severe disabilities as opposed to a more costly school program the parent requested. The eleven-year-old had severe psychomotor retardation, no self-help skills, functioned at a one-month level, and breathed through a tracheotomy tube, Thomas v. Cincinnati Bd. of Educ., 918 F.2d 618 (6th Cir. 1990).
117. The Supreme Court has ruled that under the eleventh amendment federal courts cannot enforce state law claims, Pennhurst State School and Hosp. v. Halderman, 465 U.S. 89 (1984). Prior to 1989 some federal courts used the IDEA, rather than state laws, to enforce higher state requirements for the disabled because the IDEA incorporated existing state standards. However, unless Congress specifically abrogates states' eleventh amendment immunity when enacting legislation, states cannot be sued under a federal law. In *Dellmuth v. Muth,* 491 U.S. 223 (1989), the Court held that states could not be sued under the IDEA because Congress did not unmistakably abrogate states' eleventh amendment immunity with the enactment of the law. Responding to this decision, in 1990 Congress specified in the IDEA that states are *not* immune from suit for violations of the Act, 20 U.S.C.A. § 1403 (1991). Thus, suits can be initiated under the IDEA, seeking enforcement of more stringent state standards regarding entitlements of children with disabilities.
118. *See* text with note 129, Chapter 3.
119. Board of Educ. of Cabell County v. Dienelt, 843 F.2d 813, 815 (4th Cir. 1988), quoting Hall v. Vance, 774 F.2d 629, 635 (4th Cir. 1985). *See also* Cordrey v. Euckert, 917 F.2d 1460 (6th Cir. 1990) (parents also must operate within the IDEA's procedural requirements; parents, with benefit of counsel, were found to have voluntarily relinquished their right to an appropriate IEP meeting when they rejected school officials' attempt to schedule the meeting).
120. A parent's right to tape-record meetings of the planning and placement team was found to be an aspect of meaningful parental involvement under the Act, E.H. v. Tirozzi, 735 F. Supp. 53 (D. Conn. 1990). Failure to follow precise, detailed technical requirements does not violate procedural rights of the parents and student if there has been full participation of the parents in the process, Doe v. Defendant I, 898 F.2d 1186 (6th Cir. 1990). Under the Rehabilitation Act, deaf parents were entitled to a sign language interpreter to enable them to participate in school-initiated conferences related to the child's education, Rothschild v. Grottenthaler, 907 F.2d 286 (2d Cir. 1990).

121. *See* text with note 129, Chapter 3.

122. Bonadonna v. Cooperman, 619 F. Supp. 401 (D.N.J. 1985).

123. Spielberg v. Henrico County Pub. Schools, 853 F.2d 256 (4th Cir. 1988), *cert. denied,* 489 U.S. 1016 (1989).

124. The Second Circuit Court of Appeals cited three possible exceptions speci-fied by Congress: "(1) it would be futile to use the due process procedures . . . ; (2) an agency has adopted a policy or pursued a practice of general applicability that is contrary to the law; (3) it is improbable that adequate relief can be obtained by pursuing administrative remedies (e.g., the hearing officer lacks the authority to grant the relief sought)," Mrs. W. v. Tirozzi, 832 F.2d 748, 756 (2d Cir. 1987). *See also* Kerr Center Parents Ass'n v. Charles, 897 F.2d 1463 (9th Cir. 1990); Christopher W. v. Portsmouth School Comm., 877 F.2d 1089 (1st Cir. 1989).

125. Doe v. Maher, 793 F.2d 1470 (9th Cir. 1986).

126. 20 U.S.C. § 1415(e)(3) (1988). *See* Stock v. Massachusetts Hosp. and School, 467 N.E.2d 448 (Mass. 1984), *cert. denied,* 474 U.S. 844 (1985) (graduation is a change in placement requiring the full procedural protections of the Act; under the requirement that a student remain in his or her current educational placement during review proceedings, special education services could not be discontinued if parents objected to this change in their child's status). *See also* Cronin v. Board of Educ. of East Ramapo Cent. School Dist., 689 F. Supp. 197 (S.D.N.Y. 1988).

127. *See* Honig v. Doe, 484 U.S. 305 (1988); text with note 172, *infra.*

128. 20 U.S.C.A. § 1412 (5) (1991).

129. Daniel R.R. v. State Bd. of Educ., 874 F.2d 1036, 1045 (5th Cir. 1989). *See also* Lachman v. Illinois State Bd. of Educ., 852 F.2d 290 (7th Cir. 1988), *cert. denied,* 488 U.S. 925 (1988).

130. Wilson v. Marana Unified School Dist. No. 6 of Pima County, 735 F.2d 1178 (9th Cir. 1984). *See also* Briggs v. Board of Educ. of State of Connecticut, 882 F.2d 688 (2d Cir. 1989) (a public school segregated program, rather than a mainstreamed private school program, was found to be appropriate because of the student's dual disabilities); Barnett v. Fairfax County School Bd., 721 F. Supp. 757 (E.D. Va. 1989), *aff'd,* 927 F.2d 146 (4th Cir. 1991) (school system that operated mainstreamed, small, resource-intensive programs for hearing-impaired students in centralized locations was not required to pro-vide students such programs in their neighborhood schools).

131. Devries by DeBlaay v. Fairfax County School Bd., 882 F.2d 876 (4th Cir 1989). *See also* A. W. v. Northwest R-1 School Dist., 813 F.2d 158 (8th Cir. 1987), *cert. denied,* 484 U.S. 847 (1987) (cost of placement of a severely retarded student in regular public school must be balanced against the benefit to the student); Board of Educ. v. Diamond, 808 F.2d 987 (3d Cir. 1986) (residential placement may be the least restrictive program depending on a student's disability); Mark A. v. Grant Wood Area Educ. Agency, 795 F.2d 52 (8th Cir. 1986), *cert. denied,* 480 U.S. 936 (1987) (upheld placement in a special public school class for students with disabilities as opposed to par-ents' request for a mainstreamed class in a private program).

132. Department of Educ., State of Hawaii v. Katherine D., 727 F.2d 809 (9th Cir. 1983), *cert. denied,* 471 U.S. 1117 (1985). *See* Evans v. District No. 17 of Douglas County, Nebraska, 841 F.2d 824 (8th Cir. 1988).

133. Roncker v. Walter, 700 F.2d 1058, 1063 (6th Cir. 1983), *cert. denied,* 464 U.S.

864 (1983). While favoring mainstreaming, the court stated that the cost of providing such a program is a legitimate consideration; "excessive spending on one handicapped child deprives other handicapped children," *id. See also* A.W. v. Northwest R-1 School Dist., 813 F.2d 158 (8th Cir. 1987).

134. Daniel R.R. v. State Bd. of Educ., 874 F.2d 1036 (5th Cir. 1989).

135. *See also* St. Louis Developmental Disabilities Treatment Center Parents' Ass'n v. Mallory, 767 F.2d 518 (8th Cir. 1985) (Missouri's system of separate schools for the severely disabled does not *per se* violate the Act; whether a less restrictive appropriate placement is available to children who might benefit from it was not addressed).

136. *See, e.g.,* Board of Educ. v. Diamond, 808 F.2d 987 (3d Cir. 1986); Parks v. Pavkovic, 753 F.2d 1397 (7th Cir. 1985), *cert. denied,* 473 U.S. 906 (1985); Abrahamson v. Hershman, 701 F.2d 223 (1st Cir. 1983). *See also* Taylor v. Honig, 910 F.2d 627 (9th Cir. 1990) (court issued a preliminary injunction ordering the placement of a student in a residential facility operating as a school and psychiatric hospital; placement was primarily for educational purposes); Clovis Unified School Dist. v. California Office of Admin. Hearings, 903 F.2d 635 (9th Cir. 1990) (school district was not obligated to pay for a child's care at a psychiatric hospital because the hospitalization was for medical and psychiatric reasons).

137. Abrahamson, *id. But see* Tice v. Botetourt County School Bd., 908 F.2d 1200 (4th Cir. 1990) (only costs for educational services and counseling were recoverable while hospitalized); Metropolitan Gov't of Nashville v. Tennessee Dep't of Educ., 771 S.W.2d 427 (Tenn. Ct. App. 1989) (placement of a student with learning and social difficulties in a private psychiatric facility was for medical and not educational purposes and therefore not subject to public funding).

138. Prior to 1985, most federal courts agreed that absent unusual circumstances the IDEA barred the recovery of tuition costs. *See* Department of Educ., State of Hawaii v. Katherine D., 727 F.2d 809 (9th Cir. 1983), *cert. denied,* 471 U.S. 1117 (1985); Zvi D. v. Ambach, 694 F.2d 904 (2d Cir. 1982).

139. 471 U.S. 359 (1985).

140. *Id. See also* Doe v. Defendant I, 898 F.2d 1186 (6th Cir. 1990); Roland M. v Concord School Comm., 910 F.2d 983 (1st Cir. 1990), *cert. denied,* 111 S. Ct. 1122 (1991); Tice v. Botetourt County School Bd., 908 F.2d 1200 (4th Cir. 1990); Gregory K. v. Longview School Dist., 811 F.2d 1307 (9th Cir. 1987); Matta v. Board of Educ., Indian Hill Exempted Village Schools, 731 F. Supp. 253 (S.D. Ohio 1990).

141. *See, e.g.,* Tucker v. Bay Shore Union Free School Dist., 873 F.2d 563 (2d Cir. 1989); Antkowiak v. Ambach 838 F.2d 635 (2d Cir. 1988), *cert. denied,* 488 U.S. 850 (1988); Schimmel v. Spillane, 819 F.2d 477 (4th Cir. 1987).

142. *See, e.g.,* Drew P. v. Clarke County School Dist., 877 F.2d 927 (11th Cir. 1989), *cert. denied,* 110 S. Ct. 1510 (1990); Board of Educ. of Cabell County v. Dienelt, 843 F.2d 813 (4th Cir. 1988); Jefferson County Bd. of Educ. v. Breen, 853 F.2d 853 (11th Cir. 1988); Hudson v. Wilson, 828 F.2d 1059 (4th Cir. 1987).

143. *See, e.g.,* Leonard v. McKenzie, 869 F.2d 1558 (D.C. Cir. 1989); Cain v. Yukon Pub. Schools, 775 F.2d 15 (10th Cir. 1985); Matta v. Board of Educ. Indian Hill Exempted Village Schools, 731 F. Supp. 253 (S.D. Ohio 1990).

144. Cain, *id.*
145. Geis v. Board of Educ. of Parsippany–Troy Hills, 774 F.2d 575 (3d Cir. 1985). *See also* Board of Educ. v. Diamond, 808 F.2d 987 (3d Cir. 1986).
146. David D. v. Dartmouth School Comm., 775 F.2d 411, 423 (1st Cir. 1985), *cert. denied,* 475 U.S. 1140 (1986).
147. 20 U.S.C.A, § 1401(17) (1991).
148. *See* Polk v. Central Susquehanna Intermediate Unit 16, 853 F.2d 171 (3d Cir. 1988), *cert. denied,* 488 U.S. 1030 (1989) (for students with severe physical disabilities, physical therapy may be a prerequisite to classroom instruction or may constitute the major portion of a program).
149. *See, e.g.,* Macomb County Intermediate School Dist. v. Joshua S., 715 F. Supp. 824 (E.D. Mich. 1989) (transportation of a medically fragile student is required, but not if the attention of a physician is needed during transport).
150. Hurry v. Jones, 734 F.2d 879 (1st Cir. 1984). *See also* Alamo Heights Indep. School Dist. v. State Bd. of Educ., 790 F.2d 1153 (5th Cir. 1986) (special circumstances necessitated transporting a child with disabilities one mile outside the district boundary; the only available custodian to care for the child while his mother worked lived outside the school district).
151. *See, e.g.,* Birmingham and Lamphere School Dists. v. Superintendent of Pub. Instruction, State of Michigan, 328 N.W.2d 59 (Mich. Ct. App. 1982). *But see* Rettig v. Kent City School Dist., 788 F.2d 328 (6th Cir. 1986), *cert. denied,* 478 U.S. 1005 (1986) (extracurricular activities are not required if a student does not receive a significant educational benefit from participation).
152. Espino v. Besteiro, 520 F. Supp. 905 (S.D. Tex. 1981).
153. *See* Seals v. Loftis, 614 F. Supp. 302 (E.D. Tenn. 1985) (parents could not be required to reduce their available lifetime insurance benefits to cover neurological and psychological examinations requested by the school system during the evaluation process).
154. 468 U.S. 883 (1984).
155. *Id.* at 891.
156. *Id.* at 892, citing 34 C.F.R. § 300.13(b) (1990). *See* Macomb County Intermediate School Dist. v. Joshua S., 715 F. Supp. 824 (E.D. Mich. 1989); Metropolitan Gov't of Nashville and Davidson County v. Tennessee Dep't of Educ., 771 S.W.2d 427 (Tenn. Ct. App. 1989).
157. *See also* Department of Educ., State of Hawaii v. Katherine D., 727 F.2d 809 (9th Cir. 1984), *cert. denied,* 471 U.S. 1117 (1985) (periodic replacement of a tracheostomy tube, which could be performed by a nurse or trained layperson, is a related service).
158. Detsel v. Board of Educ. of the Auburn Enlarged City School Dist., 820 F.2d 587 (2d Cir. 1987), *cert. denied,* 484 U.S. 981 (1987). The appellate court, however, later ruled that the student was entitled to Medicaid payment for private-duty nursing services during the school day, Detsel v. Sullivan, 895 F.2d 58 (2d Cir. 1990).
159. Bevin H. v. Wright, 666 F. Supp. 71 (W.D. Pa. 1987).
160. *See also* B.G. v. Cranford Bd. of Educ., 882 F.2d 510 (3d Cir. 1989); A.A. v. Cooperman, 526 A.2d 1103 (N.J. Super. Ct. App. Div. 1987).
161. McNair v. Oak Hills Local School Dist., 872 F.2d 153 (6th Cir. 1989).
162. *See, e.g.,* Papacoda v. State of Connecticut, 528 F. Supp. 68 (D. Conn. 1981); In the Matter of the "A" Family, 602 P.2d 157 (Mont. 1979).

163. T. G. v. Board of Educ. of Piscataway, 738 F.2d 420 (3d Cir.1984), *cert. denied,* 469 U.S. 1086 (1984). *See also* Doe v. Anrig, 651 F. Supp. 424 (D. Mass. 1987) (related services do not have to be primarily for educational purposes; they must simply assist the child to benefit from special education).

164. Darlene L. v. Illinois State Bd. of Educ., 568 F. Supp. 1340 (N.D. Ill. 1983). *See also* McKenzie v. Jefferson, 566 F. Supp. 404 (D.D.C. 1983).

165. Max M. v. Thompson, 592 F. Supp. 1437 (N.D. Ill. 1984) (reimbursement of physicians' fees was restricted to the cost that would be charged by qualified health care professionals). *See also* Max M. v. Illinois State Bd. of Educ., 629 F. Supp. 1504 (N.D. Ill. 1986) (court ordered full reimbursement of the physician-provided care since the school district did not offer proof that the services could be provided for less).

166. Cordrey v. Euckert, 917 F.2d 1460 (6th Cir. 1990); Johnson v. Independent School Dist. No. 4 of Bixby, Tulsa County, Oklahoma, 921 F.2d 1022 (10th Cir. 1990), *cert. denied,* 111 S. Ct. 1685 (1991); Alamo Heights Indep. School Dist. v. State Bd. of Educ., 790 F.2d 1153 (5th Cir. 1986); Yaris v. Special School Dist. of St. Louis, 728 F.2d 1055 (8th Cir. 1984); Crawford v. Pittman, 708 F.2d 1028 (5th Cir. 1983); Georgia Ass'n of Retarded Citizens v. McDaniel, 716 F.2d 1565 (11th Cir. 1983), *cert. denied,* 469 U.S. 1228 (1985); Battle v. Commonwealth of Pennsylvania, 629 F.2d 269 (3d Cir. 1980), *cert. denied,* 452 U.S. 968 (1981).

167. *See* B. G. v. Cranford Bd. of Educ., 882 F.2d 510 (3d Cir. 1989) (although the student's academic progress met the minimum federal standards under *Rowley,* a year-round residential placement was required to meet the state's requirement of a program that assures a student the fullest opportunity to develop).

168. Battle v. Commonwealth of Pennsylvania, 629 F.2d 269 (3d Cir. 1980), *cert. denied,* 452 U.S. 968 (1981).

169. Georgia Ass'n of Retarded Citizens v. McDaniel, 716 F.2d 1565 (11th Cir. 1983), *cert. denied,* 469 U.S. 1228 (1985).

170. *Id.,* Georgia Ass'n of Retarded Citizens, 716 F.2d at 1576.

171. The Tenth Circuit Court of Appeals held that this analysis must include not only retrospective data related to regression but also predictive data, Johnson v. Independent School Dist. No. 4 of Bixby, Tulsa County, Oklahoma, 921 F.2d 1022 (10th Cir. 1990), *cert. denied,* 111 S. Ct. 1685 (1991).

172. Cordrey v. Euckert, 917 F.2d 1460 (6th Cir. 1990).

173. Doe by Gonzales v. Maher, 793 F.2d 1470 (9th Cir. 1986), *aff'd as modified sub nom.* Honig v. Doe, 484 U.S. 305 (1988); School Bd. of the County of Prince William, Virginia v. Malone, 762 F.2d 1210 (4th Cir. 1985); Kaelin v. Grubbs, 682 F.2d 595 (6th Cir. 1982); S-1 v. Turlington, 635 F.2d 342 (5th Cir. 1981), *cert. denied,* 454 U.S. 1030 (1981).

174. 484 U.S. 305 (1988).

175. *See* cases listed in note 169, *supra.*

176. *See, e.g.,* Doe by Gonzales v. Maher, 793 F.2d 1470 (9th Cir. 1986), *aff'd as modified sub nom.* Honig v. Doe, 484 U.S. 305 (1988).

177. Kaelin v. Grubbs, 682 F.2d 595 (6th Cir. 1982); S-l v. Turlington, 635 F.2d 342 (5th Cir. 1981), *cert. denied,* 454 U.S. 1030 (1981). *See also* Board of Trustees Pascagoula Mun. Separate School Dist. v. Doe, 508 So. 2d 1081 (Miss. 1987).

178. *See* Gail Sorenson, ''Special Education Discipline in the 1990s,'' *Education*

Law Reporter, vol. 62 (1990), pp. 387–398; Jordan Dey, "Expelled Disabled Students Must Be Served, ED Says," *Education Daily,* February 20, 1991, p. 3.

179. The stance of the Office of Special Education and Rehabilitative Services regarding termination of services under IDEA provides students greater protection than provided under Section 504. The Office of Civil Rights has stated that under Section 504 services can be terminated if the misconduct is not related to the student's disability. OCR Senior Staff Memorandum, 3 EHLR (CRR) 307:05 (1988).

180. Thomas, *Legal Issues in Special Education,* p. 44. Any change in placement, however, must be preceded by due process. An Ohio school district violated due process procedures by unilaterally moving two students from a classroom to home instruction for disciplinary reasons, Lamont X. v. Quisenberry, 606 F. Supp. 809 (S.D. Ohio 1984).

181. The Supreme Court also noted the discretion of school officials to use these techniques, Honig v. Doe, 484 U.S. 305 (1988).

182. Cole v. Greenfield-Cent. Community Schools, 657 F. Supp. 56 (S.D. Ind. 1986).

183. Wise v. Pea Ridge School Dist., 855 F.2d 560 (8th Cir. 1988).

184. Dickens v. Johnson County Bd. of Educ., 661 F. Supp. 155 (E.D. Tenn. 1987).

185. Hayes v. Unified School Dist. No. 377, 877 F.2d 809 (10th Cir. 1989).

186. School Comm. of Town of Burlington, Massachusetts v. Department of Educ. of Massachusetts, 471 U.S. 359 (1985).

187. *See, e.g.,* Lester H. v. Gilhool, 916 F.2d 865 (3d Cir. 1990); Burr. v. Sobol, 888 F.2d 258 (2d Cir. 1989), *cert. denied,* 110 S. Ct. 1298 (1990); Mrs. C. v. Wheaton, 916 F.2d 69 (2d Cir. 1990); Jefferson County Bd. of Educ. v. Breen, 853 F.2d 853 (11th Cir. 1988); Board of Educ. of Strongsville City School Dist. v. Theado, 566 N.E.2d 667 (Ohio 1991).

188. Miener v. Missouri, 800 F.2d 749 (8th Cir. 1986).

189. 20 U.S.C.A. § 1415 (1991).

190. 468 U.S. 992 (1984).

191. *See* Moore v. District of Columbia, 907 F.2d 165 (D.C. Cir. 1990), *cert. denied,* 111 S. Ct. 556 (1990); McSomebodies v. Burlingame Elementary School Dist., 886 F.2d 1558 (9th Cir. 1989); Mitten v. Muscogee County School Dist., 877 F.2d 932 (11th Cir. 1989), *cert. denied,* 110 S. Ct. 1117 (1990); Duane M. v. Orleans Parish School Bd., 861 F.2d 115 (5th Cir. 1988); Eggers v. Bullitt County School Dist., 854 F.2d 892 (6th Cir. 1988). *See also* Shelly C. v. Venus Indep. School Dist., 878 F.2d 862 (5th Cir. 1989), *cert. denied,* 110 S. Ct. 729 (1990) (attorneys' fees are available even if dispute is settled before an administrative hearing).

192. 483 F.2d 791 (9th Cir. 1973), *rev'd,* 414 U.S. 563 (1974).

193. *Id.,* 483 F.2d at 798.

194. Lau, 414 U.S. at 566.

195. *Id.* Following the Supreme Court's decision in Regents of the Univ. of California v. Bakke, 438 U.S. 265 (1978), substantial doubt has been raised regarding the viability of Title VI as a basis to challenge the adequacy of programs for language-deficient students. While the Supreme Court in *Bakke* did not specifically overrule *Lau,* it appears that Title VI, like the equal

protection clause, is violated only with evidence of *intentional* discrimination. Several lower counts have rejected claims of alleged Title VI violations in the absence of proof of purposeful discrimination in structuring bilingual education programs, Gomez v. Illinois State Bd. of Educ., 811 F.2d 1030 (7th Cir. 1987); Castaneda v. Pickard, 648 F.2d 989 (5th Cir. 1981); Keyes v. School Dist. No. 1, Denver, Colo., 576 F. Supp. 1503 (D. Colo. 1983). *But see* Guardians Ass'n v. Civil Service Comm'n of the City of New York, 463 U.S. 582 (1983) (discriminatory intent is not required for *equitable* relief).

196. United States v. Texas, 342 F. Supp. 24 (E.D. Tex. 1971), *aff'd,* 466 F.2d 518 (5th Cir. 1972).
197. Arvizu v. Waco Indep. School Dist., 373 F. Supp. 1264 (W.D. Tex. 1973).
198. *See, e.g.,* Otero v. Mesa County School Dist. No. 51, 408 F. Supp. 162 (D. Colo. 1975)
199. *See, e.g.,* Rios v. Read, 73 F.R.D. 589 (E.D.N.Y. 1977).
200. Morales v. Shannon, 516 F.2d 411, 414-415 (5th Cir. 1975), *cert. denied,* 423 U.S. 1034 (1975).
201. Guadalupe Org., Inc. v. Tempe Elementary School Dist. No. 3, 587 F.2d 1022 (9th Cir. 1978). *See also* Serna v. Portales Mun. Schools, 351 F. Supp. 1279 (D.N.M. 1972), *aff'd,* 499 F.2d 1147 (10th Cir. 1974).
202. 20 U.S.C. § 1703(f) (1988).
203. Castaneda v. Pickard, 648 F.2d 989, 1009 (5th Cir. 1981) (bilingual programs found to be nondiscriminatory); Castaneda II, 781 F.2d 456 (5th Cir. 1986) (affirmed district court's decision on remand that ability grouping did not discriminate against Mexican-American students).
204. *Id.,* 648 F.2d at 1009-1010.
205. *See* Castaneda, *id.*; Keyes v. School Dist. No. 1, Denver, Colo., 576 F. Supp. 1503 (D. Colo. 1983).
206. Keyes, *id.* at 1520. *See also* Teresa P. v. Berkeley Unified School Dist., 724 F. Supp. 698 (N.D. Cal. 1989) (school system had taken appropriate action to address language barriers).
207. Gomez v. Illinois State Bd. of Educ., 811 F.2d 1030, 1043 (7th Cir. 1987).
208. 20 U.S.C. § 880b *et seq.* (1988).
209. 20 U.S.C. § 880b-1(a)(4)(A) (1988).
210. Ind. Code Ann. § 20-10.1-5.5-1 (1984).
211. Although most legal activity has focused on LEP students, a Michigan federal court addressed the special needs of students who speak various English dialects. The court ruled that school districts must offer students who speak "black English" assistance in learning to use standard English. The students' rights under the EEOA were held to have been violated because the education agencies failed to take appropriate action to overcome the students' language deficiencies, Martin Luther King Junior Elementary School Children v. Ann Arbor School Dist. Bd., 473 F. Supp. 1371 (E.D. Mich. 1979).

6
Student Discipline

One of the most persistent and troublesome problems confronting educators is student misconduct. With the increased incidence of drug and alcohol abuse among teenagers, greater public attention has been focused on school disciplinary problems, and the efficacy of various discipline techniques has evoked volatile debate.[1] The range of strategies employed by educators to address these concerns is examined in this chapter from a legal perspective. The analysis focuses on the development of conduct regulations, the imposition of sanctions for noncompliance, and the procedures required in the administration of pupil punishments.

The law clearly authorizes the state and its agencies to establish and enforce reasonable conduct codes to protect the rights of students and school districts and to ensure school environments conducive to learning. Historically, courts exercised limited review of student disciplinary regulations, and pupils were seldom successful in challenging policies governing their behavior. In 1923 the Arkansas Supreme Court upheld the expulsion of a student who wore talcum powder on her face in violation of a school rule forbidding pupils to wear transparent hosiery, low-necked dresses, face paint, or cosmetics.[2] In another early case, the Michigan Supreme Court endorsed the suspension of a female high school student for smoking and riding in a car with a young man.[3] In these and similar cases, courts were reluctant to interfere with the judgment of school officials because public education was considered to be a privilege bestowed by the state.

While there has been a quantum leap from the posture espoused during the first third of the twentieth century to the active protection of students' rights characterized by the litigation of the late 1960s and early 1970s,[4] judicial developments have not eroded educators' rights or their responsibilities.[5] Reasonable disciplinary regulations, even those impairing students' protected liberties, have been upheld if justified by a legitimate educational interest. Educators have not only the authority but also the *duty* to maintain discipline in public schools. While rules made at any level cannot conflict with higher authorities (e.g., constitutional and statutory provisions), building administrators and teachers retain considerable latitude in establishing and enforcing conduct codes that are necessary for instructional activities to take place. In the subsequent sections of this chapter, educators' prerogatives and students' rights are explored in connection with conduct regulations, expulsions and suspensions, disciplinary transfers, corporal punishment, academic sanctions, search and seizure, and remedies for unlawful disciplinary actions.

CONDUCT REGULATIONS

School boards are granted considerable latitude in establishing and interpreting their own disciplinary rules and regulations. The Supreme Court has held that the interpretation of a school regulation resides with the body that adopted it and is charged with its enforcement.[6] Disciplinary policies, however, have been struck down if unconstitutionally vague. Policies prohibiting "improper conduct" and behavior "inimical to the best interests of the school" have been invalidated because they have not specified the precise nature of the impermissible conduct.[7] A vague school district discipline policy prohibiting the consumption of alcohol prior to the school day or a school event was found to be overly broad in an Arkansas case; it could be arbitrarily interpreted as minutes, hours, or even days before attending a school activity.[8] While policies should be precise, courts have recognized that disciplinary regulations do not have to satisfy the stringent criteria or level of specificity required in criminal statutes.[9]

In addition to reviewing the validity of the conduct regulation upon which a specific punishment is based, courts evaluate the nature and extent of the penalty imposed in relation to the gravity of the offense. In deciding whether a given punishment is appropriate, courts also consider the age, gender, mental condition, and past behavior of the student. Punishments such as the denial of privileges, suspension, expulsion, corporal punishment, and detention after school have been judicially sanctioned. Any of these punishments, however, could be considered unreasonable under a specific set of circumstances. Consequently, courts study each unique factual situation; they do not evaluate the validity of student punishments in the abstract.

Litigation challenging disciplinary practices often has focused on the procedures followed in administering punishments, rather than on the substance of disciplinary rules or the nature of the sanctions imposed. Implicit in all judicial declarations regarding school discipline is the notion that severe penalties require more formal procedures while minor punishments necessitate only minimal due process. Nonetheless, any disciplinary action should be accompanied by some procedure to ensure the rudiments of fundamental fairness and to prevent mistakes in the disciplinary process. The Fifth Circuit Court of Appeals has recognized that "the quantum and quality of procedural due process to be afforded a student varies with the seriousness of the punishment to be imposed."[10]

Courts have prohibited school authorities from punishing students because of the acts of others, such as their parents. For example, the Fifth Circuit Court of Appeals held that two children could not be suspended indefinitely from school simply because their mother struck the assistant principal.[11] In reaching its conclusion, the appellate court noted that a fundamental principle of justice is that personal guilt must be present before an individual can be punished. Similarly, an Indiana federal district court held that a student could not be suspended for the parent's failure to pay textbook fees.[12]

The judiciary also has recognized that punishments imposed for student conduct *off school grounds* must be supported by evidence that the student behavior outside of school has a detrimental impact on other pupils, teachers, or school activities. In an early case, the Connecticut Supreme Court held that student conduct outside school hours and off school property could be regulated by school officials if such conduct affected the management of the school.[13] Courts have upheld sanctions imposed on students for engaging in assault or criminal acts off school grounds,[14] attending a party where alcohol was served,[15] engaging in the gang rape of a female student at the home of a student,[16] stealing automobile parts,[17] and making an offensive remark about a teacher to a group of students at a shopping center.[18] Courts, however, have prohibited school authorities from punishing students for misbehavior off school grounds if pupils had not been informed that such conduct would result in sanctions[19] or if the misbehavior had no direct relationship to the welfare of the school.[20]

School personnel should be careful not to place *unnecessary* constraints on student behavior. In developing disciplinary policies, all possible means of achieving the desired outcomes should be explored, and means that are least restrictive of students' personal freedoms should be selected. Once it is ascertained that a certain conduct regulation is necessary, the rule should be clearly written so that it is not open to multiple interpretations. Each regulation should include the rationale for enacting the rule as well as penalties for infractions. It may be advisable to require students to sign a form indicating that they have read the conduct regulations. With such documentation, pupils would be unable to plead ignorance of the rules as a defense for their misconduct.

In general, educators would be wise to adhere to the following guidelines:

- Any conduct regulation adopted should be necessary in order to carry out the school's educational mission; rules should not be designed merely to satisfy the preferences of school board members, administrators, or teachers.

- The rules should be publicized to students and their parents.
- The rules should be specific and clearly stated so that students know what behaviors are expected and what behaviors are prohibited.
- The regulations should not impair constitutionally protected rights unless there is an overriding public interest, such as a threat to the safety of other students.
- A rule should not be "ex post facto"; it should not be adopted to prevent a specific activity that school officials know is being planned or has already occurred.
- The regulations should be consistently enforced and uniformly applied to all students without discrimination.
- Punishments should be appropriate to the offense, taking into consideration the child's age, sex, mental condition, and past behavior.
- Some procedural safeguards should accompany the administration of all punishments; the formality of the procedures should be in accord with the severity of the punishment.

In designing and enforcing pupil conduct codes, it is important that school personnel bear in mind the distinction between students' substantive and procedural rights. If a disciplinary regulation or the administration of punishment violates substantive rights (e.g., restricts protected speech), the regulation cannot be enforced nor the punishment imposed. If only procedural rights are impaired, however, the punishment eventually can be administered after the student has been provided an appropriate hearing.

EXPULSIONS AND SUSPENSIONS

Expulsions and suspensions are among the most widely used disciplinary measures. Courts uniformly have upheld educators' authority to use such measures as punishments, but due process is required to ensure that students are afforded fair and impartial treatment. This section focuses on disciplinary action in which students are removed from the instructional program; suspensions and expulsions from extracurricular activities are addressed in Chapter 4.

EXPULSIONS

State laws and/or school board regulations are usually quite specific regarding the grounds for expulsions, that is, the removal of students from school for a lengthy period of time (usually in excess of ten days). Such grounds are not limited to occurrences during school hours, but generally include infractions on school property immediately before or after school or at any time the school is being used for a school-related activity. Also, expulsions can result from infractions occurring en route to or from school or during school functions held off school premises. While specific grounds vary from state to state, the following Indiana law illustrates infractions that are typically considered legitimate grounds for expulsion, as long as the offense occurs while the student is under the school's jurisdiction:

- using or encouraging others to use violence, force, noise, coercion, or comparable conduct that interferes with school purposes;
- stealing or vandalizing valuable school or private property or repeatedly damaging or stealing school or private property of small value;
- causing or attempting to cause physical injury to a fellow student or school employee;
- possessing a weapon;
- knowingly possessing, using, or transmitting intoxicants of any kind (except for prescriptions from authorized physicians);
- repeatedly refusing to comply with reasonable directives of school personnel; and
- engaging in criminal activity or other behavior forbidden by state laws.[21]

State statutes specify limitations on the length of student expulsions. Generally, a student cannot be expelled beyond the end of the current academic year unless the expulsion takes place near the close of the term. A teacher or administrator may initiate expulsion proceedings, but usually only the school board itself can expel a pupil. Although the details of required procedures must be gleaned from state statutes and school board regulations, courts have held that students facing expulsion from school are guaranteed at least minimum due process under the fourteenth amendment. It is advisable to provide the following safeguards:

- Written notice of the charges, the intention to expel, and the place, time, and circumstances of the hearing, with sufficient time for a defense to be prepared[22]
- A full and fair hearing before an impartial adjudicator[23]
- The right to legal counsel or some other adult representation
- The opportunity to present witnesses or evidence
- The opportunity to cross-examine opposing witnesses[24]
- Some type of written record demonstrating that the decision was based on the evidence presented at the hearing

Procedural safeguards required, however, may vary depending on the circumstances of a particular situation. In a Mississippi case, a student and his parents claimed that prior to an expulsion hearing they should have been given a list of the witnesses and a summary of their testimony.[25] Although recognizing that these procedural protections should generally be afforded prior to a long-term expulsion, the Fifth Circuit Court of

Appeals held that they were not requisite in this case. The parents had been fully apprised of the charges, the facts supporting the charges, and the nature of the hearing. Consequently, the court concluded that the student suffered no material prejudice from the school board's failure to provide a list of witnesses; the witnesses provided no surprises or interference with the student's ability to present his case. In a later case involving expulsion for possession of drugs, the same court found no impairment of a student's rights when he was denied an opportunity to confront and rebut witnesses who accused him of selling drugs.[26] The names of student witnesses had been withheld to prevent retaliation against them. Similarly, the Sixth Circuit Court of Appeals noted that it is critical to protect the anonymity of students who "blow the whistle" on classmates involved in serious offenses such as drug dealing. Although the right to cross-examine witnesses did not constitute a denial of due process in this case, the court held that the superintendent's disclosure of evidence in the school board's closed deliberations that was not introduced during the open hearing violated the student's procedural rights.[27] Given this violation, the appellate court remanded the case to determine if the student was entitled to injunctive and compensatory relief.

State laws and school board regulations often provide students facing expulsion with more elaborate procedural safeguards than the constitutional protections noted above. Once such expulsion procedures are established, courts will require that they be followed.[28] In a Texas case, an expulsion decision was invalidated because the student was not given proper notice that his behavior would result in expulsion, and the applicable school policy was not followed in making the expulsion decision.[29] The student was expelled for possession of marijuana in his car (parked off school grounds), but the school regulation did not stipulate that such behavior off school property would constitute grounds for expulsion. Furthermore, the school district policy on expulsion specified that other means of correcting a student's misbehavior had to be employed before expulsion could be recommended. Since there was no evidence that any other disciplinary measures were used, the Texas civil appeals court ordered the student's reinstatement. More recently, a Louisiana appeals court ruled that a student's possession of marijuana *off* school property did not justify expulsion under a state law proscribing the possession of controlled substances *on* school property.[30]

Often, expulsions are challenged as excessive for certain offenses. Unless actions are arbitrary, capricious, or oppressive, school officials have broad discretionary powers in establishing disciplinary penalties. An Illinois student, expelled for the remainder of the school year for possession of caffeine pills, challenged the punishment as too harsh for a first offense.[31] The trial court agreed that the punishment far outweighed the crime, but the appellate court found the action reasonable and justified in light of the dangers posed by unauthorized drugs in the schools. Permanent expulsion of an Alabama student was upheld based on the student's extensive history of behavioral problems, which included threats to a teacher and a physical attack upon a classmate.[32] A Pennsylvania commonwealth court held that a ten-day suspension followed by a twenty-four-calendar-day expulsion for drinking on school property after a football game may have been "harsh" but was supported by substantial evidence.[33] Several months later, however, the same court affirmed a trial court's modification of a three-month expulsion of two students who had a couple of sips of a soft drink mixed with whiskey at a football game.[34] The punishment was found to be excessive for students with no prior history of discipline problems.

Several federal courts have addressed the special considerations involved in the expulsion of children with disabilities. In addition to constitutional procedural safeguards, the Individuals with Disabilities Education Act (IDEA) assures all children with disabilities a free appropriate public education in the least restrictive environment (see Chapter 5). While the IDEA is silent on the issue of expulsion, federal courts have regarded such action as a change in placement when children with disabilities are involved.[35] Prior to any change in a student's program, a special review committee must determine if the misconduct is related to the disability. If a relationship is found, expulsion is prohibited, and the appropriate action would be placement of the student in a more restrictive setting. Even if no connection is found between misbehavior and disability, it appears that all educational services cannot be terminated.[36]

SUSPENSIONS

Suspensions are frequently used to punish students for violating school rules and standards of behavior when the infractions are not of sufficient magnitude to warrant expulsion. Suspensions include the short-term denial of school attendance as well as the denial of participation in regular courses and activities (in-school suspension). Most legal controversies have focused on out-of-school suspensions, but it is advisable to apply the same legal principles to any disciplinary action that separates the student from the regular instructional program even for a short period of time.

In contrast to expulsions, historically state laws and judicial decisions differed widely in identifying and interpreting procedural safeguards for suspensions. In 1975, however, the Supreme Court provided substantial clarification regarding the constitutional rights of students confronting short-term suspensions. The Court majority in *Goss v. Lopez* held that minimum due process must be provided before a student is suspended for even a brief period of time.[37] Recognizing that a student's state-created property right to an education is protected by the fourteenth amendment, the Court ruled that such a right cannot be impaired unless the student is afforded notice of the charges and an opportunity to refute them. The

Supreme Court also emphasized that suspensions implicate students' constitutionally protected liberty interests because of the potentially damaging effects that the disciplinary process can have on a student's reputation and permanent record:

> School authorities here suspended appellees from school for periods of up to ten days based on charges of misconduct. If sustained and recorded, those charges could seriously damage the students' standing with their fellow pupils and their teachers as well as interfere with later opportunities for higher education and employment.[38]

The *Goss* majority strongly suggested that its holding applied to *all* short-term suspensions, including those of only one class period. Consequently, many school boards have instituted policies that require informal procedures for every brief suspension and more formal procedures for longer suspensions. In the absence of greater specificity in state statutes or administrative regulations, students have a constitutional right to the following protections prior to suspension:

- Oral or written notification of the nature of the violation and the intended punishment
- An opportunity to refute the charges before an objective decisionmaker (such a discussion may immediately follow the alleged rule infraction)
- An explanation of the evidence upon which the disciplinarian is relying

The requirement of an impartial decisionmaker does not imply that an administrator or teacher who is familiar with the facts cannot serve in this capacity. The decisionmaker simply must judge the situation fairly and on the basis of valid evidence.

The Supreme Court's *Goss* decision established the rudimentary procedural requirements for short-term suspensions, but students continue to seek an expansion of their procedural rights. The Supreme Court specifically noted that such formal procedures as the right to secure counsel, to confront and cross-examine witnesses, and to call witnesses were not constitutionally required. The Court reiterated this stance in a later case by noting that a two-day suspension "does not rise to the level of a penal sanction calling for the full panoply of procedural due process protections applicable to a criminal prosecution."[39] Decisions by lower state and federal courts indicate a reluctance to impose these additional requirements unless mandated by state law. In a Maine case, a student claimed a violation of procedural due process because the school administrator denied him permission to leave during questioning and failed to advise him of his right to remain silent or to have his parents present during the interrogation.[40] The court rejected all claims, noting that there was no legal authority to substantiate any of the asserted rights. The court reasoned that to rule otherwise would, in fact, contradict the informal procedures outlined in *Goss* allowing for immediate questioning and disciplinary action. Also relying on *Goss*, the Tenth Circuit Court of Appeals held that the removal of a student from class for twenty minutes for questioning did not constitute the denial of a property right to an education without due process.[41]

Although the Supreme Court in *Goss* recognized the possibility of "unusual situations" that would require more formal procedures than those outlined, little guidance was given as to what these circumstances might be. The only suggestion offered in *Goss* was that a disciplinarian should adopt more extensive procedures in instances involving factual disputes "and arguments about cause and effect."[42] Courts have declined to expand on this brief listing. A student's contention that drug charges constituted such an "unusual situation" because of their stigmatizing affect on his reputation was rejected by the Sixth Circuit Court of Appeals. The court did not believe that an eighth-grade student suspended for ten days for possessing a substance that resembled an illegal drug is "forever faced with a tarnished reputation and restricted employment opportunities."[43] More extensive procedures also were found unnecessary in a ten-day academic suspension, coupled with a sixty-day athletic suspension, imposed on a high school senior for smoking marijuana and drinking beer at the school radio station during evening hours.[44] Although the student argued that greater safeguards were required because of the significant adverse effect of the suspension on his chances for a college football career, the court concluded that such a loss did not necessitate additional procedures or support a claim for a separate disciplinary process for athletes.

It has been argued that suspensions involving loss of course credit or occurring during exam periods might require greater due process than outlined in *Goss*. The Fifth Circuit Court of Appeals, however, did not find persuasive the argument that the loss incurred for a ten-day suspension during final examinations required more than a mere give-and-take discussion between the principal and the student. In refusing to require more formal proceedings, the court noted that *Goss* makes no distinction as to when a short-term suspension occurs, and a contrary ruling would "significantly undermine, if not nullify, its definitive holding."[45] Similarly, the Seventh Circuit Court of Appeals rejected a student's claim that additional procedures were required because a suspension occurred at the end of the school year and precluded the student from taking his final exams and graduating.[46]

Suspensions, however, may require additional procedural protections under state laws. For example, the Ohio statute, earlier found to be constitutionally defective in *Goss*, now requires that prior to suspension each student must be provided written notice of the intent to suspend and the reasons for the intended suspension.[47] Pennsylvania law also mandates written notification to parents prior to the informal hearing.[48] A Pennsylvania commonwealth court declared that a seven-day suspension violated a student's due process rights because the parents received only oral notification of the reasons for suspension.[49]

In-school suspensions or isolation may be equivalent to an out-of-school suspension, thereby necessitating minimal due process procedures. A Mississippi federal district court noted that whether procedural due process is required is dependent upon the extent to which the student is deprived of instruction or the opportunity to learn.[50] The physical presence of a student at school does not conclusively relieve school officials of their duty to provide due process for disciplinary measures that exclude a student from the learning process. A Tennessee federal district court found that a student's placement in a classroom "time-out box" did not require due process because he continued to work on class assignments and could hear and see the teacher from the confined area.[51] The court emphasized that teachers must be free to administer minor forms of classroom discipline such as time out, denial of privileges, and special assignments.

Courts have continued to resist attempts to elaborate or formalize the minimal due process requirements outlined in *Goss* for short-term suspensions. As the Supreme Court noted, "further formalizing the suspension process and escalating its formality and adversary nature may not only make it too costly as a regular discipline tool but also destroy its effectiveness as part of the teaching process."[52]

DISCIPLINARY TRANSFERS

Closely related to suspensions are involuntary student transfers for disciplinary reasons. Legal challenges to the use of disciplinary transfers primarily have addressed the adequacy of the procedures followed. Recognizing that students do not have an inherent right to attend a given school, courts nonetheless have held that pupils facing involuntary reassignment are entitled to a hearing if such transfers are occasioned by alleged misbehavior.

For example, a New Jersey superior court ruled that a hearing was required before a student could be assigned to home instruction because of misconduct occurring off school premises after school hours.[53] The court noted that school officials had the authority to suspend the student and place him in homebound instruction, if it were determined at a proper hearing that he was dangerous to himself or others. The court declared, however, that the student could not be denied the right to attend school without first being given an opportunity to present a full defense regarding the incident precipitating the disciplinary action. Similarly, a New York court held that a student could not be assigned to homebound instruction for disruptive behavior and truancy without procedural due process.[54] The court rejected the assertion that the student was merely being afforded alternative education, and equated the assignment to homebound instruction with a suspension from school.

Courts also have held that disciplinary transfers to special schools or programs necessitate some type of procedural safeguards to ensure that the students are not being relegated to inferior programs. The judiciary has required due process prior to reassigning students to a school for habitual truants or to a program for pupils with behavior problems.[55] Transfer policies allowing the receiving program or school to refuse to admit the child also have been disallowed.[56]

A Pennsylvania federal district court ruled that "lateral transfers" for disciplinary reasons affected personal interests of sufficient magnitude to require procedural due process. Even though such transfers involved comparable schools, the court reasoned that a disciplinary transfer carried with it a stigma, and thus implicated a protected liberty right. Noting that a transfer of a student "during a school year from a familiar school to a strange and possibly more distant school would be a terrifying experience for many children of normal sensibilities," the court concluded that such transfers were more drastic punishments than suspensions, and thus necessitated due process.[57] As to the nature of the procedures required, the court held that the student and parents must be given notice of the proposed transfer and that a prompt informal hearing before the school principal must be provided. The court stipulated that if parents were still dissatisfied with the arrangement after the informal meeting, they had the right to contest the transfer recommendation at a more formal hearing, with the option of being represented by legal counsel.

CORPORAL PUNISHMENT

Corporal punishment in American public schools has evoked litigation for several decades, and historically it has been the most frequently challenged student punishment. Many states permit educators to administer corporal punishment, but a growing number have banned the practice either by law or state regulation. The total number prohibiting the practice grew from one in 1971 to twenty-one in 1991.[58] Generally, where state law permits corporal punishment, courts have upheld its reasonable application and have placed the burden on the aggrieved students to prove otherwise. In evaluating the reasonableness of a teacher's actions in a given situation, courts have assessed the child's age, maturity, and past behavior; the nature of the offense; the instrument used; any evidence of lasting harm to the child; and the motivation of the person inflicting the punishment.[59]

CONSTITUTIONAL ISSUES

In 1977 the Supreme Court addressed the constitutionality of corporal punishment that resulted in the severe injury of two students. The Supreme Court held in *Ingraham v. Wright* that the use of corporal punishment in public schools does not violate the eighth amendment or fourteenth amendment procedural due process guarantees.[60] While recognizing that corporal punishment implicates students' constitutionally protected liberty interests, the Court emphasized that state remedies are available, such as assault and battery suits, if students are excessively or arbitrarily punished by school personnel. In essence, the Court majority concluded that cases dealing with corporal punishment should be handled by state courts under provisions of state laws. The majority distinguished corporal punishment from a suspension by noting that the denial of school attendance is a more severe penalty that deprives students of a property right and, thus, necessitates procedural safeguards. Furthermore, the majority reasoned that the purpose of corporal punishment would be diluted if elaborate procedures had to be followed prior to its use.[61]

The Supreme Court's ruling in *Ingraham,* however, does not foreclose a successful constitutional challenge to the use of unreasonable corporal punishment. Several federal appellate courts have held that students' substantive due process right to be free of brutal and harmful state intrusions into realms of personal privacy and bodily security might be impaired by the use of excessive corporal punishment.[62] The Fourth Circuit Court of Appeals concluded that while *Ingraham* bars federal litigation on procedural due process issues, excessive or cruel corporal punishment may violate students' substantive due process rights. According to the appellate court, the standard for determining if such a violation has occurred is "whether the force applied caused injury so severe, was so disproportionate to the need presented, and was so inspired by malice or sadism rather than a merely careless or unwise excess of zeal that it amounted to a brutal and inhumane abuse of official power literally shocking to the conscience."[63] The Eighth Circuit Court of Appeals assessed a substantive due process claim by evaluating: "(1) the need for the application of corporal punishment; (2) the relationship between the need and the amount of punishment administered; (3) the extent of injury inflicted; and (4) whether the punishment was administered in a good faith effort to maintain discipline or maliciously and sadistically for the very purpose of causing harm."[64]

Courts have found the threshold for recovery for the violation of a student's substantive due process rights to be high. Minor pain, embarrassment, and hurt feelings do not rise to this level; actions must literally be "shocking to the conscience."[65] Actions courts have found *not* to rise to this level include the paddling of a nine-year-old girl seven times within thirty minutes,[66] two licks with a paddle that resulted in bruises to a sixth-grade boy,[67] and the piercing of a student's upper arm with a straight pin.[68] In contrast, the Tenth Circuit Court of Appeals ruled that substantive due process rights were implicated where a nine-year-old girl was paddled with a split paddle while she was held upside down by another teacher, resulting in severe bruises, cuts, and permanent scarring.[69] Also, the Third Circuit Court of Appeals found a substantive due process violation in the physical restraint of a student that caused him to lose consciousness and fall to the ground, suffering significant injuries.[70]

STATE LAW

Although the Supreme Court has ruled that the Federal Constitution does not prohibit corporal punishment in public schools, its use may conflict with state constitutional provisions or statutes or local administrative regulations. In West Virginia, the doctrine of *in loco parentis* (in place of parent), insofar as it permitted corporal punishment, was challenged under the state constitution.[71] Declining to address the constitutionality of *in loco parentis,* the state high court concluded that the doctrine does not permit corporal punishment by mechanical devices (e.g., paddles, whips, sticks) but does permit spanking by hand or physical restraint and removal of unruly students. The court reasoned that because a liberty interest is implicated when the state attempts to use even manual corporal punishment, minimal due process must be provided. The court noted that this would include at least an opportunity for the student to explain his or her version of the disruptive event and the administration of the punishment in the presence of another adult.

In addition to statutory prohibitions on corporal punishment, many school boards, especially in large urban districts, place explicit restrictions or conditions on the use of this disciplinary measure. Local school boards, however, cannot prohibit corporal punishment if a state law specifically authorizes educators to use it. In the absence of statutory language, corporal punishment is permissible, but local boards may develop policies restricting or banning its use.

Teachers can be discharged for violating state laws or board policies regulating corporal punishment. Several courts have upheld dismissals based on insubordination for failure to comply with reasonable school board requirements in administering corporal punishment.[72] In a typical case, a Michigan teacher was dismissed because he violated board policy by using corporal punishment after having been warned repeatedly to cease.[73] Teachers also have been dismissed under the statutory cause of "cruelty" for improper use of physical force with students. In Illinois, a tenured teacher was dismissed on this ground for using a cattle prod in punishing students.[74] A Pennsylvania teacher was dismissed for "cruelty" because she threw a student against a blackboard and then pulled him upright by his hair.[75]

In the absence of statutory or board restrictions, there are other legal means available to challenge the use of unreasonable corporal punishment in public schools. Teachers can be charged with criminal assault and battery which might result in fines and/or imprisonment. Civil assault and battery suits for monetary damages also can be initiated against school personnel. For example, a Louisiana appeals court awarded a student $1,000 for pain, suffering, and humiliation associated with an excessive and unreasonable whipping administered by a teacher.[76]

Educators should use caution in administering corporal punishment since improper administration can result in dismissal, monetary damages, and even imprisonment. Corporal punishment should never be administered with malice, and the use of excessive force should be avoided. Teachers would be wise to keep a record of incidents involving corporal punishment and to adhere to minimum procedural safeguards such as notifying students of behavior that will result in a paddling, asking another staff member to witness the act, and providing parents upon request written reasons for the punishment. Moreover, teachers should become familiar with relevant state laws and school board policies before attempting to use corporal punishment in their classrooms.

ACADEMIC SANCTIONS

It is indisputable that school authorities have the right to use academic sanctions for poor academic performance. Consistently, courts have been reluctant to substitute their own judgment for that of educators in assessing students' academic accomplishments. Failing grades, denial of credit, academic probation, retention, and expulsion from particular programs have been upheld as legitimate means of dealing with poor academic performance.[77] The Supreme Court (1985) stated:

> When judges are asked to review the substance of a genuinely academic decision, . . . they should show great respect for the faculty's professional judgment. Plainly, they may not override it unless it is such a substantial departure from accepted academic norms as to demonstrate that the person or committee responsible did not actually exercise professional judgment.[78]

Courts usually have granted broad discretionary powers to school personnel in establishing academic standards,[79] but there has been less agreement regarding the use of grade reductions or academic sanctions as punishments for student misbehavior and/or absences.[80] More complex legal issues are raised when academic penalties are imposed for *nonacademic* reasons. These issues are explored below in connection with grade reductions for absences and misconduct.

ABSENCES

Excessive student absenteeism is a growing concern and has led many school boards to impose academic sanctions for absences. These practices have generated legal challenges related to students' substantive due process rights. To meet the due process requirements the sanction must be reasonable—that is, rationally related to a valid educational purpose. Since students must attend class to benefit from the educational program, most courts have found that academic penalties for absenteeism serve a valid educational goal.

In an Illinois case, a student claimed that protected rights were impaired by a school regulation stipulating that grades would be lowered one letter grade per class for an unexcused absence.[81] In defending the rule, school officials asserted that it was the most appropriate punishment for the serious problem of truancy. They argued that students could not perform satisfactorily in their classwork if they were absent, as grades reflected class participation in addition to other standards of performance. The appeals court was not persuaded by the student's argument that grades should reflect only scholastic achievement, and therefore concluded that the regulation was reasonable.

The Supreme Court of Connecticut upheld a schoolwide policy that provided for a five-point reduction in course grades for each unapproved absence and denied course credit for absences in excess of twenty-four. The court drew a sharp distinction between academic and disciplinary sanctions, noting that the school board's policy was academic in intent and effect rather than disciplinary. Specifically, the court found that a board's determination that academic grades should reflect more than examinations and papers "constitutes an academic judgment about academic requirements."[82]

Even policies that do not differentiate between excused and unexcused absences in imposing academic penalties have been upheld by some courts. For example, the Supreme Court of Arkansas upheld a board policy that disallowed course credit and permitted expulsion of students who accumulated more than twelve absences.[83] The court, in refusing to substitute its judgment for the school board's, concluded that under state law this action was within the board's power to make reasonable rules and regulations for the administration of the schools. A Michigan appellate court upheld a school board's authority to require students with more than three days of excused absences to attend after-school study sessions or have their letter grades reduced.[84] Similarly, a New York appellate court found that a policy denying course credit for absences in excess of nine classes for semester courses and eighteen absences for full-year courses was rational; students were permitted and encouraged to make up the classes before they exceeded the limit.[85]

To ensure procedural fairness, however, students must be informed that absences will result in academic penalties. In a Missouri case, a student received a failing grade for half of a semester in a music course for failure to attend the last two performances of the semester.[86] The court upheld the grade reduction because students were informed the first day of class that attendance at all performances was required to complete the course and that unexcused absences would result in a failing grade. Where grade reductions are part of academic evaluations, courts generally do not require additional procedural safeguards beyond notice.

Although courts usually have supported sanctions that link attendance and scholastic achievement, state laws may limit the use of academic penalties or require other responses to the problem of truancy. For example, a Colorado appeals court found that academic sanctions for absenteeism were impermissible under state law.[87] The contested school board policy stipulated that any student who missed more than seven days during a semester would not receive academic credit for the courses taken; it did not matter whether the absences were because of illness, family problems, or any other reasons. Two students, denied academic credit for exceeding seven absences in a semester, filed suit challenging the policy as inconsistent with a state law that required attendance for 172 days excluding absences for illness and disciplinary suspensions. The court invalidated the school board's regulation, holding that the board had exceeded its authority in enacting such a policy.

Given the serious truancy problem confronting many school districts, it seems likely that school boards will continue to consider the imposition of academic sanctions. The legality of such policies will depend primarily on judicial interpretation of applicable state law.

MISCONDUCT

Academic sanctions imposed for student misconduct also have been challenged. It is generally accepted that students can be denied credit for work missed while suspended from school. In fact, if students could make up such work without penalty, a suspension might be viewed as a vacation rather than a punishment. More controversy has surrounded policies that impose an additional grade reduction for suspension days, and courts have not agreed regarding the legality of this practice.

For example, a Kentucky appeals court voided a regulation whereby grades were reduced because of unexcused absences resulting from student suspensions.[88] The school board policy stated that work missed because of unexcused absences could not be made up, and that five points would be deducted for every unexcused absence from each class during the grading period. The court held that the use of suspensions or expulsions for misconduct was permissible, but the additional lowering of grades as a punitive measure was not. Similarly, a Pennsylvania court found grade reductions for suspensions to be beyond a school board's authority.[89] In the court's opinion, it was a clear misrepresentation of students' scholastic achievement; the penalty went beyond the five-day suspension and downgraded achievement for a full grading period.

A Texas appellate court, however, upheld a school system's right to lower course grades for suspension days imposed for misconduct.[90] Relying on a state attorney general's opinion approving grade reductions, the court found the pivotal question to be whether the board had actually adopted a policy that would authorize grade reductions. According to the court, oral announcements in school assemblies explaining grade penalties constituted a valid policy. Further, the court noted that the grade reduction did not impair constitutionally protected property or liberty rights.

Generally, courts have ruled that academic course credit or high school diplomas cannot be withheld solely for disciplinary reasons. As early as 1921, the Supreme Court of Iowa held that students who had completed all academic requirements had the right to receive a high school diploma even though they refused to wear graduation caps during the ceremony.[91] The court ruled that the school board was obligated to issue a diploma to a pupil who had satisfactorily completed the prescribed course of study and who was otherwise qualified to graduate from high school. More recently a Pennsylvania court held that a student who was permanently expelled from school after completing all coursework and final examinations, but prior to graduation, could not be denied a diploma.[92]

Courts have issued conflicting decisions regarding the legality of denying a student the right to participate in graduation ceremonies as a disciplinary measure. A New York appeals court held that a student could not be denied such participation on disciplinary grounds,[93] whereas a North Carolina federal district court held that a student could be denied the privilege of participating in the graduation ceremony as a penalty for misconduct.[94] In the latter case, the federal court concluded that the student was not deprived of any property right, since he received his high school diploma even though he was not allowed to take part in the ceremony.

Although the use of grade reductions as sanctions for student misconduct and truancy is prevalent, students seem likely to continue to challenge such practices. Even if the Supreme Court should declare that grades need not reflect only academic performance, any regulation stipulating that grades will be lowered for nonacademic reasons should be reasonable, related to absences from class, and serve a legitimate school purpose. Furthermore, the rules should be made known to all students through the school's official student handbook or some similar means.

SEARCH AND SEIZURE

Search and seizure cases involving public schools have increased in recent years, with the majority resulting from the confiscation of illegal drugs. Students have asserted that warrantless searches conducted by school officials impair their rights under the fourth amendment of the Federal Constitution. Through an extensive line of decisions, the United States Supreme Court has affirmed that the basic purpose of the amendment is to "safeguard the privacy and security of individuals against arbitrary invasions by governmental officials."[95] This amendment protects individuals against unreasonable searches by requiring state agents to obtain a warrant based on probable cause prior to conducting a search. Under the probable cause standard, a governmental official must have reasonable grounds of suspicion, supported by sufficient evidence, to cause a cautious person to believe that the suspected individual is guilty of the alleged offense and that the search will produce evidence of the crime committed. Governmental officials violating fourth amendment rights are subject to criminal or civil liability, but the most important remedy for the aggrieved individual is the exclusionary rule.[96] This rule renders evidence of an illegal search inadmissible in criminal prosecutions.[97]

Significant fourth amendment questions have been raised in the public school setting.[98] Since fourth amendment protections apply only to searches conducted by agents of the state, a fundamental issue in education cases is whether school authorities function as private individuals or as state agents. Most courts have found the fourth amendment applicable to public schools, but it was not until 1985 in *New Jersey v. T.L.O.*, that the Supreme Court finally held that the amendment's prohibition on unreasonable searches applies to school officials.[99] The Court concluded that school officials are state agents, and all governmental actions—not merely those of law enforcement officers—come within the constraints of the fourth amendment.[100]

Although finding the fourth amendment applicable, the Court in *T.L.O.* concluded that school officials' substantial interest in maintaining discipline required "easing" the warrant and probable cause requirements imposed on police officers. The Court reasoned that "requiring a teacher to obtain a warrant before searching a child suspected of an infraction of school rules (or of the criminal law) would unduly interfere with the maintenance of the swift and informal disciplinary procedures needed in the schools."[101] In modifying the level of suspicion required to conduct a search, the Court found the public interest was best served in the school setting with a standard less than probable cause. Accordingly, the Court held that the legality of a search should depend "simply on the reasonableness, under all the circumstances, of the search."[102]

The Court in *T.L.O.* advanced two tests for determining reasonableness. First, is the search justified at its inception? That is, are there "reasonable grounds for suspecting that the search will turn up evidence that the student has violated or is violating either the law or the rules of the school?"[103] Second, is the scope of the search reasonable? In the Court's words, are "the measures adopted reasonably related to the objectives of the search and not excessively intrusive in light of the age and sex of the student and the nature of the infraction?"[104]

The "reasonableness" standard allows courts substantial latitude in interpreting fourth amendment rights.[105] Among factors courts have considered in assessing reasonable grounds for a search are the child's age, history, and record in the school; prevalence and seriousness of the problem in the school to which the search is directed; exigency to make the search without delay and further investigation; probative value and reliability of the information used as a justification for the search; the school officials' experience with the student and with the type of problem to which the search is directed; and the type of search.[106] Courts have differed, however, in the rigor applied in making these assessments, with some essentially imposing the stringency of the probable cause standard and others accepting a mere hunch as substantiating reasonable grounds to search.[107]

Clearly, reasonable suspicion requires more than a hunch, good intentions, or good faith. The Supreme Court, in upholding an exception to the warrant requirement for a "stop and frisk" search for weapons by police officers, concluded that to justify the intrusion the police officer must be able to point to "specific and articulable facts."[108] In recognizing school searches also as special exceptions, it appears that, at a minimum, the judiciary will require searches to be supported by objective facts.[109]

A further requirement of reasonableness appears to be *individualized* suspicion. While the Supreme Court in *T.L.O.* did not address individualized suspicion, the Court stated that "exceptions to the requirement of individualized suspicion are generally appropriate only where the privacy interests implicated by a search are minimal and where 'other safeguards' are available 'to assure that the individual's reasonable expectation of privacy is not subject to the discretion of the official in the field.' "[110] In the absence of exigency requiring an immediate search, courts have been reluctant to support searches void of individualized suspicion.[111]

In assessing the constitutionality of searches in the public schools, two questions are central: What constitutes a search, and what types of searches are reasonable? What constitutes a search must be appraised in the context of the Supreme Court's statement that:

> the fourth amendment protects people, not places. What a person knowingly exposes to the public, even in his own home or office, is not a subject of fourth amendment protection. But what he seeks to preserve as private, even in an area accessible to the public, may be constitutionally protected.[112]

According to the Court's rulings, essential considerations in determining whether an action is a search are an individual's reasonable expectation of privacy (reasonable in the sense that society is prepared to recognize the privacy)[113] and the extent of governmental intrusion.[114] The reasonableness of a specific type of search must be evaluated in terms of all the circumstances surrounding the search.[115] This would include variables such as who initiated the search, who conducted the search, need for the search, purpose of the search, information or factors prompting the search, what or who was searched, and use of the evidence. In the following sections, various types of school searches are examined within this framework.

LOCKERS AND OTHER PROPERTY

In singling out school lockers as generating a lower expectation of privacy, courts have usually distinguished locker searches on the basis that a locker is school property, and a student does not retain exclusive possession. Under the view of joint control, school officials have been allowed to inspect lockers or even to consent to searches by law enforcement officers.[116] The judiciary, however, has not given school personnel blanket approval to make indiscriminate locker searches; any search must be based on reasonable suspicion that contraband disruptive to the educational process will be uncovered. If the purpose of the search is to gather criminal evidence, a search warrant is required.

A Kansas case illustrates the prevalent judicial view toward locker searches. The Supreme Court of Kansas held that the right of inspection is inherent in the authority granted school officials to manage the schools.[117] The court maintained that it is a proper function of school personnel to inspect the lockers under their control and to prevent the use of lockers in illicit ways or for illegal purposes. Earlier, the New York high court proclaimed that "not only have the school authorities a right to inspect but this right becomes a duty when suspicion arises that something of an illegal nature may be secreted there."[118] The Tenth Circuit Court of Appeals also concluded that "school authorities have, on behalf of the public, an interest in these lockers and a duty to police the school, particularly where possible serious violations of the criminal laws exist."[119] All three courts noted that school officials had a list of the combinations and had occasionally inspected the lockers. These points have been emphasized in other cases to support the nonexclusive nature of lockers.[120]

Applying the *T.L.O.* standards for reasonableness, the West Virginia Supreme Court upheld a locker search that produced evidence of drug use.[121] An administrator initiated the search of the student's locker for alcohol based on information that a friend of the student had consumed alcohol at the suspected student's home that morning. Finding that this constituted reasonable grounds for conducting the search, the court concluded that discovery of drugs in a jacket found in the locker was reasonably related to the search for alcoholic beverages.

A decision of the New Jersey high court, however, departed from the general judicial view of locker privacy.[122] In this situation, the court held that the student did have an expectation of privacy in the contents of his locker. The locker was characterized as a "home away from home," a place to store personal items. Although the existence of a master key did not lower the expectation of privacy, the court noted that a policy of regularly inspecting the students' lockers might have that effect.

In some cases students have contested locker searches on the basis of state constitutional provisions or state statutes. A Washington appeals court interpreted the state constitution as affording students no greater protection from locker searches by school officials than is guaranteed by the fourth amendment.[123] Although the Washington high court has found that state law provides almost a complete bar to warrantless searches and arrests, the appellate court declined to extend this holding to school searches.[124]

Statutes in some states address students' rights in connection with locker searches. Indiana law, for example, indicates that a student's locker is property of the school district and that a student is presumed to have no expectation of privacy in the locker or its contents. The law, however, also stipulates that other than a general search of all lockers, "where possible," locker searches will be conducted in the presence of the affected students.[125] If a state law provides greater privacy protections than the Federal Constitution, school authorities must adhere to the statutory mandates.

Students' personal property or effects usually entail a greater expectation of privacy than school lockers. The constitutionality or reasonableness of searches of personal effects is determined by assessing the grounds for the search and the circumstances surrounding it. In the Supreme Court's *T.L.O.* decision, a teacher had reported that a student was smoking in the restroom. Upon questioning by the assistant principal, the student denied smoking and, in fact, denied that she even smoked. The assistant principal then opened the student's purse seeking evidence to substantiate that she did smoke. In the process of removing a package of cigarettes, he spotted rolling papers, and subsequently found marijuana and other evidence implicating her in drug dealing. Using the "reasonable suspicion" test, the Supreme Court found that the search in *T.L.O.* was reasonable. The school official had a basis for suspecting that the student had cigarettes in her purse. Although possession was not a violation of a school rule, it was not irrelevant; discovery of cigarettes provided evidence to corroborate that she had been smoking and challenged her credibility. No direct evidence existed that the student's purse contained cigarettes, but, based on a teacher's report that the student had been smoking, it was logical to suspect that she might have had cigarettes in her purse.

Characterizing this as a "common sense" conclusion, the Court noted that "the requirement of reasonable suspicion is not a requirement of absolute certainty: 'sufficient probability, not certainty, is the touchstone of reasonableness under the fourth amendment.' "[126]

A Florida district court upheld the search of a student's car after a school aide observed a waterpipe, commonly used to smoke marijuana, in plain view.[127] The aide regularly patrolled the school parking lot to ensure enforcement of school regulations and to supervise students during their lunch break. In the court's opinion, patrolling the lot fell within the school's duty to maintain order and discipline and did not constitute a search. A Texas federal district court, however, declined to uphold a general dragnet search of a school parking lot.[128] The school's interest in the contents of the cars was viewed as minimal since students did not have access to their cars during the school day. Furthermore, the search was indiscriminate, lacking any evidence of individualized suspicion. The Supreme Court of California also declined to uphold the search of a student's calculator case in the absence of articulable facts to support individualized suspicion.[129] The vice principal's search was based on the student's tardiness for class, his "furtive gestures" to hide the calculator, and his comment that the principal needed a warrant.

PERSONAL SEARCHES

Warrantless searches of a student's person raise significant legal questions. Unlike locker searches, it cannot be asserted that there is a lower expectation of privacy. The Fifth Circuit Appellate Court noted that "the fourth amendment applies with its fullest vigor against any intrusion on the human body."[130] In personal searches not only is it necessary to have reasonable cause to search, but also the search itself must be reasonable. Reasonableness is assessed in terms of the specific facts and circumstances of a case.

A California appellate court found the search of a student's pockets reasonable under the *T.L.O.* standard.[131] In this case, a school official found a student in a restroom without a pass during class time. Because the student appeared to be nervous and was acting suspiciously, the administrator requested that he empty his pockets, which led to the discovery of drugs. The court held that the search was justified on the basis of suspicious behavior and that the scope of the search was not excessive or intrusive. Similarly, the Alabama Supreme Court found the search of two fifth-grade students for the alleged theft of nine dollars reasonable based on the fact that they had been alone in the classroom at the time the money disappeared.[132]

An individual may waive entitlement to fourth amendment protection by consenting to a search or volunteering requested evidence. The consent, however, is valid only if voluntarily given in the absence of coercion.

Serious questions arise as to whether a student's consent is actually voluntary. Did the student have a free choice? Was the student aware of his or her fourth amendment rights? A Texas federal district court reasoned that the very nature of the school setting diminishes the assumption of consent.[133] Students are accustomed to receiving and following orders of school officials; refusal to obey a request is considered insubordination. In this case, the threat to call the students' parents and the police if they did not cooperate further substantiated a coercive atmosphere. In another case, the Sixth Circuit Court of Appeals stated that there is "a presumption against the waiver of constitutional rights," placing the burden on school officials to show that students knowingly and intelligently waived their constitutional rights.[134] Although some courts have found student consent valid,[135] the inherent pitfalls of pursuing such a search in the absence of reasonable cause must be duly considered.

STRIP SEARCHES

It is doubtful that strip searches of students can ever be justified on the basis of reasonable suspicion. The Second Circuit Court of Appeals noted that "as the intrusiveness of the search intensifies, the standard of fourth amendment 'reasonableness' approaches probable cause, even in the school context."[136] The Seventh Circuit Appellate Court, in a strongly worded statement, proclaimed in an Indiana case:

> It does not require a constitutional scholar to conclude that a nude search of a thirteen-year-old child is an invasion of constitutional rights of some magnitude. More than that: it is a violation of any known principle of human decency.[137]

Litigation indicates that substantial evidence must exist to conduct strip searches. The Ninth Circuit Court of Appeals found a "pat-down" search and subsequent strip search to be unlawful.[138] Such an invasion of privacy could not be justified on the basis that a bus driver saw the student exchange "what appeared to be money" for an unidentified object. Similarly, a New York federal district court held that a strip search of a fifth-grade class to find three dollars that had been stolen was unreasonable.[139] Factors considered by the court were the lack of danger in the situation, the intrusiveness of the search, and the age of the students. The court did imply that a more dangerous situation, such as drug possession, might support a strip search. The New York high court voiced similar reasoning in suppressing evidence obtained from the search of a student's wallet and follow-up strip search for lack of reasonable grounds for the action.[140] The court noted, however, that if there had been a reasonable basis to conduct the search, the discovery of drugs in the wallet would have warranted a strip search.

In contrast to the general trend in judicial decisions, a Kentucky appeals court found the strip search of a student reasonable because it was based on sufficient evidence.[141] Such evidence included the student's passing of prescription drugs and marijuana to other students and his admission that he had grown marijuana and smoked it frequently. Other influential facts in this case were that no criminal charges were filed; law enforcement officers were not involved; and the search was initiated for a specific reason rather than an indiscriminate search of all students.

Although courts have not prohibited strip searches of students, enough caveats exist to alert school officials of the inherent risks of such intrusive personal searches. The judicial trend indicates that reasonable suspicion alone may be inadequate to justify strip searches; rather, the required standard approaches probable cause. Except for emergency situations, few circumstances appear to necessitate such intrusions.

USE OF CANINES TO SEARCH

The use of drug-detecting dogs in searches raises a number of controversial questions regarding fourth amendment rights. Does the presence of a dog sniffing students constitute a search? Must reasonable suspicion exist to justify the use of dogs? Does the alert of a dog establish reasonable suspicion? A few courts have addressed these issues.

The Tenth Circuit Court of Appeals upheld the use of trained police dogs in the sniffing of lockers but did not directly address the constitutional issues presented by the use of dogs.[142] Rather, the court discussed generally the school administrator's duty to inspect, even to the point that an inspection may violate fourth amendment rights. Under this broad grant of authority, the alert of a dog three times at a locker established reasonable suspicion to conduct a search.

The Fifth Circuit Court of Appeals, on the other hand, confronted the question of whether sniffing by a dog is a search in terms of an individual's reasonable expectation of privacy.[143] The appellate court noted that the vast majority of courts have held that law enforcement use of canines for sniffing objects does not constitute a search. Specifically, the court referenced cases involving checked luggage, shipped packages, public lockers, and cars on public streets.[144] According to the court, a reasonable expectation of privacy does not extend to the airspace surrounding these objects. The court maintained that what has evolved is a doctrine of "public smell," equivalent to the "plain view" theory (that is, an object in plain view can be seized under certain circumstances). This point was illustrated by the example of a police officer detecting the odor of marijuana from an object or property. No search is involved because the odor is considered to be in "public view" and thus unprotected.

From this line of reasoning, the appellate court noted that the use of canines has been viewed as merely enhancing the ability to detect an odor, as the use of a flashlight improves vision. Accordingly, the court concluded that sniffing of student lockers and cars in public view was not a search, and, therefore, the fourth amendment did not apply.[145] While permitting the use of dogs to detect drugs, the court held that reasonable suspicion is required for a further search of a locker or car by school officials, and that such suspicion can be established only upon showing that the dogs are reasonably reliable in detecting the actual presence of contraband.[146]

In most instances, judicial support for the use of dogs has been limited to the sniffing of objects. The Seventh Circuit Court of Appeals, however, concluded that the presence of dogs in a classroom was not a search.[147] In this well-publicized Indiana case, school officials, with the assistance of police officers, conducted a schoolwide inspection for drugs in which trained dogs were brought into each classroom for approximately five minutes. When a dog alerted beside a student, school officials requested that the student remove the contents of his or her pockets or purse. A continued alert by the dog resulted in a strip search. The appellate court, in weighing the minimal intrusion of the dogs against the school's desire to eliminate a significant drug problem, concluded that sniffing of the students by the dogs did not constitute a search invoking fourth amendment protections. Search of pockets and purses, however, did involve an invasion of privacy, but was justified on the basis that the dog's alert constituted reasonable cause to believe that the student possessed drugs. However, as discussed previously, the court drew the line at conducting a strip search based on a dog's alert.

In contrast to the reasoning of the Seventh Circuit Court of Appeals, a Texas federal district court concluded that the use of dogs in a blanket "sniffing" (or inspection) of students did constitute a search. The court noted that drug-detecting dogs posed a greater intrusion upon personal privacy than electronic surveillance devices that have been found to constitute searches. According to the court, "the dog's inspection was virtually equivalent to a physical entry into the students' pockets and personal possessions."[148] In finding the dog's sniffing to be a search, the court further held that for school authorities to use dogs in a search they must have *prior* individualized suspicion that a student possesses contraband that will disrupt the educational process.[149] In essence, a dog alert cannot be used to establish such suspicion.

Similarly, the Fifth Circuit Court of Appeals held that sniffing of students by dogs significantly intrudes on an individual's privacy, thereby constituting a search.[150] While recognizing that the sniffing of a person is a search, the court did not prohibit such searches, but held that their intrusiveness must be weighed against the school's need to conduct the search. The court concluded that even a significant need to search requires individualized suspicion prior to the use of dogs because of the degree of intrusion on personal dignity and security.

Given the scope of the drug problem in public schools, it seems likely that other school districts will consider the use of drug-detecting canine units. Until the Supreme Court addresses whether such a practice constitutes a search (requiring individualized suspicion) or whether a dog alert can establish reasonable grounds for a personal search, different interpretations among lower courts seem destined to persist.

Drug Testing

In an effort to control drug use among students, some districts have considered school-wide drug-testing programs. Such programs raise serious questions about students' privacy rights. The Supreme Court has held that urinalysis, the most frequently used means for drug testing, is a search under the fourth amendment.[151] Although the Court upheld the testing of government employees for drug use in two separate decisions, the holdings were narrowly drawn and based on a compelling governmental interest. The Court upheld the testing of railroad employees who are involved in certain types of accidents, emphasizing the highly regulated nature of the industry and the need to ensure the safety of the public.[152] In the second case, drug testing of customs employees seeking promotion to positions involving the interdiction of illegal drugs or requiring the use of firearms was justified based on safety and security concerns.[153] Individualized suspicion was not a precondition for conducting the urinalysis in these cases, but the narrow circumstances justifying the testing programs minimized the discretion of supervisors and the potential for arbitrariness.

Relying on the Supreme Court's conclusion that drug-testing programs must be justified by a compelling governmental interest, a Texas federal district court found unconstitutional a requirement that all seventh-through twelfth-grade students who participate in extracurricular activities be subjected to urinalysis.[154] School officials were unable to demonstrate a compelling interest that would justify the interference with students' legitimate expectation of privacy. The court emphasized that under *ordinary* circumstances individualized suspicion must exist to support the search of a student. Due to the lack of a drug problem within the school as well as the failure to show a relationship between drug use and extracurricular activities, extraordinary circumstances could not be established.

In contrast, the Seventh Circuit Court of Appeals, prior to the Supreme Court's drug-testing decisions, upheld a random urine testing program for interscholastic athletes and cheerleaders in an Indiana school district.[155] Among the factors that the court noted in support of the random drug-testing policy were the diminished expectation of privacy resulting from the elective nature of athletic participation and the highly regulated nature of interscholastic athletics, evidence of a drug problem within the school system, and the danger drug usage poses for the health and safety of athletes. Further, the court noted that the drawing of random numbers to select students for testing limited the discretion of school officials, and the test results would not be used for criminal prosecution. This policy was more narrowly defined than the Texas policy, but it might not meet the more stringent requirements subsequently articulated by the Supreme Court.

Although blanket or random drug testing of students is not likely to withstand judicial challenge, many schools subject students to urinalysis based on *individualized* suspicion, and such practices have not been invalidated by courts. Any drug-testing program, however, must be carefully constructed to avoid impairing students' fourth amendment privacy rights. The policy must be clearly developed, specifically identifying reasons for testing. Data collection procedures must be precise and well defined. Students and parents should be informed of the policy, and it is advisable to request students' consent prior to testing. If the test indicates drug use, the student must be given an opportunity to explain the results. Providing for the rehabilitation of the student rather than punishment strengthens the policy.

POLICE INVOLVEMENT

A "reasonable suspicion" or "reasonable cause to believe" standard is generally invoked in assessing the legality of school searches, but it appears that a higher standard may be required when police officers are involved. The nature and extent of such involvement are important considerations in determining whether a search is reasonable. If the police role is one of finding evidence of a crime, probable cause would be required.[156] If, on the other hand, it is simply providing school officials assistance in a disciplinary action, reasonable suspicion may be adequate.[157] Early decisions generally supported police participation in searches initiated and conducted by school officials,[158] but more recent decisions have tended to draw a sharp distinction between searches with and without police assistance.[159]

The more stringent judicial posture is represented in an Illinois decision.[160] In that case, the school principal received a call that led him to suspect that three girls possessed illegal drugs. Upon the superintendent's advice, he called the police to assist in the investigation. After the police arrived, each girl was searched by the school nurse and the school psychologist; however, no drugs were discovered. Subsequently, the students filed suit alleging that their civil rights had been violated. The court found that the police were not called merely to assist in maintaining school discipline but to search for evidence of a crime. Under the circumstances, the court concluded that the students had a constitutional right not to be searched unless the police had a warrant based on probable cause.

In contrast, the same Illinois court held that a police officer's involvement in persuading a student to relinquish the contents of his pockets did not violate fourth amendment rights under the *T.L.O.* standard.[161] The police officer's role was quite limited in this case. He was in the school building on another matter, and his role in the search was restricted simply to requesting that the student empty his pockets. There was no police involvement in the investigation that led to detaining the student nor was the evidence used for criminal prosecution. Furthermore, the facts did not indicate that the school and the police officer were attempting to avoid the warrant and probable cause requirements.

Similarly, the Eighth Circuit Court of Appeals held that the assistance of a police officer assigned as a liaison officer in a high school did not subject a search for stolen property to the fourth amendment's probable cause standard.[162] Relying on *T.L.O.*, the court found no evidence that the search activities were at *the behest of* a police official. Rather, the vice principal had initiated and conducted the investigation with limited assistance from the police officer. While the police officer had participated in a pat-down search, it occurred only after the vice principal had discovered evidence of drug involvement in a student's purse. The court found this search by a school official working in conjunction with a police officer to be permissible.

The Washington Supreme Court ruled that a call from the chief of police informing a principal that two high school students were selling speed did not constitute "police action" or "joint action."[163] The court emphasized that the chief of police did not initiate the search or request that the principal search the students. Furthermore, the court noted that there would have been a duty to search the students and to report the results to the police regardless of the source of the information. In a strongly worded dissent, one justice argued that the standard in this case should have been probable cause since the search was used for criminal prosecution, not for school disciplinary action.

In a number of decisions applying the reasonable suspicion standard to school searches, courts have specifically noted or implied that this lower standard is not applicable if law enforcement officials are involved. A Florida district court stated: "The reasonable suspicion standard does not apply in cases involving a search directed or participated in by a police officer."[164] Similarly, a Kentucky appellate court found the lower standard appropriate for searches in school settings *in the absence* of police participation.[165]

Troubling questions are raised when the fruits of warrantless searches result in the criminal prosecution of students.[166] Classifying searches on the basis of who conducts the search and for what purpose is inadequate. Searches cannot be discreetly classified as either administrative (school related) or criminal. A search may be clearly criminal when the purpose is to find evidence of a crime, thereby necessitating probable cause prior to the search. But administrative searches undertaken strictly for disciplinary or safety purposes may result in prosecution of students if evidence of a crime is uncovered and reported to the police. In fact, school authorities have a duty to alert the police if evidence of a crime is discovered, even though the search was initiated for school purposes.

Although many legal issues involving search and seizure in schools are still evolving, school personnel can generally protect themselves from a successful legal challenge by adhering to a few basic guidelines. First, students and parents should be informed at the beginning of the school term of the procedures for conducting locker and personal searches. Any search conducted should be based on "reasonable suspicion" that the student possesses contraband that may be disruptive to the educational process. Further, the authorized person conducting a search should have another staff member present who can verify the procedures used in the search. School personnel should refrain from using strip searches or mass searches of groups of students. And finally, if police officials conduct a search in the school, either with or without the school's involvement, it is advisable to ensure that they first obtain a search warrant.

REMEDIES FOR UNLAWFUL DISCIPLINARY ACTIONS

There are several remedies available to students who are unlawfully disciplined by school authorities. Where physical punishment is involved, students can seek damages through assault and battery suits against those who inflicted the harm.[167] For unwarranted suspensions or expulsions, students are entitled to reinstatement without penalty to grades and to have their school records expunged of any reference to the illegal disciplinary action.[168] If academic penalties are unlawfully imposed, grades must be restored and transcripts altered accordingly.[169] For unconstitutional searches, illegally seized evidence may be suppressed, school records may be expunged, and damages may be awarded if the unlawful search results in substantial injury to the student.[170]

The Supreme Court has held that school officials can be sued for monetary damages in state courts as well as federal courts under the Civil Rights Act of 1871 if they arbitrarily violate students' federally protected rights in disciplinary proceedings.[171] In *Wood v. Strickland,* the Court declared that ignorance of the law is not a valid defense to shield school officials from liability if they should have known that their actions would impair students' *clearly established* federal rights.[172] Under *Wood,* a showing of malice is not always required to prove that the actions of school officials were taken in bad faith, but a mere mistake in carrying out duties does not render school authorities liable. The Court also recognized in *Wood* that educators are not charged with predicting the future direction of constitutional law. An Arkansas federal district court, however, concluded that even in the absence of substantial case law firmly identifying a specific constitutional right, certain actions are "so inherently invasive as to be obviously suspect in the school setting."[173] The court classified a urinalysis procedure (seminude body fluid search) as such an action.

Other courts have reiterated school officials' potential liability in connection with student disciplinary proceedings, but to date students have not been as successful as teachers in obtaining monetary awards for constitutional violations. Courts have been reluctant to delineate students' "clearly established" rights, the impairment of which would warrant compensatory damages.

In 1978 the Supreme Court placed restrictions on the amount of damages that could be awarded to students in instances involving the impairment of procedural due process rights. In *Carey v. Piphus* the Court declared that students who were suspended without a hearing, but were not otherwise injured, could recover only nominal damages (not to exceed one dollar).[174] This case involved two Chicago students who had been suspended without hearings for allegedly violating school regulations. They brought suit against the school district, claiming an abridgment of their constitutional rights. The Supreme Court ruled that substantial damages could be recovered only if the suspensions were unjustified. Accordingly, the case was remanded for the district court to determine whether the students would have been suspended if correct procedures had been followed.

This decision may appear to have strengthened the position of school boards in exercising discretion in disciplinary proceedings, but the Supreme Court indicated that students *might* be entitled to substantial damages if suspensions are proven to be unwarranted. To illustrate, an Arkansas federal district court assessed punitive damages against a high school coach for intentionally impairing students' free speech rights in a disciplinary action.[175] Also, students have received damages when subjected to unlawful searches. For example, the Seventh Circuit Court of Appeals assessed damages against school officials for an intrusive body search.[176] In addition to damages, students also may be awarded attorneys' fees.

Educators should take every precaution to afford fair and impartial treatment to students. School personnel would be wise to provide at least an informal hearing if in doubt as to whether a particular situation necessitates due process. Liability never results from the provision of too much due process, whereas damages possibly could be assessed in situations involving violations of procedural rights that result in unjustified suspensions, expulsions, or other disciplinary actions. Although constitutional and statutory due process requirements do not mandate that a specific procedure be followed in every situation, courts will carefully study the record to ensure that any procedural deficiencies do not impede the student's efforts to present a full defense.

Also, school authorities should ensure that constraints placed on student conduct are necessary for the proper functioning of the school. Educators have considerable latitude in controlling student behavior to maintain an appropriate educational environment, but courts will award students relief where restrictions are clearly unreasonable. School personnel, however, should not feel that their authority to discipline students has been curtailed by the judiciary. As noted in *Goss,* courts "have imposed requirements which are, if anything, less than a fair-minded principal would impose."[177]

CONCLUSION

In 1969 Justice Black noted that "school discipline, like parental discipline, is an integral and important part of training our children to be good citizens—to be better citizens."[178] Accordingly, school personnel have been empowered with the authority and duty to regulate pupil behavior in order to protect the interests of the student body and the school. Reasonable sanctions can be imposed if students do not adhere to legitimate conduct regulations. Courts, however, will intervene if disciplinary procedures are arbitrary or impair students' protected rights. Although the law pertaining to certain aspects of student discipline remains in a state of flux, judicial decisions support the following generalizations.

1. School authorities must be able to substantiate that any disciplinary regulation enacted is reasonable and necessary for the management of the school or for the welfare of pupils and school employees.
2. All regulations should be stated in precise terms and disseminated to students and parents.
3. Punishments for rule infractions should be appropriate for the offense and the characteristics of the offender (e.g., age, mental condition, prior behavior).
4. Students cannot be punished for the acts of others (such as their parents).
5. Some type of due process should be afforded to students prior to the imposition of punishments. For minor penalties, an informal hearing suffices; for serious punishments, more formal procedures are required (e.g., notification of parents, representation by counsel, opportunity to cross-examine witnesses).
6. Students can be punished for misbehavior occurring off school grounds if the conduct directly relates to the welfare of the school.
7. Suspensions and expulsions are legitimate punishments if accompanied by appropriate procedural safeguards and not arbitrarily imposed.

8. The transfer of students to different classes, programs, or schools for disciplinary reasons must be accompanied by due process procedures.

9. If not prohibited by state law or school board policy, reasonable corporal punishment can be used as a disciplinary technique.

10. Academic sanctions for nonacademic reasons should be reasonable, related to absences from class, and serve a legitimate school purpose.

11. School personnel can search students' lockers or personal effects for educational purposes upon reasonable suspicion that the students possess contraband that will disrupt the school.

12. Strip searches should be avoided unless evidence substantiates that there is probable cause to search or an emergency exists.

13. The use of canines to sniff objects is generally not viewed as a search, but courts are not in agreement regarding whether their use with students is a search and that requires individualized suspicion.

14. Chemical screening of students comes within the purview of the fourth amendment and requires reasonable suspicion that an individual student is using drugs.

15. If students are unlawfully punished, they are entitled to be restored (without penalty) to their status prior to the imposition of the punishment and to have their records expunged of any reference to the illegal punishment.

16. School officials can be held liable for compensatory damages if unlawful punishments result in substantial injury to the students involved (e.g., unwarranted suspensions from school); however, only nominal damages, not to exceed one dollar, can be assessed against school officials for the abridgment of students' procedural rights (e.g., the denial of an adequate hearing).

ENDNOTES

1. *See* Janet Price, Alan Levine, and Eve Cary, *The Rights of Students,* 3d ed. (Carbondale: Southern Illinois University Press, 1988).

2. Pugsley v. Sellmeyer, 250 S.W. 538 (Ark. 1923). *See also* Jones v. Day, 89 So. 906 (Miss. 1921).

3. Tanton v. McKenney, 197 N.W. 510 (Mich. 1924).

4. *See* Tinker v. Des Moines Indep. School Dist., 393 U.S. 503 (1969); text with note 45, Chapter 4.

5. *See* Bethel School Dist. No. 403 v. Fraser, 478 U.S. 675 (1986); New Jersey v. T.L.O., 469 U.S. 325 (1985).

6. *See* Board of Educ. of Rogers, Arkansas v. McCluskey, 458 U.S. 966 (1982); Wood v. Strickland, 420 U.S. 308 (1975).

7. *See* Soglin v. Kauffman, 418 F.2d 163 (7th Cir. 1969).
8. Caliborne v. Beebe School Dist., 687 F. Supp. 1358 (E.D. Ark. 1988). *See also* Warren County Bd. of Educ. v. Wilkinson, 500 So. 2d 455 (Miss. 1986) (in the absence of a board rule prohibiting the consumption of beer at home, a school board could not impose loss of credit for the semester when a student drank a few sips of beer at her home before going to school the last day of the semester).
9. *See* Bethel School Dist. No. 403 v. Fraser, 478 U.S. 675 (1986); text with note 21, Chapter 4.
10. Pervis v. LaMarque Indep. Dist., 466 F.2d 1054, 1057 (5th Cir. 1972).
11. St. Ann v. Palisi, 495 F.2d 423, 426 (5th Cir. 1974).
12. Carder v. Michigan City School Corp., 552 F. Supp. 869 (N.D. Ind. 1982).
13. O'Rourke v. Walker, 102 Conn. 130 (1925).
14. *See* Pollnow v. Glennon, 757 F.2d 496 (2d Cir. 1985); Smith v. Little Rock School Dist., 582 F. Supp. 159 (E.D. Ark. 1984).
15. Bush v. Dassel-Cokato Bd. of Educ., 745 F. Supp. 562 (D. Minn. 1990) (sanction did not violate student's first amendment right to freedom of association; a rational relationship existed between the school board's rule and the board's interest in deterring alcohol use among students).
16. Brands v. Shelton Community School, 671 F. Supp. 627 (N.D. Iowa 1987).
17. Felton v. Fayette School Dist., 875 F.2d 191 (8th Cir. 1989).
18. Fenton v. Stear, 423 F. Supp. 767 (W.D. Pa. 1976). *But see* Klein v. Smith, 635 F. Supp. 1440 (D. Me. 1986); text with note 27, Chapter 4.
19. Galveston Indep. School Dist. v. Boothe, 590 S.W.2d 553 (Tex. Civ. App. 1979).
20. Klein v. Smith, 635 F. Supp. 1440 (D. Me. 1986); Anable v. Ford, 653 F. Supp. 22 (W.D. Ark. 1985).
21. *See* Ind. Code Ann. § 20-8.1-5-5 (West Supp. 1990).
22. *See, e.g.,* Draper v. Columbus Pub. Schools, 760 F. Supp. 131 (S.D. Ohio 1991); Brands v. Sheldon Community School, 671 F. Supp. 627 (N.D. Iowa 1987).
23. *See, e.g.,* Newsome v. Batavia Local School Dist., 842 F.2d 920 (6th Cir. 1988).
24. *See, e.g.,* Dillon v. Pulaski County Special School Dist., 594 F.2d 699 (8th Cir. 1979); Warren County Bd. of Educ. v. Wilkinson, 500 So. 2d 455 (Miss. 1986); Aquirre v. San Bernardino City Unified School Dist., 170 Cal. Rptr. 206 (Cal. Ct. App.1980) (under the California Constitution, students must be allowed to confront and cross-examine witnesses). *But see* Newsome v. Batavia Local School Dist., 842 F.2d 920 (6th Cir. 1988); Brewer v. Austin Indep. School Dist., 779 F.2d 260 (5th Cir. 1985) (names of witnesses could be withheld to prevent retaliation).
25. Keough v. Tate County Bd. of Educ., 748 F.2d 1077 (5th Cir. 1984).
26. Brewer v. Austin Indep. School Dist., 779 F.2d 260 (5th Cir. 1985).
27. Newsome v. Batavia Local School Dist., 842 F.2d 920 (6th Cir. 1988). *See also* Jones v. Board of Trustees of the Pascagoula Mun. Separate School Dist., 524 So. 2d 968 (Miss. 1988).
28. The failure to enact required state rules or to follow them would violate state law rather than the Federal Constitution. *See, e.g.,* White v. Salisbury Township School Dist., 588 F. Supp. 608 (E.D. Pa. 1984); Rutz v. Essex Junction Prudential Comm., 457 A.2d 1368 (Vt. 1983).

29. Galveston Indep. School Dist. v. Boothe, 590 S.W.2d 553 (Tex. Civ. App. 1979).

30. Labrosse v. St. Bernard Parish School Bd., 483 So. 2d 1253 (La. Ct. App. 1986).

31. Wilson v. Collinsville Community Unit School Dist., 451 N.E.2d 939 (Ill. App. Ct. 1983). *See also* McEntire v. Brevard County School Bd., 471 So. 2d 1287 (Fla. Dist. Ct. App. 1985) (expulsion of student for selling caffeine pills was overturned because evidence did not support that the student represented the pills as speed; school board policy prohibited the selling of counterfeit pills only if represented as speed).

32. Scoggins v. Henry County Bd. of Educ., 549 So. 2d 99 (Ala. Civ. App. 1989).

33. In re McClellan, 475 A.2d 867 (Pa. Commw. Ct. 1984).

34. Tomlinson v. Pleasant Valley School Dist., 479 A.2d 1169 (Pa. Commw. Ct. 1984).

35. S-1 v. Turlington, 635 F.2d 342 (5th Cir. 1981), *cert. denied,* 454 U.S. 1030 (1981); School Bd. of the County of Prince William, Virginia v. Malone, 762 F.2d 1210 (4th Cir. 1985); Kaelin v. Grubbs, 682 F.2d 595 (6th Cir. 1982). *See also* Honig v. Doe, 484 U.S. 305 (1988) (IDEA's "stay put" provision prohibits school officials from unilaterally excluding students with disabilities from their assigned placement for dangerous or disruptive behavior during pendency of expulsion proceedings); text with note 174, Chapter 5.

36. *See* S-1, *id.;* text with note 176, Chapter 5.

37. 419 U.S. 565 (1975).

38. *Id.* at 574–575.

39. Bethel School Dist. No. 403 v. Fraser, 478 U.S. 675, 686 (1986).

40. Boynton v. Casey, 543 F. Supp. 995 (D. Me. 1982). The "right to remain silent" also has been advanced in other cases, with students arguing that school disciplinary proceedings should be governed by the principle established by the Supreme Court in Miranda v. Arizona, 384 U.S. 436 (1966) (persons subjected to custodial interrogation must be advised of their right to remain silent, that any statement made may be used against them, and that they have the right to legal counsel). Courts have readily dismissed these claims, finding that discussions with school administrators are noncustodial. Clearly, in the *Miranda* decision, the Supreme Court was interpreting an individual's fifth amendment right against self-incrimination when first subjected to police questioning in connection with criminal charges. *See* Cason v. Cook, 810 F.2d 188 (8th Cir. 1987), *cert. denied,* 482 U.S. 930 (1987); Pollnow v. Glennon, 757 F.2d 496 (2d Cir. 1985).

41. Edwards v. Rees, 883 F.2d 882 (10th Cir. 1989).

42. Goss, 419 U.S. at 583–584.

43. Paredes v. Curtis, 864 F.2d 426, 429 (6th Cir. 1988).

44. Palmer v. Merluzzi, 868 F.2d 90 (3d Cir. 1989).

45. Keough v. Tate County Bd. of Educ., 748 F.2d 1077, 1081 (5th Cir. 1984).

46. Lamb v. Panhandle Community Unit School Dist. No. 2, 826 F.2d 526 (7th Cir. 1987).

47. Ohio Rev. Code § 3313.66 (1990).

48. 24 Pa. Stat. Ann. § 13-1318 (Purdon, West Supp. 1991).

49. Mifflin County School Dist. v. Stewart, 503 A.2d 1012 (Pa. Commw. Ct. 1986).

50. Cole v. Newton Special Mun. Separate School Dist., 676 F. Supp. 749 (S.D.

Miss. 1987), *aff'd,* 853 F.2d 924 (5th Cir. 1988). *See also* Heimberger v. School Dist. of the City of Saginaw, 881 F.2d 242 (6th Cir. 1989) (student lacked standing to challenge lunch period suspension, which deprived him of federally subsidized school lunches, since district could legally impose full-day suspension for the same misconduct).

51. Dickens v. Johnson County Bd. of Educ., 661 F. Supp. 155 (E.D. Tenn. 1987).

52. Goss, 419 U.S. at 583.

53. R.R. v. Board of Educ. of Shore Regional High School Dist., 263 A.2d 180 (N.J. Super. Ct. App. Div. 1970).

54. Johnson v. Board of Educ., Union Free School Dist. No. 6, Manhasset, 393 N.Y.S.2d 510 (N.Y. App. Div. 1977).

55. *See* Chicago Bd. of Educ. v. Terrile, 361 N.E.2d 778 (Ill. App. Ct. 1977); Betts v. Board of Educ. of Chicago, 466 F.2d 629, 633 (7th Cir. 1972).

56. *See* Jordan v. School Dist. of the City of Erie, Pennsylvania, 615 F.2d 85 (3d Cir. 1980).

57. Everett v. Marcase, 426 F. Supp. 397, 400 (E.D. Pa. 1977). *See also* Hobson v. Bailey, 309 F. Supp. 1393 (W.D. Tenn. 1970).

58. *Education Daily,* Special Supplement, February 1990, p. 1. Two additional states banned corporal punishment after this report identifying nineteen. In 1991, proposed legislation was introduced in the U.S. House of Representatives to prohibit corporal punishment in educational institutions receiving federal financial assistance, H.R. 1522, 102d Cong., 1st Sess. (1991).

59. *See* Burton v. Kirby, 775 S.W.2d 834 (Tex. Civ. App. 1989); Gaspershon v. Harnett County Bd. of Educ., 330 S.E.2d 489 (N.C. Ct. App. 1985); LeBoyd v. Jenkins, 381 So. 2d 1290 (La. Ct. App. 1980), *writ denied,* 386 So. 2d 341 (La. 1980).

60. 430 U.S. 651 (1977). *See also* Cunningham v. Beavers, 858 F.2d 269 (5th Cir. 1988), *cert. denied,* 489 U.S. 1067 (1989) (Texas law permitting corporal punishment does not violate the equal protection clause of the Federal Constitution).

61. The Court noted that procedures outlined earlier by a federal district court, although desirable, were not required under the Federal Constitution. *See* Baker v. Owen, 395 F. Supp. 294 (M.D.N.C. 1975), *aff'd,* 430 U.S. 651 (1977).

62. *See* Metzger v. Osbeck, 841 F.2d 518 (3d Cir. 1988); Wise v. Pea Ridge School Dist., 855 F.2d 560 (8th Cir. 1988); Garcia v. Miera, 817 F.2d 650 (10th Cir. 1987), *cert. denied,* 485 U.S. 959 (1988); Webb v. McCullough, 828 F.2d 1151 (6th Cir. 1987); Hall v. Tawney, 621 F.2d 607 (4th Cir. 1980). The Fifth Circuit Court of Appeals has held that substantive due process rights are not implicated if states proscribe unreasonable student discipline and provide adequate postpunishment remedies for abuse, Fee v. Herndon, 900 F. 2d 804 (5th Cir. 1990), *cert. denied,* 111 S. Ct. 279 (1990); Cunningham v. Beavers, 858 F.2d 269 (5th Cir. 1988), *cert. denied,* 489 U.S. 1067 (1989). *See also* Jefferson v. Ysleta Indep. School Dist., 817 F.2d 303 (5th Cir. 1987) (tying a second-grade student to a chair for an entire day as an instructional technique implicated substantive due process rights).

63. Hall v. Tawney, 621 F.2d 607, 613 (4th Cir. 1980).

64. Wise v. Pea Ridge, 855 F.2d 560, 564 (8th Cir. 1988) ("two licks" with a wooden paddle did not violate a student's substantive due process rights).

65. *Id.*; Garcia v. Miera, 817 F.2d 650 (10th Cir. 1987), *cert. denied,* 485 U.S. 959

(1988); Woodard v. Los Fresnos Indep. School Dist., 732 F.2d 1243 (5th Cir. 1984).

66. Brown v. Johnson, 710 F. Supp. 183 (E.D. Ky. 1989).

67. Wise v. Pea Ridge, 855 F.2d 560 (8th Cir. 1988).

68. Brooks v. School Bd. of City of Richmond, Virginia, 569 F. Supp. 1534 (E.D. Va. 1983).

69. Garcia v. Miera, 817 F.2d 650 (10th Cir. 1987), *cert. denied,* 485 U.S. 959 (1988).

70. Metzger v. Osbeck, 841 F.2d 518 (3d Cir. 1988). *See also* Webb v. McCullough, 828 F.2d 1151 (6th Cir. 1987) (case was remanded for determination of substantive due process claim).

71. Smith v. West Virginia State Bd. of Educ., 295 S.E.2d 680 (W. Va. 1982).

72. *See, e.g.,* Burton v. Kirby, 775 S.W.2d 834 (Tex. Civ. App. 1989); Simmons v. Vancouver School Dist., 704 P.2d 648 (Wash. Ct. App. 1985).

73. Tomczik v. State Tenure Comm'n, 438 N.W.2d 642 (Mich. Ct. App. 1989).

74. Rolando v. School Directors of Dist. No. 125, 358 N.E.2d 945 (Ill. App. Ct. 1976).

75. Landi v. West Chester Area School Dist., 353 A.2d 895 (Pa. Commw. Ct. 1976).

76. Johnson v. Horace Mann Mutual Ins. Co., 241 So. 2d 588 (La. Ct. App. 1970). *See also* Commonwealth v. Douglass, 588 A.2d 53 (Pa. Super. Ct. 1991) (principal was convicted for assault for administering excessive corporal punishment—50 to 60 swats).

77. *See, e.g.,* Fiacco v. Santee, 421 N.Y.S.2d 431 (N.Y. App. Div. 1979); Barnard v. Inhabitants of Shelburne, 102 N.E. 1095 (Mass. 1913).

78. Regents of Univ. of Michigan v. Ewing, 474 U.S. 214, 225 (1985).

79. In Horowitz v. Board of Curators of the Univ. of Missouri, 435 U.S. 78 (1978), the United States Supreme Court reiterated that school authorities can establish and enforce academic standards. In this case, a medical student who was dismissed without notice of the charges or a formal hearing alleged that her constitutional rights were violated. The high court, however, concluded that neither the student's liberty nor property interests were impaired by the academic dismissal without a hearing. *See also* Regents of the Univ. of Michigan v. Ewing, 474 U.S. 214 (1985); Spencer v. New York City Bd. of Higher Educ., 502 N.Y.S.2d 358 (N.Y. App. Div. 1986).

80. *See* Emily Bernheim, "Academic Penalties for Misconduct and Nonattendance," *School Law Bulletin,* vol. 16 (1985), pp. 18–28.

81. Knight v. Board of Educ. of Tri-Point Community Unit School Dist., 348 N.E.2d 299 (Ill. App. Ct. 1976).

82. Campbell v. Board of Educ. of New Milford, 475 A.2d 289, 294 (Conn. 1984).

83. Williams v. Board of Educ. for the Marianna School Dist., 626 S.W.2d 361 (Ark. 1982).

84. Slocum v. Holton Bd. of Educ., 429 N.W.2d 607 (Mich. Ct. App. 1988).

85. Bitting v. Lee, 564 N.Y.S.2d 791 (N.Y. App. Div. 1990).

86. R.J.J. by Johnson v. Shineman, 658 S.W.2d 910 (Mo. Ct. App. 1983).

87. Gutierrez v. School Dist. R-1, Otero County, 585 P.2d 935 (Colo. Ct. App. 1978).

88. Dorsey v. Bale, 521 S.W.2d 76 (Ky. Ct. App. 1975).

89. Katzman v. Cumberland Valley School Dist., 479 A.2d 671 (Pa. Commw. Ct.

1984). *See also* In re Angela, 340 S.E.2d 544 (S.C. 1986) (under state law, absences for suspension could not be counted as unexcused absences for determining delinquency).

90. New Braunfels Indep. School Dist. v. Armke, 658 S.W.2d 330 (Tex. Civ. App. 1983).

91. Valentine v. Independent School Dist. of Casey, 183 N.W. 434 (Iowa 1921).

92. Shuman v. Cumberland Valley School Dist. Bd. of Directors, 536 A.2d 490 (Pa. Commw. Ct. 1988).

93. Ladson v. Board of Educ. of Union Free School Dist. No. 9, 323 N.Y.S.2d 545 (N.Y. App. Div. 1971).

94. Fowler v. Williamson, 448 F. Supp. 497 (W.D.N.C. 1978). There also have been a few challenges to school board policies prohibiting students from participating in graduation activities if they have completed graduation requirements in less than the normal four years. *See, e.g.,* Clark v. Board of Educ., Hamilton Local School Dist., 367 N.E.2d 69 (Ohio 1977) (public school officials could not deny an early graduate the right to participate in graduation ceremonies).

95. Camara v. Municipal Court of the City and County of San Francisco, 387 U.S. 523, 528 (1967). *See generally* Nelda Cambron-McCabe and Stephen B. Thomas, "Search and Seizure in the Public Schools," in *Current Issues in School Law,* W. Camp, J. Underwood, and M. Connelly, eds. (Topeka, KS: National Organization on Legal Problems of Education, 1989).

96. *See* Mapp v. Ohio, 367 U.S. 643 (1961).

97. Evidence seized by a private person, however, is admissible since the exclusionary rule does not apply. *See, e.g.,* People v. Stewart, 313 N.Y.S.2d 253 (N.Y. 1970).

98. Search and seizure issues are problematic beyond educational settings. These issues in the law enforcement area pose perplexing dilemmas for police officers and receive frequent review by the Supreme Court.

99. 469 U.S. 325 (1985).

100. *Id.* at 336. Although the Supreme Court rejected the *in loco parentis* (in place of parent) doctrine, the Sixth Circuit Court of Appeals found it applicable in a search that occurred on a class trip. Recognizing school officials' supervisory duties away from the school, the court concluded that they must be given the authority necessary to intervene in a range of activities and to protect students from harm, Webb v. McCullough, 828 F.2d 1151 (6th Cir. 1987).

101. T.L.O., 469 U.S. at 340.

102. *Id.* at 341.

103. *Id.* at 342.

104. *Id.*

105. As Justice Brennan noted in his dissent in *T.L.O.,* the "only definite content [of reasonableness] is that it is *not* the same test as the 'probable cause' standard. . . ." He argued that the departure from probable cause was unclear and unnecessary, creating an "amorphous" standard that will promote more litigation and uncertainty among school officials, *id.* at 354.

106. *See, e.g.,* State v. D.T.W., 425 So. 2d 1383, 1387 (Fla. Civ. App. 1983); State v. McKinnon, 558 P.2d 781, 784 (Wash. 1977); People v. D., 315 N.E.2d 466, 470 (N.Y. 1974); In the Interest of L.L., 280 N.W.2d 343, 351 (Wis. Ct. App. 1979).

107. *See, e.g.,* Edwards v. Rees, 883 F.2d 882 (10th Cir. 1989); M. v. Board of Educ. Ball-Chatham, 429 F. Supp. 288 (S.D. Ill. 1977); In re William G., 709 P.2d 1287 (Cal. 1985); State v. Baccino, 282 A.2d 869 (Del. Super. Ct. 1971).
108. Terry v. Ohio, 392 U.S. 1, 21 (1968).
109. *See, e.g.,* Tarter v. Raybuck, 742 F.2d 977 (6th Cir. 1984), *cert. denied,* 470 U.S. 1051 (1985); State v. McKinnon, 558 P.2d 781 (Wash. 1977); Coronado v. State, 806 S.W.2d 302 (Tex. Ct. App. 1991); People v. Frederick B., 237 Cal. Rptr. 338 (Cal. Ct. App. 1987); State v. D.T.W., 425 So. 2d 1383 (Fla. Civ. App. 1983).
110. T.L.O., 469 U.S. at 342 n. 8.
111. *See, e.g.,* Burnham v. West, 681 F. Supp. 1160 (E.D. Va. 1987); Cales v. Howell Pub. Schools, 635 F. Supp. 454 (E.D. Mich. 1985); Jones v. Latexo Indep. School Dist., 499 F. Supp. 223 (E.D. Tex. 1980).
112. Katz v. United States, 389 U.S. 347, 351–352 (1967).
113. *Id.* at 361 (Harlan, J., concurring).
114. United States v. Chadwick, 433 U.S. 1, 7 (1977).
115. Terry v. Ohio, 392 U.S. 1, 9 (1968).
116. *But see* text with note 156, *infra,* for recent cases addressing the involvement of law enforcement personnel.
117. State v. Stein, 456 P.2d 1, 2 (Kan. 1969), *cert. denied,* 397 U.S. 947 (1970).
118. People v. Overton, 229 N.E.2d 596, 598 (N.Y. 1967).
119. Zamora v. Pomeroy, 639 F.2d 662, 670 (10th Cir. 1981).
120. *See* Commonwealth v. Carey, 554 N.E.2d 1199 (Mass. 1990); In re Donald-son, 75 Cal. Rptr. 220 (Cal. Ct. App. 1969).
121. State v. Joseph T., 336 S.E.2d 728 (W. Va. 1985). *See also* State v. Brooks, 718 P.2d 837 (Wash. Ct. App. 1986) (reasonable grounds for search were established by tip from a student informant; search was further supported by teachers' previous reports of suspected drug use and observations of adminis-trator).
122. State in the Interest of T.L.O., 463 A.2d 934 (N.J. 1983).
123. State v. Brooks, 718 P.2d 837 (Wash. Ct. App. 1986).
124. The court relied on an earlier Washington Supreme Court decision holding that state law does not afford greater protection than the fourteenth amend-ment in connection with school searches, State v. McKinnon, 558 P.2d 781 (Wash. 1977). *See* text with note 149, *infra.*
125. Indiana Code § 20-8.1-5-17(c) (1988).
126. T.L.O., 469 U.S. at 346 (1985).
127. State v. D.T.W., 425 So. 2d 1383 (Fla. Civ. App. 1983). *See also* Common-wealth v. Carey, 554 N.E.2d 1199 (Mass. 1990) (search of locker for a gun was upheld based on report by two student informants); State v. Slattery, 787 P.2d 932 (Wash. Ct. App. 1990) (reliable informant and student's past involvement in drugs justified search of student, his locker, and his car); Shamberg v. State, 762 P.2d 488 (Alaska Ct. App. 1988) (a student's extremely intoxicated condition warranted the search of his car).
128. Jones v. Latexo Indep. School Dist., 499 F. Supp. 223 (E.D. Tex. 1980). *See also* Burnham v. West, 681 F. Supp. 1160 (E.D. Va. 1987).
129. In re William G., 709 P.2d 1287 (Cal. 1985).
130. Horton v. Goose Creek Indep. School Dist., 690 F.2d 470, 478 (5th Cir. 1982), *cert. denied,* 463 U.S. 1207 (1983).

131. In re Bobby B., 218 Cal. Rptr. 253 (Cal. Ct. App. 1985).

132. Wynn v. Board of Educ. of Vestavia Hills, 508 So. 2d 1170 (Ala. 1987).

133. Jones v. Latexo Indep. School Dist., 499 F. Supp. 223 (E.D. Tex. 1980).

134. Tarter v. Raybuck, 742 F.2d 977, 980 (6th Cir. 1984), *cert. denied*, 470 U.S. 1051 (1985).

135. *See, e.g.*, Commonwealth v. Carey, 554 N.E.2d 1199 (Mass. 1990); Rone v. Daviess County Bd. of Educ., 655 S.W.2d 28 (Ky. Ct. App. 1983); State in the Interest of Feazell, 360 So. 2d 907 (La. Ct. App. 1978).

136. M.M. v. Anker, 607 F.2d 588, 589 (2d Cir. 1979). *See* Williams v. Ellington, 936 F.2d 881 (6th Cir. 1991) (substantial evidence existed to justify search).

137. Doe v. Renfrow, 631 F.2d 91, 92–93 (7th Cir. 1980), *cert. denied*, 451 U.S. 1022 (1981).

138. Bilbrey v. Brown, 738 F.2d 1462 (9th Cir. 1984).

139. Bellnier v. Lund, 438 F. Supp. 47 (N.D.N.Y. 1977).

140. People v. D., 315 N.E.2d 466 (N.Y. 1974). *See also* Cales v. Howell Pub. Schools, 635 F. Supp. 454 (E.D. Mich. 1985) (required reasonable suspicion that a *specific* rule or law had been violated).

141. Rone v. Daviess County Bd. of Educ. 655 S.W.2d 28 (Ky. Ct. App. 1983).

142. Zamora v. Pomeroy, 639 F.2d 662, 670 (10th Cir. 1981).

143. Horton v. Goose Creek Indep. School Dist., 690 F.2d 470 (5th Cir. 1982), *cert. denied*, 463 U.S. 1207 (1983). *See also* Jennings v. Joshua Indep. School Dist., 877 F.2d 313 (5th Cir. 1989), *cert. denied*, 110 S. Ct. 3212 (1990); Jones v. Latexo Indep. School Dist., 499 F. Supp. 223 (E.D. Tex. 1980).

144. *See* Horton, *id.* at 477 for a list of case cites.

145. The Fifth Circuit Appellate Court's position is bolstered by the Supreme Court's decision in a law enforcement case, United States v. Place, 462 U.S. 696 (1983). The Court concluded that the brief detention of a passenger's luggage at an airport for the purpose of subjecting it to a "sniff" test by a trained narcotics detection dog did not constitute a search under the fourth amendment. Use of canines was characterized as unique, involving a very limited investigation and minimal disclosure.

146. Subsequently, in denying a rehearing, the court clarified the issue of the dogs' reliability. According to the court, a school district does not have to establish with "*reasonable certainty* that contraband is present . . . or even that there is *probable cause* to believe that contraband will be found." Rather, there must be some evidence to indicate that the dogs' performance is reliable enough to give rise to a reasonable suspicion, Horton, 693 F.2d 524, 525 (5th Cir. 1982), *cert. denied*, 463 U.S. 1207 (1983).

147. Doe v. Renfrow, 631 F.2d 91 (7th Cir. 1980), *cert. denied*, 451 U.S. 1022 (1981).

148. Jones v. Latexo Indep. School Dist., 499 F. Supp. 223, 233 (E.D. Tex. 1980).

149. *Id. See also* Kuehn v. Renton School Dist. No. 403, 694 P.2d 1078, 1081 (Wash. 1985), in which the state high court declared: "The fourth amendment demands more than a generalized probability; it requires that the suspicion be particularized with respect to each individual searched."

150. Horton, 690 F.2d 470 (5th Cir. 1982), *cert. denied*, 463 U.S. 1207 (1983).

151. Skinner v. Railway Labor Executives' Ass'n, 489 U.S. 602 (1989); National Treasury Employees Union v. Von Raab, 489 U.S. 656 (1989).

152. Skinner, *id.*

153. National Treasury Employees Union v. Von Raab, 489 U.S. 656 (1989).
154. Brooks v. East Chambers Consol. Indep. School Dist., 730 F. Supp. 759 (S.D. Tex. 1989). *See also* Odenheim v. Carlstadt-East Rutherford Regional School Dist., 510 A.2d 709 (N.J. Super. Ct. 1985); Anable v. Ford, 653 F. Supp. 22 (W.D. Ark. 1985) (urinalysis to determine if students were under the influence of drugs while on school grounds was held unconstitutional; a positive test did not necessarily mean that students were under the influence of drugs at school but simply could mean that they had used drugs during the preceding days or weeks); text with note 145, Chapter 8, for a discussion of drug testing of employees.
155. Schaill v. Tippecanoe County School Corp. 864 F.2d 1309 (7th Cir. 1988).
156. *See, e.g.,* Picha v. Wielgos, 410 F. Supp. 1214 (N.D. Ill. 1976).
157. *See, e.g.,* Cason v. Cook, 810 F.2d 188 (8th Cir. 1987), *cert. denied,* 482 U.S. 930 (1987).
158. *See* J. W. Shaw, *Admissibility, in Criminal Cases, of Evidence Obtained by Search Conducted by School Official or Teacher,* 49 A.L.R.3d 978 (1973).
159. *See, e.g.,* In the Interest of P.E.A., 754 P.2d 382 (Colo. 1988); State v. D.T.W., 425 So. 2d 1383 (Fla. Civ. App. 1983); D.R.C. v. State, 646 P.2d 252 (Alaska Ct. App. 1982). *But see* People v. Frederick B., 237 Cal. Rptr. 338 (Cal. Ct. App. 1987) (detention by a school-paid police officer is not a search).
160. Picha v. Wielgos, 410 F. Supp. 1214 (N.D. Ill. 1976).
161. Martens v. District No. 220, Bd. of Educ., 620 F. Supp. 29 (N.D. Ill. 1985). *See also* Commonwealth v. Carey, 554 N.E.2d 1199 (Mass. 1990).
162. Cason v. Cook, 810 F.2d 188 (8th Cir. 1987), *cert. denied,* 482 U.S. 930 (1987). *See also* In the Interest of P.E.A., 754 P.2d 382 (Colo. 1988).
163. State v. McKinnon, 558 P.2d 781 (Wash. 1977).
164. State v. D.T.W., 425 So. 2d 1838, 1385 (Fla. Civ. App. 1983). *See also* M.J. v. State, 399 So. 2d 996 (Fla. Civ. App. 1981).
165. Rone v. Daviess County Bd. of Educ., 655 S.W.2d 28 (Ky. Ct. App. 1983). *See also* D.R.C. v. State, 646 P.2d 252 (Alaska Ct. App. 1982) (implicit assumption that police involvement would require probable cause).
166. Other constitutional questions also may be raised. In some public schools, undercover police have been placed in classes to investigate drug trafficking. In a case before the Sixth Circuit Court of Appeals, teachers, students, and parents alleged that such action constituted an impairment of first amendment rights. Rejecting this claim, the court held that the surveillance did not disrupt classroom activities, and even though the investigation allegedly focused on classes involving students and teachers with "liberal" sociopolitical views, there was no indication that the investigation had any tangible and concrete inhibitory effect on classroom expression, Gordon v. Warren Consol. Bd. of Educ., 706 F.2d 778 (6th Cir. 1983). *See also* Labrosse v. St. Bernard Parish School Bd., 483 So. 2d 1253 (La. Ct. App. 1986).
167. *See* Ingraham v. Wright, 430 U.S. 651 (1977).
168. *See, e.g.,* McEntire v. Brevard County School Bd., 471 So. 2d 1287 (Fla. Civ. App. 1985); Quinlan v. University Place School Dist., 660 P.2d 329 (Wash. Ct. App. 1983); John A. v. San Bernardino City Unified School Dist., 654 P.2d 242 (Cal. 1982).
169. *See, e.g.,* Shuman v. Cumberland Valley School Dist. Bd. of Directors, 536 A.2d 490 (Pa. Commw. Ct. 1988); Katzman v. Cumberland Valley School Dist., 479 A.2d 671 (Pa. Commw. Ct. 1984).

170. *See, e.g.,* Anable v. Ford, 663 F. Supp. 149 (W.D. Ark. 1985); Jones v. Latexo Indep. School Dist., 499 F. Supp. 223 (E.D. Tex. 1980); People v. D., 315 N.E.2d 466 (N.Y. 1974).
171. Howlett v. Rose, 110 S. Ct. 2430 (1990), *on remand,* 571 So. 2d 29 (Fla. Dist. Ct. App. 1990); Wood v. Strickland, 420 U.S. 308 (1975). Section 1983 of the Civil Rights Act of 1871, 42 U.S.C. § 1983 (1988), provides a damages remedy for deprivations of federally protected rights under color of state law. *See also* text with note 172, Chapter 8.
172. 420 U.S. 308 (1975).
173. Anable v. Ford, 663 F. Supp. 149, 155 (W.D. Ark. 1985).
174. 435 U.S. 247 (1978).
175. Boyd v. Board of Directors of McGehee School Dist. No. 17, 612 F. Supp. 86 (E.D. Ark. 1985). *See also* text with note 70, Chapter 4.
176. Doe v. Renfrow, 631 F.2d 91 (7th Cir. 1980), *cert. denied,* 451 U.S. 1022 (1981).
177. Goss v. Lopez, 419 U.S. 565, 583 (1975).
178. Tinker v. Des Moines Indep. School Dist., 393 U.S. 503, 524 (1969) (Black, J., dissenting).

7
Terms and Conditions of Employment

As noted in Chapter 1, the control of public education resides with the states. The judiciary has clearly recognized the plenary power of the state legislature in establishing, conducting, and regulating all public education functions. The legislature, through statutory law, establishes the boundaries within which educational systems operate; however, the actual administration of school systems is delegated to state boards of education, state departments of education, and local boards of education. These agencies promulgate rules and regulations pursuant to legislative policy for the operation of public schools.

While state statutes are prominent in defining teachers' employment rights, they cannot be viewed independently of state and federal constitutional provisions, civil rights laws, and negotiated agreements between school boards and teacher unions. These provisions may restrict or modify options available under the state school code. For example, the authority to transfer teachers may be vested in the school board, but the board cannot use this power to discipline a teacher for exercising protected constitutional rights. The board's discretion may be further limited if it has agreed in the master contract with the teachers' union to follow certain procedures prior to transferring an employee.

Among the areas affected by state statutory and regulatory provisions are the terms and conditions of a public school teacher's employment. This chapter presents an overview of state requirements pertaining to teacher certification, employment, contracts, tenure, and related conditions of employment. Also, two topics of increasing interest to educators, using copyrighted materials and reporting child abuse, are included. Specific job requirements that implicate constitutional rights or antidiscrimination mandates are addressed in subsequent chapters.

CERTIFICATION

To qualify for a teaching position in public schools, prospective teachers must acquire a valid certificate or license. Certification is a state responsibility, and certificates are issued according to each state's statutory provisions. States have not only the right but also the duty to establish minimum qualifications and to ensure that teachers meet these standards. Although the responsibility for licensing resides with legislatures, administration of the process has been delegated to state boards of education and departments of education.

Certificates are granted primarily on the basis of professional preparation. In most states, educational requirements include a college degree, with minimum credit hours or courses in various curricular areas. Other prerequisites to certification may include good character, a minimum age, United States citizenship, signing of a loyalty oath, and passage of an academic examination. The following is a representative statutory requirement.

> The Department of Public Instruction shall have the power, and its duty shall be: (a) To provide for and to regulate the certificates and the registration of persons qualified to teach in such schools; (b) To certify as qualified to practice the art of teaching in such schools any applicant eighteen (18) years of age, of good moral character, not addicted to the use of intoxicating liquor or narcotic drugs and who has graduated from a college, university or institution of learning approved as herein provided, and who has completed such professional preparation for teaching as may be prescribed by the State Board of Education, and to register such person upon such proof as the State Board of Education may require that such applicant possess such qualifications.[1]

As noted in the above statutory requirement, an applicant for certification may be required to have "good moral character." The definition of what constitutes good character is often elusive, with a number of factors entering into the determination. The Supreme Court of Oregon found that conviction for burglary eight years prior to application for a teaching certificate was pertinent in assessing character for certification purposes. The court noted that character embraced all "qualities and deficiencies regarding traits of personality, behavior, integrity, temperament, consideration, sportsmanship, altruism, etc."[2] Courts generally will not rule on the wisdom of a certifying agency's assessment of character; they will intervene only if statutory or constitutional rights are abridged.

Certification of teachers by examination was common prior to the expansion of teacher education programs in colleges and universities. Then, for many years, only a few southern states required passage of an exam. With the emphasis on improving the quality of schools and teachers, the trend has been toward the reinstatement of examinations as a prerequisite to certification. By 1988, forty-seven states required some type of standardized test for entry into teacher education programs, program completion, initial certification, and/or certification renewal.[3] Most of the states have employed the National Teachers Examination, and its use has been upheld by the United States Supreme Court even though the test has been shown to disproportionately disqualify African-American applicants.[4] Constitutional and statutory challenges to employment tests are discussed in Chapter 9.

Signing a loyalty oath often is a condition of obtaining a teaching certificate, but such oaths cannot be used to restrict associational rights guaranteed under the Federal Constitution. The Supreme Court has invalidated oaths that require teacher applicants to swear that they are not members of subversive organizations;[5] however, teachers can be required to sign an oath pledging faithful performance of duties and support for the Federal Constitution and an individual state's constitution.[6] According to the Supreme Court, these oaths must be narrowly limited to affirmation of support for the government and a pledge not to act forcibly to overthrow the government.[7]

As a condition of certification, a teacher may be required to be a citizen of the United States. In 1979 the Supreme Court addressed whether such a New York statutory requirement violated the equal protection clause of the fourteenth amendment.[8] Under the New York education laws, a teacher who is eligible for citizenship but refuses to apply for naturalization cannot be certified. Although the Supreme Court has placed restrictions on the states' ability to exclude aliens from governmental employment, it has recognized that certain functions are "so bound up with the operation of the state as a governmental entity as to permit the exclusion from those functions of all persons who have not become part of the process of self-government."[9] Applying this principle, the Court held that teaching is an integral "governmental function"; thus, a state must show only a rational relationship between a citizenship requirement and a legitimate state interest. The Court concluded that New York's interest in furthering its educational goals justified the citizenship mandate for teachers.

Some litigation has focused on legislative efforts to alter certification standards by imposing new or additional requirements as a prerequisite to recertification. The Supreme Court of Texas held that teachers possessing life certificates could be required to pass an examination as a condition of continued employment.[10] Since the certificate was found to be a "license" rather than a "contract," the court held that new conditions for retention of the certificate could be imposed. The Supreme Court of Connecticut, recognizing teaching certificates as contracts, still upheld the state's authority to replace permanent certificates with five-year certificates renewable upon the completion of continuing education requirements.[11] Holding that this change was constitutionally acceptable, the court found only a minimal impairment of contractual rights, which could be justified by the state's significant interest in improving public education. Under statutory law, however, the Supreme Court of Rhode Island found that the State Board of Regents for Elementary and Secondary Education could not revoke valid five-year certificates for teachers' failure to meet new *agency* requirements.[12] Since state law provided that certificates were valid for a specified period of time and could be revoked only for cause, teachers could not be required to meet a state agency's new requirements until their certificates expired.

Certificates are issued for designated periods of time under various classifications such as emergency, temporary, provisional, professional, and permanent. Renewing or upgrading a certificate may require additional university coursework, other continuing education activities, or passage of an examination. Certificates also specify professional position (e.g., teacher, administrator, librarian), subject areas (e.g., history, English, math), and grade levels (e.g., elementary, high school). Where certification subject areas have been established, a teacher must possess a valid certificate to teach a specific subject.[13] A school district's failure to employ certified teachers may result in the loss of state accreditation and financial support.[14]

A certificate to teach is a license, not an absolute right to acquire a position. Certification indicates only that a teacher has satisfied minimum state requirements. It does not entitle an individual to employment in a particular district or guarantee employment in the state, nor does it prevent a local school board from attaching additional prerequisites for employment.[15] For example, an Iowa appellate court upheld a local school board's authority to require physical education teachers to complete training in cardiopulmonary resuscitation and water-safety instruction.[16] If a local board imposes additional standards, however, the requirements must be uniformly applied to all teachers in the district.[17]

Teaching credentials must be in proper order to ensure full employment rights. Where a state law required a teacher's certificate to be on file in the district of employment, the failure to file the certificate rendered the teacher's contract voidable.[18] Failure to renew a certificate prior to expiration[19] or to meet educational requirements necessary to maintain or acquire a higher grade certification[20] can result in loss of employment. Without proper certification, a teaching contract is unenforceable.[21]

The state is empowered not only to certify teachers but also to revoke certification. Although a local board may initiate charges against a teacher, only the state can revoke a teacher's certificate.[22] Revocation of a certificate is a harsh penalty, generally foreclosing future employment as a teacher in the state.[23] As such, it must be based on statutory cause with full procedural rights provided to the teacher.[24] The most frequently cited grounds for revoking certification are immorality, incompetency, contract violation, and neglect of duty.

When revocation of a certificate is being considered, assessment of a teacher's competency encompasses not only classroom performance but also actions outside the school setting that may impair the teacher's effectiveness. The California Supreme Court found that a teacher's participation in a "swingers club" and disguised appearance on television discussing nonconventional sexual behavior justified revocation of certification on grounds of unfitness to teach.[25] In an earlier case, however, the same court held that an isolated incident of private homosexuality did not justify license revocation; no connection was shown between the teacher's activity and effectiveness to teach.[26] Similarly, the Supreme Court of Iowa found an extramarital affair insufficient to warrant revoking the certificate of an effective, highly respected teacher.[27] A Florida appellate court, however, ruled that two teachers' possession of marijuana plants established "moral turpitude" justifying revocation of their certificates.[28] In a Pennsylvania case, a teacher's conviction for mail fraud was considered a crime involving "moral turpitude," which by state law required revocation of his teaching certificate.[29]

EMPLOYMENT BY LOCAL SCHOOL BOARDS

As noted, certification does not guarantee employment in a state; it attests only that the teacher has met minimum state requirements. The decision to employ a certified teacher is among the discretionary powers of local school boards. While such powers are broad, school board actions cannot be arbitrary, capricious, or in violation of an individual's statutory or constitutional rights.[30] Employment decisions must be neutral as to race, religion, national origin, and gender.[31] Unless protected individual rights are abridged, courts will not review the wisdom of a local school board's judgment in employment decisions made in good faith.

The responsibility for hiring teachers is vested in the school board as a collective body and cannot be delegated to the superintendent or board members individually.[32] In most states, binding employment agreements between a teacher and school board must be approved at legally scheduled board meetings. Procedurally, a number of state laws specify that the superintendent must make employment recommendations to the board; however, the board is not compelled to follow these recommendations unless mandated to do so by law.[33]

School boards possess extensive authority in establishing job requirements and conditions of employment for school personnel. The following sections examine the school board's power to impose specific conditions on teacher employment and to assign personnel.

EMPLOYMENT REQUIREMENTS

The state's establishment of minimum certification standards for teachers does not preclude the local school board from requiring higher professional or academic standards as long as they are applied in a uniform and nondiscriminatory manner. For example, school boards often establish continuing education requirements for teachers and a board's right to dismiss teachers for failing to satisfy such requirements has been upheld by the Supreme Court.[34] The Court concluded that school officials merely had to establish that the requirement was rationally related to a legitimate state objective, which in this case was to provide competent, well-trained teachers.

School boards also may require teachers to live within the school district as a condition of employment. Such residency requirements have been challenged as impairing equal protection rights under the Federal Constitution by interfering with interstate and intrastate travel. Generally, as long as the board has a rational basis for adopting the rule, courts will uphold a residency requirement as constitutionally acceptable. Illustrative is a Sixth Circuit Court of Appeals case involving a Cincinnati school board policy that required all new employees to establish residency in the school district within ninety days of employment.[35] A teacher challenged the rule on equal protection grounds. Declining to extend constitutional protection to intrastate travel, the court held that the district produced a rational basis to support the regulation. Among the reasons advanced by the school system for establishing the residency requirement were that teachers living in the community were more likely to be involved in community affairs, have a commitment to urban education, and support district tax increases.

Shortly after the Sixth Circuit Appellate Court's decision, the United States Supreme Court upheld a municipal regulation requiring all employees hired after a certain date in Philadelphia to be residents of the city.[36] Those already employed were not required to alter their residence. The requirement was challenged as unconstitutionally interfering with interstate travel by a fire department employee who was terminated when he moved to New Jersey. In upholding the regulation, the Court distinguished a requirement of residency of a given duration *prior* to employment (which violates the right to interstate travel) from a continuing residency requirement applied *after* employment. The Court concluded that a continuing residency requirement, if "appropriately defined and uniformly applied," does not violate an individual's constitutional rights.[37]

Although residency requirements after employment do not violate the Federal Constitution, public employees have urged state courts to hold such provisions impermissible under state law. Following the majority of other courts, in 1988 the Supreme Court of Arkansas concluded that a school district policy requiring personnel to live within the district or within a ten-mile radius did not violate the state's equal protection clause, even though it applied only to certified personnel.[38] Individual states, however, may have statutory or constitutional provisions prohibiting residency requirements. For example, Indiana school boards, by statute, are not permitted to adopt any requirements pertaining to employee residence.[39] In states with such restrictions, the laws would have to be repealed or amended to enable school boards to establish residency regulations.

Unlike residency requirements, school board policies requiring employees to send their children to public schools have been declared unconstitutional. Parents have a constitutionally protected right to direct the upbringing of their children that cannot be restricted without a compelling state interest. The Eleventh Circuit Appellate Court held that a school board policy requiring employees to enroll their children in public schools could not be justified to promote an integrated public school system and good relationships among teachers when weighed against the right of parents to direct the education of their children.[40]

School boards can adopt reasonable health and physical requirements for teachers. Courts have recognized that such standards are necessary to safeguard the health and welfare of students and other employees. The First Circuit Court of Appeals held that a school board could compel an administrator to submit to a psychiatric examination as a condition of continued employment; a reasonable basis existed for the board members to believe that the administrator might jeopardize the safety of students.[41] Although courts have not condoned blanket drug testing of teachers as a condition of employment, the District of Columbia Court of Appeals found a mandatory drug test, as part of a routine, job-related medical examination, permissible under the fourth amendment for employees whose duties related to the safety of children—in this instance, school bus attendants.[42]

Health and physical requirements imposed on school personnel, however, must not be applied in an arbitrary manner. The Second Circuit Court of Appeals found arbitrary and unreasonable a New York school board's insistence that a female teacher on extended sick leave for a back ailment be examined by the district's male physician rather than a female physician (to be selected by the board).[43] School board standards for physical fitness also must be rationally related to ability to perform teaching duties. A New York appellate court found that obesity *per se* was not reasonably related to ability to teach or maintain discipline.[44]

In addition, regulations must not contravene various state and federal laws designed to protect the rights of persons with disabilities. For example, in a Pennsylvania case the Third Circuit Court of Appeals ruled that school officials could not refuse to consider blind individuals as teachers for sighted students.[45] A New York trial court similarly held that blindness *per se* cannot disqualify one as a teacher.[46] The United States Supreme Court ruled that tuberculosis, a contagious disease, is a disability under federal antidiscrimination provisions that protect otherwise qualified individuals with disabilities from adverse employment consequences. Accordingly, a school district could not dismiss a teacher for chronic recurrences of tuberculosis without evidence that the teacher was otherwise unqualified to perform her job or that accommodations would place undue hardships on the school district.[47]

A school board's authority in employment also can extend to prohibiting employees from engaging in outside employment during the school year. The Fifth Circuit Court of Appeals reviewed the constitutionality of a board policy, incorporated into employment contracts, providing that employees could not engage in any other business full- or part-time during the contract period.[48] The school board relied on this policy in declining to renew the contracts of a principal and his wife, an elementary teacher, after they purchased a dry goods store. Although finding the policy related to a legitimate state purpose—"assuring that public school employees devote their professional energies to the education of children"—the court concluded that the rule was arbitrarily and discriminatorily applied to the couple.[49] A number of employees in the district were involved in outside employment, but the policy had never been applied to anyone else. Acknowledging the school board's "wide latitude" in adopting policies necessary for effective administration of schools, the court emphasized that a restriction must be applied equally to all who are similarly situated.

ASSIGNMENT OF PERSONNEL AND DUTIES

The authority to assign teachers to schools within a district resides with the board of education.[50] As with employment in general, these decisions can be challenged only if arbitrary or made in bad faith.[51] Within the limits of certification, a teacher can be assigned to teach in any school at any grade level.[52] Assignments designated in the teacher's contract, however, cannot be changed during a contractual period without the teacher's consent. That is, a board cannot reassign a teacher to a first-grade class if the contract specifies a fifth-grade assignment. If the contract designates only a teaching assignment within the district, the assignment still must be in the teacher's area of certification. Also, objective, nondiscriminatory standards must be used in any employment or assignment decision.[53] Assignments to achieve racial balance may be permitted in school districts that have not eliminated the effects of school segregation; however, any racial classification must be temporary and necessary to eradicate the effects of prior discrimination.[54]

School boards retain the authority to assign or transfer teachers, but such decisions often are challenged as demotions requiring procedural due process. Depending on statutory law, factors considered in determining whether a reassignment is a demotion may include reduction in salary, responsibility, and stature of position.[55] A Pennsylvania teacher contested a transfer from a ninth- to a sixth-grade class as a demotion.[56] The court, noting the equivalency of the positions, stated that "there is no less importance, dignity, responsibility, authority, prestige, or compensation in the elementary grades than in secondary."[57] In another instance, however, the reassignment of a Montana band instructor to a teaching position in an ungraded rural school without a band was held to be a demotion.[58] Similarly, the reassignment of an Ohio classroom teacher as a permanent substitute or floating teacher was found to be a demotion in violation of the state tenure law.[59] The court recognized the pervasive authority of the superintendent and board to make teaching assignments, but noted that this power may be limited by other statutory provisions, such as the state tenure law. This reduction in status without a notice and hearing was found to deprive the teacher of due process guarantees.

Administrative reassignments frequently are challenged as demotions because of reductions in salary, responsibility, and stature of position. An Alabama high school principal asserted that his transfer to an elementary principalship with a $4,000 reduction in salary violated state law that prohibited transfers involving a "loss of status."[60] According to a state appellate court, the only factor to be considered in determining "status" is tenure status. Since the principal's tenure was not affected, there was no loss in status. A Michigan principal also was unsuccessful in challenging a salary freeze as a demotion.[61] Although other administrators were given raises each year, the court found that under state law compensation must be actually reduced for an action to be considered a demotion. A Pennsylvania school district increased administrative salaries, but a simultaneous increase in the number of workdays resulted in a reduction in compensation per day. Under state law, however, this did not constitute a demotion since the annual salary was not reduced.[62] A reassignment from an administrative to a teaching position because of financial constraints or good faith reorganization is not a demotion requiring due process unless procedural protections are specified in state law.[63]

Statutory procedures and agency regulations established for transferring or demoting employees must be strictly followed.[64] For example, under a West Virginia State Board of Education policy, school boards cannot initiate a disciplinary transfer unless there has been a prior evaluation informing the individual that specific conduct can result in a transfer.[65] Furthermore, there must be an opportunity for employees to improve their performance. Under Pennsylvania law, demotions related to declining enrollment involve a realignment of staff, and to assure proper realignment of positions, procedural protections are required.[66]

The assignment of noninstructional duties often is defined in a teacher's contract or the master contract negotiated between the school board and the teachers' union. In the absence of such specification, it is generally held that boards can make reasonable and appropriate assignments.[67] Courts usually restrict assignments to activities that are an integral part of the school program and, in some situations, to duties related to the employee's teaching responsibilities.[68] A California teacher claimed that being required to supervise six athletic events during the school year was both unprofessional and beyond the scope of his duties.[69] The court determined that the assignment was within the scope of the contract and reasonable, since it was impartially distributed and did not place an onerous time burden on the teacher. An Illinois appellate court concluded that requiring teachers to submit typed copies of class examinations for duplication is not demeaning or detrimental to a teacher's professional standing; the board has the right to assign nonclassroom duties.[70] A New Jersey appellate court stated that the reasonableness of an assignment should be evaluated in terms of time involvement, teachers' interests and abilities, benefits to students, and the professional nature of the duty.[71] Refusal to accept assigned duties can result in dismissal.[72]

CONTRACTS

The employment contract defines the rights and responsibilities of the teacher and the school board in the employment relationship. The general principles of contract law apply to this contractual relationship. Like all other legal contracts, it must contain the basic elements of (1) offer and acceptance, (2) competent parties, (3) consideration, (4) legal subject matter, and (5) proper form.[73] Beyond these basic elements, it also must meet the requirements specified in state law and administrative regulations.

The authority to contract with teachers is an exclusive right of the board. The school board's offer of a position to a teacher, including (1) designated salary, (2) specified period of time, and (3) identified duties and responsibilities, creates a binding contract when accepted by the teacher. In most states, only the board can make an offer, and this action must be approved by a majority of the board members in a properly called meeting. In a South Dakota case, the superintendent and chairperson of the school board extended a teacher an offer of employment at the beginning of the school year, pending approval by the board two weeks later.[74] Because of teaching problems the teacher encountered during that brief period, the board refused to approve the contract. The Supreme Court of South Dakota concluded that no contract existed between the teacher and the district since the statutorily mandated procedure for contract approval had not been met.

Contracts also can be invalidated because of lack of competent parties. To form a valid, binding contract, both parties must have the legal capacity to enter into an agreement. The school board has been recognized as a legally competent party with the capacity to contract. A teacher who lacks certification or is under the statutorily required age for certification is not considered a competent party for contractual purposes. Consequently, a contract made with such an individual is not enforceable.[75]

Consideration is another essential element of a valid contract. Consideration is something of value that one party pays in return for the other party's performance. Also, the contract must pertain to a legal subject matter and follow the proper form required by law. Most states prescribe that a teacher's contract must be in writing to be enforceable. If there is no statutory specification, an oral agreement is legally binding on both parties.

In addition to employment rights derived from the teaching contract, other rights accrue from collective bargaining agreements in effect at the time of employment. Also, statutory provisions and school board rules and regulations may be considered as part of the terms and conditions of the contract. If not included directly, the provisions existing at the time of the contract may be implied. Moreover, the contract cannot be used as a means of waiving teachers' statutory rights.[76]

Two basic types of employment contracts are issued to teachers: term contracts and tenure contracts. Term contracts are valid for a fixed period of time (e.g., one or two years). At the end of the contract period, renewal is at the discretion of the school board, and nonrenewal requires no explanation, unless statutorily mandated. Generally, a school board is required only to provide notice prior to the expiration of the contract that employment will not be renewed. Tenure contracts, created through state legislative action, ensure teachers that employment will be terminated only for adequate cause and that procedural due process will be provided. After the award of tenure or *during* a term contract, school boards cannot unilaterally abrogate teachers' contracts. At a minimum, the teacher must be provided with notice of the dismissal charges and a hearing.[77]

Since tenure contracts involve statutory rights, specific procedures and protections vary among the states. Consequently, judicial interpretations in one state provide little guidance in understanding another state's law. Most tenure statutes specify requirements and procedures for obtaining tenure and identify causes and procedures for dismissing a tenured teacher. In interpreting tenure laws, courts have attempted to protect teachers' rights while simultaneously preserving school officials' flexibility in personnel management.

Prior to a school board awarding a tenure contract to a teacher, most states require a probationary period of approximately three years to assess a teacher's ability and competence. During this probationary period, teachers receive term contracts, and there is no guarantee of employment beyond each contract. Tenure statutes generally require regular and continuous service to complete the probationary period. For example, the Massachusetts tenure law requires three consecutive school years of teaching service immediately prior to the award of tenure. Interpreting this mandate, a Massachusetts appellate court held that a teacher who taught for approximately three-fourths of a school term could not count such teaching service toward tenure because it was less than a year.[78] However, part-time employment of a continuous and regular nature was interpreted as meeting probationary requirements under the Massachusetts statute, because the law required only continuous service and did not designate a separate classification for part-time service.[79]

The authority to grant a tenure contract is a discretionary power of the local school board that cannot be delegated.[80] Although the school board confers tenure, it cannot alter the tenure terms established by the legislature; the legislature determines the basis for tenure, eligibility, and the procedures for acquiring tenure status.[81] Thus, if a statute requires a probationary period, this term of service must be completed prior to acquisition of tenure. Also, if areas in which school personnel may accrue tenure are identified, school boards can grant tenure only in those areas.[82] A tenure contract provides a certain amount of job security, but it does not guarantee permanent employment, nor does it convey the right to teach in a particular school, grade, or subject area.[83] Teachers may be dismissed for the causes specified in the tenure law, and may be reassigned to positions for which they are certified.

In establishing tenure, a legislature may create a contractual relationship that cannot be altered without violating constitutional guarantees. The Federal Constitution, Article I, Section 10, provides that the obligation of a contract cannot be impaired. The United States Supreme Court found such a contractual relationship in the 1927 Indiana Teacher Tenure Act, which prevented the state legislature from subsequently depriving teachers of rights conveyed under the Act.[84] However, a statutory relationship that does not have the elements of a contract can be altered or repealed at the legislature's discretion.[85] Some state tenure laws are clearly noncontractual, containing provisos that the law may be altered, while other state laws are silent on revisions. If a tenure law is asserted to be contractual, the language of the act is critical in the judiciary's interpretation of legislative intent.

A number of states limit the award of tenure to teaching positions, thereby excluding administrative and supervisory positions. Where tenure is available for administrative positions, probationary service and other specified statutory terms must be met.[86] Although tenure as a teacher usually does not imply tenure as an administrator, most courts have concluded that continued service as a certified professional employee, albeit as an administrator, does not alter tenure rights acquired as a teacher.[87] The Supreme Court of Wyoming noted: "It is desirable—and even important—to have people with extensive classroom teaching experience in administrative positions. It would be difficult to fill administrative positions with experienced teachers if the teachers would have to give up tenure upon accepting administrative positions."[88] In contrast to the prevailing view, the Supreme Court of New Mexico held that an individual who voluntarily resigned a teaching position for advancement to an administrative position forfeited tenure rights.[89] According to the court, tenure rights attach to a position rather than to an individual.

Supplemental service contracts are usually considered outside the scope of tenure protections. Coaches, in particular, have asserted that supplemental contracts are an integral part of the teaching position and thereby must be afforded the procedural and substantive protections of state tenure laws. Several courts have noted that tenure rights apply only to employment in certified areas and that the lack of certification requirements for coaches in a state negates tenure claims for such positions.[90] The Supreme Court of Iowa held that even a requirement that coaches must be certified did not confer teachers' tenure rights on coaching positions.[91] In this case, the coaching assignment was found to be clearly an extra duty, requiring a separate contract and compensation based on an extra-duty pay scale. Other courts also have distinguished coaching and various extra duties from teaching duties based on the extracurricular nature of the assignment and supplemental compensation.[92] However, the Supreme Court of South Dakota held that the position of head coach came under the continuing contract law, since state administrative rules defined certification requirements for the job.[93]

Because coaching assignments generally require execution of a supplemental contract, a teacher can usually resign a coaching position and maintain the primary teaching position.[94] School boards having difficulty in filling coaching positions, however, may tender an offer to teach on the condition that an individual assume certain coaching responsibilities. If a single teaching and coaching contract is found to be indivisible, a teacher cannot unilaterally resign the coaching duties without relinquishing the teaching position.[95] Individual state laws must be consulted to determine the status of such contracts.

Where teaching and coaching positions are combined, a qualified teaching applicant who cannot assume the coaching duties may be rejected. This practice, however, may be vulnerable to legal challenge if certain classes of applicants, such as women, are excluded from consideration. In an Arizona case, female plaintiffs successfully established that a school district was guilty of gender discrimination by coupling a high school biology teaching position with a football coaching position. The school board was unable to demonstrate a business necessity for the practice that resulted in female applicants for the teaching position being eliminated from consideration.[96]

Contracts may specify various types of leaves of absence. Within the parameters of state law, school boards have discretion in establishing requirements for these leaves. This topic often is the subject of collective negotiations, with leave provisions specified in bargained agreements. School boards, however, cannot negotiate leave policies that impair rights guaranteed by the Federal Constitution and various federal and state antidiscrimination laws.[97] Similarly, where state law confers specific rights, local boards do not have the discretion to deny or alter these rights. Generally, statutes identify employees' rights related to various kinds of leaves such as sick leave, personal leave, sabbatical leave, disability leave, and military leave. State laws pertaining to leaves of absence usually specify eligibility for benefits, minimum days that must be provided, whether leave must be granted with or without pay, and restrictions that may be imposed by local school boards. If a teacher meets all statutory and procedural requirements for a specific leave, a school board cannot deny the request.[98]

PERSONNEL EVALUATION

To ensure a quality teaching staff, many states have enacted laws requiring periodic appraisal of teaching performance. Beyond the purposes of faculty improvement and remediation, results of evaluations may be used in a variety of employment decisions including retention, tenure, dismissal, promotion, salary, reassignment, and reduction in force. When adverse personnel decisions are based on evaluations, legal concerns of procedural fairness arise. Were established state and local procedures followed? Did school officials employ equitable standards? Was sufficient evidence collected to support the staffing decision? Were evaluations conducted in a uniform and consistent manner?

School systems have broad discretionary powers to establish teacher performance criteria, but state statutes may impose specific evaluation requirements. More than half of the states have enacted laws governing teacher evaluation. Content and requirements vary substantially across states, with some states merely mandating the establishment of an appraisal system and others specifying procedures and criteria to be employed. Iowa law notes only that the local board must establish an evaluation system.[99] California, on the other hand, specifies the intent of evaluations, areas to be assessed, frequency of evaluations, notice to employees of deficiencies, and an opportunity to improve performance.[100] Florida requires the superintendent of schools to establish criteria and procedures for appraisal including evaluation at least once a year by the principal, written record of assessment, prior notice to teachers of criteria and procedures, and a meeting with the principal to discuss the results of the evaluation.[101] Although a few evaluation systems are established at the state level,[102] state laws usually require local officials to develop evaluation criteria, often in conjunction with teachers or other professionals.[103]

Teacher evaluation also may be required by state administrative regulations rather than by statute. For example, a West Virginia Board of Education policy entitles a teacher to an "open and honest evaluation of his performance on a regular basis."[104] Failure of school officials to follow the state board procedures will nullify demotion, promotion, transfer, or dismissal of a teacher.[105] Under this policy, the West Virginia Supreme Court overturned the discharge of a teacher who was not afforded an opportunity to improve his performance[106] and ordered reinstatement of two teachers in the absence of honest and open evaluations.[107]

When evaluation procedures are identified in statutes, board policies, or employment contracts, courts generally require strict compliance with these provisions. A California appeals court found that the nonrenewal of a teacher's contract violated the statutory notification deadline and requirement for a written evaluation.[108] A Washington appellate court required the reinstatement of a principal because the school board had not adopted evaluation criteria and procedures as required by law.[109] The court noted that in the absence of evaluation criteria the principal would serve at the whim of the superintendent and would be deprived of guidelines to improve his performance. The West Virginia Supreme Court held that a school system could not transfer an individual because the decision was not based on performance evaluations as required by state board policy.[110]

Where school boards have been attentive to evaluation requirements, courts have upheld challenged employment decisions.[111] A California appellate court found that a teacher's dismissal comported with state evaluation requirements because he received periodic appraisals noting specific instances of unsatisfactory performance.[112] The evaluation reports informed the teacher of the system's expectations, his specific teaching weaknesses, and actions needed to correct deficiencies. An Iowa court found a school district's policy requiring a formal evaluation every three years for nonprobationary teachers to be adequate under a statutory requirement that "the board shall establish evaluation criteria and shall implement evaluation procedures."[113] The court denied a teacher's claim that the law required an additional evaluation whenever termination of employment was contemplated. According to the Supreme Court of South Dakota, violation of an evaluation procedure *per se* does not require reinstatement of a teacher.[114] Reinstatement is justified only if the violation substantially interfered with a teacher's ability to improve deficiencies.

Courts are reluctant to interject their judgment into the teacher evaluation process. Judicial review generally is limited to the procedural issues of fairness and reasonableness. Several principles emerge from case law to guide educators in developing equitable systems: Standards for assessing teaching adequacy must be defined and communicated to teachers; criteria must be applied uniformly and consistently; an opportunity and direction for improvement must be provided; and procedures specified in state laws and school board policies must be followed.

PERSONNEL RECORDS

Because several or more statutes in each state as well as employment contracts govern school records, it is difficult to generalize as to the specific nature of teachers' privacy rights regarding personnel files. Personnel information is generally protected by state privacy laws that place restrictions on maintenance and access to the records. Among other provisions, these laws typically require school boards to maintain only necessary and relevant information, provide individual employees access to their files, inform employees of the various uses of the files, and provide a procedure for challenging the accuracy of information. Collective bargaining contracts may impose additional and more stringent requirements regarding access and dissemination of personnel information.

A central issue in the confidentiality of personnel files is whether the information constitutes a public record that must be reasonably accessible to the general public. Public-record, or right-to-know, laws that grant broad access to school records may directly conflict with privacy laws, requiring courts to balance the interests of the teacher, school officials, and the public. The specific provisions of state laws determine the level of confidentiality granted personnel records. Several courts have concluded that any doubt as to the appropriateness of disclosure should be decided in favor of public disclosure.[115] Ruling that teachers' personnel files are subject to the open-records law, the Supreme Court of North Dakota held that governmental records are open to the public unless *specifically* exempt by law.[116] The Supreme Court of Washington noted that the public disclosure act mandated disclosure of information that is of legitimate public concern.[117] As such, the state superintendent of public instruction was required to provide a newspaper publisher records specifying the reasons for teacher certificate revocations. In several instances, state laws have been amended to protect from disclosure personal information, such as performance evaluations and college transcripts, while lawsuits seeking disclosure were pending.[118]

Educators have not been successful in asserting that privacy interests in personnel records are protected under the Family Educational Rights and Privacy Act of 1974 (FERPA) and the Federal Constitution. The FERPA has been found to apply only to students and their educational records, not to employees' personnel records.[119] Similarly, employees' claims that their constitutional privacy rights bar disclosure of their personnel records have been unsuccessful. In a case where a teacher's college transcript was sought by a third party under the Texas Open Records Act, the Fifth Circuit Court of Appeals ruled that even if a teacher had a recognizable privacy interest in her transcript, that interest "is significantly outweighed by the public's interest in evaluating the competence of its school teachers."[120]

Access to personnel files also has been controversial in situations involving allegations of employment discrimination. Personnel files must be relinquished if subpoenaed by a court. The Equal Employment Opportunity Commission (EEOC) also is authorized to subpoena *relevant* personnel files to enable the Commission to investigate thoroughly allegations that a particular individual has been the victim of discriminatory treatment. The Supreme Court, in holding that confidential peer review materials used in university promotion and tenure decisions are not protected from disclosure to the EEOC, ruled that under the provisions of Title VII of the Civil Rights Act of 1964 the Commission must only show relevance, not special reasons or justifications, in demanding specific records. Regarding access to peer review materials, the Court noted that "if there is a 'smoking gun' to be found that demonstrates discrimination in tenure decisions, it is likely to be tucked away in peer review files."[121]

Regarding maintenance of records, information clearly cannot be placed in personnel files in retaliation for the exercise of constitutional rights. Courts have ordered letters of reprimand expunged from files when they have been predicated on protected speech and association activities. Reprimands, while not a direct prohibition on protected activities, may present a constitutional violation because of their potentially chilling effect on the exercise of constitutional rights.[122]

Public Concern

OTHER EMPLOYMENT ISSUES

In addition to the terms and conditions of employment already discussed, other reasonable requirements can be attached to public employment as long as civil rights laws are respected and constitutional rights are not impaired without a compelling governmental justification. Public educators are expected to comply with such reasonable requirements as a condition of maintaining their jobs. Some requirements, such as those pertaining to the instructional program and prohibitions against proselytizing students, are discussed in other chapters. Requirements pertaining to two topics have received substantial attention since the 1980s and warrant discussion here—using copyrighted materials and reporting child abuse.

USE OF COPYRIGHTED MATERIALS

Educators' extensive use of published materials and various media in the classroom raises issues relating to the federal copyright law. As a condition of employment, educators are expected to comply with restrictions on the use of copyrighted materials. Although the law grants the owner of a copyright exclusive control over the protected material, courts since the 1800s have recognized exceptions to this control under the doctrine of "fair use." The fair use doctrine cannot be precisely defined, but a common definition frequently used is the "privilege in others than the owner of the copyright to use the copyrighted material in a reasonable manner without his consent, notwithstanding the monopoly granted to the owner. . . ."[123]

Congress incorporated the judicially created fair use concept into the 1976 revisions of the Copyright Act.[124] In identifying the purposes of the fair use exception, Congress specifically noted teaching. The exception provides needed flexibility for teachers but by no interpretation grants them exemption from copyright infringement. The law stipulates four factors to assess whether the use of specific material constitutes fair use or an infringement:

> (1) the purpose and character of the use, including whether such use is of a commercial nature or is for non-profit educational purposes; (2) the nature of the copyrighted work; (3) the amount and substantiality of the portion used in relation to the copyrighted work as a whole; and (4) the effect of the use upon the potential market for or value of the copyrighted work.[125]

To clarify fair use pertaining to photocopying from books and periodicals, Congress incorporated into the committees' conference report a set of guidelines developed by a group representing educators, authors, and publishers.[126] These guidelines are only part of the legislative history of the Act and do not have the force of law, but they have been widely used in assessing the legality of reproducing printed materials in the educational environment. The guidelines permit making single copies of copyrighted material for teaching or research but are quite restrictive on the use of multiple copies. To use multiple copies of a work, the tests of brevity, spontaneity, and cumulative effect must be met. *Brevity* is precisely defined according to type of publication. For example, reproduction of a poem cannot exceed 250 words; copying from longer works cannot exceed 1,000 words or 10 percent of the work (whichever is less); only one chart or drawing can be reproduced from a book or an article. *Spontaneity* requires that the copying be initiated by the individual teacher (not an administrator or supervisor) and that it occur in such a manner that does not reasonably permit a timely request for permission. *Cumulative effect* restricts use of the copies to one course; limits material reproduced from the same author, book, and journal during the term; and sets a limit of nine instances of multiple copying for each course during one class term. Furthermore, the guidelines do not permit copying to substitute for anthologies or collective works or to replace consumable materials such as workbooks.

Publishers have taken legal action to ensure compliance with these guidelines. In 1991 a New York federal district court awarded eight publishers $510,000 in damages in a claim against Kinko's Graphics, a national photocopying chain, for the reproduction of course packets for faculty at Columbia University, New York University, and the New School for Social Research.[127] In assessing fair use, the court found that the character and purpose of the copying were commercial, not educational; the materials reproduced were critical sections of the publications and were substantial in length; and the copying had a detrimental impact on the market for the books. The court noted that Kinko's had created a nationwide business by impermissibly usurping the publishing industry's copyrights and profits. This ruling does not prevent faculty use of course packets, or anthologies, in the classroom, but it does require that profit-making businesses request permission from publishers prior to photocopying.

The fair use doctrine and congressional guidelines have been strictly construed in educational settings. Although the materials reproduced meet the first factor in determining fair use—educational purpose—the remaining factors must be met. The Ninth Circuit Court of Appeals held that a teacher's use of a copyrighted booklet to make a learning activity packet abridged the copyright law.[128] The court concluded that fair use was not met in this case because the learning packet was used for the same purpose as the protected booklet, the nature of the work reproduced was a "creative" effort rather than "information," and one-half of the packet was verbatim copy of the copyrighted material. Furthermore, the copying was found to violate the guideline of spontaneity in that it was reproduced several times over two school years. The appeals court did not find the absence of personal profit on the part of the teacher to lessen the violation.

Rapid developments in instructional technology pose a new set of legal questions regarding use of videotapes and computer software. Recognizing the need for guidance related to videotaping, Congress issued guidelines for educational use in 1981.[129] These guidelines specify that taping must be made at the request of the teacher. The taped material must be used for relevant classroom activities only once within the first ten days of taping. Additional use is limited to instructional reinforcement or evaluation purposes. After forty-five calendar days the tape must be erased. A New York federal district court held that a school system violated the fair use standards by extensive off-the-air taping and replaying of entire television programs.[130] The taping interfered with the producers' ability to market the tapes and films. In a subsequent appeal, the school system sought permission for temporary taping; however, because of the availability of these programs for rental or lease, even temporary recording and use was held to violate fair use by interfering with the marketability of the films.[131]

Taping television broadcasts on home video recorders for later classroom use may constitute copyright infringement if off-the-air taping guidelines are not followed. Under the legal principles advanced by the Supreme Court in *Sony Corporation v. Universal City Studios,* "even copying for noncommercial purposes may impair the copyright holder's ability to obtain the rewards that Congress intended him to have."[132] In this case, the Court found that personal video recording for the purpose of "time shifting" was a legitimate, unobjectionable purpose, posing minimal harm to marketability. Home taping for broader viewing by students in the classroom, however, would be beyond the purposes envisioned by the Court in *Sony* and would necessitate careful adherence to the guidelines for limited use discussed above.

Illegal copying of computer software in the school environment has generated significant concern among software publishers. Limited school budgets and the high cost of software have led to abuse of copyrighted software. In 1980 the copyright law was amended to include software.[133] Established copyright principles provide guidance in analyzing fair use. It is clear from the amended law that only one duplicate or backup copy can be made of the master computer program by the owner. This is to ensure a working copy of the program if the master copy is damaged. Application of the fair use exception does not alter this restriction for educators. While duplicating multiple copies would be clearly for educational purposes, other factors of fair use would be violated: The software is readily accessible for purchase (not impossible to obtain), programs can only be duplicated in their entirety, and copying substantially reduces the potential market.

A question not answered by the copyright law but plaguing schools is the legality of multiple use of a master program. That is, can a program be loaded in a number of computers in a laboratory for simultaneous use, or can a program by modified for use in a network of microcomputers? Again, application of the fair use concept would indicate that this is impermissible.[134] The most significant factor is that the market for the educational software would be greatly diminished. A number of students using the master program one at a time (serial use), however, would appear not to violate the copyright law. School boards are being urged to adopt guidelines or policies to prohibit illegal duplication of software.

Technological advances have given teachers and their school systems the means to access a wide range of instructional materials and products, but many of them are protected by the federal copyright law that restricts unauthorized reproduction. Because violation of the law can result in school district and educator liability, school boards should adopt policies or guidelines to prohibit infringement and to alert individuals to practices that violate the law.[135]

REPORTING SUSPECTED CHILD ABUSE

Child abuse and neglect are recognized as national problems, with the number of reported cases approaching two million annually.[136] Because the majority of these children are school age, teachers are in a unique role to detect signs of potential abuse. States, recognizing the daily contact teachers have with students, have imposed certain *duties* for reporting suspected abuse.

All states have enacted some type of child abuse law, and teachers are identified among the professionals required to report signs of abuse. Most state laws impose criminal liability for failure to report suspected child abuse. Penalties may include fines ranging from $500 to $1,000, prison terms up to one year, or both. Civil suits also may be initiated against teachers for negligence in failing to report suspected abuse.[137] Additionally, school systems may impose disciplinary measures against a teacher who does not follow the mandates of the law. The Seventh Circuit Court of Appeals upheld the suspension and demotion of a teacher-psychologist for not promptly reporting suspected abuse.[138] The court rejected the teacher's claim to a federal right of confidentiality, noting the state's compelling interest to protect children from abuse.

Although specific aspects of the laws may vary from one state to another, definitions of abuse and neglect often are based on the federal Child Abuse Prevention and Treatment Act of 1974. The Act identifies child abuse and neglect as:

> the physical or mental injury, sexual abuse or exploitation, negligent treatment, or maltreatment of a child under the age of eighteen, or the age specified by the child protection law of the state in question, by a person who is responsible for the child's welfare under the circumstances which indicate that the child's health or welfare is harmed or threatened thereby. . . .[139]

Several common elements are found in state child abuse statutes. The laws mandate that certain professionals such as doctors, nurses, and teachers report suspected abuse. Statutes do not require that reporters have absolute knowledge, but rather "reasonable cause to believe" or "reason to believe," that a child has been abused or neglected.[140] Once abuse is suspected, the report must be made immediately to the designated child protection agency, department of welfare, or law enforcement unit. All states grant immunity from civil and criminal liability to individuals if reports are made in good faith.[141] In Ohio, absolute immunity exists even for reports made in bad faith.[142]

Although state laws are explicit as to reporting requirements for suspected child abuse, it is difficult to prove that a teacher had sufficient knowledge of abuse to trigger legal liability for failure to report. Therefore, it is desirable for school officials to establish policies and procedures to encourage effective reporting. The pervasiveness of the problem and the lack of reporting by teachers[143] also indicate a need for in-service programs to assist teachers in recognizing signs of abused and neglected children.

Although sanctions have rarely been imposed on educators for failure to report abuse inflicted by *parents*, recent litigation has involved allegations that *school employees* are the abusers. These cases have received substantial publicity and raised questions regarding the duties of teachers, administrators, and school boards to report suspicions of abuse and to prevent such abuse from occurring in the school setting.

Several recent cases also have addressed whether a school district's failure to protect students from suspected abuse by school employees violates students' constitutional rights.[144] Damages can be sought under the Civil Rights Act of 1871, Section 1983, if a claimant has been deprived of a federally protected right by an individual acting under official state policy or custom. Although the Supreme Court did not find a violation of a federal right in a case involving a social worker's failure to intervene when she knew a child was being severely beaten by his father, abuse in the school setting involves actions by public rather than private individuals.[145] The Third Circuit Court of Appeals found a clearly established constitutional right to bodily security—to be free from sexual abuse—and that school districts may violate this right by maintaining a policy, practice, or custom reflecting "deliberate indifference" to this right. The court concluded that the student's evidence showing that school officials' actions in discouraging and minimizing reports of sexual misconduct by teachers and failing to take action on complaints may have established a custom or practice in violation of Section 1983.[146] If school officials have not had knowledge of abuse or acted with indifference to complaints, courts have not assessed liability.[147] However, the Eighth Circuit Court of Appeals in a 1991 case cautioned that it will "closely scrutinize bureaucratic hierarchies which, in their operation, tend to insulate its policymaking officials from knowledge of events which may subject them to Section 1983 liability."[148] The court noted the need for school boards to ensure that procedures provide adequate lines of communication to the board regarding suspected abuse.

With the judicial recognition that sexual abuse by school employees can result in federal liability for school districts, it can be anticipated that an increased number of suits will be filed in this area. At the same time school boards are developing and implementing policies for handling child abuse complaints, they also are enacting policies to prevent teachers and other school employees from becoming the targets of false child abuse charges. It is becoming increasingly common for school boards to prohibit physical contact between teachers and students in the absence of another adult and to place restrictions on private meetings between students and teachers before or after school. Employees can face disciplinary action for failing to comply with such directives, even if they are not found guilty of actual child abuse.

CONCLUSION

Except for certain limitations imposed by constitutional provisions and federal civil rights laws, the employment of teachers is governed by state statutes. The state prescribes general requirements for certification, contracts, tenure, and employment. Local school boards must follow state mandates and, in addition, may impose other requirements. In general, the following terms and conditions govern teacher employment.

1. The state establishes minimum qualifications for certification, which may include professional preparation, a minimum age,

United States citizenship, good moral character, signing a loyalty oath, and passing an academic examination.

2. A teacher must acquire a valid certificate to teach in public schools.
3. Certification does not assure employment in a state.
4. Certification may be revoked for cause, generally identified in state law.
5. School boards are vested with the power to appoint teachers and to establish professional and academic employment standards above the state minimums.
6. Courts generally have upheld school board residency requirements, reasonable health and physical standards, and limitations on outside employment if formulated on a reasonable basis.
7. A teacher may be assigned or transferred to any school or grade at the board's discretion, as long as the assignment is within the teacher's certification area and not circumscribed by contract terms.
8. School officials can make reasonable and appropriate extracurricular assignments.
9. Teacher contracts must satisfy the general principles of contract law, as well as conform to any additional specifications contained in state law.
10. Tenure is a statutory right ensuring that dismissal is based on adequate cause and accompanied by procedural due process.
11. Tenure must be conferred in accordance with statutory provisions.
12. Supplemental contracts for extra duty assignments are generally outside the scope of tenure laws.
13. A school board's broad authority to determine teacher performance standards may be restricted by state-imposed evaluation requirements.
14. Maintenance, access, and dissemination of personnel information must conform to state law and contractual agreements.
15. Personnel records can be subpoenaed to assess discrimination charges.
16. Educators must comply with the federal copyright law; copyrighted materials may be used for instructional purposes without the publisher's permission if "fair use" guidelines are followed.
17. All states have laws requiring teachers to report suspected child abuse and granting immunity from liability if reports are made in good faith.
18. Schools districts can be held liable for a policy or practice of deliberate indifference to reports of child abuse by school employees.

ENDNOTES

1. Pa. Stat. Ann. 24 § 1225 (Purdon, West Supp. 1991).
2. Bay v. State Bd. of Educ., 378 P.2d 558, 561 (Or. 1963). *See also* Reguero v. Teacher Standards and Practices Comm'n, 789 P.2d 11 (Or. Ct. App. 1990) (a teacher guilty of gross neglect of duty and gross unfitness based on sexual contact with sixth-grade female students lacked good moral character necessary for the reinstatement of his teaching certificate).
3. *See* Martha McCarthy, "Teacher-Testing Programs," in *Educational Reform Movement of the 1980s*, Joseph Murphy, ed. (Berkeley, CA: McCutchan Publishing, 1990), pp. 189–214.
4. *See* United States v. South Carolina, National Educ. Ass'n v. South Carolina, 445 F. Supp. 1094 (D.S.C. 1977), *aff'd*, 434 U.S. 1026 (1978); text with note 20, Chapter 9.
5. Keyishian v. Board of Regents of Univ. of State of New York, 385 U.S. 589 (1967).
6. Ohlson v. Phillips, 397 U.S. 317 (1970).
7. Cole v. Richardson, 405 U.S. 676 (1972); Connell v. Higginbotham, 403 U.S. 207 (1971).
8. Ambach v. Norwick, 441 U.S. 68 (1979).
9. *Id.* at 73-74.
10. State v. Project Principle, Inc., 724 S.W.2d 387 (Tex. 1987). *See also* Fields v. Hallsville Indep. School Dist., 906 F.2d 1017 (5th Cir. 1990); text with note 37, Chapter 9.
11. Connecticut Educ. Ass'n v. Tirozzi, 554 A.2d 1065 (Conn. 1989).
12. Reback v. Rhode Island Bd. of Regents for Elementary and Secondary Educ., 560 A.2d 357 (R.I. 1989).
13. *See, e.g.,* Tate v. Livingston Parish School Bd., 444 So. 2d 219 (La. Ct. App. 1983), *writ denied*, 446 So. 2d 314 (La. 1984).
14. *See, e.g.,* Wagenblast v. Crook County School Dist., 707 P.2d 69 (Or. Ct. App. 1985).
15. *See, e.g.,* Wardwell v. Board of Educ. of the City School Dist. of Cincinnati, 529 F.2d 625, 629 (6th Cir. 1976); Steiner v. Independent School Dist., 262 N.W.2d 173 (Minn. 1978).
16. Pleasant Valley Educ. Ass'n v. Pleasant Valley Community School Dist., 449 N.W.2d 894 (Iowa Ct. App. 1989).
17. *See, e.g.,* Moore v. Board of Educ. of Chidester School Dist. No. 59, 448 F.2d 709 (8th Cir. 1971).
18. Johnson v. School Dist. No. 3 of Clay County, 96 N.W.2d 623 (Neb. 1959). *But see* Woodrum v. Rolling Hills Bd. of Educ., 421 N.E.2d 859 (Ohio 1981) (failure to file a renewal certificate with the board did not result in a loss of tenure rights where the board had been notified of the renewal by the state).
19. *See, e.g.,* Frey v. Adams County School Dist. No. 14, 771 P.2d 27 (Colo. Ct. App. 1989), *aff'd*, 804 P.2d 851 (Colo. 1991); Wagenblast v. Crook County School Dist., 707 P.2d 69 (Or. Ct. App. 1985).
20. *See, e.g.,* Smith v. Andrews, 504 N.Y.S.2d 286 (N.Y. App. Div. 1986), *appeal denied*, 513 N.Y.S.2d 1025 (N.Y. App. Div. 1987); Occhipinti v. Board of School Directors of Old Forge School Dist., 464 A.2d 631 (Pa. Commw. Ct. 1983).

21. *See* Travers v. Cameron County School Dist., 544 A.2d 547 (Pa. Commw. Ct. 1988) (damages may be available where a person accepts a position and is assured by school officials that credentials meet certification requirements).
22. *See* Hunt v. Sanders, 554 N.E.2d 285 (Ill. App. Ct. 1990) (under Illinois law, authority to revoke a teacher's license is vested in the state board of education, not the state superintendent of education).
23. *See, e.g.,* Longenecker v. Turlington, 464 So. 2d 1249 (Fla. Dist. Ct. App. 1985).
24. *See* text with note 46, Chapter 10, for details of procedural due process. *See also* Brown v. South Carolina State Bd. of Educ., 391 S.E.2d 866 (S.C. 1990) (cancellation of National Teachers' Examination scores by Educational Testing Service could not result in invalidation of teaching certificate without procedural due process); Couch v. Turlington, 465 So. 2d 557 (Fla. Dist. Ct. App. 1985) (state education practices commission has the power to reject a teacher's voluntary surrender of teaching certificate to avoid revocation).
25. Pettit v. State Bd. of Educ., 513 P.2d 889 (Cal. 1973). *See also* Ulrich v. State, 555 N.E.2d 172 (Ind. Ct. App. 1990) (rape of student warranted revocation of teacher's license).
26. Morrison v. State Bd. of Educ., 461 P.2d 375 (Cal. 1969); text with note 135, Chapter 10.
27. Erb v. Iowa State Bd. of Public Instruction, 216 N.W.2d 339 (Iowa 1974).
28. Adams v. State Professional Practices Council, 406 So. 2d 1170 (Fla. Dist. Ct. App. 1981). *See also* Ambus v. Utah State Bd. of Educ., 800 P.2d 811 (Utah 1990) (drug charges, which were dismissed, sealed, and expunged by a court, were inadmissible in revocation hearing).
29. Startzel v. Commonwealth Dep't of Educ., 562 A.2d 1005 (Pa. Commw. Ct. 1989), *appeal denied,* 574 A.2d 76 (Pa. 1990).
30. *See generally* Chapter 8 for a discussion of teachers' constitutional rights.
31. *See generally* Chapter 9 for a discussion of discriminatory employment practices.
32. *See, e.g.,* Crawford v. Board of Educ., Barberton City Schools, 453 N.E.2d 627 (Ohio 1983); Fortney v. School Dist. of West Salem, 321 N.W.2d 225 (Wis. 1982); Lindemuth v. Jefferson County School Dist. R-1, 765 P.2d 1057 (Colo. Ct. App. 1988).
33. *See, e.g.,* Bonar v. City of Boston, 341 N.E.2d 684 (Mass. 1976); Armstead v. Starkville Mun. Separate School Dist., 331 F. Supp. 567 (D. Miss. 1971).
34. Harrah Indep. School Dist. v. Martin, 440 U.S. 194 (1979) (policy required teachers to earn an additional five semester hours of college credit every three years while employed).
35. Wardwell v. Board of Educ. of the City School Dist. of Cincinnati, 529 F.2d 625 (6th Cir. 1976). *See also* Meyers v. Newport Consol. Joint School Dist., 639 P.2d 853 (Wash. Ct. App. 1982). *But see* Angwin v. City of Manchester, 386 A.2d 1272, 1273 (N.H. 1978) (invalidating a school district's residency requirement, finding no "public interest which is important enough to justify the restriction on the private right").
36. McCarthy v. Philadelphia Civil Service Comm'n, 424 U.S. 645 (1976).
37. *Id.* at 647. In several later cases, the Supreme Court has reiterated that *prior residency requirements* for conferring certain benefits or employment preference violate the equal protection clause and the constitutional right to

travel. *See* Attorney General of New York v. Soto-Lopez, 476 U.S. 898 (1986); Hooper v. Bernalillo County Assessor, 472 U.S. 612 (1985); Zobel v. Williams, 457 U.S. 55 (1982).

38. McClelland v. Paris Public Schools, 742 S.W.2d 907 (Ark. 1988).

39. Ind. Code Ann. 20 § 6.1-6-12 (1984). *See also* Pa. Stat. Ann. 24 § 11-1106 (Purdon, West Supp. 1991).

40. Stough v. Crenshaw County Bd. of Educ., 744 F.2d 1479 (11th Cir. 1984). *See also* Curlee v. Fyte, 902 F.2d 401 (5th Cir. 1990); Brantley v. Surles, 804 F.2d 321 (5th Cir. 1986).

41. Daury v. Smith, 842 F.2d 9 (1st Cir. 1988).

42. Jones v. Jenkins, 878 F.2d 1476 (D.C. Cir. 1989). For further discussion of fourth amendment rights of employees, *see* text with note 141, Chapter 8.

43. Gargiul v. Tompkins, 704 F.2d 661 (2d Cir. 1983). The teacher, however, was not ultimately successful in obtaining back pay for the period in which she was suspended for failing to submit to the exam because she had not appealed the commissioner of education's decision in state legal proceedings. *See* Gargiul v. Tompkins, 790 F.2d 265 (2d Cir. 1986).

44. Parolisi v. Board of Examiners of City of New York, 285 N.Y.S.2d 936 (N.Y. Sup. Ct. 1967).

45. Gurmankin v. Costanzo, 556 F.2d 184 (3d Cir. 1977), *cert. denied,* 450 U.S. 923 (1981).

46. Bevan v. New York State Teachers' Retirement System, 345 N.Y.S.2d 921 (N.Y. Sup. Ct. 1973).

47. School Bd. of Nassau County, Florida v. Arline, 480 U.S. 273 (1987). *See* Chapter 9 for discussion of discrimination based on disabilities.

48. Gosney v. Sonora Indep. School Dist., 603 F.2d 522 (5th Cir. 1979).

49. *Id.* at 526.

50. *See, e.g.,* Thomas v. Smith, 897 F.2d 154 (5th Cir. 1989); Stevenson v. Lower Marion County School Dist., 327 S.E.2d 656 (S.C. 1985).

51. *See, e.g.,* Alabama State Tenure Comm'n v. Phenix City Bd. of Educ., 467 So. 2d 263 (Ala. Civ. App. 1985) (under state law, transfers must not be personal, political, or arbitrarily unjust); Glanville v. Hickory County Reorganized School Dist. No. 1, 637 S.W.2d 328 (Mo. Ct. App. 1982) (teachers cannot be transferred for exercising constitutional rights).

52. *See, e.g.,* Adlerstein v. Board of Educ. City of New York, 485 N.Y.S.2d 1 (N.Y. 1984); Wells v. Del Norte School Dist. C-7, 753 P.2d 770 (Colo. Ct. App. 1987); Olson v. Board of School Directors Methacton School Dist., 478 A.2d 954 (Pa. Commw. Ct. 1984). *See also* Kelleher v. Flawn, 761 F.2d 1079 (5th Cir. 1985) (no entitlement to teach specific courses).

53. *See, e.g.,* Moore v. Board of Educ. of Chidester School Dist. No. 59, 448 F.2d 709 (8th Cir. 1971); Singleton v. Jackson Mun. Separate School Dist., 419 F.2d 1211 (5th Cir. 1970), *cert. denied,* 396 U.S. 1032 (1970); Bolin v. San Bernardino City Unified School Dist., 202 Cal. Rptr. 416 (Cal. Ct. App. 1984).

54. *See* Wygant v. Jackson Bd. of Educ., 476 U.S. 267 (1986).

55. *See, e.g.,* Rockdale County School Dist. v. Weil, 266 S.E.2d 919 (Ga. 1980) (individual must claim reduction in salary, responsibility level, and prestige of position—one factor alone is insufficient); Elam v. Waynesville R-VI School Dist., 676 S.W.2d 880 (Mo. Ct. App. 1984) (reduction in longevity salary increments to all teachers in a classification—nonresidents of districts—is not

a demotion); Wagner v. West Perry School Dist., 480 A.2d 1336 (Pa. Commw. Ct. 1984) (salary loss from discontinuance of summer programs is not a demotion); Glanville v. Hickory County Reorganized School Dist. No. 1, 637 S.W.2d 328 (Mo. Ct. App. 1982) (only factor to be considered under state law is reduction in salary).

56. *In re* Santee Appeal, 156 A.2d 830 (Pa. 1959). *See also* Hood v. Alabama State Tenure Comm'n, 418 So. 2d 131 (Ala. Civ. App. 1982).

57. *In re* Santee, *id.* at 832.

58. Smith v. School Dist. No. 18, Pondera County, 139 P.2d 518 (Mont. 1943).

59. Mroczek v. Board of Educ. of the Beachwood City School Dist., 400 N.E.2d 1362 (Ohio C.P. 1979).

60. Alabama State Tenure Comm'n v. Shelby County Bd. of Educ., 474 So. 2d 723 (Ala. Civ. App. 1985). *See also* Williams v. Board of Educ. of Plainfield, 422 A.2d 461 (N.J. Super. Ct. App. Div. 1980).

61. LeGalley v. Bronson Community Schools, 339 N.W.2d 223 (Mich. Ct. App. 1983). *But see* Vilelle v. Reorganized School Dist. No. R-l, Benton County, 689 S.W.2d 72 (Mo. Ct. App. 1985) (under state law, teacher's salary could not be frozen if other teachers received raises).

62. Ahern v. Chester-Upland School Dist., 582 A.2d 741 (Pa. Commw. Ct. 1990).

63. *See, e.g.,* Breslin v. School Comm. of Quincy, 478 N.E.2d 149 (Mass. Ct. App. 1985), *review denied,* 481 N.E.2d 197 (Mass. 1985); Philadelphia Ass'n of School Adm'rs v. School Dist. of Philadelphia, 471 A.2d 581 (Pa. Commw. Ct. 1984) (temporary reassignment of administrators to teaching assignments during a teachers' strike was not a demotion in rank or salary requiring due process).

64. *See, e.g.,* Ex parte Ezell, 545 So. 2d 52 (Ala. 1989); Powers v. Freetown-Lakeville Regional School Dist. Comm., 467 N.E.2d 203 (Mass. 1984); Chester-Upland School Dist. v. Brown, 447 A.2d 1068 (Pa. Commw. Ct. 1982).

65. *See* Hosaflook v. Nestor, 346 S.E.2d 798 (W. Va. 1986); Holland v. Board of Educ. of Raleigh County, 327 S.E.2d 155 (W. Va. 1985). *See also* Hahn v. Board of Educ. of Alvord Unified School Dist., 252 Cal. Rptr. 471 (Cal. Ct. App. 1988).

66. *See* Fry v. Commonwealth, 485 A.2d 508 (Pa. Commw. Ct. 1984).

67. *See, e.g.,* Lewis v. Board of Educ. of North Clay Community Unit School Dist. No. 25, 537 N.E.2d 435 (Ill. App. Ct. 1989) (assignments cannot be unreasonable, onerous, or burdensome); Pleasant Valley Educ. v. Pleasant Valley Community School Dist., 449 N.W.2d 894 (Iowa Ct. App. 1989) (school boards have extensive authority in assigning personnel); Ballard v. Board of Educ. of Goshen Local School Dist., 469 N.E.2d 951 (Ohio Ct. App. 1984) (additional duties can be assigned to teachers without providing supplemental pay).

68. *See* Wolf v. Cuyahoga Falls City School Dist. Bd. of Educ., 556 N.E.2d 511 (Ohio 1990) (although supervision of the student newspaper was related to teaching journalism, supplemental contract was required for the newspaper sponsor because other teachers who performed similar class-related duties were paid).

69. McGrath v. Burkhard, 280 P.2d 864 (Cal. Ct. App. 1955).

70. Thomas v. Board of Educ. of Community Unit School Dist. No. 1 of Pope County, 453 N.E.2d 150 (Ill. App. Ct. 1983). *See also* Penns Grove–Carneys

Point Educ. Ass'n v. Board of Educ. of Penns Grove–Carneys Point Regional School Dist., 506 A.2d 1289 (N.J. Super. Ct. App. Div. 1986), *cert. denied*, 517 A.2d 430 (N.J. 1986) (band instructor could be assigned extra duties on weekends).

71. Board of Educ. v. Asbury Park Educ. Ass'n, 368 A.2d 396 (N.J. Super. Ct. Ch. Div. 1976).

72. *See, e.g.*, Howell v. Alabama State Tenure Comm'n, 402 So. 2d 1041 (Ala. 1981) (teacher refused to participate in a program to improve classroom management); Jones v. Alabama State Tenure Comm'n, 408 So. 2d 145 (Ala. 1981) (counselor refused to supervise students before school hours).

73. *See* Kern Alexander and David Alexander, *American Public School Law* (St. Paul, MN: West Publishing Co., 1985), pp. 551–553, for a discussion of contract elements.

74. Minor v. Sully Buttes School Dist. No. 58-2, 345 N.W.2d 48 (S.D. 1984). *See also* Branch v. Greene County Bd. of Educ., 533 So. 2d 248 (Ala. Civ. App. 1988) (superintendent's promise of contract made without concurrence of school board does not create a contract); Lindemuth v. Jefferson County School Dist. R-1, 765 P.2d 1057 (Colo. Ct. App. 1988) (a head coach's offer of a coaching position to an individual could be revoked by the coach since the school board had not acted on the recommendation); Ogbunugafor v. St. Christopher's Union Free School Dist., 473 N.Y.S.2d 517 (N.Y. App. Div. 1984) (superintendent's promise to recommend a teacher to the board does not create a contract).

75. *See, e.g.*, Nelson v. Doland Bd. of Educ., 380 N.W.2d 665 (S.D. 1986); Floyd County Bd. of Educ. v. Slone, 307 S.W.2d 912 (Ky. 1957).

76. *See, e.g.*, Bruton v. Ames Community School Dist., 291 N.W.2d 351 (Iowa 1980).

77. *See* text with note 46, Chapter 10, for discussion of procedural due process requirements.

78. Brodie v. School Comm. of Easton, 324 N.E.2d 922 (Mass. Ct. App. 1975). *See also* Burns v. State Bd. of Elementary and Secondary Educ., 529 So. 2d 398 (La. Ct. App. 1988), *writ denied*, 533 So. 2d 374 (La. 1988) (time spent in federally funded teaching position did not apply to probationary period); Schmidt v. Unified School Dist. No. 497, Douglas County, 644 P.2d 396 (Kan. 1982) (a one-month gap in employment due to uncertainty of federal funding rendered a teacher ineligible for tenure under statutory requirement of two consecutive years of employment).

79. Brodie, *id. See also* State *ex rel.* Williams v. Belpre City School Dist., 534 N.E.2d 96 (Ohio Ct. App. 1987) (regular and substantial part-time employment rendered teacher eligible for tenure).

80. *See, e.g.*, Board of Educ. of Carroll County v. Carroll County Educ. Ass'n, 452 A.2d 1316 (Md. Ct. App. 1982) (school board cannot enter a negotiated agreement delegating authority to another party).

81. *See, e.g.*, James v. Board of Educ. of School Dist. #189, East St. Louis, 549 N.E.2d 1001 (Ill. App. Ct. 1990); Fleice v. Chualar Union Elementary School Dist., 254 Cal. Rptr. 54 (Cal. Ct. App. 1988).

82. In New York, for example, tenure may be acquired by special area, general area, vertical (subject area across junior and senior high), or horizontal (junior *or* senior high only). *See* Cole v. Board of Educ. of South Huntington Union

Free School Dist., 457 N.Y.S.2d 547 (N.Y. App. Div. 1982), *aff'd,* 471 N.Y.S.2d 84 (N.Y. 1983).

83. *See, e.g.,* Belanger v. Warren Consol. School Dist., 443 N.W.2d 372 (Mich. 1989).

84. Indiana *ex rel.* Anderson v. Brand, 303 U.S. 95 (1938). Under such legislation, the status of teachers who have received tenure cannot be altered, but the legislature is not prohibited from changing the law for future employees.

85. *See, e.g.,* State v. Project Principle, Inc., 724 S.W.2d 387 (Tex. 1987) (teaching certificate was a license rather than a contract and thus could be subject to future restrictions by the state).

86. *See, e.g.,* Wooten v. Alabama State Tenure Comm'n, 421 So. 2d 1277 (Ala. Civ. App. 1982).

87. *See, e.g.,* Burke v. Lead-Deadwood School Dist. No. 40-1, 347 N.W.2d 343 (S.D. 1984); Wolfe v. Sierra Vista Unified School Dist. No. 68, 722 P.2d 389 (Ariz. Ct. App. 1986); Wahlquist v. School Bd. of Liberty County, 423 So. 2d 471 (Fla. Dist. Ct. App. 1982).

88. Spurlock v. Board of Trustees, Carbon County School Dist. No. 4, 699 P.2d 270, 272 (Wyo. 1985).

89. Atencio v. Board of Educ. of Penasco Indep. School Dist. No. 4, 655 P.2d 1012 (N.M. 1982). *See also* Rose v. Currituck County Bd. of Educ., 350 S.E.2d 376 (N.C. Ct. App. 1986) (principal retains tenure as teacher during the probationary period as principal).

90. Smith v. Board of Educ. of Urbana School Dist. No. 116, 708 F.2d 258 (7th Cir. 1983); Coles v. Glenburn Public School Dist. 26, 436 N.W.2d 262 (N.D. 1989); Neal v. School Dist. of York, 288 N.W.2d 725 (Neb. 1980); Bryan v. Alabama State Tenure Comm'n, 472 So. 2d 1052 (Ala. Civ. App. 1985).

91. Slockett v. Iowa Valley Community School Dist., 359 N.W.2d 446 (Iowa 1984).

92. *See, e.g.,* Lagos v. Modesto City Schools Dist., 843 F.2d 347 (9th Cir. 1988), *cert. denied,* 488 U.S. 926 (1988); Issaquah Educ. Ass'n v. Issaquah School Dist. No. 411, 706 P.2d 618 (Wash. 1985); Lexington County School Dist. v. Bost, 316 S.E.2d 677 (S.C. 1984). *But see* Smith v. Board of Educ. of County of Logan, 341 S.E.2d 685 (W. Va. 1985) (failure of a school board to renew a coaching contract was considered a transfer, which under state law required procedural due process).

93. Reid v. Huron Bd. of Educ., Huron School Dist. No. 2-2, 449 N.W.2d 240 (S.D. 1989).

94. *See, e.g.,* Lewis v. Board of Educ. of North Clay Community Unit School Dist. No. 25, 537 N.E.2d 435 (Ill. App. Ct. 1989); Hachiya v. Board of Educ. Unified School Dist. No. 307, 750 P.2d 383 (Kan. 1988); Babitzke v. Silverton Union High School, 695 P.2d 93 (Or. Ct. App. 1985), *writ denied,* 700 P.2d 251 (Or. 1985).

95. *See, e.g.,* Munger v. Jesup Community School Dist., 325 N.W.2d 377 (Iowa 1982).

96. Civil Rights Div. of the Arizona Dep't of Law v. Amphitheater Unified School Dist. No. 10, 706 P.2d 745 (Ariz. Ct. App. 1985).

97. Charges of discrimination in connection with leave policies pertaining to pregnancy-related absences and the observance of religious holidays are discussed in Chapter 9.

98. *See, e.g.,* Bristol Township School Dist. v. Karafin, 478 A.2d 539 (Pa. Commw. Ct. 1984), *aff'd,* 498 A.2d 824 (Pa. 1985); Collins v. Orleans Parish School Bd., 384 So. 2d 336 (La. 1980).

99. Iowa Code Ann. § 279.14 (1988). *See also* Ark. Code Ann. § 6-17-1504 (1987).

100. Cal. Educ. Code §§ 44660, 44662, 44664 (West Supp. 1991).

101. Fla. Stat. Ann. § 231.29 (West Supp. 1991).

102. *See* La. Rev. Stat. Ann. § 17:391.5 (West Supp. 1991); Pa. Stat. Ann. 24, § 11-1123 (Purdon, West Supp. 1991).

103. *See* Ariz. Rev. Stat. Ann. § 15-537 (1991); Or. Rev. Stat. Ann. § 342.850 (Butterworth Supp. 1990); Conn. Gen. Stat. Ann. § 10-151b (West Supp. 1991).

104. West Virginia Bd. of Educ. Policy No. 5300 (6)(a).

105. *See* Hosaflook v. Nestor, 346 S.E.2d 798 (W. Va. 1986); Trimboli v. Board of Educ. of Wayne County, 280 S.E.2d 686 (W. Va. 1981).

106. Wren v. McDowell County Bd. of Educ., 327 S.E.2d 464 (W. Va. 1985).

107. Lipan v. Board of Educ., County of Hancock, 295 S.E.2d 44 (W. Va 1982); Wilt v. Flanigan, 294 S.E.2d 189 (W. Va. 1982).

108. Anderson v. San Mateo Community College Dist., 151 Cal. Rptr. 111 (Cal. Ct. App. 1978). *But see* Retzlaff v. Grand Forks Public School Dist. No. 1, 424 N.W.2d 637 (N.D. 1988) (a "supervisory report" containing specific educational goals for a teacher substantially complied with state requirement of a written performance review).

109. Hyde v. Wellpinit School Dist. 49, 611 P.2d 1388 (Wash. Ct. App. 1980).

110. Holland v. Board of Educ. of Raleigh County, 327 S.E.2d 155 (W. Va. 1985).

111. *See, e.g.,* Kudasik v. Board of Directors, Port Allegany School Dist., 455 A.2d 261 (Pa. 1983). *See also* Roberts v. Houston Indep. School Dist., 788 S.W.2d 107 (Tex. Civ. App. 1990) (board's policy permitting involuntary videotaping of teachers for evaluation purposes did not violate privacy rights).

112. Perez v. Commission on Professional Competence, 197 Cal. Rptr. 390 (Cal. Ct. App. 1983).

113. Johnson v. Board of Educ. of the Woden-Crystal Lake Community School Dist., 353 N.W.2d 883, 887 (Iowa Ct. App. 1984).

114. Schaub v. Chamberlain Bd. of Educ., 339 N.W.2d 307 (S.D. 1983). It must be emphasized that failure to follow established evaluation procedures does not necessarily result in a denial of *constitutional due process* rights in termination actions if the minimum notice, specification of charges, and opportunity for a hearing are provided. *See also* Goodrich v. Newport News School Bd., 743 F.2d 225 (4th Cir. 1984); text with note 49, Chapter 10.

115. *See, e.g.,* Brouillet v. Cowles Publishing Co., 791 P.2d 526 (Wash. 1990); Sargent School Dist. No. RE-33J v. Western Services, Inc., 751 P.2d 56 (Colo. 1988); Wooster Republican Printing Co. v. City of Wooster, 383 N.E.2d 124 (Ohio 1978); Rathie v. Northeastern Wisconsin Technical Institute, 419 N.W.2d (Wis. Ct. App. 1987).

116. Hovet v. Hebron Public School Dist., 419 N.W.2d 189 (N.D. 1988).

117. Brouillet v. Cowles Publishing Co., 791 P.2d 526 (Wash. 1990).

118. *See, e.g.,* Houston Indep. School Dist. v. Houston Chronicle Publishing Co., 798 S.W.2d 580 (Tex. 1990); Board of Educ. of Town of Somers v. Freedom of Information Comm'n, 556 A.2d 592 (Conn. 1989), *overruled by* Chairman,

Criminal Justice Comm'n v. Freedom of Information Comm'n, 585 A.2d 96 (Conn. 1991).

119. *See, e.g.,* Klein Indep. School Dist. v. Mattox, 830 F.2d 576 (5th Cir. 1987), *cert. denied,* 485 U.S. 1008 (1988); Brouillet v. Cowles Publishing Co., 791 P.2d 526 (Wash. 1990).

120. Klein, *id.* at 580. *See also* Hovet v. Hebron Public School Dist., 419 N.W.2d 189 (N.D. 1988).

121. University of Pennsylvania v. Equal Employment Opportunity Comm'n, 110 S. Ct. 577, 584 (1990) (university's contention that access to peer review materials violated academic freedom by interfering with the university's process for determining who may teach was rejected). *See also* Equal Employment Opportunity Comm'n v. Maryland Cup Corp. 785 F.2d 471 (4th Cir. 1986), *cert. denied,* 479 U.S. 815 (1986); Equal Employment Opportunity Comm'n v. Franklin and Marshall College, 775 F.2d 110 (3d Cir. 1985), *cert. denied,* 476 U.S. 1163 (1986).

122. *See, e.g.,* Aebisher v. Ryan, 622 F.2d 651 (2d Cir. 1980); Columbus Educ. Ass'n v. Columbus City School Dist., 623 F.2d 1155 (6th Cir. 1980); Swilley v. Alexander, 629 F.2d 1018 (5th Cir. 1980).

123. Marcus v. Rowley, 695 F.2d 1171, 1174 (9th Cir. 1983).

124. 17 U.S.C. § 101 *et seq.* (1988). *See also* Virginia Helm, *What Educators Should Know About Copyright,* Fastback 233 (Bloomington, IN: Phi Delta Kappa, 1986).

125. *Id.,* 17 U.S.C. at § 107.

126. *See* Mark Merickel, "The Educator's Rights to Fair Use of Copyrighted Works," *Education Law Reporter,* vol. 51 (1989), pp. 711–724, for a summary of the guidelines.

127. Basic Books Inc. v. Kinko's Graphics Corp., 758 F. Supp. 1522 (S.D.N.Y. 1991). *See also* Sheldon E. Steinbach, "Photocopying Copyrighted Course Materials: Doesn't Anyone Remember the NYU Case?" *Education Law Reporter,* vol. 50 (1989), pp. 317–330 for a discussion of a 1983 consent decree between Addison-Wesley Publishing Company and New York University.

128. Marcus v. Rowley, 695 F.2d 1171 (9th Cir. 1983).

129. Guidelines for Off-The-Air Recording of Broadcast Programming for Educational Purposes, Cong. Rec. § E4751, October 14, 1981.

130. Encyclopedia Britannica Educ Corp. v. Crooks, 542 F. Supp. 1156 (W.D.N.Y. 1982).

131. Encyclopedia Brittanica Educ. Corp. v. Crooks, 558 F. Supp. 1247 (W.D.N.Y. 1983).

132. 464 U.S. 417, 450 (1984).

133. 17 U.S.C. § 117 (1988).

134. *See* Virginia Helms, "Copyright Issues in Computer-Assisted Instruction," *School Law Update 1985,* Thomas Jones and Darel Semler, eds. (Topeka, KS: National Organization on Legal Problems of Education, 1985); John Soma and Dwight Pringle, "Computer Software in the Public Schools," *Education Law Reporter,* vol. 28 (1985), pp. 315–324.

135. *See* 17 U.S.C.A. § 511(a) (1991). In response to several appellate court decisions holding that under the eleventh amendment states and their agents were not subject to suit in federal courts for the infringement of copyrights, Congress amended the copyright law (Copyright Remedy Clarification) spe-

cifically abrogating immunity. *See also* BV Engineering v. University of California, Los Angeles, 858 F.2d 1394 (9th Cir. 1988), *cert. denied,* 109 S. Ct. 1537 (1989); Richard Anderson Photography v. Brown, 852 F.2d 114 (4th Cir. 1988), *cert. denied,* 109 S. Ct. 1171 (1989).

136. House Select Committee on Children, Youth and Families, Abused Children in America: Victims of Official Neglect, 100th Cong., 2d Sess. 10–18 (March 1987).

137. The California Supreme Court, finding liability against a physician for failure to report, commented that other professionals identified as mandated report-ers by law, such as teachers, also could be held liable. Landeros v. Flood, 551 P.2d 389, 392 n. 5 (Cal. 1976). *See also* Chapter 12 for discussion of the elements of negligence.

138. Pesce v. J. Sterling Morton High School Dist. 201, Cook County, Illinois, 830 F.2d 789 (7th Cir. 1987). *See also* State v. Grover, 437 N.W.2d 60 (Minn. 1989) (principal was charged with criminal negligence for failure to report child abuse by teacher).

139. 42 U.S.C.A § 5102 (1991).

140. *See* Roman v. Appleby, 558 F. Supp. 449, 459 (E.D. Pa. 1983).

141. *See, e.g.,* Davis v. Durham City Schools, 372 S.E.2d 318 (N.C. Ct. App. 1988); McDonald v. Children's Services Div., 694 P.2d 569 (Or. Ct. App. 1985), *review denied,* 698 P.2d 964 (Or. 1985) (immunity existed for good-faith reporting). *See also* Landstrom v. Illinois Dep't of Children and Family Services, 892 F.2d 670 (7th Cir. 1990) (school personnel and social worker who questioned and examined child regarding abuse were entitled to qualified immunity from civil rights claim filed by parents).

142. Ohio Rev. Code Ann. § 2151.421 (1990); Bishop v. Ezzone, No. WD-80-63 (Wood County AP, June 26, 1981). While school authorities and health and child-care professionals have absolute immunity, other persons who report abuse are entitled to immunity only if the report is made in good faith, Ohio Rev. Code § 2151.421 (amended 1990).

143. Various reports show that fewer than 10 percent of suspected child abuse reports are made by teachers. Research studies of teachers' reporting prac-tices indicate that teachers understand their legal obligation to report sus-pected abuse but do not know the correct procedures or where to report the information. Furthermore, they focus primarily on physical abuse as op-posed to sexual and psychological abuse. *See* Robert Shoop and Lyn Fire-stone, "Mandatory Reporting of Suspected Child Abuse: Do Teachers Obey the Law?" *Education Law Reporter,* vol. 46 (1988), pp. 1115–1122.

144. *See* William Valente, "School District and Official Liability for Teacher Sexual Abuse of Students Under 42 U.S.C. § 1983," *Education Law Re-porter,* vol. 57 (1990), pp. 645–659.

145. DeShaney v. Winnebago County Dep't of Social Services, 489 U.S. 189 (1989).

146. Stoneking v. Bradford Area School Dist., 882 F.2d 720 (3d Cir. 1989), *cert. denied,* 110 S. Ct. 840 (1990). *See* City of Canton, Ohio v. Harris, 489 U.S. 378 (1989) ("deliberate indifference" standard was articulated by Supreme Court). *See also* Pagano v. Massapequa Public Schools, 714 F. Supp. 641 (E.D.N.Y. 1989) (school officials' knowledge of abuse of student by classmates was actionable under Section 1983); J.O. v. Alton Community

Unit School Dist. 11, 909 F.2d 267 (7th Cir. 1990) (the court found no affirmative constitutional duty for school authorities to protect a child from harm of which they had no knowledge, but the case was remanded to allow parents to amend pleadings to attempt to establish a claim that the district through its policies or practices permitted abuse to occur).

147. *See* D. T. v. Independent School Dist. No. 16 Pawnee County Oklahoma, 894 F.2d 1176 (10th Cir. 1990); Spann v. Tyler Indep. School Dist., 876 F.2d 437 (5th Cir. 1989); Jane Doe "A" v. Special School Dist. of St. Louis County, 901 F.2d 642 (8th Cir. 1990); Thelma D. v. Board of Educ. of City of St. Louis, 934 F.2d 929 (8th Cir. 1991); Jarrett v. Butts, 379 S.E.2d 583 (Ga. Ct. App. 1989); Scott v. Willis, 543 A.2d 165 (Pa. Commw. Ct. 1988).

148. Thelma D. v. Board of Educ. of City of St. Louis, 934 F.2d 929, 936 (8th Cir. 1991).

8

Teachers' Substantive Constitutional Rights

Although statutory law is prominent in defining specific terms and conditions of employment, substantive rights also are conferred on public employees by the Federal Constitution. These rights cannot be abridged by state or school board action without an overriding governmental interest, nor can employment be conditioned on their relinquishment. The exercise of these protected rights often results in a conflict between school officials and teachers, requiring judicial resolution.

This chapter presents an overview of the scope of teachers' constitutional rights as defined by the judiciary in connection with free expression, academic freedom, freedom of association, freedom of choice in appearance, and privacy rights. The concluding section focuses on remedies available to aggrieved individuals when their constitutional rights have been violated by school officials or school boards. Constitutional rights pertaining to equal protection, due process, and religious guarantees are discussed in other chapters.

FREEDOM OF EXPRESSION

Until the mid-twentieth century, it was generally accepted that public school teachers could be dismissed or disciplined for expressing views considered objectionable by the school board. The private-sector practice of firing such employees was assumed to apply to public employment as well. During the past few decades, however, the Supreme Court has recognized that the first amendment places restrictions on public employers' discretion to condition employment on the expression of certain views, including those critical of governmental policies. Although it is now clearly established that the right to free expression is not relinquished by accepting public school employment, courts have acknowledged that this right must be weighed against the school district's interest in maintaining an effective and efficient school system. The federal judiciary is continually refining judicial tests in an attempt to achieve an appropriate balance between these interests. In this section, the evolution of legal principles and their application to specific school situations are reviewed.

LEGAL PRINCIPLES: FROM *PICKERING* TO *CONNICK*

In the landmark 1968 decision, *Pickering v. Board of Education*, the Supreme Court recognized that teachers have a first amendment right to air their views on matters of public concern.[1] The case focused on a teacher's letter to a local newspaper, criticizing the school board's fiscal policies, especially the allocation of funds between the education and athletic programs. The school board dismissed Pickering because of the letter, which included false statements allegedly damaging the reputations of school board members and district administrators, and the Illinois courts upheld the dismissal.

Reversing the state courts, the Supreme Court first identified expression pertaining to matters of public concern as constitutionally protected and reasoned that the funding and allocation issues raised by Pickering were clearly questions of public interest requiring free and open debate. The Court then applied a balancing test, weighing the teacher's interest in expressing his views on public issues against the school board's interest in providing educational services. The Court recognized that if the exercise of protected expression jeopardized Pickering's relationship with his immediate supervisor, harmony with coworkers, classroom performance, or school operations, the school board's decision to curtail the expression would prevail. Concluding that Pickering's letter did not have a detrimental effect in any of these areas, the Court found no justification for limiting his contribution to public debate. Indeed, the Court noted that a teacher's role provides a special vantage point from which to formulate an "informed and definite opinion" on the allocation of school district funds, thus making it essential for teachers to be able to speak about public issues without fear of reprisal.[2] Furthermore, the Court held that false statements about public matters, without proof that they were "knowingly or recklessly" made, cannot be the basis for dismissal.

Since *Pickering*, teachers often have challenged dismissals or other disciplinary actions on grounds that their exercise of protected expression in part precipitated the adverse employment consequences. In 1977, however, the Supreme Court established the principle that even if a teacher's expression is constitutionally protected, school officials are not prevented from discharging the employee if sufficient cause exists *independent* of the protected speech. In *Mt. Healthy City School District v. Doyle,* a school board voted not to renew the contract of a nontenured teacher who had made a telephone call to a local radio station concerning a proposed teacher grooming code. The teacher had been involved in several previous incidents; however, in not renewing his contract the board cited "lack of tact in handling professional matters" with reference only to the radio call and obscene gestures made to several female students.[3] Both the trial court and Sixth Circuit Court of Appeals concluded that reinstatement was warranted because the telephone call was protected speech and was a substantial reason for the adverse personnel action.

Reversing and remanding the decision, the Supreme Court instructed the lower court to assess whether the school board would have reached the same decision in the absence of the teacher's exercise of protected speech. The Court reasoned that protected expression should not place an employee in a better or worse position with regard to continued employment. On remand, the board clearly established that there were sufficient grounds other than the radio station call to justify the teacher's nonrenewal.[4]

Under the *Mt. Healthy* test, the burden is on the employee to show that the conduct was constitutionally protected and was a "substantial or motivating" factor in the school board's adverse employment decision.[5] Once established, the burden then shifts to the board to show by a preponderance of evidence that it would have reached the same decision if the protected expression had not occurred. Even if proven that the school board's decision was predicated on the exercise of expression related to matters of public concern, the decision might still be upheld if shown that the expression interfered with working relationships or disrupted school operations.

For over a decade after the *Pickering* decision, it was unclear whether public employees' *private* communications enjoyed first amendment protection. In 1979 the Supreme Court addressed this issue in *Givhan v. Western Line Consolidated School District,* concluding that as long as the expression pertains to matters of public concern (in contrast to personal grievances), statements made in private or through a public medium are constitutionally protected.[6] The Court reasoned that the forum where the expression occurs does not determine whether it is of public or personal interest. In this case, the teacher made critical comments to her principal regarding race relations in the school. Although these private comments were found to be constitutionally protected, the Court did note that the balancing process may involve additional considerations when private speech is involved. Whereas public expression is generally evaluated on its content and impact, private expression—because of the nature of the employer–employee relationship—should also be assessed based on the time, place, and manner of the remarks.

In a significant 1983 decision, *Connick v. Meyers,* the Supreme Court's interpretation of the *Pickering* balancing test narrowed the circumstances under which public employees can prevail in free expression cases.[7] The Court reiterated that the threshold inquiry is whether the expression involves matters of public concern, since personal grievances are not protected by the first amendment. Of particular importance was the Court's conclusion that the *form* and *context* as well as the content of the expression should be considered in assessing whether it relates to public matters. Thus, the Court indicated that the factors applied under the *Pickering* balancing test to determine whether speech adversely affects governmental interests can be considered in the *initial* assessment of whether the expression informs public debate or is simply part of a personal employment grievance. For expression in the latter category, no additional constitutional scrutiny is required.

In *Connick,* an assistant district attorney was dissatisfied with her proposed transfer and circulated to coworkers a questionnaire concerning transfer policy, office morale, need for a grievance committee, level of confidence in supervisors, and pressure to work in political campaigns. She was subsequently terminated and challenged the action as violating her first amendment rights. Both the federal district court and Fifth Circuit Court of Appeals ruled in favor of the employee, finding that the primary reason for the discharge was the survey involving matters of public policy and that the state had not "clearly demonstrated" that the questionnaire "substantially interfered" with operations of the district attorney's office.[8]

Reversing the lower courts, the Supreme Court ruled by a one-vote margin that the questionnaire related primarily to a personal employment grievance rather than matters of public interest. Only one question (regarding pressure to participate in political campaigns) was found to involve a public issue. Weighing various factors—the importance of close working relationships to fulfill public responsibilities, the employee's attempt to precipitate a vote of no confidence in the district attorney, distribution of the questionnaire during office hours, the district attorney's conclusion that the functioning of his office was endangered, and the questionnaire's very limited connection to a public concern—the Court concluded that the employee's dismissal did not offend the first amendment.

The *Connick* majority recognized that the state's burden of justifying a given discharge varies according to the nature of the employee's expression; the employer's burden of proof increases as the employee's speech more directly involves public issues and decreases as the expression interferes with close working relationships that are essential to fulfilling public responsibilities. The majority did concede, however, that this "particularized balancing" of competing interests is a difficult task.[9]

APPLICATION OF THE LEGAL PRINCIPLES

During the 1970s and early 1980s, courts relied on the *Pickering* guidelines in striking down a variety of restrictions on teachers' rights to express views on matters of public interest. Courts ordered reinstatement or nullified transfers when evidence substantiated that dismissals or other disciplinary actions were based on the exercise of protected expression, such as wearing black arm bands as a symbolic protest against the Vietnam War, making public comments favoring a collective bargaining contract, and criticizing the instructional program and other school policies.[10] While most of these cases involved challenges to terminations or involuntary transfers, courts also have ordered letters of reprimand, prompted by employees' exercise of protected speech, to be expunged from personnel files.[11]

Since the early 1980s, however, courts have seemed increasingly inclined to view public employees' expression as relating to *private* employment disputes rather than to matters of public concern. To illustrate, the Sixth Circuit Court of Appeals found no first or fourteenth amendment violation in the suspension, transfer, and ultimate nonrenewal of a guidance counselor after she revealed her bisexuality to various school employees.[12] Relying on *Connick,* the appellate court concluded that the counselor's statements did not enjoy first amendment protection as they pertained to a personal interest, not a public concern. Also rejecting the equal protection claim, the appeals court noted that to establish discrimination, the counselor would have to prove that she had performed her job properly and was released for no apparent legitimate reason. However, evidence indicated improper job performance as she had breached the confidence of two advisees by disclosing their homosexuality to a third party. Furthermore, no evidence was presented indicating that heterosexual employees would be treated differently for airing their personal sexual preferences in the high school community. The Supreme Court declined to review this decision, but two justices dissented, admonishing the appellate court for condoning the dismissal of a teacher for merely speaking about her bisexuality when no adverse consequences resulted from the expression.[13]

The Supreme Court also declined to review a case in which the Eleventh Circuit Court of Appeals upheld a school board's decision not to rehire a nontenured teacher who had filed a grievance after being assigned a job-sharing position that meant part-time employment. The court ruled that the teacher's expression pertained to personal dissatisfaction over her assignment and that her reference to the negative impact of the job-sharing position on students' welfare was "not sufficient to bring her grievance within the rubric of matters of 'public concern.' "[14]

Other courts have relied on *Connick* in concluding that specific expression pertains primarily to a private grievance, based on an assessment of its context and form as well as content. The Seventh Circuit Court of Appeals held that a former high school basketball coach's comments to the local newspaper, voicing dissatisfaction with the school board's decision to replace him as coach, involved a personal grievance and could be the basis for retaliatory action.[15] The First Circuit Court of Appeals held that a teacher could be disciplined for posting letters of reprimand in her classroom on parents' night because her act pertained to a private dispute.[16] The teacher had received the reprimands for refusing to give her principal a case history she had written on one of her students for a college course. Courts also have found the following expression to involve personal employment disputes rather than matters of public interest: statements accusing the superintendent of inciting student disturbances;[17] sarcastic, critical memoranda sent to school officials;[18] private complaints of sexual harassment;[19] and protests about unfavorable performance evaluations.[20]

In post-*Connick* cases, courts have considered the *impact* of expression in the initial determination of whether it is protected, even if the expression touches on issues of public concern. For example, in 1989 the Tenth Circuit Court of Appeals ruled that a school nurse's criticism of the school district's student medication policy, an issue of undeniable public interest, was not constitutionally protected because the expression disrupted the school's health service program.[21] The court considered the expression's detrimental impact in denying constitutional protection and thus did not have to address whether the expression was a motivating factor in nonrenewal of the plaintiff's contract. Similarly considering the impact of expression, the Eighth Circuit Court of Appeals held that a teacher's "frequent, lengthy, and uncompromising criticisms of the administration, faculty, and students" were not protected by the first amendment "when balanced against the needs of the board for efficient operation and internal harmony in its schools."[22]

Although *Connick* has made it more difficult for public employees to establish that their expression is constitutionally protected, this burden can be satisfied. If the expression clearly relates to the welfare of students, it is afforded first amendment protection. To illustrate, the Tenth Circuit Court of Appeals ruled that critical expression regarding the school district's method of disciplining students was constitutionally protected.[23] The First Circuit Court of Appeals held that a teacher could not be dismissed for criticizing a cutback in the district's high school reading program and filing several grievances with the teachers' union.[24] Also, the Eighth Circuit Court of Appeals held that nonrenewal of a teacher's contract for writing a letter to the newspaper protesting the school board's decision to drop junior high school track, which he had coached, abridged first amendment rights as the expression pertained to a public issue.[25] The same court held that a letter written by teachers to the state department of education, complaining about the school district's delay in implementing programs for children with disabilities, pertained to a matter of public concern and was protected by the first amendment.[26]

Courts have ruled that expression pertaining to other school district concerns also is constitutionally protected. For example, federal appellate courts have afforded first amendment protection to school employees in opposing the superintendent's campaign for a tax referendum,[27] opposing a bond issue,[28] and voicing vocal support for the principal receiving tenure.[29] Also, a teacher's publication of a satirical letter in the high school newspaper (regarding allegations of sex discrimination in the physical education department) was found to involve a matter of public concern and, thus, could not be the basis for reprisal.[30]

The Seventh Circuit Court of Appeals discussed *Connick* at length in reviewing a teacher's claim that he was harassed, given negative evaluations, denied a personal leave day, removed as an assistant baseball coach, and transferred to a grade school assignment for exercising protected speech.[31] The appellate court concluded that the teacher's speech pertaining to classroom assignment and his evaluations was clearly personal and not constitutionally protected. However, his expression of views regarding inequities in mileage allowances and liability insurance coverage for coaches and parent volunteers was found to pertain to issues of public concern. The appeals court held that if any of the speech was considered protected, the court must move to the next stage of the *Connick* test and balance the school district's interests in maintaining efficient school operations against the employee's right to address matters of public concern. Finding that the teacher's protected speech was a substantial factor in the adverse employment decisions and that the school district's interests did not justify the disciplinary action, the district was ordered to reinstate the teacher and pay him compensatory damages. The Supreme Court subsequently dismissed an appeal of this decision.

In a 1987 case outside the school domain, the Supreme Court reiterated that *Connick* requires the content, form, and context of statements to be considered in determining whether expression relates to issues of public concern. This case involved a clerical worker, McPherson, in a county constable's office who was discharged for making the following comment to a coworker after hearing the news of an attempt on President Reagan's life: "If they go for him again, I hope they get him."[32] Recognizing that an actual threat to kill the President would not be protected by the first amendment, the Court held that McPherson's remark could not properly be criminalized. Considering the statement in its context, which was a conversation addressing the policies of President Reagan's administration, the Court concluded that it plainly dealt with a matter of public concern. Thus, the Court applied the balancing test and found that the remark did not interfere with office operations or work relationships or impede McPherson's performance of her duties; McPherson's first amendment rights outweighed the constable's interest in dismissing her. The court noted that although McPherson was a probationary employee, she could not be dismissed for the exercise of constitutionally protected expression.

Terminations predicated on political expression or union activities are clearly impermissible.[33] For example, the Eighth Circuit Court of Appeals affirmed a jury's verdict that a teacher had been improperly dismissed because of her labor union activities. The board asserted that the teacher had used indecent language with a student, but the jury concluded that the dismissal was based on protected union-related expression.[34] Espousing similar logic, the Sixth Circuit Court of Appeals rejected the nonrenewal of a probationary teacher for declining teaching evaluations and a personality conflict with the principal, finding that these asserted reasons were due to the teacher's constitutionally protected union activities.[35]

Even if protected speech is involved, however, courts have relied on *Mt. Healthy* to uphold terminations or transfers where other legitimate reasons justify the personnel actions. In an illustrative case, the Fifth Circuit Court of Appeals upheld a teacher's dismissal based on a confrontation with the assistant coach during a basketball game and repeated threats toward the athletic director. The fact that the teacher also had criticized the athletic program and voiced disagreement with an unsatisfactory evaluation did not negate the legitimate grounds for dismissal.[36] The Eleventh Circuit Court of Appeals recognized that *Mt. Healthy* applies regardless of whether a teacher has tenure, finding that there were sufficient grounds independent of protected speech to dismiss a tenured university faculty member. The court noted, however, that when a tenured teacher is involved, an educational institution must "make a considerably stronger showing" to justify dismissal than was made in *Mt. Healthy*.[37]

School authorities cannot rely on *Mt. Healthy* to justify termination or other adverse employment action if the school officials' stated reasons for personnel decisions are merely a pretext to restrict protected expression. For example, the Tenth Circuit Court of Appeals ruled that a Wyoming teacher, who was terminated for alleged lack of satisfactory progress and enthusiasm and failure to cooperate with other teachers, was in fact impermissibly terminated for protected speech involving public criticism of the new superintendent's recommendations for changes in teaching methods.[38] Similarly, the Fifth Circuit Court of Appeals concluded that the motivating factor in a school board's decision not to hire teachers for summer term positions was their support for defeated candidates for the school board.[39]

In applying the principles articulated by the Supreme Court, the threshold question is whether the speech pertains to a public issue.[40] Considering the content, form, and context of the expression in making this determination, courts have concluded that comments related to political advocacy, collective bargaining, and policies governing the welfare of the school and student body are of public interest. However, complaints about individual work assignments or conditions of employment and personal attacks on superiors have not been considered public issues. During the 1970s it was generally assumed that even educators' expression involving matters of *personal* rather than public interest could not be the basis for adverse personnel action unless the expression posed some threat of disrupting the educational process. But post-*Connick* cases indicate that sanctions can be imposed for such expression regarding personal concerns in the absence of any disruptive effect.[41] Thus, the threshold determination of whether the speech pertains to public or private issues has become increasingly important.

If determined that expression is protected, the employee then has the burden of demonstrating that it was a substantial or motivating factor in the adverse employment decision. Even if established that expression on matters of public concern was the sole basis for adverse action, the public employer may still prevail by showing that its interests in protecting the public agency outweigh the individual's free speech rights.[42] Under *Connick,* the employer's burden varies according to the nature of the employee's expression. This balancing process has generated a steady stream of first amendment litigation, with state and individual interests weighed in light of the circumstances of each case.

PRIOR RESTRAINT AND CHANNEL RULES

Although *reprisals* for expression have been the focus of most of the litigation, courts also have addressed *prior restraints* on public employees' expression and restrictions on the channels through which views may be aired. The judiciary has been more reluctant to condone such prior restraints on expression than it has to uphold disciplinary action after the expression has occurred.

For example, the Tenth Circuit Appellate Court struck down a portion of an Oklahoma law authorizing the termination of teachers for "advocating . . . public or private homosexual activity in a manner that creates a substantial risk that such conduct will come to the attention of school children or school employees."[43] The appellate court held that such restrictions on teachers' expression could not be imposed unless shown to be necessary to prevent "a material or substantial interference or disruption in the normal activities of the school."[44] The Supreme Court divided evenly in this case, thus affirming the appellate court's ruling.

The Fifth Circuit Court of Appeals also invalidated a school board policy requiring prior approval of all political, sectarian, or special interest materials distributed in the schools. The board had invoked the policy to prevent distribution of the teachers' association's documents that were critical of a proposed teacher competency testing program. Literature written by the school board supporting the program had been distributed in the schools. The court reasoned that "school administrators and principals may not permit one side to promote its position while denying the other side the same opportunity."[45] The court noted, however, that the policies were not invalidated simply because they required prior approval; rather, they were unconstitutional because they did not "furnish sufficient guidance" to prohibit school administrators from exercising "unbridled discretion" in curtailing communication within the schools.[46]

Subsequently, the Supreme Court affirmed a Fifth Circuit Appellate Court's conclusion that a Texas school district had not created a public forum in either its schools or school mail facilities; therefore, the district could deny school access during school hours to representatives of teachers' organizations and could bar their use of the school mail system.[47] However, the court invalidated school policies that denied teachers the right to discuss employee organizations during nonclass time or to use school mail facilities for communications including *any* mention of employee organizations. The latter policies were found to impair first amendment rights.

In a significant 1983 decision, *Perry Education Association v. Perry Local Educators' Association,* the Supreme Court ruled that a school district is not constitutionally obligated to allow a rival teachers' union access to internal school mailboxes although the exclusive bargaining agent is granted such access. Holding that a public school's internal mail system is not a public forum for expression, the Court declared that "the state may reserve the forum for its intended purposes, communicative or otherwise, as long as the regulation on speech is reasonable and not an effort to suppress expression merely because public officials oppose the speaker's view."[48] The Court determined that alternative communication channels were available to the rival union.

Under certain circumstances, however, a school's mail system might be considered a public forum because it has been designated as such by school officials. Applying the principle articulated in *Perry,* the Fifth Circuit Court of Appeals reasoned that although a school was not obligated to open its internal mail system to the general public or to employee organizations, in this case the school had designated its mail system as a forum for all employee organizations and thus could not selectively deny access.[49] The court also found the school district's guidelines, requiring prior clearance of material distributed through the mail system, to be unconstitutionally vague.

Most controversies have focused on teachers' organizations using school facilities and mail systems, but other prior restraints on expression also have been challenged. An Indiana case involved a school board's denial of a request by a group of teachers to hold religious meetings in the public school before students arrived in the morning. Upholding the board's action, the Seventh Circuit Court of Appeals reasoned that employees cannot assert an inherent free speech right to use public school facilities for expressive purposes not related to school business.[50] Distinguishing private conversations during noninstructional time from group meetings, the court concluded that the public school is not a forum for employees to hold meetings on matters of personal concern.

In addition to controversies over restrictions on employees' rights to distribute literature and hold meetings in public schools, policies limiting teachers' access to the school board also have generated legal disputes.

Several courts have struck down policies prohibiting individual teachers from communicating with the school board. In 1976 the Supreme Court held that a nonunion teacher has a free speech right to comment on a bargaining issue at a public school board meeting.[51] Also, the Ninth Circuit Court of Appeals awarded a teacher-coach damages for his suspension as a coach because of writing a letter to school board members without giving advance notice to the superintendent.[52] The school district was enjoined from prohibiting teachers' communication with the school board on matters of public concern. Similarly, the Seventh Circuit Court of Appeals struck down a policy requiring all communication to the school board to be directed through the superintendent and ordered a reprimand for violating the policy to be removed from a teacher's personnel file.[53]

Although prior restraints on teachers' free speech rights are vulnerable to legal attack, courts have upheld reasonable time, place, and manner regulations. For example, the Supreme Court of Louisiana recognized that such restrictions may be placed on expression as long as they (1) are not based on the content of speech, (2) serve significant governmental interests, and (3) leave alternative communication channels open. Accordingly, the court upheld a ban on hand-held signs in the school board offices, reasoning that the regulation served the legitimate governmental interest of ensuring that school board meetings were conducted in an orderly fashion.[54] In general, time, place, and manner restrictions will be upheld if justified to prevent a disruption of the educational environment and if other avenues are available for employees to express their views.

ACADEMIC FREEDOM

From its origin in German universities, the concept of academic freedom historically was applied to postsecondary education and embodied the principle that faculty members should be free from governmental controls in conducting research and imparting knowledge to students. The concept has undergone substantial change in American universities, where faculty members have claimed a first amendment right to academic freedom in research and teaching as well as activities away from the classroom.[55]

Public school teachers have asserted a similar right to academic freedom, but courts have not extended the broad protections found in higher education to public elementary and secondary schools. Teachers possess judicially recognized academic interests, but courts have refrained from establishing precise legal principles in this domain. Rather, controversies have been resolved on a case-by-case basis, involving a delicate balancing of teachers' interests in academic freedom against school boards' interests in assuring an appropriate instructional program and efficient school operations. Valente has referred to academic freedom as a "subset" of free expression rights, noting that the "constitutional contours of academic freedom at the public school level are not clearly fixed, or harmonized with the state's control over the curriculum.''[56]

Controversies pertaining to censorship of the school curriculum are addressed in Chapter 3, so this section concentrates specifically on public educators' academic freedom within the classroom setting. Can a teacher determine the most appropriate materials for classroom use? Does the first amendment protect a teacher's expression of personal ideas and philosophies? Is a teacher free to determine teaching methodologies? What topics or issues can a teacher discuss in a course?

COURSE CONTENT

In contrast to the discretion enjoyed by university faculty in curriculum matters, public school teachers in elementary and secondary schools do not have a right to determine the content of the instructional program. Legislatures in all states have granted local school boards considerable authority to establish programs of study and prescribe course content, including the scope and sequence of materials. Several courts have declared that school boards are not legally obligated to accept teachers' curricular recommendations in the absence of a board policy to that effect. For example, the Tenth Circuit Court of Appeals recognized the school board's authority to determine the curriculum and rejected the notion that teachers "have an unlimited liberty as to structure and content of the courses."[57] Subsequently, the same court upheld a school board that rejected a proposal from teachers for books to use in the English curriculum, "even though the decision was a political one influenced by the personal views of the [board] members."[58] In 1989 the Fifth Circuit Court of Appeals held that teachers cannot assert a first amendment right to substitute their own supplemental reading list for the official list without securing administrative approval.[59]

Teachers also are not permitted to ignore or omit prescribed course content under the guise of academic freedom. To illustrate, the Seventh Circuit Court of Appeals upheld a school board's dismissal of a kindergarten teacher who refused to teach patriotic topics for religious reasons.[60] The Supreme Court of Washington similarly found no first amendment impairment in a school board prohibiting two teachers from team-teaching a history course. The teachers characterized the dispute as one involving freedom to select teaching methodology; however, the board focused on the significant loss of course content between the traditional teaching method and the proposed alternative. The court reasoned that "course content is manifestly a matter within the board's discretion," and requiring teachers to cover this content in a conventional manner does not violate their academic freedom.[61]

Other courts have rendered similar decisions regarding school board requirements for conformity in content coverage. For example, the Eighth

Circuit Court of Appeals upheld the dismissal of a teacher who ignored her principal's warnings to cover prescribed material in her economics course. The teacher had structured her course to allow substantial student input in the selection of topics for class discussion, resulting in considerable instructional time being devoted to internal school disputes. According to the appellate court, academic freedom does not include the right to disregard a superior's valid instructional directives regarding appropriate course content.[62] Similarly, the Seventh Circuit Court of Appeals rejected a teacher's claim that he had a first amendment right to determine the content of his social studies courses; the board's prohibition on religious advocacy, including the teaching of creation science, was upheld.[63] The Supreme Court of Alaska endorsed a school board's rule requiring the superintendent's approval of supplementary materials used in the classroom.[64] A teacher, who refused to comply with this rule in selecting materials to teach about homosexual rights in a unit on American minorities, asserted that the rule abridged the first amendment. Noting that the issue was not whether the materials selected by the teacher were appropriate, but rather where the authority to make such a determination resides, the court concluded that the school board—not teachers—has the authority to control the curriculum.

TEACHING STRATEGIES

State laws and school board policies establish the basic contours of the curriculum, but teachers retain some discretion in choosing *strategies* to convey prescribed content.[65] In reviewing school board restrictions on teachers' classroom activities, the judiciary considers a number of factors, such as whether teachers have been provided adequate notice that use of specific teaching methodologies or materials will result in disciplinary action, the relevance of the method to the course of study, the threat of disruption posed by the method, and the impact of the strategy on community mores.

Adequate Notice. Courts in general have recognized teachers' discretion to select appropriate teaching methods that serve a demonstrated educational purpose. If a particular method is supported by professional educators, the teacher has no reason to anticipate that its use might result in disciplinary action unless there is a regulation forbidding its use. This procedural right of notice that specific methods are prohibited often is the decisive factor in academic freedom cases.

In an early case one of the central issues was the board's failure to notify the teacher that certain conduct was forbidden. The controversy involved the suspension and pending dismissal of a high school English teacher for using an article from the *Atlantic Monthly,* which parents asserted contained vulgar words.[66] The teacher sought an injunction to bar dismissal, alleging that his right to academic freedom was impaired. The First Circuit Court of Appeals conceded that some regulation of classroom speech is inherent in public education but found the "rigorous censorship" in this situation to have a chilling effect on the teacher's constitutional rights. The potential due process violation coupled with the academic freedom claim convinced the appeals court that the teacher would likely prevail when the case was heard by the trial court on remand.

In a Massachusetts case, a high school English teacher was dismissed for the illustrative use of a slang term for sexual intercourse in a discussion of taboo words.[67] The federal district court concluded that use of the word could be the basis for dismissal because it did not have the "support of the preponderant opinion of the teaching profession."[68] However, since no regulation existed prohibiting the teaching method, the teacher's reinstatement was ordered. The court noted that a teacher should not be placed in a position of guessing whether certain conduct will result in dismissal, and this decision was affirmed by the First Circuit Court of Appeals.

Failure to provide notice also was questioned in a Texas case, where a high school civics teacher was dismissed for discussing controversial topics such as interracial marriages and antiwar protests in his classes.[69] The court upheld the teacher's right to select valid teaching methods and found that the lack of notice regarding prohibited subject matter denied the teacher procedural due process. The school board had not adopted regulations or issued a statement to forewarn the teacher that the topics in question were considered inappropriate.

Similarly, adequacy of notice of prohibited activities was at issue in a 1990 Pennsylvania case. The Third Circuit Court of Appeals held that a teacher could not assert a first amendment right to disregard school board instructions and continue to use a classroom management technique (Learnball) that gave students responsibility for establishing class rules and grading procedures.[70] However, the case was remanded to give the teacher an opportunity to establish that the ban on her classroom management strategies was vague and overbroad, leaving ambiguity as to what strategies could be used.

Courts addressing the procedural due process issue have indicated that while teachers enjoy some measure of discretion, certain classroom conduct may be restricted by the school board if proper notice of proscribed methods is given. Behavior that lacks strong support from the education profession would certainly be more susceptible to restrictions.

Relevancy. A primary consideration in reviewing the legitimacy of classroom activities is whether instructional strategies are related to course objectives. In the absence of such a relationship, the teacher's behavior is not constitutionally protected. Relevancy applies not only to objectives but also to the age and maturity of the students; a controversial topic appropriate for high school students would not necessarily be suitable for elementary and junior high pupils. Even though a certain method may be considered relevant, if it lacks the general support of the profession, a school board still may prevail in barring its use.[71]

The Seventh Circuit Court of Appeals found that teachers' distribution of a brochure on the pleasures of drug use and sex to an eighth-grade class lacked a legitimate educational purpose.[72] In upholding dismissal of the teachers, the court asserted that the materials, which were distributed without any explanation or discussion, were unrelated to course objectives and totally inappropriate for eighth-grade students. Relevance to course objectives similarly was found lacking in a high school teacher's use of an R-rated movie on the last day of school[73] and a photography teacher's showing of a pornographic film to high school students.[74] Also, a Louisiana appeals court found that a teacher's statements regarding the sexual behavior of African Americans lacked instructional relevance and thus were outside the scope of protected academic freedom.[75]

In contrast, the Fifth Circuit Court of Appeals ruled that a teacher's use of a simulation to teach about post–Civil War American history was related to legitimate educational objectives and therefore could not be the basis for dismissal.[76] Parents had complained that the simulation aroused racial feelings, and the school board subsequently dismissed the teacher after he refused to stop using the simulation. Ruling that the board's action violated the teacher's academic rights, the appellate court recognized that teachers cannot be forced to discontinue instructionally relevant activities solely because of parental displeasure.

Similarly, the Sixth Circuit Court of Appeals ordered reinstatement of a teacher who had been effectively discharged when citizens complained to the school board regarding the teacher's instruction in a life science course. The teacher was suspended and told that he would be terminated after he refused to accept a letter of reprimand. The court upheld the teacher, finding that his classroom behavior was appropriate and relevant to the course objectives.[77] The court noted that the films and text used by the teacher had been approved by the school board and used for several years.

Threat of Disruption. Among the factors courts examine in assessing restrictions on classroom instruction is whether a teacher's action poses a threat of disruption to the operation of the school. An Alabama federal district court singled out this factor and the appropriateness of instructional strategies for the age of students in reviewing the dismissal of an eleventh-grade English teacher for using a Kurt Vonnegut story that allegedly encouraged "the killing off of elderly people and free sex."[78] The court found the teacher's dismissal unwarranted since the story was not considered inappropriate for high school students and did not pose "a material and substantial threat of disruption."[79] An Oregon federal district court found a school board's policy, banning all political speakers from the high school, unreasonable on several grounds, including the fact that no disruptions had occurred or could be anticipated from political discussions.[80] In a case discussed previously, the Fifth Circuit Court of Appeals concluded that numerous complaints from parents and students about use of a simulation to teach history did not constitute a sufficient disruption to destroy the teacher's effectiveness in the classroom. The court stated that the "test is not whether substantial disruption occurs but whether such disruption overbalances the teacher's usefulness as an instructor."[81] Similarly, a Texas federal court found that community objections to a teacher's administration of a survey regarding sex roles did not equate to disruption of the school system.[82]

However, an Illinois federal district court recognized that a school board does not necessarily have to show that instructional materials actually caused a disruption to justify nonrenewal of a teacher's contract. Materials may be considered inappropriate for classsroom use (e.g., an R-rated film with vulgarity and sexually explicit scenes), even though students "quietly acquiesce" to their use.[83] Also, the Supreme Court of Maine held that a school board's decision to cancel a "Tolerance Day" program was based on a legitimate concern for safety, order, and security due to bomb threats that had been received.[84] The court found no impairment of teachers' academic freedom or students' free speech rights in canceling the program at which a homosexual was scheduled to speak, noting that teachers and students were not precluded from discussing tolerance and prejudice against homosexuals in classes.

Community Standards. Courts have been protective of school boards' authority to design the curriculum to reflect community values. In 1980 the Seventh Circuit Court of Appeals recognized that school board members represent the community, which "has a legitimate, even a vital and compelling, interest in the choice [of] and adherence to a suitable curriculum for the benefit of our young citizens."[85] Similarly, the Tenth Circuit Court of Appeals acknowledged that community standards can be considered in determining the appropriateness of teaching materials and methods.[86]

However, the judiciary also has recognized that school boards cannot suppress first amendment rights simply to placate angry citizens. In a case discussed previously, the Sixth Circuit Court of Appeals held that complaints regarding a teacher's instruction in a life science course, taught in conformance with school board directives, did not justify the school board placing restrictions on the teacher's classroom activities.[87] A parent had organized a community protest against the teacher, and neither the administrators, who had approved the course materials, nor the school board came to the teacher's defense. Concluding that the teacher's "exercise of 'academic freedom' had followed rather than violated his superior's instructions," the court held that a community uproar does not justify school board action that stigmatizes a teacher and inflicts pain and suffering for impermissible reasons.[88]

In the Oregon case also cited earlier, a civics teacher had invited political speakers representing four viewpoints to address his class.[89] Severe community objection to the invited Communist speaker (e.g., petitions and threats to defeat the school budget and incumbent board members) resulted in the school board's ban on all *political* speakers. The court noted that teachers' first amendment rights may be restricted in light of the special circumstances of the school environment if the restrictions are reasonable. In this case, however, the suppression of selected viewpoints was not considered reasonable; the only basis for the board's action appeared to be fear of voter reaction.

Because of the school board's legitimate interest in advancing community mores, the judiciary has considered community standards in evaluating challenges to various teaching methods. However, if a particular strategy is instructionally relevant and supported by the profession, it likely will survive judicial review even though it might disturb some school patrons.

FREEDOM OF ASSOCIATION

Although freedom of association is not specifically addressed in the first amendment, the Supreme Court has recognized that associational rights are "implicit in the freedoms of speech, assembly, and petition."[90] Accordingly, public educators cannot be disciplined for forming or joining political, labor, religious, or social organizations. However, limitations may be placed on associational activities that disrupt school operations or interfere with teachers' professional duties. This section presents an overview of teachers' associational rights in connection with political affiliations and activities. Public educators' rights in connection with labor unions are addressed in Chapter 11.

POLITICAL AFFILIATIONS

[handwritten: membership is not grounds for firing, but refusing to cooperate is]

States have made frequent attempts to prohibit or limit teachers' affiliations with subversive political organizations. These restrictions have been imposed to protect public schools from treasonable and seditious acts. In early cases, the Supreme Court held that associational rights could be restricted when a public employee was fully knowledgeable of an organization's subversive purpose,[91] but in the mid-1960s this stance was rejected. While teachers can be required to affirm their support of the federal and state constitutions,[92] the Supreme Court has invalidated loyalty oaths requiring individuals to deny membership in subversive organizations as unduly vague or imposing sanctions for "guilt by association."[93] Recognizing the state's legitimate interest in protecting schools from subversion, courts have not allowed this interest to infringe on fundamental associational rights. The Supreme Court in *Keyishian v. Board of Regents* firmly established that mere membership in an organization, such as the Communist Party, without the specific intent to further the unlawful aims of the organization could not disqualify an individual for public school employment.[94]

Thus, state statutes specifically barring members of subversive or controversial organizations from public employment are clearly unconstitutional.[95] Neither can a school system impose restrictions, directly or indirectly, on teachers' memberships or their lawful activities in certain organizations. As with protected speech, dismissal of a teacher will not be supported if the motivating factor behind the decision is the teacher's exercise of associational rights.

Governmental action need not proscribe organizational membership to impair associational rights. Courts will scrutinize challenged laws that *inhibit* the free exercise of constitutional guarantees unless the state can show that such measures are substantially related to a compelling governmental interest. The Supreme Court overturned an Arkansas law that required all teachers to submit annually a list of every organization they had joined or regularly supported during the prior five years.[96] The Court found that this law went well beyond the state's interest in determining the fitness and competence of teachers and constituted "comprehensive interference with associational freedom."[97] Similarly, teachers relied on first amendment associational rights to challenge a Texas statute that allowed county judges to compel disclosure of membership lists by certain organizations engaged in activities designed to disrupt public schools.[98] As in the Arkansas case, this law also was found to sweep too broadly; the required disclosure exposed to public recrimination those members who did not participate in disruptive activities.

The fact that associational rights are protected by the first amendment, however, does not preclude school administrators from questioning a teacher about associational activities that may adversely affect teaching. In *Beilan v. Board of Public Education of Philadelphia,* the Supreme Court held that questions regarding a teacher's activities in the Communist Party were relevant to an assessment of his fitness to serve as a classroom teacher and that refusal to answer the superintendent's inquiries could result in dismissal.[99] Although organizational membership *per se* is protected, a teacher must respond to queries about associational activities related to fitness to teach.

Membership in controversial political organizations has not been the only source of litigation; partisan political affiliation also has been controversial. Historically, public employment was characterized by the patronage system; when the controlling political party changed, non–civil service employees belonging to the defeated party lost their jobs. In 1976 the Supreme Court examined the constitutionality of such a patronage system in an Illinois sheriff's office.[100] The Court viewed the practice as a severe restriction on political association and belief, noting that nonpolicy-making, nonconfidential individuals are not in a position to undermine policies of the new administration and the constant threat of replacement is detrimental to governmental effectiveness and efficiency. In 1980 the Supreme Court reiterated that the democratic process would be preserved by limiting patronage dismissals to policymaking positions.[101] A decade later the Court extended the principle established in the political firing cases to all aspects of public employment, ruling that party affiliation cannot influence promotion, transfer, recall, and other decisions pertaining to employees who do not establish policies.[102]

Although state statutes substantially insulate public educators from partisan politics, in some instances teachers have asserted that employment decisions have been based on partisan affiliation. In such cases, the burden has been placed on the school employee to substantiate that protected political affiliation was the motivating factor in the board's employment decision.[103] If an employee satisfies this burden, then the board must demonstrate by a preponderance of evidence that it would have reached the same decision in the absence of the political association.

POLITICAL ACTIVITY

Teachers, like all citizens, are guaranteed the right to participate in the political process. Yet, active participation often has prompted school officials to place limitations on the exercise of this right, surfacing difficult legal questions. Can teachers run for political offices? What types of political activities are permitted in the school setting? Can certain political activities outside the school be restricted?

Risky!

Campaigning for Issues and Candidates. First amendment associational as well as free speech rights have been invoked to protect teachers in expressing political views and campaigning for candidates. While such political activity is constitutionally protected, restrictions can be placed on teachers' activities in the school setting. Making campaign speeches in the classroom is clearly prohibited; teachers cannot take advantage of their position of authority with an impressionable captive audience to impose their political views. However, if campaign issues are related to the class topic, a teacher can present election issues and candidates in a nonpartisan manner.

In general, political activity in schools that would cause divisiveness among faculty members also can be restricted. But school officials cannot impose unnecessary constraints; there must be a legitimate threat that the activity will interfere with school operations. In a California case, a school board refused to allow teachers to circulate a petition in the school lounge regarding school funding matters, asserting that the issue would create dissension in the faculty. The California Supreme Court rejected the board's claim, noting that any restraint on teachers' political activities must be justified as "a practical necessity" to meet a "compelling public need to protect efficiency and integrity of the public service."[104]

Courts have tended to reject restrictions affecting teachers' political activities *outside* the school. Public employees are constitutionally protected from retaliation for participation in political affairs at the local, state, and federal levels. For example, the New Jersey Federal District Court prevented the dismissal of a tenured teacher based on clear evidence that the charges were brought only for the purpose of harassment and retaliation for the teacher's statements at a political rally and his activities supporting a political faction that was opposed by the current school board majority.[105] Other courts also have overturned dismissals, transfers, or demotions predicated on the support or nonsupport of particular candidates in school board elections where protected political activity was a motivating or substantial factor in the adverse employment action.[106]

Holding Public Office. Limitations have been upheld on certain categories of public employees running for political office, but the status of public educators in this regard is somewhat unclear. In 1973 the Supreme Court upheld a federal law (the Hatch Act) that prevents federal employees from holding formal positions in political parties, playing substantial roles in partisan campaigns, and running for partisan office.[107] The Court recognized that legitimate reasons exist for restricting political activities of public employees, such as the need to ensure impartial and effective government, to remove employees from political pressure, and to prevent employee selection based on political factors. In a companion case, the Court upheld an Oklahoma law forbidding classified civil servants from running for paid political offices.[108]

Other courts also have endorsed certain restrictions on state and municipal employees running for elective office. For example, the Georgia Supreme Court reasoned that a state law, prohibiting legislators from being employed by a state agency, was necessary to ensure efficient governmental services.[109] The Rhode Island Supreme Court also upheld a state law forbidding municipal employees from holding elective public office in the city or town where employed, declaring that the "government has a strong interest in protecting its employees from entanglements caused by dual positions or even the appearance of such entanglements."[110] But the court struck down the portion of the city charter prohibiting *all* elected officers from holding any other local, state, or federal partisan or nonpartisan office, finding this restriction unconstitutionally overbroad. Similarly, an Oregon court struck down as overly broad a state law prohibiting all public employees from running for political office.[111]

Several courts have held that public educators, unlike public employees who are directly involved in the operation of governmental agencies, have the right to run for and hold public office. The Utah Supreme Court, for example, ruled that public school teachers and administrators were not disqualified from serving in the state legislature.[112] Also, the Ohio Supreme Court upheld a public school principal's right to serve as a county commissioner.[113]

Restrictions can be imposed, however, to protect the integrity of the educational system. To illustrate, courts have recognized that certain offices are incompatible with public school employment, especially if they involve an employer–employee relationship. Common law has established that such incompatibility exists when a teacher seeks a position on the school board where employed. The Supreme Court of Wyoming recognized that if the teacher is both employer and employee, it is "inimical to the public interest."[114] Moreover, the court noted that this infirmity cannot be remedied by the teacher's abstention from voting on certain financial and personnel issues. According to the court, for the teacher "to hold office as trustee while acting as teacher would deprive the citizens of the school district of independent judgment of a full and impartial board of trustees elected to represent the entire public interest."[115] Of course, a teacher would not be prevented from serving on the school board of another school district.[116]

The Supreme Court of Virginia held that a city council member also employed as a principal was disqualified from voting on appointments to the school board because of the personal interest involved.[117] The court noted that the statutory prohibition on conflicts of interests does not require proof that decisions on specific issues are affected by personal considerations; individuals are disqualified from voting on matters where there is a *danger* that judgments may be compromised for personal reasons.

Also, public educators can be required to take a leave of absence before running for a public office, if campaigning would interfere with their job responsibilities.[118] However, some leave requirements have been judicially struck down where there has been insufficient justification for the policies. A Kentucky appellate court overturned a school board regulation requiring all employees who were political candidates to take a one-month leave of absence prior to the election.[119] This policy was found to violate teachers' associational and expression rights since there was no evidence that the political activities would hinder job performance. The court further noted that an individual determination should be made to assess whether certain types of political participation would have an adverse effect on teaching duties.

The Supreme Court affirmed a lower court's decision striking down a Georgia school board's policy requiring any school employee who became a candidate for public office to take a leave of absence without pay for the duration of the candidacy. Finding this policy to be a violation of the federal Voting Rights Act, the Court recognized that it created a substantial economic deterrent to seeking elective public office and was potentially discriminatory since it was adopted after an African-American employee announced his candidacy for the state legislature.[120] However, the school board's revised policy, denying special leaves of absence for political purposes, was subsequently upheld by the Supreme Court.[121] The modified policy was considered a legitimate reaffirmation of the board's authority to require employees to fulfill their contracts, which did not impair federally protected rights.

Although school boards must respect employees' associational rights, they also are obligated to ensure that the political activities of public school personnel do not adversely affect the school. If educators neglect instructional duties to campaign for issues or candidates, use the classroom as a political forum, or disrupt school operations because of their political activities, disciplinary actions can be imposed. But school boards must be certain that constraints imposed on employees' freedom of association are not based on mere disagreement with the political orientation of the activities. Personnel actions must be justified as necessary to protect the interests of students and the school.

PERSONAL APPEARANCE

Historically, school boards often imposed rigid grooming restrictions on teachers.[122] In the 1970s, such attempts to regulate teachers' appearance generated considerable litigation, as did grooming standards for students.[123] Controversies have subsided somewhat, but constraints on school employees' appearance continue to be challenged. School boards have defended their efforts to regulate teacher appearance on the perceived need to set an appropriate tone in the classroom and enforce similar appearance and dress codes for students. Teachers have contested these requirements as abridgments of their constitutionally protected privacy, liberty, and free expression rights.

A few courts have declared that the right to govern one's own appearance is a fundamental constitutional right. A Mississippi federal district court held that governmental restrictions on the personal appearance of adults as a condition of employment must be viewed with close judicial scrutiny.[124] The court found no legitimate state interest to justify applying a school board's student grooming policy to teachers in the absence of evidence that a certain manner of grooming would disrupt the educational process. A California appeals court also ruled that school staff members could not be prohibited from wearing beards without evidence that beards would have an adverse effect on the learning environment,[125] and a Florida federal district court ordered reinstatement of a teacher whose contract was not renewed for failure to comply with the principal's request to remove his goatee.[126]

In contrast to the above cases, most courts since the mid-1970s have supported school officials in imposing reasonable grooming and dress restrictions on teachers.[127] The Supreme Court provided significant clarification of public employers' authority regarding regulation of employee appearance in a 1976 decision upholding a hair grooming regulation for police officers. The Court acknowledged that personal appearance does involve a constitutional right but "implicates only the more general contours of the substantive liberty interest protected by the fourteenth amendment."[128] According to the Court, the protected interest would be impaired only if a regulation were "so irrational that it [could] be branded 'arbitrary.'"[129] The Court placed the burden on the individual to demonstrate the lack of a rational connection between the regulation and accomplishment of a legitimate public purpose.

The Supreme Court's rationale in upholding the grooming regulation for police officers has been followed by other courts assessing dress and appearance restrictions for teachers. For example, the Second Circuit Court of Appeals held that a Connecticut school board was justified in requiring all male teachers to wear a tie.[130] The court did not find the dress code arbitrary but accepted it as a rational means of promoting respect for authority, traditional values, and classroom discipline. Because of the uniquely influential role of teachers, the court noted that they may be subjected to restrictions in their professional lives that otherwise would not be acceptable. The Fifth Circuit Court of Appeals also found a Louisiana school board's prohibition against wearing beards to be rationally related to the board's "undeniable interest in teaching hygiene, instilling discipline, asserting authority, and compelling uniformity."[131] Applying similar reasoning, the First Circuit Appellate Court upheld a school board's dismissal of a teacher for wearing short skirts.[132]

Restrictions will not be upheld, however, if found to be unrelated to a legitimate governmental concern. To illustrate, the Seventh Circuit Court of Appeals found that a regulation prohibiting school bus drivers from wearing mustaches lacked a valid purpose and, accordingly, overturned the school board's suspension of a driver for violating the rule.[133] The only justification the school board offered for the policy was conservative community attitudes. There was no indication in this case that the bus driver's mustache affected his ability to perform his job. The court noted that the irrationality of this policy was exemplified by the fact that the bus driver also was a full-time teacher but was not suspended from his teaching position.

Although courts generally acknowledge that the right to govern personal appearance is a protected interest, it has not been declared a fundamental right requiring heightened judicial scrutiny. School officials thus can restrict employees' appearance as long as there is a rational basis for the regulation and the rules are not arbitrary.

PRIVACY RIGHTS

Public employees have asserted the right to be free from unwarranted governmental intrusions in their personal affairs. Protections of personal privacy flow from both constitutional and statutory provisions.[134] Litigation covered in this section focuses on constitutional privacy claims initiated under the fourth amendment (protection against unreasonable searches and seizures), the ninth amendment (personal privacy as an unenumerated right reserved to the people), and the fourteenth amendment (protection against state action impairing personal liberties without due process of law).

Although the Federal Constitution does not explicitly address personal privacy rights, the Supreme Court has recognized that certain *implied* fundamental rights warrant constitutional protection because of their close relationship to explicit constitutional guarantees. Protected privacy rights have been interpreted as encompassing personal choices in matters such as marriage, contraception, procreation, family relations, and childrearing.[135]

Interpreting teachers' privacy rights, the Fifth Circuit Court of Appeals recognized that a teacher's interest in breast-feeding her child at school during noninstructional time is sufficiently close to fundamental rights regarding family relationships and childrearing to trigger constitutional privacy protection. The court, however, also acknowledged that, if necessary, fundamental liberties can be restricted to further compelling state interests. The case was remanded for a trial to ascertain if the school board's interests in avoiding disruption of the educational process, ensuring that teachers perform their duties without distraction, and avoiding liability for potential injuries were strong enough to justify the restriction imposed on the teacher's privacy interests.[136]

The Second Circuit Court of Appeals upheld a teacher's privacy claim in her refusal to submit to a physical examination by the school district's male physician, noting that the teacher offered to go at her own expense to any female physician selected by the board. The court found it unnecessary to determine whether there is a fundamental constitutional right to be examined by a physician of the same sex because the school board's action was considered so unreasonable to be unconstitutionally arbitrary.[137]

In some instances the governmental interest in ensuring the welfare of students and the school overrides teachers' privacy interests. For example, a tenured teacher did not prevail in claiming that her privacy rights were violated when the school board refused to allow her to return from an extended medical absence without providing medical records from the treating physician and submitting to a physical examination by the school board doctor. Recognizing the school board's strong interest in safeguarding the health and welfare of students, the Second Circuit Court of Appeals found no invasion of privacy in the legitimate requests for medical information.[138] The First Circuit Court of Appeals also held that a principal's constitutional right to privacy was not impaired when he was required to undergo a psychiatric examination before returning to work. The court declared that a teacher or administrator may be compelled to submit to such an examination as a condition of continued employment if there is reason to believe that the welfare of students may be jeopardized.[139]

Teachers also have not succeeded in asserting that observations by superiors and other strategies used to assess teaching competence violate protected privacy rights. For example, in 1990 a Texas appeals court upheld videotaping a teacher's performance for evaluative purposes, concluding that teachers' privacy rights do not shield them from legitimate performance evaluations.[140]

Although courts have shown sensitivity toward educators' claims involving matters of personal privacy, the judiciary also has recognized that the school board's interest in maintaining an appropriate educational environment justifies some constraints on teachers' personal freedoms. School officials have defended such restrictions on the grounds that teachers serve as role models for students and therefore should conform to community norms. Although regulations are far less restrictive today than in the early 1900s, when some school districts prohibited female teachers from marrying or even dating, school boards still attempt to proscribe aspects of teachers' personal lives that are inimical to community values. The remainder of this section focuses on litigation in which courts have assessed the competing interests of employees and employers in connection with search and seizure and lifestyle choices.

SEARCH AND SEIZURE

Public educators, like all citizens, are shielded by the fourth amendment against unreasonable governmental invasions of their personal property. This amendment requires police officers and other state agents to secure a search warrant (based on probable cause that evidence of a crime will be found) before conducting a search of an individual's person or effects. As discussed in Chapter 6, most search and seizure controversies in public schools have focused on whether warrantless *student* searches are justified to maintain a proper educational environment. The Supreme Court has ruled that although school authorities are considered agents of the state under the fourth amendment, they can conduct personal searches of students without a warrant as long as they have *reasonable suspicion* that contraband detrimental to the educational process is concealed.[141]

The Supreme Court has not addressed teachers' rights in connection with searches initiated by school authorities, but in 1987 it upheld a warrantless search by state hospital supervisors of an employee physician's office. Noting the scant case law on the appropriate fourth amendment standard of reasonableness for a public employer's work-related search of its employees' offices, desks, or file cabinets, the Court held that such searches should be governed by a standard of reasonableness in that both the basis for the search and the scope of the intrusion must be reasonable.[142] In this case, hospital officials were concerned about possible improprieties in the physician's management of the residency program, and items seized from his desk and file cabinets were used in administrative proceedings that resulted in his dismissal. Although recognizing that public employees have a reasonable expectation of privacy in their desks and files, the Court concluded that a warrant is not required for work-related searches that are necessary to carry out the business of the agency. The case was remanded for a determination of whether the search in question met this standard of reasonableness.

In the public school context, the judiciary has recognized that the reasonableness of a job-related search or seizure by a supervisor rests on whether educational interests outweigh the individual employee's expectation of privacy. The Third Circuit Court of Appeals held that a school board member's search of a school guidance counselor's desk violated the fourth amendment because sufficient work-related justification for the search was not presented.[143] The search was conducted to find evidence that the counselor had submitted to the local newspaper a cartoon ridiculing the school board's fiscal and personnel policies. The court held that teachers and counselors have a legitimate expectation of privacy in the contents of their school desks, noting that the school district had not established a regulation or practice dispelling such an expectation.

In contrast, the First Circuit Court of Appeals rejected a teacher's fourth amendment claim that she had a reasonable expectation of privacy in withholding from the school administration a term paper she had written about a child with disabilities in her class. Although the paper was written for a college course, the court determined that the teacher extinguished any expectation of privacy when she shared the paper with the professor of the course and offered it to the school official in charge of the committee convened to design an educational program for the child. Concluding that the school principal had a legitimate interest in the contents of the paper as it pertained to a student under his charge, the court held that disciplinary action resulting from the teacher's initial refusal to relinquish the paper did not violate fourth amendment rights.[144] Although the fourth amendment prohibits *arbitrary* invasions of teachers' personal effects by school officials, courts have recognized that in some situations educational interests justify interference with the individual's expectation of privacy.

Public school employees' fourth amendment rights also have been asserted in connection with drug screening programs. School boards can require employees to have physical examinations as a condition of employment, but mandatory screening for drugs has been challenged as impairing privacy rights. Teachers in a New York school district secured a restraining order prohibiting the school board from forcing probationary teachers to submit urine samples for purposes of determining whether they were using controlled substances. The school district defended its policy as part of an effort to reduce substance abuse, but the state high court affirmed the lower courts' conclusion that the "compulsory extraction of bodily fluids is a search and seizure within the meaning of the fourth amendment."[145] Noting that the school board can conduct warrantless searches based on reasonable suspicion of conduct detrimental to the school environment, the appeals court concluded that the drug-testing program did not satisfy this standard. Since there was no *individualized suspicion* of wrongdoing, the drug-testing program was found to violate teachers' privacy rights.

In 1990 a Georgia federal district court also struck down a statewide drug-testing law that would have required all new state employees and veteran employees transferring to another school district or state agency to submit to urinalysis screening.[146] The court found no compelling governmental interest to justify testing *all* job applicants. The general interest in maintaining a drug-free workplace was not sufficient; the governmental objective must be related to risks associated with particular job duties.

The District of Columbia Court of Appeals, however, upheld the school district's policy requiring all employees whose duties involve safety of children to submit to a drug test as part of routine medical examinations.[147] The program was instituted after school officials found evidence suggesting drug use among some attendants who assisted in transporting children with disabilities. The court declared that the "drug-testing program bears a close and substantial relationship" to the legitimate governmental goal of deterring drug use.[148]

Support for *limited* drug testing of employees can be found in two 1989 Supreme Court decisions upholding the mandatory drug testing of railroad employees involved in accidents[149] and customs employees who carry firearms or are involved in interdiction of illegal drugs.[150] The Court found that the safety and security interests served by the programs outweighed employees' privacy concerns. Given these rulings, it seems that mandatory drug testing can be required for certain public school employees, such as bus drivers, where justified by overriding safety considerations.

LIFESTYLE CHOICES

In recent years, teachers frequently have challenged school officials' authority to restrict personal lifestyle choices. Although the right to such personal freedom is not an enumerated constitutional guarantee, it is a right implied in the concept of personal liberty embodied in the fourteenth amendment. Constitutional protection afforded to teachers' privacy rights is determined not only by the *location* of the conduct, but also by the *nature* of the activity.[151] The judiciary has attempted to balance teachers' privacy interests against the school board's legitimate interests in safe-guarding the welfare of students and the effective management of the school. Sanctions cannot be imposed solely because school officials disapprove of teachers' personal and private conduct, but restrictions can be placed on unconventional behavior that is detrimental to job performance or harmful to students.

The precise contours of public educators' constitutional privacy rights have not been clearly delineated; constitutional claims involving pregnancies out of wedlock, unconventional living arrangements, homosexuality, and other alleged sexual improprieties usually have been decided on a case-by-case basis. Since many of these cases also are discussed in Chapter 10 in connection with dismissals based on charges of immorality, the following discussion is confined to an overview of the constitutional issues.

Recognizing that decisions pertaining to marriage and parenthood involve constitutionally protected privacy rights, courts have been reluctant to support dismissal actions based on teachers' unwed, pregnant status in the absence of evidence that the condition impairs fitness to teach. In a typical case, the Fifth Circuit Court of Appeals invalidated a Mississippi school district's rule prohibiting the employment of unwed parents in order to promote a "properly moral scholastic environment."[152] According to the court, the policy equating birth of an illegitimate child with immoral conduct precluded an individual determination of each applicant's qualifications, thereby violating equal protection and due process guarantees. Compelled leaves of absence for pregnant, unmarried employees similarly have been invalidated as violating constitutional privacy rights.[153]

Most courts also have reasoned that public employees, including educators, have a protected privacy right to engage in consenting sexual relationships out of wedlock and that such relationships cannot be the basis for dismissal unless teaching effectiveness is impaired. For example, the Supreme Court of Iowa held that a teacher's adulterous relationship was insufficient to justify revocation of his teaching certificate, since it was not substantiated that the teacher's private conduct had a harmful effect on his teaching.[154] Likewise, a Florida court overturned a school board's termination of a teacher for lacking good moral character based on her personal romantic relationship.[155] The Supreme Court declined to review a case in which the Sixth Circuit Court of Appeals ruled that a school board's nonrenewal of a nontenured teacher because of her involvement in a divorce abridged constitutional privacy rights.[156]

Some courts, however, have upheld dismissals or other disciplinary actions based on public employees' lifestyle choices, finding no impairment of protected privacy rights. The Supreme Court declined to review two nonschool decisions in which federal appellate courts upheld dismissals of public employees for engaging in adulterous relationships that allegedly impaired job performance.[157] The Eighth Circuit Court of Appeals also upheld the dismissal of an unmarried female teacher who was living with a male friend in a mobile home close to the school, reasoning that the arrangement offended community norms and had an adverse effect on students.[158]

Whether employment decisions can be based on a teacher's sexual orientation has become increasingly controversial, and the scope of constitutional protections afforded to teachers who select a homosexual lifestyle has not yet been clarified.[159] Among factors courts consider are the nature of the homosexual conduct (public or private), the notoriety surrounding the conduct, and its impact on teaching effectiveness.

In 1984 the Tenth Circuit Court of Appeals upheld an Oklahoma statute permitting a teacher to be discharged for engaging in public homosexual activity, finding that this provision was neither vague nor a violation of equal protection rights.[160] However, as discussed previously, the Court struck down the portion of the law authorizing the dismissal or nonrenewal of teachers for *advocating* public or private homosexuality. The court found the latter section to be overbroad in restricting teachers' free speech rights, declaring that the first amendment protects advocacy of legal as well as illegal conduct as long as such advocacy does not incite imminent, lawless action. Since the Supreme Court divided evenly in this case, the appellate ruling was affirmed, but it does not establish a precedent that is binding on courts in other federal circuits.

A Georgia law attaching criminal penalties to public *or private* consensual sodomy resulted in a widely publicized Supreme Court decision in 1986. An individual challenged the law's constitutionality after being charged with violating the statute by committing sodomy with another adult male in the privacy of his home. The Court by a narrow margin upheld the law, stating that legislation reflecting the citizenry's view that sodomy is immoral and unacceptable has a rational basis.[161] Declaring that homosexuals do not have a constitutional right to engage in sodomy, the Court majority focused its opinion on the homosexual nature of the conduct at issue, even though the law's prohibition applies to heterosexual sodomy as well. A number of other states currently have laws similar to the contested Georgia statute, but criminal sanctions for *private* sodomy have not generally been enforced.

Educators can be dismissed for convictions under state antisodomy laws, but dismissals based solely on an individual's sexual orientation, in the absence of criminal charges, have generated a range of judicial interpretations. According to the Supreme Court of California, mere disapproval of private conduct does not constitute adequate grounds for dismissing a teacher. In several decisions, the California high court has suggested that evidence of impaired teaching effectiveness must accompany a teacher's discharge for private homosexuality.[162] Other courts, however, have not universally adopted this reasoning.

The Ninth Circuit Court of Appeals affirmed a trial court's conclusion that a teacher who was unconstitutionally dismissed for being a homosexual was entitled only to damages and attorneys' fees, but not to reinstatement.[163] Although finding the dismissal for alleged immorality to be unconstitutionally vague, the court held that the nature of the constitutional right at stake can be considered in determining whether reinstatement is required. Concluding that unconstitutional dismissals predicated on the exercise of protected speech or racial considerations would necessitate reinstatement, the appellate court held that choice of a nonconventional lifestyle does not trigger such a remedy.

Some courts have upheld dismissals based on mere knowledge of a teacher's homosexuality, suggesting that such knowledge is sufficient to establish an impairment of teaching effectiveness that overrides any protected privacy interest. For example, the Washington Supreme Court upheld a teacher's dismissal after he admitted to a school administrator that he was a homosexual, and the Supreme Court declined to review the case.[164] In a case discussed previously, the Supreme Court also declined to review a decision in which the Sixth Circuit Court of Appeals upheld the nonrenewal of a guidance counselor who told other school personnel about her bisexuality.[165] Since the Supreme Court has not recognized a constitutional privacy right to engage in homosexual conduct, a range of interpretations among lower courts regarding homosexual educators' rights will likely persist.

REMEDIES FOR VIOLATIONS OF SUBSTANTIVE CONSTITUTIONAL RIGHTS

When established that school districts or officials have violated an employee's constitutional rights, several remedies are available to the aggrieved individual. In some situations, the employee may seek a court injunction ordering the unlawful action to cease. This remedy might be sought if a school board has unconstitutionally imposed prior restraints on teachers' expression. As discussed in Chapter 10, where terminations, transfers, or other adverse employment consequences have been unconstitutionally imposed, courts will order school districts to return the affected employees to their original status with back pay.

In addition to these remedies, educators are increasingly bringing suits to recover damages for actions that violate their constitutional rights. Suits are usually based on Section 1983 of the Civil Rights Act of 1871—a federal law rarely invoked until the 1960s. Section 1983 provides that any person who acts under color of state law to deprive another individual of rights secured by the Federal Constitution or laws is subject to personal liability.[166] This law, which was originally enacted to prevent discrimination against African-American citizens, has been broadly interpreted as conferring liability on school personnel and school districts, not only for racial discrimination, but also for actions that may result in the impairment of other federally protected rights.[167] In 1989 the Supreme Court ruled that Section 1983 provides the exclusive federal damages remedy for violation of other Reconstruction-era civil rights laws when the alleged violation is by a state actor.[168]

Suits alleging Section 1983 violations can be initiated in federal or state courts,[169] and exhaustion of state administrative remedies is not required before initiating a federal suit.[170] However, where a federal law authorizes an exclusive nondamages remedy, a Section 1983 suit is precluded.[171] The remainder of this section focuses on the liability of school officials and districts under Section 1983 and the types of damages available to aggrieved employees. Awards of attorneys' fees in connection with civil rights violations are discussed in Chapter 10.

LIABILITY OF SCHOOL OFFICIALS

Under Section 1983, public school employees acting under color of state law can be held personally liable for actions abridging a student's or teacher's federal rights.[172] However, the Supreme Court has recognized that government officials cannot be held liable under Section 1983 for the actions of their subordinates, thus rejecting the doctrine of *respondeat superior,* even where school officials have general supervisory authority over the activities of the wrongdoers. In order to be held liable, the officials must have personally participated in, or had personal knowledge of, the unlawful acts or promulgated official policy under which the acts were taken.[173]

The Supreme Court has recognized that in some circumstances school officials can claim qualified immunity to shield them from personal liability when they have acted in good faith. The burden of establishing good-faith immunity clearly resides with the official claiming the protection; the plaintiff does not have to prove that immunity is not applicable.[174] In a 1975 student discipline case, *Wood v. Strickland,* the Supreme Court declared:

> A school board member is not immune from liability for damages under Section 1983 if he knew or reasonably should have known that the action he took within his sphere of official responsibility would violate the constitutional rights of the student affected, or if he took the action with the malicious intention to cause a deprivation of constitutional rights or other injury to the student.[175]

Subsequently, in *Harlow v. Fitzgerald* the Court eliminated the subjective test (i.e., an assessment of whether the defendants acted with malicious intentions) from the qualified-immunity standard. Under *Har-*

low, "government officials performing discretionary functions generally are shielded from liability for civil damages insofar as their conduct does not violate clearly established statutory or constitutional rights of which a reasonable person would have known."[176] When a school official claims qualified immunity, this objective test is applied by a judge prior to the trial.[177] In 1988 the Sixth Circuit Court of Appeals noted that school officials generally have qualified immunity "unless plaintiffs' rights were so clearly established when the acts were committed that any officer in the defendant's position, measured objectively, would have clearly understood that he was under an affirmative duty to have refrained from such conduct."[178]

In several cases qualified immunity has been denied because of the disregard of well-established legal principles. For example, school officials were not entitled to qualified immunity where they reasonably should have known that retaliating against a teacher for using her union's grievance procedure violated constitutional rights.[179] Similarly, a superintendent was not protected by qualified immunity for refusing to recommend a teacher's reemployment based on constitutionally impermissible reasons pertaining to her involvement in a divorce.[180] Public officials are not expected to predict the future course of constitutional law, but they are expected to adhere to principles of law that were clearly established at the time of the violation.[181]

LIABILITY OF SCHOOL DISTRICTS

In 1978 the Supreme Court departed from precedent[182] and ruled that local governments are considered "persons" under Section 1983.[183] In essence, school districts can be assessed damages when action taken pursuant to official policy violates federally protected rights.

However, the governmental unit (like the individual official) cannot be held liable under the *respondeat superior* doctrine for the wrongful acts committed solely by its employees. Liability under Section 1983 against the agency can be imposed only when execution of official policy by an individual with final authority impairs a federally protected right.[184] The Supreme Court has held that a single egregious act of a low-level employee does not infer an official policy of inadequate training and supervision,[185] but an agency can be liable if "deliberate indifference" in ensuring adequately trained employees is established.[186]

In 1989 the Court also rejected the *respondeat superior* theory under Section 1981 of the Civil Rights Act of 1866, which prohibits discrimination in making and enforcing contracts.[187] In this case a white athletic director and head football coach was relieved of his duties and sought damages from the school district and African-American principal for alleged violations of Sections 1981 and 1983. Recognizing that the remedial provisions of Section 1983 are controlling in Section 1981 damages suits against state actors, the Court held that the school district would be liable under Section 1983 only if unlawful decisions were made by individuals who had been delegated policymaking authority or had acted pursuant to a well-settled custom that represented official policy.

Although school *officials* can plead good-faith immunity, this defense is not available to school *districts*. The Supreme Court has ruled that school districts and other governmental subdivisions cannot claim qualified immunity based on good-faith actions of their officials. The Court acknowledged that under certain circumstances sovereign immunity can shield municipal corporations from state tort suits,[188] but concluded that Section 1983 abrogated governmental immunity in situations involving the impairment of federally protected rights.[189]

To avoid liability for constitutional violations, school districts have introduced claims of eleventh amendment immunity.[190] The eleventh amendment, prohibiting citizens of one state from bringing suit against another state without its consent, has been interpreted as also precluding federal lawsuits against a state by its own citizens.[191] A state can waive this immunity by specifically consenting to be sued, and Congress can abrogate state immunity through legislation enacted to enforce the fourteenth amendment. However, such congressional intent must be explicit in the federal legislation.[192]

School districts have asserted eleventh amendment protection based on the fact that they perform a state function. Admittedly, education is a state function, but it does not necessarily follow that school districts gain eleventh amendment immunity against claims of constitutional abridgments. For the eleventh amendment to be invoked in a suit against a school district, the state must be the "real party in interest." The Third Circuit Court of Appeals identified the following factors in determining if a governmental agency, such as a school district, is entitled to eleventh amendment protection: (1) whether payment of the judgment will be from the state treasury; (2) whether a governmental or proprietary function is being performed;[193] (3) whether the agency has autonomy over its operation; (4) whether it has the power to sue and be sued; (5) whether it can enter into contracts; (6) and whether the agency's property is immune from state taxation.[194] The most significant of these factors in determining if a district is shielded by eleventh amendment immunity has been whether or not the judgment will be recovered from state funds. If funds are to be paid from the state treasury, courts have declared the state to be the real party in interest.[195]

For many states, the eleventh amendment question with respect to school district immunity was resolved in the *Mt. Healthy* case.[196] The Supreme Court concluded that the issue in this case hinged on whether, under Ohio law, a school district is considered an arm of the state as opposed to a municipality or other political subdivision. Considering the taxing power and autonomy of school district operations, the Supreme

Court found school districts to be more like counties or cities than an extension of the state.

DAMAGES

When a school official or school district is found liable for violating an individual's federally protected rights, an award of damages is assessed to compensate the claimant for the injury. For example, the Fifth Circuit Court of Appeals found that a $250,000 damages award to a superintendent, who had been suspended in retaliation for voicing support for a particular slate of school board candidates, was not excessive to compensate him for mental anguish, loss of reputation, personal expenses, and other monetary harm he suffered.[197] However, actual injury must be shown for the aggrieved party to recover damages; without evidence of monetary or mental injury, the plaintiff is entitled only to nominal damages (not to exceed one dollar), even though an impairment of federal rights is established.[198]

In 1986 the Supreme Court emphasized that compensatory damages cannot to be based on a jury's perception of the value or importance of constitutional rights.[199] In this case, involving the award of compensatory damages to a teacher for his unconstitutional dismissal, the Supreme Court declared that while individuals are entitled to full compensation for the injury suffered, they are not entitled to supplementary damages based on the perceived value of the constitutional rights that have been abridged. The Court remanded the case for a determination of the amount of damages necessary to compensate the teacher for the *actual* injury suffered.

In some instances, aggrieved individuals have sought punitive as well as compensatory damages. The judiciary has ruled that school officials can be liable for punitive damages (to punish the wrongdoer) if a jury concludes that the individual's conduct is willful or in reckless and callous disregard of federally protected rights.[200] Punitive as well as compensatory damages were assessed against a principal and superintendent who, without authority, discharged a teacher in retaliation for the exercise of protected speech.[201] Punitive damages, however, must be assessed on an individual basis against each defendant and cannot be imposed jointly against several officials.[202]

In 1981 the Supreme Court ruled that Section 1983 does not authorize the award of punitive damages against a municipality.[203] Recognizing that compensation for injuries is an obligation of a municipality, the Court held that *punitive* damages were appropriate only for the *individual* wrongdoers and not for the municipality itself. The Court also noted that punitive damages constitute punishment against individuals to deter similar conduct in the future, but they are not intended to punish innocent taxpayers. This ruling does not bar claims for punitive damages for violations of federal rights in school cases, but such claims must be brought against individuals rather than against the school district itself.

CONCLUSION

Although public educators do not shed their constitutional rights as a condition of public employment, under certain circumstances restrictions on these freedoms are justified by overriding governmental interests. Protections afforded to educators' constitutional rights continue to be delineated by the judiciary; the following generalizations reflect the current status of the law in the substantive areas discussed in this chapter.

1. Public educators have a first amendment right to express their views on public issues related to the welfare of the school and students; dismissal or other retaliatory personnel action, such as transfers, demotions, or written reprimands, cannot be predicated solely on protected speech.
2. Expression pertaining to personal employment disputes, attacks on supervisors, or speech intended to disrupt the school is not constitutionally protected.
3. The exercise of protected speech will not invalidate a dismissal action if the school board can show by a preponderance of evidence that it would have reached the same decision had the protected speech not occurred.
4. Even if expression on public issues is the sole basis for adverse employment action, the school board might still prevail if established that its interests in providing effective and efficient educational services outweigh the individual's free expression rights.
5. A school's internal mail system is not a traditional open forum for expression, and, unless designated as such, access to the mail system can be restricted to business relating to the school's educational function as long as restrictions are not viewpoint-based.
6. Reasonable time, place, and manner restrictions can be imposed on educators' expression, but arbitrary prior restraints on the content and channel of communication violate the first amendment.
7. Public school teachers do not have the right to determine the content of the instructional program, but they do have some latitude in selecting appropriate strategies to convey the prescribed content.

8. In evaluating the appropriateness of teaching materials and strategies, courts consider relevance to course objectives, threat of disruption, age and maturity of students, and community standards.

9. Public employees cannot be retaliated against because of their membership in labor unions, political groups, or organizations with unlawful purposes.

10. Educators' participation in political activities outside the classroom cannot be the basis for employment decisions related to promotion, transfer, or dismissal.

11. State laws can impose restrictions on the types of elected offices that public educators can hold (e.g., two incompatible positions cannot be held).

12. Employees can be required to take temporary leave from their positions to campaign for political office if established that campaign demands would interfere with professional responsibilities.

13. School officials can impose reasonable restrictions on educators' personal appearance if there is a rational basis for such regulations.

14. Educators' school desks and other personal effects at school can be searched based on reasonable suspicion that the search is necessary for educational reasons.

15. Public educators enjoy protected privacy rights in their lifestyle choices; however, adverse employment consequences may be justified if private choices have a detrimental effect on job performance.

16. School officials and school districts can be held liable for compensatory damages in connection with actions that impair educators' constitutional rights.

17. An individual can recover only nominal damages for the impairment of constitutional rights unless monetary, emotional, or mental injury can be proven.

18. School officials can plead immunity to protect themselves from liability if their actions were taken in good faith; ignorance of clearly established principles of law is evidence of bad faith.

19. School districts cannot plead good faith as a defense against liability for compensatory damages in connection with the impairment of federally protected civil rights.

20. Punitive damages to punish the wrongdoer can be assessed against individual school officials but not against school districts.

21. Most courts have *not* considered school districts an arm of the state for purposes of eleventh amendment immunity from federal suits initiated by the state's citizens.

ENDNOTES

1. 391 U.S. 563 (1968).
2. *Id.* at 572. *See also* Perry v. Sinderman, 408 U.S. 593 (1972) (professor's lack of tenure, taken alone, did not defeat his claim that nonrenewal of his contract was in retaliation for his public criticism of the Board of Regents); text with note 19, Chapter 10.
3. 429 U.S. 274, 282 (1977).
4. Doyle v. Mt. Healthy City School Dist., 670 F.2d 59 (6th Cir. 1982).
5. *Id.*, 429 U.S. at 286.
6. 439 U.S. 410 (1979).
7. 461 U.S. 138 (1983).
8. *Id.* at 142.
9. *Id.* at 150. For the Supreme Court's subsequent application of *Connick, see* Rankin v. McPherson, 483 U.S. 378 (1987); text with note 32, *infra.*
10. *See, e.g.,* Lemons v. Morgan, 629 F.2d 1389 (8th Cir. 1980); McGill v. Board of Educ. of Pekin Elementary School Dist. No. 108, 602 F.2d 774 (7th Cir. 1979); Bernasconi v. Tempe Elementary School Dist. No. 3, 548 F.2d 857 (9th Cir. 1977), *cert. denied,* 434 U.S. 825 (1977); James v. Board of Educ. of Cent. Dist. No. 1, 461 F.2d 566 (2d Cir. 1972), *cert. denied,* 409 U.S. 1042 (1972).
11. *See* Aebisher v. Ryan, 622 F.2d 651 (2d Cir. 1980); Columbus Educ. Ass'n v. Columbus City School Dist., 623 F.2d 1155 (6th Cir. 1980); Swilley v. Alexander, 629 F.2d 1018 (5th Cir. 1980).
12. Rowland v. Mad River Local School Dist., 730 F.2d 444 (6th Cir. 1984), *cert. denied,* 470 U.S. 1009 (1985).
13. *Id.*, 470 U.S. at 1012 (Brennan and Marshall, J.J., dissenting).
14. Renfroe v. Kirkpatrick, 722 F.2d 714, 715 (11th Cir. 1984), *cert. denied,* 469 U.S. 823 (1984). *See also* Patterson v. Masem, 774 F.2d 251 (8th Cir. 1985) (teacher's denial of a promotion to a supervisory role was not in retaliation for recommending that a play she found racially offensive not be performed).
15. Vukadinovich v. Bartels, 853 F.2d 1387 (7th Cir. 1988). *See also* Hall v. Ford, 856 F.2d 255 (D.C. Cir. 1988); Berg v. Hunter, 854 F.2d 238 (7th Cir. 1988), *cert. denied,* 489 U.S. 1053 (1989) (dismissals were upheld because employees' expression jeopardized relationships with superiors and fulfillment of job responsibilities).
16. Alinovi v. Worcester School Comm., 766 F.2d 660 (1st Cir. 1985), *cert. denied,* 479 U.S. 816 (1986). *See* text with note 144, *infra,* for a discussion of the privacy issue raised in this case.
17. Stevenson v. Lower Marion County School Dist. No. 3, 327 S.E.2d 656 (S.C. 1985). *See also* Rabon v. Bryan County Bd. of Educ., 326 S.E.2d 577 (Ga. Ct. App. 1985), *cert. denied,* 474 U.S. 855 (1985) (termination of a principal based on his sexual remarks that intimidated teachers and reduced his competency did not impair free speech rights).
18. Hesse v. Board of Educ. of Township High School Dist. No. 211, Cook County, Illinois, 848 F.2d 748 (7th Cir. 1988), *cert. denied,* 489 U.S. 1015 (1989). *See also* Ferrara v. Mills, 781 F.2d 1508 (11th Cir. 1986) (complaints about class assignments, a policy allowing students to select their own courses, and the hiring of coaches to teach social studies did not pertain to matters of public concern).

19. Callaway v. Hafeman, 832 F.2d 414 (7th Cir. 1987). *But see* Wren v. Spurlock, 798 F.2d 1313 (10th Cir. 1986), *cert. denied*, 479 U.S. 1085 (1987) (allegations of sexual harassment of students and teachers in a letter signed by most of the school's faculty members involved a public issue).

20. Day v. South Park Indep. School Dist., 768 F.2d 696 (5th Cir. 1985), *cert. denied*, 474 U.S. 1101 (1986). *See also* Roberts v. Van Buren Pub. Schools, 773 F.2d 949 (8th Cir. 1985) (a grievance, expressing elementary teachers' dissatisfaction with the way parental complaints concerning a field trip had been handled, pertained more to the teacher–principal relationship than to a public concern).

21. Johnsen v. Independent School Dist. No. 3 of Tulsa County, Oklahoma, 891 F.2d 1485 (10th Cir. 1989). *See also* Saye v. St. Vrain Valley School Dist., 785 F.2d 862 (10th Cir. 1986), *on remand*, 650 F. Supp. 716 (D. Colo. 1986) (a teacher's discussion of her allocation of teacher aide time with parents was not constitutionally protected in part because the subject was raised in a *manner* that had an adverse impact on working relationships and school operations; however, teacher's second claim that her nonrenewal was in retaliation for union activities involved constitutionally protected expression requiring a jury to address whether such activity was a motivating factor in the adverse employment decision).

22. Derrickson v. Board of Educ. of the City of St. Louis, 738 F.2d 351, 352–353 (8th Cir. 1984). *See also* Anderson v. Evans, 660 F.2d 153 (6th Cir. 1981) (teacher's racially derogatory comments made to the principal and assistant principal were not constitutionally protected). *But see* Lewis v. Harrison School Dist. No. 1, 805 F.2d 310 (8th Cir. 1986), *cert. denied*, 482 U.S. 905 (1987) (principal's criticism to the school board of superintendent's decision to transfer the principal's wife from high school to junior high school was a matter of public concern).

23. Rankin v. Independent School Dist., 876 F.2d 838 (10th Cir. 1989), *cert. denied*, 111 S. Ct. 786 (1991).

24. Fishman v. Clancy, 763 F.2d 485 (1st Cir. 1985). *See* text with note 201, *infra*.

25. McGee v. South Pemiscot School Dist. R-V, 712 F.2d 339 (8th Cir. 1983). *See also* Cox v. Dardanelle Pub. School Dist., 790 F.2d 668 (8th Cir. 1986) (nonrenewal of teacher's contract for criticizing the principal's administrative style of discouraging teacher input, inhibiting creativity, and adversely affecting morale violated the teacher's first amendment rights); Bowman v. Pulaski County Special School Dist., 723 F.2d 640 (8th Cir. 1983) (public statements about the severity of the head coach's disciplinary practices could not be the basis for transferring plaintiffs to undesirable coaching assignments).

26. Southside Pub. Schools v. Hill, 827 F.2d 270 (8th Cir. 1987).

27. Stewart v. Baldwin County Bd. of Educ., 908 F.2d 1499 (11th Cir. 1990).

28. Ware v. Unified School Dist. No. 492, 902 F.2d 815 (10th Cir. 1990).

29. Piver v. Pender County Bd. of Educ., 835 F.2d 1076 (4th Cir. 1987), *cert. denied*, 487 U.S. 1206 (1988).

30. Seemuller v. Fairfax County School Bd., 878 F.2d 1578 (4th Cir. 1989).

31. Knapp v. Whitaker, 757 F.2d 827 (7th Cir. 1985), *appeal dismissed*, 474 U.S. 803 (1985). The case was remanded to reconsider the award of compensatory damages and evidence regarding the teacher's certification status for a high school science position.

32. Rankin v. McPherson, 483 U.S. 378, 380 (1987).

33. *See, e.g.*, Morfin v. Albuquerque Pub. Schools, 906 F.2d 1434 (10th Cir. 1990); Stellmaker v. DePetrillo, 710 F. Supp. 891 (D. Conn. 1989); Thompson v. Board of Educ. of City of Chicago, 711 F. Supp. 394 (N.D. Ill. 1989).
34. Hinkle v. Christensen, 733 F.2d 74 (8th Cir. 1984).
35. Hickman v. Valley Local School Dist. Bd. of Educ., 619 F.2d 606 (6th Cir. 1980).
36. White v. South Park Indep. School Dist., 693 F.2d 1163 (5th Cir. 1982). *See also* Coats v. Pierre, 890 F.2d 728 (5th Cir. 1989), *cert. denied*, 111 S. Ct. 70 (1990); Kelleher v. Flawn, 761 F.2d 1079 (5th Cir. 1985); Hughes v. Whitmer, 714 F.2d 1407 (8th Cir. 1983), *cert. denied*, 465 U.S. 1023 (1984).
37. Harden v. Adams, 841 F.2d 1091, 1094 (11th Cir. 1988), *cert. denied*, 488 U.S. 967 (1988).
38. Simineo v. School Dist. No. 16, Park County, Wyoming, 594 F.2d 1353 (10th Cir. 1979).
39. Solis v. Rio Grande City Indep. School, 734 F.2d 243 (5th Cir. 1984). *See also* Wells v. Hico Indep. School Dist., 736 F.2d 243 (5th Cir. 1984), *cert. dismissed*, 473 U.S. 901 (1985) (teachers' criticism of administration of a special reading program was the motivating factor in their nonrenewal).
40. The inappropriate or controversial nature of the expression is irrelevant to determining whether it deals with a matter of public concern. *See* Rankin v. McPherson, 483 U.S. 378 (1987); text with note 32, *supra*.
41. Prior to *Connick,* courts often relied on the principle that undifferentiated fear of disruption was not sufficient to curtail free expression rights. *See* Tinker v. Des Moines Indep. Community School Dist., 393 U.S. 503 (1969); text with note 45, Chapter 4.
42. For a discussion of this three-stage analysis to determine whether retaliation against a public employee violates the first amendment, *see* Schneider v. Indian River Community College Found., 875 F.2d 1537 (11th Cir. 1989).
43. National Gay Task Force v. Board of Educ. of City of Oklahoma City, 729 F.2d 1270, 1274 (10th Cir. 1984), *aff'd by an equally divided court,* 470 U.S. 903 (1985).
44. *Id.,* 729 F.2d at 1274, citing in part, Pickering v. Board of Educ., 391 U.S. 563, 568 (1968) and Tinker v. Des Moines Indep. Community School Dist., 393 U.S. 503, 513 (1969).
45. Hall v. Board of School Comm'rs of Mobile County, Alabama, 681 F.2d 965, 968 (5th Cir. 1982).
46. *Id.* at 969.
47. Texas State Teachers Ass'n v. Garland Indep. School Dist., 777 F.2d 1046 (5th Cir. 1985), *aff'd mem.,* 479 U.S. 801 (1986). The school's selective visitation policy, under which certain groups of educators and representatives of textbook companies and civic and charitable groups were allowed to meet with teachers on education business during school hours, did not create a public forum. *See also* Texas State Teachers Ass'n v. Garland Indep. School Dist., 489 U.S. 782 (1989) (since unions prevailed on first amendment claims that materially altered the school district's policies, they were entitled to attorneys' fees); text with note 231, Chapter 10.
48. Perry Educ. Ass'n v. Perry Local Educators' Ass'n, 460 U.S. 37, 46 (1983).
49. Ysleta Fed'n of Teachers v. Ysleta Indep. School Dist., 720 F.2d 1429 (5th Cir. 1983). The court further held that the school board had not produced evidence

of a compelling interest for limiting employee organizations to one distribution of recruitment literature per year through the school mail system. The case was remanded for development of the record on this issue.

50. May v. Evansville-Vanderburgh School Corp., 787 F.2d 1105 (7th Cir. 1986).

51. City of Madison, Joint School Dist. No. 8 v. Wisconsin Employment Relations Comm'n, 429 U.S. 167 (1976).

52. Anderson v. Central Point School Dist., 746 F.2d 505 (9th Cir. 1984).

53. Knapp v. Whitaker, 757 F.2d 827 (7th Cir. 1985), *appeal dismissed,* 474 U.S. 803 (1985). *See also* Unified School Dist. No. 503 v. McKinney, 689 P.2d 860 (Kan. 1984) (school board was found guilty of unconstitutional prior restraint by forbidding teachers from speaking at school board meetings or holding press conferences in school buildings).

54. Godwin v. East Baton Rouge Parish School Bd., 408 So. 2d 1214, 1216 (La. 1981), *appeal dismissed,* 459 U.S. 807 (1982). *See also* Heffron v. International Society of Krishna Consciousness, 452 U.S. 640 (1981) (upholding restriction on literature distribution at a fairgrounds to ensure order).

55. For a discussion of the evolution of the concept of academic freedom, *see* Mark Yudof, "Three Faces of Academic Freedom," *Loyola Law Review,* vol. 32 (1987), pp. 831–858; Ralph Fuchs, "Academic Freedom—Its Basic Philosophy, Function, and History," *Law and Contemporary Problems,* vol. 28 (1968), pp. 431–446.

56. William Valente, *School Law* (St. Paul, MN: West Publishing Co., 1985), pp. 276, 278.

57. Adams v. Campbell County School Dist., 511 F.2d 1242, 1247 (10th Cir. 1975). Distinguishing school boards' broad discretion to determine the curriculum from the more limited discretion of college administrators to override faculty decisions, *see* DiBona v. Matthews, 269 Cal. Rptr. 882 (Cal. Ct. App. 1990), *cert. denied,* 111 S. Ct. 557 (1990).

58. Cary v. Board of Educ. of the Adams-Arapahoe School Dist. 28-J, 598 F.2d 535, 544 (10th Cir. 1979).

59. Kirkland v. Northside Indep. School Dist., 890 F.2d 794 (5th Cir. 1989), *cert. denied,* 110 S. Ct. 2620 (1990).

60. Palmer v. Board of Educ. of the City of Chicago, 603 F.2d 1271, 1274 (7th Cir. 1979), *cert. denied,* 444 U.S. 1026 (1980). *See also* Roberts v. Madigan, 921 F.2d 1047 (10th Cir. 1990) (requirement that a teacher remove religiously oriented books from his classroom library and refrain from silently reading his Bible during class did not impair his academic freedom); text with note 58, Chapter 2.

61. Millikan v. Board of Directors of Everett School Dist. No. 2, 611 P.2d 414, 418 (Wash. 1980).

62. Ahern v. Board of Educ. of School Dist. of Grand Island, 456 F.2d 399 (8th Cir. 1972).

63. Webster v. New Lenox School Dist. No. 122, 917 F.2d 1004 (7th Cir. 1990).

64. Fisher v. Fairbanks North Star Borough School Dist., 704 P.2d 213 (Alaska 1985).

65. Teachers also retain some discretion in assessing student performance. *See* In re Proposed Termination of James Johnson's Teaching Contract with Indep. School Dist. No. 709, 451 N.W.2d 343 (Minn. Ct. App. 1990) (school district's directive to a mathematics teacher that his grade distribution not deviate by

more than 2 percent from distributions in similar classes was an inappropriate interference with the teacher's legitimate academic need for classroom flexibility).

66. Keefe v. Geanakos, 418 F.2d 359 (1st Cir. 1969).
67. Mailloux v. Kiley, 323 F. Supp. 1387 (D. Mass. 1971), *aff'd,* 448 F.2d 1242 (1st Cir. 1971).
68. *Id.,* 323 F. Supp. at 1392.
69. Sterzing v. Fort Bend Indep. School Dist., 376 F. Supp. 657 (S.D. Tex. 1972), *vacated and remanded* (regarding denial of reinstatement), 496 F.2d 92 (5th Cir. 1974).
70. Bradley v. Pittsburgh Bd. of Educ., 910 F.2d 1172 (3d Cir. 1990).
71. *See* Mailloux v. Kiley, 323 F. Supp. 1387 (D. Mass. 1971), *aff'd,* 448 F.2d 1242 (1st Cir. 1971).
72. Brubaker v. Board of Educ., School Dist. 149, 502 F.2d 973 (7th Cir. 1974), *cert. denied,* 421 U.S. 965 (1975).
73. Fowler v. Board of Educ., Lincoln County, Kentucky, 819 F.2d 657 (6th Cir. 1987), *cert. denied,* 484 U.S. 986 (1987). *See also* text with note 83, *infra.*
74. Shurgin v. Ambach, 436 N.E.2d 1324 (N.Y. 1982).
75. Simon v. Jefferson Davis Parish School Bd., 289 So. 2d 511 (La. Ct. App. 1974).
76. Kingsville Indep. School Dist. v. Cooper, 611 F.2d 1109 (5th Cir. 1980).
77. Stachura v. Memphis Community School Dist., 763 F.2d 211 (6th Cir. 1985), *rev'd and remanded* (regarding award of compensatory damages), 477 U.S. 299 (1986). For a discussion of the damages issue, *see* text with note 199, *infra.*
78. Parducci v. Rutland, 316 F. Supp. 352, 353–354 (M.D. Ala. 1970).
79. *Id.,* citing the standard adopted by the Supreme Court in Tinker v. Des Moines Indep. Community School Dist., 393 U.S. 503 (1969). *See* text with note 45, Chapter 4.
80. Wilson v. Chancellor, 418 F. Supp. 1358 (D. Or. 1976).
81. Kingsville Indep. School Dist. v. Cooper, 611 F.2d 1109, 1113 (5th Cir. 1980).
82. Dean v. Timpson Indep. School Dist., 486 F. Supp. 302 (E.D. Tex. 1979).
83. Krizek v. Board of Educ., Cicero-Stickney Township High School Dist. 201, 713 F. Supp. 1131, 1141 (N.D. Ill. 1989) (the court noted that the severity of the action against the teacher also must be considered in assessing the legitimacy of the board's sanctions).
84. Solmitz v. Maine School Admin. Dist. No. 59, 495 A.2d 812 (Me. 1985).
85. Zykan v. Warsaw Community School Corp., 631 F.2d 1300, 1304 (7th Cir. 1980), citing Palmer v. Board of Educ. of the City of Chicago, 603 F.2d 1271, 1274 (7th Cir. 1979), *cert. denied,* 444 U.S. 1026 (1980).
86. Adams v. Campbell County School Dist., 511 F.2d 1242 (10th Cir. 1975).
87. Stachura v. Memphis Community School Dist., 763 F.2d 211 (6th Cir. 1985), *rev'd and remanded* (regarding award of compensatory damages), 477 U.S. 299 (1986).
88. *Id.,* 763 F.2d at 215. In a related suit, combined on appeal, the teacher sued the parent who initiated the protests, but the court concluded that the parent's expression was made to the public body charged with administering the schools, and thus the action was protected by the first amendment right to petition, Stachura v. Truszkowski, 763 F.2d 211 (6th Cir. 1985).
89. Wilson v. Chancellor, 418 F. Supp. 1358 (D. Or. 1976).

90. Healy v. James, 408 U.S. 169, 181 (1972).

91. *See* Adler v. Board of Educ. of City of New York, 342 U.S. 485 (1952); Wieman v. Updegraff, 344 U.S. 183 (1952).

92. *See* Cole v. Richardson, 405 U.S. 676 (1972); Connell v. Higginbotham, 403 U.S. 207 (1971). Employees also can be required to pledge that they will oppose the overthrow of the government and that they will fulfill their job responsibilities. *See* text with note 5, Chapter 7.

93. *See* Keyishian v. Board of Regents of the Univ. of the State of New York, 385 U.S. 589, 606 (1967); Elfbrandt v. Russell, 384 U.S. 11, 19 (1966); Baggett v. Bullitt, 377 U.S. 360 (1964).

94. Keyishian, *id. See also* Woodward v. Hereford Indep. School Dist., 421 F. Supp. 93 (N.D. Tex. 1976) (a nontenured teacher was reinstated because nonrenewal was based on active membership in the American Civil Liberties Union).

95. *See* National Ass'n for the Advancement of Colored People v. Alabama, 357 U.S. 449 (1958).

96. Shelton v. Tucker, 364 U.S. 479 (1960).

97. *Id.* at 490.

98. Familias Unidas v. Briscoe, 619 F.2d 391 (5th Cir. 1980).

99. 357 U.S. 399 (1958).

100. Elrod v. Burns, 427 U.S. 347 (1976).

101. Branti v. Finkel, 445 U.S. 507 (1980).

102. Rutan v. Republican Party of Illinois, 110 S. Ct. 2729 (1990).

103. *See* Piazza v. Aponte Roque, 909 F.2d 35 (1st Cir. 1990) (nonrenewal of teachers' aides because of their political party affiliation impaired associational rights); Burris v. Willis Indep. School Dist., 713 F.2d 1087 (5th Cir. 1983) (nonrenewal of an administrator's contract was predicated on his association with previous "old-line" board members and thereby violated his associational rights).

104. Los Angeles Teachers Union v. Los Angeles City Bd. of Educ., 455 P.2d 827, 832 (Cal. 1969). *See also* Martinez v. Cotulla Indep. School Dist., 922 F.2d 839 (5th Cir. 1990). *But see* Connick v. Myers, 461 U.S. 138 (1983) (questionnaire that did not relate to matters of public concern was not protected expression); text with note 7, *supra.*

105. Wichert v. Walter, 606 F. Supp. 1516 (D.N.J. 1985).

106. *See, e.g.,* Kercado-Melendez v. Aponte Roque, 829 F.2d 255 (1st Cir. 1987), *cert. denied,* 486 U.S. 1044 (1988); Banks v. Burkich, 788 F.2d 1161 (6th Cir. 1986); Alaniz v. San Isidro Indep. School Dist., 742 F.2d 207 (5th Cir. 1984); Childers v. Independent School Dist. No. 1 of Bryan County, 676 F.2d 1338 (10th Cir. 1982).

107. United States Civil Service Comm'n v. National Ass'n of Letter Carriers, 413 U.S. 548 (1973). *See* 5 U.S.C. § 7324 (1988).

108. Broadrick v. Oklahoma, 413 U.S. 601 (1973).

109. Galer v. Board of Regents of the Univ. System, 236 S.E.2d 617 (Ga. 1977).

110. Cranston Teachers Alliance, Local No. 1704 v. Miele, 495 A.2d 233, 237 (R.I. 1985). *See also* Fletcher v. Marino, 882 F.2d 605 (2d Cir. 1989) (a New York law prohibiting certain municipal employees, political party office holders, and elected officials from serving as community school board members was found to be a valid exercise of the state's power and did not violate associational rights).

111. Minielly v. State, 411 P.2d 69 (Or. 1966).
112. Jenkins v. Bishop, 589 P.2d 770 (Utah 1978) (per curiam).
113. State *ex rel.* Gretick v. Jeffrey, 465 N.E.2d 412 (Ohio 1984).
114. Haskins v. State *ex rel.* Harrington, 516 P.2d 1171, 1178 (Wyo. 1973). *See also* Visotcky v. City Council of the City of Garfield, 273 A.2d 597 (N.J. Super. Ct. App. Div. 1971); City of Kingsport v. Lay, 459 S.W.2d 786 (Tenn. Ct. App. 1970) (after being elected a city alderman, an individual could not continue to receive a salary as a public school administrator beyond the end of his current contract).
115. Haskins, *id.* at 1179. *See also* LaBosco v. Dunn, 502 N.Y.S.2d 200 (N.Y. 1986), *appeal denied*, 494 N.E.2d 112 (N.Y. 1986) (though disqualified from serving on the school board of his employing district, the teacher could serve on the board in another district).
116. *See* LaBosco, *id.* In addition to prohibitions on individuals holding two incompatible roles, courts have ruled that states can prohibit the practice of more than one member of a family serving concurrently on a school board. *See* Rosenstock v. Scaringe, 357 N.E.2d 347 (N.Y. 1976).
117. West v. Jones, 323 S.E.2d 96 (Va. 1984). *See also* Town of Cheshire v. McKenney, 438 A.2d 88 (Conn. 1980) (under town charter, public school teachers were ineligible to hold a position on the town council).
118. *See, e.g.,* Chatham v. Johnson, 195 So. 2d 62 (Miss. 1967).
119. Allen v. Board of Educ. of Jefferson County, 584 S.W.2d 408 (Ky. Ct. App. 1979).
120. White v. Dougherty County Bd. of Educ., 431 F. Supp. 919 (M.D. Ga. 1977), *aff'd*, 439 U.S. 32 (1978).
121. White v. Dougherty County Bd. of Educ., 579 F. Supp. 1480 (M.D. Ga. 1984), *aff'd*, 470 U.S. 1067 (1985).
122. One district went so far as to require female teachers to wear at least two petticoats and dresses no shorter than two inches above the ankle. *See* Michael LaMorte, *School Law: Cases and Concepts* (Englewood Cliffs, NJ: Prentice-Hall, 1982), p. 216. For a discussion of cases pertaining to employees' wearing religious attire in public schools, *see* text with note 194, Chapter 9.
123. For a discussion of restrictions on student appearance, *see* text with note 97, Chapter 4.
124. Conard v. Goolsby, 350 F. Supp. 713 (N.D. Miss. 1972).
125. Finot v. Pasadena City Bd. of Educ., 58 Cal. Rptr. 520 (Cal. Ct. App. 1967).
126. Braxton v. Board of Public Instruction of Duval County, Florida, 303 F. Supp. 958 (M.D. Fla. 1969) (wearing a beard is a constitutionally protected liberty interest under the fourteenth amendment, and, in this case, it also implicated first amendment rights since it was worn as an expression of the teacher's heritage, culture, and racial pride).
127. *See, e.g.,* Miller v. School Dist. No. 167, Cook County, Illinois, 495 F.2d 658, 666 (7th Cir. 1974) (rule prohibiting teachers from wearing beards and sideburns was found to be, at best, a "relatively minor deprivation of protected rights").
128. Kelley v. Johnson, 425 U.S. 238, 245 (1976).
129. *Id.* at 248.
130. East Hartford Educ. Ass'n v. Board of Educ. of the Town of East Hartford, 562 F.2d 838 (2d Cir. 1977). Although the teacher asserted that his refusal to

wear a tie involved "symbolic speech," the court reasoned that "as conduct becomes less and less like 'pure speech' the showing of governmental interest required for its regulation is progressively lessened," *id.* at 858.

131. Domico v. Rapides Parish School Bd., 675 F.2d 100, 102 (5th Cir. 1982). *See also* Ball v. Board of Trustees of the Kerrville Indep. School Dist., 584 F.2d 684 (5th Cir. 1978), *cert. denied,* 440 U.S. 972 (1979).

132. Tardif v. Quinn, 545 F.2d 761 (1st Cir. 1976).

133. Pence v. Rosenquist, 573 F.2d 395 (7th Cir. 1978).

134. Most states have laws giving employees access to their personnel files and safeguarding the confidentiality of the records. However, such files can be subpoenaed by the Equal Employment Opportunity Commission if needed to assess charges of hiring or promotion discrimination. *See* text with note 121, Chapter 7.

135. *See* Thornburgh v. American College of Obstetricians and Gynecologists, 476 U.S. 747 (1986); Loving v. Virginia, 388 U.S. 1 (1967); Griswold v. Connecticut, 381 U.S. 479 (1965); Skinner v. Oklahoma, 316 U.S. 535 (1942); Pierce v. Society of Sisters, 268 U.S. 510 (1925). The Supreme Court in 1973 ruled that the decision to have an abortion also was among these protected privacy rights, Roe v. Wade, 410 U.S. 113 (1973), but the Court recently has allowed states to put some restrictions on the individual's discretion to have an abortion. *See* Webster v. Reproductive Health Services, 492 U.S. 490 (1989).

136. Dike v. School Bd. of Orange County, Florida, 650 F.2d 783 (5th Cir. 1981). Public school employees also have asserted privacy rights in connection with the decision to send their own children to private schools. For a discussion of this issue, *see* text with note 40, Chapter 7.

137. Gargiul v. Tompkins, 704 F.2d 661 (2d Cir. 1983), *vacated and remanded,* 465 U.S. 1016 (1984). However, the teacher was subsequently dismissed on other grounds and denied pay for the period of suspension for refusing to submit to the examination because she had not appealed the commissioner of education's adverse decision in state legal proceedings involving the same injury. Thus, a federal civil rights action for back pay was barred, Gargiul v. Tompkins, 790 F.2d 265 (2d Cir. 1986).

138. Strong v. Board of Educ. of Uniondale Free School Dist., 902 F.2d 208 (2d Cir. 1990), *cert. denied,* 111 S. Ct. 250 (1990) (also rejected was the teacher's due process claim; she had ample notice of the request, and there was no factual dispute necessitating a hearing).

139. Daury v. Smith, 842 F.2d 9 (1st Cir. 1988). *See also* Sweeney v. Board of Educ. of Mundelein Consol. High School Dist. 120, Lake County, 746 F. Supp. 758 (N.D. Ill. 1990).

140. Roberts v. Houston Indep. School Dist., 788 S.W.2d 107 (Tex. Ct. App. 1990).

141. New Jersey v. T.L.O., 469 U.S. 325 (1985). *See* text with note 103, Chapter 6, for a discussion of the reasonable suspicion standard.

142. O'Connor v. Ortega, 764 F.2d 703 (9th Cir. 1985), *rev'd,* 480 U.S. 709 (1987). *See also* United States v. Collins, 349 F.2d 863 (2d Cir. 1965), *cert. denied,* 383 U.S. 960 (1966).

143. Gillard v. Schmidt, 579 F.2d 825 (3d Cir. 1978).

144. Alinovi v. Worcester School Comm., 766 F.2d 660 (1st Cir. 1985), *cert. denied,* 479 U.S. 816 (1986). *See* text with note 16, *supra,* regarding the free expression claim in this case.

145. Patchogue-Medford Congress of Teachers v. Board of Educ. of Patchogue-Medford Union Free School Dist., No. 85-8759 (N.Y. Sup. Ct. 1985), slip opinion, p. 5, *aff'd,* 505 N.Y.S.2d 888 (N.Y. App. Div. 1986), *aff'd,* 510 N.E.2d 325 (N.Y. 1987).

146. Georgia Ass'n of Educators v. Harris, 749 F. Supp. 1110 (N.D. Ga. 1990). *See also* Glover v. Eastern Nebraska Community Office of Retardation, 867 F.2d 461 (8th Cir. 1989), *cert. denied,* 110 S. Ct. 321 (1989) (county health services agency's policy requiring mandatory screening of employees for hepatitis B and AIDS was unreasonable under the fourth amendment); Charles Curran, "Mandatory Testing of Public Employees for the Human Immunodeficiency Virus," *Columbia Law Review,* vol. 90 (1990), pp. 720–759.

147. Jones v. Jenkins, 878 F.2d 1476 (D.C. Cir. 1989). *See also* Leckelt v. Board of Comm'rs of Hosp. Dist. No. 1, 909 F.2d 820 (5th Cir. 1990) (dismissal of a nurse for failure to submit results of test for AIDS did not violate fourth amendment rights; public safety concerns outweighed the nurse's expectation of privacy).

148. Jones, *id.* at 1477.

149. Skinner v. Railway Executives' Ass'n, 489 U.S. 602 (1989) (alcohol testing of employees also was upheld).

150. National Treasury Employees Union v. Von Raab, 489 U.S. 656 (1989).

151. *See* Lile v. Hancock Place School Dist., 701 S.W.2d 500, 508 (Mo. Ct. App. 1985).

152. Andrews v. Drew Mun. Separate School Dist., 507 F.2d 611, 614 (5th Cir. 1975), *cert. dismissed,* 425 U.S. 559 (1976). *See also* Avery v. Homewood City Bd. of Educ., 674 F.2d 337 (5th Cir. 1982), *cert. denied,* 461 U.S. 943 (1983); Eckmann v. Board of Educ. of Hawthorn School Dist. No. 17, 636 F. Supp. 1214 (N.D. Ill. 1986).

153. *See* Ponton v. Newport News School Bd., 632 F. Supp. 1056 (E.D. Va. 1986).

154. Erb v. Iowa State Bd. of Pub. Instruction, 216 N.W.2d 339 (Iowa 1974).

155. Sherburne v. School Bd. of Suwannee County, 455 So. 2d 1057 (Fla. Dist. Ct. App. 1984). *See also* Briggs v. North Muskegon Police Dep't, 746 F.2d 1475 (6th Cir. 1984), *cert. denied,* 473 U.S. 909 (1985) (dismissal of a married police officer for cohabiting with a married woman who was not his wife impaired fundamental privacy and associational rights).

156. Littlejohn v. Rose, 768 F.2d 765 (6th Cir. 1985), *cert. denied,* 475 U.S. 1045 (1986). *See* text with note 180, *infra.*

157. Shawgo v. Spradlin, 701 F.2d 470 (5th Cir. 1983), *cert. denied,* 464 U.S. 965 (1983) (upheld disciplinary action against two members of a police department for their off-duty cohabitation which allegedly violated department regulations); Hollenbaugh v. Carnegie Free Library, 578 F.2d 1374 (3d Cir. 1978), *cert. denied,* 439 U.S. 1052 (1978) (cohabiting couple was fired by a public library after it became public knowledge that the employees were expecting a child).

158. Sullivan v. Meade Indep. School Dist. No. 101, 530 F.2d 799 (8th Cir. 1976).

159. In addition to asserting protected privacy rights, some homosexual employees have claimed discrimination under the fourteenth amendment. The judiciary in general has declined to apply heightened scrutiny under the equal protection clause to discrimination based on homosexuality, concluding that sexual orientation is not an immutable characteristic. *See* High Tech Gays v. Defense Indus. Sec. Clearance Office, 895 F.2d 563, 573 (9th Cir. 1990);

Woodward v. United States, 871 F.2d 1068, 1076 (Fed. Cir. 1989); Ben-Shalom v. Marsh, 881 F.2d 454, 463–464 (7th Cir. 1989). Departing from the judicial trend, however, a Kansas federal district court held that an individual's allegations that he was denied employment as a public school teacher because of the principal's perception that the applicant had "homosexual tendencies" should be subjected to heightened judicial scrutiny and thus rejected defendants' motion for summary judgment, Jantz v. Muci, 759 F. Supp. 1543 (D. Kan. 1991).

160. National Gay Task Force v. Board of Educ. of City of Oklahoma City, 729 F.2d 1270 (10th Cir. 1984), *aff'd by an equally divided court,* 470 U.S. 903 (1985). *See* text with note 43, *supra.* Statutes in some states, however, prohibit employment discrimination based on sexual orientation. *See* Mass. Ann. Laws ch. 151B, §§ 1,3,4 (1991); Collins v. Secretary of the Commonwealth, 407 Mass. 837 (Mass. 1990).

161. Bowers v. Hardwick, 478 U.S. 186 (1986).

162. *See* Board of Educ. of Long Beach Unified School Dist. v. Jack M., 566 P.2d 602 (Cal. 1977); Morrison v. State Bd. of Educ., 461 P.2d 375 (Cal. 1969); Sarac v. State Bd. of Educ., 57 Cal. Rptr. 69 (Cal. Ct. App. 1967); text with note 135, Chapter 10.

163. Burton v. Cascade School Dist., Union High School No. 5, 512 F.2d 850 (9th Cir. 1975), *cert. denied,* 423 U.S. 839 (1975). A dissenting justice, however, argued that reinstatement is the appropriate remedy for an individual who has been unconstitutionally dismissed, regardless of the personal right impaired, and asserted that any disruption resulting from such reinstatement should not be a consideration, *id.,* 512 F.2d at 854–856 (Lumbard, J., dissenting). *See also* Acanfora v. Board of Educ., 359 F. Supp. 843 (D. Md. 1973) (teacher who had been unjustifiably transferred because of his homosexuality went beyond the needs of his defense by making radio and television appearances; thus, refusal to renew his contract was not arbitrary or capricious).

164. Gaylord v. Tacoma School Dist. No. 10, 559 P.2d 1340 (Wash. 1977), *cert. denied,* 434 U.S. 879 (1977).

165. Rowland v. Mad River Local School Dist., 730 F.2d 444 (6th Cir. 1984), *cert. denied,* 470 U.S. 1009 (1985). *See* text with note 12, *supra.*

166. 42 U.S.C. § 1983 (1988).

167. *See* Maine v. Thiboutot, 448 U.S. 1 (1980).

168. Jett v. Dallas Indep. School Dist., 491 U.S. 701 (1989).

169. In 1990 the Supreme Court rejected the assertion that school officials are immune from a Section 1983 suit initiated in a state court, Howlett v. Rose, 110 S. Ct. 2430 (1990).

170. *See* Patsy v. Board of Regents of the State of Florida, 457 U.S. 496 (1982).

171. *See* Middlesex County Sewerage Auth. v. National Sea Clammers Ass'n, 453 U.S. 1 (1981).

172. William Valente, "School District and Official Liability for Teacher Sexual Abuse of Students under 42 U.S.C. § 1983," *Education Law Reporter,* vol. 57 (1990), pp. 645–659. *See also* Jeffrey Horner, "The Anatomy of a Constitutional Tort," *Education Law Reporter,* vol. 47 (1988), pp. 1–14.

173. *See* Rizzo v. Goode, 423 U.S. 362 (1976). *See* Chapter 12 for a discussion of the application of *respondeat superior* in state tort cases.

174. Gomez v. Toledo, 446 U.S. 635 (1980).

175. 420 U.S. 308, 322 (1975).
176. 457 U.S. 800, 818 (1982). *See also* Anderson v. Creighton, 483 U.S. 635, 640–641 (1987) (objectively reasonable conduct in light of existing legal principles is entitled to qualified immunity).
177. *See, e.g.,* Alvarado v. Picur, 859 F.2d 448, 451 (7th Cir. 1988).
178. Garvie v. Jackson, 845 F.2d 647, 649–650 (6th Cir. 1988), quoting Ramirez v. Webb, 835 F.2d 1153, 1156 (6th Cir. 1987).
179. Gavrilles v. O'Connor, 611 F. Supp. 210 (D. Mass. 1985).
180. Littlejohn v. Rose, 768 F.2d 765 (6th Cir. 1985), *cert. denied,* 475 U.S. 1045 (1986).
181. *See* Davis v. Scherer, 468 U.S. 183 (1984).
182. *See* Monroe v. Pape, 365 U.S. 167 (1961).
183. Monell v. Department of Social Services of the City of New York, 436 U.S. 658 (1978).
184. *See* City of St. Louis v. Praprotnik, 485 U.S. 112 (1988); Pembaur v. City of Cincinnati, 475 U.S. 469 (1986).
185. City of Oklahoma City v. Tuttle, 471 U.S. 808 (1985).
186. City of Canton, Ohio v. Harris, 489 U.S. 378 (1989). For a discussion of school district liability in connection with sexual abuse of students by school employees, *see* text with note 145, Chapter 7.
187. Jett v. Dallas Indep. School Dist., 491 U.S. 701 (1989).
188. Owen v. City of Independence, Missouri, 445 U.S. 622 (1980). *See* Chapter 12 for a discussion of tort law.
189. Owen, *id.* at 647–648.
190. Under certain circumstances, school districts may be able to use other defenses to preclude liability in a Section 1983 suit. Claims that have already been decided in a state case (res judicata) or could have been litigated between the same parties in a prior state action (collateral estoppel) may be barred in a federal suit under Section 1983. *See* Migra v. Warren City School Dist., 465 U.S. 75 (1984); Allen v. McCurry, 449 U.S. 90 (1980).
191. *See* Hans v. Louisiana, 134 U.S. 1 (1890).
192. *See* note 115, Chapter 5; note 162, Chapter 9.
193. Governmental functions are those performed in discharging the agency's official duties; proprietary functions are often for profit and could be performed by private corporations.
194. Urbano v. Board of Managers of the New Jersey State Prison, 415 F.2d 247, 250–251 (3d Cir. 1969), *cert. denied,* 397 U.S. 948 (1970).
195. Eleventh amendment immunity covers only federal suits; it does not have any bearing on immunity in state tort actions.
196. Mt. Healthy City School Dist. v. Doyle, 429 U.S. 274 (1977). *See also* Stewart v. Baldwin County Bd. of Educ., 908 F.2d 1499 (11th Cir. 1990); Blackburn v. Floyd County Bd. of Educ., 749 F. Supp. 159 (E.D. Ky. 1990). *But see* Garcia v. Board of Educ. of Socorro Consol. School Dist., 777 F.2d 1403 (10th Cir. 1985), *cert. denied,* 479 U.S. 814 (1986) (in New Mexico the state has such extensive administrative and financial control over local school districts that local systems are considered arms of the state and entitled to eleventh amendment immunity).
197. Kinsey v. Salado Indep. School Dist., 916 F.2d 273 (5th Cir. 1990), *rehearing ordered en banc,* 925 F.2d 118 (5th Cir. 1991). *See also* McGee v. South

Pemiscot School Dist. R-V, 712 F.2d 339 (8th Cir. 1983) (even though the teacher-coach who was dismissed for exercising protected speech found a higher paying job, he was entitled to $10,000 in damages for mental anguish, loss of professional reputation, and expenses incurred in obtaining new employment).

198. *See* Carey v. Piphus, 435 U.S. 247 (1978) (pupils who were denied procedural due process in a disciplinary proceeding would be entitled only to nominal damages unless established that lack of proper procedures resulted in actual injury to the students), text with note 174, Chapter 6; Rogers v. Kelly, 866 F.2d 997 (8th Cir. 1989) (teacher was entitled only to one dollar for violation of procedural rights based on evidence that the same termination decision would have been reached in proper proceedings), text with note 216, Chapter 10.

199. Memphis Community School Dist. v. Stachura, 477 U.S. 299 (1986). *See* text with note 77, *supra.*

200. *See* Smith v. Wade, 461 U.S. 30 (1983). *See also* text with note 222, Chapter 10, for examples of damages awards for unlawful terminations. In 1991 the Supreme Court refused to place a limit on the amount of punitive damages that properly instructed juries can award in common-law suits, but it did note that extremely high awards might be viewed as unacceptable under the due process clause of the fourteenth amendment, Pacific Mutual Life Ins. Co. v. Haslip, 111 S. Ct. 1032 (1991).

201. Fishman v. Clancy, 763 F.2d 485 (1st Cir. 1985). *See* text with note 24, *supra.*

202. *See* McFadden v. Sanchez, 710 F.2d 907 (2d Cir. 1983), *cert. denied,* 464 U.S. 961 (1983).

203. City of Newport v. Fact Concerts, Inc., 453 U.S. 247 (1981).

9
Discrimination in Employment

Since the 1960s, legislative bodies have enacted numerous laws to protect individuals against bias in hiring, promotion, compensation, and other employment practices. Courts also have been active in reviewing discrimination claims under the Federal Constitution and civil rights statutes. Following a brief discussion of constitutional and statutory standards of review, this chapter focuses on allegations of employment discrimination based on race and national origin, gender, age, disabilities, and religion.[1] Because legal principles applicable to educators often have been established outside the school domain, relevant nonschool cases are discussed.

CONSTITUTIONAL AND STATUTORY STANDARDS OF REVIEW

The federal judiciary has applied several tests in assessing claims of discrimination in public employment. These judicially created standards vary depending on the type of discrimination alleged, the nature of the contested policies or practices, and whether constitutional or statutory grounds are used to challenge the governmental action.

CONSTITUTIONAL STANDARDS

Most constitutional suits involving discrimination in public employment are initiated under the fourteenth amendment's guarantee that states must provide each person equal protection of the laws. Governmental action that facially discriminates against individuals on the basis of a *suspect* classification, such as race or national origin, cannot be justified under the equal protection clause unless substantiated that a compelling state interest is being served. Rarely have legislative bodies been able to justify the creation of a suspect class.[2] However, if legislation does not involve a suspect classification or affect a fundamental interest (i.e., an explicit or implicit constitutional right), courts traditionally have required only a rational relationship between the governmental classification and a legitimate goal, a standard most legislation can satisfy. This lenient rational basis test generally has been used to evaluate the constitutionality of challenged governmental classifications based on traits such as age and disabilities.

As discussed in Chapter 5, dissatisfaction with having to choose between the stringent and lenient equal protection tests has caused the Supreme Court since the 1970s to apply an intermediate standard in some cases where neither a suspect class nor a fundamental right is involved. This test requires that the challenged classification serve "important governmental objectives" and be "substantially related to the achievement of those objectives."[3] The Court has applied this middle-tier standard in assessing equal protection claims involving gender-based classifications.

Although the equal protection clause offers significant protections to victims of invidious governmental discrimination, most allegations of discrimination in public employment do not involve overt classifications based on race, gender, or other immutable traits. Rather, suits usually assert that an individual has been treated less favorably than others solely because of an inherent characteristic or that facially neutral employment policies adversely affect certain classes of employees. To establish a constitutional violation in such suits, aggrieved individuals must prove that they have been victims of *purposeful* governmental discrimination. The Supreme Court has recognized that mere awareness of a policy's adverse impact on a protected class does not constitute proof of unlawful motive; a discriminatory purpose "implies that the decisionmaker . . . selected or reaffirmed a particular course of action at least in part 'because of,' not merely 'in spite of,' its adverse effects upon an identifiable group."[4] The Court, however, has also acknowledged that the foreseeable discriminatory consequences of acts can be considered by courts in assessing intent, even though foreseeable consequences alone cannot substantiate unlawful motive.[5]

STATUTORY STANDARDS

Because of the difficulty in proving discriminatory intent in constitutional cases, plaintiffs have recently relied primarily on federal civil rights statutes to challenge allegedly biased employment practices; some civil rights laws apply to private as well as public employers, so they have broader application than the equal protection clause. Substantial litigation has been based on Title VII of the Civil Rights Act of 1964, which prohibits employers with fifteen or more employees, employment agencies, and labor organizations from discriminating against employees on the basis of race, color, religion, sex, or national origin. Title VII covers hiring, promotion, and compensation practices as well as fringe benefits and other terms and conditions of employment.[6] The law allows employers to impose hiring restrictions based on gender, national origin, or religion (but not race), if such characteristics are bona fide occupational qualifications.

Plaintiffs must satisfy procedural requisites to initiate a Title VII suit. Time limitations are specified for complaints to be filed with the Equal Employment Opportunity Commission (EEOC), which conducts an investigation. A lawsuit can be filed after applicable administrative remedies have been exhausted without relief.[7] In 1989 the Supreme Court held that Title VII's 180-day time limit for filing a charge with the EEOC (or 300 days if proceedings have been initiated with local or state agencies) starts running at the time the discriminatory policy was enacted rather than when the employee was affected.[8] Thus, employees who do not experience the adverse effects of a policy soon after its enactment may not be able to satisfy Title VII's procedural requisites.

Assuming that a plaintiff has standing to file a Title VII suit, there remains the difficult substantive task of proving that specific employment practices have violated the Act. Two legal doctrines have been developed to assess employment discrimination claims under Title VII, and these doctrines also have been applied under civil rights laws prohibiting discrimination based on age and disabilities. The first pertains to allegations of *discriminatory treatment* predicated on a protected characteristic (e.g., race or gender). In such cases, proof of the employer's discriminatory motive is required, which is similar to the constitutional standard under the equal protection clause.

Once a prima facie case or initial inference of disparate treatment is established,[9] the employer can rebut this inference by explaining the nondiscriminatory reason for the action.[10] If the employer produces such a reason, the plaintiff still has an opportunity to prove that the reason is a mere pretext for discrimination. The burden of persuasion usually remains with the plaintiff to prove intentional discrimination by a preponderance of evidence.[11] However, if a plaintiff presents direct evidence that the employer placed substantial reliance on an impermissible factor (e.g., gender) in making a decision, the burden shifts to the employer to show that the decision would have been justified by wholly legitimate reasons.[12]

The second Title VII doctrine pertains to cases involving neutral employment policies that have a *disparate impact* on a protected group. In these cases, proof of discriminatory intent is not necessary. In 1971 the Supreme Court declared that "the consequences of employment practices, not simply motivation," must be considered in assessing the legality of requirements having an adverse impact on minorities.[13] Once an employee establishes that an employment practice has a disparate impact on a protected group, the employer must produce evidence of a business justification for the challenged practice. Even if there is such a business justification, the plaintiff might still prevail by showing that the employer's legitimate interest can be served through less discriminatory means.[14]

Prior to 1988, it was generally assumed that the disparate impact theory would be applied only when objective employment practices (e.g., tests) were at issue. However, in 1988 the Supreme Court held that a Title VII challenge to subjective promotion practices (i.e., leaving promotion decisions to the unchecked discretion of supervisors who may apply subconscious stereotypes and prejudices) could be analyzed under the disparate impact doctrine. The Court majority recognized that "the necessary premise of the disparate impact approach is that some employment practices, adopted without a deliberately discriminatory motive, may in operation be functionally equivalent to intentional discrimination."[15]

Yet, a 1989 Supreme Court decision, *Wards Cove Packing Company v. Atonio,* made it more difficult for employees to substantiate a claim of disparate impact through statistical evidence and made it easier for employers to satisfy the business necessity standard.[16] The Court majority rejected the contention that differences in racial composition between skilled and nonskilled jobs could be used to establish a prima facie case of disparate impact, noting that the appropriate basis for comparison is not between job categories but between the percentage of qualified minorities in the relevant labor force and the percentage hired in the jobs in question. Furthermore, the majority held that if such a racial disparity is established in a given job, it must be directly linked to specific employment practices to establish a Title VII violation. The majority also seemed to dilute the "business necessity" standard, holding that employers need only show that the challenged practice serves legitimate employment goals; proof that the practice is a valid predictor of success in the job is not required.

By increasing the aggrieved employee's burden in disparate impact cases, *Wards Cove* somewhat blurred the distinction between the two Title VII doctrines. Judicial interpretations pertaining to the burden of proof under both approaches are still evolving and may stimulate additional congressional action to clarify Title VII protections. The remainder of this chapter reviews the current status of the law in connection with specific allegations of discrimination in employment.

DISCRIMINATION BASED ON RACE OR NATIONAL ORIGIN

The criteria discussed in the preceding section have been applied in assessing claims of racial or national origin discrimination in a variety of employment contexts: prerequisites to employment; hiring, promotion, and dismissal decisions; compensation practices; and the application of seniority systems. In addition, affirmative action programs have resulted in claims of discrimination against the racial majority or "reverse discrimination."[17]

TEST REQUIREMENTS AS A CONDITION OF EMPLOYMENT

Although other prerequisites to employment have been challenged as racially discriminatory,[18] controversies have focused primarily on the use of examinations that eliminate a disproportionate number of minorities from the applicant pool. Such tests have been upheld under the equal protection clause if substantiated that they are rationally related to legitimate objectives and not accompanied by discriminatory motive. In the leading case, the Supreme Court in 1976 endorsed the use of a written skills test as an entrance requirement for the Washington, D.C., police training program, even though the test had an adverse impact on African-American applicants. The Court reasoned that the test was directly related to requirements of the training program; a positive correlation between test results and training-school performance was sufficient to validate the test. Finding no intentional discrimination, the Court held that the practice did not violate the Federal Constitution.[19]

Subsequently, the Supreme Court affirmed a lower court's conclusion that South Carolina's use of the National Teachers Examination (NTE) for teacher certification and salary purposes satisfied the equal protection clause. The test was found to have a rational relationship to the legitimate purpose of improving the effectiveness of the state's teaching force and was not administered with any intent to discriminate against minority applicants for teacher certification.[20] The trial court was satisfied that the test was valid since it measured knowledge of course content in teacher preparation programs. The court also found sufficient evidence to establish a relationship between the use of the test scores in determining teachers' placement on the salary scale and legitimate employment objectives such as encouraging teachers to upgrade their skills.

In 1986 the Fifth Circuit Court of Appeals upheld use of a basic skills competency test as a prerequisite to enrollment in teacher education programs in Texas.[21] The appeals court reasoned that a state is not obligated to educate or certify teachers who cannot pass a valid test of skills necessary for professional training. Noting that the state presented considerable evidence to establish the test's validity, the court concluded that plaintiffs would have to prove intentional discrimination to substantiate a constitutional violation.

Although plaintiffs carry a heavy burden of proof in establishing that a testing program violates the equal protection clause, some employment testing programs have been invalidated as lacking a rational relationship to legitimate governmental objectives. The Fifth Circuit Court of Appeals found that the use of a specified score on the Graduate Record Examination (GRE) as a prerequisite to employment in a Mississippi school district was not rationally related to the objective of ensuring competent teachers, noting that the GRE is not a valid measure of teacher effectiveness.[22]

Similarly, a Georgia federal district court struck down the use of a minimum NTE score as an alternative criterion for attaining advanced certification, reasoning that the practice was arbitrary and not rationally related to its intended purpose.[23]

Relatively few plaintiffs have established that prerequisites to employment abridge the Federal Constitution,[24] but they have been more successful in proving Title VII violations in connection with facially neutral requirements that have a disparate impact on minorities. In *Griggs v. Duke Power Company,* the Supreme Court found that the use of a test of general intelligence as a prerequisite to employment violated Title VII since the practice disproportionately eliminated minority applicants and the employer did not produce a business necessity for the testing program.[25] In this case, the Court did not prohibit the use of tests *per se,* but concluded that the employer must substantiate that tests used as a condition of employment are related to job performance in order to satisfy Title VII.

Subsequently, the Court elaborated on the Title VII requirement that tests must be validated for the specific jobs for which they are used. The Court concluded that a company's test validation study, which used experienced, white workers, could not be used to validate a test designed for job applicants who were primarily inexperienced and nonwhite. Also, the Court noted that a test can be used only for jobs for which it has been professionally validated.[26] Furthermore, in validating the test, if employee rankings by supervisors are compared with employees' test scores, there must be clear job performance criteria applied by all supervisors.

In several school cases, courts have relied on Title VII and guidelines issued by the EEOC[27] in concluding that specific tests with an adverse racial impact cannot be used in making employment decisions unless justified as a business necessity. For example, the Second Circuit Court of Appeals upheld a district court's ruling that examinations for supervisory positions in the New York City school district had a disparate impact on minorities and were not empirically shown to be job related.[28] The Fourth Circuit Court of Appeals also enjoined a school district's use of a specified score on the NTE in making hiring and retention decisions in the absence of proper validation studies and job analyses.[29]

Employers in other cases, however, have successfully articulated a business necessity for policies with a disparate racial impact. In the South Carolina case discussed previously, the Supreme Court affirmed the trial court's ruling that neither Title VII nor the equal protection clause precluded the use of the NTE for certification and salary purposes to further the legitimate objective of assuring more competent teachers.[30] Similarly, the Fourth Circuit Court of Appeals found no constitutional or Title VII violation in connection with a school district determining teachers' salaries by using certification levels based on NTE scores.[31] Despite the fact that the use of certification grades resulted in the denial of pay raises to a disproportionate number of African-American teachers, the appellate court reasoned that the practice was justified by the job necessity of attracting the most qualified teachers and encouraging self-improvement among low-rated instructional personnel.

In future Title VII challenges to testing programs, individuals may find it more difficult to use statistical data in substantiating discrimination, and employers may find it easier to show a business justification based on the 1989 *Wards Cove* decision discussed previously.[32] Although this case did not deal with test requirements, the Court's treatment of the disparate impact doctrine casts some doubt on the principle established in *Griggs* and has implications for challenges to a range of prerequisites to employment. *Wards Cove* eliminated any ambiguity regarding burden of proof that may have been created by earlier disparate impact decisions. Once a prima facie case is established, the employer only has the burden of producing evidence of a legitimate business justification; the burden of persuasion remains with the challengers.[33]

A number of recent challenges to employment testing programs have been resolved through consent decrees. For example, in 1984 the Golden Rule Insurance Company, the Educational Testing Service, and the state of Illinois reached a settlement that has implications for teacher-testing programs. Two of the four licensing tests used by the Illinois Department of Insurance were challenged as abridging Title VII, and the state agreed in an out-of-court settlement to review the tests in a systematic fashion to reduce racial bias.[34] Legislation requiring a similar review of tests in public employment testing programs has been introduced in a number of states,[35] and the "Golden Rule" strategy has been sought as a remedy in recent cases involving challenges to teacher testing programs.[36]

Test requirements applied to *practicing* educators, who have not taken precertification tests, to determine whether they will *retain* their jobs have generated litigation in each state that has adopted such a mandate. State courts in Texas and Arkansas have upheld test requirements to validate certificates, finding no impairment of due process, equal protection, or contractual rights.[37] In 1990 the Fifth Circuit Court of Appeals rejected an employment discrimination suit initiated by teachers who were terminated for failing the Texas examination.[38] In 1988 a challenge to the Georgia certification test, applicable to initial applicants as well as those holding renewable or provisional certificates, was resolved through a settlement in which the state agreed among other things to provide free study courses and to provide study grants for teachers who were terminated for failure to pass the test.[39]

With increasing legislative interest in assuring teacher competence, it seems likely that additional state and local education agencies will consider the imposition of tests as a requirement for admission to teacher education programs, a prerequisite to certification, a criterion for merit pay, and a condition for recertification. Although several teacher testing programs have withstood legal challenges, the recent trend appears to be for parties to settle the controversies through consent decrees. No settlement has yet barred the use of a properly validated test as a condition of employment, but modifications in the test instruments, validation process, and scoring procedures have been required. Thus, both sides have claimed partial victories in the consent decrees.[40]

SCREENING, DISMISSAL, AND COMPENSATION PRACTICES

In addition to challenges to prerequisites to employment, individuals often have claimed that employment decisions have been racially motivated. Discrimination charges in hiring and promotion procedures have been particularly troublesome for the judiciary because of the subjective judgments involved. Courts have been reluctant to divest employers of their prerogatives to base decisions on personality and other factors, but also have recognized that greater possibilities for masking racial discrimination "are inherent in subjective definitions of employment selection and promotion criteria."[41]

In a 1973 decision, *McDonnell Douglas v. Green*, the Supreme Court provided criteria for establishing a prima facie case of disparate treatment in hiring under Title VII: a plaintiff must be from a racial minority group, show rejection for a position for which qualified, and show that the employer continued to seek similarly qualified applicants after rejecting the plaintiff.[42] This prima facie case does not mean that discrimination ultimately will be established. It only raises an inference of discriminatory hiring practices that, if unexplained by a legitimate, nondiscriminatory reason, can be used to substantiate a Title VII violation. As noted previously, the burden of persuasion usually remains with the plaintiff, but it can shift to the employer where direct evidence establishes that the employer has placed substantial reliance on an impermissible factor.[43]

Courts have accepted employers' asserted nondiscriminatory reasons for denying employment or promotion to racial and ethnic minorities if the individuals have not been qualified for the positions sought or the decisions have been based on quality of performance or other considerations unrelated to race and ethnic background. In an illustrative case, the Ninth Circuit Court of Appeals ruled that even if a Mexican-American curriculum supervisor had been able to establish an inference of discrimination, the school board's evidence that she was unable to work well with other employees was a sufficient nondiscriminatory reason for nonrenewal of her contract.[44] Similarly, the Fifth Circuit Court of Appeals found no discrimination in a school board's demotion of an African-American principal to a teaching position at a reduced salary for willful neglect of duty and incompetence. The principal had instructed teachers to prevent certain students from participating in a mandatory proficiency testing program.[45]

Plaintiffs have prevailed, however, upon showing that an avowed nondiscriminatory reason was merely pretextual to mask a discriminatory motive. For example, the Eleventh Circuit Court of Appeals affirmed a lower court's finding that a school board's nondiscriminatory reasons for its employment practices were pretextual. The court reasoned that over a period of years the school board appointed less qualified white persons to administrative positions and refused to consider seriously the minority plaintiff.[46] The plaintiff was awarded back pay and compensatory damages; in addition, punitive damages were assessed against the superintendent for intentional racial discrimination.

Employees need not be racial minorities to invoke Title VII's protection against discrimination; in several school cases, white employees have gained relief for racially motivated personnel actions.[47] In addition, national origin discrimination has been established where individuals have suffered adverse employment consequences because of their foreign accents without any evidence that such accents impeded job performance.[48]

Compensation discrepancies based on race clearly offend Title VII. In 1986 the Supreme Court ruled in a nonschool case that a public employer was guilty of violating Title VII by paying African Americans less than whites occupying the same positions. Even though the salary disparity originated before Title VII became applicable to public employment, the Court determined that the employer's subsequent failure to remedy the disparity constituted a Title VII violation.[49]

Statistical analyses have proven useful to both plaintiffs and defendants in hiring discrimination cases. Minority employees have used statistics pertaining to the racial composition of the labor market in establishing either a pattern of discrimination or a prima facie case, and employers have rebutted discrimination charges by establishing that the racial mix of their employees reflects the composition of the work force. The Supreme Court has cautioned that the usefulness of statistics depends on the circumstances of each case, and it is commonly known that statistics can be used selectively to prove almost any point. This has been demonstrated in cases where the plaintiffs and defendants, by comparing different population groups and time periods, have used the same data to support claims of both discriminatory and nondiscriminatory practices.

Title VII does not require that a work force mirror the racial composition of the local labor market, but a notable discrepancy may be a strong indicator of employment discrimination. In a Missouri school district, for example, the Supreme Court held that a significant discrepancy between the racial composition of the teaching staff and the composition of the teacher applicant pool in the area established a pattern and practice of discriminatory hiring practices. The Court declared that a comparison between the minority teaching force and the minority pupils in the district was irrelevant in establishing a Title VII violation.[50] As discussed previously, in 1989 the Court also ruled that racial disparities between job categories cannot be used to establish a prima facie case of disparate impact; the appropriate comparison is between the racial composition of the job in question and the relevant labor pool.[51]

Although most employment discrimination cases have been initiated under Title VII, some cases have been based on Section 1981 of the Civil Rights Act of 1866, which prohibits racial discrimination in making and enforcing contracts.[52] In 1976 the Supreme Court held that Section 1981 covers private conduct and, thus, prohibits discrimination in contractual matters in private schools.[53] In 1989 the Court reiterated that the Act can be used to challenge discrimination by private employers but rejected the contention that Section 1981 protections extend beyond contractual matters. The Court narrowly interpreted the reach of Section 1981, concluding that a claim of racial harassment was not actionable under the law. The Court held that Section 1981 covers the formation of a contract, but not problems that may arise from the conditions of continuing employment.[54]

In another 1989 decision the Supreme Court affirmed a Fifth Circuit Appellate Court's decision that a principal and superintendent violated Section 1981 by relieving the athletic director/head football coach of his duties.[55] The white plaintiff had been involved in a number of confrontations with the African-American principal over school policies, and the appeals court reasoned that his removal was racially motivated. However, the Supreme Court did not allow an award of damages, ruling that a local governmental body cannot be held liable for damages under Section 1981 for unlawful actions of its employees.

SENIORITY ADJUSTMENTS FOR DISCRIMINATION VICTIMS

The importance of job seniority is well established as a basis for determining fringe benefits, priority lists for promotions and other job opportunities, and the order of personnel layoffs and recall privileges. Seniority rights often have become the focus of controversy after an employer has been found guilty of employment discrimination under Title VII. Victims of discriminatory hiring and promotion practices have sought retroactive or constructive seniority to restore them to their proper place in relation to other employees.

Title VII insulates seniority systems from disparate impact suits to the extent that employers are allowed to "apply different standards of compensation, or different terms, conditions, or privileges of employment pursuant to a bona fide seniority or merit system" as long as intentional discrimination is not involved.[56] Several cases have focused on the scope of immunity provided to seniority systems under Title VII and whether equitable relief to compensate for prior discrimination can include seniority adjustments.

In a significant 1976 decision, the Supreme Court held that minority plaintiffs who were denied employment on racial grounds after the effective date of Title VII were entitled to priority hiring with retroactive seniority to the date of their rejected applications.[57] The Court did not order the employer to modify its negotiated seniority system, but rather to award plaintiffs the seniority they would have earned in the absence of the discriminatory practice. Without retroactive seniority for the hiring discrimination, the Court held that the plaintiffs could never obtain their rightful place in the seniority hierarchy. The burden was placed on the company to prove that individuals who reapplied for the jobs in question had not been victims of hiring discrimination.

In the latter 1960s and early 1970s, several federal appellate courts awarded retroactive seniority to individuals where seniority systems perpetuated discrimination, even though the discriminatory practices occurred *prior* to the effective date of Title VII. However, in 1977 the Supreme Court ruled that a bona fide seniority system does not become unlawful simply because it operates to "freeze" the adverse impact of pre–Title VII discrimination.[58] Although barring relief for minority applicants who suffered only pre-Act discrimination, the Court held that victims of post-Act discrimination in a specific job category were entitled to seniority adjustments to restore them to their rightful place in the seniority hierarchy. Subsequently, the Supreme Court recognized that proof of discriminatory intent is necessary to invalidate seniority systems established before or *after* the effective date of Title VII.[59] The federal judiciary seems increasingly deferential to negotiated collective bargaining agreements in concluding that challenged seniority systems are bona fide, but it is possible for plaintiffs to establish a Title VII violation where a given seniority system was established with the clear intent to discriminate against minority workers.[60]

Since legal proceedings in discrimination suits often are quite lengthy, some employers charged with hiring discrimination have attempted to reduce their potential liability by remedying the alleged discriminatory practice before being ordered to do so by a court. In 1982 the Supreme Court ruled that an employer can stop the continuing accrual of back pay liability under Title VII by unconditionally offering the claimant the job previously denied, and the offer need not include retroactive seniority to the date of the alleged refusal to hire.[61] The Court majority reasoned that without such an opportunity to reduce back pay liability, employers charged with discrimination have no incentive to initiate corrective action before the suit is resolved. Of course, if the claimant accepts the unconditional job offer and ultimately proves hiring discrimination, the court then may award retroactive seniority and back pay to the date of the unlawful refusal to hire.

AFFIRMATIVE ACTION PLANS

Affirmative action is a concept that has been embodied in presidential executive orders, legislation, and court rulings. The United States Commission on Civil Rights has defined affirmative action as "steps taken to remedy the grossly disparate staffing and recruitment patterns that are the present consequences of past discrimination and to prevent the occurrence of employment discrimination in the future."[62] Initial executive orders were general pronouncements prohibiting discrimination in federal employment and in companies and institutions holding federal contracts. By the 1960s, however, it was clear that employment discrimination could not be curbed without affirmative steps to recruit and retain employees from underrepresented groups. Thus, executive orders signed by Presidents Kennedy and Johnson placed specific requirements on federal contractors to develop affirmative action plans with numerical goals and timetables.

In addition to executive orders, federal antidiscrimination laws and funding provisions and their regulations have included affirmative action requirements. School boards often have developed affirmative action plans in response to a judicial finding of unconstitutional school segregation or prior intentional discrimination in personnel practices. In other instances, employers voluntarily have adopted such plans or agreed to affirmative action goals and timetables in collective bargaining agreements in the absence of a judicial finding of legal liability for prior discrimination. Affirmative action plans designed to expand employment opportunities for underrepresented groups have been broadly supported; disputes have focused on plans entailing preferential treatment that results in the denial of employment opportunities to nonminorities.[63]

Affirmative action plans have been challenged under the equal protection clause and Title VII as causing "reverse discrimination"—that is, discrimination against nonminorities that results from efforts to remedy the effects of prior bias against minorities.[64] Suits have focused on modifications in seniority systems to give preference to minorities regarding eligibility for promotion and other job benefits or in protection from personnel reductions. Such affirmative action plans, similar to awards of retroactive seniority, affect employees' competitive status. However, in contrast to seniority adjustments for *individual* discrimination victims, *class* remedies benefit certain class members who have not personally suffered discrimination.

Challenges to affirmative action plans raise complex questions that do not lend themselves to simple answers. Can employers voluntarily adopt affirmative action plans that would not be permissible for courts to impose? Is there a legal distinction between preferential treatment in hiring practices and personnel reduction plans? Can employment quotas in school settings be defended as necessary to guarantee students' rights to equal educational opportunities? Can nonminorities challenge a court-approved affirmative action plan that was adopted without their involvement? To date, the Supreme Court has provided only partial answers to these and related questions.

In 1979 the Supreme Court confronted the matter of "reverse discrimination" under Title VII in connection with a company's voluntary affirmative action program that imposed racial quotas in an on-the-job training program. In this case, *Kaiser Aluminum and Chemical Corporation v. Weber,* the Court held that Title VII's prohibition of racial discrimination does not condemn all private, voluntary, race-conscious affirmative action plans to correct a racial imbalance in traditionally segregated jobs.[65] Upholding the company's plan, the Court concluded that its purposes mirrored those of Title VII and did not "unnecessarily trammel" the interests of white employees. It neither required white workers to be discharged and replaced with African-American hirees nor created an absolute bar to the advancement of white employees because half of those trained in the program were white. Moreover, the plan was a temporary measure, intended not to maintain a specific racial balance but simply to eliminate a manifest racial imbalance. Although *Weber* involved a private company, several federal appellate courts during the next decade upheld voluntary affirmative action plans entailing minority preferences in hiring, promotion, and assignment of *public* employees as long as the plans were temporary and did not require the discharge of nonminorities or bar their advancement.[66]

However, the federal judiciary has not looked favorably on court-ordered or voluntary *layoff* quotas that disregard seniority rights to *preserve* a designated percentage of minority employees. In 1984 the Supreme Court held that a federal district court had exceeded its powers by entering an injunction and modifying a consent decree, which required a city to disregard its negotiated seniority system and release white employees with greater seniority than African-American employees who were retained. Observing that both parties who had agreed to the original decree did not contemplate such a nullification of seniority rights, the majority rejected the contention that the court order was justified by the unanticipated fiscal exigency requiring layoffs that threatened gains made under the negotiated affirmative action plan.[67] The Court recognized that where an employer has been found guilty of a pattern or practice of racial discrimination, *individual* discrimination victims can be awarded competitive seniority to restore them to their rightful place, but a trial court cannot disregard a seniority system in fashioning a *class* remedy.

In 1986 the Supreme Court resolved the conflict among lower courts regarding the legality of layoff quotas in *voluntary* affirmative action plans. The Court in *Wygant v. Jackson Board of Education* struck down a Michigan school district's collective bargaining agreement that protected minority teachers from layoffs to preserve the percentage of minority personnel employed prior to any reductions in force.[68] The *Wygant* plurality reasoned that the layoff quota system, resulting in the release of some white teachers with greater seniority than African-American teachers who were retained, violated the equal protection clause. "Societal discrimination" alone was found to be insufficient to justify the class preferential treatment. Recognizing that racial classifications in employment must be justified by a compelling governmental purpose and that means must be narrowly tailored to accomplish that purpose, the plurality concluded that the layoff provision in question did not satisfy either of these conditions.

The plurality further rejected the lower courts' reliance on the "role model" theory (tying the percentage of minority teachers to the percentage of minority students to ensure appropriate role models), noting that the proper comparison for determining employment discrimination is between the racial composition of the teaching staff and the relevant labor market.[69] The plurality reasoned that use of the role model theory would allow school boards to go far beyond legitimate remedial purposes. The plurality voiced a strong preference for hiring goals in contrast to layoff quotas to remedy prior discriminatory practices, indicating that the former would be easier to justify in the absence of liability for past discrimination: "Denial of a future employment opportunity is not as intrusive as loss of an existing job."[70] However, the *Wygant* ruling did not clarify whether "convincing evidence of prior discrimination" to justify layoff quotas could be established where a school district is operating under a court-ordered desegregation plan and *students* rather than employees are the identified discrimination victims.

In several decisions rendered in 1986 and 1987, the Supreme Court endorsed the concept of both voluntary and court-ordered, race-conscious remedies in hiring and promotion practices, lending support to the distinction between hiring and layoff preferences suggested in *Wygant*. In one case, the Court upheld a consent decree between the city of Cleveland and an organization of African-American and Hispanic firefighters.[71] The decree called for the creation of additional promotion opportunities for all firefighters and specified promotion goals in terms of racial percentages for each rank of firefighters. The Court held that, regardless of whether Title VII precludes a court from imposing certain forms of race-conscious relief after a trial, such relief is not barred in a consent decree. In a companion case, the Court held that federal courts can order remedies entailing racial preferences if necessary to dissipate the effects of pervasive discrimination.[72] The federal district court had found a labor union guilty of a pattern of discrimination against nonwhite workers in recruitment, selection, training, and admission to the union. The Supreme Court majority reasoned that Congress did not intend to limit a court in exercising its remedial authority under Title VII where an employer or union has engaged in blatant intentional discrimination. The following year the Supreme Court upheld an affirmative action plan that included temporary promotion quotas in the Alabama Department of Public Safety as appropriate to remedy prior hiring discrimination against African Americans.[73]

Several lower courts also have endorsed temporary hiring and assignment quotas in school districts to achieve integrated faculties and assure students' constitutional rights to equal educational opportunities. Both court-ordered and voluntary plans have survived legal attacks if justified to eliminate the effects of prior school segregation and provide students with a multicultural education.[74]

Two 1989 decisions, however, call into question the legitimacy of many affirmative action plans that are not part of desegregation orders. In one case the Court held that white firefighters were entitled to challenge a city's affirmative action settlement that had been approved by the federal district court.[75] The consent decree, negotiated between the city of Birmingham, Alabama, and the NAACP to settle a Title VII claim, set goals and timetables for the promotion of African Americans to supervisory positions. The Court majority held that white workers could not be bound by the terms of an affirmative action plan that they had had no part in developing. In the public school context, this case may be relied on by nonminorities to reopen some consent decrees that were previously considered settled.[76]

The second decision involved racial quotas in awarding public contracts but has implications for racial preferences in hiring and promotion practices as well. The Court invalidated a racial quota system used to award public contracts in Richmond, Virginia, because the city had not identified its past discriminatory practices with sufficient specificity to justify the plan.[77] Finding similar constitutional defects as in the teacher layoff program in *Wygant,* the majority reaffirmed that affirmative action plans entailing quotas must address a compelling governmental goal and be narrowly designed to attain that goal to satisfy the equal protection clause. The majority reiterated that societal discrimination is an inadequate basis for race-conscious remedies; there must be evidence of specific discriminatory action to justify such relief.

These decisions may have the effect of making employers more reluctant to establish affirmative action plans that involve racial preferences in hiring and promotion practices. Where such plans have been adopted, they seem more vulnerable to reverse discrimination challenges than they did a decade ago.[78] However, a clear judicial pattern has not yet emerged as the Supreme Court has continued to show deference to congressional authority to establish affirmative action programs with preferences for minority businesses.[79] The legality of specific affirmative action plans will depend on a judicial assessment of a number of factors, including the justification for the plans and their impact on workers who are not accorded preferences.

GENDER DISCRIMINATION

Until the 1970s, employment discrimination based on gender was legally sanctioned, reflected in sex-based differences in working conditions, compensation, prerequisites to employment, and work-related benefits. A statement from an 1873 case is illustrative of the prevailing judicial attitude through much of the twentieth century toward differential treatment of men and women.

> Man is, or should be, woman's protector and defender. The natural and proper timidity and delicacy which belong to the female sex evidently unfits it for many of the occupations of civil life. The constitution of the family organization, which is founded in the divine ordinance, as well as in the nature of things, indicates the domestic sphere as that which properly belongs to the domain and functions of womanhood. . . .[80]

Along with gains in securing equal rights for racial minorities, the earlier status of women has given way to greater equality in employment. Extensive litigation based on constitutional and statutory guarantees has challenged gender-based classifications that impose unequal employment burdens on female employees.

Although many discriminatory practices have been invalidated under the fourteenth amendment, gender, unlike race, has *not* been designated a "suspect class," and thus does not trigger strict judicial scrutiny under the equal protection clause. This distinction is critical in judicial review, for if gender were elevated to a "suspect class," a compelling justification would be required for any governmental classifications based on this trait. In gender discrimination cases since the latter 1970s, the Supreme Court has *not* reverted to the lenient equal protection standard of review that requires the government to show only a rational relationship between classifications and a legitimate governmental purpose. Instead, the Court has applied an intermediate standard, requiring gender classifications to bear a "close and substantial relationship to important governmental objectives."[81]

For example, in 1982 the Supreme Court struck down a state university's policy that restricted enrollment in its nursing school to women. Noting that the policy was not substantially related to important governmental objectives, the Court majority declared that there must be "an exceedingly persuasive justification" for such classifications. The majority rejected the contention that the single-sex admission policy was a justifiable affirmative action effort to compensate for past discrimination against women, finding instead that the policy "tends to perpetuate the stereotyped view of nursing as an exclusively woman's job."[82]

Sec. 1983 1873 civil rights Act
"Remedies for discrimination"
Discrimination in Employment **339**

Although discriminatory gender classifications have been invalidated under the intermediate equal protection standard, the mere disparate impact of a facially neutral law on men or women is not sufficient to abridge equal protection guarantees. To illustrate, in 1979 the Supreme Court ruled that the Massachusetts Veterans Preference Statute with a disparate impact on women satisfied the equal protection clause.[83] The statute, giving absolute preference to veterans (98 percent male) in civil service positions, was found to be gender neutral because it classified individuals on veteran status rather than on gender. Recognizing that the law's adverse impact on women was foreseeable when the statute was written, the Court nonetheless concluded that the legislation was not *designed* to exclude women from civil service positions.

As with claims of racial discrimination, the difficult burden of establishing unconstitutional intent has caused most plaintiffs in gender-bias suits to rely on federal statutory guarantees. Some suits have been brought under Title IX of the Education Amendments of 1972, which bars gender discrimination against participants in or beneficiaries of federally assisted educational programs.[84] Individuals have a right to bring suit to force institutions to comply with Title IX,[85] and federal funds can be withdrawn from institutions that are not in compliance.[86]

Without question, Title IX has motivated many schools and colleges to reassess institutional policies and take steps to curb gender bias. However, the imposition of federal sanctions for violations has been impeded by disputes over the scope of Title IX coverage. In 1982 the Supreme Court resolved the controversy among lower courts regarding the meaning of "participants in and beneficiaries of" educational programs, ruling that Congress intended the law to cover *employees* as well as students.[87] Two years later the Court addressed a second controversial issue, finding Title IX to be *program-specific,* applying only to programs or activities receiving direct federal assistance.[88] Immediately following this decision, legislation was introduced in Congress to nullify the Supreme Court's interpretation and clarify that Title IX and three other civil rights laws with similar language were intended to apply to *institutional recipients* of federal funds (rather than only to programs or activities within institutions). Although it took four years to pass the measure, in 1988 the Civil Rights Restoration Act (CRRA) was signed into law.[89]

Partly because of the disputes over Title IX's application and the prevailing judicial stance that personal damages cannot be awarded under that law, most suits alleging gender discrimination in employment have been brought under Title VII of the Civil Rights Act of 1964. Also, some compensation claims have been initiated under the Equal Pay Act of 1963. These provisions have generated substantial litigation, and several topics of particular importance to educators are discussed in this section.

HIRING AND PROMOTION PRACTICES

Charges of gender bias in hiring, promotion, job assignment, and other conditions of employment have generally been initiated under Title VII. As mentioned previously, employers can defend a facially discriminatory hiring policy under Title VII with proof that gender is a bona fide occupational qualification (BFOQ) necessary to the normal operation of the business. The BFOQ exception to Title VII has generated a few school cases. For example, in 1971 the Supreme Court ruled that an employer could not deny employment to women with preschool-age children while hiring men with such children without establishing that the policy was justified as a BFOQ.[90] However, the Supreme Court of Montana held that gender was a bona fide occupational qualification for a second guidance counselor position because of the compelling need to give students an opportunity to discuss very private and personal matters with either a male or a female counselor.[91]

Most gender-bias suits in public employment have involved allegations that women have been treated unfairly solely because of their gender, thus requiring proof of intentional discrimination. Plaintiffs often have attempted to establish a prima facie case of disparate treatment by presenting evidence that they were better qualified for positions awarded to males and/or that a pattern of gender bias existed in the institution. However, statistical disparity data have been rejected where gender-neutral factors that might account for the employment decision have not been considered.

Public employers have successfully rebutted a prima facie case of gender discrimination by providing nondiscriminatory reasons for personnel decisions, such as showing that positions were filled by males who were equally or better qualified than females who were rejected. The Supreme Court declared in 1981 that employers are not legally obligated under Title VII to give preference to a female applicant when choosing between a male and female with similar credentials.[92] Employers also have prevailed by showing that hiring, promotion, or dismissal decisions were based on factors other than gender, such as inability to get along with coworkers or inadequate experience, scholarship, or performance.[93]

Plaintiffs, however, have obtained relief where employers have been unable to articulate a legitimate, nondiscriminatory reason for their actions. Title VII violations have been found with evidence that female applicants were better qualified for specific jobs but were rejected in favor of males because of stereotypic attitudes about the capabilities of women.[94] Courts similarly have awarded equitable relief where job advertisements have included the phrase, "prefer male," or job descriptions have been specifically drafted to exclude qualified women.[95] In addition, courts have intervened where women have been barred from specific positions, such as coaching boys' sports.[96]

Even if the employer does produce a nondiscriminatory reason for the employment decision, it is possible for the employee to prove that the asserted reason is merely a pretext.[97] For example, in 1990 the Eighth Circuit Court of Appeals found that a teacher who was passed over eight times for promotion to an administrative position was the victim of intentional gender discrimination and entitled to back pay to the date of the first rejection.[98] The Sixth Circuit Court of Appeals reached a similar conclusion regarding a female teacher who had been passed over numerous times for promotion while males with similar or lesser qualifications had been promoted.[99]

In a significant 1989 decision, *Price Waterhouse v. Hopkins,* the Supreme Court made it somewhat easier for individuals to establish discrimination in connection with certain types of disparate treatment, noting that Title VII was designed to prohibit employment decisions based on a mixture of legitimate and illegitimate motives.[100] In this gender-bias case involving the denial of promotion in an accounting firm, the majority concluded that an employer could prevail only by substantiating that it would have reached the same promotion decision even if it had not taken gender into account. In essence, if the plaintiff demonstrates that an employer substantially relied on a forbidden factor (e.g., gender stereotypes), the burden shifts to the employer to show that the decision would have been justified based only on legitimate reasons. The *Price Waterhouse* majority, however, also held that the correct standard to assess the employer's action is by a preponderance of evidence (i.e., evidence when fairly considered produces the stronger impression) rather than by the more rigorous standard of clear and convincing evidence. The case was remanded to ascertain if the employer could justify its promotion decision under the less stringent standard. Thus, although grounds were strengthened to attack employment decisions in mixed-motive cases, these gains were partially offset by the lower standard announced to assess whether employers have engaged in discriminatory treatment.

PREGNANCY-RELATED POLICIES

Since pregnancy affects only women, employment disadvantages that accrue because of this condition have generated numerous charges of gender bias under federal and state constitutional and statutory provisions. The law is clearly settled that pregnancy *per se* is an impermissible basis for refusing to hire applicants or for terminating employees. For example, the Fourth Circuit Court of Appeals invalidated a school board's practice of not renewing teachers' contracts where a foreseeable period of absence could be predicted for the ensuing year; the policy had been applied only to pregnant employees, thus imposing a disproportionate burden on female teachers.[101]

The treatment of pregnancy-related disabilities in employee disability benefits programs elicited two Supreme Court rulings and stimulated congressional action in the mid-1970s. The Court found no constitutional or Title VII violation in denying benefits for pregnancy-related conditions in such programs.[102] The Court held that the classification involved was based on pregnancy, not on gender, noting that nonpregnant employees included both men and women. In reaction to the Supreme Court's interpretation of Title VII, Congress amended the law in 1978 specifically to prohibit employers from excluding pregnancy-related conditions in comprehensive medical and disability insurance plans.[103]

Under this amendment, the Pregnancy Discrimination Act (PDA), employers cannot treat pregnancy-related conditions less favorably than other medical conditions. For example, employees are entitled to use sick leave for pregnancy-related illnesses.[104] Also, maternity leave cannot be considered an interruption in employment for the purposes of accumulating credit toward tenure.[105] Even before enactment of the PDA, the Supreme Court found a Title VII violation in the denial of accumulated seniority upon return from maternity leave, where employees retained seniority rights when on leave for all other disabilities.[106]

For almost a decade it was unclear whether the PDA prevented employers from treating pregnancy-related illness more favorably than other illnesses (e.g., granting special leave and other benefits to pregnant employees). However, in 1987 the Supreme Court affirmed a decision in which the Ninth Circuit Court of Appeals interpreted the PDA as allowing a state to enact a law requiring employers to grant employees up to four months of unpaid pregnancy leave. The Court reasoned that the PDA's prohibition against less favorable treatment of pregnancy-related conditions does not preclude a state from affording greater protections than required by Title VII.[107] According to the appeals court, the PDA was intended "to construct a floor beneath which pregnancy disability benefits may not drop" rather than "a ceiling above which they may not rise."[108]

Although special benefits can be given to pregnant employees, in 1990 the Third Circuit Court of Appeals invalidated a leave policy that permitted female employees, but not male employees, to use up to one year of combined sick leave and unpaid leave for childrearing.[109] Noting that the leave was not tied to any continuing disability related to pregnancy or childbirth, the court held that denial of a year's unpaid leave for childrearing to a male teacher, when the collective bargaining agreement authorized such leaves for female teachers, constituted gender discrimination under Title VII.

Like benefits for pregnancy-related absences, mandatory pregnancy leave policies have been the subject of litigation. The Supreme Court in 1974 ruled that a compulsory maternity leave policy, requiring every pregnant teacher to take a leave of absence five months prior to the birth of her child and specifying a return date of the next semester after the child reached three months of age, violated the teacher's fourteenth amendment due process rights.[110] The Court recognized the need for continuity in classroom instruction but found the arbitrary five-month date to have no relationship to that purpose. The other justification for the policy—that teachers beyond the fifth month would be physically unable to perform their jobs—was rejected because it made an "irrebuttable presumption" that all pregnant teachers were physically incompetent as of a specified date. The Court also found that the three-month return date following the birth of the child suffered the same deficiencies.

The Supreme Court, however, did not prohibit school boards from establishing maternity leave policies that are justified by a business necessity. Accordingly, the Ninth Circuit Court of Appeals upheld as reasonable a leave policy that required all teachers to take maternity leave at the beginning of the ninth month of pregnancy.[111] The board adequately demonstrated that the business necessity of obtaining a replacement teacher justified the policy.

School boards are not required to ignore pregnancy in designing personnel policies, but they must ensure that pregnancy is not singled out for less favorable treatment in leave policies, disability benefits programs, or other conditions of employment. Only if justified by a valid business necessity will courts uphold policies that disadvantage pregnant employees.

RETIREMENT BENEFITS PROGRAMS

Unlike some stereotypic assumptions, longevity is an accurate generalization of women as a class; statistically, women outlive men. Recognition of female longevity traditionally resulted in differential treatment of women with respect to retirement benefits. Employers either required women to make a higher contribution as they paid into a pension system or awarded them lower benefits upon retirement. Such differential treatment was defended as based on differences in longevity rather than on gender.

Since the late 1970s, however, this justification has not been persuasive; on two occasions the United States Supreme Court has struck down the use of sex-segregated actuarial tables in retirement benefits programs as constituting gender discrimination in violation of Title VII. In 1978 the Court invalidated a retirement program requiring women to make a higher contribution to receive equal benefits upon retirement, noting that gender was the only factor considered in predicting life expectancy.[112] The Court, however, specifically limited its ruling to retirement plans requiring unequal contributions to an employer-operated pension plan.

In a subsequent decision, the Court enjoined the state of Arizona from administering a deferred compensation program by contracting with insurance companies that used sex-segregated actuarial tables to determine benefits.[113] The program was found to violate Title VII because upon retirement, female employees received lower monthly annuity payments than male employees who contributed the same amount. The Court concluded that it is as discriminatory "to pay a woman lower benefits when she has made the same contributions as a man as it is to make her pay larger contributions to obtain the same benefits."[114] However, a majority of the justices concluded that relief should not be retroactive in that contributions already made to the fund could be subjected to sex-segregated tables in determining benefits. Given these Supreme Court rulings, most insurance companies have adopted unisex actuarial tables.

COMPENSATION PRACTICES

Claims of gender discrimination in compensation have been litigated under the Equal Pay Act of 1963 (EPA) and Title VII. The EPA stipulates that all employees are entitled to equal pay for equal work; jobs performed do not have to be identical but must be substantially equal with regard to skills, effort, and responsibilities. Employers can defend compensation differentials under the EPA on the basis of "a seniority system, a merit system, a system which measures earnings by quantity or quality of production, or a differential based on any factor other than sex."[115] Relying on the EPA, courts have invalidated pay differentials between male and female coaches who perform substantially equivalent duties[116] and have struck down other gender differences such as male teachers receiving a "head of household" supplement.[117]

In 1981 the Supreme Court ruled that the application of Title VII in compensation controversies is not confined by the Equal Pay Act's "equal pay for equal work" standard. In this case, *Gunther v. County of Washington,* female prison matrons challenged the pay discrepancy between matrons and male guards, even though their duties were not equivalent.[118] The employer had conducted a job evaluation study, assessing the responsibilities and working conditions of various positions, and concluded that female guards should be paid 95 percent as much as male guards. Since the matrons were actually paid only 70 percent as much as their male counterparts, the appellate court, and subsequently the Supreme Court, found evidence of intentional gender discrimination under Title VII.

Although the Supreme Court in *Gunther* cautioned that its decision was not based on the controversial notion of "comparable worth," the decision left the door open for subsequent Title VII claims of compensation discrimination beyond claims of unequal pay for equivalent work. A basic premise of the "comparable worth" concept is that the marketplace alone should *not* govern compensation practices. Instead, compensation should be based on an evaluation of the training and skills required, responsibilities, and working conditions. Proponents of the comparable worth theory claim that wage differentials among job classifications reflect gender discrimination rather than an objective assessment of the positions.[119]

To date, however, the judiciary has not found the "comparable worth" doctrine persuasive. Reasoning that the evidence of a pay disparity between jobs that are only "comparable" does not establish a Title VII violation, the Ninth Circuit Court of Appeals concluded that intentional discrimination must be proven, even if the employer's own study indicates that the jobs receiving unequal pay are comparable based on objective criteria.[120] Other courts also have rejected the notion of comparable worth in holding that employers do not have to disregard market considerations in establishing wage rates for different jobs. For example, the Eighth Circuit Court of Appeals declared that mere evidence that "employees of different sexes receive disparate compensation for work of differing skills that may, subjectively, be of equal value to the employer, but does not command an equal price in the labor market" is not sufficient to establish a prima facie Title VII violation.[121]

It seems unlikely that the judiciary will endorse the comparable worth theory, but this notion has motivated many employers to implement pay equity studies involving an evaluation of positions as to level of training and skills required, responsibilities, and working conditions. Thus, the argument that comparable jobs should be compensated equally is having some impact on employment practices, even though compensation based on the comparable worth doctrine has not been required under Title VII.

SEXUAL HARASSMENT

Claims of sexual harassment in employment have generated particularly sensitive legal activity. Sexual harassment generally refers to "repeated and unwelcomed sexual advances, derogatory statements based on . . . sex, or sexually demeaning gestures or acts."[122] Both men and women have been victims of sexual harassment, inflicted by members of the opposite as well as their own sex. Although sexual harassment is not a new phenomenon, Title VII litigation involving such harassment has a relatively brief history.

In the mid-1970s, courts began interpreting Title VII as providing a remedy to victims of sexual harassment resulting in adverse employment consequences such as termination, demotion, or denial of other job benefits. Back pay and accompanying employment benefits have been awarded where employers have not successfully rebutted charges that an employee was terminated or otherwise disadvantaged because of rejecting sexual advances.[123] Employers also have been found in violation of Title VII for failing to investigate employee complaints of adverse employment consequences stemming from sexual harassment by individuals in supervisory positions.[124]

In 1986 the Supreme Court delivered its first and only opinion to date involving a claim of sexual harassment, *Meritor Savings Bank v. Vinson*.[125] The Court recognized that a Title VII violation can be predicated on harassment that creates a hostile or offensive working environment as well as harassment that involves conditioning concrete employment benefits (e.g., promotions) on sexual favors. The Court rejected the employer's claim that Title VII's prohibition of sex discrimination is intended to prevent only tangible losses of an economic character, rather than injury from psychological aspects of the workplace. The Court noted that the 1980 guidelines issued by the EEOC stipulate that conduct with "the purpose or effect of unreasonably interfering with an individual's work performance or creating an intimidating, hostile, or offensive working environment" is actionable under Title VII.[126] The Court concluded that the EEOC guidelines allowing redress for noneconomic injuries are fully consistent with existing case law. However, the Court cautioned that "for sexual harassment to be actionable, it must be sufficiently severe or pervasive 'to alter the conditions of [the victim's] employment and create an abusive working environment.' "[127]

The Supreme Court further agreed with the appellate court that the employer could not use as a defense "the fact that sex-related conduct was 'voluntary,' in the sense that the complainant was not forced to participate against her will."[128] However, it rejected the appeals court's conclusion that evidence regarding the victim's sexual fantasies and provocative dress was inadmissible. Finding the crucial consideration to be whether the alleged sexual advances were "unwelcomed," the Supreme Court reasoned that evidence regarding the victim's conduct could be relevant in making this determination on remand.[129]

Since *Meritor,* several courts have considered evidence of a hostile environment in sexual harassment cases.[130] The assertion that sexual advances represent personal desire for an individual rather than gender discrimination has not been persuasive.[131] While most of these cases have involved allegations of unwelcomed sexual advances,[132] in some cases, a hostile environment in violation of Title VII has been created by abusive language, physical aggression, and other demeaning behavior toward women.[133]

The Supreme Court in *Meritor* left some ambiguity regarding the employer's liability for acts of supervisors; it declined to endorse the appellate court's position that an employer is automatically liable for a hostile environment created by a supervisor's sexual advances, even though the employer could not have reasonably been aware of the alleged misconduct.[134] The Court noted that Congress surely intended to place some limits on the acts of employees for which employers are liable under Title VII. However, the Court also recognized that an aggrieved employee's failure to invoke an available grievance procedure would not preclude liability in all circumstances. For example, in *Meritor* the company's nondiscriminatory policy did not specifically address sexual harassment, and, more importantly, the grievance procedure apparently required employees to complain first to their supervisors, which in this situation was the alleged perpetrator.

Most sexual harassment litigation involving the workplace has been initiated under Title VII because aggrieved employees can seek a damages remedy, but the federal government also is authorized to investigate complaints of sexual harassment in federally funded education programs under Title IX of the Education Amendments of 1972. In addition, states have discretion to go beyond federal mandates in providing remedies for sexual harassment.[135]

Although charges of sexual harassment are problematic, administrative agencies and courts have become increasingly inclined to address this subject. The judiciary has interpreted civil rights mandates as placing an obligation on employers to assure that employees are not subjected to harassment based on gender as well as race, religion, or national origin.[136] Stakes are particularly high in sexual harassment cases because, in addition to the threat of legal sanctions, reputations and family harmony can be jeopardized.

AGE DISCRIMINATION

Unlike other characteristics that generate charges of discrimination, age is unique in that everyone is subject to the aging process. The mean age of the American population has climbed steadily in recent years, and this phenomenon has been accompanied by an increase in legal activity pertaining to age discrimination. Although legislative enactments that classify individuals on the basis of age can satisfy the equal protection clause if rationally related to a legitimate governmental objective,[137] in recent years plaintiffs have not had to rely on constitutional protections in challenging age-based employment discrimination.

In 1967 Congress enacted the Age Discrimination in Employment Act (ADEA), prohibiting age-based discrimination against employees forty to sixty-five years old in hiring, promotion, and compensation.[138] The upper limit on the protected group was extended to seventy in 1978 and completely removed in 1986.[139] Thus, employees over forty are now protected under the ADEA. Remedies for ADEA violations include: (1) injunctive relief, (2) offer of employment or reinstatement, (3) back pay, and (4) liquidated damages (equal to the back pay award) where established that age discrimination was unlawfully motivated.[140] If reinstatement is impossible or impractical, courts can award "front pay" to compensate for the loss of future earnings. Successful plaintiffs also can be awarded attorneys' fees.

In 1983 the Supreme Court resolved the conflict among lower courts regarding the constitutionality of the 1974 ADEA amendments, which extend the Act's protections to state and local government employees. The Court ruled that the amendments constitute a valid exercise of congressional power under the commerce clause of the Federal Constitution.[141] Noting that the state retains the authority to assess the fitness of employees and to dismiss those considered unfit, the majority declared that "the Act requires the state to achieve its goals in a more individualized and careful manner than would otherwise be the case, but it does not require the state to abandon those goals, or to abandon the public policy decisions underlying them."[142]

In 1991 the Supreme Court held that workers who allege age bias cannot bring an ADEA suit if they signed an agreement to arbitrate such claims out of court.[143] The Court held that neither the text nor the legislative history of the ADEA explicitly precludes arbitration, and there is no inconsistency between the ADEA's underlying purposes and enforcement of arbitration agreements. The Court noted that the EEOC can still investigate complaints even though the complainant who has agreed to use arbitration cannot initiate a federal suit.

The substantive provisions of the ADEA are almost identical to those of Title VII of the Civil Rights Act of 1964, and the judicial criteria developed in Title VII cases often are adapted to evaluate age discrimination charges under the ADEA.[144] Some employees have established intentional age discrimination by presenting evidence that younger, less qualified individuals were hired for positions they sought.[145] However, employers have been able to rebut a prima facie ADEA violation by articulating nondiscriminatory reasons for declining to hire or for dismissing older individuals, such as inferior qualifications, excessive tardiness, poor performance, or inability to relate to a supervisor.[146]

In 1986 the Ninth Circuit Court of Appeals affirmed a federal district court's conclusion that a former school administrator did not prove age-based disparate treatment under the ADEA.[147] Rejecting the assertion that the plaintiff's age was a motivating factor in the elimination of his position as assistant superintendent, the trial court reasoned that the school district articulated a nondiscriminatory basis for its action. Even though one of the school district's defenses—that administrative reorganization was necessitated by a fiscal crisis—was not considered credible, the court found that the district's desire to create a new administrative team provided a legitimate justification for eliminating the plaintiff's position. More recently, the Seventh Circuit Court of Appeals ruled that reassignment of a principal over age sixty-five to a more distant principalship spanning two schools was not a "materially adverse" change in employment that would be actionable under the ADEA.[148]

Although most courts have adopted the disparate treatment standard of review in ADEA cases, in 1980 the Second Circuit Court of Appeals recognized that plaintiffs could establish an ADEA violation with evidence that employment practices, regardless of motive, have a disparate impact on older employees.[149] In this case, the defendant school board adopted a cost-cutting policy of preferentially hiring teachers with less than five years' experience. The court concluded that the policy, with a disparate impact on older teachers, had to be justified as a job necessity to satisfy the

ADEA. A Missouri federal district court applied similar logic in evaluating a prima facie case of age discrimination in connection with a university's policy reserving a certain portion of faculty positions for nontenured professors.[150] The court rejected the economic rationale offered in defense of this practice as an insufficient business necessity to justify the adverse impact of the policy on older faculty members.

The United States Department of Labor and several courts have interpreted the ADEA as prohibiting age discrimination among employees *within* the protected age group in that an employer cannot discriminate against employees who are sixty years old by preferring those who are forty-five. To illustrate, the First Circuit Court of Appeals ruled that an employee need not show that he or she was replaced by a person under forty years of age to establish a prima facie case of discrimination under the ADEA.[151] An employee may not even need to show replacement by a younger person to substantiate an inference of age discrimination; the Seventh Circuit Court of Appeals recognized that evidence of an age-based termination would be sufficient to establish an ADEA violation.[152]

Given that mandatory retirement for most employees has been eliminated, employers have attempted to entice employees to retire through attractive retirement benefits packages. Under the ADEA, employers can observe the terms of a bona fide retirement benefits plan as long as the plan is not a subterfuge to evade the purposes of the Act.[153] An ADEA amendment that became effective in 1988 prohibits employers from reducing annual benefits or ceasing the accrual of benefits after employees attain a certain age as an inducement for them to retire.[154]

In a significant 1989 decision, *Public Employees Retirement System of Ohio v. Betts,* the Supreme Court invalidated the EEOC regulation requiring employers to justify any age-based reduction in benefits with evidence that additional costs would be incurred to provide equal benefits.[155] Under this ruling, a retirement plan will be considered bona fide unless it intentionally discriminates against older employees in some *nonfringe* aspect of the employment relationship. Of course, employers can still use cost justifications to show that a plan is bona fide, but it is not the sole justification that can be used.

In light of *Betts,* plaintiffs carry a heavier burden than before in challenging age-based differentials in retirement plans, but it is a burden that can be met. The *Betts* case was remanded for a determination of whether the plaintiff's retirement was "involuntary" in violation of the ADEA, and the Sixth Circuit Court of Appeals concluded that it was. Recognizing that the employee's ill health precipitated her retirement, the appeals court found that because she was over sixty years old she was not offered the option of receiving disability benefits (with the possibility of being rehired). Her only retirement option was to receive benefits based on age and length of service, which were considerably lower than disability benefits. The fact that more desirable retirement options were available to younger employees in similar circumstances rendered her retirement "involuntary" in violation of the ADEA.[156]

"Voluntariness" is also a critical factor is assessing the legality of early retirement incentive programs (ERIPs).[157] In 1988 the Fifth Circuit Court of Appeals held that an ERIP was not rendered involuntary even though employees were given only a fifteen-day period in which to accept or reject the early retirement offer.[158] The court further held that the employer's decision to offer the incentive only to salaried employees who were eligible for early retirement under the company's pension plan did not violate the ADEA. The court reasoned that a plan need not extend to all potentially eligible employees as long as objective factors explain the exclusions. While the ADEA protects employees against adverse consequences if they decline to participate in an ERIP, incentive programs should be able to withstand ADEA challenges as long as they are clearly voluntary and do not affect normal retirement benefits.[159]

Although federal and state statutes have removed mandatory retirement ages, exceptions may be permissible for certain job categories.[160] Employers, however, must be able to produce a legitimate rationale for such exceptions. With the graying of American society, it seems likely that legal protections for older employees and incentives for voluntary early retirement will receive increasing attention.

DISCRIMINATION BASED ON DISABILITIES

Since the 1970s considerable attention has focused on protecting the employment rights of individuals with physical and mental disabilities. Federal and state laws have sought to eliminate barriers to the employment of qualified individuals with disabilities and have provided financial assistance for the rehabilitation of disabled persons.[161] The most significant federal laws are Section 504 of the Vocational Rehabilitation Act of 1973 and the Americans with Disabilities Act (ADA) of 1990. Section 504 provides in part that "no otherwise qualified handicapped individual" shall be excluded from participation in a program receiving federal financial assistance solely because of disabilities.[162] The ADA protects individuals with physical or mental impairments that substantially limit one or more major life activities; the law applies to employment, public transportation and accommodations, and telecommunications.[163] The ADA is modeled in part after Title VII of the Civil Rights Act of 1964 and extends Section 504 protections beyond federally assisted institutions.

In 1979 the Supreme Court rendered its first interpretation of Section 504 requirements in *Southeastern Community College v. Davis.*[164] The suit was initiated by a licensed practical nurse who was denied admission to a college training program for registered nurses because of her serious hearing disability. College officials asserted that her disability precluded participation in all aspects of the program and might endanger future patients. Finding that the applicant's inability to communicate would have necessitated close supervision and substantial alteration of the curriculum to accommodate her disability, the Court ruled that she was not "otherwise qualified" under Section 504.[165] The Court determined that Section 504 does not require institutions to lower or substantially modify their standards to accommodate individuals with disabilities.

However, under Section 504 reasonable accommodations must be made for individuals with disabilities who are otherwise qualified for participation. A deaf graduate student, who claimed that the University of Texas violated Section 504 by failing to provide him a sign-language interpreter, was granted a preliminary injunction because of his likelihood of prevailing on the merits of his claim.[166] On appeal, the Supreme Court ruled that the issue was moot (since the student had graduated), but the case was remanded for a trial regarding who should bear the cost of the interpreter. In a subsequent decision, the Eleventh Circuit Court of Appeals held that university students with disabilities were entitled to auxiliary aids (e.g., sign-language interpreters) regardless of their financial need.[167] The court also held that the denial of such aids to students in noncredit or nondegree programs violated Section 504. Furthermore, the provision of lift-equipped bus service only four hours a day was found to be an inadequate accommodation for students with physical disabilities.

In employment cases, courts have reiterated that Section 504 protects otherwise qualified persons with disabilities but does not require special accommodations for individuals who are not qualified for the positions sought. In a California case, a blind teacher was unsuccessful in challenging the school board's failure to appoint him to an administrative position; the board produced evidence that the plaintiff did not possess the requisite administrative skills or leadership experience for an administrative job.[168] The court rejected both equal protection and Section 504 claims, finding that the individual was not otherwise qualified for an administrative position and that there was a rational basis for the board's decision. In addition, the court was not persuaded that the board's action violated due process guarantees by creating an irrebuttable presumption that blind persons were unqualified to serve as administrators; the board did not impose a blanket ban on hiring blind employees in leadership roles. The Eighth Circuit Court of Appeals also found that a legally blind applicant who was rejected for a librarian position was not the victim of unlawful discrimination because the school board articulated a legitimate nondiscriminatory reason for its action. Concluding that the applicant was not rejected solely because of her blindness, the court accepted the evidence that the candidate selected by the board was better qualified.[169]

However, individuals have successfully challenged employment decisions by establishing that they were qualified for the job and disadvantaged solely because of their disabilities or were not provided an individual assessment of their ability to perform the job being sought.[170] For example, a rejected applicant for a preschool teaching position was awarded attorneys' fees and damages for mental anguish and loss of earnings because of the school board's violation of Section 504. Evidence showed that the multiply handicapped applicant was better qualified for the job than the individual subsequently hired and was denied employment solely because of his disabilities.[171] A New York federal district court also ruled that a school district's preemployment inquiries about an applicant's prior mental problems were impermissible under Section 504 because the questions were not related to his present fitness for a teacher's aide position.[172]

In 1987 the Supreme Court affirmed an Eleventh Circuit Appellate Court's decision that a teacher with physical impairments resulting from her susceptibility to tuberculosis, a communicable disease, was "handicapped" within the meaning of Section 504 and could not be summarily dismissed because of the disease.[173] The Court rejected the contention that Congress intended to allow discrimination based on the contagious effects of a physical impairment. The lower court was instructed to determine whether risks of infection precluded the teacher from being considered otherwise qualified for her job and whether her condition could be reasonably accommodated without an undue burden on the school district.[174] On remand, the teacher was found to be otherwise qualified and to pose little risk of infecting others; thus, her reinstatement with back pay was ordered.[175]

Although Section 504 does not specify that individuals with acquired immune deficiency syndrome (AIDS) are considered "handicapped," several courts have interpreted Section 504 as protecting such individuals from employment discrimination.[176] For example, the Ninth Circuit Court of Appeals ordered a school district to restore teaching duties to an AIDS victim, admonishing the lower court for not following the consensus in medical evidence when rendering its decision.[177] The legislative history of the ADA also indicates that its definition of individuals with disabilities applies to AIDS victims.[178]

The ADA and its regulations will likely replace Section 504 as the grounds for most employment discrimination litigation involving individuals with disabilities. The ADA specifically protects those who have impairments, such as severe burns, that do not actually interfere with life functions but can result in discrimination because the individuals are *regarded* as disabled. However, persons *currently* using illegal drugs and alcoholics, whose use of alcohol interferes with job performance, are not considered individuals with disabilities under the ADA.[179]

Even though there is some evidence of more relaxed judicial enforcement of civil rights provisions pertaining to race and gender, actions of Congress and the federal judiciary reflect a strong commitment to protecting employees with disabilities. Employment opportunities cannot be denied solely on a person's disabilities as long as the individual is otherwise qualified to perform the job and does not require unreasonable accommodations.

RELIGIOUS DISCRIMINATION

Religious discrimination as opposed to title VII [handwritten]

The Federal Constitution affords citizens explicit protection against governmental interference with their religious freedom. As discussed in Chapter 2, the first amendment in part prohibits Congress from enacting any law respecting an establishment of religion or interfering with the free exercise of religious beliefs. These provisions have been made applicable to the states through the fourteenth amendment.

On numerous occasions the Supreme Court has recognized that while the freedom to believe is absolute, the freedom to act on those beliefs is subject to reasonable governmental regulations.[180] Public educators cannot use their positions to spread their faith or disregard aspects of the state-prescribed curriculum for religious reasons.[181] However, requiring a profession of faith as a prerequisite to public employment clearly abridges the first amendment. In 1961 the Supreme Court invalidated a Maryland law requiring notary publics to sign an oath affirming their belief in God.[182] Public employees also have a free exercise right to abstain from certain observances and activities that conflict with their religious beliefs as long as such abstention does not impede their work performance. To illustrate, public school teachers have a first amendment right to refrain from saluting the American flag and pledging their allegiance, even though they cannot deny students the opportunity to engage in these observances.[183]

In addition to constitutional guarantees, employees are protected from religious discrimination under Title VII. In the 1972 amendments to Title VII, Congress stipulated that the protection against religious discrimination includes "all aspects of religious observance and practice, as well as belief, unless an employer demonstrates that he is unable to reasonably accommodate an employee's or prospective employee's religious observance or practice without undue hardship on the conduct of the employer's business."[184] The EEOC has promulgated guidelines with suggested religious accommodations such as accepting voluntary substitutes and assignment exchanges, using flexible scheduling, and changing job assignments.

Many controversies have arisen over the degree of religious accommodation required in work schedules to satisfy Title VII. In a significant 1977 case involving an airline company, a plaintiff challenged his dismissal for refusing to work on Saturdays in contravention of his religious beliefs.[185] The employer asserted that the plaintiff could not be accommodated because shift assignments were based on seniority in conformance with the collective bargaining agreement. Evidence also showed that supervisors had taken appropriate steps in meeting with the plaintiff and attempting to find someone to exchange shifts. The Supreme Court found no Title VII violation, reasoning that an employer need not bear more than minimal costs in making religious accommodations. The Court further noted that the employer is not required to disregard a bona fide seniority system in the absence of proof of intentional discrimination.

In a 1986 school case, the Supreme Court ruled that while an employer is obligated to offer reasonable accommodations to enable employees to practice their religious beliefs, a school board is not required to prove that an employee's proposal for religious accommodations would create an undue hardship.[186] The plaintiff teacher asserted that a Connecticut school board's negotiated agreement violated Title VII by permitting employees to use only three days of paid leave for religious purposes, while three additional days of paid personal business leave could be used for specified *secular* activities. The plaintiff proposed either to take personal leave for religious observances required by his faith beyond the three days allowed or to receive full pay and hire a substitute for these religious absences. Reversing the court below, the Supreme Court held that once an employer fulfills its obligation of providing a reasonable religious accommodation, it is not required to justify its rejection of an employee's proposal. On remand to determine whether the district's leave policy constituted a reasonable accommodation, the Second Circuit Court of Appeals upheld the negotiated agreement as administered, finding no religious discrimination.[187]

Although employers are not obligated to make costly religious accommodations to satisfy Title VII, in several school cases plaintiffs have proven that they suffered adverse employment consequences for unauthorized religious absences that should have been accommodated by unpaid leave.[188] In addition to federal safeguards, some school employees also have relied on state constitutional or statutory prohibitions against religious discrimination in challenging dismissals based on unauthorized religious absences.[189]

The obligation on public employers to reasonably accommodate religious absences does not mean that *paid* leave must be provided for this purpose. In 1984 the Tenth Circuit Court of Appeals rejected a teacher's claim that the school district's leave policy violated Title VII and burdened his free exercise of religion because he occasionally had to take unpaid leave to observe Jewish holidays. The policy allowed teachers two days of paid leave ("special leave") that could be used for religious observances and other purposes.[190] The court concluded that the availability of unpaid leave for additional religious observances constituted a reasonable accommodation under Title VII and did not place a substantial burden on free-exercise rights.

Whether paid leave tied specifically to religious observances implicates the establishment clause has not been clarified. Some decisions suggest that such leave would unconstitutionally advance religion. For example, in a New Jersey case, public school teachers were allowed to use personal leave days for religious reasons as well as other purposes, but the teachers' association sought paid leave specifically for religious observances.[191] The state supreme court ruled that the establishment clause prohibits the school board from granting such religious leave, and, therefore, negotiations over this item would be unconstitutional. Similarly, in 1976 a California appeals court found unconstitutional a proposed order of the governor that granted state employees paid leave on Good Friday for religious worship.[192]

The Supreme Court, however, has not ruled that school boards are precluded from providing paid religious leave. In the Connecticut case discussed previously, the Court did not invalidate the school board's allowance of three days' paid leave for religious ceremonies. While noting that a policy requiring employees to take unpaid leave for religious observances would satisfy Title VII, the Court declared that it would not be a reasonable accommodation if paid leave were provided "for all purposes except religious ones."[193]

In addition to requests for religious absences, the wearing of religious attire also has been controversial. In 1990 the Third Circuit Court of Appeals held that a school board's refusal to accommodate a public school teacher who sought to wear religious attire in the classroom did not violate Title VII.[194] The board's action was pursuant to a state statute proscribing such attire, and the court found that the statute advanced the compelling governmental interest of maintaining the appearance of religious neutrality in public schools. However, the Supreme Court of Mississippi invalidated the denial of unemployment benefits to a public school teacher who was dismissed for wearing "inappropriate" dress. Finding a violation of the teacher's first amendment rights, the court reasoned that her African headwrap was an expression of her sincerely held religious beliefs.[195]

Public employees, like all citizens, enjoy constitutional and statutory protection of their religious freedoms. Employers are expected to make reasonable accommodations to enable individuals to practice their faith. Yet, a minimal infringement on the practice of sectarian beliefs may be required in public school settings to ensure that religion is not being advanced under the auspices of the state.

CONCLUSION

Equal employment opportunity has been an elusive concept, continually refined through legislative enactments and judicial opinions. In general, it means that employment decisions should be based on qualifications, merit, seniority, and similar factors rather than on an individual's inherent traits such as race, gender, age, or disabilities. Courts have applied varying standards in assessing discriminatory employment practices. The appropriate standard of judicial review depends on the classification challenged (e.g., race, gender, disability) and the basis for the litigation (i.e., constitutional or statutory grounds). Although the applicable principles continue to be refined, generalizations reflecting the current status of the law are enumerated below.

1. The Federal Constitution and various civil rights laws protect employees from discrimination in employment based on race, national origin, gender, age, disabilities, and religion.

2. Governmental classifications based on race rarely can be justified; overt discrimination based on other characteristics, such as gender or age, can be justified only if the characteristic is a bona fide occupational qualification or the classification is substantially related to an important governmental interest.

3. The foreseeable adverse impact of a facially neutral employment practice on a protected group does not establish a federal constitutional violation unless the practice lacks a rational basis or is accompanied by unlawful intent; however, such disparate impact can violate Title VII of the Civil Rights Act of 1964 if the employer cannot show that the challenged practice serves legitimate employment goals.

4. Mere statistical disparities in racial composition between two job categories does not establish a prima facie case of disparate impact under Title VII; the disparities must be shown to be a direct result of the challenged employment practices.

5. A standardized test can be used to screen teacher applicants, even though it has a disproportionate impact on minorities, as long as the test is used to advance legitimate job objectives.

6. In challenging disparate treatment under Title VII, plaintiffs must establish discriminatory intent; employers can rebut an inference of discrimination by articulating a legitimate, nondiscriminatory basis for the practice.

7. In a disparate treatment case, if the employee proves that an employer's decision was based in part on impermissible reasons (e.g., sexual stereotypes), the burden shifts to the employer to show that the decision would have been justified based only on legitimate grounds.

8. Employers can *voluntarily* establish affirmative action plans involving racial or gender preferences in hiring and promotion practices as long as such plans are temporary, designed to remedy specific acts of prior discrimination, and do not foreclose employment opportunities for specific groups.

9. Courts can *order* hiring and promotion preferences based on race or gender to remedy intentional prior discrimination.

10. Layoff quotas based on race that abrogate seniority rights cannot be judicially imposed or voluntarily adopted unless justified by a

compelling governmental purpose and less intrusive means are not available to accomplish that purpose.

11. Pregnancy-related conditions cannot be treated less favorably than other temporary disabilities in medical and disability insurance plans or leave policies.

12. Employees cannot be required to take maternity leave at a specified date during pregnancy unless the policy is justified as a business necessity.

13. Employers cannot make a distinction between men and women in retirement contributions and benefits.

14. Employees can gain relief under Title VII for sexual harassment that results in the loss of tangible benefits or creates a hostile working environment; the fact that an individual has submitted to sexual advances cannot be used as a defense if the advances were unwelcomed.

15. Title VII provides remedies for gender discrimination in compensation that extend beyond the Equal Pay Act's guarantee of equal pay for substantially equivalent work; however, the judiciary has not endorsed the theory of "comparable worth."

16. The antidiscrimination provisions contained in Title IX of the Educational Amendments of 1972, Title VI of the Civil Rights Act of 1964, Section 504 of the Rehabilitation Act of 1973, and the Age Discrimination Act of 1975 protect individuals in entire institutions that house any programs or activities receiving federal aid.

17. School boards can establish bona fide retirement benefits programs, but the Age Discrimination in Employment Act precludes mandatory retirement based on age.

18. An otherwise qualified individual cannot be excluded from employment solely on the basis of a disability, but employers are not obligated to make substantial adjustments in working conditions to accommodate employees with disabilities or to hire persons who are not qualified.

19. Employers must make reasonable accommodations to enable employees to practice their religious beliefs as long as an undue business hardship is not created; however, accommodations that advance religion are barred by the establishment clause.

ENDNOTES

1. For a discussion of remedies under Section 1983 of the Civil Rights Act of 1871 for impairments of federally protected rights, *see* Chapter 8.

2. *See* Hirabayashi v. United States, 320 U.S. 81 (1943) (a wartime restriction on citizens of Japanese descent served a sufficiently compelling governmental interest).

3. Craig v. Boren, 429 U.S. 190, 197 (1976).
4. Personnel Adm'r of Massachusetts v. Feeney, 442 U.S. 256, 279 (1979), *on remand,* 475 F. Supp. 109 (D. Mass. 1979), *aff'd,* 445 U.S. 901 (1980). *See also* Washington v. Davis, 426 U.S. 229 (1976).
5. *See* Dayton Bd. of Educ. v. Brinkman, 443 U.S. 526, 536 n. 9 (1979).
6. 42 U.S.C. § 2000e *et seq.* (1988). Originally, Title VII did not apply to educational institutions, but in 1972 this exemption was substantially repealed. The only remaining exemption pertains to the employment by educational institutions of "individuals of a particular religion." 42 U.S.C. § 2000e-1 (1988).
7. *See* 42 U.S.C. § 2000e-5 (1988) for procedural requirements in filing Title VII claims. A claimant is not entitled to a federal trial on a Title VII claim if the issue has already been litigated in a state court under state antidiscriminatory provisions. *See* Alexander v. Gardner-Denver Co., 415 U.S. 36 (1974).
8. Lorance v. AT&T Technologies, 490 U.S. 900 (1989) (employees filed their claim too late to challenge a seniority system because the time limitation was calculated from 1979, when the system was adopted, rather than from 1982, when the employees learned that they would be demoted under provisions of the system).
9. A prima facie case raises an inference of discrimination, which if unexplained, is "more likely than not based on the consideration of impermissible factors," Furnco Constr. Corp. v. Waters, 438 U.S. 567, 577 (1978).
10. *See* Texas Dep't of Community Affairs v. Burdine, 450 U.S. 248, 258–259 (1981).
11. Pullman-Standard v. Swint, 456 U.S. 273, 289–290 (1982).
12. Price Waterhouse v. Hopkins, 490 U.S. 228 (1989).
13. Griggs v. Duke Power Co., 401 U.S. 424, 432 (1971). *See also* New York City Transit Auth. v. Beazer, 440 U.S. 568 (1979).
14. *See* Dothard v. Rawlinson, 433 U.S. 321, 329 (1977).
15. Watson v. Fort Worth Bank and Trust, 487 U.S. 977, 987 (1988).
16. 490 U.S. 642 (1989). *See* note 33, *infra.*
17. Most of the cases have involved alleged discrimination against African Americans, but the legal principles apply to other racial and ethnic minorities as well. Title VII explicitly prohibits employment discrimination based on national origin; however, some nineteenth-century civil rights statutes limit protections specifically to race, such as 42 U.S.C. § 1981 (1988) (affording nonwhites equal rights to make and enforce contracts, sue, and receive full and equal benefit of the laws) and 42 U.S.C. § 1982 (1988) (affording nonwhites equal rights to acquire and hold property). The Supreme Court has broadly interpreted "race" under these laws. *See* Saint Francis College v. Al-Khazraji, 481 U.S. 604 (1987) (Arabs are protected under Section 1981); Shaare Tefila Congregation v. Cobb, 481 U.S. 615 (1987) (Jews are protected under Section 1982).
18. *See, e.g.,* Thomas v. Washington County School Bd., 915 F.2d 922 (4th Cir. 1990) (a school board's strong reliance on nepotism in filling teaching positions had a disparate impact on minorities, warranting prospective injunctive relief).
19. Washington v. Davis, 426 U.S. 229 (1976). This case was brought under the fifth amendment, rather than the fourteenth, because the latter provision applies only to state action. Although the fifth amendment does not include an equal protection clause, the Supreme Court has interpreted its

due process clause as prohibiting the federal government from denying citizens equal protection of the law. *See* Bolling v. Sharpe, 347 U.S. 497 (1954).

20. National Educ. Ass'n v. South Carolina, 445 F. Supp. 1094 (D.S.C. 1977), *aff'd,* 434 U.S. 1026 (1978). *See* text with note 30, *infra,* for discussion of the Title VII claim. *See also* Moore v. Tangipahoa Parish School Bd., 594 F.2d 489 (5th Cir. 1979).
21. United States v. Texas, 628 F. Supp. 304 (E.D. Tex. 1985), *rev'd sub nom.* United States v. Lulac, 793 F.2d 636 (5th Cir. 1986).
22. Armstead v. Starkville Mun. Separate School Dist., 461 F.2d 276 (5th Cir. 1972).
23. Georgia Ass'n of Educators v. Nix, 407 F. Supp. 1102 (N.D. Ga. 1976).
24. *See* Michael Rebell, "Disparate Impact of Teacher Competency Testing on Minorities: Don't Blame the Test-Takers or the Tests," *Yale Law & Policy Review,* vol. 4 (1986), pp. 384–391. Most constitutional challenges to employment test requirements have focused on equal protection guarantees, whereas challenges to student proficiency testing programs have relied on due process protections as well. *See* text with note 115, Chapter 3.
25. 401 U.S. 424 (1971). *See also* Guardians Ass'n v. Civil Serv. Comm'n of the City of New York, 633 F.2d 232 (2d Cir. 1980), *aff'd,* 463 U.S. 582 (1983), holding that the practice of conditioning employment eligibility on tests, which had not been validated as job related and had a disparate impact on African-Americans and Hispanics, was a continuing policy of discrimination that ended only when the last person was hired off the list. While granting back pay and retroactive seniority to minority employees who had suffered from the discriminatory practice since the effective date of Title VII, the Court denied the request for compensatory damages under Title VI of the Civil Rights Act of 1964 (prohibiting racial and national origin discrimination in federally assisted programs), reasoning that plaintiffs are entitled only to injunctive relief for *unintentional* discrimination under Title VI.
26. Albemarle Paper Co. v. Moody, 422 U.S. 405 (1975). A test validated for one job can be used with a different job only if there are "no significant differences" between the jobs, *id.* at 432. *See also* Connecticut v. Teal, 457 U.S. 440 (1982) (if prerequisites to employment or promotion, such as tests, have a disparate impact on minorities and are not substantiated as job related, they abridge Title VII even though the "bottom line" of the hiring or promotion process results in an appropriate racial balance).
27. In 1978 the EEOC issued *Uniform Guidelines on Employee Selection Procedures,* stipulating that evidence of adverse impact will be established if a selection rate of any racial or ethnic group or either gender is less than 80 percent of the group with the highest rate, 29 C.F.R. § 1607 *et seq.* (1990). The EEOC prefers test validation by correlating job performance with test scores, but the agency has allowed other types of validation that meet recognized standards of the American Psychological Association and textbooks and journals in the field of personnel selection.
28. Chance v. Board of Examiners, 458 F.2d 1167 (2d Cir. 1972).
29. Walston v. School Bd. of City of Suffolk, 566 F.2d 1201 (4th Cir. 1977). *See also* Ensley Branch, NAACP v. Seibels, 616 F.2d 812 (5th Cir. 1980), *cert. denied,* 449 U.S. 1061 (1980).

30. National Educ. Ass'n v. South Carolina, 445 F. Supp. 1094 (D.S.C. 1977), *aff'd,* 434 U.S. 1026 (1978). *See* text with note 20, *supra.*
31. Newman v. Crews, 651 F.2d 222 (4th Cir. 1981).
32. 490 U.S. 642 (1989). *See* text with note 16, *supra.*
33. Partly in response to *Wards Cove* and its apparent erosion of the principle enunciated in *Griggs,* a bill was introduced in Congress to require employers to show that challenged practices with a disparate impact are essential to effective job performance. Under the measure, employees could establish an inference of disparate impact by showing that practices result in statistical disparities; employees would not be required to show a causal relationship between a *specific* practice and the disparity. Civil Rights Act of 1990, H.R. 4000, 101st Cong., 2d Sess. (1990); 136 Cong. Rec. H6746 (daily ed. Aug. 3, 1990). Although Congress passed this bill in 1990, President Bush vetoed the measure and a congressional override failed by one vote. Proponents of the bill have voiced optimism that the measure eventually will become law.
34. Golden Rule Ins. Co. v. Washburn, No. 419-76 (Ill. Cir. Ct. 1984) (the procedure entails identifying the rate of correct responses to each item for minorities and nonminorities and selecting items from a pool of equally difficult items that display the least difference between majority and minority test-takers).
35. *See* S. E. Phillips, "The Golden Rule Remedy for Disparate Impact of Standardized Testing: Progress or Regress?" *Education Law Reporter,* vol. 63 (1990), pp. 383–428; "Golden Rule in the States," *FairTest Examiner,* vol. 1, no. 1 (1987), pp. 1, 3.
36. For example, a consent decree to settle a challenge to the Alabama statewide certification testing program included, among other remedies, the use of a modified version of the Golden Rule strategy to evaluate test items for bias, Allen v. Alabama State Bd. of Educ., 816 F.2d 575 (11th Cir. 1987). As the legislature did not provide funds to revise the tests, in 1988 the Alabama Board of Education announced that efforts to design a new certification examination were being abandoned. However, in 1991 the state passed legislation calling for a new teacher certification test under supervision of the Professional Teachers Standards Commission. *See* Millicent Lawton, "Alabama Governor, Union Reach Accord on Teacher Testing," *Education Week,* June 5, 1991, p. 22.
37. Stanfield v. Turnbow, Chancery Ct., Pulaski County, Arkansas, March 22, 1985; State v. Project Principle, 724 S.W.2d 387 (Tex. 1987); Texas State Teachers' Ass'n v. Texas, 711 S.W.2d 421 (Tex. Ct. App. 1986).
38. Fields v. Hallsville Indep. School Dist., 906 F.2d 1017 (5th Cir. 1990), *cert. denied,* 111 S. Ct. 676 (1991). *See also* Swanson v. Houston Indep. School Dist., 800 S.W.2d 630 (Tex. Ct. App. 1990) (test requirement applied to practicing teachers and administrators did not impair constitutional or contractual rights).
39. Georgia Ass'n of Educators v. State, No. C86-2234A, N.D. Ga. 1988. More controversial has been the Georgia Teacher Performance Assessment Instrument (TPAI), used to assess teachers' on-the-job performance as a prerequisite to receipt of renewable certificates. Use of the TPAI was eliminated by the state legislature in 1990, and in 1991 a state court required reinstatement of teachers who had lost their jobs based on poor ratings under the program. *See* "Update," *Education Week,* March 6, 1991, p. 3.
40. *See* Martha McCarthy, "Teacher-Testing Programs," in *The Educational*

Reform Movement of the 1980s, Joseph Murphy, ed. (Berkeley, CA: McCutchan, 1990), pp. 189–214.

41. Rogers v. International Paper Co., 510 F.2d 1340, 1345 (8th Cir. 1975), *vacated,* 423 U.S. 809 (1975), *modified,* 526 F.2d 722 (8th Cir. 1975).

42. 411 U.S. 792, 802 (1973). Once a prima facie case is established, questions of fact are to be resolved by a jury. *See* Equal Employment Opportunity Comm'n v. Board of Regents of Univ. of Oklahoma, 774 F.2d 999 (10th Cir. 1985), *cert. denied,* 475 U.S. 1120 (1986).

43. Price Waterhouse v. Hopkins, 490 U.S. 228 (1989). *See* text with note 12, *supra.*

44. Correa v. Nampa School Dist. No. 131, 645 F.2d 814 (9th Cir. 1981). *See also* Chambers v. Wynne School Dist., 909 F.2d 1214 (8th Cir. 1990) (African-American elementary teacher was not hired as a guidance counselor because she lacked requisite certification); Torrence v. Oxford Mun. School Dist., 615 F. Supp. 321 (N.D. Miss. 1985), *aff'd mem.,* 793 F.2d 1289 (5th Cir. 1986), *cert. denied,* 479 U.S. 985 (1986) (African-American band director's discharge was based on declining band performance and failure to maintain discipline); Morgan v. South Bend Community School Corp., 797 F.2d 471 (7th Cir. 1986) (African-American principal's demotion was because of substandard performance rather than race).

45. Hammond v. Rapides Parish School Bd., 757 F.2d 284 (5th Cir. 1985), *cert. denied,* 474 U.S. 829 (1985). *See also* Morton v. City School Dist. of City of New York, 742 F. Supp. 145 (S.D.N.Y. 1990) (superior performance by white candidate in interview constituted nondiscriminatory reason for not hiring African-American candidate as assistant principal).

46. Stallworth v. Shuler, 777 F.2d 1431 (11th Cir. 1985). *See also* Johnson v. Chapel Hill Indep. School Dist., 853 F.2d 375 (5th Cir. 1988); Webb v. Board of Educ. of Dyer County, 715 F.2d 254 (6th Cir. 1983), *aff'd,* 471 U.S. 234 (1985).

47. *See, e.g.,* Lincoln v. Board of Regents of Univ. System of Georgia, 697 F.2d 928 (11th Cir. 1983), *cert. denied,* 464 U.S. 826 (1983) (white professor established that she would have received a new contract "but for" her race); Covington v. Beaumont Indep. School Dist., 714 F. Supp. 1402 (E.D. Tex. 1989) (racial composition of student body did not justify reassigning white and Hispanic football coaches and replacing them with African-American coaches). *See also* Jett v. Dallas Indep. School Dist., 491 U.S. 701 (1989) (white athletic director's reassignment was racially motivated in violation of Section 1981 of the Civil Rights Act of 1866 and Section 1983 of the Civil Rights Act of 1871); text with note 55, *infra.*

48. *See* Carino v. University of Oklahoma Bd. of Regents, 750 F.2d 815 (10th Cir. 1984); Berke v. Ohio Dep't of Public Welfare, 628 F.2d 980 (6th Cir. 1980).

49. Bazemore v. Friday, 478 U.S. 385 (1986), *on remand,* 848 F.2d 476 (4th Cir. 1988). *See also* Pittman v. Hattiesburg Mun. Separate School Dist., 644 F.2d 1071 (5th Cir. 1981) (African-American employee established that a pay differential was primarily based on racial considerations).

50. Hazelwood School Dist. v. United States, 433 U.S. 299 (1977). *See also* Wygant v. Jackson Bd. of Educ., 476 U.S. 267, 275-276 (1986); text with note 68, *infra;* Castaneda v. Pickard, 648 F.2d 989 (5th Cir. 1981).

51. Wards Cove Packing Co. v. Atonio, 490 U.S. 642 (1989). *See* text with note 16, *supra.*

52. 42 U.S.C. § 1981 (1988).
53. Runyon v. McCrary, 427 U.S. 160 (1976).
54. Patterson v. McLean Credit Union, 491 U.S. 164 (1989), *on remand,* 887 F.2d 484 (4th Cir. 1989), *on remand,* 729 F. Supp. 35 (M.D.N.C. 1990) (Section 1981 claim of discriminatory failure to promote was dismissed). The Supreme Court ruling caused Justice Brennan to observe that "what the Court declines to snatch away with one hand, it takes with the other," *id.* at 189 (Brennan, J., concurring in part, dissenting in part). The civil rights act that was vetoed by the president in 1990 would have amended Section 1981 specifically to protect the "making, performance, modification and termination of contracts, and the enjoyment of all benefits, privileges, terms, and conditions of the contractual relationship." Civil Rights Act of 1990, H.R. 4000, 101st Cong., 2d Sess. (1990). *See* note 33, *supra.*
55. Jett v. Dallas Indep. School Dist., 491 U.S. 701 (1989). *See* text with note 187, Chapter 8, for a discussion of the liability issue. *See also* Bennun v. Rutgers, The State Univ., 737 F. Supp. 1393 (D.N.J. 1990) (professor's denial of promotion was actionable under Section 1981; retroactive promotion was ordered because university's nondiscriminatory reasons were pretextual).
56. 42 U.S.C. § 2000e-2(h) (1988).
57. Franks v. Bowman Transp. Co., 424 U.S. 747 (1976).
58. International Bhd. of Teamsters v. United States, 431 U.S. 324 (1977).
59. American Tobacco Co. v. Patterson, 634 F.2d 744 (4th Cir. 1980), *vacated and remanded,* 456 U.S. 63 (1982). The majority noted that if post-Act seniority systems were subjected to disparate impact suits, employers would be discouraged from modifying pre-Act systems to make them more equitable. *See also* Pullman-Standard v. Swint, 456 U.S. 273 (1982) (federal appeals court cannot substitute its judgment for that of the trial court in determining whether a seniority system is bona fide).
60. *See, e.g.,* International Bhd. of Boilermakers v. Wattleton, 686 F.2d 586 (7th Cir. 1982), *cert. denied,* 459 U.S. 1208 (1983).
61. Ford Motor Co. v. Equal Employment Opportunity Comm'n, 458 U.S. 219 (1982). Although this case involved alleged gender discrimination, the principle announced by the Court is applicable to charges of discrimination in hiring practices against other groups protected by Title VII.
62. United States Comm'n on Civil Rights, "Statement of Affirmative Action for Equal Employment Opportunities," 1973.
63. *See* Ruth Siegel, "Requisites for Affirmative Action," *Education Law Reporter,* vol. 38 (1987), pp. 399–415; Arval Morris, "Developing Standards for Affirmative Action," *Education Law Reporter,* vol. 32 (1986), pp. 883–896.
64. The issue of "reverse discrimination" was first addressed by the Supreme Court in Regents of the Univ. of California v. Bakke, 438 U.S. 265 (1978). The Court concluded that the admissions policy of the University of California Medical School at Davis violated Title VI of the Civil Rights Act of 1964. The university reserved a designated number of openings in each class for minority students; thus, minority applicants were accepted while white applicants with higher scores were rejected. Although invalidating the rigid quota system, a majority of the Court also reasoned that race could be a consideration in making admissions decisions.
65. 443 U.S. 193 (1979). Subsequently, in Fullilove v. Klutznick, 448 U.S. 448 (1980), the Supreme Court upheld the Minority Business Enterprise provision

of the Public Works Employment Act of 1977, which requires at least 10 percent of federal funds granted for local public works projects to be "set aside" to ensure participation by minority contractors; the Court reasoned that Congress was authorized to fashion a remedy with a racial factor in light of a history of prior discrimination. *See also* Metro Broadcasting, Inc. v. F.C.C., 110 S. Ct. 2997 (1990); note 79, *infra*.

66. *See, e.g.*, Bratton v. City of Detroit, 704 F.2d 878 (6th Cir. 1983), *modified on rehearing*, 712 F.2d 222 (6th Cir. 1983), *cert. denied*, 464 U.S. 1040 (1984); Valentine v. Smith, 654 F.2d 503 (8th Cir. 1981), *cert. denied*, 454 U.S. 1124 (1981); Detroit Police Officers' Ass'n v. Young, 608 F.2d 671 (6th Cir. 1979), *cert. denied*, 452 U.S. 938 (1981).

67. Firefighters Local Union No. 1784 v. Stotts, 467 U.S. 561 (1984).

68. 476 U.S. 267 (1986). *But see* Morgan v. Burke, 926 F.2d 86 (1st Cir. 1991) (upholding racial preferences in laying off teachers where the school district was under a court-ordered desegregation plan because it had not achieved unitary status).

69. *Id.*, 476 U.S. at 275–276.

70. *Id.* at 282–283.

71. Local No. 93, Int'l Ass'n of Firefighters v. City of Cleveland, 478 U.S. 501 (1986).

72. Local 28 of the Sheet Metal Workers' Int'l Ass'n and Local 28 Joint Apprenticeship Comm. v. Equal Employment Opportunity Comm'n, 478 U.S. 421 (1986).

73. United States v. Paradise, 480 U.S. 149 (1987). *See also* Johnson v. Transportation Agency, 480 U.S. 616 (1987) (upholding an employer's affirmative action plan giving promotion preferences to women because they were underrepresented in a particular position; the employer was acting within the spirit of Title VII to remedy a manifest imbalance in a traditionally segregated job category).

74. *See, e.g.*, Morgan v. Burke, 926 F.2d 86 (1st Cir. 1991); Kromnick v. School Dist. of Philadelphia, 739 F.2d 894 (3d Cir. 1984), *cert. denied*, 469 U.S. 1107 (1985); Zaslawsky v. Board of Educ. of Los Angeles City Unified School Dist., 610 F.2d 661 (9th Cir. 1979); Vaughns v. Board of Educ. of Prince George's County, 742 F. Supp. 1275 (D. Md. 1990); text with note 97, Chapter 13.

75. Martin v. Wilks, 490 U.S. 755 (1989). A year earlier, the justices had divided evenly on the question of whether white employees could challenge a court-approved consent decree in a Title VII case, Marino v. Ortiz, 484 U.S. 301 (1988).

76. *See* Joseph Beckham, *School Officials and the Courts* (Arlington, VA: Educational Research Service, 1989). Federal legislation has been introduced, but not yet enacted, to nullify this decision and protect consent decrees from such challenges, Civil Rights Act of 1990, H.R. 4000, 101st Cong., 2d Sess. *See* text with note 33, *supra*.

77. Richmond v. J. A. Croson Co., 488 U.S. 469 (1989). *See also* Associated Builders and Contractors of Louisiana v. Orleans Parish School Bd., 919 F.2d 374 (5th Cir. 1990) (plaintiffs who challenged a school board's construction program, establishing set-asides for women and minority contractors, were entitled to attorneys' fees even though the program was repealed after the constitutional suit was initiated).

78. *See* Barbara Lee, "Recent Supreme Court Rulings Could Disrupt or Halt

Affirmative Action Recruitment and Hiring in Academe," *The Chronicle of Higher Education,* June 28, 1989, p. B1.

79. Metro Broadcasting, Inc. v. F.C.C., 110 S. Ct. 2997 (1990) (upholding the Federal Communications Commission's policy, awarding preference to minorities in obtaining new licenses and allowing a limited category of existing radio and television stations to be transferred only to minority-controlled firms; the strict scrutiny test applied to a municipal minority set-aside program in *Croson* does not apply to benign racial classifications employed by Congress).

80. Bradwell v. Illinois, 83 U.S. 130, 141 (1873).

81. Craig v. Boren, 429 U.S. 190, 197 (1976). Most courts have subjected claims of alleged discrimination based on sexual orientation to the rational basis test rather than to the intermediate standard of review. *See, e.g.,* Ben-Shalom v. Marsh, 881 F.2d 454 (7th Cir. 1989); note 159, chapter 8.

82. Mississippi Univ. for Women v. Hogan, 458 U.S. 718, 729 (1982).

83. Personnel Adm'r of Massachusetts v. Feeney, 442 U.S. 256 (1979).

84. 20 U.S.C. § 1681(a) (1988).

85. *See* Cannon v. University of Chicago, 441 U.S. 677 (1979).

86. Currently before the Supreme Court is the question of whether individuals can secure personal damages for Title IX violations, Franklin v. Gwinnett County Pub. Schools, 911 F.2d 617 (11th Cir. 1990), *cert. granted,* 111 S. Ct. 2795 (1991). Holding that such damages are not available under Title IX, *see* Franklin, *id.;* Lieberman v. University of Chicago, 660 F.2d 1185 (7th Cir. 1981), *cert. denied,* 456 U.S. 937 (1982). *But see* Pfeiffer v. Marion Center Area School Dist., 917 F.2d 779 (3d Cir. 1990) (compensatory damages can be awarded under Title IX).

87. North Haven Bd. of Educ. v. Bell, 456 U.S. 512 (1982). The Court observed that Title IX's drafters did not specify "employment" among the law's exceptions and that Congress did not approve proposed bills to amend Title IX specifically to exclude employees from its coverage.

88. Grove City College v. Bell, 465 U.S. 555 (1984) (the college was subject to Title IX compliance, but *only* in its student financial aid program, since the only federal aid flowing to the institution was through student aid).

89. Civil Rights Restoration Act of 1987, P.L. 100-259, 102 Stat. 28, amending 20 U.S.C. §§ 1681, 1687, 1688; 29 U.S.C. §§ 706, 794; 42 U.S.C. § 2000d-4a. *See* DeVargas v. Mason & Hanger–Silas Mason Co., 911 F.2d 1377 (10th Cir. 1990), *cert. denied,* 111 S. Ct. 799 (1991) (the CRRA cannot be applied retroactively to claims that were initiated prior to its effective date as Congress did not express its clear intent to include retroactive application). For a discussion of complaints that the Office of Civil Rights had put on hold since the *Grove City* decision, *see* Courtney Leatherman, "Congress Overrides President's Veto of Civil-Rights Bill, Countering High Court's 'Grove City' Decision," *The Chronicle of Higher Education,* March 30, 1988, p. A-1.

90. Phillips v. Martin Marietta Corp., 400 U.S. 542 (1971). *See also* Sprogis v. United Airlines, 444 F.2d 1194 (7th Cir. 1971), *cert. denied,* 404 U.S. 991 (1971) (airline's policy requiring only female flight attendants to be unmarried was not justified as a BFOQ).

91. Stone v. Belgrade School Dist. No. 44, 703 P.2d 136 (Mont. 1985). *See also* Chambers v. Omaha Girls Club, 834 F.2d 697 (8th Cir. 1987), *rehearing denied,* 840 F.2d 583 (8th Cir. 1988) (discharge of unmarried pregnant employee of girls

club was upheld as a business necessity; employees being appropriate role models also was considered a legitimate BFOQ).

92. Texas Dep't of Community Affairs v. Burdine, 450 U.S. 248, 259 (1981).
93. *See, e.g.,* Jennings v. Tinley Park Community Consol. School Dist. No. 146, 864 F.2d 1368 (7th Cir. 1988); McCarthney v. Griffin-Spalding County Bd. of Educ., 791 F.2d 1549 (11th Cir. 1986); Wardwell v. School Bd. of Palm Beach County, Florida, 786 F.2d 1554 (11th Cir. 1986).
94. *See, e.g.,* Farber v. Massillon Bd. of Educ., 917 F.2d 1391 (6th Cir. 1990), *cert. denied,* 111 S. Ct. 952 (1991); Joshi v. Florida State Univ. Health Center, 763 F.2d 1227 (11th Cir. 1985), *cert. denied,* 474 U.S. 948 (1985).
95. *See, e.g.,* Coble v. Hot Springs School Dist. No. 6, 682 F.2d 721 (8th Cir. 1982); Rodriguez v. Board of Educ. of Eastchester Union Free School Dist., 620 F.2d 362 (2d Cir. 1980); Schoneberg v. Grundy County Special Educ. Coop., 385 N.E.2d 351 (Ill. App. Ct. 1979).
96. *See, e.g.,* Burkey v. Marshall County Bd. of Educ., 513 F. Supp. 1084 (N.D. W. Va. 1981).
97. *See, e.g.,* Sweeney v. Board of Trustees of Keene State College, 604 F.2d 106, 113 (1st Cir. 1979), *cert. denied,* 444 U.S. 1045 (1980) (female university professor established that the asserted legitimate reasons offered for her denial of promotion were a pretext for gender bias).
98. Willis v. Watson Chapel School Dist., 899 F.2d 745 (8th Cir. 1990), *on remand,* 749 F. Supp. 923 (E.D. Ark. 1990) (she also was awarded front pay to the time that an appropriate administrative position becomes available).
99. Spears v. Board of Educ. of Pike County, Kentucky, 843 F.2d 882 (6th Cir. 1988).
100. 490 U.S. 228 (1989).
101. Mitchell v. Board of Trustees of Pickens County School Dist. A., 599 F.2d 582 (4th Cir. 1979), *cert. denied,* 444 U.S. 965 (1979). *See also* Ohio Civil Rights Comm'n v. Dayton Christian Schools, 477 U.S. 619 (1986), *on remand mem.,* 802 F.2d 457 (6th Cir. 1986); Zuniga v. Kleberg County Hosp., Kingsville, Texas, 692 F.2d 986 (5th Cir. 1982). Dismissals based on unwed, pregnant status are covered in Chapters 8 and 10, as challenges to such terminations are usually based on asserted constitutional privacy rights.
102. General Electric Co. v. Gilbert, 429 U.S. 125 (1976) (no Title VII violation); Geduldig v. Aiello, 417 U.S. 484 (1974) (no constitutional violation under the equal protection clause).
103. Pregnancy Discrimination Act, 42 U.S.C. § 2000e(k) (1978). A health care plan that covered pregnancy for employees but limited spouses' coverage for pregnancy was struck down as violating this law, Newport News Shipbuilding and Dry Dock Co. v. Equal Employment Opportunity Comm'n, 667 F.2d 448 (4th Cir. 1982), *aff'd,* 462 U.S. 669 (1983).
104. *See, e.g.,* Hoeflinger v. West Clermont Local Bd. of Educ., 478 N.E.2d 251 (Ohio Ct. App. 1984) (school board could not require a physician's statement from an employee desiring to use sick leave for pregnancy-related absences, while not requiring such a statement for other types of illnesses).
105. *See, e.g.,* Solomon v. School Comm. of Boston, 478 N.E.2d 137 (Mass. 1985).
106. Nashville Gas Co. v. Satty, 434 U.S. 136 (1977). However, employees who voluntarily quit their jobs because of pregnancy are not entitled to unem-

ployment benefits. *See* Wimberly v. Labor and Indus. Relations Comm'n of Missouri, 688 S.W.2d 344 (Mo. 1985), *aff'd*, 479 U.S. 511 (1987).

107. California Fed. Savings and Loan Ass'n v. Guerra, 758 F.2d 390 (9th Cir. 1985), *aff'd*, 479 U.S. 272 (1987).

108. *Id.*, 758 F.2d at 396.

109. Schafer v. Board of Pub. Educ. of the School Dist. of Pittsburgh, 903 F.2d 243 (3d Cir. 1990).

110. Cleveland Bd. of Educ. v. LaFleur, 414 U.S. 632 (1974).

111. deLaurier v. San Diego Unified School Dist., 588 F.2d 674 (9th Cir. 1978).

112. City of Los Angeles Dep't of Water and Power v. Manhart, 435 U.S. 702 (1978).

113. Arizona Governing Comm. v. Norris, 463 U.S. 1073 (1983).

114. *Id.* at 1086.

115. 29 U.S.C. § 206(d)(1) (1988).

116. *See, e.g.,* Burkey v. Marshall County Bd. of Educ., 513 F. Supp. 1084 (N.D. W. Va. 1981). *See also* United Teachers of Seaford v. New York State Human Rights Appeal Bd., 414 N.Y.S.2d 207 (N.Y. App. Div. 1979) (relying on state law to strike down pay discrimination against female coaches).

117. *See, e.g.,* Equal Employment Opportunity Comm'n v. Fremont Christian School, 609 F. Supp. 344 (N.D. Cal. 1984), *aff'd*, 781 F.2d 1362 (9th Cir. 1986). A willful violation of the EPA was found where a college could not justify the difference between the wages of male and female teachers in the same discipline who were performing substantially equivalent duties, Brock v. Georgia Southwestern College, 765 F.2d 1026 (11th Cir. 1985).

118. 452 U.S. 161 (1981).

119. *See* Martha McCarthy, "Comparable Worth," *Educational Horizons,* vol. 64 (1986), pp. 109–111.

120. American Fed'n of State, County, and Mun. Employees (AFSCME) v. Washington, 770 F.2d 1401 (9th Cir. 1985); Spaulding v. University of Washington, 740 F.2d 686 (9th Cir. 1984), *cert. denied,* 469 U.S. 1036 (1984). In both cases, the appeals court rejected the assertion that market-driven compensation practices could be challenged under the disparate impact model; plaintiffs were required to prove discriminatory intent.

121. Christensen v. State of Iowa, 563 F.2d 353, 356 (8th Cir. 1977). *See also* Lemons v. City and County of Denver, 620 F.2d 228 (10th Cir. 1980), *cert. denied,* 449 U.S. 888 (1980); American Nurses Ass'n v. State of Illinois, 783 F.2d 716 (7th Cir. 1986) (while rejecting the claim based on the state's failure to alter salaries according to its comparable worth study, allegations of *intentional* gender discrimination constituted a cause of action).

122. Dayle Nolan, "Sexual Harassment in Public and Private Employment," *Education Law Reporter,* vol. 3 (1982), p. 227. *See also* Martha McCarthy, "Recent Developments Pertaining to Sexual Harassment," *Education Law Reporter,* vol. 36 (1987), pp. 7–14. To be actionable under Title VII, the harassment must be based on an individual's gender, rather than sexual orientation. *See* Williamson v. A. G. Edwards and Sons, Inc., 876 F.2d 69 (8th Cir. 1989), *cert. denied,* 110 S. Ct. 1158 (1990); DeSantis v. Pacific Tel. and Tel. Co., Inc., 608 F.2d 327 (1979).

123. *See, e.g.,* Barnes v. Costle, 561 F.2d 983 (D.C. Cir. 1977); Tomkins v. Public Serv. Elec. and Gas Co., 568 F.2d 1044 (3d Cir. 1977).

124. *See, e.g.*, Miller v. Bank of America, 600 F.2d 211, 213 (9th Cir. 1979) (a Title VII violation was found where the alleged harassment was by a supervisor authorized to hire, fire, discipline or promote, or at least to participate in such decisions, even though what the supervisor was said to have done violated company policy).
125. 477 U.S. 57 (1986).
126. *Id.* at 65. *See* 29 C.F.R. § 1604.11(a)(3) (1985).
127. Meritor Savings Bank, *id.* at 67, quoting Henson v. City of Dundee, 682 F.2d 897, 904 (11th Cir. 1982). *See also* Sparks v. Pilot Freight Carriers, Inc., 830 F.2d 1554 (11th Cir. 1987) (trucking company was found liable for the sexually hostile environment caused by a supervisor who was considered an agent of the company).
128. Meritor Savings Bank, *id.* at 68. *But see* Trautvetter v. Quick, 916 F.2d 1140 (7th Cir. 1990) (a private consensual sexual relationship in the workplace was not actionable as sexual harassment under Title VII).
129. The case was remanded for further proceedings since the district court's findings were insufficient to dispose of the merits of the hostile environment claim and the employer's liability. On remand, the plaintiff was not allowed to amend her complaint to assert new claims to substantiate the unwelcomed nature of the sexual activity, Vinson v. Taylor, 51 Empl. Prac. Dec. (CCH) ¶39,275 (D.C. Cir. 1989).
130. *See* Hawkins v. Hennepin Technical Center, 900 F.2d 153 (8th Cir. 1990), *cert. denied,* 111 S. Ct. 150 (1990); Huddleston v. Roger Dean Chevrolet, Inc., 845 F.2d 900 (11th Cir. 1988); Sparks v. Pilot Freight Carriers, Inc., 830 F.2d 1554 (11th Cir. 1987); Hicks v. Gates Rubber Co., 833 F.2d 1406 (10th Cir. 1987).
131. *See, e.g.*, King v. Board of Regents of the Univ. of Wisconsin System, 898 F.2d 533 (7th Cir. 1990).
132. *See, e.g.*, Jones v. Wesco Investments, Inc., 846 F.2d 1154 (8th Cir. 1988); Hall v. Gus Constr., 842 F.2d 1010 (8th Cir. 1988); Yates v. Avco Corp., 819 F.2d 630 (6th Cir. 1987).
133. *See, e.g.*, Huddleston v. Roger Dean Chevrolet, Inc., 845 F.2d 900 (11th Cir. 1988); Hicks v. Gates Rubber Co., 833 F.2d 1406 (10th Cir. 1987).
134. Meritor Savings Bank v. Vinson, 477 U.S. 57 (1986). All justices agreed that harassment creating a hostile environment is actionable under Title VII and that the victim's consent in submitting to unwelcomed advances cannot be used as a defense. However, only four justices argued that the Court should have resolved the liability issue by holding that "sexual harassment by a supervisor of an employee under his supervision, leading to a discriminatory work environment, should be imputed to the employer for Title VII purposes regardless of whether the employee gave 'notice' of the offense," *id.* at 78 (Marshall, J., concurring).
135. *See, e.g.*, Continental Can Co., Inc. v. Minnesota, 297 N.W.2d 241 (Minn. 1980) (under state law, employers are obligated to curb sexual harassment among coworkers); Downie v. Independent School Dist. No. 141, 367 N.W.2d 913 (Minn. Ct. App. 1985) (under state law, guidance counselor was not entitled to be warned of his deficiencies prior to dismissal for sexual harassment that violated professional ethics); Philips v. Plaquemines Parish School Bd., 465 So. 2d 53 (La. Ct. App. 1985) (upholding a principal's

discharge under state law for incompetence, based on evidence of his sexual harassment of a former teacher and a teacher applicant). *But see* Board of Educ. of Alamogordo Pub. School Dist. No. 1 v. Jennings, 651 P.2d 1037 (N.M. Ct. App. 1982) (sexual harassment constitutes unsatisfactory work performance under state education law; accordingly, two work conferences and the opportunity to eliminate the unsatisfactory conduct were required before dismissal).

136. *See, e.g.*, Rogers v. Equal Employment Opportunity Comm'n, 454 F.2d 234, 238 (5th Cir. 1971), *cert. denied,* 406 U.S. 957 (1972); Brown v. City of Guthrie, 22 FEP Cases 1627, 1631 (W.D. Okla. 1980).

137. *See* Gregory v. Ashcroft, 111 S. Ct. 2395 (1991); Palmer v. Ticcione, 576 F.2d 459 (2d Cir. 1978), *cert. denied,* 440 U.S. 945 (1979). *But see* Gault v. Garrison, 569 F.2d 993 (7th Cir. 1977), *cert. denied,* 440 U.S. 945 (1979) (fitness to teach should be determined on an individual basis; mandatory retirement per se violates the employee's due process rights).

138. 29 U.S.C. § 621 *et seq.* (1988). This law applies to all employers, employment agencies, and labor unions. The Age Discrimination Act of 1975, 42 U.S.C. § 6101 *et seq.* (1988), also prohibits age discrimination in federally assisted programs or activities. In addition, most states have enacted legislation protecting employees against age discrimination.

139. Age Discrimination in Employment Amendment of 1986, P.L. 99-592, 29 U.S.C. § 621 (1991). Among exceptions, this amendment allowed (1) employers to adhere to collective bargaining agreements in effect until January 1, 1990, and (2) colleges and universities to compel tenured faculty members to retire at age seventy until December 31, 1993. A study was commissioned to analyze the potential consequences of eliminating mandatory retirement on institutions of higher education.

140. *See, e.g.*, Loeb v. Textron, Inc., 600 F.2d 1003 (1st Cir. 1979).

141. Equal Employment Opportunity Comm'n v. Wyoming, 460 U.S. 226 (1983).

142. *Id.* at 239. *But see* Gregory v. Ashcroft, 111 S. Ct. 2395 (1991) (upholding provision of the Missouri Constitution mandating retirement of state judges at age seventy; appointed judges are not considered employees under the ADEA).

143. Gilmer v. Interstate Johnson Lane Corp., 111 S. Ct. 1647 (1991).

144. *See* text with notes 11–18, *supra.* For a discussion of the similarities between ADEA and Title VII, *see* Oscar Meyer Co. v. Evans, 441 U.S. 750 (1979); Lorillard v. Pons, 434 U.S. 575 (1978).

145. *See, e.g.*, Farber v. Massillon Bd. of Educ., 917 F.2d 1391 (6th Cir. 1990), *cert. denied,* 111 S. Ct. 952 (1991) (plaintiff also claimed sex discrimination in being passed over for administrative positions in favor of younger, less-qualified males).

146. *See, e.g.*, Wooden v. Board of Educ. of Jefferson County, Kentucky, 931 F.2d 376 (6th Cir. 1991) (inferior qualifications to those hired for teaching positions); Schwager v. Sun Oil Co. of Pennsylvania, 591 F.2d 58 (10th Cir. 1979) (poor performance); Kerwood v. Mortgage Bankers Ass'n, 494 F. Supp. 1298 (D.D.C. 1980) (inability to relate to supervisor); Brennan v. Reynolds and Co., 367 F. Supp. 440 (N.D. Ill. 1973) (excessive tardiness).

147. Sherlock v. Merced Union High School Dist., 788 F.2d 1566 (9th Cir. 1986),

cert. denied, 479 U.S. 876 (1986). For a discussion of the employee's burden of proving that age was a determining factor in the employer's decision, *see, e.g.,* Equal Employment Opportunity Comm'n v. University of Oklahoma, 774 F.2d 999, 1002 (10th Cir. 1985), *cert. denied,* 475 U.S. 1120 (1986); Murray v. Mount Pleasant Indep. School Dist., 754 F. Supp. 535 (E.D. Tex. 1990).

148. Spring v. Sheboygan Area School Dist., 865 F.2d 883, 886 (7th Cir. 1989). Courts also have rejected ADEA challenges to university compensation practices using market rates to set salaries of new faculty members. *See* MacPherson v. University of Montevallo, 922 F.2d 766 (11th Cir. 1991) (however, a trial was ordered to determine whether specific senior faculty had received discriminatory treatment in pay raises); Davidson v. Board of Governors of State Colleges and Univ., 920 F.2d 441 (7th Cir. 1990).

149. Geller v. Markham, 635 F.2d 1027 (2d Cir. 1980), *cert. denied,* 451 U.S. 945 (1981).

150. Leftwich v. Harris-Stowe State College, 540 F. Supp. 37 (E.D. Mo. 1982), *modified,* 702 F.2d 686 (8th Cir. 1983).

151. Loeb v. Textron, 600 F.2d 1003 (1st Cir. 1979). *See* 29 C.F.R. § 1625.2(a) (1990).

152. Stumph v. Thomas & Skinner, Inc., 770 F.2d 93 (7th Cir. 1985).

153. *See* United Air Lines v. McMann, 434 U.S. 192 (1977); Patterson v. Independent School Dist. No. 709, 742 F.2d 465 (8th Cir. 1984).

154. 29 U.S.C. § 623 (i)(1) (1988). *See* Karlen v. City Colleges of Chicago, 837 F.2d 314 (7th Cir. 1988).

155. 492 U.S. 158 (1989). An amendment to ADEA has been proposed to nullify this ruling, Older Workers Benefit Protection Act, S. 1293, S. 151, H.R. 3200, H.R. Rep. No. 664, 101st Cong., 2d Sess. (Aug. 3, 1990).

156. Betts v. Hamilton County Bd. of Mental Retardation and Developmental Disabilities, 897 F.2d 1380 (6th Cir. 1990), *cert. denied,* 111 S. Ct. 397 (1990).

157. *See* Scott Tarter and Martha McCarthy, "Early Retirement Incentive Programs for Teachers," *Journal of Education Finance,* vol. 15 (1989), pp. 119–133.

158. Bodnar v. Synpol, 843 F.2d 190 (5th Cir. 1988), *cert. denied,* 488 U.S. 908 (1988).

159. *See* Henn v. National Geographic Society, 819 F.2d 824 (7th Cir. 1987), *cert. denied,* 484 U.S. 964 (1987); Dorsch v. L. B. Foster Co., 782 F.2d 1421 (7th Cir. 1986); Equal Employment Opportunity Comm'n v. City Colleges of Chicago, 740 F. Supp. 508 (N.D. Ill. 1990) ("positive" incentives for early retirement such as lump-sum payments or increased benefits are valid under the ADEA).

160. *See* Vance v. Bradley, 440 U.S. 93 (1979) (federal government produced a rational basis for requiring foreign service employees to retire at age sixty); Ten Hoeve v. Board of Educ. of Dundee Cent. School Dist., 489 N.Y.S.2d 59 (N.Y. 1985) (age restriction for school bus drivers was upheld).

161. The Developmentally Disabled Assistance and Bill of Rights Act, 42 U.S.C. § 601 *et seq.* (1988), provides federal funds to participating states to create programs for the developmentally disabled. *See* Pennhurst State School and Hosp. v. Halderman, 451 U.S. 1 (1981) (the law was enacted pursuant to

congressional spending powers, rather than to enforce the fourteenth amendment; the bill of rights section does not create substantive rights for the developmentally disabled).

162. 29 U.S.C. § 794 (1988). State agencies may be able to avoid liability under Section 504 by pleading immunity under the eleventh amendment which bars federal suits against a state by its citizens. The Supreme Court has ruled that states do not waive eleventh amendment immunity by accepting funds under the Rehabilitation Act, Atascadero State Hosp. v. Scanlon, 473 U.S. 234 (1985). For a discussion of the application of eleventh amendment immunity to school districts, *see* text with note 190, Chapter 8.

163. 42 U.S.C.A. § 12101 *et seq.* (1991). Unlike Section 504, the ADA specifically waives eleventh amendment immunity regarding actions in federal or state courts, 42 U.S.C.A. § 12202 (1991).

164. 442 U.S. 397 (1979).

165. *Id.* at 406. This conclusion is reinforced by Section 504's regulations pertaining to program admissions, which specify that an individual must meet academic *and* technical standards, with technical standards defined as all nonacademic criteria. *See also* Doherty v. Southern College of Optometry, 862 F.2d 570 (6th Cir. 1988).

166. Camenisch v. University of Texas, 616 F.2d 127 (5th Cir. 1980), *vacated and remanded,* 451 U.S. 390 (1981). *See also* Wynne v. Tufts Univ. School of Medicine, 932 F.2d 19 (1st Cir. 1990) (material issues of fact precluded summary judgment as to whether school could dismiss student with disabilities for failing multiple-choice examination without providing alternative methods of testing him).

167. United States v. Board of Trustees for Univ. of Alabama, 908 F.2d 740 (11th Cir. 1990).

168. Upshur v. Love, 474 F. Supp. 332 (N.D. Cal. 1979). *See also* Coleman v. Darden, 595 F.2d 533, 537 (10th Cir. 1979), *cert. denied,* 444 U.S. 927 (1979).

169. Norcross v. Sneed, 755 F.2d 113 (8th Cir. 1985). *See also* DeVargas v. Mason & Hanger-Silas Mason Co., 911 F.2d 1377 (10th Cir. 1990), *cert. denied,* 111 S. Ct. 799 (1991) (Department of Energy's regulation barring one-eyed individuals from security inspector duties has a rational basis and does not deprive sight-impaired applicants of substantive due process); Beck v. James, 793 S.W.2d 416 (Mo. Ct. App. 1990) (a learning-disabled teacher is not considered "handicapped" under state law); School Dist. of Philadelphia v. Friedman, 507 A.2d 882 (Pa. Commw. Ct. 1986) (personality disorder causing an employee to be chronically late is not a mental disability under state law; and even if it is a disability, the employer is not required to accommodate chronic lateness).

170. Individuals with disabilities also can establish disparate impact under Section 504 by showing that an employer has created insurmountable barriers to their employment. *See* Prewitt v. United States Postal Service, 662 F.2d 292 (5th Cir. 1981).

171. Fitzgerald v. Green Valley Area Educ. Agency, 589 F. Supp. 1130 (S.D. Iowa 1984). *See also* Board of Trustees of the Univ. of Illinois v. Human Rights Comm'n, 485 N.E.2d 33 (Ill. App. Ct. 1985).

172. Doe v. Syracuse School Dist., 508 F. Supp. 333 (N.D.N.Y. 1981). Plaintiffs with physical disabilities also have prevailed in challenging their exclusion

from employment as school bus drivers, if established that they can perform the job with reasonable accommodations. *See, e.g.,* Longoria v. Harris, 554 F. Supp. 102 (S.D. Tex. 1982); Coleman v. Casey County Bd. of Educ., 510 F. Supp. 301 (W.D. Ky. 1980).

173. Arline v. School Bd. of Nassau County, 772 F.2d 759 (11th Cir. 1985), *aff'd,* 480 U.S. 273 (1987), *on remand,* 692 F. Supp. 1286 (M.D. Fla. 1988).

174. The Civil Rights Restoration Act of 1988 clarifies that Sections 503 and 504 of the Rehabilitation Act of 1973 do not protect an employee who currently has a contagious disease or who, by reason of such disease, cannot perform job duties or poses a health threat to others, 29 U.S.C. § 706(8)(c)(1988).

175. Arline v. School Bd. of Nassau County, Florida, 692 F. Supp. 1286 (M.D. Fla. 1988).

176. *See* Leckelt v. Board of Comm'rs of Hosp. Dist. No. 1, 909 F.2d 820 (5th Cir. 1990); Chalk v. United States Dist. Ct., 840 F.2d 701 (9th Cir. 1988); Doe v. Attorney General of United States, 723 F. Supp. 452 (N.D. Cal. 1989).

177. Chalk v. United States District Court, *id.* (rejecting the lower court's suggestion that not enough was known about AIDS to ascertain if the teacher posed a threat of spreading the disease). *But see* Leckelt v. Board of Commn'rs, *id.* (nurse was not discriminated against under Section 504 by being discharged for failure to submit results of a test for AIDS).

178. H.R. Rep. No. 101-485, 101st Cong., 2d Sess. (1990), pt. II at 52.

179. 42 U.S.C.A. § 12114 (1991). Amendments to Section 504 also have incorporated these provisions. *See* Traynor v. Turnage, 485 U.S. 535 (1988) (Veteran's Administration Rules defining alcoholism as willful misconduct do not violate the Rehabilitation Act). However, individuals with current disabilities resulting from *prior* addictions are protected under the Rehabilitation Act and the ADA. Also, some state antidiscrimination laws consider alcoholics to be "handicapped" and protected from adverse employment decisions as long as they perform their jobs satisfactorily and safely. Interpreting such an Ohio statute, *see* Greater Cleveland Regional Transit Auth. v. Ohio Civil Rights Comm'n, 567 N.E.2d 1325 (Ohio Ct. App. 1989).

180. *See* Torcaso v. Watkins, 367 U.S. 488 (1961); Cantwell v. Connecticut, 310 U.S. 296, 303–304 (1940).

181. *See* text with notes 55–72, chapter 2.

182. Torcaso v. Watkins, 367 U.S. 488 (1961). *See also* Beauregard v. City of St. Albans, 450 A.2d 1148 (Vt. 1982) (membership on the public school board of trustees could not be conditioned on religious preference).

183. *See* Russo v. Central School Dist. No. 1, 469 F.2d 623 (2d Cir. 1972), *cert. denied,* 411 U.S. 932 (1973); text with note 88, Chapter 2. *See also* Frazee v. Illinois Dep't of Employment Security, 489 U.S. 829 (1989) (free exercise clause precludes a state from denying unemployment compensation benefits to an individual who refuses to work on his Sabbath for sincere religious reasons, even if the person is not a member of an established religious sect that opposes Sabbath work).

184. 42 U.S.C. § 2000e(j) (1988). Title VII exempts religious institutions, including secular activities of such institutions, from its ban on religious discrimination. *See* Corporation of Presiding Bishop of Church of Jesus Christ of Latter Day Saints v. Amos, 483 U.S. 327 (1987).

185. Trans World Airlines v. Hardison, 432 U.S. 63 (1977).

186. Ansonia Bd. of Educ. v. Philbrook, 757 F.2d 476 (2d Cir. 1985), *aff'd and remanded,* 479 U.S. 60 (1986).

187. Philbrook v. Ansonia Bd. of Educ., 925 F.2d 47 (2d Cir. 1991), *cert. denied,* 111 S. Ct. 2828 (1991).

188. *See, e.g.,* Edwards v. School Bd. of Norton, Virginia, 483 F. Supp. 620 (W.D. Va. 1980), *vacated and remanded,* 658 F.2d 951 (4th Cir. 1981); Niederhuber v. Camden County Vocational-Technical School Dist., 495 F. Supp. 273 (D.N.J. 1980), *aff'd mem.,* 671 F.2d 496 (3d Cir. 1981).

189. *See, e.g.,* Rankins v. Commission on Professional Competence, 593 P.2d 852 (Cal. 1979), *appeal dismissed,* 444 U.S. 986 (1979) (interpreting California law, reinstatement was ordered of a teacher who had been terminated for unauthorized religious absences that were not proven to have a detrimental effect on the educational program). *But see* School Dist. No. 11, Joint Counties of Archuleta and LaPlata v. Umberfield, 512 P.2d 1166 (Colo. Ct. App. 1973), *modified,* 522 P.2d 730 (Colo. 1974) (upholding dismissal of a tenured teacher for unauthorized religious absences that interfered with his students' academic progress and disrupted management of the school).

190. Pinsker v. Joint Dist. No. 28J of Adams and Arapahoe Counties, 735 F.2d 388 (10th Cir. 1984).

191. Hunterdon Cent. High School Bd. of Educ. v. Hunterdon Cent. High School Teachers' Ass'n, 429 A.2d 354 (N.J. 1981). A 1985 Supreme Court decision lends support to the contention that paid leave tied specifically to religious observances might unconstitutionally advance religion. The Court struck down a Connecticut law (giving employees the unqualified right not to work on their chosen sabbath) as entailing an absolute preference based on religious beliefs in violation of the establishment clause, Estate of Thornton v. Caldor, 472 U.S. 703 (1985).

192. Mandel v. Hodges, 127 Cal. Rptr. 244 (Cal. Ct. App. 1976). *But see* California School Employment Ass'n v. Sequoia Union High School Dist., 136 Cal. Rptr. 594 (Cal. Ct. App. 1977) (upholding a school district's collective bargaining agreement designating Good Friday as a paid holiday for all employees; the paid holiday was designed to afford teachers a longer spring vacation and was not expressly tied to religious worship).

193. Ansonia Bd. of Educ. v. Philbrook, 479 U.S. 60, 71 (1986).

194. United States v. Board of Educ. for the School Dist. of Philadelphia, 911 F.2d 882 (3d Cir. 1990). *See also* Cooper v. Eugene School Dist. No. 4J, 723 P.2d 298 (Or. 1986), *appeal dismissed,* 480 U.S. 942 (1987); note 66, Chapter 2.

195. Mississippi Employment Security Comm'n v. McGlothin, 556 So. 2d 324 (Miss. 1990), *cert. denied,* 111 S. Ct. 211 (1990).

10

Termination of Employment

State laws delineate the authority of school boards in terminating school personnel. Generally, these laws specify the causes for which a teacher may be terminated and the procedures that must be followed. The school board's right to determine the fitness of teachers is well established; in fact, courts have declared that school boards have a duty as well as a right to make such determinations. According to the United States Supreme Court:

> A teacher works in a sensitive area in a schoolroom. There he shapes the attitude of young minds towards the society in which they live. In this, the state has a vital concern. It must preserve the integrity of the schools. That the school authorities have *the right and the duty to screen* the officials, teachers, and employees as to their fitness to maintain the integrity of the schools as a part of ordered society, cannot be doubted.[1] [emphasis added]

Numerous factors surround the school board's screening process. This chapter addresses the procedures that must be followed in termination of a teacher's employment and the grounds for dismissal. The first section provides an overview of due process in connection with non-retention and dismissal. Since due process is required only if a teacher is able to establish that a protected property or liberty interest is at stake, this section explores the dimensions of teachers' property and liberty rights in the context of employment termination. In the next section, specific procedural requirements are identified and discussed. A survey of judicial interpretations of state laws regarding causes for dismissal is presented in the third section. The concluding section provides an overview of remedies available to teachers for wrongful termination.

DUE PROCESS IN GENERAL

Basic due process rights are embodied in the fourteenth amendment, which guarantees that no state shall "deprive any person of life, liberty, or property without due process of law."[2] Due process safeguards apply not only in judicial proceedings but also to acts of governmental agencies such as school boards. As discussed in Chapter 1, constitutional due process entails *substantive* protections against arbitrary governmental action and *procedural* protections when the government threatens an individual's life, liberty, or property interests. Most teacher termination cases have focused on procedural due process requirements.

The nature of procedural due process required is influenced by the individual and governmental interests at stake and applicable state laws. Courts have established that a teacher's interest in public employment may entail significant "property" and "liberty" rights necessitating due process prior to employment termination. A property interest is a "legitimate claim of entitlement" to continued employment that is created by state law.[3] The granting of tenure conveys such a right to a teacher. Also, a contract establishes a property right to employment within its stated terms.

The judiciary has recognized that fourteenth amendment liberty rights encompass fundamental constitutional guarantees, such as freedom of speech. Procedural due process is always required when terminations implicate such fundamental liberties. A liberty interest also is involved when termination creates a stigma or damages an individual's reputation in a manner that forecloses future employment opportunities. If protected liberty or property interests are implicated, the fourteenth amendment entitles the teacher at least to notice of the reasons for the school board's action and an opportunity for a hearing.

Employment terminations are classified as either dismissals or nonrenewals. The distinction between the two has significant implications for the procedural rights that must be accorded a teacher. In this section, the procedural safeguards that must be provided the tenured teacher and the nontenured teacher are distinguished. Specific attention is given to the conditions that may give rise to a nontenured teacher's acquiring a protected liberty or property interest in employment, thereby establishing a claim to procedural due process.

DISMISSAL

The term "dismissal" refers to the termination for cause of any tenured teacher or a probationary teacher within the contract period. Both tenure statutes and employment contracts establish a property interest entitling teachers to full procedural protection. Beyond the basic constitutional requirements of appropriate notice and an opportunity to be heard, state laws and school board policies often contain detailed procedures that must be followed. However, failure to provide these additional procedures results in a violation of state law, rather than constitutional law.[4] Statutory procedures vary as to specificity, with some states enumerating detailed steps and others identifying only broad parameters. In addition to complying with state law, a school district must abide by its own procedures, even if they exceed state law. For example, if school board policy provides for a preliminary notice of teaching inadequacies and an opportunity to correct remediable deficiencies prior to dismissal, the board must follow these steps.

A critical element in dismissal actions is a showing of justifiable cause for termination of employment. If causes are identified by state law, a school board must base dismissal on those grounds. Failure to relate the charges to statutory grounds can invalidate the termination decision. Because statutes typically list broad causes such as incompetency, insubordination, immorality, unprofessional conduct, and neglect of duty, notice of discharge must indicate specific conduct substantiating the legal charges. Procedural safeguards ensure not only that a teacher is informed of the specific reasons and grounds for dismissal, but also that the school board bases its decision on evidence substantiating those grounds. Detailed aspects of procedural due process requirements and dismissal for cause are addressed in subsequent sections of this chapter.

NONRENEWAL

In most states, procedural protections are not accorded the probationary teacher when the employment contract is not renewed.[5] At the end of the contract period, employment can be terminated for any or no reason, as long as the reason is not constitutionally impermissible (e.g., denial of protected speech).[6] Generally, the only statutory requirement is notification of nonrenewal on or before a specified date prior to the expiration of the contract. Courts strictly construe the timeliness of nonrenewal notices. When a statute designates a deadline for nonrenewal, a school board must notify a teacher on or before the established date. The fact that the school board has set in motion notification (e.g., mailed the notice) generally does not satisfy the statutory requirement; the teacher's actual receipt of the notice is critical.[7] For example, in a situation where a statutory deadline was April 30 and the notice was mailed on April 29 but not received until May 2, notice was held to be inadequate.[8] A teacher, however, cannot avoid or deliberately thwart delivery of notice and then claim insufficiency of notice.[9] Failure of school officials to observe the notice deadline may result in a teacher's reinstatement for an additional year or even the granting of tenure in some jurisdictions.[10]

In the nonrenewal of teachers, a few states require a written statement of reasons and may even require, on the teacher's request, an opportunity for a hearing. Such provisions do not usually imply the right to an evidentiary hearing requiring the school board to show cause for termination;[11] a teacher is simply provided the reasons underlying the nonrenewal and an opportunity to address the school board.[12] Where state law establishes specific requirements and procedures for nonrenewal, failure to abide by these provisions may invalidate a termination. In Arizona, for example, if nonrenewal is based primarily on inadequate classroom performance, teachers must be given a preliminary notice of the school board's intent not to renew their contracts and ninety days to remedy the inadequacies.[13] Likewise, the judiciary will not condone a school board's failure to comply substantially with its own nonrenewal procedures.[14]

Although state laws may not provide the probationary teacher specific procedural protections, a teacher's interest in continued public employment may be constitutionally protected if established that a liberty or property right has been abridged. The United States Supreme Court addressed the scope of protected interests encompassed by the fourteenth amendment in two significant decisions in 1972, *Board of Regents of State Colleges v. Roth*[15] and *Perry v. Sindermann*.[16] These decisions established that the infringement of a liberty or property interest entitles a probationary teacher to due process rights similar to the rights of tenured teachers. The cases involved faculty members at the postsecondary level, but the rulings are equally applicable to public elementary and secondary school teachers.

In *Roth,* the question presented to the Court was whether a nontenured teacher had a constitutional right to a statement of reasons and a hearing prior to nonreappointment. Roth was hired on a one-year contract, and the university elected not to rehire him for a second year. Since Roth did not have tenure, there was no entitlement under Wisconsin law to an explanation of charges or a hearing; the university simply did not reemploy him for the succeeding year. Roth challenged the nonrenewal, alleging that failure to provide notice of reasons and an opportunity for a hearing impaired his due process rights.

The Supreme Court held that nonrenewal did not require procedural protection unless impairment of a protected liberty or property interest could be shown. To establish infringement of a liberty interest, the Court held that the teacher must show that the employer's action (1) resulted in damage to his or her reputation and standing in the community, or (2) imposed a stigma that foreclosed other employment opportunities. The evidence presented by Roth indicated that there was no such damage to his reputation or future employment. Accordingly, the Court concluded that "it stretches the concept too far to suggest that a person is deprived of 'liberty' when he simply is not rehired in one job but remains as free as before to seek another."[17]

The Court also rejected Roth's claim that he had a protected property interest to continued employment. The Court held that in order to establish a valid property right an individual must have more than an "abstract need or desire" for a position; there must be a "legitimate claim of entitlement."[18] Property interests are not defined by the Federal Constitution, but rather by state laws or employment contracts that secure specific benefits. An abstract desire or unilateral expectation of continued employment alone does not constitute a property right. The terms of Roth's one-year appointment and the state law precluded any claim of entitlement.

On the same day it rendered the *Roth* decision, the Supreme Court in the *Sindermann* case explained the circumstances that might create a legitimate expectancy of reemployment for a nontenured teacher.[19] Sindermann was a nontenured faculty member in his fourth year of teaching when he was notified, without a statement of reasons or an opportunity for a hearing, that his contract would not be renewed. He challenged the lack of procedural due process, alleging that nonrenewal deprived him of a property interest protected by the fourteenth amendment and violated his first amendment right to freedom of speech.

In advancing a protected property right, Sindermann claimed that the college, which lacked a formal tenure system, had created an informal or *de facto* tenure system through various practices and policies. Specifically, Sindermann cited a provision in the faculty guide stating that "the College wishes the faculty member to feel that he has permanent tenure as long as his teaching services are satisfactory."[20] The Supreme Court found that Sindermann's claim, unlike Roth's, may have been based on a legitimate expectancy of reemployment promulgated by the college. According to the Court, the lack of a formal tenure system did not foreclose the possibility of an institution fostering an entitlement to a position through its personnel policies.

In assessing Sindermann's free speech claim, the Supreme Court confirmed that a teacher's lack of tenure does not void a claim that nonrenewal was based on the exercise of constitutionally protected conduct. Procedural due process must be afforded when a substantive constitutional right is violated. In a later case, however, the Supreme Court held that if a constitutional right is implicated in a nonrenewal, the teacher bears the burden of showing that the protected conduct was a substantial or motivating factor in the school board's decision.[21] The establishment of this inference of a constitutional violation then shifts the burden to the school board to show by a preponderance of evidence that it would have reached the same decision in the absence of the protected activity.

The *Roth* and *Sindermann* cases are the legal precedents for assessing the procedural rights of nontenured teachers. To summarize, the Supreme Court held that a nontenured teacher does not have a constitutionally protected property right to employment requiring procedural due process before denial of reappointment. However, certain actions of the school board may create conditions entitling a nontenured teacher to notice and a hearing similar to the tenured teacher. Such actions would include:

- Nonrenewal decisions damaging an individual's reputation and integrity
- Nonrenewal decisions foreclosing other employment opportunities
- Policies and practices creating a valid claim to reemployment

- Nonrenewal decisions violating fundamental constitutional guarantees

Since the Supreme Court has held that impairment of a nontenured teacher's property or liberty interests triggers procedural protections, the question arises as to what constitutes a violation of these interests. Courts have purposely avoided precisely defining the concepts of liberty and property, preferring to allow experience and time to shape their meanings.[22] Since 1972 the Supreme Court and federal appellate courts have rendered a number of decisions that provide some guidance in understanding these concepts.

Property Interest. In general, a nontenured employee does not have a property claim to reappointment unless state or local governmental action has clearly established such a right.[23] A federal district court found that a Delaware school board created a reasonable expectancy of reemployment, requiring procedural protection, when it advised a principal that his contract would be renewed if his performance was satisfactory.[24] The court concluded that the principal was justified in believing that he would be reappointed after receiving a satisfactory rating. Similarly, the Seventh Circuit Court of Appeals found that a promise of two years of employment to a coach/athletic director established a legitimate expectation of continued employment.[25] To persuade the athletic director to accept the position, the board had assured him that his one-year contract would be extended for a second year. Based on such an implied contract, the court found that unilateral termination of the contract after one year violated due process rights.

Protected property interests are not created by mere longevity in employment. Both the Fourth and Tenth Circuit Appellate Courts found that issuing an employee a series of annual contracts did not constitute a valid claim to continued employment in the absence of a guarantee in state law, local policy, or an employment contract.[26] Similarly, a statute or collective bargaining agreement providing a teacher, upon request, a hearing and statement of reasons for nonrenewal does not confer a property interest in employment requiring legally sufficient cause for termination.[27] Such a provision simply gives the teacher an opportunity to present reasons why the contract should be renewed.[28]

Establishing a legitimate expectancy of reemployment in a school district with a formal tenure system is difficult.[29] If a tenure system exists, courts have refused to consider *de facto* tenure arguments except in "extraordinary circumstances."[30] An Arizona federal district court decision illustrates the unique conditions that must exist to present a valid property claim. In this case, an individual was offered a faculty position with tenure, but because of personal considerations, he rejected the tenure offer and secured written assurance that it would be awarded automatically at the beginning of his third year or perhaps sooner if mutually agreed.[31] Prior to awarding the teacher tenure, the university decided, without a statement of reasons or a hearing, not to renew his contract. The federal court concluded that the offer of employment promising tenure was an exceptional situation that would lead the faculty member legitimately to expect continued employment, thereby necessitating procedural safeguards prior to termination.

As noted, property rights are created by state laws or contracts but also may emanate from policies, regulations, or implied contracts. The sufficiency of the claim, however, must be interpreted in light of a state's laws, irrespective of the claim's origin. In some instances, reference to state law can narrowly restrict or limit alleged property interests. For example, the United States Supreme Court, in construing a North Carolina employee's property rights, relied on the state supreme court's opinion that "an enforceable expectation of continued public employment in that state can exist only if the employer, by *statute or contract* has actually granted some form of guarantee" (emphasis added).[32] Although in this case a city ordinance gave rise to an expectancy of reemployment after the successful completion of a six-month probationary period, the Supreme Court reasoned that, in the absence of a statutory or contractual obligation, the employee worked at the will and pleasure of the city. To establish a property right, then, it is necessary to prove not only that the employer's actions create an expectancy of employment but also that state law does not limit the claim.

Liberty Interest. As noted previously, liberty interests encompass fundamental constitutional guarantees such as freedom of expression and privacy rights. If the reason given for a nonrenewal implicates such fundamental liberties, procedural due process must be afforded. Most nonrenewals, however, do not overtly implicate fundamental rights, and thus, the burden is on the aggrieved employee to prove that the proffered reason is pretextual to mask impermissible grounds. Teachers' substantive constitutional rights are discussed at length in Chapter 8.

A liberty interest also may be implicated if the nonrenewal of employment damages an individual's reputation. The Supreme Court established in *Roth* that damage to a teacher's reputation or employability could infringe fourteenth amendment liberty rights. In subsequent decisions, the Supreme Court has identified the factors that are prerequisite to establishing that a constitutionally impermissible stigma has been imposed. According to the Court, procedural protections must be afforded only if stigma or damaging statements are:

- Related to loss of employment
- Publicly disclosed
- Alleged to be false[33]

Governmental action damaging a teacher's reputation, standing alone, is insufficient to invoke the fourteenth amendment's procedural safeguards. The Supreme Court has held that a liberty interest must be raised in connection with a loss of a governmental benefit such as employment. Generally, under this "stigma-plus" test, a teacher who has been defamed by reassignment, a transfer, suspension, or loss of a promotion cannot claim violation of a liberty interest.[34] The Fifth Circuit Court of Appeals noted that "the internal transfer of an employee, unless it constitutes such a change of status as to be regarded essentially as a loss of employment, does not provide the additional loss of a tangible interest necessary to give rise to a liberty interest meriting protection under the due process clause of the fourteenth amendment."[35] Similarly, the nonrenewal of coaching contracts does not involve a liberty interest when individuals retain their teaching positions.[36] While many of these employment actions may stigmatize and affect a teacher's reputation, they do not constitute a deprivation of liberty in the absence of loss of employment.

Likewise, liberty interests are not affected unless damaging reasons are publicly communicated.[37] The primary purpose of a hearing is to enable individuals to clear their name. Without public knowledge of the reasons for nonreappointment, such a hearing is not required. Neither is a protected liberty interest affected by statements that are disclosed in a public meeting requested by the teacher, since the board's action does not publicize the comments.[38] Further, rumors or hearsay remarks surfacing as a result of nonrenewal do not impair liberty interests. The First Circuit Court of Appeals noted that "in terms of likely stigmatizing effect, there is a world of difference between official charges (say, of excessive drinking) made publicly and a campus rumor based upon hearsay."[39] Even when a school board publicly announces stigmatizing reasons for its action, there must be a factual dispute regarding the truth of the allegations for a hearing to be required. If a teacher does not challenge the truth of the statements, a name-clearing hearing serves no purpose.[40]

The primary issue in these terminations is determining what charges constitute stigmatization. Nonrenewal alone is insufficient. As the Ninth Circuit Court of Appeals noted, "nearly any reason assigned for dismissal is likely to be to some extent a negative reflection on an individual's ability, temperament, or character," but circumstances giving rise to a liberty interest are narrow.[41] Charges must be serious implications against character, such as immorality and dishonesty, to create a stigma of constitutional magnitude. According to the Fifth Circuit Appellate Court, a charge must give rise to "a 'badge of infamy,' public scorn, or the like."[42] Such a liberty violation was clearly illustrated by the termination of a life-science teacher after public attacks on his teaching of human reproduction.[43] In this case, the appellate court found that the teacher was subjected to extensive, embarrassing publicity in the local, national, and even international media (being referred to as a sex maniac); incurred substantial personal harassment; and suffered permanent damage to his professional career.

Among the accusations that lower federal courts have found to necessitate a hearing are: (1) a serious drinking problem, (2) apparent emotional instability, (3) mental illness, and (4) immoral conduct.[44] Reasons held to pose no threat to a liberty interest include: (1) job-related comments such as personality differences and difficulty in getting along with others, (2) hostility toward authority, (3) incompetence, (4) aggressive behavior, (5) ineffective leadership, and (6) poor performance.[45] Charges relating to job performance may have an impact on future employment but do not create a stigma of constitutional magnitude.

PROCEDURAL REQUIREMENTS IN DISCHARGE PROCEEDINGS

Since termination of a tenured teacher or a nontenured teacher during the contract period requires procedural due process, the central question becomes *what process is due?* Courts have noted that no fixed set of procedures apply under all circumstances. Rather, due process entails a balancing of the individual and governmental interests affected in each situation. According to the Supreme Court, a determination of the specific aspects of due process requires consideration of:

> first, the private interest that will be affected by the official action; second, the risk of an erroneous deprivation of such interest through the procedures used, and the probable value, if any, of additional or substitute procedural safeguards; and finally, the government's interest, including the function involved and the fiscal and administrative burdens that the additional or substitute procedural requirement would entail.[46]

Application of these standards would require only minimum procedures in suspending a student but a more extensive, formal process in dismissing a teacher.

Minimally, the fourteenth amendment requires that dismissal proceedings be based on established rules or standards. Actual procedures will depend on state law and school board regulations, but they cannot drop below constitutional minimums. For example, a statute requiring tenured teachers to pay half the cost of a hearing that constitutionally must be provided by the school board violated federal rights.[47] In assessing the adequacy of procedural safeguards, the judiciary looks for the provision of certain basic elements to meet constitutional guarantees. Courts generally have held that a teacher facing a severe loss such as termination must be afforded procedures encompassing the following elements:[48]

- Notification of charges
- Opportunity for a hearing

- Adequate time to prepare a rebuttal to the charges
- Access to evidence and names of witnesses
- Hearing before an impartial tribunal
- Representation by legal counsel
- Opportunity to present evidence and witnesses
- Opportunity to cross-examine adverse witnesses
- Decision based on evidence and findings of the hearing
- Transcript or record of the hearing
- Opportunity to appeal an adverse decision

Beyond these constitutional considerations, courts also strictly enforce any additional procedural protections conferred by state laws and local policies. Examples of such requirements might be providing detailed performance evaluations prior to termination, notifying teachers of weaknesses, and allowing an opportunity for improvement before dismissal. While failure to comply with these stipulations may invalidate the school board's action under state law, federal due process rights *per se* are not violated if minimal constitutional procedures are provided.[49]

Various elements of due process proceedings may be contested as inadequate. Questions arise regarding issues such as the sufficiency of notice, impartiality of the board members, and placement of the burden of proof. The aspects of procedural due process that courts frequently scrutinize in assessing the fundamental fairness of school board actions are examined below.

NOTICE

In general, a constitutionally adequate notice is timely, informs the teacher of specific charges, and allows the teacher sufficient time to prepare a response.[50] Beyond the constitutional guarantees, state laws and regulations and school board policies usually impose very specific requirements relating to form, timeliness, and content of notice. In legal challenges, the adequacy of a notice is assessed in terms of whether it meets constitutional as well as other requirements. Failure to comply substantially with mandated requisites will void school board action.

The form or substance of notice is usually stipulated in statutes. In determining appropriateness of notice, courts generally have held that substantial compliance with form requirements (as opposed to strict compliance required for notice deadlines) is sufficient. Under this standard, the decisive factor is whether the notice adequately informs the teacher of the pending action rather than the actual form of the notice.[51] For example, if a statute requires notification by certified mail and the notice is mailed by registered mail or is personally delivered, it substantially complies with the state requirement. However, oral notification will not suffice if the law requires written notification.[52] If the form of the notice is not specified in statute, any timely notice that informs a teacher is adequate.[53]

Form and timeliness are important concerns in issuing a notice, but the primary consideration is the statement of reasons for an action. With termination of a tenured or nonprobationary teacher's contract, school boards must bring specific charges against the teacher, including not only the factual basis for the charges but also names of accusers.[54] If the state law identifies grounds for dismissal, charges must be based on the statutory causes. A teacher, however, cannot be forced to defend against vague and indefinite statutory charges such as incompetency or neglect of duty. Notice must include specific accusations to enable the teacher to prepare a proper defense. To illustrate, the Supreme Court of Nebraska held that a listing of statutory causes and witnesses did not inform the teacher of the factual allegations underlying the charges.[55] A Missouri appellate court found charges such as poor organization and failure to seek remediation to lack the specificity a teacher needed to rebut the charges.[56] Similarly, a federal district court found conclusory statements identifying the teacher's need to improve and ways to improve to be inadequate notice.[57] In some instances, state law may further require that the notice delineate the nexus between the teacher's conduct and responsibilities and duties as a teacher.[58] Finally, only charges identified in the notice can form the basis for dismissal.[59]

HEARING

In addition to notice, some type of hearing is required *before* an employer makes the initial termination decision; post-termination hearings do not satisfy federal constitutional due process requirements. In a significant 1985 decision, *Cleveland Board of Education v. Loudermill,* the United States Supreme Court recognized the necessity for some kind of a pretermination hearing. While the Court emphasized that a full evidentiary hearing to resolve the propriety of the discharge is not required, an initial hearing must be provided to serve as a check against wrong decisions.[60] This would entail determining if there are reasonable grounds to believe that the charges are true and that they support the dismissal. Essentially, in such a pretermination hearing, an employee is entitled to notice of the charges and evidence and an opportunity to respond, orally or in writing, as to why the proposed action should not be taken.[61] If only the minimal pretermination procedures outlined by the Supreme Court are provided, a full evidentiary post-termination hearing is required. Even extenuating circumstances involving severe disruption to the educational process cannot justify the omission of a preliminary determination. Under emergency conditions, however, teachers can be suspended with pay pending a termination hearing.

Courts have not prescribed in detail the procedures to be followed in administrative hearings. Basically, the fundamental constitutional requirement is fair play, that is, an opportunity to be heard at a meaningful time and in a meaningful manner.[62] Beyond this general requirement, the specific aspects of a hearing are influenced by the circumstances of the case, with the potential for grievous losses necessitating more extensive safeguards. According to the Missouri Supreme Court, a hearing generally should include a meaningful opportunity to be heard, to state one's position, to present witnesses, and to cross-examine witnesses; the accused also has the right to counsel and access to written reports in advance of the hearing.[63] Implicit in these rudimentary requirements are the assumptions that the hearing will be conducted by an impartial decisionmaker and will result in a decision based on the evidence presented.[64] This section examines issues that may arise in adversarial hearings before the school board.

Adequate Notice of Hearing. As noted, due process rights afford an individual the opportunity to be heard at a meaningful time. This implies sufficient time between notice of the hearing and the scheduled meeting. Unless state law designates a time period, the school board can establish a reasonable date for the hearing, taking into consideration the specific facts and circumstances. In a termination action, the school board would be expected to provide ample time for the teacher to prepare a defense; however, the teacher bears the burden of requesting additional time if the length of notice is insufficient to prepare an adequate response. A notice as short as two days was upheld as satisfying due process requirements where the teacher participated in the hearing and did not object to the time or request a postponement.[65] Similarly, a one-day notice was found constitutionally sufficient when the teacher did not attend the meeting to raise objections.[66] A teacher who participates fully in the hearing process or waives the right to a hearing by failure to attend cannot later assert "lack of adequate time" to invalidate the due process proceeding.

Waiver of Hearing. Although a hearing is an essential element of due process, a teacher can waive this right by refusing to attend a hearing or by walking out of a hearing.[67] If state law provides an opportunity for a hearing upon a teacher's request, failure to make such a request also constitutes a waiver. In some states, a hearing before the school board may be waived by an employee's election of an alternative hearing procedure such as a grievance mechanism or an impartial referee. For example, the Third Circuit Court of Appeals held that an employee's choice of *either* a hearing before the school board or arbitration under the collective bargaining agreement met the constitutional requirements of due process; the school board was not required to provide the individual a hearing in addition to the arbitration proceeding.[68] Similarly, an Ohio federal district court ruled that a teacher who selected a hearing before an impartial referee was not entitled to be heard by the school board prior to its decision on the referee's report.[69]

Impartial Hearing. A central question raised regarding hearings is the school board's impartiality as a hearing body. This issue arises because school boards often perform multiple functions in a hearing; they may investigate the allegations against a teacher, initiate the proceedings, and render the final judgment. Teachers have contended that such expansive involvement violates their right to an unbiased decisionmaker. Rejecting the idea that combining the adjudicative and investigative functions violates due process rights, courts generally have determined that prior knowledge of the facts does not disqualify school board members.[70] In addition, the fact that the board makes the initial decision to terminate employment does not render subsequent review impermissibly biased. Neither is a hearing prejudiced by a limited, preliminary inquiry to determine if there is a basis for terminating a teacher. The Colorado Supreme Court noted that since hearings are costly and time consuming, such a preliminary investigation may save time as well as potential embarrassment.[71]

In *Hortonville Education Association v. Hortonville Joint School District No. 1,* the United States Supreme Court firmly established that the school board is a proper review body to conduct dismissal hearings.[72] The Court held that a school board's involvement in collective negotiations did not disqualify it as an impartial hearing board in the subsequent dismissal of striking teachers. The Court noted that "a showing that the Board was 'involved' in the events preceding this decision, in light of the important interest in leaving with the board the power given by the state legislature, is not enough to overcome the presumption of honesty and integrity in policymakers with decisionmaking power."[73]

Although the school board is the proper hearing body, bias on the part of the board or its members is constitutionally unacceptable. A teacher challenging the impartiality of the board has the burden of proving actual, not merely potential, bias. This requires the teacher to show more than board members' predecision involvement or prior knowledge of the issues.[74] A high probability of bias, however, can be shown if a board member has a personal interest in the outcome of the hearing or has suffered personal abuse or criticism from a teacher.

Several cases illustrate instances of unacceptable bias. For example, the Alabama Supreme Court invalidated a teacher termination hearing for "intolerably high bias" created by a school board member's son testifying against the teacher; the son had been the target of alleged personal abuse by the teacher.[75] The Tenth Circuit Court of Appeals also ruled that bias was shown in the termination of a superintendent because one of the board members had campaigned to remove the superintendent from his position, and two other board members had made unfavorable statements to the effect that the superintendent "had to go."[76] The Iowa Supreme Court concluded that a school board's role of "investigation, instigation, prosecution, and verdict rendering" denied a teacher an impartial hearing, since the board used no witnesses and relied solely on its personal knowledge of the case in reaching a decision.[77] Other instances showing lack of impartiality or inferences of partiality include board members testifying as witnesses, prior announcements by board members of views and positions showing closed minds, and board members assuming adversarial or prosecutorial roles.[78]

If a teacher elects a hearing before an impartial hearing officer, the hearing officer also must avoid any suggestion of partiality in practice and appearance. The Colorado Court of Appeals ordered a new hearing for a teacher when the hearing officer ate lunch at the same table with the counsel for the school board and the witness who was testifying when the group broke for lunch. The court stated that "this blatant appearance of impropriety casts such a doubt on the impartiality of the decision as to vitiate the proceedings."[79]

An individual serving as prosecutor and also as advisor or counsel to the board may impair due process rights. The Supreme Court of Colorado cautioned that "not only is actual fairness mandated, but the integrity of the administrative process also requires that the appearance of fairness be preserved."[80] In this case, the court found that the presence of the superintendent and principal (who initiated the charges and served as witnesses) during the board's closed deliberations undermined the appearance of impartiality. In addition, a school board's legal counsel serving both prosecutorial and advisory roles may create an unacceptable risk of bias or appearance of prejudice.[81] Such a situation also may be created when a hearing officer and the board's counsel are from the same law firm.[82]

Evidence. Under teacher tenure laws, the burden of proof is placed on the school board to show cause for dismissal. The standard of proof generally applied to administrative bodies is to produce a "preponderance of evidence."[83] Administrative hearings are not held to the more stringent standards applied in criminal proceedings (i.e., clear and convincing evidence beyond a reasonable doubt).[84] Proof by a preponderance of evidence simply indicates that the majority of the evidence supports the board's decision or, as the New York high court stated, "such relevant evidence as a reasonable mind might accept as adequate to support a conclusion."[85] If the board fails to meet this burden of proof, the judiciary will not uphold the termination decision. For example, the Nebraska Supreme Court, in overturning a school board's dismissal decision, concluded that dissatisfaction of parents and school board members was not sufficient evidence to substantiate incompetency charges against a teacher who had received above-average performance evaluations during her entire term of employment.[86]

The objective of school board hearings is to ascertain the relevant facts of the situation;[87] these hearings are not encumbered by technical, judicial rules of evidence even if charges also carry criminal liability.[88] Termination proceedings are separate from the criminal proceedings, and, as such, dismissal might be warranted based on the evidence presented, even though such evidence would not satisfy the more stringent requirements to sustain a criminal conviction.

Only relevant, well-documented evidence presented at the hearing can be the basis for the board's decision.[89] Unlike formal judicial proceedings, hearsay evidence may be admissible in administrative hearings.[90] Courts have held that such evidence provides the background necessary for understanding the situation. While comments and complaints of parents have been considered relevant, hearsay statements of students have been given little weight.[91]

Findings of Fact. At the conclusion of the hearing, the board must make specific findings of fact. A written report of the findings on which the board based its decision is essential. Without a report of the findings of fact, appropriate administrative or judicial review would be impeded. The Minnesota Supreme Court noted that "if the trial court were to review the merits of the case without findings of fact, there would be no safeguard against judicial encroachment on the school board's function since the trial court might affirm on a charge rejected by the school board."[92] Similarly, the Oklahoma Supreme Court held that a probationary teacher's statutory entitlement to a hearing includes the right to know the rationale for the board's decision. The court admonished that "an absence of required findings is fatal to the validity of administrative decisions even if the record discloses evidence to support proper findings."[93] The findings of fact need not be issued in technical language but simply in a form that explains the reasons for the action.

DISMISSAL FOR CAUSE

Tenure laws are designed to assure competent teachers continued employment as long as their performance is satisfactory. With the protection of tenure, a teacher can be dismissed only for cause, and only in accordance with the procedures specified by law. Although acquiring tenure status gives a teacher a vested interest in continued employment that cannot be denied without due process, it does not guarantee permanent employment. The school district may discharge a tenured teacher for cause or due to conditions within the district, such as financial exigencies or declining enrollment, that necessitate reductions in the teaching force. Tenure rights accrue under state laws and therefore must be interpreted in light of each state's provisions.

Dismissal safeguards generally emanate from tenure statutes and are not applicable to the nontenured teacher. Within a contract period, however, certain procedural rights are constitutionally guaranteed. That is, a probationary teacher with an annual contract cannot be dismissed during the term of the contract except for cause and must be provided procedural due process. The contract itself establishes a property right to due process that extends throughout the contract period.

Where grounds for dismissal of a permanent teacher are identified by statute, a school board cannot base dismissal on reasons other than those specified.[94] To cover unexpected matters, statutes often include a catch-all phrase such as "other good and just cause." Causes included in statutes vary considerably among states and range from an extensive listing of individual grounds to a simple statement that dismissal must be based on cause. The most frequently cited causes are incompetency, neglect of duty, insubordination, and immorality.

Since grounds for dismissal are statutorily determined, it is difficult to provide generalizations for all teachers. The causes are broad in scope and application; in fact, individual causes often have been attacked for impermissible vagueness. It is not unusual to find dismissal cases with similar factual situations based on different grounds. In addition, a number of grounds often are introduced and supported in a single termination case. Illustrative case law is examined below in relation to several of the more frequently cited grounds for dismissal. Claims that dismissals impair constitutional rights are discussed in Chapter 8.

INCOMPETENCY

Courts have broadly defined incompetency. Although it usually refers to classroom performance, it has been extended in some instances to a teacher's private life. The term is legally defined as "lack of ability, legal qualifications, or fitness to discharge the required duty."[95] While incompetency has been challenged as unconstitutionally vague, courts have found the term sufficiently precise to give fair warning of prohibited conduct.[96] Incompetency cases often involve issues relating to teaching methods, grading procedures, classroom management, and professional relationships.

Two Pennsylvania cases illustrate the range of conduct courts have found to constitute incompetency. An early case dealt with a teacher working in her husband's "beer garden," where she occasionally had a drink of beer, served beer, and played a pinball machine with customers.[97] The Pennsylvania Supreme Court held that the loss of respect and good will of the community that resulted from her outside activities was evidence of incompetency. In a later Pennsylvania case, the United States Supreme Court reiterated that classroom performance alone was not the only basis for determining a teacher's fitness.[98] The superintendent in this case sought information concerning a teacher's loyalty relating to alleged prior activities in the Communist Party. Since the teacher refused to answer the superintendent's questions, he was dismissed on the ground of incompetency.[99] The Supreme Court, in upholding the dismissal, agreed with the Pennsylvania high court that incompetency included the teacher's "deliberate and insubordinate refusal to answer the questions of his administrative superior in a vitally important matter pertaining to his fitness."[100]

In general, dismissals for incompetency are based on a number of factors or a pattern of behavior rather than isolated incidents. A Louisiana appeals court noted that a teacher's repeated violations of rules in the administrative handbook, lack of control of students, and neglect of the principal's instructions as to grading procedures, lesson plans, and lunch counts constituted incompetence.[101] Similarly, in a Minnesota case, indicators of incompetency included poor rapport with students, inappropriate use of class time, irrational grading of students, and lack of student progress.[102] A Pennsylvania court interpreted incompetency as deficiencies in personality, composure, judgment, and attitude that have a detrimental effect on a teacher's performance.[103] Incompetency in this case was supported by evidence that the teacher was a disruptive influence in the school; could not maintain control of students; and failed to maintain her composure in dealing with students, other professionals, and parents.

Courts frequently examine dismissals based on incompetency to determine if the teacher received adequate notice of the need to improve performance. Illinois law requires that a teacher must be given notice of deficiencies and provided an opportunity to correct them. The Supreme Court of Illinois invalidated a teacher's dismissal because of lack of warning of deficiencies.[104] The teacher had failed to submit lesson plans and attendance reports and to perform football duties adequately. In finding these causes remediable, the court held that the teacher should have been notified and given an opportunity to correct the problems. Where a school board provided notice and an opportunity for remediation, however, a Missouri appellate court upheld the dismissal of a teacher.[105] The Washington Supreme Court held that a teacher's striking of students in the genitals did not constitute a remediable teaching deficiency and found the conduct was "so patently unacceptable that the school district was entitled to discharge the teacher for his actions in this case regardless of prior warnings."[106]

Dismissals for incompetency have included a wide range of charges. To illustrate, dismissals have been upheld for incompetency where a teacher required two eleven-year-old girls to write a vulgar word one thousand times,[107] a teacher brandished a starter pistol in an attempt to gain control of a group of students,[108] a principal sexually harassed a job applicant,[109] and a teacher provided inadequate supervision of the school newspaper and dressed improperly.[110] Two Arkansas teachers, hired primarily as coaches, were dismissed for unsatisfactory performance because of their inability to field competitive teams.[111] However, a Montana teacher, who was being considered for reassignment after her position was eliminated, could not be dismissed for incompetency based on poor performance in four interviews with superiors, because she had performed satisfactorily in the classroom for thirteen years.[112]

Frequently, school boards have based charges of incompetency on teachers' lack of proper classroom management and control. Such dismissals often have been contested on the grounds that the penalty of discharge is too severe for the offense. Courts generally have held that school boards have latitude in determining penalties, and their decisions will be overturned only if disproportionate to the offense.[113] As long as evidence is presented to substantiate the board's charge, poor classroom management can result in termination.[114]

An Iowa school board dismissed a teacher for incompetency, in part because her students scored poorly on standardized basic skills tests. The Eighth Circuit Court of Appeals noted that the school board has responsibility for evaluating teachers and that such evaluations are not subject to judicial review.[115] With the current emphasis on teacher accountability, the consideration of pupil performance in evaluating teacher competence may become increasingly controversial.

IMMORALITY

Immorality, the most frequently cited cause for dismissal, is generally not defined in state laws. In defining the term, the judiciary has tended to interpret "immorality" broadly as unacceptable conduct that affects a teacher's fitness. Traditionally, the teacher has been viewed as an exemplar whose conduct is influential in shaping the lives of young students. This high standard was noted by the Supreme Court of Pennsylvania:

> It has always been the recognized duty of the teacher to conduct himself in such a way as to command the respect and good will of the community, though one result of the choice of a teacher's vocation may be to deprive him of the same freedom of action enjoyed by persons in other vocations. Educators have always regarded the example set by the teacher as of great importance. . . .[116]

Sexually related conduct *per se* between a teacher and student has consistently been held to constitute sufficient cause for dismissal.[117] The Supreme Court of Colorado stated that when a teacher engages in sexually provocative or exploitative conduct with students, "a strong presumption of unfitness arises against the teacher."[118] Similarly, a Washington appeals court found that a male teacher's sexual relationship with a minor student justified dismissal.[119] The court declined to hold that an adverse effect on fitness to teach must be shown. Rather, the court concluded that when a teacher and a minor student are involved, the board may reasonably decide that such conduct is harmful to the school district. A Michigan appellate court also held that school officials were not required to show that a female teacher's relationship with a male student had an adverse affect on the school or students; discharge was supported by the very existence of the unprofessional relationship.[120] An Illinois appellate court, however, noted that damage to the students, faculty, or the school must be shown; the fondling of third-grade female students by a male teacher presented such damage.[121]

Faller v. Ill. B. of E.

Teachers discharged for sexually related conduct have challenged the statutory grounds of "immorality" or "immoral conduct" as impermissibly vague. An Alabama teacher, dismissed for sexual advances toward female students, asserted that the term "immorality" did not adequately warn a teacher as to what behavior would constitute an offense. The court acknowledged the lack of clarity but rejected the teacher's contention, reasoning that his behavior fell "squarely within the hard core of the statute's proscriptions."[122] The court noted that the teacher should have been aware that his conduct was improper, and the claim of vagueness or overbreadth could not invalidate his dismissal. A Missouri federal district court conceded that the term "immoral conduct" is abstract, but, when construed in the overall statutory scheme, can be precisely defined as any conduct rendering a teacher unfit to teach.[123] The Supreme Court of Missouri concurred and upheld a teacher's dismissal for sexual harassment of the only female member of his class and for permitting male students also to harass her.[124]

In addition to sexual improprieties with students, which clearly are grounds for dismissal, other conduct that sets a bad example for students may be considered immoral under the "role model" standard. Recently, however, courts have become more restrictive in construing immoral conduct and have required that school officials show that misconduct has an adverse impact on fitness to teach. Courts have recognized that allowing dismissal merely upon a showing of immoral behavior without consideration of the nexus between the conduct and fitness to teach would be an unwarranted intrusion upon a teacher's right to privacy.[125]

Constitutional privacy rights may protect a teacher's sexual conduct outside school, but the teacher does not have the freedom to select any desired lifestyle if there is a potential for adverse impact on students. An Eighth Circuit Court of Appeals decision exemplifies the judiciary's reasoning in circumscribing the teacher's freedom outside the classroom.[126] In this case, an unmarried teacher was living with a male friend in a mobile home in close proximity to the school. School officials gave her several opportunities to alter her living arrangements, but she declined, claiming that this demand violated her rights to privacy and free association. In upholding the teacher's dismissal, the appellate court found that the conduct offended community mores and had an adverse effect on students. A strong connection was established between the teacher's actions and her classroom effectiveness. In contrast, a Florida appellate court found that school officials had not produced evidence to show that an off-campus sexual relationship between a teacher and an adult of the opposite sex adversely affected the teacher's ability to teach.[127]

Community disapproval of a teacher's sexual conduct outside of school is not sufficient to justify termination of employment. An Oregon court noted that "no amount of public opposition" can override an individual's tenure rights if statutory grounds for dismissal are not met.[128] In a Nebraska case, a middle-aged divorced teacher was occasionally visited by friends of her son. Because of the lack of motel accommodations, these guests stayed in her apartment. One young man, who was a frequent visitor, spent one week with the teacher while attending classes to complete college course requirements. Following his visit, the teacher was notified that her contract would not be renewed. The Eighth Circuit Court of Appeals, rejecting the board's assertion that the teacher's behavior exhibited a "strong potential for sexual misconduct," found the dismissal to be arbitrary and capricious.[129]

School boards have attempted to use the ground of immorality as the basis for dismissing unwed, pregnant employees. Whether such a pregnancy is sufficient to justify termination depends on the resulting harm to students, other teachers, and the school itself.[130] If an adverse impact can be demonstrated, adequate cause for dismissal can be established.[131] Most courts, however, have invalidated dismissals based on a teacher's unwed, pregnant status. In an Alabama case, an unmarried, pregnant teacher was reinstated when the board failed to establish a connection between her condition and her fitness to teach.[132] The New Mexico Supreme Court held that a school board's decision to dismiss an unwed, pregnant teacher was arbitrary and unreasonable considering that (1) at the time of dismissal five other unwed mothers were teaching in the school system, and (2) the teacher had been rated above average in performance, recommended for reemployment by the principal, and supported by the community for continued employment.[133] As discussed in Chapter 8, several courts have found that dismissals of unwed, pregnant teachers abridge the fourteenth amendment.

The issue of teacher homosexuality has been the focus of a number of controversial dismissal cases. While these cases often have raised constitutional issues related to freedom of expression and privacy, courts also have confronted the question of whether homosexuality *per se* is evidence of unfitness to teach or whether it must be shown that this lifestyle impairs teaching effectiveness. Teachers, like other citizens, can be prosecuted for violating antisodomy laws;[134] diverse opinions, however, have been rendered by courts regarding the status of homosexual teachers when criminal charges are not involved. According to the Supreme Court of California, immoral or unprofessional conduct or moral turpitude must be related to unfitness to teach to justify termination.[135] Consequently, the school board does not possess the right to dismiss an employee simply because it does not approve of a particular private lifestyle. In a case where a male teacher had been involved in a one-week relationship with another male, the California court enumerated the following criteria for evaluating the fitness of a teacher.

> The board may consider such matters as the likelihood that the conduct may have adversely affected students or fellow teachers, the degree of such adversity anticipated, the proximity or remoteness in time of the conduct, the type of teaching certificate held by the party involved, the extenuating or aggravating circumstances, if any, surrounding the conduct, . . . the likelihood of the recurrence of the questioned conduct, and the extent to which disciplinary action may inflict an adverse impact or chilling effect upon the constitutional rights of the teacher involved or other teachers.[136]

The particular circumstances of a case are important in determining whether a teacher can be dismissed for homosexual conduct. Two California decisions are illustrative. In the first case, a teacher's certificate was revoked for immoral conduct after he made sexual advances to a plain-clothes police officer on a public beach.[137] Upholding the revocation, an appellate court noted that the teacher had a history of homosexual behavior which justified barring him from contact with students. In contrast, the state supreme court overturned the dismissal of a teacher who was charged with immoral conduct for making sexual advances to a police officer in a public restroom.[138] Evidence indicated that this was an isolated incident, posed no threat to students, and did not attract public attention.

Although the California decisions suggest that evidence of impaired teaching effectiveness must accompany a teacher's dismissal for homosexuality, not all courts have agreed. In 1977 the Washington Supreme Court upheld a teacher's dismissal for immorality after he admitted his homosexuality to a school administrator.[139] The board's dismissal action was based entirely on the fact that the teacher was homosexual; immoral conduct was not alleged. The Washington high court concluded that mere knowledge of the teacher's homosexuality was sufficient to establish an impairment of teaching effectiveness, and the United States Supreme Court declined to review the case.

Many dismissals for immorality involve sexual conduct, but immorality is broader in meaning and scope. As one court noted, it covers "conduct which is hostile to the welfare of the school community."[140] Such hostile conduct has included, among other things, dishonest acts, criminal conduct, and drug-related conduct. The range of misconduct resulting in charges of immorality can be seen in the cases noted below.

The Supreme Court of Nebraska found a teacher's disparaging statements in a classroom that subjected African-American students to humiliation and public ridicule to be immoral.[141] The court considered it immoral for the teacher to teach students by example that it is proper to engage in such conduct. A Pennsylvania court found a teacher's reference to a student as a "slut" and "prostitute" in the presence of other students also to be immoral. The court noted that "such statements are crude and ill-advised when used by a teacher in a public school environment."[142]

State laws often stipulate that engaging in criminal conduct constitutes immorality. For example, Alaska statutes define immorality as "an act which, under the laws of the state, constitutes a crime involving moral turpitude."[143] The state high court held that a conviction for unlawfully diverting electricity was such a crime. Under Georgia law, conviction for submitting false tax documents was sufficient grounds to dismiss a principal for moral turpitude.[144] Other dishonest conduct found to substantiate charges of immorality has included misrepresenting absences from school as illness when in fact the teacher attended a conference unrelated to work,[145] taking school property without permission (return of the property did not mitigate the charge),[146] and instructing a student to lie and cheat during a wrestling tournament.[147] In the absence of a statutory specification, however, the West Virginia Supreme Court held that a school board could not conclude that a conviction for a misdemeanor was *per se* immoral conduct.[148] The Washington high court held that even a conviction for grand larceny, standing alone, was generally not sufficient cause for dismissal; evidence that a teacher pled *nolo contendere* to a charge of shoplifting did not establish that the teacher was unfit to teach.[149]

INSUBORDINATION

Insubordination, another frequently cited cause for dismissal, is generally defined as the willful disregard of or refusal to obey school regulations and official orders. Teachers can be dismissed for violation of administrative regulations and policies even though classroom performance is satisfactory; school officials are not required to establish a relationship between the conduct and fitness to teach.[150]

With the plethora of regulations enacted by school districts, wide diversity is found in types of behavior adjudicated as insubordination. Dismissals based on insubordination have been upheld in cases involving refusal to abide by specific school directives, unwillingness to cooperate with superiors, unauthorized absences, and numerous other actions. Since conduct is measured against the existence of a rule or policy, a school board may more readily document insubordination than most other legal causes for dismissal.

Many state laws and court decisions require that acts be "willful and persistent" to be considered insubordinate. In general, a single incident, unless severe or substantial, is inadequate for dismissal action.[151] A Minnesota teacher's continuous refusal to complete program evaluation forms resulted in insubordination charges. The Minnesota Supreme Court, upholding the dismissal, defined insubordination as "constant or continuing intentional refusal to obey a direct or implied order, reasonable in nature, and given by and with proper authority."[152] The Wyoming Supreme Court presented an opposing view, finding that repeated refusals to obey orders were not required to justify dismissal.[153] The court concluded that termination of a teacher who refused a split assignment between two schools was proper; repeated refusals were unnecessary if other elements of insubordination were present, such as reasonableness of the order and direct refusal to obey. Similarly upheld were a Kansas teacher's dismissal for a one-time refusal to obey the superintendent's direct order to supervise recess,[154] a Missouri teacher's termination after she refused to teach an assigned course,[155] and a Colorado teacher's dismissal for using abusive and offensive language toward a student after being directed not to use profanity when dealing with students.[156]

Numerous dismissal cases involving insubordination have resulted from the inappropriate use of corporal punishment. Corporal punishment is not limited to actions involving "paddlings" but is defined broadly to include all types of physical punishments, such as slapping, pinching, and kicking.[157] If the school board has prohibited corporal punishment or prescribed procedures for its administration, teachers must strictly adhere to board requirements. Dismissal of an Illinois teacher was upheld because he failed to follow procedures specifying that a teacher must explain the reasons for the punishment to the child and must have another adult present while administering corporal punishment.[158] Repeatedly failing to follow official directives in administering corporal punishment resulted in the termination of a Texas teacher.[159] In contrast to the preceding cases, the Colorado Supreme Court invalidated a teacher's dismissal for insubordination in connection with excessive use of corporal punishment because the school board had not adopted regulations pertaining to this disciplinary technique.[160] A Pennsylvania court also found that a single infraction of a policy prohibiting corporal punishment was neither severe nor willful and persistent to warrant dismissal.[161]

Insubordination charges often have resulted from conflicts arising from the administrator–teacher relationship. For example, a Florida teacher's discharge was upheld for refusal to meet with her principal to discuss concerns about her leaving her class unattended.[162] An Arizona teacher's continuing refusal to meet with his principal for the purpose of improving teaching skills supported dismissal.[163] The dismissal of an Arkansas teacher who engaged in frequent belligerent "verbal fights" with his principal was upheld.[164] However, a Tennessee teacher, who was unable to work because of stress, fear, and intimidation resulting from events in the school, could not be terminated for insubordination when she failed to return to work as directed by the superintendent.[165]

Teachers cannot ignore reasonable directives and policies of administrators or school boards. The Fifth Circuit Appellate Court found that insubordination was established because a teacher allowed boycotting students to attend classes in violation of school policy and refused to attend two football games, as all male teachers were required to do.[166] The dismissal of an Iowa teacher was supported by a preponderance of evidence that he "persistently violated, ignored and demonstrated a nonsupportive attitude toward administrative policies, procedures, rules and directives."[167] Violations included numerous incidents (misuse of copying machine, failure to notify administrators that he would be absent, creation of schedule conflicts) that showed a persistent pattern of insubordination. Other instances of insubordination justifying dismissal have included violating a school directive to retain final examination papers, taking personal leave without permission, abusing sick leave, refusal to perform hall supervision duties, failure to follow directives designed to improve instruction, refusal to sign an attachment to a contract, refusal to cease residing with a sixteen-year-old student, failure to acquire board approval of supplementary materials used in the classroom, and refusal to cease religious exercises in the classroom.[168] The key determinant is whether the teacher has persisted in disobeying a *reasonable* school policy or directive.

NEGLECT OF DUTY

Neglect of duty arises when a teacher fails to carry out assigned duties. This may involve an intentional omission or may result from ineffectual performance. In a Colorado case, neglect of duty was found when a teacher permitted high school cheerleaders to drink beer in a hotel room following a basketball tournament.[169] A Louisiana appeals court upheld a teacher's discharge for willful neglect of duty after she locked three preschool children with disabilities in a room while attending to chores unrelated to her classroom.[170] The Supreme Court of North Carolina found that a teacher's habitual use of alcohol during the school day supported dismissal.[171] Neglect of duty also was found when a teacher persistently refused to update students' cumulative files for an accreditation review and was unable to keep her students inside the classroom.[172]

The United States Supreme Court upheld the dismissal of an Oklahoma teacher for "willful neglect of duty" in failing to comply with the school board's continuing education requirement.[173] For a period of time, lack of compliance was dealt with through denial of salary increases. Upon enactment of a state law requiring salary increases for all teachers, the board notified teachers that noncompliance with the requirement would result in termination. Affirming the board's action, the Supreme Court found the sanction of dismissal to be rationally related to the board's objective of improving its teaching force through continuing education requirements.

The Supreme Court of Nebraska addressed what constitutes "just cause" in a dismissal for neglect of duty where a teacher had failed on several occasions to perform certain duties and at other times had not performed duties competently.[174] Evidence revealed that the teacher had not violated any administrative orders or school laws, had received good evaluations, and had been recommended for retention by the administrators. The court concluded that the facts did not support just cause for dismissal. The court cautioned that in evaluating a teacher's performance, neglect of duty is not measured "against a standard of perfection, but, instead, must be measured against the standard required of others performing the same or similar duties."[175] It was not demonstrated that the teacher's performance was below that expected of other teachers in similar positions.

The West Virginia Supreme Court held that missing one parent–teacher conference did not justify dismissal for neglect of duty.[176] In a later case, the same court also held that a teacher's unintentional distribution of pornographic cartoons to eighth-grade students was insufficient to establish neglect of duty.[177] Having failed to review the materials, the teacher was unaware of their objectionable content. Similarly, a Georgia appellate court held that a teacher's showing of an R-rated film may have been negligent but did not warrant dismissal for willful neglect of duty.[178] A Louisiana appellate court also concluded that a teacher's removal of a gun from his car when physically attacked by a student did not warrant dismissal for neglect of duty.[179]

UNPROFESSIONAL CONDUCT

A number of states identify either "unprofessional conduct" or "conduct unbecoming" a teacher as cause for dismissal. A teacher's activities both inside and outside of school can be used to substantiate this charge. Dismissals for unprofessional conduct, neglect of duty, and unfitness to teach often are based on quite similar facts. For instance, a New York teacher was dismissed for unprofessional conduct for being absent after having been denied permission for a leave, whereas a Colorado teacher in a similar situation was charged with neglect of duty.[180] A Maine school board classified a teacher's unauthorized absences as unfitness to teach.[181] It must be remembered that causes for dismissal are identified in state statutes, but are defined through case law and various administrative rulings in individual states. Consequently, across states there are wide variances in the meaning of the same legal cause.

Courts have upheld dismissal for unprofessional conduct based on a number of grounds, such as conviction for criminally negligent homicide,[182] serving liquor to two female students,[183] permitting students to kick or hit each other for violations of classroom rules,[184] being indicted for possession of cocaine with intent to distribute,[185] smoking marijuana with two fifteen-year-old students in the teacher's apartment,[186] showing a sexually explicit film to a classroom of adolescents without previewing it,[187] and engaging in public sexually suggestive behavior with a mannequin.[188] As with dismissals based on incompetency, courts often require prior warning that the behavior may result in dismissal.[189]

UNFITNESS TO TEACH

Unfitness to teach covers a wide array of teacher behavior.[190] An Illinois appellate court, defining unfitness as "conduct detrimental to the operation of the school," held that improper sexual conduct toward students constituted unfitness.[191] A New Jersey court addressed the question of incapacity as unfitness, upholding the dismissal of a male teacher who underwent a sex change operation. The court concluded that dismissal was appropriate because the teacher's continued presence could potentially result in emotional harm to students.[192] The judiciary has recognized that a determination of fitness or capacity may extend beyond actual classroom performance.

Two decisions from the Supreme Court of Maine dealt with dismissals for one-time incidents that allegedly affected fitness to teach. In the first case, a teacher who was also a licensed gunsmith inadvertently brought a gun and ammunition to school in his jacket. The gun was stolen from his room but later returned. The school board initiated dismissal proceedings for "grave lack of judgment." Overturning the board action, the court held that one isolated incident does not represent such "moral impropriety, professional incompetence, or unsuitability" to constitute unfitness to teach.[193] The second case involved a teacher striking a student across the face with his hand during a basketball game.[194] The blow was severe, causing the loss of one tooth, damage to another, and extensive bruises. Here the court concluded that the single incident was sufficient to justify dismissal because of its direct impact on the teacher's effectiveness as a coach. Dismissals for one-time incidents, regardless of the grounds, are always scrutinized closely by courts.

Mental, emotional, or physical disorders can constitute unfitness or incapacity to teach.[195] To establish incapacity, health conditions must be severe and interfere with a teacher's ability to perform in the classroom.[196] It should be noted, however, that dismissals based on physical disabilities can, under certain circumstances, impair federally protected rights of disabled employees. As discussed in Chapter 9, the United States Supreme Court held that a teacher with tuberculosis was "handicapped" under federal antidiscrimination provisions and thus could not be summarily dismissed because of the disease.[197]

OTHER GOOD AND JUST CAUSE

Not unexpectedly, "other good and just cause" as a ground for dismissal often has been challenged as vague and overbroad. Courts have been faced with the task of determining whether the phrase's meaning is limited to the specific grounds enumerated in the statute or whether it is a separate, expanded cause. An Indiana appellate court interpreted it as permitting termination for reasons other than those specified in the tenure law, if evidence indicated that the board's decision was based on "good cause."[198] As such, dismissal of a teacher convicted of a misdemeanor was upheld even though the teacher had no prior indication that such conduct was sufficient cause. Similarly, an Ohio appellate court concluded that "other good and just cause" was separate and distinct from other causes listed in the statute identifying reasons for terminating tenured teachers' contracts; a teacher's refusal to report to work during a labor dispute was found to establish "other good and just cause" justifying discharge.[199]

The Second Circuit Court of Appeals found "other due and sufficient cause" as a ground for dismissal to be "appropriate in an area such as discipline of teachers, where a myriad of uncontemplated situations may arise and it is not reasonable to require a legislature to elucidate in advance every act that requires sanction."[200] The court declined to rule on the vagueness of "other due and sufficient cause," but rather noted that courts generally assess the teacher's conduct in relation to the statutory grounds for dismissal. That is, if the specific behavior is sufficiently related to the causes specified in state law, it is assumed that the teacher should have reasonably known that the conduct was improper. In this case, where a teacher repeatedly humiliated and harassed students (and school administrators had discussed the problem with him), the court concluded that the teacher was aware of the impropriety of his conduct.

REDUCTION IN FORCE

In addition to dismissal for causes related to teacher performance and fitness, legislation generally permits the release of teachers for reasons related to declining enrollment, financial exigency, and school district consolidation. While most state statutes provide for such terminations, a number of states also have adopted legislation that specifies the basis for selection of released teachers, procedures to be followed, and provisions for reinstatement. These terminations, characterized as "reductions in force" (RIF), also may be governed by board policies and negotiated bargaining agreements.

Unlike other termination cases, the burden of proof is shouldered by the employee challenging a RIF decision. There is a presumption that the board has acted in good faith with permissible motives. Legal controversies in this area usually involve questions related to the necessity for the reductions, board compliance with mandated procedures, and possible subterfuge for impermissible termination (such as denial of constitutional rights or subversion of tenure rights).

If statutory or contractual restrictions exist for teacher layoffs, there must be substantial compliance with the provisions. One of the provisions most frequently included is a method for selecting teachers for release. In general, reductions are based on seniority, and a tenured teacher must be retained rather than a nontenured teacher if both are qualified to fill the same position. Oregon statutes require that both certification and seniority be considered; a teacher lacking certification would not be permitted to teach while a permanent teacher with proper certification, but less seniority, was dismissed.[201] Along with seniority, merit rating systems often are included in the determination of reductions. School districts in Pennsylvania use a combination of ratings and seniority; ratings are the primary determinant unless no substantial difference exists in ratings, and then seniority becomes the basis for layoff.[202] The Nebraska Supreme Court concluded that a school board could include noneducational factors such as contribution to the school activity program in selecting teachers for release.[203] Guidelines or criteria established by state or local education agencies must be applied in a uniform and nondiscriminatory manner.

While the fourteenth amendment requires minimal procedural protections in dismissals for cause, courts have not clearly defined the due process requirements for RIF. Thus, procedural rights of employees vary according to interpretations of state law, bargaining agreements, and board policy. A Michigan court found no need for a hearing over staff reductions, because there were no charges to refute.[204] The court emphasized that the law protected the released teacher, who, subject to qualifications, was entitled to the next vacancy. In contrast, a Pennsylvania commonwealth court held that a hearing must be provided to assure the teacher (1) that termination is for reasons specified by law, and (2) that the board followed the correct statutory procedures in selecting the teacher for discharge.[205]

Preference in reemployment often is given to the teacher who is released because of unavoidable staff reductions. A teacher, however, must be certified for the available position. A French teacher whose tenure was in the secondary academic area was found to be unqualified to teach English or science because of lack of certification in those subjects.[206] Although statutes often require that a teacher be appointed to the first vacancy for which certified and qualified, courts have held that reappointment is still at the board's discretion. A Michigan appeals court recognized that a teacher could be certified in an area, but in the opinion of the board, not necessarily qualified.[207] Additionally, a board is generally not obligated to realign or rearrange teaching assignments to create a position for a released teacher.[208]

REMEDIES FOR WRONGFUL TERMINATIONS

An important element of due process is the right to appeal a school board's adverse employment decision to a higher authority, such as a court of law. The cases cited in this chapter illustrate the variety of issues appealed to courts and the remedies available for wrongful employment decisions. Several points are important to note regarding judicial review. First, courts generally will not interject themselves into school board review proceedings until all aspects of the administrative appeal process have been exhausted. A teacher alleging denial of due process must first use established administrative procedures prior to resorting to judicial review. Second, in reviewing teacher termination actions, the judiciary does not substitute its judgment for that of the school board. Rather, courts examine cases to determine if the school board failed to accord the teacher procedural protections, impaired substantive constitutional rights, or was arbitrary and capricious in its decision. If it is found that protected rights have been violated, courts attempt to redress the wrong by framing an appropriate remedy.

Depending on employment status, judicial remedies for the violation of employment rights may include reinstatement with back pay, compensatory and punitive damages, and attorneys' fees. The specific nature of the award depends on individual state statutory provisions and the discretion of courts. State laws often identify damages that may be recovered or place limitations on types of awards. Unless state provisions restrict specific remedies, courts have broad discretionary power to formulate equitable settlements.

REINSTATEMENT

Whether or not a court orders reinstatement as a remedy for school board action depends on the protected interests involved and the discretion of the court, unless specific provision for reinstatement is specified in state law. If a tenured teacher is unjustly dismissed, the property interest gives rise to an expectation of reemployment; reinstatement in such instances is usually the appropriate remedy. However, a nontenured teacher, wrongfully dismissed during the contract period, is normally entitled only to damages, not reinstatement.

A valid property or liberty claim entitles a teacher to procedural due process, but the teacher can still be dismissed for cause after proper procedures have been followed. However, if a teacher is terminated without proper procedures and can establish that the action is not justified, reinstatement will be ordered.[209] If proven that the actual reason for the nonrenewal of a teacher's contract is retaliation for the exercise of constitutional rights (e.g., protected speech), reinstatement would be warranted, although substantiation of such a claim is difficult.[210]

The failure to comply with statutory requirements in nonrenewals and dismissals may result in reinstatement. When statutory dates are specified for notice of nonrenewal, failure to strictly comply with the deadline provides grounds for reinstatement of the teacher. Courts may interpret this as continued employment for an additional year[211] or reinstatement with tenure if nonrenewal occurs at the end of the probationary period.[212]

In contrast to the remedy for lack of proper notice, the remedy for failure to provide an appropriate hearing is generally a remand for a hearing, not reinstatement.[213]

DAMAGES

As discussed in Chapter 8, judicial decisions in recent years have increased the potential for teachers to recover monetary damages when their constitutional rights, such as freedom of speech, are violated. Under Section 1983 of the Civil Rights Act of 1871, both school officials and school boards can be liable for damages for violations of federally protected rights. Individual school officials may claim qualified immunity for actions taken in "good faith"; however, disregard of constitutionally protected rights or impermissible motivation may demonstrate a lack of good faith. While *individuals* possess a certain degree of immunity, *school boards* are not protected against liability for the impairment of federal rights, even if their members or employees have acted in good faith. The Supreme Court's interpretations of Section 1983 have significantly expanded the likelihood of teachers recovering damages from school systems;[214] therefore, teachers increasingly are turning to federal courts for restitution.

The United States Supreme Court has held that deprivation of protected rights requires only an award of nominal damages (not to exceed one dollar) unless actual injury is shown.[215] Accordingly, the Eighth Circuit Court of Appeals held that an award of one dollar was appropriate for the denial of procedural rights when the evidence indicated an individual would have been terminated even if procedural due process had been followed.[216] However, significant monetary damages may be awarded for a wrongful termination if a teacher is able to demonstrate substantial losses.

A Delaware federal district court decision cited earlier illustrates the range of factors a court may consider in ordering relief.[217] The failure of the school board to provide procedural protection to a principal who had been assured of contract renewal if his performance was satisfactory resulted in a judgment against the board and its members. The court held that the injured individual should be compensated for lost salary, out-of-pocket expenses, physical and mental stress, and injury to reputation in the amount of $51,000. In addition to the compensatory damages to repay the principal for harm inflicted by the board, the court found that punitive damages against board members in the amount of $7,750 were appropriate.[218] The sole purpose of punitive awards is to deter school officials and others from committing similar offenses in the future.[219]

The following cases illustrate the diverse circumstances that have resulted in awards of damages. An Illinois school board was required to pay a teacher $750,000 in compensatory damages for wrongfully terminating her for an out-of-wedlock pregnancy.[220] Back pay for five years and all other emoluments and fringe benefits were awarded in the wrongful dismissal of a Louisiana teacher for displaying a gun to defend himself when physically attacked by a student.[221] Denial of a continuing contract to a Florida teacher for her relationship with a member of the opposite sex entitled the teacher to reimbursement for "any economic loss sustained," including legal expenses.[222] A Tennessee teacher who was unable to work because of stress and intimidation as a direct result of the wrongful action of a school board was restored to all rightful privileges, benefits, and perquisites.[223] The termination of a tenured New York teacher without due process merited consideration of back pay and other employment benefits but not damages for emotional distress and mental anguish because only subjective evidence of such injury was presented.[224] However, a North Carolina teacher received $78,000 in damages based on mental distress evidenced by depression and insomnia following procedural violations in his termination.[225]

Given the success teachers have had in securing damages to compensate for injuries associated with wrongful terminations, school officials should ensure that dismissals or other disciplinary actions are based on legitimate reasons and accompanied by appropriate procedural safeguards. Courts, however, have not awarded damages unless the evidence shows that a teacher has suffered actual injury. As the Supreme Court has noted, compensatory damages are intended to provide full compensation for the loss or injury suffered but are not to be based simply on a jury's perception of the value of the constitutional rights impaired.[226]

ATTORNEYS' FEES

Attorneys' fees are not automatically granted to the teacher who prevails in a lawsuit, but are generally dependent on statutory authorization.[227] At the federal level, the Civil Rights Attorneys' Fees Award Act gives federal courts discretion to award fees in civil rights suits.[228] In congressional debate concerning attorneys' fees, it was stated that "private citizens must be given not only the right to go to court, but also the legal resources. If the citizen does not have the resources his day in court is denied him."[229]

To receive attorneys' fees the teacher must be the prevailing party; that is, damages or some form of equitable relief must be granted to the teacher. The Supreme Court has held that a prevailing party is one who is successful in achieving some benefit on any significant issue in the case, but not necessarily the primary issue. At a minimum, the Court ruled that "the plaintiff must be able to point to a resolution of the dispute which changes the legal relationship between itself and the defendant."[230]

Because Section 1983 does not require exhaustion of state administrative proceedings before initiating litigation, the Supreme Court has denied the award of attorneys' fees for school board administrative proceedings conducted prior to filing a federal suit. Unlike Title VII's explicit requirement that individuals must pursue administrative remedies, plaintiffs can bring a Section 1983 claim directly to a federal court. In a wrongful termination case, a Tennessee teacher was awarded attorneys' fees as a prevailing litigant for the time spent on the judicial proceedings but was unsuccessful in persuading the Supreme Court that the local administrative proceedings were part of the preparation for court action.[231]

Although it has been established that the plaintiff who prevails in a civil rights suit may, at the court's discretion, be entitled to attorneys' fees, the same standard is not applied to defendants. When a plaintiff teacher is awarded attorneys' fees, the assessment is against a party who has violated a federal law. Different criteria must be applied when a prevailing defendant seeks attorneys' fees. The Supreme Court has held that such fees cannot be imposed on a plaintiff unless the claim was "frivolous, unreasonable, or groundless."[232] While awards of damages to prevailing defendants have not been common, in some situations such awards have been made to deter groundless lawsuits.[233]

CONCLUSION

Employment security is an area of general concern among teachers. Through state laws and the Federal Constitution, extensive safeguards are provided to prevent school officials' arbitrary or capricious actions. Most states have adopted tenure laws that precisely delineate teachers' employment rights in termination proceedings. Additionally, in the absence of specific state guarantees, the fourteenth amendment ensures that teachers will be afforded procedural due process when property or liberty interests are implicated. Legal decisions interpreting both state and federal rights in dismissal actions have established broad guidelines as to when due process is required, the types of procedures that must be provided, and the legitimate causes required to substantiate dismissal action. Generalizations applicable to teacher employment termination are enumerated below.

1. A teacher is entitled to procedural due process if dismissal impairs a property or liberty interest.
2. Tenure status, defined by state law, confers upon teachers a property interest in continued employment; tenured teachers can be dismissed only for cause.
3. Courts generally have held that probationary employment does not involve a property interest, except within the contract period.
4. A probationary teacher may establish a liberty interest, and thus entitlement to a hearing, if nonrenewal imposes a stigma, forecloses opportunities for future employment, or implicates constitutional rights.

5. When a liberty or property interest is implicated, the fourteenth amendment requires that a teacher be notified of charges and provided with an opportunity for a hearing that includes representation by counsel, examination and cross-examination of witnesses, and a record of the proceedings; however, formal trial procedures are not required.

6. An adequate notice of dismissal must adhere to statutory deadlines, follow designated form, allow the teacher time to prepare for a hearing, and specify charges.

7. The school board is considered an impartial hearing tribunal unless bias of its members can be clearly established.

8. The school board bears the burden of proof to introduce sufficient evidence to support a teacher's dismissal.

9. Causes for dismissal vary widely among the states, but usually include such grounds as incompetency, neglect of duty, immorality, insubordination, unprofessional conduct, and other good and just cause.

10. Incompetency is generally defined in relation to classroom performance—classroom management, teaching methods, grading, pupil–teacher relationships, and general attitude.

11. Immoral conduct, as the basis for dismissal, includes dishonest acts, improper sexual conduct, criminal acts, drug-related conduct, and other improprieties that have a negative impact on the teacher's effectiveness in the school system.

12. Dismissal for insubordination is based on a teacher's refusal to follow school regulations and policies.

13. Declining enrollment and financial exigencies constitute adequate cause for dismissing tenured teachers.

14. An improper dismissal can result in an award of damages, reinstatement, and/or attorneys' fees.

ENDNOTES

1. Adler v. Board of Educ. of City of New York, 342 U.S. 485, 493 (1952).
2. *See* Nelda Cambron-McCabe, "Procedural Due Process," in *Legal Issues in Public Employment,* Joseph Beckham and Perry Zirkel, eds. (Bloomington, IN: Phi Delta Kappa, 1983). As noted in Chapter 1, the fourteenth amendment restricts state, in contrast to private, action. For employees in a private school to assert a constitutional right to due process in connection with termination proceedings, they must establish that the private school is sufficiently involved in state activity to trigger the limitations imposed by the fourteenth amendment. The Supreme Court has recognized that mere regulation by the state may be insufficient to evoke constitutional protections in private school personnel matters. The Court rejected a suit for damages against a private school for

allegedly unconstitutional dismissals, reasoning that there was no "symbiotic relationship" between the private school and the state, Rendell Baker v. Kohn, 457 U.S. 830 (1982). Although the private school received some public funds and had to comply with a variety of governmental regulations, the Court reasoned that the school was not fundamentally different from other private contractors performing services for the state. It is not impossible to establish that a private school is sufficiently entwined with the state to constitute "state action"; however, such determinations must be made on a case-by-case basis.

3. *See* Board of Regents of State Colleges v. Roth, 408 U.S. 564 (1972).

4. *See* Goodrich v. Newport News School Bd., 743 F.2d 225 (4th Cir. 1984); Atencio v. Board of Educ. of Penasco Indep. School Dist. No. 4, 658 F.2d 774 (10th Cir. 1981).

5. *See, e.g.,* Provoda v. Maxwell, 808 P.2d 28 (N.M. 1991); Blum v. Quinones, 526 N.Y.S.2d 611 (N.Y. App. Div. 1988).

6. *See* Chapter 8 for a discussion of teachers' constitutional rights.

7. This general rule of actual receipt of notice would not apply, of course, if a statutory provision indicated other means of satisfying the deadline, such as requiring the notice to be postmarked by a certain date. *See, e.g.,* Andrews v. Howard, 291 S.E.2d 541 (Ga. 1982). *See also* Martinez v. Anchorage School Dist., 699 P.2d 330 (Alaska 1985) (a notice picked up by the teacher after the statutory deadline but on the day a registered letter probably would have arrived met the statutory intent).

8. State *ex rel.* Peake v. Board of Educ. of South Point Local School Dist., 339 N.E.2d 249 (Ohio 1975). *See also* School Dist. RE-11J, Alamosa County v. Norwood, 644 P.2d 13 (Colo. 1982).

9. *See, e.g.,* Stollenwerck v. Talladega County Bd. of Educ., 420 So. 2d 21 (Ala. 1982); Ledbetter v. School Dist. No. 8, El Paso County, 428 P.2d 912 (Colo. 1967).

10. *See, e.g.,* Francu v. Windham Exempted Village School Dist., 496 N.E.2d 902 (Ohio 1986); Lipka v. Brown City Community Schools, 271 N.W.2d 771 (Mich. 1978).

11. *See, e.g.,* Perkins v. Board of Directors of School Admin. Dist. No. 13, 686 F.2d 49 (1st Cir. 1982).

12. *See, e.g.,* Birgenheier v. Trustees, Yellowstone County School Dist. No. 2, 791 P.2d 1388 (Mont. 1990) (an explanation of reasons must be provided; it is inadequate to state simply that one year contract has expired); Bridger Educ. Ass'n v. Board of Trustees, 678 P.2d 659 (Mont. 1984) (school board's proffered reason that it "could find a better teacher" was inadequate to meet the statutory requirement that teachers be given reasons for nonrenewal); Gibson v. Board of Educ. of Jackson County, 805 S.W.2d 673, 674 (Ky. Ct. App. 1991) (teacher must be furnished with true grounds for nonrenewal action to meet the statutory requirement that a school board must provide "a written statement containing the specific, detailed and complete statement of grounds").

13. Wheeler v. Yuma School Dist. No. One of Yuma County, 750 P.2d 860 (Ariz. 1988). *See also* Wren v. McDowell County Bd. of Educ., 327 S.E.2d 464 (W. Va. 1985) (state board of education procedures required opportunity for probationary teachers to correct teaching inadequacies).

14. *See, e.g.,* Struthers City Schools Bd. of Educ. v. Struthers Educ. Ass'n, 453 N.E.2d 613 (Ohio 1983); Maxwell v. Southside School Dist., 618 S.W.2d 148 (Ark. 1981).

15. 408 U.S. 564 (1972).
16. 408 U.S. 593 (1972).
17. Roth, 408 U.S. at 575.
18. *Id.* at 577. *See also* Hemmige v. Chicago Pub. Schools, 786 F.2d 280 (7th Cir. 1986) (one-year temporary teaching certificate did not establish a property interest in continued employment).
19. 408 U.S. 593 (1972).
20. *Id.* at 600.
21. Mt. Healthy City School Dist. Bd. of Educ. v. Doyle, 429 U.S. 274 (1977). *See* text with note 3, Chapter 8 for a discussion of the first amendment issue in this case.
22. *See* Board of Regents of State Colleges v. Roth, 408 U.S. 564, 572 (1972).
23. *See, e.g.,* Goudeau v. Independent School Dist. No. 37 of Oklahoma County, Oklahoma, 823 F.2d 1429 (10th Cir. 1987); Hatcher v. Board of Pub. Educ. and Orphanage for Bibb County, 804 F.2d 1546 (11th Cir. 1987); Longarzo v. Anker, 578 F.2d 469 (2d Cir. 1978).
24. Schreffler v. Board of Educ. of Delmar School Dist., 506 F. Supp. 1300 (D. Del. 1981).
25. Vail v. Board of Educ. of Paris Union School Dist. No. 95, 706 F.2d 1435 (7th Cir. 1983), *aff'd by an equally divided court,* 466 U.S. 377 (1984). *See also* Thomas v. Board of Examiners, Chicago Pub. Schools, 866 F.2d 225 (7th Cir. 1988), *cert. denied,* 490 U.S. 1035 (1989) (entitlement to consideration for a promotion does not constitute a property right).
26. Martin v. Unified School Dist. No. 434, Osage County, Kansas, 728 F.2d 453 (10th Cir. 1984); Robertson v. Rogers, 679 F.2d 1090 (4th Cir. 1982).
27. *See, e.g.,* Perkins v. Board of Directors of School Admin. Dist. No. 13, 686 F.2d 49 (1st Cir. 1982); New Castle–Gunning Bedford Educ. Ass'n v. Board of Educ. of New Castle–Gunning Bedford School Dist., 421 F. Supp. 960 (D. Del. 1976); Schaub v. Chamberlain Bd. of Educ., 339 N.W.2d 307 (S.D. 1983). *See also* Wells v. Hico Indep. School Dist., 736 F.2d 243 (5th Cir. 1984), *cert. denied,* 473 U.S. 901 (1985) (grievance policy and procedures did not create a property interest).
28. *See, e.g.,* Schaub v. Chamberlain Bd. of Educ., 339 N.W.2d 307 (S.D. 1983) (a hearing may be available to a nontenured teacher, but the board is not required to speak, produce evidence, or even answer questions at the hearing).
29. *See, e.g.,* Ryan v. Aurora City Bd. of Educ., 540 F.2d 222 (6th Cir. 1976), *cert. denied,* 429 U.S. 1041 (1977).
30. *See, e.g.,* Haimowitz v. University of Nevada, 579 F.2d 526, 528 (9th Cir. 1978).
31. Harris v. Arizona Bd. of Regents, 528 F. Supp. 987 (D. Ariz. 1981).
32. Bishop v. Wood, 426 U.S. 341, 345 (1976).
33. *See* Codd v. Velger, 429 U.S. 624 (1977); Bishop v. Wood, 426 U.S. 341 (1976); Paul v. Davis, 424 U.S. 693 (1976).
34. *See, e.g.,* Thomas v. Smith, 897 F.2d 154 (5th Cir. 1989); Thomas v. Board of Examiners, Chicago Pub. Schools, 866 F.2d 225 (7th Cir. 1988), *cert. denied,* 490 U.S. 1035 (1989); Hardiman v. Jefferson County Bd. of Educ., 709 F.2d 635 (11th Cir. 1983); Moore v. Otero, 557 F.2d 435 (5th Cir. 1977).
35. Moore, *id.* at 438.
36. *See, e.g.,* Lagos v. Modesto City Schools Dist., 843 F.2d 347 (9th Cir. 1988),

cert. denied, 488 U.S. 926 (1988); Diehl v. Albany County School Dist. No. 1, 694 F. Supp. 1534 (D. Wyo. 1988).

37. *See, e.g.,* Hayes v. Phoenix-Talent School Dist. No. 4, 893 F.2d 235 (9th Cir. 1990); Rankin v. Independent School Dist. No. I-3, Noble County, Oklahoma, 876 F.2d 838 (10th Cir. 1989), *cert. denied,* 111 S. Ct. 786 (1991); Brandt v. Board of Cooperative Educ. Services, 845 F.2d 416 (2d Cir. 1988); Noel v. Andrus, 810 F.2d 1388 (5th Cir. 1987).

38. *See, e.g.,* Cato v. Collins, 539 F.2d 656 (8th Cir. 1976).

39. Beitzell v. Jeffrey, 643 F.2d 870, 879 (1st Cir. 1981). *See also* Peterson v. Unified School Dist. No. 418, 724 F. Supp. 829 (D. Kan. 1989).

40. *See* Codd v. Velger, 429 U.S. 624 (1977).

41. Gray v. Union County Intermediate Educ. Dist., 520 F.2d 803, 806 (9th Cir. 1975). *See also* Adams v. School Dist. No. 5 of Jackson County, Oregon, 699 F. Supp. 243 (D. Or. 1988).

42. Ball v. Board of Trustees of Kerrville Indep. School Dist., 584 F.2d 684, 685 (5th Cir. 1978), *cert. denied,* 440 U.S. 972 (1979).

43. Stachura v. Memphis Community School Dist., 763 F.2d 211 (6th Cir. 1985), *rev'd on damages issue,* 477 U.S. 299 (1986).

44. *See* Vanelli v. Reynolds School Dist. No. 7, 667 F.2d 773 (9th Cir. 1982); Dennis v. S & S Consol. Rural High School Dist., 577 F.2d 338 (5th Cir. 1978); Lombard v. Board of Educ. of City of New York, 502 F.2d 631 (2d Cir. 1974), *cert. denied,* 420 U.S. 976 (1975); Bomhoff v. White, 526 F. Supp. 488 (D. Ariz. 1981).

45. *See* Hayes v. Phoenix-Talent School Dist. No. 4, 893 F.2d 235 (9th Cir. 1990); Robertson v. Rogers, 679 F.2d 1090 (4th Cir. 1982); Gray v. Union County Intermediate Educ. Dist., 520 F.2d 803 (9th Cir. 1975); Bomhoff v. White, 526 F. Supp. 488 (D. Ariz. 1981); Harris v. Arizona Bd. of Regents, 528 F. Supp. 987 (D. Ariz. 1981); Blum v. Quinones, 526 N.Y.S.2d 611 (N.Y. App. Div 1988); Bristol, Virginia School Bd. v. Quarles, 366 S.E.2d 82 (Va. 1988).

46. Mathews v. Eldridge, 424 U.S. 319, 335 (1976).

47. Rankin v. Independent School Dist. No. I-3, Noble County, Oklahoma, 876 F.2d 838 (10th Cir. 1989), *cert. denied,* 111 S. Ct. 786 (1991).

48. This chapter focuses on procedural protections required in teacher termina tions. It should be noted, however, that other school board decisions, such a transfers, demotions, or mandatory leaves, may impose similar constraints oi decisionmaking. For example, an Ohio court found that the transfer of a tenured teacher from a regular classroom position to a position as a permanent itinerant substitute violated the teacher's due process rights, Mroczek v. Board of Educ. of Beachwood City School Dist., 400 N.E.2d 1362 (Ohio C.P. 1979). *See also* Dusanek v. Hannon, 677 F.2d 538 (7th Cir. 1982), *cert. denied,* 459 U.S. 1017 (1982).

49. *See* Ray v. Birmingham City Bd. of Educ., 845 F.2d 281 (11th Cir. 1988); Goodrich v. Newport News School Bd., 743 F.2d 225 (4th Cir. 1984). *See also* Levitt v. University of Texas at El Paso, 759 F.2d 1224 (5th Cir. 1985), *cert. denied,* 474 U.S. 1034 (1985) (under certain circumstances, a constitutional deprivation might occur when an omission of state or local procedures results in a denial of the minimal constitutional procedures).

50. The West Virginia high court specified that the notice should include instructions as to where to file a request for a hearing, Duruttya v. Board of Educ. of

County of Mingo, 382 S.E.2d 40 (W. Va. 1989). *See also* Farley v. Board of Educ. of County of Mingo, 365 S.E.2d 816 (W. Va. 1988) (notice of termination received by teachers one to two days prior to hearing date set by school board was not a "meaningful notice" to prepare for a hearing).

51. *See, e.g.,* Hoover v. Wagner Community School Dist. No. 11-4, 342 N.W.2d 226 (S.D. 1984); Lee v. Big Flat Pub. Schools, 658 S.W.2d 389 (Ark. 1983); Andrews v. Howard, 291 S.E.2d 541 (Ga. 1982). *But see* Hoyme v. Board of Educ. ABC Unified School Dist., 165 Cal. Rptr. 737 (Cal. Ct. App. 1980).

52. *See, e.g.,* McDonald v. East Jasper County School Dist., 351 So. 2d 531 (Miss. 1977).

53. *See, e.g.,* Griffin v. Galena City School Dist., 640 P.2d 829 (Alaska 1982).

54. *See, e.g.,* Casada v. Booneville School Dist. No. 65, 686 F. Supp. 730 (W.D. Ark. 1988).

55. Benton v. Board of Educ., 361 N.W.2d 515 (Neb. 1985). *See also* Gardner v. Alabama State Tenure Comm'n, 553 So. 2d 606 (Ala. Civ. App. 1989).

56. Jefferson Consol. School Dist. C-123 v. Carden, 772 S.W.2d 753 (Mo. Ct. App. 1989). *See also* Iven v. Hazelwood School Dist., 710 S.W.2d 462 (Mo. Ct. App. 1986).

57. Wagner v. Little Rock School Dist., 373 F. Supp. 876 (E.D. Ark. 1973). *See also* Stein v. Board of Educ. of City of New York, 792 F.2d 13 (2d Cir. 1986), *cert. denied,* 479 U.S. 984 (1986) (notice specifying only date and time was inadequate).

58. *See, e.g.,* Shipley v. Salem School Dist., 669 P.2d 1172 (Or. Ct. App. 1983), *review denied,* 675 P.2d 492 (Or. 1984).

59. *See, e.g.,* Allen v. Texarkana Pub. Schools, 794 S.W.2d 138 (Ark. 1990); Haddock v. Board of Educ., 661 P.2d 368 (Kan. 1983); Turk v. Franklin Special School Dist., 640 S.W.2d 218 (Tenn. 1982).

60. 470 U.S. 532 (1985). *See also* Fields v. Durham, 909 F.2d 94 (4th Cir. 1990); Runge v. Dove, 857 F.2d 469 (8th Cir. 1988); Matthews v. Harney County, Oregon, School Dist. No. 4, 819 F.2d 889 (9th Cir. 1987); Degnan v. Bering Strait School Dist., 753 P.2d 146 (Alaska 1988); Short v. Kiamichi Area Vocational-Technical School Dist. No. 7 of Choctaw County, 761 P.2d 472 (Okla. 1988), *cert. denied,* 489 U.S. 1066 (1989); Leslie Gerstman, "Minimal Procedural Safeguards for Dismissal of Tenured Public Employees," *Education Law Reporter,* vol. 24 (1985), pp. 695–710.

61. *See, e.g.,* Adams v. School Dist. No. 5 Jackson County, Oregon, 699 F. Supp. 243 (D. Or. 1988) (due process only requires that employees be given an opportunity to state their side).

62. *See, e.g.,* Brouillette v. Board of Directors of Merged Area IX, 519 F.2d 126 (8th Cir. 1975).

63. Valter v. Orchard Farm School Dist., 541 S.W.2d 550 (Mo. 1976). *See also* Casada v. Booneville School Dist. No. 65, 686 F. Supp. 730 (W.D. Ark. 1988) (teacher was deprived of due process rights when he was not allowed to cross-examine witnesses at hearings); Gaulden v. Lincoln Parish School Bd., 554 So. 2d 152 (La. Ct. App. 1989), *writ denied,* 559 So. 2d 126 (La. 1990) (no requirement to swear witnesses at tenure hearing); *In re* Wolf, 555 A.2d 722 (N.J. Super. Ct. App. Div. 1989), *certification denied,* 564 A.2d 862 (N.J. 1989) (new hearing ordered because teacher was excluded from courtroom while students testified).

64. *See, e.g.,* Heithoff v. Nebraska State Bd. of Educ., 430 N.W.2d 681 (Neb. 1988) (termination decision cannot be made prior to hearing to consider the action).

65. Ahern v. Board of Educ. of School Dist. of Grand Island, 456 F.2d 399 (8th Cir. 1972).

66. Birdwell v. Hazelwood School Dist., 491 F.2d 490 (8th Cir. 1974). *See also* Crane v. Mitchell County Unified School Dist. No. 273, 652 P.2d 205 (Kan. 1982).

67. *See, e.g.,* Birdwell, *id.;* Crane, *id.;* Ferguson v. Board of Trustees of Bonner County Unified School Dist. No. 82, 564 P.2d 971 (Idaho 1977), *cert. denied,* 434 U.S. 939 (1977). *But see* Wertz v. Southern Cloud Unified School Dist. No. 334, 542 P.2d 339 (Kan. 1975) (teacher's refusal to participate in a post-termination or "after the fact" hearing did not constitute a waiver of due process rights).

68. Pederson v. South Williamsport Area School Dist., 677 F.2d 312 (3d Cir. 1982), *cert. denied,* 459 U.S. 972 (1982).

69. Jones v. Morris, 541 F. Supp. 11 (S.D. Ohio 1981), *aff'd,* 455 U.S. 1009 (1982). *See also* Bates v. Sponberg, 547 F.2d 325 (6th Cir. 1976) (hearing before authority with ultimate responsibility for discharge decision is not required); Pagano v. Board of Educ. of City of Torrington, 492 A.2d 197 (Conn. Ct. App. 1985), *certification denied,* 499 A.2d 60 (Conn. 1985) (due process is fulfilled by full, trial-type evidentiary hearing held before impartial hearing panel).

70. *See* Withrow v. Larkin, 421 U.S. 35 (1975); Rouse v. Scottsdale Unified School Dist. No. 48, 752 P.2d 22 (Ariz. Ct. App. 1987).

71. Weissman v. Board of Educ. of Jefferson County School Dist., 547 P.2d 1267 (Colo. 1976). *See also* Ferguson v. Board of Trustees of Bonner County School Dist. No. 82, 564 P.2d 971 (Idaho 1977), *cert. denied,* 434 U.S. 939 (1977).

72. 426 U.S. 482 (1976).

73. *Id.* at 496–497.

74. *See, e.g.,* Strain v. Rapid City School Bd., 447 N.W.2d 332 (S.D. 1989); Kizer v. Dorchester County Vocational Educ. Bd. of Trustees, 340 S.E.2d 144 (S.C. 1986). *But see* Crump v. Board of Educ. of Hickory Admin. School Unit, 378 S.E.2d 32 (N.C. Ct. App. 1989) (prehearing knowledge of the board members coupled with denial of such knowledge at the hearing substantiated impermissible bias).

75. *Ex parte* Greenberg v. Alabama State Tenure Comm'n, 395 So. 2d 1000 (Ala. 1981). *But see* Danroth v. Mandaree Pub. School Dist. No. 36, 320 N.W.2d 780 (N.D. 1982) (teacher was not denied fair and proper hearing even though a board member's wife was a principal critic).

76. Staton v. Mayes, 552 F.2d 908 (10th Cir. 1977), *cert. denied,* 434 U.S. 907 (1977). *But see* Welch v. Barham, 635 F.2d 1322 (8th Cir. 1980), *cert. denied,* 451 U.S. 971 (1981) (statements by two board members at trial that they could not think of any evidence that would have changed their minds about terminating the individual did not show the degree of bias necessary to disqualify a decisionmaker).

77. Keith v. Community School Dist. of Wilton, 262 N.W.2d 249, 260 (Iowa 1978).

78. *See* Withrow v. Larkin, 421 U.S. 35 (1975); Cook v. Board of Educ. for County of Logan, 671 F. Supp. 1110 (S.D. W. Va. 1987); *Ex parte* Conecuh County Bd. of Educ., 495 So. 2d 1108 (Ala. 1986); Ferrario v. Board of Educ. of Escanaba

Area Pub. Schools, 395 N.W.2d 195 (Mich. 1986); Dale v. Board of Educ., 316 N.W.2d 108 (S.D. 1982).

79. Wells v. Del Norte School Dist. C-7, 753 P.2d 770, 772 (Colo. Ct. App. 1987).

80. deKoevend v. Board of Educ. of West End School Dist. RE-2, 688 P.2d 219, 228 (Colo. 1984).

81. *See, e.g.*, McIntyre v. Tucker, 490 So. 2d 1012 (Fla. Dist. Ct. App. 1986); Board of Educ. v. Lockhart, 687 P.2d 1306 (Colo. 1984); Schmidt v. Independent School Dist. No. 1, Aitkin, 349 N.W.2d 563 (Minn. Ct. App. 1984). *But see* Holley v. Seminole County School Dist., 755 F.2d 1492 (11th Cir. 1985) (board's attorney was permitted to sit as hearing examiner).

82. *See, e.g.*, Hagerty v. State Tenure Comm'n, 445 N.W.2d 178 (Mich. Ct. App. 1989) (court did not find bias in this case but alerted the state bar association that if a similar situation occurs in the future, a *per se* rule of reversal would be adopted because of the potential for prejudice).

83. *See, e.g.*, Martin v. Ambach, 502 N.Y.S.2d 991 (N.Y. 1986); Munger v. Jesup Community School Dist., 325 N.W.2d 377 (Iowa 1982). *See also* Harris v. Bailey, 798 P.2d 96 (Mont. 1990) (state law required substantial credible evidence).

84. *See, e.g.*, Board of Educ. of City of Chicago v. State Bd. of Educ., 497 N.E.2d 984 (Ill. 1986) (preponderance of evidence is required in teacher dismissal proceedings even when conduct that might violate criminal law is alleged).

85. Altsheler v. Board of Educ. of Great Neck Union Free School Dist., 476 N.Y.S.2d 281, 281 (N.Y. 1984).

86. Schulz v. Board of Educ. of the School Dist. of Freemont, 315 N.W.2d 633 (Neb. 1982).

87. *See, e.g.*, Alabama State Tenure Comm'n v. Tuscaloosa County Bd. of Educ., 401 So. 2d 84 (Ala. Civ. App. 1981), *review denied,* 401 So. 2d 87 (Ala. 1981); Doran v. Board of Educ. of Western Boone County Community Schools, 285 N.E.2d 825 (Ind. Ct. App. 1972).

88. *See, e.g.*, Libe v. Board of Educ. of Twin Cedars Community School Dist., 350 N.W.2d 748 (Iowa Ct. App. 1984) (board could consider polygraph results).

89. *See* Goldberg v. Kelly, 397 U.S. 254, 271(1970).

90. *See, e.g.*, Rogliano v. Fayette County Bd. of Educ., 347 S.E.2d 220 (W. Va. 1986); Benke v. Neenan, 658 P.2d 860 (Colo. 1983); Hinkle v. Garrett-Keyser-Butler School Dist., 567 N.E.2d 1173 (Ind. Ct. App. 1991); Vorm v. David Douglas School Dist. No. 40, 608 P.2d 193 (Or. Ct. App. 1980).

91. *See, e.g.*, Hollingsworth v. Board of Educ., 303 N.W.2d 506 (Neb. 1981).

92. Morey v. School Bd. of Indep. School Dist. No. 492, 128 N.W.2d 302, 307 (Minn. 1964).

93. Jackson v. Independent School Dist. No. 16, 648 P.2d 26, 31 (Okla. 1982). *See also* Caldwell v. Blytheville, Arkansas School Dist. No. Five, 746 S.W.2d 381 (Ark. Ct. App. 1988).

94. 78 Corpus Juris Secundum § 202 (1952).

95. Henry Black, *Black's Law Dictionary,* 6th ed. (St. Paul, MN: West Publishing Co., 1990), p. 765.

96. *See, e.g.*, Benke v. Neenan, 658 P.2d 860 (Colo. 1983).

97. Horosko v. School Dist. of Township of Mt. Pleasant, 6 A.2d 866 (Pa. 1939), *cert. denied,* 308 U.S. 553 (1939).

98. Beilan v. Board of Pub. Educ. of Philadelphia, 357 U.S. 399 (1958).

99. *See also* text with note 165, *infra*.

100. Beilan, 357 U.S. at 408.

101. Mims v. West Baton Rouge Parish School Bd., 315 So. 2d 349 (La. Ct. App. 1975).

102. Whaley v. Anoka-Hennepin Indep. School Dist. No. 11, 325 N.W.2d 128 (Minn. 1982). *See also* Saunders v. Anderson, 746 S.W.2d 185 (Tenn. 1987).

103. Hamburg v. North Penn School Dist., 484 A.2d 867 (Pa. Commw. Ct. 1984).

104. Aulwurm v. Board of Educ. of Murphysboro Community Unit School Dist. No. 186, 367 N.E.2d 1337 (Ill. 1977). *See also* Iven v. Hazelwood School Dist., 710 S.W.2d 462 (Mo. Ct. App. 1986); Board of Directors of Sioux City Community School Dist. v. Mroz, 295 N.W.2d 447 (Iowa 1980).

105. Cozad v. Crane School Dist. R-3, 716 S.W.2d 408 (Mo. Ct. App. 1986).

106. Mott v. Endicott School Dist., No. 308, 713 P.2d 98, 101 (Wash. 1986).

107. Celestine v. Lafayette Parish School Bd., 284 So. 2d 650 (La. Ct. App. 1973).

108. Myres v. Orleans Parish School Bd., 423 So. 2d 1303 (La. Ct. App. 1983), *review denied*, 430 So. 2d 657 (La. 1983).

109. Phillips v. Plaquemines Parish School Bd., 465 So. 2d 53 (La. Ct. App. 1985), *review denied*, 467 So. 2d 540 (La. 1985).

110. Jergeson v. Board of Trustees of School Dist. No. 7, 476 P.2d 481 (Wyo. 1970).

111. Lamar School Bd. Dist. No. 39 v. Kinder, 642 S.W.2d 885 (Ark. 1982).

112. Trustees, Missoula County School Dist. No. 1 v. Anderson, 757 P.2d 1315 (Mont. 1988).

113. *See, e.g.,* Kinsella v. Board of Educ. of Cent. School Dist. No. 7, 407 N.Y.S.2d 78 (N.Y. App. Div. 1978); Hatta v. Board of Educ., Union Endicott Cent. School Dist., Broome County, 394 N.Y.S.2d 301 (N.Y. App. Div. 1977).

114. *See, e.g.,* Jones v. Jefferson Parish School Bd., 533 F. Supp. 816 (E.D. La. 1982), *aff'd*, 688 F.2d 837 (5th Cir. 1982), *cert. denied*, 460 U.S. 1064 (1983); Board of Educ. of School Dist. of Philadelphia v. Kushner, 530 A.2d 541 (Pa. Commw. Ct. 1987); Combs v. Board of Educ. of Avon Center School Dist. No. 47, 498 N.E.2d 806 (Ill. App. Ct. 1986), *appeal denied*, 505 N.E.2d 351 (Ill. 1987); Rainwater v. Board of Educ. of Greenville R-2 School Dist., 645 S.W.2d 172 (Mo. Ct. App. 1982).

115. Scheelhaase v. Woodbury Cent. Community School Dist., 488 F.2d 237 (8th Cir. 1973), *cert. denied*, 417 U.S. 969 (1974).

116. Horosko v. School Dist. of Mt. Pleasant, 6 A.2d 866, 868 (Pa. 1939), *cert. denied*, 308 U.S. 553 (1939).

117. *See generally* Floyd Delon, "A Teacher's Sexual Involvement with Pupils: 'Reasonable Cause' for Dismissal," *Education Law Reporter*, vol. 22 (1985), pp. 1085–1093.

118. Weissman v. Board of Educ. of Jefferson County School Dist. No. 1, 547 P.2d 1267, 1273 (Colo. 1976). *See also* Strain v. Rapid City School Bd., 447 N.W.2d 332 (S.D. 1989); Manheim Cent. Educ. Ass'n v. Manheim Cent. School Dist., 572 A.2d 31 (Pa. Commw. Ct. 1990), *appeal denied*, 582 A.2d 326 (1990) (love letters to two students resulted in dismissal for immorality); Sauter v. Mount Vernon School Dist. No. 320, 791 P.2d 549 (Wash. Ct. App. 1990) (attempted seduction of student supported dismissal for immoral conduct); Board of Educ. of City of Chicago v. Box, 547 N.E.2d 627 (Ill. App. Ct.

1989) (improper touching of female elementary students was irremediable);
Katz v. Ambach, 472 N.Y.S.2d 492 (N.Y. App. Div. 1984) (touching and
kissing of sixth-grade female students supported dismissal).

119. Denton v. South Kitsap School Dist. No. 402, 516 P.2d 1080 (Wash. Ct. App.
1973).

120. Clark v. Ann Arbor School Dist., 344 N.W.2d 48 (Mich. Ct. App. 1983),
appeal denied, 357 N.W.2d 659 (Mich. 1984). *See also* Coupeville School
Dist. v. Vivian, 677 P.2d 192 (Wash. Ct. App. 1984) (dismissal was supported
by one-time incident of male teacher permitting two female students to drink
alcohol in his home); Shipley v. Salem School Dist. 24J, 669 P.2d 1172 (Or.
Ct. App. 1983), *review denied,* 675 P.2d 492 (Or. 1984) (negative impact of
sexual contact with student on teaching effectiveness was obvious); Potter v.
Kalama Pub. School Dist., 644 P.2d 1229 (Wash Ct. App. 1982) (inappropriate
physical contact with female students was adequate basis for dismissal).

121. Fadler v. Illinois State Bd. of Educ., 506 N.E.2d 640 (Ill. App. Ct. 1987). *See
also* Pesce v. J. Sterling Morton High School Dist. 201, 830 F.2d 789 (7th Cir.
1987) (psychologist was suspended for failure to report a student's disclosure
of sexual activity with a teacher).

122. Kilpatrick v. Wright, 437 F. Supp. 397, 399 (M.D. Ala. 1977).

123. Thompson v. Southwest School Dist., 483 F. Supp. 1170 (W.D. Mo. 1980).

124. Ross v. Robb, 662 S.W.2d 257 (Mo. 1983).

125. *See, e.g.,* Golden v. Board of Educ. of Harrison County, 285 S.E.2d 665 (W.
Va. 1981); Stephens v. Board of Educ. of School Dist. No. 5, 429 N.W.2d 722
(Neb. 1988); Massie v. East St. Louis School Dist. #189, 561 N.E.2d 940 (Ill.
App. Ct. 1990).

126. Sullivan v. Meade Indep. School Dist. No. 101, 530 F.2d 799 (8th Cir. 1976).
See also Yanzick v. School Dist. No. 23, Lake County Montana, 641 P.2d 431
(Mont. 1982) (teacher's cohabitation was known throughout the small com-
munity and had become a matter of class discussion).

127. Sherburne v. School Bd. of Suwannee County, 455 So. 2d 1057 (Fla. Dist. Ct.
App. 1984).

128. Ross v. Springfield, 691 P.2d 509, 513 (Or. Ct. App. 1984), *rev'd,* 716 P.2d 724
(Or. 1986) (case was remanded for the Fair Dismissal Appeals Board to
articulate criteria for assessing immorality).

129. Fisher v. Snyder, 476 F.2d 375, 377 (8th Cir. 1973).

130. *See, e.g.,* Reinhardt v. Board of Educ. of Alton Community Unit School Dist.
No. 11, 311 N.E.2d 710 (Ill. App. Ct. 1974).

131. *See, e.g.,* Brown v. Bathke, 416 F. Supp. 1194 (D. Neb. 1976).

132. Drake v. Covington County Bd. of Educ., 371 F. Supp. 974 (M.D. Ala. 1974).

133. New Mexico State Bd. of Educ. v. Stoudt, 571 P.2d 1186 (N.M. 1977). *See
also* Ponton v. Newport News School Bd., 632 F. Supp. 1056 (E.D. Va. 1986)
(forced leave of absence violated a pregnant, unwed teacher's constitutional
right to privacy and statutory rights under Title VII).

134. *See* Bowers v. Hardwick, 478 U.S. 186 (1986).

135. Morrison v. State Bd. of Educ., 461 P.2d 375 (Cal. 1969).

136. *Id.* at 386. It should be noted that this case dealt with the revocation of a
teacher's certificate because of homosexual conduct. Although it was not a
dismissal case, the criteria listed have been relied on in dismissals for immorality.

137. Sarac v. State Bd. of Educ., 57 Cal. Rptr. 69 (Cal. Ct. App. 1967).

138. Board of Educ. of Long Beach v. Jack M., 566 P.2d 602 (Cal. 1977).
139. Gaylord v. Tacoma School Dist. No. 10, 559 P.2d 1340 (Wash. 1977), *cert. denied,* 434 U.S. 879 (1977). *See also* Rowland v. Mad River Local School Dist., 730 F.2d 444 (6th Cir. 1984), *cert. denied,* 470 U.S. 1009 (1985) (non-renewal of guidance counselor who revealed her homosexuality was upheld); text with note 12, Chapter 8.
140. Jarvella v. Willoughby–Eastlake City School Dist., 233 N.E.2d 143, 145 (Ohio 1967).
141. Clarke v. Board of Educ. of School Dist. of Omaha, 338 N.W.2d 272 (Neb. 1983).
142. Bovino v. Board of School Directors of Indiana Area School Dist., 377 A.2d 1284, 1288 (Pa. Commw. Ct. 1977). *See also* Fiscus v. Board of School Trustees of Cent. School Dist., 509 N.E.2d 1137 (Ind. Ct. App. 1987) (single utterance of an obscene word in a fifth-grade classroom supported dismissal for immorality).
143. *See* Kenai Peninsula Borough Bd. of Educ. v. Brown, 691 P.2d 1034, 1036 (Alaska 1984).
144. Logan v. Warren County Bd. of Educ., 549 F. Supp. 145 (S.D. Ga. 1982).
145. Bethel Park School Dist. v. Krall, 445 A.2d 1377 (Pa. Commw. Ct. 1982), *cert. denied,* 464 U.S. 851 (1983). *See also* Dohanic v. Commonwealth Dep't of Educ., 533 A.2d 812 (Pa. Commw. Ct. 1987), *appeal denied,* 541 A.2d 1392 (Pa. 1988) (lying to school officials constituted immoral conduct).
146. Kimble v. Worth County R.-III Bd. of Educ., 669 S.W.2d 949 (Mo. Ct. App. 1984), *cert. denied,* 469 U.S. 933 (1984).
147. Florian v. Highland Local School Dist. Bd. of Educ., 493 N.E.2d 249 (Ohio Ct. App. 1983).
148. Golden v. Board of Educ. of Harrison County, 285 S.E.2d 665 (W. Va. 1981).
149. Hoagland v. Mount Vernon School Dist. No. 320, 623 P.2d 1156 (Wash. 1981).
150. *See, e.g.,* Sutherby v. Gobles Bd. of Educ., 348 N.W.2d 277 (Mich. Ct. App. 1984).
151. *See, e.g.,* Belasco v. Board of Pub. Educ., 486 A.2d 538 (Pa. Commw. Ct. 1985), *aff'd,* 510 A.2d 337 (Pa. 1986); Sims v. Board of Trustees, Holly Springs, 414 So. 2d 431 (Miss. 1982).
152. Ray v. Minneapolis Bd. of Educ., Special School Dist. No. 1, 202 N.W.2d 375, 378 (Minn. 1972). *See also* Blackwell v. Wyoming County Bd. of Educ., 375 S.E.2d 25 (W. Va. 1988).
153. Board of Trustees of School Dist. No. 4 v. Colwell, 611 P.2d 427 (Wyo. 1980). *See also* Gaylord v. Board of Educ., Unified School Dist. No. 218, 794 P.2d 307 (Kan. Ct. App. 1990).
154. Warner v. U.S.D. #468, 604 P.2d 295 (Kan. Ct. App. 1979).
155. McLaughlin v. Board of Educ., 659 S.W.2d 249 (Mo. Ct. App. 1983).
156. Ware v. Morgan County School Dist. No. RE-3, 748 P.2d 1295 (Colo. 1988).
157. *See, e.g.,* Tomczik v. State Tenure Comm'n, 438 N.W.2d 642 (Mich. Ct. App. 1989); Simmons v. Vancouver School Dist. No. 37, 704 P.2d 648 (Wash. Ct. App. 1985).
158. Welch v. Board of Educ. of Bement Community Unit School Dist. No. 5, 358 N.E.2d 1364 (Ill. App. Ct. 1977).
159. Burton v. Kirby, 775 S.W.2d 834 (Tex. Ct. App. 1989).
160. Nordstrom v. Hansford, 435 P.2d 397 (Colo. 1967).

161. Belasco v. Board of Pub. Educ., 486 A.2d 538 (Pa. Commw. Ct. 1985), *aff'd*, 510 A.2d 337 (Pa. 1986).
162. Seitz v. Duval County School Bd., 346 So. 2d 644 (Fla. Dist. Ct. App. 1977), *review denied*, 354 So. 2d 985 (Fla. 1978).
163. Siglin v. Kayenta Unified School Dist. No. 27, 655 P.2d 353 (Ariz. Ct. App. 1982).
164. Caldwell v. Blytheville, Arkansas School Dist. No. 5, 746 S.W.2d 381 (Ark. Ct. App. 1988).
165. McGhee v. Miller, 753 S.W.2d 354 (Tenn. 1988).
166. Blair v. Robstown Indep. School Dist., 556 F.2d 1331 (5th Cir. 1977).
167. Johnson v. Board of Educ. of Woden–Crystal Lake Community School Dist., 353 N.W.2d 883, 884 (Iowa Ct. App. 1984).
168. *See* Meckley v. Kanawha County Bd. of Educ., 383 S.E.2d 839 (W. Va. 1989); Fisher v. Fairbanks North Star Borough School, 704 P.2d 213 (Alaska 1985); Board of Trustees of the Hattiesburg Mun. Separate School Dist. v. Gates, 461 So. 2d 730 (Miss. 1984); Moffitt v. Batesville School Dist., 643 S.W.2d 557 (Ark. 1982); Sims v. Board of Trustees, Holly Springs Mun. Separate School Dist., 414 So. 2d 431 (Miss. 1982); In re Proposed Termination of James E. Johnson, 451 N.W.2d 343 (Minn. Ct. App. 1990); Weaver v. Board of Educ. of Pine Plains Cent. School Dist., 514 N.Y.S.2d 473 (N.Y. App. Div. 1987), *appeal denied*, 519 N.Y.S.2d 1031 (N.Y. 1987); Lockhart v. Board of Educ. of Araphahoe County School Dist. No. 6, 735 P.2d 913 (Colo. Ct. App. 1986); Ward v. Board of Educ. of the School Dist. of Philadelphia, 496 A.2d 1352 (Pa. Commw. Ct. 1985); Fink v. Board of Educ., 442 A.2d 837 (Pa. Commw. Ct. 1983), *appeal dismissed*, 460 U.S. 1048 (1983).
169. Blaine v. Moffat County School Dist. RE No. 1, 748 P.2d 1280 (Colo. 1988). *See also* Jefferson County School Dist. No. 509-J v. Fair Dismissal Appeals Bd., 793 P.2d 888 (Colo. Ct. App. 1990).
170. Cunningham v. Franklin Parish School Bd., 457 So. 2d 184 (La. Ct. App. 1984), *review denied*, 461 So. 2d 319 (La. 1984). *See also* Thomas v. Cascade Union High Schol Dist. No. 5, 780 P.2d 780 (Or. Ct. App. 1989) (one incident of kicking a student substantiated neglect of duty).
171. Faulkner v. New Bern–Craven County Bd. of Educ., 316 S.E.2d 281 (N.C. 1984).
172. Gaulden v. Lincoln Parish School Bd., 554 So. 2d 152 (La. Ct. App. 1989), *writ denied*, 559 So. 2d 126 (La. 1990). *See also* Franklin v. Alabama State Tenure Comm'n, 482 So. 2d 1214 (Ala. Civ. App. 1985) (failure to report to school at the beginning of school year was sufficient to establish neglect of duty).
173. Harrah Indep. School Dist. v. Martin, 440 U.S. 194 (1979).
174. Sanders v. Board of Educ. of the South Sioux City Community School Dist. No. 11, 263 N.W.2d 461 (Neb. 1978).
175. *Id.* at 465. *See also* Eshom v. Board of Educ. of School Dist. No. 54, 364 N.W.2d 7 (Neb. 1985) (dismissal was supported by detailed evaluations comparing terminated teacher with other teachers).
176. Fox v. Board of Educ. of Doddridge County, 236 S.E.2d 243 (W. Va. 1977).
177. DeVito v. Board of Educ., 317 S.E.2d 159 (W. Va. 1984). *But see* Shurgin v. Ambach, 451 N.Y.S.2d 722 (N.Y. 1982) (knowingly exhibiting a pornographic film to students established adequate cause for the dismissal of a teacher).
178. Terry v. Houston County Bd. of Educ., 342 S.E.2d 774 (Ga. Ct. App. 1986).

179. Landry v. Ascension Parish School Bd., 415 So. 2d 473 (La. Ct. App. 1982), *review denied*, 420 So. 2d 448 (La. 1982). *See also* Board of Educ. of Gilmer v. Chaddock, 398 S.E.2d 120 (W. Va. 1990) (failure to remove student with loaded gun from classroom did not substantiate willful neglect of duty).

180. Pell v. Board of Educ. of Union Free School Dist. No. 1, 313 N.E.2d 321 (N.Y. 1974); School Dist. No. 11, Joint Counties of Archuleta and La Plata v. Umberfield, 512 P.2d 1166 (Colo. Ct. App. 1973).

181. Fernald v. City of Ellsworth Superintending School Comm., 342 A.2d 704 (Me. 1975).

182. Ellis v. Ambach, 508 N.Y.S.2d 624 (N.Y. App. Div. 1986), *appeal denied*, 514 N.Y.S.2d 1023 (N.Y. 1987).

183. Coupeville School Dist. No. 204 v. Vivian, 677 P.2d 192 (Wash. Ct. App. 1984).

184. Roberts v. Santa Cruz Valley Unified School Dist. No. 35, 778 P.2d 1294 (Ariz. Ct. App. 1989).

185. Dupree v. School Comm. of Boston, 446 N.E.2d 1099 (Mass. App. Ct. 1983), *review denied*, 451 N.E.2d 1166 (Mass. 1983).

186. Board of Educ. of Hopkins County v. Wood, 717 S.W.2d 837 (Ky. 1986).

187. Fowler v. Board of Educ. of Lincoln County, Kentucky, 819 F.2d 657 (6th Cir. 1987), *cert. denied*, 484 U.S. 986 (1987).

188. Wishart v. McDonald, 500 F.2d 1110 (1st Cir. 1974).

189. *See, e.g.,* Board of Trustees of the Clark County School Dist. v. Rathbun, 556 P.2d 548 (Nev. 1976).

190. *See* William D. Valente, *Education Law: Public and Private*, vol. I (St. Paul, MN: West Publishing Co., 1985), pp. 437–439; Hagerty v. State Tenure Comm'n, 445 N.W.2d 178 (Mich. Ct. App. 1989) (unfitness to teach was established through a range of factors related to deficiencies in teaching).

191. Lombardo v. Board of Educ. of School Dist. No. 27, 241 N.E.2d 495, 498 (Ill. App. Ct. 1968). *See also* Elvin v. City of Waterville, 573 A.2d 381 (Me. 1990) (female teacher's sexual relationship with a fifteen-year-old male student rendered her unfit to teach); Johnson v. Board of Trustees, Beaverhead County High School Dist., 771 P.2d 137 (Mont. 1989) (sexual contact with two students resulted in dismissal for unfitness to teach and immorality).

192. In re Grossman, 316 A.2d 39 (N.J. Super. Ct. App. Div. 1974), *certification denied*, 321 A.2d 253 (N.J. 1974).

193. Wright v. Superintending Comm., City of Portland, 331 A.2d 640, 647 (Me. 1975).

194. McLaughlin v. Machias School Comm., 385 A.2d 53 (Me. 1978).

195. *See, e.g.,* Dusanek v. Hannon, 677 F.2d 538 (7th Cir. 1982), *cert. denied*, 459 U.S. 1017 (1982); Fitzpatrick v. Board of Educ. of the Mamaroneck Union Free School Dist., 465 N.Y.S.2d 240 (N.Y. App. Div. 1983), *appeal denied*, 463 N.E.2d 1235 (N.Y. 1984) (serious personality disorder established incapacity to teach).

196. *See, e.g.,* Smith v. Board of Educ. of Fort Madison Community School Dist., 293 N.W.2d 221 (Iowa 1980) (temporary mental illness was inadequate basis for dismissal). *But see* Clarke v. Shoreline School Dist. No. 412, 720 P.2d 793 (Wash. 1986) (dismissal of sight and hearing impaired teacher was upheld because he could not perform essential functions of teaching position).

197. Arline v. School Bd. of Nassau County, 480 U.S. 273 (1987).

198. Gary Teachers Union, Local No. 4, AFT v. School City of Gary, 332 N.E.2d 256, 263 (Ind. Ct. App. 1975). *But see* Trustees Lincoln County School Dist. No. 13 v. Holden, 754 P.2d 506 (Mont. 1988) (two instances of calling students crude names did not support good cause for dismissal).

199. Wheeler v. Mariemont City School Dist., 467 N.E.2d 552 (Ohio Ct. App. 1983).

200. diLeo v. Greenfield, 541 F.2d 949, 954 (2d Cir. 1976). *See also* Wilson v. Des Moines Indep. Community School Dist., 389 N.W.2d 681 (Iowa Ct. App. 1986).

201. Cooper v. Fair Dismissal Appeals Bd., 570 P.2d 1005 (Or. Ct. App. 1977). *See also* In the Matter of Nelson, 416 N.W.2d 848 (Minn. Ct. App. 1987).

202. Pa. Stat. Ann. tit. 24 § 11-1124 (Purdon, West Supp. 1991).

203. Dykeman v. Board of Educ., 316 N.W.2d 69 (Neb. 1982).

204. Steeby v. School Dist. of the City of Highland Park, 224 N.W.2d 97 (Mich. Ct. App. 1974). *See also* Martin v. School Comm. of Natick, 480 N.E.2d 625 (Mass. 1985); Downs v. Henry County Bd. of Educ., 769 S.W.2d 49 (Ky. Ct. App. 1988).

205. Fatscher v. Board of School Directors Springfield School Dist., 367 A.2d 1130 (Pa. Commw. Ct. 1977). *See also* Harris v. Trustees, Cascades County School Dist., 786 P.2d 1164 (Mont. 1990); Farley v. Board of Educ. of County of Mingo, 365 S.E.2d 816 (W. Va. 1988).

206. Chauvel v. Nyquist, 371 N.E.2d 473 (N.Y. 1977).

207. Chester v. Harper Woods School Dist., 273 N.W.2d 916 (Mich. Ct. App. 1978). *See also* Dinan v. Board of Educ., 426 N.Y.S.2d 86 (N.Y. App. Div. 1980).

208. *See, e.g.,* Palmer v. Board of Trustees Crook County School Dist. 1, 785 P.2d 1160 (Wyo. 1990); Zurlo v. Ambach, 442 N.Y.S.2d 486 (N.Y. 1981). *But see* Beeman v. Board of Educ., Oyster Bay-East Norvich Pub. Schools, 494 N.Y.S.2d 27 (N.Y. App. Div. 1985); Pennell v. Board of Educ. of Equality Community Unit School Dist. No. 4, 484 N.E.2d 445 (Ill. App. Ct. 1985) (while restructuring positions may not be required, bad-faith realignment of positions to avoid existence of a position for a tenured teacher is prohibited).

209. *See, e.g.,* McGhee v. Draper, 639 F.2d 639 (10th Cir. 1981).

210. *See, e.g.,* Sterzing v. Fort Bend Indep. School Dist., 496 F.2d 92 (5th Cir. 1974).

211. *See, e.g.,* State *ex rel.* v. Grant Valley Local Schools Bd. of Educ., 375 N.E.2d 48 (Ohio 1978); Board of Trustees of Nogales Elementary School Dist. v. Cartier, 559 P.2d 216 (Ariz. Ct. App. 1977); Jackson v. Board of Educ. of Oktibbeha County, 349 So. 2d 550 (Miss. 1977).

212. *See, e.g.,* Weckerly v. Mona Shores Bd. of Educ., 202 N.W.2d 777 (Mich. 1972).

213. *See, e.g.,* deKoevend v. Board of Educ., 688 P.2d 219 (Colo. 1984); DiCello v. Board of Directors of Riverside School Dist., 380 A.2d 944 (Pa. Commw. Ct. 1977).

214. *See* Maine v. Thiboutot, 448 U.S. 1 (1980); Owen v. City of Independence, 445 U.S. 622 (1980); Monell v. Department of Social Services of the City of New York, 436 U.S. 658 (1978).

215. Memphis Community School Dist. v. Stachura, 477 U.S. 299 (1986); Carey v. Piphus, 435 U.S. 247 (1978).

216. Rogers v. Kelly, 866 F.2d 997 (8th Cir. 1989).

217. Schreffler v. Board of Educ. of Delmar School Dist., 506 F. Supp. 1300 (D. Del. 1981).

218. The Supreme Court held in City of Newport v. Fact Concerts, 453 U.S. 247 (1981) that punitive awards cannot be assessed against governmental bodies such as school boards.

219. In 1991, the Supreme Court, in a noneducation case, refused to place a limit on the amount of punitive damages awards but did recognize that extreme awards could be unacceptable under the fourteenth amendment, Pacific Mutual Life Ins. Co. v. Haslip, 111 S. Ct. 1032 (1991).

220. Eckmann v. Board of Educ. of Hawthorn School Dist. No. 17, 636 F. Supp. 1214 (N.D. Ill. 1986).

221. Landry v. Ascension Parish School Bd., 415 So. 2d 473 (La. Ct. App. 1982), *review denied,* 420 So. 2d 448 (La. 1982). *See also* Carpenter v. Catahoula Parish School Bd., 566 So. 2d 1013 (La. Ct. App. 1990) (in addition to reinstatement and back pay, a teacher may seek damages in a state tort action).

222. Sherburne v. School Bd. of Suwanee County, 455 So. 2d 1057, 1062 (Fla. Dist. Ct. App. 1984).

223. McGhee v. Miller, 753 S.W.2d 354 (Tenn. 1990).

224. Cohen v. Board of Educ., Smithtown Cent. School Dist. No. 1, 728 F.2d 160 (2d Cir. 1984). *But see* Alaniz v. San Isidro Indep. School Dist., 589 F. Supp. 17 (S.D. Tex. 1983), *aff'd,* 742 F.2d 207 (5th Cir. 1984) (jury award of $50,000 as compensation for mental anguish and emotional distress was upheld because evidence substantiated injury).

225. Crump v. Board of Educ. of Hickory Admin. School Unit, 392 S.E.2d 579 (N.C. 1990) (damages were awarded for procedural violation even though discharge was upheld). *See also* Jacobs v. Meister, 775 P.2d 254 (N.M. Ct. App. 1989), *cert. denied,* 775 P.2d 1299 (N.M. 1989) (expert testimony is not required to substantiate emotional distress; trial court must judge credibility of claim).

226. Memphis Community School Dist. v. Stachura, 477 U.S. 299 (1986). *See* text with note 77, Chapter 8.

227. *See, e.g.,* Harris v. Bauer, 749 P.2d 1068 (Mont. 1988) (in the absence of a specific statutory provision, fees can be awarded only if the board's action was in bad faith or frivolous).

228. 42 U.S.C. § 1988 (1988).

229. 122 Cong. Rec. 33,313 (1976).

230. Texas State Teachers Ass'n v. Garland Indep. School Dist., 489 U.S. 782, 792 (1989).

231. Webb v. Board of Educ. of Dyer County, Tennessee, 471 U.S. 234 (1985). *See also* North Carolina Dep't of Transp. v. Crest Street Community, 479 U.S. 6 (1986) (attorneys' fees could not be recovered in administrative proceedings independent of enforcement of Title VI of the Civil Rights Act of 1964).

232. Christiansburg Garment Co. v. Equal Employment Opportunity Comm'n, 434 U.S. 412, 422 (1978).

233. *See, e.g.,* Hershinow v. Bonamarte, 772 F.2d 394 (7th Cir. 1985).

11
Collective Bargaining

Employment of teachers has been dramatically affected by collective bargaining in the public sector. Traditionally, boards of education had unilateral control over the management and operation of public schools. As employees of the school board, teachers were only minimally involved in the decisionmaking process. To achieve a balance of power and a voice in school affairs, teachers turned to collective action during the 1960s and acquired significant labor rights.

Diversity in labor laws and bargaining practices among the states makes it difficult to generalize about collective bargaining and teachers' labor rights. State labor laws, state employment relations board rulings, and court decisions must be consulted to determine specific rights, because there is no federal labor law covering public school employees.[1] Over two-thirds of the states have enacted bargaining laws, varying widely in coverage from very comprehensive laws controlling most aspects of negotiations to laws granting the minimal right to meet and confer. Still other states, in the absence of legislation, rely on judicial rulings to define the basic rights of public employees in the labor relations arena. This chapter presents an overview of the legal structure in which bargaining occurs and public school teachers' employment rights under state labor laws.

EMPLOYEES' BARGAINING RIGHTS IN THE PRIVATE AND PUBLIC SECTORS

Although there are basic differences in employment between the public and private sectors, collective bargaining legislation in the private sector has been significant in shaping statutory and judicial regulation of public negotiations. Similarities between the two sectors can be noted in a number of areas, such as unfair labor practices, union representation, and impasse procedures. Because of the influence of private-sector legislation on the public sector, a brief overview of major legislative acts is warranted.

Prior to the 1930s, labor relations in the private sector were dominated by the judiciary, which strongly favored management. The extensive use of judicial injunctions against strikes and boycotts effectively countered employee efforts to obtain recognition for purposes of bargaining.[2] Consequently, courts reinforced the powers of management and substantially curtailed the development and influence of unions. To bolster the position of the worker, Congress enacted the Norris-LaGuardia Act in 1932.[3] The purpose of this federal law was to circumscribe the role of courts in labor disputes by preventing the use of the injunction, except where union activities were unlawful or jeopardized public safety and health. In essence, the legislation did not confer any new rights on employees or unions but simply restricted judicial authority that had impeded the development of unions.

Following the Norris-LaGuardia Act, Congress in 1935 passed the National Labor Relations Act (NLRA), commonly known as the Wagner Act.[4] This Act created substantial rights for private-sector employees, but one of the most important outcomes was that it granted legitimacy to the collective bargaining process. In addition to defining employees' rights to organize and bargain collectively, the Act established a mechanism to safeguard these rights—the National Labor Relations Board (NLRB). The NLRB was created specifically to monitor claims of unfair labor practices such as interference with employees' rights to organize, discrimination against employees in hiring or discharge because of union membership, and failure to bargain in good faith.[5]

The NLRA was amended in 1947 by the Labor Management Relations Act (commonly known as the Taft-Hartley Act).[6] While the Wagner Act regulated employers' activities, the Taft-Hartley Act was an attempt to balance the scales in collective bargaining by regulating abusive union practices, such as interfering with employees' organizational rights and refusing to bargain in good faith. Since 1947 other amendments to the Taft-Hartley Act have further limited union abuses. Federal legislation has restricted interference from both the employer and the union, thereby ensuring the individual employee greater freedom of choice in collective bargaining.

Although the NLRA specifically exempted bargaining by governmental employees, a number of state public employee statutes have been modeled after this law, and judicial decisions interpreting the NLRA have been used to define certain provisions in public-sector laws. The recognition of the sovereign power of public employers, however, is clearly present in public labor laws. For example, many public laws require employers to bargain over "wages, hours, and other terms and conditions of employment" as in the NLRA, but this requirement is then restricted by "management rights" clauses limiting the scope of bargaining.[7]

There are several basic differences in bargaining between the public and private sectors. First, the removal of decisionmaking authority from public officials through bargaining has been viewed as an infringement on the government's sovereign power, which has resulted in the enactment of public labor laws strongly favoring public employers. Public employees' rights have been further weakened by prohibitions of work stoppages. Whereas employees' ability to strike is considered *essential* to the effective operation of collective decisionmaking in the private sector, this view has been rejected in the public sector because of the nature and structure of governmental services.

Bargaining rights developed slowly for public employees who historically had been deprived of the right to organize and bargain collectively. President Kennedy's Executive Order 10988 in 1962, which gave federal employees "the right, freely and without fear of penalty or reprisal, to form, join, and assist any employee organization,"[8] was a significant milestone for all public employees. The granting of organizational rights to federal employees provided the impetus for similar gains at the state and local levels.

Until the late 1960s, however, public employees' constitutional right to join a union had not been fully established. A large number of public employees actively participated in collective bargaining, but statutes and regulations in some states prohibited union membership. These restrictions against union membership were challenged as impairing association freedoms protected by the first amendment. Although not addressing union membership, the Supreme Court held in 1967 that public employment could not be conditioned on the relinquishment of free association rights.[9] In a later decision, the Seventh Circuit Court of Appeals clearly announced that "an individual's right to form and join a union is protected by the first amendment."[10] Other courts followed this precedent by invalidating state statutory provisions that blocked union membership.[11]

The judiciary has continued to reinforce teachers' constitutional rights to participate fully in union activities. School officials have been prohibited from imposing sanctions or denying benefits to discourage protected association rights. For example, the Sixth Circuit Court of Appeals overturned a school board's dismissal of a teacher because of union activities.[12] An Illinois federal district court held that a school board infringed on teachers' rights by abolishing a differentiated staffing system and appointing only nonunion members to certain positions after a union was reestablished in the district.[13] Similarly, the Connecticut Federal District Court found that the transfer of a teacher to another school in retaliation for using the negotiated grievance procedure was constitutionally prohibited.[14]

The United States Constitution has been interpreted as protecting public employees' rights to organize, but the right to form and join a union does not ensure the right to bargain collectively with a public employer; individual state statutes and constitutions govern such bargaining rights. Whether identified as professional negotiations, collective negotiations, or collective bargaining, the process entails bilateral decisionmaking in which the teachers' representative and the school board attempt to reach mutual agreement on matters affecting teacher employment. This process is governed in the majority of the states by legislation granting specific bargaining rights to teachers and their professional associations. Courts, viewing collective bargaining as within the scope of legislative authority, have restricted their role primarily to interpreting statutory and constitutional provisions. The judiciary has been reluctant to interfere with legislative authority to define the collective bargaining relationship between public employers and employees unless protected rights have been compromised.

Because of the variations in labor laws, as well as the lack of such laws in some states, substantial differences exist in bargaining rights and practices. A few states, such as New York, have a detailed, comprehensive collective bargaining statute that delineates specific bargaining rights. In contrast, negotiated contracts between teachers' organizations and school boards are prohibited in North Carolina. Under North Carolina law, all contracts between public employers and employee associations are invalid.[15] Similarly, in 1977 the Virginia Supreme Court declared that a negotiated contract between a teachers' organization and the school board was null and void in the absence of enabling legislation.[16] The board maintained that its power to enter into contracts allowed it also to bargain collectively with employee organizations, but the court concluded that such implied power was contrary to legislative intent.

In contrast to North Carolina and Virginia, other states without legislation have permitted negotiated agreements. The Kentucky Supreme Court has ruled that a public employer may recognize an employee organization for the purpose of collective bargaining, even though state law is silent regarding public employee bargaining rights.[17] The decision does not impose a duty on local school boards to bargain but merely allows a board the discretion to negotiate. This ruling is consistent with a number of other decisions permitting negotiated contracts in the absence of specific legislation. The board's power and authority to enter into contracts for the operation and maintenance of the school system have been construed to include the ability to enter into negotiated agreements with employee organizations.

Unless bargaining is mandated by statute, courts have not compelled school boards to negotiate. Whether or not to negotiate is thus at the school board's discretion. Once a school board extends recognition to a bargaining agent and commences bargaining, however, the board's actions in the negotiation process are governed by established judicial principles. Although the employer maintains certain prerogatives, such as recognition of the bargaining unit and determination of bargainable items, specific judicially recognized rights also are conferred on the employee organization. For example, there is a legal duty for the board to bargain in good faith. Furthermore, if negotiations reach an impasse, the board may not unilaterally terminate the bargaining process. Also, after signing a contract, the board is bound by the provisions and cannot abrogate the agreement on the basis that no duty to bargain existed. Hence, the school board is subject to a number of legal constraints after it enters into the negotiation process.

The diversity across states in protected bargaining rights for public employees has led many individuals and groups to advocate a federal bargaining law for all state and local employees. Supporting such a proposal are a number of national organizations, including the National Education Association, the American Federation of Teachers, and the American Federation of State, County, and Municipal Employees. In the mid-1970s a federal law appeared imminent, but was abandoned by Congress with the Supreme Court's decision in *National League of Cities v. Usery* interpreting congressional authority under the commerce clause and the tenth amendment.[18] The Court ruled that congressional amendments to the Fair Labor Standards Act (FLSA), extending the federal minimum wage and maximum hour provisions to state and local government employees, unconstitutionally interfered with the states' rights to structure the public employer–employee relationship.

However, the Supreme Court overturned *Usery* in 1985, concluding in *Garcia v. San Antonio Metropolitan Transit Authority* that state and municipal governments must comply with the minimum wage and overtime requirements in the FLSA.[19] The Court noted that nothing in these requirements was destructive of state sovereignty and that various checks on congressional power existed within the states. With this recognition of congressional authority, uniform collective bargaining legislation may again be considered by Congress. But for the immediate future, bargaining rights seem destined to be controlled by individual state legislation or, in the absence of such legislation, by court rulings.

STATUTORY BARGAINING RIGHTS OF TEACHERS

In the states that have enacted statutes governing teachers' bargaining rights, school boards must negotiate with teachers in accordance with the statutorily prescribed process. Generally, public employee bargaining laws address employer and employee rights, bargaining units, scope of bargaining, impasse resolution, grievance procedures, unfair labor practices, and penalties for prohibited practices. Many states have established labor relations boards to monitor bargaining under their statutes. Although the specific functions of these boards vary widely, their general purpose is to resolve questions arising from the implementation of state law. Functions assigned to such boards include determination of membership in bargaining units, resolution of union recognition claims, investigation of unfair labor practices, and interpretation of the general intent of statutory bargaining clauses. Decisions of labor boards are an important source of labor law since many of the issues addressed by boards are never appealed to courts.

Most state laws define the broad criteria for determining appropriate groupings of employees for bargaining purposes. Among the factors considered in assessing the appropriateness of bargaining units are the similarity in skills, wages, hours, and other working conditions of the employees; the effect of overfragmentation; the efficiency of operations of the employer; and the employer's administrative structure. Of these factors, similarity in skills and working conditions has been the most significant requirement. Disputes over the appropriateness of bargaining units are usually resolved by state labor boards.[20]

State laws generally provide that the school board will negotiate with an exclusive representative selected by the teachers. Procedures are specified for certification of the bargaining representative, election of the representative by employees, and recognition by the employer. Once an exclusive representative is recognized by the state labor relations board, an employer must bargain with that representative. In addition to certification, state laws also address cause and process for decertification of the exclusive representative.

Like the NLRA, state statutes require bargaining "in good faith." Good-faith bargaining has been interpreted as requiring parties to meet at reasonable times and attempt to reach mutual agreement without compulsion on either side to agree. A number of states have followed the federal law in stipulating that this "does not compel either party to agree to a proposal or to require the making of a concession."[21] Good-faith bargaining has been open to a range of interpretations, and judicial decisions in the public sector have relied extensively on private-sector rulings that have clarified the phrase. Failure of the school board or teachers' organization to bargain in good faith can result in the imposition of penalties.

Statutes impose certain restrictions or obligations on both the school board and the employee organization. Violation of the law by either party can result in an unfair labor practice claim. Allegations of unfair labor practices are brought before the state public employee relations board for a hearing and judgment. Specific unfair labor practices, often modeled after those in the NLRA, are included in state statutes. The most common prohibited labor practice in both public and private employment is that an employer or union will not interfere with, restrain, or coerce public employees in exercising their rights under the labor law. Among other prohibited employer practices are interference with the union's operations, discrimination against employees because of union membership, refusal to bargain collectively with the exclusive representative, and failure to bargain in good faith. Unions are prevented from causing an employer to discriminate against employees on the basis of union membership, refusing to bargain or failing to bargain in good faith, failing to represent all employees in the bargaining unit, and engaging in unlawful activities such as strikes or boycotts identified in the bargaining law.

SCOPE OF NEGOTIATIONS

Should the teachers' organization have input into class size? Who will determine the length of the school day? How will extra-duty assignments be determined? Will reductions in force necessitated by declining enrollment be based on seniority or merit? These questions and others are raised in determining the scope of negotiations. "Scope" refers to the range of issues or subjects that are negotiable, and determining scope is one of the most difficult tasks in public-sector bargaining. Public employers argue that issues must be narrowly defined to protect the government's policymaking role, while employee unions counter that bargaining subjects must be defined broadly for negotiations to be meaningful.[22]

Restrictions on scope of bargaining vary considerably among the states. Consequently, to determine negotiable items in a particular state, the state's collective bargaining law, other statutes, and litigation interpreting these laws must be examined.[23] The specification of negotiable items in labor laws may include broad guidelines or detailed enumerations. Many states have modeled their bargaining statutes after the NLRA, which stipulates that representatives of the employer and employees must meet and confer "with respect to wages, hours, and other terms and conditions of employment."[24] A few states have elected to deal directly with the scope of bargaining by identifying each item that must be negotiated.[25] In general, if specific statutory rights have been granted to teachers, they cannot be preempted by negotiation.[26] For example, the state tenure law may require extensive procedural protections for the termination of a teacher's employment that cannot be altered through a collective bargaining contract.

All proposed subjects for negotiation can be classified as either mandatory, permissive, or prohibited. Mandatory items must be negotiated. Failure of the school board to meet and confer on such items is evidence of lack of good-faith bargaining. Permissive items can be negotiated if both parties agree; however, there is no legal duty to consider the items. Furthermore, in most states permissive items cannot be pursued to the point of negotiation impasse, and an employer can make unilateral changes with respect to these items if a negotiated agreement is not reached. Prohibited items are beyond the power of the board to negotiate; an illegal delegation of power results if the board agrees to negotiate regarding these items. Since most statutory scope provisions are general in nature, courts often have been called upon to differentiate between negotiable and nonnegotiable items. The following sections highlight issues related to governmental policy and specific bargaining topics.

GOVERNMENTAL POLICY

Defining managerial rights is one of the key elements in establishing limitations on negotiable subjects at the bargaining table. State laws specify that public employers cannot be required to negotiate governmental policy matters, and courts have held that it is impermissible for a school board to bargain away certain rights and responsibilities in the public policy area.[27] Generally, educational policy matters are defined through provisions in collective bargaining statutes, such as "management rights" and "scope of bargaining" clauses. Policy issues such as class size and decisions related to the granting of tenure to teachers are totally excluded as negotiable items in a few states; however, most states stipulate only that employers will not be *required* to bargain such policy rights.

Public employee bargaining laws requiring the negotiation of "conditions of employment" can include far-reaching policy matters since most decisions made by a school board either directly or indirectly affect the teacher at the classroom level. The difficulty in distinguishing between educational policy and matters relating to teachers' employment was noted by the Maryland high court:

> Virtually every managerial decision in some way relates to "salaries, wages, hours, and other working conditions," and is therefore arguably negotiable. At the same time, virtually every such decision also involves educational policy considerations and is therefore arguably nonnegotiable.[28]

Judicial decisions interpreting negotiability illustrate the range in bargainable matters. The Supreme Court of New Jersey narrowly interpreted the phrase to mean wages, benefits, and work schedules, thereby removing governmental policy items such as teacher transfers, course offerings, and evaluations.[29] A number of courts, however, have construed conditions of employment in broader terms. The South Dakota Supreme Court held that subjects that *materially* affect teachers' employment are negotiable.[30] Similarly, the Nevada Supreme Court ruled that items *significantly* related to wages, hours, and working conditions are negotiable.[31] The Pennsylvania Supreme Court concluded that an issue's *impact* on conditions of employment must be weighed in determining whether it should be considered outside the educational policy area.[32]

While courts are in agreement that school boards cannot be *required* to negotiate inherent managerial rights pertaining to policy matters, these rights are viewed as *permissive* subjects of bargaining in some states. That is, the board may agree to negotiate a particular "right" in the absence of statutory or judicial prohibitions.[33] If the board does negotiate the policy item, it is bound by the agreement in the same manner as if the issue were a mandatory item.[34]

SELECTED BARGAINING SUBJECTS

Beyond wages, hours, and fringe benefits, there is a lack of agreement among states as to what is negotiable. Similar enabling legislation has been interpreted quite differently among states, as illustrated by the subjects discussed below.

Class Size. Class size has been one of the most controversial policy subjects, and one that courts and state legislatures have been reluctant to designate as negotiable. It is not specifically identified as a mandatory bargaining item in any state law, and the majority of courts reviewing the issue have found it to be a nonmandatory item. In Alaska, the state high court declared class size a nonnegotiable item because of its effect on educational policy.[35] The Nevada Supreme Court interpreted the state collective bargaining statute as including class size among mandatory subjects by implication,[36] but the legislature responded by revising the state law to exclude class size from a detailed list of bargainable items.[37] However, an Illinois appellate court held that class size is a mandatory issue for bargaining,[38] and several other courts have found it to be a *permissive* subject of bargaining.[39] Although the Wisconsin Supreme Court found class size to be such a permissive subject, the court held that negotiations on the *impact* of class size on teachers' conditions of employment would be mandatory.[40] Similarly, a Florida appellate court concluded that class size and staffing levels were not mandatorily bargainable but noted that bargaining on the impact or effect of the implementation of these decisions would be mandatory.[41]

School Calendar. Establishment of the school calendar generally has been held to be a managerial prerogative.[42] Reflecting the judicial trend that it is a nonnegotiable managerial decision, the Maine high court stated:

> The commencement and termination of the school year and the scheduling and length of intermediate vacations during the school year, at least insofar as students and teachers are congruently involved, must be held matters of "educational policies" bearing too substantially upon too many and important non-teacher interests to be settled by collective bargaining.[43]

An Indiana appellate court agreed, noting that the impact of the school calendar on students and other public interests outweighed teachers' interests.[44] In a later case, another Indiana appellate court concurred that mandatory bargaining of the school calendar is not required, but under state law it is a "working condition" that must be discussed.[45] Departing from the prevailing view, the Wisconsin Supreme Court upheld a ruling of the Wisconsin Employment Relations Commission declaring the school calendar mandatorily bargainable; calendar issues were found to be more closely related to terms of employment than to policy matters.[46]

Teacher Evaluation. Employee unions have made significant gains in securing the right to negotiate various aspects of teacher performance evaluations. Most states have not specified evaluation as a mandatory bargaining item, but a number of courts have found it to be significantly related to conditions of employment and thus negotiable. Although courts have been receptive to union proposals to negotiate the technical and procedural elements of evaluation, they have been reluctant to mandate the negotiation of evaluation criteria. The Supreme Court of New Jersey, concluding that criteria for evaluation cannot be negotiated, recognized that "while the policy established for evaluating tenured teachers intimately and directly affects the work and welfare of those public employees, it also involves the exercise of inherent management prerogatives."[47] The court, however, did uphold negotiation of procedural aspects beyond those required by the state board of education. Similarly, the Supreme Court of Kansas distinguished between managerial policies and the mechanics of such policies; the mechanics of developing the evaluation procedures were found to be mandatorily negotiable, but not the evaluation criteria, which were designated as a managerial prerogative.[48] The Supreme Court of Iowa, however, found a statutory requirement to negotiate *evaluation procedures* to encompass substantive criteria for evaluation because the term "procedures" had been interpreted broadly in previous judicial rulings.[49]

Reduction in Force. With declining student enrollments and financial exigency faced by many school districts, staff reductions in force (RIF) have become a threat to tenured as well as nontenured teachers. The threat has resulted in employee unions demanding input into decisions to reduce staff, criteria for reductions, and procedures for selecting teachers for release. Generally, courts have held that the decision to reduce staff and the criteria used to make that decision are educational policy matters and thus not negotiable.[50] The *impact* of reductions on employee rights, however, may necessitate negotiation of RIF procedures. The Supreme Court of Kansas held that the decision to reduce teaching positions was a nonnegotiable managerial decision, but concluded that the mechanics of staff reductions, such as how staff would be selected and procedures for recall, were mandatorily negotiable.[51] The Supreme Court of Wisconsin developed a balancing test for weighing employees' interests in wages, hours, and conditions of employment against the employer's right to make managerial policy decisions. If an item is "primarily related" to wages, hours, and conditions of employment, the item is a mandatory subject of bargaining; if not, there is no duty to bargain. Accordingly, the court found that notice and timing of layoffs had to be bargained as they were primarily related to employees' interest and had "a direct impact on wages and job security."[52] The Supreme Court of New Jersey also found that procedural fairness concerning timely notice of teachers' release was negotiable; such a requirement did not pose a "significant interference with the exercise of governmental prerogative."[53] In contrast to these decisions, an Illinois appellate court held that the decision to lay off teachers for economic reasons "greatly affects" terms and conditions of employment and, therefore, the school board has a duty to bargain regarding this matter.[54] This provides the teachers' union an opportunity to suggest other cost-reduction alternatives.

Procedures negotiated by the employer and the teachers' union for staff reductions, however, must not violate the constitutional rights of any employees. The United States Supreme Court overturned a collective bargaining agreement that was designed to protect members of certain minority groups from layoffs.[55] The agreement ensured that the percentage of minority teachers would not fall below the percentage employed before any reduction in force. Without evidence that there had been prior employment discrimination, the Court held that the plan violated the equal protection rights of nonminority teachers.

Nonrenewal and Tenure Decisions. Decisions to retain a teacher or grant tenure clearly are managerial rights and not mandatorily bargainable.[56] If a school board negotiates procedural aspects of these decisions, however, the provisions generally are binding.[57] For example, collective bargaining agreements may entitle nontenured teachers to procedural protections that ordinarily would not be required under state laws or the fourteenth amendment.[58] The Supreme Court of New Hampshire held that state law did not prevent a school board from agreeing to provide probationary teachers with a statement of reasons for nonrenewal; the board still retained its managerial prerogative not to renew the teacher's contract.[59]

Failure of school boards to follow negotiated procedures has resulted in arbitrators ordering reinstatement of discharged teachers. Permissibility of such awards, however, depends on how a school board's authority is interpreted under state law. The Supreme Court of Alaska rejected an arbitrator's reinstatement of a teacher, reasoning that school boards "possess the exclusive power, not subject to *any* appeal, to decide whether to 'nonrenew' a provisional employee."[60] The court noted that a range of other remedies was available for the board's violation of the negotiated nonretention procedures. In contrast, the Supreme Court of Montana concluded that reinstatement of teachers by an arbitrator did not usurp school board authority but simply provided appropriate relief for the board's failure to abide by negotiated procedures.[61]

UNION SECURITY PROVISIONS

To ensure their strength and viability, unions attempt to obtain various security provisions in the collective bargaining contract. The nature and extent of these provisions will depend on state laws and constitutional limitations. In this section, provisions related to union revenue and exclusive privileges are addressed.

DUES AND SERVICE FEES

Unions seek to require all employees either to join or support financially the recognized bargaining agent. It is argued that such provisions are necessary to eliminate "free riders," since a union must represent all individuals in the bargaining unit. Union security provisions take several forms. The *closed shop,* requiring an employer to hire only union members, does not exist in the public sector and is unlawful in the private sector under the NLRA and the Taft-Hartley amendments. The *union shop* agreement requires an employee to join the union within a designated period of time after employment to retain a position. While union shop agreements are prevalent in the private sector, they are not authorized by most public-sector laws and are limited or proscribed in a number of states under "right-to-work" laws. The *agency shop* and *fair share* agreements are the security provisions most frequently found in the public sector.[62] An agency shop agreement requires an employee to pay union dues but does not mandate membership. A variant of agency shop is the fair share arrangement whereby the nonmember simply pays a service fee to cover the cost of bargaining activities.

The constitutionality of mandatory payment of agency fees by public employees was upheld by the Supreme Court in 1977 in a Michigan case, *Abood v. Detroit Board of Education.*[63] The Court rejected the nonunion members' first amendment speech and association claims, noting the importance of ensuring labor peace and eliminating "free riders." The Court, however, concluded that under the protection of the first amendment, an employee could not be compelled "to contribute to the support of an ideological cause he may oppose as a condition of holding a job as a public school teacher."[64] Accordingly, the fee for a nonmember teacher who objects to forced contribution to political activities of the union must reflect only costs of bargaining and contract administration.[65]

Although the Supreme Court's decision permitted the collection of a service fee from nonunion members who raised first amendment objections, it did not resolve a number of significant issues, such as: (1) What expenditures can unions legitimately claim as related to collective bargaining activities? (2) What procedures are adequate or necessary to protect the interests of individuals challenging the union's apportionment of costs? (3) Can employees be discharged as a means to enforce an agency shop agreement?

Under the *Abood* ruling, the burden is placed on the nonunion employee to object to the union's use of the agency fee, and the union then must establish the proportionate service fee share related to employee representation. The Supreme Court noted that there would be "difficult problems in drawing lines between collective bargaining activities, for which contributions may be compelled, and ideological activities unrelated to collective bargaining, for which such compulsion is prohibited."[66] In subsequent cases, the Supreme Court and lower courts have attempted to define this dividing line as well as the procedural protections necessary to respond to nonmembers' objections.

In *Ellis v. Brotherhood of Railway, Airline, and Steamship Clerks*, a private sector case, the Supreme Court in 1984 advanced a standard for determining which union expenditures can be assessed against objecting employees:

> The test must be whether the challenged expenditures are necessarily or reasonably incurred for the purpose of performing the duties of an exclusive representative of the employees in dealing with the employer on labor–management issues. Under this standard, objecting employees may be compelled to pay their fair share of not only the direct costs of negotiating and administering a collective-bargaining contract and of settling grievances and disputes, but also the expenses of activities or undertakings normally or reasonably employed to implement or effectuate the duties of the union as exclusive representative of the employees in the bargaining unit.[67]

In applying this test, the Court upheld the assessment of costs related to union conventions, social activities, and publications, but disallowed expenditures related to organizing activities and litigation unrelated to negotiations, contract administration, and fair representation.

The *Ellis* test has been employed by courts to uphold the assessment of a range of expenditures against objecting employees in the public sector such as conventions, lobbying activities, publications, and campaigns for levies to increase funding for public education.[68] In 1991, however, the Supreme Court in *Lehnert v. Ferris Faculty Association* limited some of these charges in a Michigan public sector case.[69] Expenditures for conventions, selected sections of union publications, preparations for a strike,[70] and chargeable activities of state and national affiliates were upheld. But the Court ruled that unions may not assess nonmembers for lobbying and other political activities that are "outside the limited context of contract ratification or implementation," for litigation that does not involve the local bargaining unit, and for public relations efforts "to enhance the reputation of the teaching profession."[71] In denying charges for lobbying activities, the Court noted:

> By utilizing petitioners' funds for political lobbying and to garner the support of the public in its endeavors, the union would use each dissenter as "an instrument for fostering public adherence to an ideological point of view he

finds unacceptable.'' The first amendment protects the individual's right to participation in these spheres from precisely this type of invasion. Where the subject of compelled speech is the discussion of governmental affairs, which is at the core of our first amendment freedoms, the burden upon dissenters' rights extends far beyond the acceptance of the agency shop and is constitutionally impermissible.[72]

Significant for unions, however, was the recognition that contributions to the state and national affiliates are chargeable expenditures even in the absence of a ''direct and tangible impact'' on the local bargaining unit. As Justice O'Connor noted, this affiliation functions in much the same manner as an insurance policy—bringing to bear the substantial economic and political resources of the affiliates when there is a local need.

The constitutionality of union procedures adopted to respond to non-members who object to the agency fee has generated considerable debate. Generally, after a nonmember raises an objection, unions have provided a rebate of the portion of the fee unrelated to bargaining activities. However, in the 1984 *Ellis* decision, the Supreme Court found a *pure rebate* procedure inadequate. Characterizing this approach as an ''involuntary loan,'' the Court stated that ''by exacting and using full dues, then refunding months later the portion that it was not allowed to exact in the first place, the union effectively charges the employees for activities that are outside the scope of the statutory authorization.''[73] Because other alternatives such as advance reduction of dues and escrow accounts exist, the Court found even temporary use of dissenters' funds impermissible.[74]

In 1986 the Supreme Court provided further guidance in determining the adequacy of union procedural safeguards to protect nonmember employees' constitutional rights in the apportionment and assessment of representation fees. According to the Court in *Chicago Teachers' Union, Local No. 1 v. Hudson,* constitutional requirements for the collection of an agency fee include ''an adequate explanation of the basis for the fee, a reasonably prompt opportunity to challenge the amount of the fee before an impartial decisionmaker, and an escrow for the amounts reasonably in dispute while such challenges are pending.''[75] The contested Chicago union's plan included an advance reduction of dues, but it was found to be flawed because nonmembers were required to file an objection in order to receive any information about the calculation of the proportionate share, and they were not provided sufficient information to judge the appropriateness of the fee. The Court held that adequate disclosure required more than identification of expenditures that did not benefit objecting employees; reasons had to be provided for assessment of the fair share. In addition, the Chicago procedures did not ensure dissenting employees a prompt decision by an impartial decisionmaker.[76] The Court went further than the *Ellis* prohibition on a pure rebate procedure and held that, even if an advance reduction is made, any additional amounts in dispute must be placed in escrow. This was found to be necessary to minimize the risk that any funds of an objector would be used for impermissible ideological activities. Subsequently, several courts also have held that if it appears that the union's procedures for collecting fair share fees do not satisfy the constitutional requirements outlined in *Hudson* no fees can be collected even if they are placed in escrow.[77]

The adequacy of unions' financial reporting practices, as required in *Hudson,* has been contested. According to the Supreme Court, financial disclosure must be adequate or sufficient, not an exhaustive and detailed list of all expenditures. The Court specifically stated in *Hudson* that the union must provide enough detail to enable nonmembers to make an informed decision about the "propriety of the union's fee."[78] The Sixth Circuit Appellate Court held that this does not require unions to provide financial information audited at the "highest" available level of audit services.[79] In that case, the court concluded that the union's financial disclosure, including budgets, audited financial statements, and audited supplemental schedules of the state and national associations, was constitutionally adequate. In 1991, the Seventh Circuit Court of Appeals found the *revised* fair share notice procedures proposed by the Chicago teachers' union in response to the original *Hudson* case to be constitutionally adequate.[80] The thirty-two-page audited disclosure notice identified expenditures as chargeable or nonchargeable expenses with detailed breakdowns of expenditure items in each category. The level of specificity was found to be sufficient to enable nonmembers to determine if there was a basis for challenging the designated fair share fee.

Although the Supreme Court has upheld agency shop provisions, they may not be permitted under some state laws. The Maine high court held that forced payment of dues was "tantamount to coercion toward membership."[81] The Maine statute ensures employees the right to join a union *voluntarily*. This was interpreted by the court as including the right to *refrain* from joining. Similarly, the Vermont Supreme Court held that an agency fee was prohibited under the Vermont Labor Relations for Teachers Act, which specified that teachers have the right to join or not to join, assist, or participate in a labor organization.[82]

Representation fees do not violate the Federal Constitution and have been upheld in most states, but legal controversy surrounds enforcement of the provisions.[83] Some collective bargaining agreements require employers to discharge teachers who refuse to pay the fee. In Pennsylvania, an appellate court overturned the dismissal of two teachers, stating that refusal to pay dues did not constitute "persistent and willful violation of the school laws" to justify dismissal.[84] An Indiana appellate court concluded that school districts cannot bargain away their responsibility to discharge teachers.[85] Several courts have attempted to reconcile labor laws that authorize the negotiation of fair share fees as a condition of employment with tenure laws that permit dismissal only for specified causes. The Supreme Court of Michigan has ruled that the state labor law prevails when it conflicts with another statute.[86] Accordingly, a tenured teacher who fails to pay the agency service fee can be discharged without resort to procedural requirements of the teacher tenure law. Similarly, the California Public Employment Relations Board has held that state law authorizing a service fee permits termination of a teacher's employment.[87]

EXCLUSIVE PRIVILEGES

The designated employee bargaining representative gains security through negotiating exclusive rights or privileges such as dues checkoff, the use of the school mails, and access to school facilities. Although exclusive arrangements strengthen the majority union and may make it difficult for minority unions to survive, they often are supported by courts as a means of promoting labor peace and ensuring efficient operation of the school system.

The exclusive privilege most often found in collective bargaining contracts is dues checkoff. Over half of the states with public employee bargaining laws specify dues checkoff as a mandatory subject for bargaining.[88] However, the Supreme Court has held that employee unions do not have a constitutional right to payroll deductions.[89] The Fourth Circuit Court of Appeals ruled that state legislation permitting payroll deductions for charitable organizations but not labor unions was not an infringement of the first amendment; the law did not deny the union members the right to associate, speak, publish, recruit members, or express their views.[90] Unless prohibited by state law, most courts have upheld negotiated agreements between the designated bargaining representative and the employer that deny rival unions checkoff rights.

In 1983, the Supreme Court clarified one of the most controversial security rights—exclusive access to school mail facilities.[91] The case focused on an agreement between the exclusive bargaining representative and an Indiana school board denying all rival unions access to the interschool mail system and teacher mailboxes. One of the unions challenged the agreement as a violation of first and fourteenth amendment rights. The Supreme Court upheld the arrangement, reasoning that the first amendment does not require "equivalent access to all parts of a school building in which some form of communicative activity occurs."[92] The Court concluded that the school mail facility was not a public forum for communication and thereby its use could be restricted to official school business. The fact that several community groups (e.g., Scouts, civic organizations) used the school mail system did not create a public forum. The Court noted that, even if such access by community groups created a limited public forum, access would be extended only to similar groups—not to labor organizations. The Court's emphasis on the availability of alternative channels of communication (e.g., bulletin boards and meeting facilities), however, indicates that total exclusion of rival unions would not be permitted.

The Fifth Circuit Court of Appeals subsequently ruled, and the Supreme Court affirmed, that denial of access to the school mail to all teacher organizations did not violate the first amendment when other channels of communication were available.[93] However, the Court found unconstitutional a policy prohibiting individual teachers from discussing employee organizations during nonclass time or using the internal mail system or bulletin boards to mention employee organizations. Such limitations on an individual employee's expression would be permissible only if a threat of material and substantial disruption were shown.

It appears that exclusive use of communication facilities can be constitutionally granted to the bargaining representative or that use of facilities can be denied to all employee organizations. If rival unions are excluded from specific communication channels, other avenues must be available to avoid infringement of first amendment rights. Under state laws, however, exclusive access to use of mail and school facilities may be an unfair labor practice. For example, the Florida Public Employee Relations Commission adopted a policy prohibiting access rules that discriminated against rival unions.[94]

In most states, school boards negotiate only with the designated bargaining representative. Under this exclusive recognition, other unions and teacher groups can be denied the right to engage in official exchanges with an employer. The Supreme Court has held that nonmembers of a bargaining unit or members who disagree with the views of the representative do not have a constitutional right "to force the government to listen to their views."[95] The Court concluded that a Minnesota statute requiring employers to "meet and confer" only with the designated bargaining representative did not violate other employees' speech or associational rights as public employees or as citizens since these sessions were not a public forum. According to the Court, "the Constitution does not grant to members of the public generally a right to be heard by public bodies making decisions of policy."[96]

However, if a public forum, such as a school board meeting, is involved, a nonunion teacher has a constitutional right to address the public employer, even on a subject of negotiation. The Supreme Court concluded in a Wisconsin case that a nonunion teacher had the right to express concerns to the school board.[97] In this case, negotiation between the board and union had reached a deadlock on the issue of an agency shop provision. A nonunion teacher, representing a minority group of teachers, addressed the board at a regular public meeting and requested postponement of a decision until further study. The Court reasoned that the teacher was not attempting to negotiate, but merely to speak on an important issue before the board—a right any citizen possesses. The Court further noted that teachers have never been "compelled to relinquish their first amendment rights they would otherwise enjoy as citizens to comment on matters of public interest in connection with the operation of the public school in which they work.''[98]

While union security provisions such as agency shop fees and exclusive use of specific school facilities can be negotiated, nonunion teachers' constitutional rights cannot be infringed. Teachers must be ensured an effective mechanism for challenging financial contributions that might be used to support ideological causes or political activities to which they object. If specific communication channels for nonmembers are restricted through the negotiation process, alternative options must remain open.

NEGOTIATION IMPASSE

An impasse occurs in bargaining when an agreement cannot be reached and neither party will compromise. When negotiations reach such a stalemate, several options are available for resolution—mediation, fact finding, and arbitration. As discussed in the final section of this chapter, the most effective means for resolving negotiation impasse—the strike—is not legally available to the majority of public employees. Most comprehensive state statutes address impasse procedures, with provisions ranging from allowing impasse procedures to be negotiated to mandating detailed steps that must be followed. Alternatives that are most frequently employed to resolve impasse are identified below.

Mediation is often the first step to reopening negotiations. A neutral third party assists both sides in finding a basis for agreement. The mediator serves as a facilitator rather than a decisionmaker, thus enabling the school board's representative and the teachers' association jointly to reach an agreement. Mediation may be optional or required by law; the mediator is selected by the negotiation teams or, upon request, appointed by a public employee relations board.

Failure to reach agreement through mediation frequently results in fact finding (often called advisory arbitration). The process may be mandated by law or may be entered into by mutual agreement of both parties. Fact finding involves a third party investigating the causes for the dispute, collecting facts and testimony to clarify the dispute, and formulating a judgment. Because of the advisory nature of the process, proposed solutions are not binding on either party. However, since fact-finding reports are made available to the public, they provide an impetus to settle a contract that is not present in mediation.

In a number of states, the final step in impasse procedures is fact finding, which may leave both parties without a satisfactory solution. A few states permit a third alternative—binding interest arbitration. This process is similar to fact finding except that the decision of the arbitrator, related to the terms of the negotiated agreement, is binding on both parties.

States that permit binding arbitration often place restrictions on its use.[99] For example, Ohio and Maine permit binding arbitration on matters of mutual consent,[100] Rhode Island allows binding arbitration only on non-monetary items,[101] and Oregon merely provides that impasse procedures with final and binding arbitration may be negotiated.[102]

It is generally agreed that mediation and fact finding, because of their advisory nature, do not provide the most effective means for resolving negotiation disputes. Since strikes are prohibited among public employees in most states, conditional binding arbitration has been considered a viable alternative in resolving deadlocks. Although a greater balance of power is achieved between the school board and the teachers' association with binding arbitration, it has not been met with enthusiasm by public sector employers, who often view it as an illegal delegation of power. As a result, interest arbitration generally has occurred in the educational setting only on a voluntary or conditional basis.

GRIEVANCES

Disputes concerning employee rights under the terms of a collective bargaining agreement are resolved through the negotiated grievance mechanism. Grievance procedures usually provide for a neutral third party, an arbitrator, to conduct a hearing and render a decision. *Grievance* arbitration, which addresses enforcement of rights under the contract, is distinct from *interest* arbitration that may take place in reaching a contract agreement. Depending on state law and the negotiated contract, the decision in grievance arbitration may be advisory or binding. Public employers, adhering to the doctrine of the sovereign power of government, have been reluctant to agree to procedures that might result in a loss of public authority. Allowing grievance procedures to include final decisionmaking by a third party significantly lessens a school board's power, effectively equating the positions of the teachers' organization and the school board. Nevertheless, as bargaining has expanded, legislative bodies have favored binding arbitration as a means of settling labor disputes. Over twenty states have enacted laws permitting school boards to negotiate grievance procedures with binding arbitration, and several states require binding arbitration as the final step in the grievance procedure.[103] With the widespread acceptance of grievance arbitration, it has become one of the most contested areas in collective bargaining. Suits have challenged the arbitrator's authority to render decisions in specific disputes as well as the authority to provide certain remedies.

One of the primary issues in establishing a grievance procedure is the definition of a grievance, that is, what can be grieved. In the private sector, a grievance is usually defined as any dispute between the employer and the employee. Teachers' grievances, on the other hand, are generally limited

to controversies arising from the interpretation or application of the negotiated contract. Arbitrability of a dispute then depends on whether the
school board and union agreed to settle the issue by arbitration or whether
the agreement shows such an intent.[104] Decisions as to arbitrability are
made by arbitrators, and the decisions are presumed to be valid when
derived from the construction of the negotiated agreement. The Supreme
Court of Iowa noted:

> Because arbitration is favored as a means of settling civil disputes without the
> expense and delay of litigation, arbitrability will be recognized "unless it may
> be said with positive assurance that the arbitration clause is not susceptible of
> an interpretation that covers the asserted dispute. Doubts should be resolved
> in favor of coverage."[105]

Recent disputes held to be arbitrable based on negotiated contracts
include unsatisfactory teacher performance, suspensions resulting from
declining enrollment, procedural aspects of evaluation, eligibility for continuing contract, merit and equity pay raises, classroom observations, and
assignment of out-of-class activities.[106] Although a range of questions has
been found to be arbitrable, courts have ruled that issues related to nondel-
egable policy matters under state law are outside the scope of arbitration.
For example, impermissible issues have involved tenure decisions, employee dismissal, reappointment of nontenured teachers, evaluation of
teacher qualifications, teacher discipline, and employment discrimination
claims.[107] Also, issues that are specifically excluded in the contract cannot
be submitted to arbitration.

Arbitration awards or remedies also have been challenged. Again, as
with arbitrability, courts have adopted a narrow scope of review, with
many courts presuming the validity of awards. The deference afforded an
arbitrator's award is evident from the Supreme Court's statement that
"unless the arbitral decision does not 'draw its essence from the collective
bargaining agreement,' a court is bound to enforce the award and is not
entitled to review the merits of the contract dispute."[108] As long as an
arbitrator's award can be interpreted as rationally derived from the language and context of the agreement, courts have found that it "draws its
essence" from the agreement.[109] Courts do not interfere with arbitration
awards simply because they would have provided a different remedy.

STRIKES

Most teachers are prohibited from striking by either state statute or common law. It is argued that there can be no true collective bargaining
without the right to withhold services, which characterizes the bargaining
process in the private sector. Except in a few states, legislation and judicial

rulings have generally prohibited teacher strikes.[110] In those states that have legislation granting public employees a limited right to strike, certain conditions, specified in statute, must be met prior to the initiation of a work stoppage. Designated conditions vary but usually include: (1) exhaustion of statutory mediation and fact-finding steps, (2) expiration of the contract, (3) elapse of a certain time period prior to commencing the strike, (4) written notice of the union's intent to strike, and (5) evidence that the strike will not constitute a danger to public health or safety. In contrast to the few states permitting strikes, most states with statutes pertaining to collective bargaining for public employees have specific "no-strike" provisions.

Courts consistently have upheld "no-strike" laws and generally have denied the right to strike unless it has been affirmatively granted by the state.[111] Several early cases are still representative of the dominant judicial posture on public teachers' strikes. In a Connecticut case, the state high court stated that permitting teachers to strike could be equated with asserting that "they can deny the authority of government."[112] The court in this case denied teachers the right to strike, emphasizing that a teacher is an agent of the government, possessing a portion of the state's sovereignty. The Supreme Court of Indiana issued a restraining order against striking teachers, affirming the same public welfare issue.[113] Addressing the legality of strikes, a New Jersey appellate court declared that legislative authorization for bargaining did not reflect an intent to depart from the common law rule prohibiting strikes by public employees.[114]

In contrast to the prevailing common law position, the high courts of California and Louisiana have declared strikes permissible for some public employees. Both states have statutes that closely parallel private sector laws except that the issue of strikes is not addressed. In upholding strikes, the California court stated that:

> Strikes by public employees are not unlawful at common law unless or until it is clearly demonstrated that such a strike creates a substantial and imminent threat to the health or safety of the public. This standard allows exceptions in certain essential areas of public employment (e.g., the prohibition against firefighters and law enforcement personnel) and also requires courts to determine on a case-by-case basis whether the public interest overrides the basic right to strike.[115]

Following a similar standard, the Louisiana Supreme Court held that teachers have the right to strike.[116]

A strike is more than simply a work stoppage; states define the term broadly to include a range of concerted activities such as work slowdowns, massive absences for "sick" days, and refusal to perform certain duties. For example, the Massachusetts high court found that refusal to perform customary activities, such as grading papers and preparing lesson plans after the end of the school day, constituted a strike.[117]

State laws, in addition to prohibiting work stoppages, usually identify penalties for involvement in strikes. Such penalties can include withholding compensation for strike days, prohibiting salary increases for designated periods of time (e.g., one year), and dismissal. Penalties for illegal strikes also are imposed on unions. Sanctions may include fines, decertification of the union, and loss of certain privileges such as dues checkoff.[118]

Despite statutory prohibitions against strikes, many teachers, as well as other public employees, participate in work stoppages each year. Public employers can request a court injunction against teachers who threaten to strike or initiate such action. Most courts have granted injunctions, concluding as did the Supreme Court of Alaska that the "illegality of the strike is a sufficient harm to justify injunctive relief."[119] Failure of teachers to comply with such a restraining order can result in charges of contempt of court, with resulting fines and/or imprisonment. For example, teachers in a Maryland school district who refused to obey an injunction were found guilty of criminal contempt.[120] In Newark, New Jersey, refusal to comply with an injunction resulted in a contempt-of-court charge, with fines and imprisonment for teachers and an additional fine for the union.[121] An order imposing a fine of ten dollars per day on striking teachers was upheld by the Wisconsin Supreme Court.[122]

Even though the injunction has been the most effective response to strikes, a few courts have been reluctant to impose this sanction automatically. Other factors have been considered, such as whether the board bargained in "good faith," whether the strike constituted a clear and present danger to public safety, and whether irreparable harm would result from the strike.[123] Thus, evidence required by school boards to demonstrate sufficient cause for an injunction has varied according to the legal jurisdiction and the interpretation of applicable state statutes.

The procedures required for dismissal of striking teachers have received judicial attention. Courts have held that due process procedures must be provided, but questions arise as to the nature and type of hearing that must be afforded. The Wisconsin Supreme Court ruled that striking teachers must be provided an impartial and fair hearing and that the board of education was not sufficiently impartial to serve as the hearing panel. Reversing this decision, the United States Supreme Court maintained that the board's involvement did not overcome "the presumption of honesty and integrity in policymakers with decisionmaking power."[124] The Court further held that "permitting the Board to make the decision at issue here preserves its control over school district affairs, leaves the balance of power in labor relations where the state legislature struck it, and assures that the decision whether to dismiss the teachers will be made by the body responsible for that decision under state law."[125] While noting that the fourteenth amendment guarantees each teacher procedural due process, the Supreme Court concluded that a hearing before the school board satisfies this requirement.

State legislatures and courts generally have refused to grant public school teachers the right to strike. Even in the few states where a limited right to strike has been gained, extensive restrictions have been placed on its use.[126] Teachers participating in an illegal strike are subject to court imposed penalties and, in most states, to statutory penalties. Refusal of teachers to return to the classroom can result in dismissal.

CONCLUSION

Because of the diversity in collective bargaining laws among states, legal principles with universal application are necessarily broad. Generalizations concerning collective bargaining rights that are applicable to most teachers are set forth below.

1. Teachers have a constitutionally protected right to form and join a union.
2. Specific bargaining rights are conferred through state statutes or judicial interpretations of state constitutions, thus creating wide divergence in teachers' bargaining rights across states.
3. School boards are not required to bargain with employee organizations unless mandated to do so by state law.
4. Collective bargaining must be conducted "in good faith," which means that the school board and teachers' organization attempt to reach agreement without compulsion on either side to agree.
5. The scope of negotiations is generally defined to include wages, hours, and other terms and conditions of employment, such as teaching load, planning time, and lunch periods.
6. Governmental policy matters are not mandatorily bargainable but may be permissive subjects unless prohibited by law.
7. State legislation permitting the negotiation of an agency shop provision is constitutional; however, if a public employee objects to supporting specific ideological or political causes, the fee must reflect only the costs of bargaining and contract administration.
8. To collect a fair share fee from a nonunion teacher who raises first amendment objections, the union must provide adequate information regarding the basis of the fee, procedural safeguards to ensure a prompt response to employees who may object, and an escrow account for challenged amounts.
9. Unions may constitutionally negotiate exclusive privileges such as the use of the school mail and dues checkoff; other communication options, however, must be available to rival unions.
10. Nonunion teachers have the right to express a viewpoint before the school board on an issue under negotiation between the board and union.

11. Impasse procedures for public-sector bargaining are generally limited to mediation and fact finding, with the public employer retaining final decisionmaking authority.
12. Teacher strikes, except in limited situations in a few states, are illegal and punishable by dismissal, fines, and/or imprisonment.

ENDNOTES

1. *See* text with note 18, *infra*.
2. *See* Benjamin Taylor and Fred Witney, *Labor Relations Law* (Englewood Cliffs, NJ: Prentice-Hall, 1975), pp. 69–99, for a discussion of the use and control of labor injunctions.
3. 29 U.S.C. § 113 (1988).
4. The Wagner Act states that "employees shall have the right to self-organization, to form, join or assist labor organizations, to bargain collectively through representatives of their own choosing, and to engage in concerted activities, for the purpose of collective bargaining or other mutual aid or protection," 29 U.S.C. § 57 (1988).
5. The application of private-sector labor laws to private schools, most of which are church-related, has been controversial. Only private schools with a gross annual revenue of $1 million or more come under the jurisdiction of the National Labor Relations Board (NLRB); however, the majority of private schools do not reach this income level. Furthermore, the United States Supreme Court has held that the NLRB does not have jurisdiction over lay faculty in parochial schools in the absence of a clear expression of congressional intent to cover teachers in church-related schools under the NLRA, National Labor Relations Board v. Catholic Bishop of Chicago, 440 U.S. 490 (1979). The Second Circuit Court of Appeals, however, concluded that Catholic schools in New York come under the jurisdiction of the state labor relations board. Since the ruling involved bargaining activities of lay teachers regarding only secular employment practices, no infringement of the establishment clause or free exercise clause of the first amendment was found, Catholic High School Ass'n v. Culvert, 753 F.2d 1161 (2d Cir. 1985). *See also* Christ the King Regional High School v. Culvert, 815 F.2d 219 (2d Cir. 1987), *cert. denied,* 484 U.S. 830 (1987).
6. 29 U.S.C. § 142 (1988).
7. *See* text with note 27, *infra.* for discussion of management rights.
8. 3 C.F.R. § 521 (1962).
9. Keyishian v. Board of Regents, 385 U.S. 589 (1967).
10. McLaughlin v. Tilendis, 398 F.2d 287, 289 (7th Cir. 1968).
11. Atkins v. City of Charlotte, 296 F. Supp. 1068 (W.D.N.C. 1969); Dade County Classroom Teachers' Ass'n v. Ryan, 225 So. 2d 903 (Fla. 1969). *See also* American Fed'n of State, County, and Mun. Employees v. Woodward, 406 F.2d 137 (8th Cir. 1969).
12. Hickman v. Valley Local School Dist. Bd. of Educ., 619 F.2d 606 (6th Cir.

1980). *See also* Saye v. St. Vrain Valley School Dist. RE-1J, 785 F.2d 862 (10th Cir. 1986).

13. Lake Park Educ. Ass'n v. Board of Educ. of Lake Park High School Dist., 526 F. Supp. 710 (N.D. Ill. 1981). *See also* Georgia Ass'n of Educators v. Gwinnett County School Dist., 856 F.2d 142 (11th Cir. 1988); Jackson v. Hazlehurst Mun. Separate School Dist., 427 So. 2d 134 (Miss. 1983); Uniondale Union Free School Dist. v. Newman, 562 N.Y.S.2d 148 (N.Y. App. Div. 1990).

14. Stellmaker v. DePetrillo, 710 F. Supp. 891 (D. Conn. 1989). *See also* Morfin v. Albuquerque Pub. Schools, 906 F.2d 1434 (10th Cir. 1990); Gavrilles v. O'Connor, 611 F. Supp. 210 (D. Mass. 1985).

15. Winston-Salem/Forsyth County Unit of the North Carolina Ass'n of Educators v. Phillips, 381 F. Supp. 644 (M.D.N.C. 1974).

16. Commonwealth v. County Bd. of Arlington County, 232 S.E.2d 30 (Va. 1977).

17. Board of Trustees of Univ. of Kentucky v. Public Employees Council No. 51, American Fed'n of State, County, and Mun. Employees, 571 S.W.2d 616 (Ky. 1978). *See also* Littleton Educ. Ass'n v. Arapahoe County School Dist., 553 P.2d 793 (Colo. 1976).

18. 426 U.S. 833 (1976).

19. 469 U.S. 528 (1985). *See* text with note 30, Chapter 1.

20. *See* Ohio Rev. Code § 4117.06 (1991). State law not only provides that the Ohio State Employment Relations Board determines the appropriateness of a bargaining unit but also stipulates that the Board's decision is "final and conclusive and not appealable to the court." A similar restriction in the Indiana labor law resulted in the entire statute being declared void because the provision was nonseverable from the remainder of the statute, Indiana Educ. Employment Relations Bd. v. Benton Community School Corp., 365 N.E.2d 752 (Ind. 1977).

21. 29 U.S.C. § 158(d) (1988).

22. *See* "Developments in the Law, Public Employment," *Harvard Law Review,* vol. 97 (1984), pp. 1611–1738.

23. *See, e.g.,* United Teachers of Dade v. Dade County School Bd., 500 So. 2d 508 (Fla. 1986) (award provided by Florida's Master Teacher Program was not a "wage" and thus did not abridge collective bargaining rights guaranteed by the state constitution).

24. 29 U.S.C. § 158(d) (1988).

25. *See, e.g.,* Iowa Code 20 § 20.1 *et seq.* (1989); Nev. Rev. Stat. § 288.010 *et seq.* (1990).

26. *See, e.g.,* San Mateo City School Dist. v. Public Employment Relations Bd., 663 P.2d 523 (Cal. 1983); Ottawa Educ. Ass'n v. Unified School Dist. No. 290, 666 P.2d 680 (Kan. 1983); Spiewak v. Board of Educ. of Rutherford, 447 A.2d 140 (N.J. 1982); School Dist. of the City of Erie v. Erie Educ. Ass'n, 447 A.2d 686 (Pa. Commw. Ct. 1982). *But see* Jurcisin v. Cuyahoga County Bd. of Elections, 519 N.E.2d 347 (Ohio 1988) (the collective bargaining contract regarding wages, hours, terms, or conditions of employment prevails over state laws).

27. *See, e.g.,* Board of Educ. of City School Dist. of City of New York v. New York State Pub. Employment Relations Bd., 555 N.Y.S.2d 659, 663 (N.Y. 1990); Raines v. Independent School Dist. No. 6, 796 P.2d 303 (Okla. 1990); Montgomery County Educ. Ass'n v. Board of Educ. of Montgomery County, 534 A.2d 980 (Md. 1987).

28. Montgomery County Educ. Ass'n, *id.* at 986.

29. Ridgefield Park Educ. Ass'n v. Ridgefield Park Bd. of Educ., 393 A.2d 278 (N.J. 1978). *See also* Bay City Educ. Ass'n v. Bay City Pub. Schools, 422 N.W.2d 504 (Mich. 1988).

30. Aberdeen Educ. Ass'n v. Aberdeen Bd. of Educ., 215 N.W.2d 837 (S.D. 1974).

31. Clark County School Dist. v. Local Gov't Employee–Management Relations Bd., 530 P.2d 114 (Nev. 1974).

32. Pennsylvania Labor Relations Bd. v. State College Area School Dist., 337 A.2d 262 (Pa. 1975).

33. *But see* Montgomery County Educ. Ass'n v. Board of Educ. of Montgomery County, 534 A.2d 980 (Md. 1987); Colonial School Bd. v. Colonial Affiliate, 449 A.2d 243 (Del. 1982) (both courts interpreted their state labor law as containing no provision for permissive subjects of collective bargaining).

34. *See, e.g.,* Scranton School Bd. v. Scranton Fed'n of Teachers, 365 A.2d 1339 (Pa. Commw. Ct. 1976).

35. Kenai Peninsula Borough School Dist. v. Kenai Peninsula Educ. Ass'n, 572 P.2d 416 (Alaska 1977).

36. Clark County School Dist. v. Local Gov't Employee Management Relations Bd., 530 P.2d 114 (Nev. 1974).

37. Nev. Rev. Stat. 288 § 150 (1990).

38. Decatur Bd. of Educ., Dist. No. 61 v. Illinois Educ. Labor Relations Bd., 536 N.E.2d 743 (Ill. App. Ct. 1989). *See also* Tualatin Valley Bargaining Council v. Tigard School Dist., 808 P.2d 101 (Or. Ct. App. 1991).

39. *See, e.g.,* Fargo Educ. Ass'n v. Fargo Pub. School Dist., 291 N.W.2d 267 (N.D. 1980); National Educ. Ass'n–Kansas City v. Unified School Dist., Wyandotte County, 608 P.2d 415 (Kan. 1980); City of Beloit v. Wisconsin Employment Relations Comm'n, 242 N.W.2d 231 (Wis. 1976).

40. City of Beloit, *id.*

41. Hillsborough Classroom Teachers Ass'n v. School Bd. of Hillsborough County, 423 So. 2d 969 (Fla. Dist. Ct. App. 1982).

42. *See, e.g.,* Public Employee Relations Bd. v. Washington Teachers' Union Local 6, 556 A.2d 206 (D.C. Cir. 1989); Montgomery County Educ. Ass'n v. Board of Educ. of Montgomery County, 534 A.2d 980 (Md. 1987); Board of Educ. of the Woodstown-Pilesgrove Regional School Dist. v. Woodstown-Pilesgrove Regional Educ. Ass'n, 410 A.2d 1131 (N.J. 1980); Kenai Peninsula Borough School Dist. v. Kenai Peninsula Educ. Ass'n, 572 P.2d 416 (Alaska 1977).

43. City of Biddeford v. Biddeford Teachers Ass'n, 304 A.2d 387, 421 (Me. 1973).

44. Eastbrook Community Schools Corp. v. Indiana Educ. Employment Relations Bd., 446 N.E.2d 1007 (Ind. Ct. App. 1983). *See also* Indiana Educ. Employment Relations Bd. v. Highland Classroom Teachers Ass'n, 546 N.E.2d 101 (Ind. Ct. App. 1989) (calendar items that did not infringe upon exclusive managerial powers were negotiable under a grandfather clause in the collective bargaining law).

45. Union County School Corp. v. Indiana Educ. Employment Relations Bd., 471 N.E.2d 1191 (Ind. Ct. App. 1984).

46. City of Beloit v. Employment Relations Comm'n, 242 N.W.2d 231 (Wis. 1976).

47. Bethlehem Township Bd. of Educ. v. Bethlehem Township Educ. Ass'n, 449 A.2d 1254, 1259 (N.J. 1982). *See also* University Educ. Ass'n v. Regents of the

Univ. of Minnesota, 353 N.W.2d 534 (Minn. 1984) (evaluation criteria represent inherent managerial policy and therefore are not negotiable).

48. Board of Educ., U.S.D. No. 352, Goodland v. NEA-Goodland, 785 P.2d 993 (Kan. 1990). *See also* Board of Educ., LeRoy Community Unit School Dist. No. 2 v. Illinois Educ. Labor Relations Bd., 556 N.E.2d 857 (Ill. App. Ct. 1990), *appeal granted,* 561 N.E.2d 686 (Ill. 1990); Wethersfield Bd. of Educ. v. Connecticut State Bd. of Labor Relations, 519 A.2d 41 (Conn. 1986).

49. Aplington Community School Dist. v. Iowa Pub. Employment Relations Bd., 392 N.W.2d 495 (Iowa 1986). *See also* Northeast Community School Dist. v. Public Employment Relations Bd., 408 N.W.2d 46 (Iowa 1987); Board of School Trustees of the Gary Community School Corp. v. Indiana Educ. Employment Relations Bd., 543 N.E.2d 662 (Ind. Ct. App. 1989).

50. *See, e.g.,* Township of Old Bridge Bd. of Educ. v. Old Bridge Educ. Ass'n, 489 A.2d 159 (N.J. 1985); Unified School Dist. No. 501 v. Secretary of Kansas Dep't of Human Resources, 685 P.2d 874 (Kan. 1984).

51. Unified School Dist. No. 501, *id.*

52. West Bend Educ. Ass'n v. Wisconsin Employment Relations Comm'n, 357 N.W.2d 534, 543 (Wis. 1984).

53. Township of Old Bridge Bd. of Educ. v. Old Bridge Educ. Ass'n, 489 A.2d 159, 164 (N.J. 1985). *See also* Shenandoah Educ. Ass'n v. Shenandoah Community School Dist., 337 N.W.2d 477 (Iowa 1983); Boston Teachers Union v. School Comm. of Boston, 434 N.E.2d 1258 (Mass. 1982).

54. Central City Educ. Ass'n v. Illinois Educ. Labor Relations Bd., 557 N.E.2d 418 (Ill. App. Ct. 1990), *appeal granted,* 561 N.E.2d 687 (Ill. 1990).

55. Wygant v. Jackson Bd. of Educ., 476 U.S. 267 (1986). *See also* text with note 68, Chapter 9.

56. Under most state laws, reemployment of probationary teachers and tenure decisions have been found to be a prohibited subject of bargaining. *See, e.g.,* Mindemann v. Independent School Dist. No. 6, Caddo County, 771 P.2d 996 (Okla. 1989); Honeoye Falls-Lima Cent. School Dist. v. Honeoye Falls–Lima Educ. Ass'n, 402 N.E.2d 1165 (N.Y. 1980). *But see* State *ex rel.* Rollins v. Board of Educ., Cleveland Heights–University Heights City School Dist., 532 N.E.2d 1289 (Ohio 1988) (collective bargaining law provides that negotiated agreement prevails over another conflicting law).

57. *But see* Fontana Teachers Ass'n v. Fontana Unified School Dist., 247 Cal. Rptr. 761 (Cal. Ct. App. 1988) (negotiated procedures for terminating employment of probationary employees were preempted by Education Code).

58. *See* text with note 5, Chapter 10.

59. Appeal of Watson, 448 A.2d 417 (N.H. 1982).

60. Jones v. Wrangell School Dist., 696 P.2d 677, 680 (Alaska 1985).

61. Savage Educ. Ass'n v. Trustees of Richland County Elementary Dist., 692 P.2d 1237 (Mont. 1984).

62. *See, generally,* Perry A. Zirkel and Ellis H. Katz, "The Law on Agency Shop for School Districts," *Education Law Reporter,* vol. 26 (1985), pp. 567–577.

63. 431 U.S. 209 (1977). *See also* Mary Aslanian-Bedikian, "*Abood* and Its Progeny: Conflicting Perspectives on Safeguarding Union Security Agreements and Individual Rights in the Public Sector," *Detroit College of Law Review,* vol. 1 (1984), pp. 23–46.

64. Abood, *id.* at 235.

65. Under Title VII of the Civil Rights Act of 1964, an employee who objects to payment of a service fee on religious grounds must be accommodated by being allowed to substitute a contribution to a charitable organization. *See, e.g.,* McDaniel v. Essex Int'l, Inc., 696 F.2d 34 (6th Cir. 1982); Tooley v. Martin-Marietta Corp., 648 F.2d 1239 (9th Cir. 1981), *cert. denied,* 454 U.S. 1098 (1981).
66. Abood, 431 U.S. at 236.
67. 466 U.S. 435, 448 (1984).
68. *See, e.g.,* Champion v. State of California, 738 F.2d 1082 (9th Cir. 1984), *cert. denied,* 469 U.S. 1229 (1985); Robinson v. State of New Jersey, 741 F.2d 598 (3d Cir. 1984), *cert. denied,* 469 U.S. 1228 (1985); Matter of Bd. of Educ. of Town of Boonton, 494 A.2d 279 (N.J. 1985), *cert. denied,* 475 U.S. 1072 (1985). *But see* Cumero v. Public Employment Relations Bd., 262 Cal. Rptr. 46 (Cal. 1989) (lobbying efforts were beyond the union's representational obligations under state law).
69. Lehnert v. Ferris Faculty Ass'n, 111 S. Ct. 1950 (1991).
70. Although strikes are illegal in Michigan, preparation for a strike was viewed as a effective bargaining tool during contract negotiations, *id.*
71. *Id.* at 1961.
72. *Id.* at 1960.
73. Ellis, 466 U.S. at 444.
74. Several states by statute have specified the amount of fee reductions that must be provided. For example, in New Jersey assessed fees cannot exceed 85 percent of the regular membership dues, N.J.S.A. 34: 13A-5.5(b) (1988). *See also* Tierney v. Toledo, 824 F.2d 1497 (6th Cir. 1987); Ake v. National Educ. Ass'n–South Bend, 531 N.E.2d 1178 (Ind. Ct. App. 1988).
75. 475 U.S. 292, 310 (1986).
76. A procedure that provides for the selection of an arbitrator by the American Arbitration Association meets the requirement of an impartial decisionmaker. *See* Lehnert v. Ferris Faculty Ass'n—MEA-NEA, 893 F.2d 111 (6th Cir. 1989), *cert. denied,* 110 S. Ct. 2586 (1989); Ping v. National Educ. Ass'n, 870 F.2d 1369 (7th Cir. 1989); Andrews v. Educ. Ass'n of Cheshire, 829 F.2d 335 (2d Cir. 1987).
77. *See, e.g.,* Grunwald v. San Bernardino City Unified School Dist., 917 F.2d 1223 (9th Cir. 1990); Lowary v. Lexington Local Bd. of Educ., 854 F.2d 131 (6th Cir. 1988); Gibney v. Toledo Bd. of Educ., 532 N.E.2d 1300 (Ohio 1988).
78. Chicago Teachers' Union, Local No. 1 v. Hudson, 475 U.S. at 306.
79. Gwirtz v. Ohio Educ. Ass'n, 887 F.2d 678 (6th Cir. 1989), *cert. denied,* 110 S. Ct. 1810 (1990). *See also* Hudson v. Chicago Teachers Union, Local No. 1, 922 F.2d 1306 (7th Cir. 1991), *cert. denied,* 111 S. Ct. 2852 (1991); Ping v. National Educ. Ass'n, 870 F.2d 1369 (7th Cir. 1989); Andrews v. Education Ass'n of Cheshire, 829 F.2d 335 (2d Cir. 1987).
80. Hudson, *id.*
81. Churchill v. School Adm'r Dist. No. 49 Teachers Ass'n, 380 A.2d 186 (Me. 1977).
82. Weissenstein v. Burlington Bd. of School Comm'rs, 543 A.2d 691 (Vt. 1988). *See also* Florida Educ. Ass'n/United v. Public Employee Relations Comm'n, 346 So. 2d 551 (Fla. Dist. Ct. App. 1977).
83. *See* William Kay, Karen Reinhold, and Kathy Andreolo, "Legal Problems in

Administering Agency Shop Agreements—A Management Perspective," *Journal of Law and Education,* vol. 13 (1984), pp. 61–76.

84. Langley v. Uniontown Area School Dist., 367 A.2d 736 (Pa. Commw. Ct. 1977).

85. Anderson Fed'n of Teachers, Local 519 v. Alexander, 416 N.E.2d 1327 (Ind. Ct. App. 1981). *See also* Fort Wayne Educ. Ass'n v. Goetz, 443 N.E.2d 364 (Ind. Ct. App. 1982) (agency shop agreement that did not condition employment on payment of fees was upheld).

86. Board of Educ. of School Dist. for City of Detroit v. Parks, 335 N.W.2d 641 (Mich. 1983). *See also* Whittier Regional School Comm. v. Labor Relations Comm'n, 517 N.E.2d 840 (Mass. 1988).

87. King City Joint Union High School Dist., California Pub. Relations Bd., Order No. 197 (March 1982). Unions also have pursued enforcement of agency fee agreements in civil actions against nonmember teachers. *See, e.g.,* Jefferson Area Teachers Ass'n v. Lockwood, 433 N.E.2d 604 (Ohio 1982), *cert. denied,* 459 U.S. 804 (1982); San Lorenz Educ. Ass'n v. Wilson, 654 P.2d 202 (Cal. 1982).

88. *See* John F. Lewis and Steven Spirn, *Ohio Collective Bargaining Law* (Cleveland, OH: Banks-Baldwin Law Publishing Co., 1983).

89. City of Charlotte v. Local 660, International Ass'n of Firefighters, 426 U.S. 283 (1976).

90. South Carolina Educ. Ass'n v. Campbell, 883 F.2d 1251 (4th Cir. 1989), *cert. denied,* 110 S. Ct. 1129 (1990).

91. Perry Educ. Ass'n v. Perry Local Educators' Ass'n, 460 U.S. 37 (1983). *See* text with note 48, Chapter 8.

92. *Id.* at 44.

93. Texas State Teachers Ass'n v. Garland Indep. School Dist., 777 F.2d 1046 (5th Cir. 1985), *aff'd,* 470 U.S. 801 (1986). *See also* Ysleta Fed'n of Teachers v. Ysleta Indep. School Dist., 720 F.2d 1429 (5th Cir. 1983) (a policy granting access to the school mails to all employee organizations established a limited public forum and precluded school officials from imposing prior clearance of all materials to determine if they were in accordance with school policy).

94. *See* School Bd. of Dade County v. Dade Teachers Ass'n, 421 So. 2d 645 (Fla. Dist. Ct. App. 1982).

95. Minnesota State Bd. for Community Colleges v. Knight, 465 U.S. 271, 283 (1984).

96. *Id.*

97. City of Madison, Joint School Dist. No. 8 v. Wisconsin Employment Relations Comm'n, 429 U.S. 167 (1976).

98. *Id.* at 175, quoting Pickering v. Board of Educ., 391 U.S. 563, 568 (1968).

99. To avoid strikes among certain groups of public employees, interest arbitration may be mandatory. *See, e.g.,* Ohio Rev. Code § 4117.14 (D)(1) (1991).

100. Ohio Rev. Code § 4117 (D)(2)(1991); Me. Rev. Stat. 26 § 979.D(4) (1988).

101. R.I. Gen. Laws 28 § 9.3-9 (1986).

102. Or. Rev. Stat. 243 § 706 (1986).

103. *See* William D. Valente, *Education Law: Public and Private,* vol. 2 (St. Paul, MN: West Publishing Co., 1985), p. 543, table 25. States requiring binding arbitration are Alaska, Florida, Illinois, Minnesota, and Pennsylvania.

104. *See, e.g.,* Appeal of Westmoreland School Bd., 564 A.2d 419 (N.H. 1989);

Cloquet Educ. Ass'n v. Independent School Dist. No. 94, 344 N.W.2d 416 (Minn. 1984); East Pennsboro Area School Dist. v. Pennsylvania Labor Relations Bd., 467 A.2d 1356 (Pa. Commw. Ct. 1983).

105. Iowa City Community School Dist. v. Iowa City Educ. Ass'n, 343 N.W.2d 139, 141 (Iowa 1983), quoting Sergeant Bluff–Luton Educ. Ass'n v. Sergeant Bluff-Luton Community School Dist., 282 N.W.2d 144, 147-148 (Iowa 1979). *See also* Fortney v. School Dist. of West Salem, 321 N.W.2d 225 (Wis. 1982); Scranton Fed'n of Teachers v. Scranton School Dist., 444 A.2d 1144 (Pa. 1982); Howard County Bd. of Educ. v. Howard County Educ. Ass'n, 487 A.2d 1220 (Md. Ct. App. 1985).

106. Trustees of Boston Univ. v. Boston Univ. Chapter, American Ass'n of Univ. Professors, 746 F.2d 924 (1st Cir. 1984); Cloquet Educ. Ass'n v. Independent School Dist. No. 94, 344 N.W.2d 416 (Minn. 1984); Board of Educ. of Enlarged City School Dist. of City of Newburgh v. Newburgh Teachers' Ass'n, 537 N.Y.S.2d 250 (N.Y. App. Div. 1989); State *ex rel.* Williams v. Belpre City School Dist. Bd. of Educ., 534 N.E.2d 96 (Ohio Ct. App. 1987); Howard County Bd. of Educ. v. Howard County Educ. Ass'n, 487 A.2d 1220 (Md. Ct. App. 1985); Ridley School Dist. v. Ridley Educ. Ass'n, 479 A.2d 641 (Pa. Commw. Ct. 1984).

107. Raines v. Independent School Dist. No. 6, Craig County, 796 P.2d 303 (Okla. 1990); Mindemann v. Independent School Dist. No. 6, Caddo County, 771 P.2d 996 (Okla. 1989); Neshaminy Fed'n of Teachers v. Neshaminy School Dist., 462 A.2d 629 (Pa. 1983); Teaneck Bd. of Educ. v. Teaneck Teachers Ass'n, 462 A.2d 137 (N.J. 1983); Fontana Teachers Ass'n v. Fontana Unified School Dist., 247 Cal. Rptr. 761 (Cal. Ct. App. 1988); Proviso Council of West Suburban Teachers Union, Local 571 v. Board of Educ., Proviso Township High Schools, Dist. 209, Cook County, 513 N.E.2d 996 (Ill. App. Ct. 1987).

108. W. R. Grace and Co. v. Local 759, United Rubber Workers of America, 461 U.S. 757, 764 (1983).

109. *See, e.g.,* Greater Johnstown Area Vocational-Technical School v. Greater Johnstown Area Vocational-Technical Educ. Ass'n, 553 A.2d 913 (Pa. 1989); Iowa City Community School Dist. v. Iowa City Educ. Ass'n, 343 N.W.2d 139 (Iowa 1983); Howard County Bd. of Educ. v. Howard County Educ. Ass'n, 487 A.2d 1220 (Md. Ct. App. 1985).

110. A statutory limited right to strike exists for public employees in Alaska, Hawaii, Illinois, Minnesota, Montana, Ohio, Oregon, Pennsylvania, Vermont, and Wisconsin. Although the Alaska public employee bargaining law permits most public employees to strike, the state high court has held that since the law does not expressly grant teachers this right, they are prohibited from striking, Anchorage Educ. Ass'n v. Anchorage School Dist., 648 P.2d 993 (Alaska 1982).

111. *See, e.g.,* Jefferson County Bd. of Educ. v. Jefferson County Educ. Ass'n, 393 S.E.2d 653 (W. Va. 1990); Passaic Township Bd. of Educ. v. Passaic Township Educ. Ass'n, 536 A.2d 1276 (N.J. Super. Ct. App. Div. 1987).

112. Norwalk Teachers Ass'n v. Board of Educ. of City of Norwalk, 83 A.2d 482, 485 (Conn. 1951).

113. Anderson Fed'n of Teachers v. School City of Anderson, 251 N.E.2d 15 (Ind. 1969), *cert. denied,* 399 U.S. 928 (1970).

114. Passaic Township Bd. of Educ. v. Passaic Township Educ. Ass'n, 536 A.2d 1276 (N.J. Super Ct. App. Div. 1987).

115. County Sanitation Dist. No. 2, Los Angeles County v. Los Angeles County Employees' Ass'n, 699 P.2d 835, 850 (Cal. 1985), *cert. denied,* 474 U.S. 995 (1985).

116. Davis v. Henry, 555 So. 2d 457 (La. 1990).

117. Lenox Educ. Ass'n v. Labor Relations Comm'n, 471 N.E.2d 81 (Mass. 1984).

118. *See, e.g.,* Buffalo Teachers Fed'n v. Helsby, 676 F.2d 28 (2d Cir. 1982); East Brunswick Bd. of Educ. v. East Brunswick Educ. Ass'n, 563 A.2d 55 (N.J. Super. Ct. App. Div. 1989).

119. Anchorage Educ. Ass'n v. Anchorage School Dist., 648 P.2d 993, 998 (Alaska 1982).

120. Harford County Educ. Ass'n v. Board of Educ. of Harford County, 380 A.2d 1041 (Md. 1977).

121. Board of Educ. of Newark v. Newark Teachers Union, 276 A.2d 175 (N.J. Super. Ct. App. Div. 1971), *cert. denied,* 404 U.S. 950 (1971).

122. Joint School Dist. No. 1, City of Wisconsin Rapids v. Wisconsin Rapids Educ. Ass'n, 234 N.W.2d 289 (Wis. 1975).

123. *See, e.g.,* Jefferson County Bd. of Educ. v. Jefferson County Educ. Ass'n, 393 S.E.2d 653 (W. Va. 1990); Jersey Shore Area School Dist. v. Jersey Shore Educ. Ass'n, 548 A.2d 1202 (Pa. 1988); Joint School Dist. No. 1, City of Wisconsin Rapids v. Wisconsin Rapids Educ. Ass'n, 234 N.W.2d 289 (Wis. 1975).

124. Hortonville Educ. Ass'n v. Hortonville Joint School Dist., 225 N.W.2d 658 (Wis. 1975), *rev'd,* 426 U.S. 482, 497 (1976). *See also* text with note 72, Chapter 10.

125. *Id.,* 426 U.S. at 496.

126. *See* text with note 110, *supra.*

12

Tort Liability

Other chapters in this book focus primarily on the legal resolution of conflicts between governmental interests in maintaining public schools and individual interests in exercising constitutional and statutory rights. In contrast, this chapter examines tort law that offers remedies to individuals for harm caused by the unreasonable conduct of others. This branch of law involves civil suits, pertaining to the private rights of citizens, as opposed to criminal suits, initiated by the state to redress public offenses. Generally, a tort is defined as a civil wrong, independent of breach of contract, for which a court will provide relief in the form of damages. Tort cases primarily involve state law[1] and are grounded in the fundamental premise that all individuals are liable for the consequences of their conduct that results in injury to others.

Tort actions can be grouped into three major categories: negligence, intentional torts, and strict liability. Negligence involves conduct that falls below an acceptable standard of care and results in injury.[2] Intentional torts are committed with the desire to inflict harm, and include assault, battery, false imprisonment, and trespass.[3] Strict liability occurs when an injury results from the creation of an unusual hazard (e.g., the storage of explosives), and the injured party need not establish that the injury was knowingly or negligently caused. Seldom have allegations of strict liability appeared in education cases. Some school-related injuries have generated intentional tort actions, but the vast majority of tort cases involving school districts and educational employees have entailed allegations of negligence. Accordingly, this chapter primarily addresses the conditions necessary to establish negligence and the legal defenses employed by school personnel to rebut negligence charges. Brief discussions of assault and battery and defamation also are included.

ELEMENTS OF NEGLIGENCE

Negligence is a breach of one's legal duty to protect others from unreasonable risks of harm. A charge of negligence can result when the failure to act or an improper act causes injury to another person.[4] To constitute negligence, an injury must be avoidable by the exercise of reasonable care. The ability to foresee harm is an important factor in determining whether or not an individual's conduct is negligent; accidents do not constitute negligence.

Negligence cases include questions of law, which are determined by judges, and questions of fact, which are decided by juries. In some instances, a judge may conclude that there are no material factual issues to submit to a jury and thus return a directed verdict. When a trial does take place, a judge can reverse the jury's decision if it is considered clearly erroneous. Judges, however, will not exercise this authority unless supported by overwhelming evidence.

The following conditions are necessary to establish an individual's negligence:

1. The individual must have a *duty* to protect another from unreasonable risks.
2. The duty must be breached by the failure to *exercise an appropriate standard of care*.
3. There must be a causal connection between the negligent conduct and the resulting injury (referred to as *proximate or legal cause*).
4. There must be physical or mental *injury* resulting in an actual loss.[5]

The conditions necessary to establish negligence are discussed in the following sections.

DUTY

Under common law, school officials have a duty to anticipate foreseeable dangers and to take necessary precautions to protect students entrusted in their care from such dangers.[6] The specific duties that school personnel owe students are to provide adequate supervision and instruction, to maintain equipment and facilities in good repair, and to warn of known dangers.

While courts have acknowledged that school districts are not insurers of student safety, they have emphasized school officials' duty to exercise reasonable and ordinary care to protect students from foreseeable injuries.[7] This does not require school personnel to have every child under constant surveillance at all times during the school day. However, if circumstances indicate an unusual risk of harm or unsafe conditions, reasonable preventive measures must be taken.[8]

School officials' duty of care to students clearly encompasses activities on the school grounds during school hours, but a duty also may be owed after regular hours and away from the campus. Circumstances and the nature of the activity determine whether such a duty exists. For example, a Louisiana appellate court found that a school board was negligent in the injury of a kindergarten student for its failure to provide supervision of a track practice sponsored by a nonschool organization. Liability in this instance was created primarily by the school's distribution of a flyer assuring parents that there would be "tight supervision."[9] A New York appellate court ruled that a school district was negligent for an injury that occurred in an unsupervised schoolyard prior to the beginning of the school day. Although school officials were aware that some students congregated and played on the school grounds as early as 7:30 A.M., no supervision was provided until 8:30 A.M.[10] The Supreme Court of Minnesota held that school officials' duty to supervise the activities of cheerleaders continued through the summer months because the cheerleading squad was approved and controlled by the school. In the absence of supervision by school personnel, a cheerleader injured in an automobile accident while bannering the homes of football players prior to the beginning of the school year was awarded damages.[11] A Washington appellate court, however, ruled that school officials did not have a duty to supervise students participating in a party on senior "release day."[12] School personnel were not involved in planning the party, nor did they attend; knowledge of the party on the part of the faculty adviser and principal did not create a duty to supervise the event.

When students are injured in the school setting, teachers have a duty to provide reasonable assistance commensurate with their training and experience. Provision of emergency first aid treatment to pupils has been upheld if the treatment has been reasonable. In some states, "good Samaritan" laws shield individuals providing treatment in emergency situations from liability. Because of the special duty of care surrounding the student–teacher relationship, such laws would not relieve a teacher of liability for *unreasonable* actions. In determining reasonableness, courts have recognized that students should not be moved or treated unless such emergency aid is absolutely necessary prior to the arrival of medical personnel. Liability has been assessed in instances where injured students have been negligently moved from playing fields during athletic events or where first aid has been administered improperly.[13] The Illinois Supreme Court recognized that schools or their agents, as a matter of public policy, are obligated to ensure that medical treatment is competently rendered.[14] In a Pennsylvania case, two teachers were held personally liable for administering medical treatment to a student by holding his infected finger under boiling water.[15] The superior court held that the action was unreasonable and noted that the situation did not necessitate emergency first aid. Failure to obtain prompt medical attention for injured students also may result in liability.[16]

School districts' duty to protect pupils and employees from injuries inflicted by third parties has been addressed in cases involving criminal assault.[17] Several courts have concluded that school districts have a duty to warn students or to provide increased security measures if assaults or other violent acts are reasonably foreseeable. For example, if criminal attacks have occurred on school grounds or nearby, failure to institute measures to protect students may constitute negligence.[18] Where such risks could not be anticipated, however, liability has not been assessed against the school district or school personnel.[19]

Increasing attention has been focused on school districts' duty to protect students from sexual molestation by school employees. Courts have rejected school district liability under the doctrine of *respondeat superior* (employer is liable for actions of an employee taken within the scope of employment), finding sexual abuse outside an employee's employment.[20] The Supreme Court of California concluded that "the connection between the authority conferred on teachers to carry out their instructional duties and the abuse of that authority to indulge in personal, sexual misconduct is simply too attenuated to deem a sexual assault as falling within the range of risks allocable to a teacher's employment."[21] Liability, however, has been imposed on school districts for negligence in hiring and retaining employees if school officials had knowledge of instances of sexual abuse. In denying summary judgment to a school district, the Supreme Court of Idaho held that a question of negligence was presented when school officials permitted a teacher to continue teaching after they had knowledge that he had sexually abused students.[22] Similarly, the Massachusetts high court found that school board members had, or should have had, knowledge of a counselor's assaultive behavior.[23]

STANDARD OF CARE

The standard of care required in various school settings is governed by the reasonableness theory. In assessing the reasonableness of an individual's actions, courts determine whether a reasonable and prudent person would have acted in the same manner under similar circumstances. The reasonable person has been described as one who has "(1) the physical attributes of the defendant . . . , (2) normal intelligence, (3) normal perception and memory with a minimum level of information and experience common to the community, and (4) such superior skill and knowledge" as the defendant purports to have.[24] Under this standard, a given teacher's conduct is gauged by how a reasonable teacher, who has had special training to assume that role, would have acted in a similar situation.

The degree of care owed is determined by factors such as the age of the students, the environment, and the type of instructional activity. For example, primary grade students require closer supervision and more detailed instructions than high school students. A higher level of care is required in laboratory classes, gymnasiums, and other settings where risk of harm is great. Variability in the level of care deemed reasonable is illustrated in a Louisiana case. This case involved the fatal injury of a mentally retarded student who darted into a busy thoroughfare while being escorted with nine other classmates to a park three blocks from the school. An appellate court noted that the general level of care required for all students "becomes more onerous when the student body is composed of mentally retarded youngsters."[25] The court further noted that this higher level of care becomes even greater when such a group of children is taken away from the school campus. Accordingly, the court found negligence in that one teacher could not adequately supervise the group and the safest walking route was not selected.

PROXIMATE CAUSE

For liability to be assessed, negligent conduct of school personnel must be the proximate or legal cause of a student's injury. Even in situations where a recognized duty is breached by the failure to exercise a proper standard of care, liability will not be assessed if there is not a causal connection between the actions of school personnel and the injury sustained by a student. An intervening act, such as the negligence of a third party, may relieve school personnel of liability.[26]

Foreseeability is important in establishing proximate cause of an injury. A Maryland appeals court concluded that a teacher had no reason to predict an intervening event that caused injury to a fourth-grade pupil who was engaged in a program of calisthenics while the teacher was absent briefly from the room.[27] The injury occurred when another child moved from his position, contrary to instructions, and struck the plaintiff with his feet while performing the exercises. The court reasoned that the incident could have occurred with the teacher in the classroom; therefore, her absence was not the proximate cause of the injury sustained. Similarly, a Pennsylvania court held that a teacher who was monitoring the hallway as students returned from recess was not liable for damages when a student entering the classroom was struck in the eye by a pencil that had been thrown by a classmate. The court concluded that teachers are not "required to anticipate the myriad of unexpected acts which occur daily in classrooms."[28]

The existence of intervening events, however, does not necessarily relieve school employees of liability for negligent conduct. A Tennessee appellate court held that a student's misuse of a drill press resulting in a serious head injury to a classmate did not negate the teacher's negligence.[29] The teacher had not instructed the students in the use of the specific drill bit, had not warned of the dangers associated with its improper use, and was absent from the shop during the use of the drill. In a California case involving a student who was killed while engaging in an unsupervised "slap boxing" match on school grounds, the state supreme court held that a school employee's negligent supervision was the proximate cause of the student's fatal injury.[30] While noting that another student's misconduct was the precipitating cause of the injury, the court concluded that, with proper supervision, the dangerous "slap boxing" activity would have been curtailed.

The New York high court similarly concluded that a school district was liable for injuries to an eight-year-old student caused by improperly secured dangerous chemicals.[31] Although two fifteen-year-old unsupervised student workers had taken the chemicals from an unlocked laboratory and left them on the school grounds where the young child later discovered them, this intervening act was not considered sufficient to relieve the school district of liability. According to the court, the unauthorized removal of the chemicals by a third party was foreseeable as a consequence of the school district's negligence. Even when an intervening event actually causes a given injury, if school personnel place students in a dangerous situation, or if they reasonably should anticipate special risks of harm, they will not be relieved of liability for their negligent conduct.

INJURY

To receive an award of damages, a plaintiff must have suffered an injury from the negligent conduct of the defendant. Although conduct may be considered negligent, legal action cannot be sustained unless the conduct actually results in physical or mental injury. If an injury is caused by the negligent action of more than one individual, damages will be apportioned accordingly.[32] Compensation may cover any direct financial loss (i.e., medical expenses or loss of income) as well as remuneration for pain and suffering. In the drill press injury previously noted, the injured student was awarded a total of $25,000 in damages: approximately $4,000 for medical expenses and the remainder for pain and disability caused by a permanent weakening of the skull.[33]

EDUCATORS' LIABILITY

Courts have recognized the responsibility of school personnel to provide adequate supervision and instruction and to maintain school facilities and equipment in good repair. In suits alleging negligent conduct, plaintiffs assert that one or more of these duties have been breached. Employees' negligent performance of their duties may result in school district as well as individual liability for damages. For such liability to be imposed on a school district, however, negligent conduct must arise within the scope of an employee's employment. A school board is not liable for purely private acts.

A number of states have enacted legislation requiring school districts to indemnify or "save harmless" teachers for monetary losses for tortious actions that may occur during the performance of their assigned duties. An Ohio law, for example, requires such indemnification of teachers except for "willful and wanton" acts.[34] Generally, these laws also require school districts to assume the cost of legal representation if tort claims are filed against a teacher. In states with such laws, school employees can still be found negligent, but they are relieved of responsibility for any damages assessed by courts. Some states also have enacted statutes that provide partial immunity for teachers' negligent acts. Illinois law, for example, confers *in loco parentis* (in place of parent) status on educational employees and stipulates that willful and wanton misconduct must be established in order for liability to be assessed in connection with strictly educational activities.[35]

An overview of the general nature of school employees' duties is presented in this section. Caution should be exercised in generalizing from specific cases because slight variations in the factual circumstances can alter the final determination of negligence and liability.

SUPERVISION

One of the primary responsibilities of teachers is to provide adequate supervision of students under their care. Depending on the activity, this may entail general or specific supervision. Students completing a routine written assignment at their desks would require only general supervision, whereas students attempting a new movement in gymnastics would warrant specific supervision. As emphasized previously, teachers have a duty to safeguard students from reasonably foreseeable dangers. Proper supervision thus requires teachers to be aware of students' activities and the conditions surrounding those activities and to warn of potential dangers. Failure to provide such supervision can constitute negligent conduct.

As noted, however, a teacher does not have a duty to keep each student under constant surveillance or to anticipate every possible accident that might occur; teachers cannot be held liable for unforeseeable injuries. Even if supervision is inadequate, a teacher will not be held negligent if it is established that the injury could have occurred as easily with proper supervision.[36] A Missouri appeals court concluded that a kindergarten teacher did not breach her duty of supervision simply because she was attending to other students during recess when a child fell while attempting to swing on a jungle gym.[37] The court concluded that the teacher was not required to have each pupil in sight at all times. Similarly, a Louisiana appeals court held that a teacher was not negligent with respect to an injury sustained by a child who fell on a tree stump at recess.[38] The court reasoned that the stump was not so hazardous as to place a special duty on the teacher to anticipate harm.

Courts have not assessed damages against school personnel unless an injury might have been prevented by the exercise of proper supervision typically required by the circumstances. Two student injury cases involving rock-throwing incidents illustrate the importance of foreseeability of harm in determining the appropriateness of supervision. In one instance, where student rock-throwing had continued for almost ten minutes before the injury occurred, the court found the supervising teacher liable for negligence.[39] In contrast, in a situation where a teacher aide had walked past a group of students moments before one child threw a rock that was deflected and hit another pupil, no liability was assessed against the aide.[40] The court concluded that the teacher aide had provided adequate supervision and had no reason to anticipate the event that caused the injury.

A teacher's mere absence from the classroom is not sufficient to establish negligence. Whether a teacher exercised reasonable care in temporarily leaving a class unattended is assessed in relation to the reason for the absence, length of the absence, age and maturity of the students, classroom activity in progress, and history and make-up of the class. Recognizing that teachers do not have to be present at all times in a classroom, a North Carolina appellate court concluded that a teacher could not be held liable for a student injury that occurred in her classroom while she remained in the cafeteria to finish lunch.[41] Under the school's policy, students daily returned to the classroom in groups of six and were instructed to remain in their seats and complete class assignments noted on the chalkboard. In contrast, the Supreme Court of Wisconsin, however, held that there were legitimate issues of negligence in a situation where a teacher left fifty adolescent males unsupervised in a gymnasium for twenty-five minutes. During this absence, a fourteen-year-old pupil was injured in a rowdy game.[42]

Proper supervision is essential in settings that pose significant risks to students, such as vocational shops, gymnasiums, science laboratories, and school grounds where known dangers exist. In a Louisiana case, negligent supervision was found when a teacher left his welding class unsupervised and a student suffered a severe injury to his hand while using a power saw.[43] The state appellate court concluded that when inherently dangerous equipment is used in a class, a teacher must provide supervision at all times. The District of Columbia school system was found negligent for the injury of a six-year-old student because of its failure to supervise a construction site near the school's entrance.[44] School officials warned children daily about the dangerous site but did not provide supervision.

Supervision of students en route to and from school has generated litigation. In an Indiana case, a school district was found negligent in failing to supervise adequately the boarding of school buses. A student suffered serious injuries when struck by a school bus while he waited outside the school building. Finding that lack of supervision was the proximate cause of the injury, the appellate court upheld a substantial damages award.[45] Actual supervision of student passengers on school buses may be required if there is reason to expect misconduct that might result in injury to students.[46]

The school's duty to protect truant students from injury has generated conflicting decisions. A California case involved a student who left school without permission and was struck by a motorcycle several blocks from school.[47] The trial court concluded that the duty of school personnel to protect the student from harm terminated when he became truant. In reversing this decision, the California Supreme Court reasoned that proper supervision might have prevented the student's truancy and subsequent injury. In a similar case where a truant student was injured, a New York court reached a different conclusion. The court declared that "nothing short of a prison-like atmosphere with monitors at every exit could have prevented the [student] from leaving the school grounds."[48] The court declined to mandate such security measures and further concluded that once a truant student is beyond the legal control of the school district there is no duty of supervision.

Pupil injuries during field trips often have evoked tort actions challenging the adequacy of supervision. While greater care is required during field trips to unfamiliar places, school personnel are not held liable for every injury that occurs. For example, no liability was assessed in connection with the death of a student on a band trip who drowned when he dove into the deep end of the swimming pool at a hotel.[49] The state appeals court reasoned that appropriate supervision was provided by school personnel, who had not been informed that the student could not swim. In fact, the child's parents had given permission for him to use the pool. The court concluded that he voluntarily dove into the deep end, and thus drowned through no fault of the supervisors. The Supreme Court of Oregon, however, assessed damages against a teacher for an injury sustained by a student at a beach during a school outing.[50] The court concluded that the unusual wave action on the Oregon coast was a known hazard and that the teacher failed to take reasonable safety precautions.

Teachers and administrators, because of their special training to assume such roles, are expected to make sound judgments as to the appropriate supervision required in any given school situation. The adequacy of care is measured against the risks of harm involved. Reasonable actions in one instance may be considered unreasonable under other conditions. Courts assess the facts of each case in light of the attendant circumstances in determining whether supervision is proper.[51]

INSTRUCTION

Teachers have a duty to provide students with adequate and appropriate instruction prior to commencing an activity that may pose a risk of harm. An Indiana appellate court concluded that a jury could infer that inappropriate instruction exposed students in a physical education class to an unreasonable risk of harm.[52] A sixth-grade student injured her mouth when she collided with a wall while performing a vertical jump. Evidence indicated that the teacher did not demonstrate the exercise and provided improper directions for performing the jump. In another physical education case, a teacher was found negligent for permitting two male students to engage in boxing without proper training.[53] One of the students was fatally injured, and the teacher was held liable for failing to provide adequate instruction in the basic principles of defense. Similarly, negligent instruction was found in a New York case when a teacher failed to follow the state guidelines for conducting a physical fitness test and did not instruct students to take necessary precautions.[54] Failure to provide adequate instructions also resulted in negligence being assessed against a Tennessee shop teacher.[55] The teacher had permitted a student to use a drill bit without any prior instruction, and another student who was assisting in the operation of the machinery was severely injured.

In some situations, teachers have successfully rebutted charges of negligence by establishing that proper instructions were given to the students but were disregarded. In a case involving a shop class injury resulting from a nail thrown by a student, the South Carolina Supreme Court concluded that the teacher was not negligent, since he had forbidden students to throw objects.[56] The court emphasized that the teacher could not be held responsible for an injury caused by a student who disobeyed orders. A North Carolina shop teacher's detailed instructions in the use of power saws absolved him of any liability when a student lost several fingers in an accident.[57] Prior to students using the saw, the teacher had spent twenty minutes reviewing the safe use of the equipment and another twenty minutes demonstrating proper procedures.

Although school personnel have a duty to provide appropriate instruction to protect students from unreasonable hazards, students also must act in a reasonable manner. Liability will not be imposed against school personnel if students willfully disregard teachers' instructions and warnings.

MAINTENANCE OF FACILITIES AND EQUIPMENT

Some states by law protect frequenters of public buildings from danger to life, health, safety, or welfare. These "safe place" statutes have been used successfully by individuals to obtain damages from school districts for injuries resulting from *defective conditions* of school buildings and grounds.[58] However, such "safe place" statutes do not cover injuries occurring simply from the *use* of the facilities or the equipment contained in the buildings.

In addition to "safe place" statutes that make liability explicit for certain types of injuries, school officials have a common law duty to maintain buildings, grounds, and equipment in reasonably safe condition. Courts have awarded damages in suits involving student injuries if school employees were aware of, or should have been aware of, hazardous conditions and did not take the necessary steps to repair or correct them. The

Supreme Court of Louisiana held that a school board was negligent in permitting a plate glass panel to remain in the foyer of a gymnasium. Prior to the injury of a student who broke the glass, the board had sufficient warning that the glass was dangerous, as an identical panel in the foyer had been broken several years earlier and replaced with safety glass.[59] In an Alabama case, however, the state supreme court did not find two teachers negligent for an injury that occurred when a student slipped on a puddle of water during a physical education class; the teachers were unaware of the water or of the condition in the roof that led to the accumulation of the water.[60]

The duty to provide reasonable maintenance of facilities does not place an obligation on school personnel to anticipate every possible danger or to be aware of and correct every minor defect as soon as the condition occurs. For example, a student was unsuccessful in establishing a breach of duty in connection with an injury sustained on a defective door latch.[61] The state appeals court concluded that there was no evidence that any school employee had knowledge of, or should have had knowledge of, the broken latch. Therefore, a duty to protect the student from the resulting injury could not be imposed. In another case, an appellate court rejected a claim that, because a student was injured when a heavy metal door slammed on his thumb, the door posed such a danger that a door stop and a closure were required.[62]

Allegations that school personnel have breached their duty to maintain equipment in proper condition often have arisen in connection with student injuries sustained during athletic events. The Illinois Supreme Court held that a school district breached its duty to protect athletes from harm by providing an ill-fitting, inadequate football helmet to a student.[63] The Massachusetts high court similarly concluded that a school district was liable for supplying a defective helmet to a student hockey player who had every reason to expect to be supplied with proper equipment.[64]

Damages have been awarded to students where injuries after school hours have resulted from unsafe playground conditions.[65] A Michigan student was successful in obtaining damages for the loss of sight in one eye, sustained while playing among piles of dirt and sand on the playground after school hours.[66] The area was not fenced, and prior to the incident parents had complained to the school district about the dirt piles and "dirt fights" among children. The Michigan appeals court concluded that the school district breached its duty to maintain the school grounds in a safe condition.

However, the fact that an injury occurs on a school playground does not necessarily mean that liability will be assessed against the school district. If the conduct of the injured party, rather than the unsafe condition of the grounds, is the primary cause of the injury, the school district may not be held liable for negligence. To illustrate, a California appeals court concluded that a school district was not liable for the death of a student on school grounds after school.[67] Although the playground was accessible to the public, unsupervised, and in disrepair, the court concluded that the student's death resulted from his own conduct in performing a hazardous skateboard activity, not from the defective playground conditions.

A controversial issue related to the health and safety of students and employees has been public school districts' duty to remove asbestos materials from school buildings. During the mid-twentieth century, asbestos products were commonly used in schools and colleges, and recent medical research has linked the inhalation of airborne asbestos fibers to stomach and lung cancer and other lung diseases. Responding to the serious health risk, in 1980 Congress enacted a law requiring local education agencies to inspect buildings and take remedial action to assure the safety of students and school employees.[68] This was followed by enactment of the Asbestos Hazard Emergency Response Act (AHERA) of 1986 to ensure safe removal of asbestos and to provide financial assistance to school districts.[69] Under the AHERA, school districts were required to develop asbestos management plans prior to May 9, 1989, and to implement plans by July 1989. The regulations promulgated in response to AHERA allowed school officials, after an assessment of their buildings, to determine the least burdensome abatement methods for their circumstances.[70]

Numerous school districts are involved in individual or class-action suits against asbestos manufacturers to recover costs for asbestos removal from those who supplied the hazardous materials without testing them or warning consumers of the potential dangers.[71] Suits for damages where asbestos materials in public schools have caused personal injuries seem likely to increase in volume and complexity. In 1986 the Third Circuit Court of Appeals noted that more than 30,000 suits had been filed against manufacturers and that an additional 180,000 claims would probably be filed by 2010.[72]

DEFENSES AGAINST NEGLIGENCE

Several defenses are available to school officials to rebut charges of negligence. Traditionally, the most effective defense for school districts has been governmental immunity, which is based on the common-law notion that governmental agencies cannot be held liable for tortious actions. This defense has been employed frequently by *school districts,* but it is not available to *school employees* unless state law specifically confers immunity for acts within the scope of employment.[73] The defense of contributory negligence, which bars recovery based on evidence that the injured party's action was a substantial factor in causing the injury, also has appeared in educational litigation. In some jurisdictions, comparative negligence has been used to award damages in relation to the fault of each party involved. Procedural defects in suits, such as failure to adhere to statutory requirements regarding notice of claim, also have been used to relieve defendants of liability for damages. Other defenses in educational negligence cases have included assertions that the injured party assumed the risk of a known danger or that the injury was caused by uncontrollable events of nature. Several of these defenses that have appeared frequently in school litigation are discussed in this section.

GOVERNMENTAL IMMUNITY

The doctrine of governmental or sovereign immunity originated in the Middle Ages from the notion that "the king can do no wrong." Subsequently, this idea was translated into the common-law principle that government agencies cannot be held liable for the negligent acts of their officers, agents, or employees. Various reasons have been offered for applying sovereign immunity to school districts, such as the involuntary status of government agencies and their legal inability to pay tort claims, since public funds are to be used only for statutorily prescribed purposes.

Governmental immunity for school districts in tort actions still exists under common law, but legislative and judicial actions have partially eroded the vitality of this doctrine in approximately half of the states.[74] In many states, immunity has been abrogated by legislation, and in others, the use of immunity has been curtailed by judicial decree. A decision abolishing governmental immunity in Ohio is illustrative.[75] The state high court rejected the claim that school districts and other governmental agencies were unable to pay damages based on the lack of public funds from which such judgments could be paid, as the legislature had conferred authority to purchase liability insurance. Further, the court found archaic the notion that an injured individual should be inconvenienced rather than the government. In summary, the court noted that "personal injuries from the negligence of those into whose care they are entrusted is not a risk that school children should, as a matter of public policy, be required to bear in return for the benefit of public education."[76]

Even in the states that still enjoy governmental immunity or aspects of immunity, statutory provisions may permit recovery in connection with specific functions or activities of school districts. A frequent exception to governmental immunity involves claims related to the maintenance of school buildings and property. School districts can be held liable for injuries arising from a dangerous realty condition if authorities had knowledge of the defect and did not take corrective action.[77] The Supreme Court of Michigan found the public building exception also to include fixtures that were actually attached or constructively attached by their weight.[78] A Pennsylvania court, however, concluded that a chin-up bar did not come under the real property exception because it could be easily removed and was not essential to the use of the building.[79] An Illinois court ruled that the premises liability exception was not applicable for an injury sustained by a student playing football on an uneven playing field during a physical education class; this activity involved supervision of the school program, which falls under statutory immunity.[80]

Through workers' compensation statutes, states also can waive the immunity of school districts for employee injuries. Under such statutes, negligence on the part of the employer need not be established; employees can recover damages for accidental injuries as long as they are work related. The mere fact that an injury occurs at school does not entitle an employee to benefits, however, unless it is established that the injury is job related. For example, a teacher's widow was unsuccessful in securing benefits after her husband was murdered at school.[81] The deceased was murdered by another teacher's jealous husband, and the court ruled that the action, taken for personal reasons, was not a risk associated with employment.

Government agencies cannot plead sovereign immunity if they maintain a public nuisance that results in harm to an individual. A nuisance is defined as a material annoyance, inconvenience, and discomfort that interferes with common public rights.[82] Swimming pools or ponds on school property are classified as attractive nuisances; therefore, school districts generally are not shielded by immunity if proper precautions are not taken to prevent public access to such areas.

In some jurisdictions, a distinction has been made between governmental and proprietary functions in limiting the immunity of school districts. Governmental functions, which are performed in discharging the agency's official duties, have been considered immune from liability.[83] On the other hand, proprietary functions, which could be provided as easily by a private corporation, have been legitimate targets for tort actions. Courts have not agreed, however, as to which school functions should be considered proprietary in nature. Some courts have held that profit-making extracurricular activities are proprietary functions, while other courts have ruled that all extracurricular activities are part of the educational mission of the school district and thus protected by immunity.[84]

Several courts have rejected the governmental/proprietary distinction and have instead distinguished between ministerial (administrative) and discretionary (policymaking) functions in determining a school district's potential liability. For example, the Massachusetts high court concluded that school districts were liable for negligence involving ministerial duties in the administration of policies, but were immune from liability for negligence associated with discretionary, policymaking activities.[85]

Despite judicial and legislative action limiting governmental immunity, this defense continues to be used in many jurisdictions to protect school districts against liability for negligence. A Michigan school district successfully relied on governmental immunity to bar recovery for a student's injury resulting from a horse bite that occurred on a field trip to a farm.[86] The Supreme Court of Alabama invoked governmental immunity to preclude damages for pupil injuries alleged to have resulted from unsafe high school gymnasium facilities.[87] Similarly, governmental immunity prevented a Texas student from recovering for burns received at a homecoming bonfire.[88]

In a few states where the application of sovereign immunity has not been limited, courts have ruled that the purchase of liability insurance to indemnify school districts is unnecessary since it protects a government agency against a threat that cannot exist. Under such circumstances, courts have concluded that the use of public funds to purchase liability insurance is illegal.[89] In states authorizing the purchase of liability insurance to protect government agencies, conflicting rulings have been rendered as to whether the acquisition of such insurance waives the sovereign immunity of the school district. The Supreme Court of Missouri has held that the purchase of liability insurance does not prevent a school board from asserting the defense of governmental immunity,[90] while courts in Georgia, Montana, and North Carolina have concluded that the purchase of insurance constitutes a waiver of immunity.[91]

The extent that governmental immunity applies in the various states continues to be modified by legislatures and courts. Therefore, to understand fully school district or individual liability, educators should consult their state laws and judicial rulings.

CONTRIBUTORY NEGLIGENCE

School personnel, in defending against negligence charges, often claim that an injured student's own acts contributed to the injury. If contributory negligence is found, a student is precluded from recovering any damages. In assessing whether contributory negligence exists, students are not held to the same standard of care as an adult; rather, their actions must be reasonable for a child of similar age, maturity, intelligence, and experience. Some courts have further classified minors according to a presumption of capability for negligence: (1) children under the age of seven are considered incapable of negligence; (2) children over the age of fourteen are presumed capable of negligence; and (3) children between seven and fourteen years of age are considered incapable of negligence, but the presumption can be rebutted.[92] Clearly, age is a factor in determining the reasonableness of a student's conduct, with contributory negligence being difficult to substantiate on the part of young children.

School personnel have been successful in claiming contributory negligence if they have been able to prove that a student was aware of, or should have been aware of, the consequences of specific actions and nonetheless engaged in dangerous conduct.[93] A North Carolina appellate court concluded that a fourteen-year-old student was contributorily negligent in an injury he incurred through the misuse of a power saw.[94] Immediately prior to the injury, the teacher had provided comprehensive instructions and warnings regarding use of the equipment. Similarly, the Supreme Court of Tennessee barred damages in the fatal injury of a twelve-year-old student who was struck by a guy wire supporting a utility pole when he leaned out the window of a school bus. Considering that the student was "a bright, alert and intelligent young man" who had heard school monitors regularly warn students not to have their hands or any parts of their bodies outside the bus windows, the court found that the student's action was the proximate cause of the injury and constituted contributory negligence.[95]

School personnel have been unsuccessful in using contributory negligence as a defense if a student was not aware of the hazardous nature of an activity. For example, a student who was waiting for a teacher outside an area marked "danger" in an industrial arts class was injured when a cylinder exploded.[96] A state appeals court rejected the claim of contributory negligence, concluding that the student was acting appropriately by waiting outside the danger area and had no reason to expect the injury to occur. Another court, in remanding a student injury case for a jury trial, noted that an eleven-year-old plaintiff did not necessarily realize the dangers involved in an unfamiliar and improperly taught jump in physical education. Thus, the evidence did not support the teacher's claim of contributory negligence.[97] Also, teachers who have provided inadequate supervision or instruction cannot assert that students are contributorily negligent.[98]

ASSUMPTION OF RISK

Similar to contributory negligence, assumption of risk may be used as a defense to prevent recovery for an injury if a student is found to have assumed a risk of harm. Teachers, however, may encounter difficulties in using this defense because of students' age and maturity. The defense is based on the premise that the injured plaintiff understood that a specific situation was dangerous and could result in possible injury and still voluntarily consented to participate.

Assumption of risk often has been asserted in connection with sports injuries in educational settings. While inherent risks are associated with athletics, courts generally are not inclined to hold that students understand the risks. As a Pennsylvania court noted in a case involving an eleven-year-old student injured in a hockey game: "If by reason of his tender age and lack of intelligence, experience and information, [he] did not appreciate the dangers of floor hockey, assumption of risk is not a viable defense."[99] In an earlier Pennsylvania case, the state high court remanded a student injury case for jury determination, questioning a student's understanding of the risks involved in preseason football conditioning and the voluntariness of his participation.[100] The student suffered permanent blindness in one eye from an injury incurred in playing "jungle football," an exercise conducted without protective equipment and involving rough body blocks and tackling. Evidence indicated that the student did not understand the risks and, furthermore, felt that selection for the team was contingent on his participation in the activity.

The New York high court emphasized that in extracurricular sports school personnel must exercise "ordinary reasonable care" to protect students from "unassumed, concealed or unreasonably increased risks."[101] Accordingly, the court held that when this duty is met and participation is voluntary, with no evidence of compulsion to participate in an athletic event, a student assumes the risks inherent in the sport. The court found that a nineteen-year-old football player, who was in excellent condition, properly equipped, and well trained, assumed the risk of injury when he continued to play and did not inform his coach of his fatigued condition. A Louisiana appellate court also concluded that a high school athlete who challenged a coach to a wrestling match assumed the risk of injury.[102] The student, who was one of the strongest athletes in the school, a starting guard on the basketball team, and a starting halfback on the football team, was found to know and appreciate the risk of injury involved in wrestling.

Some educators are under the mistaken impression that parents can waive their children's right to sue for negligence by signing forms granting permission for the children to participate in particular activities. Such permission slips indicate that the students assume *normal* risks associated with the activity, but parents cannot waive their children's entitlement to appropriate supervision and instruction. For example, a child may assume some risk of potential injury by engaging in a dangerous sport such as football or by participating in a field trip (i.e., swimming or roller skating), but school personnel remain responsible for providing supervision and instruction to safeguard the child from foreseeable harm. Even though a permission slip might stipulate that the school is relieved of all liability for injuries associated with a given activity or outing, such documentation would not preclude liability if the child were subjected to unreasonable risks of harm. Furthermore, it is doubtful that participation in school-related activities can be conditioned on the signing of forms that release the school district from liability. In addressing this question, the Supreme Court of Washington held that release forms were invalid whether they were characterized as "releases" or "assumptions of risk."[103]

COMPARATIVE NEGLIGENCE

Contributory negligence and assumption of risk have been used less frequently in recent tort suits since many states have modified or replaced these defenses with comparative negligence standards. Depending on the level of fault, liability is apportioned among negligent parties, which may include the plaintiff, defendant, and other intervening actors.[104] For example, in a Louisiana case involving a severely burned child, a school board was found to have been negligent in disposing of partially full cans of flammable duplicating fluid in the school dumpster. Damages, however, were apportioned among the school board (55 percent) and the children (45 percent) who removed the cans.[105] State laws vary as to restrictions placed on recovery.[106] In some states damages are assessed in direct proportion to the various actors' relative negligence, whereas in other states damages are awarded to a negligent plaintiff only if the defendant's negligence is judged to be greater than that of the plaintiff.

NOTICE OF CLAIM

Procedural defects in the process of filing a tort action can preclude recovery by the injured party. Notice-of-claim provisions in state laws specify the form to be used when initiating a suit and the time period within which a claim must be filed. Such requirements are designed to protect governmental entities' financial resources by enabling a prompt investigation of a claim while the facts surrounding it are still relatively recent. Without substantial and meaningful justifications, deadlines for filing are enforced.[107]

Although states' general statutes that limit the time period for filing claims usually do not apply to children until they reach the age of majority, most courts have upheld notice-of-claim statutes when minors have brought civil actions for damages against public employers unless an exemption is expressly provided.[108] A few courts, however, have allowed late petitions to be filed as long as they are filed within a reasonable period of time, such as one year, from the date of the injury.[109] For example, the Supreme Court of Utah held that a minor's period of disability resulting from a shop class injury should not be considered part of the elapsed time for purposes of limiting the filing of a suit for damages.[110] In ruling that special consideration should be given to minors, the court noted that children are incapable of bringing suit and are left unprotected unless parents file the claim. A California appeals court also concluded that a minor should not be penalized because his parents neglected to initiate a timely action.[111]

ASSAULT AND BATTERY

Although negligence cases have dominated educational tort litigation, a few intentional tort actions have been initiated. An intentional tort need not be maliciously planned, but may be committed if a person intentionally acts in a manner that impairs the rights of others. Intentional tort actions in school settings mainly have involved charges of assault and battery. Assault consists of an overt attempt to place another in fear of bodily harm;

no actual physical contact need take place. When an assault is consummated and physical injury occurs, battery is committed. A person wielding a knife and threatening harm is guilty of assault; the actual stabbing constitutes battery.

Assault and battery cases in the school context generally have focused on the administration of corporal punishment by school personnel. Courts have been reluctant to interfere with a teacher's authority to discipline students and have sanctioned the use of reasonable force to control pupil behavior. For example, an Oregon appeals court ruled that a teacher was not guilty of assault and battery for using force to remove a student from the classroom.[112] After the pupil defiantly refused to leave the room, the teacher held his arms and led him toward the door. The student extricated himself, swung at the teacher, and broke a window, thereby cutting his arm. Concluding that the teacher used reasonable force with the student, the court dismissed the assault and battery charges.

A Louisiana appeals court also dismissed battery charges against a teacher who gently kicked a student.[113] Testimony revealed that the student had repeatedly disobeyed the teacher and had turned around in his chair to talk to classmates when the incident occurred. The teacher, who was holding chalk and an eraser in his hands, nudged the student with his foot in the right buttock to gain the pupil's attention. The court rejected the battery charge, reasoning that the blow was of little force and resulted more in embarrassment than pain. The court noted that this situation was one of the few circumstances where a kick would meet the test of reasonableness.

In another Louisiana case, however, a student was successful in obtaining damages for assault and battery.[114] The pupil sustained a broken arm when a teacher shook him against bleachers in the gymnasium and then let him fall to the floor. The court assessed damages against the teacher, reasoning that the teacher's action was unnecessary to discipline the student or to protect himself. Similarly, the Supreme Court of Connecticut awarded damages to a twelve-year-old student because a teacher used excessive force in disciplining him.[115] The student suffered a fractured clavicle when the teacher threw him into a movable chalkboard in the classroom and then pushed him into a wall in the hallway.

School personnel also may initiate assault and battery suits against students. For example, a Wisconsin appellate court awarded a teacher both compensatory and punitive damages in a suit for battery.[116] The teacher was physically attacked by a student outside the school building while attempting to escort the student to the school office for violating a smoking rule. Concluding that the student acted with malicious intent, the court did not find excessive a punitive damage award of $23,000. Similarly, an Oregon appellate court assessed damages against a student when he struck a teacher who was attempting to prevent him from leaving the classroom.[117] Because Oregon law stipulates that parents are financially responsible for damages caused by the intentional torts of their children, damages also were entered against the father.

DEFAMATION

Most tort actions have involved claims for damages that were due to physical injuries, but some plaintiffs have sought recovery for injuries to their reputations. Generally, *defamation* is defined as a false or misleading communication that places another person in a position of disgrace, ridicule, or contempt;[118] the statements may be made intentionally or negligently. *Slander* is spoken defamation, and *libel* is written defamation. Under certain circumstances, communication is considered privileged and cannot be the grounds for a defamation suit. Statements made by justices and state officials in carrying out governmental services are usually considered absolutely privileged. Qualified privilege is often applied to statements made by educational personnel, and such communication is immune from liability as long as it is made in good faith "upon a proper occasion, from a proper motive, in a proper manner, and based upon reasonable or probable cause."[119] Qualified privilege will not shield educators if statements are made with malicious intent. The mere transmittal of erroneous information, however, does not constitute evidence of malice, as long as the communication is believed to be accurate and is conveyed in good faith. Truth can be used as a defamation defense, but usually, even if the communication is true, educators must have made the statements with good intentions in order to thwart defamation charges.

Despite the recent interest in students' privacy rights, there have been few defamation cases involving students.[120] Most defamation claims pertaining to schools have been initiated by teachers challenging evaluations placed in their personnel files or statements made by parents to school officials. A Pennsylvania court noted that administrators are authorized and required under state law to rate school personnel. As such, they are immune to suit unless comments are motivated by malicious personal animosity.[121] A New York appellate court held that a superintendent's written reprimand to a coach for failure to follow required rules and regulations in operating the interscholastic athletic program was protected by absolute privilege. Although only qualified privilege protected the superintendent's comments to the press, the defamation claim was found to be without merit in the absence of malice.[122]

Regarding parental complaints, an Arizona appeals court held that parents were not liable for defamation of character simply because they submitted to the school board a list of grievances against a teacher.[123] Similarly, in a California case, a vice-principal was unsuccessful in a defamation suit against a group of parents who had made several allegations about him to the school board.[124] The court concluded that communications between citizens and public officials who are charged with investigating activities of employees are privileged. In another California case, an appeals court rejected libel charges against parents for writing a letter to a school principal in which they made derogatory statements about a teacher. The court stated:

> One of the crosses a public school teacher must bear is intemperate complaint addressed to school administrators by overly-solicitous parents concerned about the teacher's conduct in the classroom. Since the law compels parents to send their children to school, appropriate channels for the airing of supposed grievances against the operation of the school system must remain open.[125]

Similarly, the New York high court held that parents had a qualified privilege to present a complaint against a teacher to the school board. Under state law, such concerns must be expressed in writing. The court, emphasizing the need to maintain open communication between parents and school officials, noted that "to tell lay persons that the governing body which has ultimate responsibility for the well being of their children will not even hear their claim unless they publish a statement containing their complaint, and then subject these parents to liability for making the statement is counter productive."[126]

Public educators also have initiated defamation suits against the news media,[127] with success often depending on whether the person is viewed as a private individual or as a public figure or official.[128] The United States Supreme Court has recognized the importance of preserving citizens' rights to criticize the government and public officials.[129] Accordingly, the Court has held that a public official can recover damages for defamation only if there is proof of actual malice; that is, a statement was made "with knowledge that it was false or with reckless disregard of whether it was false or not."[130] To be considered a public official, an individual must have "substantial responsibilities for or control over the conduct of governmental affairs."[131] The Florida and Maine high courts have held that teachers are not public officials since their authority is generally limited to schoolchildren.[132] An Oklahoma appellate court, however, found that a teacher who was a well-known civil rights worker, radio show hostess, and author was a public figure.[133] The Seventh Circuit Court of Appeals concluded that an elementary principal by virtue of her great discretion in the operation of the school was a public official.[134] The Ohio Supreme Court also held that public school superintendents are public officials for purposes of defamation laws.[135] The court based its decision on the fact that a superintendent has substantial responsibilities for the operation of the school system and that the public is concerned with such an individual's performance.

Even if school personnel are deemed to be public officials or public figures, the Supreme Court has held that such individuals do not have to show actual malice to recover damages if the defamatory statements do not pertain to issues of public concern.[136] For statements involving matters of public concern, liability will be assessed against the news media only if the statements are false.[137] In 1990, the Supreme Court declined to provide special protection to media statements of opinion rather than fact, noting that even if couched as an opinion, liability may be assessed for statements that are false and malign another. However, a "statement of opinion relating to matters of public concern which does not contain a provably false factual connotation will receive full constitutional protection."[138]

CONCLUSION

All individuals, including school personnel, have a responsibility to act reasonably and to respect the rights of others, but some negligent conduct is likely to occur and to generate claims for damages. Consequently, educators should be knowledgeable about their potential liability under applicable state laws and should ensure that they have adequate insurance protection to cover any awards that might be assessed against them. To guard against liability, teachers and administrators should be cognizant of the following basic principles of tort law.

1. All individuals are responsible for any harmful consequences of their conduct.
2. The propriety of a teacher's conduct in a given situation is gauged by whether a reasonably prudent teacher (with the special skills and training associated with that role) would have acted in a similar fashion under like conditions.
3. Teachers owe students a duty to provide proper instruction and adequate supervision, to maintain equipment in proper repair, and to provide warnings regarding any known hazards.
4. Teachers are expected to exercise a standard of care commensurate with the duty owed; with more dangerous activities, greater care is required.
5. Foreseeability of harm is a crucial element in determining whether a teacher's actions are negligent in a given situation.
6. An intervening act can relieve a teacher of liability for negligence if the event caused the injury and the teacher had no reason to anticipate that the event would occur.
7. The common-law doctrine that government agencies cannot be held liable in tort actions (sovereign immunity) has been abrogated by legislative or judicial action in many states; in states still adhering to this doctrine, certain restrictions have been placed on

its use as a defense by school districts in negligence claims (e.g., "safe place" statutes, exceptions to immunity for proprietary functions or ministerial duties).

8. Although sovereign immunity generally does not protect school employees from liability in tort actions, some states by law require evidence of willful or wanton misconduct in order for school personnel to be held liable for negligent acts in connection with educational activities.

9. Contributory negligence can be used to relieve school personnel of liability if it is established that the injured party's own actions were a significant factor in producing the injury.

10. If an individual knowingly and voluntarily assumes a risk of harm, recovery for an injury is barred.

11. Under comparative negligence statutes, damages may be apportioned among negligent defendants, plaintiffs, and intervening actors.

12. Procedural defects in filing a claim can preclude recovery on the part of the injured party.

13. School personnel can be held liable for assault and battery if found to have used excessive or brutal force with students.

14. Educators are protected from defamation charges by "qualified privilege," whereby written or spoken communication cannot be the subject of tort actions as long as statements are made to appropriate persons and with proper intentions.

15. Public officials can recover damages for defamation from the news media for statements pertaining to public issues only if actual malice is shown.

ENDNOTES

1. The only exceptions involve cases brought in the District of Columbia and actions initiated under 42 U.S.C. § 1983 (1988), which entitles individuals to sue persons acting under color of state law for damages in connection with the impairment of federally protected rights. For a discussion of liability under Section 1983, *see* text with note 166, Chapter 8.

2. *See, generally,* William Prosser, John Wade, and Victor Schwartz, *Cases and Materials on Torts,* 7th ed. (St. Paul, MN: West Publishing Co., 1982).

3. False imprisonment involves the unlawful restraint of an individual's freedom of movement; trespass is the unlawful interference with one's person, property, or rights, Henry Black, *Black's Law Dictionary,* 6th ed. (St. Paul, MN: West Publishing Co., 1990), pp. 601, 1502. *See* text with note 112, *infra,* for discussion of assault and battery.

4. *See* text with note 124, Chapter 3, for a discussion of educational negligence

litigation in which plaintiffs have alleged that school districts breached their duty to assure student literacy upon high school graduation.

5. Prosser, Wade, and Schwartz, *Cases and Materials on Torts,* p. 144.
6. *See, e.g.,* Fuzie v. South Haven School Dist. No. 30, 553 N.Y.S.2d 961 (N.Y. Sup. Ct. 1990) (toothpicks used in a kindergarten project were not considered dangerous instruments that would foreseeably result in injury to a third party).
7. *See, e.g.,* Gattyan v. Scarsdale Union Free School Dist. No. 1, 543 N.Y.S.2d 732 (N.Y. App. Div. 1989); Payne v. North Carolina Dep't of Human Resources, 382 S.E.2d 449 (N.C. Ct. App. 1989); Leger v. Stockton Unified School Dist., 249 Cal. Rptr. 688 (Cal. Ct. App. 1988); District of Columbia v. Doe, 524 A.2d 30 (D.C. 1987).
8. *See, e.g.,* Logan v. City of New York, 543 N.Y.S.2d 661 (N.Y. App. Div. 1989); Comuntzis v. Pinellas County School Bd., 508 So. 2d 750 (Fla. Dist. Ct. App. 1987); District of Columbia v. Doe, *id.*
9. Augustus v. Joseph A. Craig Elementary School, 459 So. 2d 665 (La. Ct. App. 1984).
10. Chan v. Board of Educ. of City of New York, 557 N.Y.S.2d 91 (N.Y. App. Div. 1990). *See also* Bauer v. Minidoka School Dist. No. 331, 778 P.2d 336 (Idaho 1989); Fazzolari v. Portland School Dist. No. 1J, 734 P.2d 1326 (Or. 1987); Laneheart v. Orleans Parish School Bd., 524 So. 2d 138 (La. Ct. App. 1988); Leger v. Stockton Unified School Dist., 249 Cal. Rptr. 688 (Cal. Ct. App. 1988).
11. Verhel v. Independent School Dist. No. 709, 359 N.W.2d 579 (Minn. 1984). *See also* Rupp v. Bryant, 417 So. 2d 658 (Fla. 1982) (school district was responsible for supervising club activities off campus). *But see* Rollins v. Blair, 767 P.2d 328 (Mont. 1989) (school district did not have a duty of supervision to a student participating in a cheerleading summer camp operated by private individuals).
12. Rhea v. Grandview School Dist., 694 P.2d 666 (Wash. Ct. App. 1985).
13. *See, e.g.,* Welch v. Dunsmuir Joint Union High School Dist., 326 P.2d 633 (Cal. Ct. App. 1958).
14. O'Brien v. Township High School Dist. 214, 415 N.E.2d 1015 (Ill. 1980).
15. Guerrieri v. Tyson, 24 A.2d 468 (Pa. Super. Ct. 1942).
16. *See, e.g.,* Czaplicki v. Gooding Joint School Dist. No. 231, 775 P.2d 640 (Idaho 1989); Barth v. Board of Educ. of City of Chicago, 490 N.E.2d 77 (Ill. App. Ct. 1986). *But see* Gara v. Lomonaco, 557 N.E.2d 483 (Ill. App. Ct. 1990) (teachers were not guilty of willful and wanton misconduct in declining injured student's request to see the school nurse); Montgomery v. City of Detroit, 448 N.W.2d 822 (Mich. Ct. App. 1989) (principal was immune from liability in claim involving failure to provide emergency procedures; establishing rules was a discretionary function entitled to governmental immunity).
17. Given the substantial concern for individual safety at school, in 1982 California voters amended the state constitution to include the "right to safe schools." The provision stipulates in part: "All students and staff of public primary, elementary, junior high and senior high schools have the inalienable right to attend campuses which are safe, secure and peaceful." Cal. Const. art. I, § 28(C) (1983). While this provision provides students with the right to attend safe schools, a damages remedy is not available to injured individuals. *See*

Clausing v. San Francisco Unified School Dist., 271 Cal. Rptr. 72 (Cal. Ct. App. 1990); Leger v. Stockton Unified School Dist., 249 Cal. Rptr. 688 (Cal. Ct. App. 1988).

18. *See, e.g.,* Greene v. City of New York, 566 N.Y.S.2d 40 (N.Y. App. Div. 1991) (school officials had a duty to protect student from neighborhood bully who had made threats on student's life and was seen frequently on school grounds); Fazzolari v. Portland School Dist. No. 1J, 734 P.2d 1326 (Or. 1987) (sexual assault on school premises following similar incident fifteen days earlier raised question of the school district's negligence in protecting students from harm); District of Columbia v. Doe, 524 A.2d 30 (D.C. 1987) (assaults and other crimes near the school placed school officials on notice of foreseeable criminal assaults). *See also* Peterson v. San Francisco Community College Dist., 685 P.2d 1193 (Cal. 1984) (school authorities had a legal duty to warn students of known dangers).

19. *See, e.g.,* Cooper v. Baldwin County School Dist., 386 S.E.2d 896 (Ga. Ct. App. 1989) (no liability was found for the stabbing of a student in the absence of previous attacks or fights in the school courtyard); Pesek v. Discepolo, 475 N.E.2d 3 (Ill. App. Ct. 1985) (rape victim failed to state a cause of action against school district for inadequate supervision of a truant student when school district could not foresee that the student would commit violent acts); Vann v. Board of Educ. of School Dist. of Philadelphia, 464 A.2d 684 (Pa. Commw. Ct. 1983) (attack on school property after school hours was not foreseeable); Kavanaugh v. Orleans Parish School Bd., 487 So. 2d 533 (La. Ct. App. 1986) (armed robbery of teacher in classroom was not foreseeable).

20. *See* text with note 145, Chapter 7, for a discussion of school district liability under 42 U.S.C. § 1983 (1988) for its employees' sexual abuse of students; Bruce Beezer, ''School District Liability for Negligent Hiring and Retention of Unfit Employees,'' *Education Law Reporter,* vol. 56 (1990), pp. 1117–1124.

21. John R. v. Oakland Unified School Dist., 256 Cal. Rptr. 766, 774 (Cal. 1989). *See also* Kimberly M. v. Los Angeles Unified School Dist., 263 Cal. Rptr. 612 (Cal. Ct. App. 1989).

22. Doe v. Durtschi, 716 P.2d 1238 (Idaho 1986). *See also* School Bd. of Orange County v. Coffey, 524 So. 2d 1052 (Fla. Dist. Ct. App. 1988), *review denied,* 534 So. 2d 401 (Fla. 1988).

23. Doe v. Town of Blandford, 525 N.E.2d 403 (Mass. 1988).

24. Kern Alexander and David Alexander, *American Public School Law* (St. Paul, MN: West Publishing Co., 1985), p. 457.

25. Foster v. Houston General Ins. Co., 407 So. 2d 759, 763 (La. Ct. App. 1981).

26. *See, e.g.,* Fornaro v. Kerry, 527 N.Y.S.2d 61 (N.Y. App. Div. 1988) (proximate cause of an injury to a kindergarten student was the intervening act of a ten-year-old student rather than conduct of school personnel).

27. Segerman v. Jones, 259 A.2d 794 (Md. Ct. App. 1969).

28. Simonetti v. School Dist. of Philadelphia, 454 A.2d 1038, 1041 (Pa. Super. Ct. 1982), *appeal dismissed,* 473 A.2d 1015 (Pa. 1984). *See also* Allison v. Field Local School Dist., 553 N.E.2d 1383 (Ohio Ct. App. 1988); Albers v. Community Consol. #204 School, 508 N.E.2d 1252 (Ill. App. Ct. 1987).

29. Roberts v. Robertson County Bd. of Educ., 692 S.W.2d 863 (Tenn. Ct. App. 1985).

30. Dailey v. Los Angeles Unified School Dist., 470 P.2d 360 (Cal. 1970). *See also* Rupp v. Bryant, 417 So. 2d 658 (Fla. 1982) (failure of school personnel to supervise activities of a student club was proximate cause of student's injury).

31. Kush v. City of Buffalo, 462 N.Y.S.2d 831 (N.Y. 1983).

32. *See* text with note 105, *infra*, for discussion of comparative negligence damage awards.

33. Roberts v. Robertson County Bd. of Educ., 692 S.W.2d 863 (Tenn. Ct. App. 1985).

34. Ohio Rev. Code Ann., § 2744.07 (1990).

35. Ill. Rev. Stat. ch. 122 § 24-24 (1989).

36. *See, e.g.,* Segerman v. Jones, 259 A.2d 794 (Md. Ct. App. 1969); text with note 27, *supra. See also* Patterson v. Orleans Parish School Bd., 461 So. 2d 386 (La. Ct. App. 1984) (no liability was assessed for injury resulting from child catching his hand in door when orderly procedures were employed for escorting students to restroom).

37. Clark v. Furch, 567 S.W.2d 457 (Mo. Ct. App. 1978).

38. Partin v. Vernon Parish School Bd., 343 So. 2d 417 (La. Ct. App. 1977).

39. Sheehan v. Saint Peter's Catholic School, 188 N.W.2d 868 (Minn. 1971).

40. Fagan v. Summers, 498 P.2d 1227 (Wyo. 1972). *See also* Allison v. Field Local School Dist., 553 N.E.2d 1383 (Ohio Ct. App. 1988) (eye injury resulting from fourth-graders' throwing dirt balls during recess was not foreseeable).

41. James v. Charlotte-Mecklenburg Bd. of Educ., 300 S.E.2d 21 (N.C. Ct. App. 1983). *See also* Simonetti v. School Dist. of Philadelphia, 454 A.2d 1038 (Pa. Super. Ct. 1982), *appeal dismissed,* 473 A.2d 1015 (Pa. 1984) (absence from classroom to monitor hallway did not constitute negligence).

42. Cirillo v. City of Milwaukee, 150 N.W.2d 460 (Wis. 1967). *See also* Alferoff v. Casagrade, 504 N.Y.S.2d 719 (N.Y. App. Div. 1986) (it was foreseeable that the disruptive behavior that regularly occurred in teacher's absence could result in injury).

43. Lawrence v. Grant Parish School Bd., 409 So. 2d 1316 (La. Ct. App. 1982), *writ denied,* 412 So. 2d 1110 (La. 1982). *But see* Payne v. North Carolina Dep't of Human Resources, 382 S.E.2d 449 (N.C. Ct. App. 1989) (shop teacher who left a sixteen-year-old deaf student unsupervised while he answered his telephone was not negligent for an injury that occurred when the student left his assignment and attempted to add oil to a hydraulic lift; the resulting injury was unforeseeable).

44. District of Columbia v. Royal, 465 A.2d 367 (D.C. 1983).

45. School City of Gary v. Claudio, 413 N.E.2d 628 (Ind. Ct. App. 1980). *See also* Torsiello v. Oakland Unified School Dist., 242 Cal. Rptr. 752 (Cal. Ct. App. 1987).

46. *See, e.g.,* Blair v. Board of Educ., 448 N.Y.S.2d 566 (N.Y. App. Div. 1982).

47. Hoyem v. Manhattan Beach City School Dist., 585 P.2d 851 (Cal. 1978).

48. Palella v. Ulmer, 518 N.Y.S.2d 91, 93 (N.Y. Sup. Ct. 1987).

49. Powell v. Orleans Parish School Bd., 354 So. 2d 229 (La. Ct. App. 1978).

50. Morris v. Douglas County School Dist. No. 9, 403 P.2d 775 (Or. 1965).

51. *See, e.g.,* Prescott v. Newsday, Inc., 541 N.Y.S.2d 501 (N.Y. App. Div. 1989) (duty to supervise does not include protecting students from interview by newspaper reporter).

52. Dibortolo v. Metropolitan School Dist. of Washington Township, 440 N.E.2d 506 (Ind. Ct. App. 1982).
53. LaValley v. Stanford, 70 N.Y.S.2d 460 (N.Y. App. Div. 1947). *See also* Brahatcek v. Millard School Dist. No. 17, 273 N.W.2d 680 (Neb. 1979).
54. Ehlinger v. Board of Educ. of New Hartford Cent. School Dist., 465 N.Y.S.2d 378 (N.Y. App. Div. 1983).
55. Roberts v. Robertson County Bd. of Educ., 692 S.W.2d 863 (Tenn. Ct. App. 1985).
56. Hammond v. Scott, 232 S.E.2d 336 (S.C. 1977).
57. Izard v. Hickory City Schools Bd. of Educ., 315 S.E.2d 756 (N.C. Ct. App. 1984).
58. *See, e.g.,* Monfils v. City of Sterling Heights, 269 N.W.2d 588 (Mich. Ct. App. 1978); Hudson v. Union Free School Dist. No. 2, 391 N.Y.S.2d 487 (N.Y. App. Div. 1977).
59. Wilkinson v. Hartford Accident and Indemnity Co., 411 So. 2d 22 (La. 1982). *See also* Bielaska v. Town of Waterford, 491 A.2d 1071 (Conn. 1985); Gump v. Chartiers-Houston School Dist., 558 A.2d 589 (Pa. Commw. Ct. 1989), *appeal denied,* 565 A.2d 1168 (Pa. 1989); Johnson v. City of Boston, 490 N.E.2d 1204 (Mass. App. Ct. 1986). *See also* Kirby v. Macon Pub. School Dist. No. 5, 523 N.E.2d 643 (Ill. App. Ct. 1988) (injury involving lack of guard rails on a twelve-foot-high slide over an asphalt surface stated a cause of action against school district); Highfield v. Liberty Christian Academy, 518 N.E.2d 592 (Ohio Ct. App. 1987) (negligence found for failure to warn individuals of steel cable suspended across access to school playground).
60. Best v. Houtz, 541 So. 2d 8 (Ala. 1989). *But see* Morris v. Orleans Parish School Bd., 553 So. 2d 427 (La. 1989) (injury from water accumulated under a water fountain knowingly in need of repair resulted in negligence).
61. Lewis v. Saint Bernard Parish School Bd., 350 So. 2d 1256 (La. Ct. App. 1977).
62. Narcisse v. Continental Ins. Co., 419 So. 2d 13 (La. Ct. App. 1982).
63. Gerrity v. Beatty, 373 N.E.2d 1323 (Ill. 1978). *But see* Thomas v. Chicago Bd. of Educ., 395 N.E.2d 538 (Ill. 1979) (coaches were immune from liability in inspecting and furnishing defective helmets).
64. Everett v. Bucky Warren, Inc., 380 N.E.2d 653 (Mass. 1978). *See also* Tiemann v. Independent School Dist. No. 740, 331 N.W.2d 250 (Minn. 1983) (use of vaulting horses with exposed holes where pommels had been removed posed question of negligence); Parisi v. Harpursville Cent. School Dist., 553 N.Y.S.2d 566 (N.Y. App. Div. 1990) (duty existed to provide student baseball catcher a mask and instruct as to proper use); Massie v. Persson, 729 S.W.2d 448 (Ky. Ct. App. 1987) (coach's failure to install a ground fault interrupter in modifying the wiring of a whirlpool was held to be negligence in the death of a student).
65. *See, e.g.,* Pichette v. Manistique Pub. Schools, 269 N.W.2d 143 (Mich. 1978); Zaepfel v. City of Yonkers, 392 N.Y.S.2d 336 (N.Y. App. Div. 1977).
66. Monfils v. City of Sterling Heights, 269 N.W.2d 588 (Mich. Ct. App. 1978).
67. Bartell v. Palos Verdes Peninsula School Dist., 147 Cal. Rptr. 898 (Cal. Ct. App. 1978).
68. Asbestos School Hazard Detection and Control Act, 20 U.S.C. 3601, *et seq.* (1988). Additionally, most states have enacted asbestos abatement legis-

lation. *See* Edgar Bittle and Jane McAllister, "Contracting for Asbestos Abatement: What You Need to Know," *Education Law Reporter,* vol. 57 (1990), pp. 1123–1135; Charles Russo, "Asbestos in the Schools: Health Hazard for the Eighties," *Education Law Reporter,* vol. 46 (1988), pp. 499–508.

69. 15 U.S.C. § 2641 *et seq.* (1988).

70. *See* 40 C.F.R. §§ 763.80–.99 (1990); Safe Buildings Alliance v. Environmental Protection Agency, 846 F.2d 79 (D.C. Cir. 1988).

71. *See, e.g.,* In re School Asbestos Litigation, 921 F.2d 1330 (3d Cir. 1990); In re School Asbestos Litigation, 789 F.2d 996 (3d Cir. 1986), *cert. denied,* 479 U.S. 852 (1986); Board of Educ. of City of Chicago v. A, C and S, Inc., 546 N.E.2d 581 (Ill. 1989); National Gypsum v. Kirbyville Indep. School Dist., 770 S.W.2d 621 (Tex. Ct. App. 1989)

72. In re School Asbestos Litigation, *id.,* 789 F.2d at 1000.

73. *See* Lentz v. Morris, 372 S.E.2d 608 (Va. 1988) (governmental immunity extended to teachers by the state high court for actions taken within the scope of their employment; court expressly overruled earlier precedents denying immunity to teachers, noting that they perform a vitally important governmental function that involves the exercise of judgment and discretion and is closely supervised and controlled by the governmental entity).

74. *See* William D. Valente, *Education Law: Public and Private,* vol. 2 (St. Paul, MN: West Publishing Co., 1985), p. 224. For a discussion of the abrogation of school district immunity in connection with abridgments of federal rights under 42 U.S.C. § 1983 (1988), *see* text with note 182, Chapter 8.

75. Carbone v. Overfield, 451 N.E.2d 1229 (Ohio 1983). In 1985, the Ohio legislature enacted a statute granting modified immunity to school districts, Ohio Rev. Code Ann. § 2744 (1990).

76. *Id.,* 451 N.E.2d at 1230.

77. *See, e.g.,* Giosa v. School Dist. of Philadelphia, 562 A.2d 411 (Pa. Commw. Ct. 1989), *appeal denied,* 578 A.2d 416 (Pa. 1990) (snow and ice can create a "dangerous condition" under the sidewalk exception to immunity); Prest v. Sparta Community Unit School Dist. #140, 510 N.E.2d 595 (Ill. App. Ct. 1987) (student injury claim related to a concrete riser in the gymnasium could be based on landowners' premises liability); Stahl v. Cocalico School Dist., 534 A.2d 1141 (Pa. Commw. Ct. 1987) (plaintiff stated a cause of action within real property exception to immunity based on known defective physical condition of skylight). *See also* text with note 58, *supra,* for a discussion of "safe place" statutes.

78. Velmer v. Baraga Area Schools, 424 N.W.2d 770 (Mich. 1988). *See also* Stretton v. City of Lewiston, 588 A.2d 739 (Me. 1991) (unimproved public athletic field did not come within the public building exception).

79. Gore v. Bethlehem Area School Dist., 537 A.2d 913 (Pa. Commw. Ct. 1988), *appeal denied,* 546 A.2d 60 (Pa. 1988).

80. Brock v. Rockridge Community Unit Dist. #300, 539 N.E.2d 445 (Ill. App. Ct. 1989).

81. Gutierrez v. Artesia Pub. Schools, 583 P.2d 476 (N.M. Ct. App. 1978).

82. Black, *Black's Law Dictionary,* p. 1065. *See also* Prosser, Wade, and Schwartz, *Cases and Materials on Torts,* p. 852.

83. *See, e.g.,* Taylor v. Klund, 739 S.W.2d 592 (Mo. Ct. App. 1987).

84. *See, e.g.,* Richards v. School Dist. of City of Birmingham, 83 N.W.2d 643 (Mich. 1957); Sawaya v. Tucson High School Dist., 281 P.2d 105 (Ariz. 1955).

85. Whitney v. City of Worcester, 366 N.E.2d 1210 (Mass. 1977). *See also* Heigl v. Board of Educ. of Town of New Canaan, 587 A.2d 423 (Conn. 1991) (school board's establishment of an open campus policy was a discretionary activity entitled to governmental immunity); Greider v. Shawnee Mission Unified School Dist. #512, 710 F. Supp. 296 (D. Kan. 1989) (discretionary immunity exception does not apply when school district fails to fulfill its legally prescribed duty).

86. Davis v. Homestead Farms, Inc., 359 N.W.2d 1 (Mich. Ct. App. 1984).

87. Hutt v. Etowah County Bd. of Educ., 454 So. 2d 973 (Ala. 1984).

88. McManus v. Anahuac Indep. School Dist., 667 S.W.2d 275 (Tex. Ct. App. 1984).

89. *See* Board of Educ. of County of Raleigh v. Commercial Casualty Ins. Co., 182 S.E. 87 (W. Va. 1935).

90. Lehmen v. Wansing, 624 S.W.2d 1 (Mo. 1981).

91. Crowell v. School Dist. No. 7, Gallatin County, 805 P.2d 522 (Mont. 1991); Dugger v. Sprouse, 364 S.E.2d 275 (Ga. 1988) (immunity waived only to the extent of the insurance coverage; if a particular claim is not covered by the policy, no waiver exists); James v. Charlotte-Mecklenburg Bd. of Educ., 300 S.E.2d 21 (N.C. Ct. App. 1983). *See also* School Bd. of Orange County v. Coffey, 524 So. 2d 1052 (Fla. Dist. Ct. App. 1988), *review denied,* 534 So. 2d 401 (Fla. 1988) (waiver of immunity was found even though school district was insured only for awards in excess of $100,000).

92. *See* Berman v. Philadelphia Bd. of Educ., 456 A.2d 545 (Pa. Super. Ct. 1983).

93. *See, e.g.,* Brazell v. Board of Educ. of Niskayuna Pub. Schools, 557 N.Y.S.2d 645 (N.Y. App. Div. 1990); Branch v. Stehr, 461 N.Y.S.2d 346 (N.Y. App. Div. 1983); District of Columbia v. Royal, 465 A.2d 367 (D.C. 1983).

94. Izard v. Hickory City Schools Bd. of Educ., 315 S.E.2d 756 (N.C. Ct. App. 1984).

95. Arnold v. Hayslett, 655 S.W.2d 941, 946 (Tenn. 1983).

96. Danos v. Foret, 354 So. 2d 667 (La. Ct. App. 1977), *cert. denied,* 356 So. 2d 1010 (La. 1978). *See also* Lawrence v. Grant Parish School Bd., 409 So. 2d 1316 (La. Ct. App. 1982), *cert. denied,* 412 So. 2d 1110 (La. 1982) (simply warning fourteen-year-old student not to use power saw without explaining dangers did not render student contributorily negligent for subsequent injury).

97. Dibortolo v. Metropolitan School Dist. of Washington Township, 440 N.E.2d 506 (Ind. Ct. App. 1982).

98. *See, e.g.,* Foster v. Houston General Ins. Co., 407 So. 2d 759 (La. Ct. App. 1981), *cert. denied,* 409 So. 2d 660 (La. 1982).

99. Berman v. Philadelphia Bd. of Educ., 456 A.2d 545, 550 (Pa. Super. Ct. 1983).

100. Rutter v. Northeastern Beaver County School Dist., 437 A.2d 1198 (Pa. 1981).

101. Benitez v. New York City Bd. of Educ., 543 N.Y.S.3d 29, 33 (N.Y. 1989).

102. Kluka v. Livingston Parish School Bd., 433 So. 2d 302 (La. Ct. App. 1983), *cert. denied,* 440 So. 2d 728 (La. 1983). *See also* Beckett v. Clinton Prairie School Corp., 504 N.E.2d 552 (Ind. 1987).

103. Wagenblast v. Odessa School Dist. No. 105-157-166J, 758 P.2d 968 (Wash. 1988).

104. *See, e.g.,* Brown v. Tesack, 566 So. 2d 955 (La. 1990); Chan v. Board of Educ. of City of New York, 557 N.Y.S.2d 91 (N.Y. App. Div 1990); Cooks v. Normandy School Dist., 778 S.W.2d 339 (Mo. Ct. App. 1989).

105. Brown, *id.*

106. Valente, *Education Law: Public and Private,* pp. 215–218.

107. *See, e.g.,* Gardner v. City of Biddeford, 565 A.2d 329 (Me. 1989).

108. 54 Corpus Juris Secundum § 112(b).

109. *See, e.g.,* Rocha v. Lodi Unified School Dist., 152 Cal. Rptr. 307 (Cal. Ct. App. 1979).

110. Scott v. School Bd. of Granite School Dist., 568 P.2d 746 (Utah 1977).

111. Williams v. Mariposa County Unified School Dist., 147 Cal. Rptr. 452 (Cal. Ct. App. 1978). *See also* John R. v. Oakland Unified School Dist., 256 Cal. Rptr. 766 (Cal. 1989) (time period for filing suit for a sexual assault could be tolled during period that teacher's threats prevented student from reporting incident).

112. Simms v. School Dist. No. 1, Multnomah County, 508 P.2d 236 (Or. Ct. App. 1973). *See* Chapter 6 for a more detailed discussion of the legal issues involved in the administration of corporal punishment.

113. Thompson v. Iberville Parish School Bd., 372 So. 2d 642 (La. Ct. App. 1979), *writ denied,* 374 So. 2d 650 (La. 1979).

114. Frank v. Orleans Parish School Bd., 195 So. 2d 451 (La. Ct. App. 1967).

115. Sansone v. Bechtel, 429 A.2d 820 (Conn. 1980).

116. Anello v. Savignac, 342 N.W.2d 440 (Wis. Ct. App. 1983). Punitive damages are awarded for intentional torts when the action is wilful and wanton or reckless, or prompted by ill will or malice.

117. Garrett v. Olsen, 691 P.2d 123 (Or. Ct. App. 1984).

118. *See* Alexander and Alexander, *American Public School Law,* pp. 499-501.

119. Baskett v. Crossfield, 228 S.W. 673, 675 (Ky. 1920).

120. *See, e.g.,* Morrison v. Mobile County Bd. of Educ., 495 So. 2d 1086 (Ala. 1986) (board members' statement in school board meeting regarding suspension of student for possession of marijuana was privileged); Rich v. Kentucky Country Day, Inc., 793 S.W.2d 832 (Ky. Ct. App. 1990) (statements to parents regarding student's performance or activities are qualifiedly privileged).

121. Malia v. Monchak, 543 A.2d 184 (Pa. Commw. Ct. 1988). *See also* Grostick v. Ellsworth, 404 N.W.2d 685 (Mich. Ct. App. 1987).

122. Santavicca v. City of Yonkers, 518 N.Y.S.2d 29 (N.Y. App. Div. 1987).

123. Sewell v. Brookbank, 581 P.2d 267 (Ariz. Ct. App. 1978).

124. Brody v. Montalbano, 151 Cal. Rptr. 206 (Cal. Ct. App. 1978), *cert. denied,* 444 U.S. 844 (1979). *See also* Stevens v. Tillman, 855 F.2d 394 (7th Cir. 1988) (president of the parent–teacher association calling an elementary principal a racist was not defamation under Illinois law).

125. Martin v. Kearney, 124 Cal. Rptr. 281, 283 (Cal. Ct. App. 1975). *See also* Nodar v. Galbreath, 462 So. 2d 803 (Fla. 1984) (parent's statement before school board concerning teacher's performance was conditionally privileged).

126. Weissman v. Mogol, 462 N.Y.S.2d 383, 386 (N.Y. 1983). *See also* Stachura v. Truszkowski, 763 F.2d 211 (6th Cir. 1985), *rev'd on issue of damages,* 477 U.S. 299 (1986) (parent has first amendment right to petition government for

redress of grievances); State v. Reyes, 700 P.2d 1155 (Wash. 1985) (statute prohibiting individuals from insulting or abusing a teacher on school grounds found unconstitutional); Commonwealth v. Ashcraft, 691 S.W.2d 229 (Ky. Ct. App. 1985) (statute providing that "no person shall upbraid, insult or abuse any teacher of the public schools in the presence of the school or in the presence of a pupil of the school" was held to violate a parent's constitutional right to free speech).

127. *See, e.g.,* O'Brien v. Williamson Daily News, 735 F. Supp. 218 (E.D. Ky. 1990) (group libel action by twenty-seven teachers against news media could not be maintained in the absence of showing that libelous article applied to each teacher).

128. A media personality would be an example of a public figure, whereas an elected office holder would be a public official. For a discussion of the distinctions between public figures and public officials, *see* Gertz v. Robert Welch, Inc., 418 U.S. 323 (1974); Rosenblatt v. Baer, 383 U.S. 75 (1966); New York Times Co. v. Sullivan, 376 U.S. 254 (1964).

129. New York Times Co. v. Sullivan, 376 U.S. 254 (1964).

130. *Id.* at 279-280. *See also* O'Neil v. Peekskill Faculty Ass'n Local No. 2916, 549 N.Y.S.2d 41 (N.Y. App. Div. 1989), *appeal dismissed,* 564 N.E.2d 673 (N.Y. 1990) (faculty association's press release falsely and maliciously accusing school district's negotiator of uttering a racial slur resulted in damages for libel).

131. Rosenblatt v. Baer, 383 U.S. 75, 85 (1966).

132. True v. Ladner, 513 A.2d 257 (Me. 1986); Nodar v. Galbreath, 462 So. 2d 803 (Fla. 1984). *See also* Milkovich v. News Herald, 473 N.E.2d 1191 (Ohio 1984), *cert. denied,* 474 U.S. 953 (1985) (teacher/coach was not a public figure nor a public official). Justice Brennan, dissenting in the Supreme Court's denial of *certiorari* in *Milkovich,* noted that public school teachers, as role models, exert significant influence in communities.

133. Luper v. Black Dispatch Publishing Co., 675 P.2d 1028 (Okla. Ct. App. 1983).

134. Stevens v. Tillman, 855 F.2d 394 (7th Cir. 1988), *cert. denied,* 489 U.S. 1065 (1989).

135. Scott v. News-Herald, 496 N.E.2d 699 (Ohio 1986). *See also* Garcia v. Board of Educ. of Socorro Consol. School Dist., 777 F.2d 1403 (10th Cir. 1985), *cert. denied,* 479 U.S. 814 (1986) (school board members are public officials).

136. Dun and Bradstreet, Inc. v. Greenmoss Building, Inc., 472 U.S. 749 (1985).

137. Philadelphia Newspapers, Inc. v. Hepps, 475 U.S. 767 (1986).

138. Milkovich v. Lorain Journal Co., 110 S. Ct. 2695, 2706 (1990), *cause dismissed,* 571 N.E.2d 137 (Ohio 1991). While the newspaper had maintained that an article concerning a high school wrestling coach was "opinion," the Court found that statements implying that the coach committed perjury in a judicial proceeding could be proven true or false. On remand, Milkovich requested and received a dismissal of the case.

13
School Desegregation

Since 1954 school desegregation has generated a steady stream of litigation and dramatically influenced the direction of education law. Claims of discrimination based on gender, disabilities, age, and other inherent traits often rely on precedents established in desegregation cases. Moreover, federal courts have assumed a more assertive posture in reviewing a range of public school policies and practices as a result of legal principles established in this arena. This chapter provides an overview of the evolving law governing efforts to eradicate racial segregation in public education.

FROM *PLESSY* TO *BROWN*

In 1896 the United States Supreme Court interpreted the fourteenth amendment's guarantee of equal protection of the laws as permitting state-imposed segregation by race. In this case, *Plessy v. Ferguson,* the Court reasoned that as long as different races were treated equally, integration was not constitutionally required.[1] Although *Plessy* involved segregated railway accommodations rather than schools, the Court cited an earlier Massachusetts case in which the state high court endorsed racial segregation in public schools.[2] Subsequently, the Supreme Court explicitly ruled that the "separate but equal" doctrine applied in the public school context.[3]

By 1950, however, serious questions had surfaced regarding the "separate but equal" precedent. In several higher education cases, the Supreme Court concluded that separate educational programs offered for African-American and white students were in fact not equivalent and thus violated the equal protection clause.[4] Perhaps realizing that federal courts might be placed in the unrealistic position of evaluating whether segregated public schools throughout the nation were indeed equal, the Supreme Court finally agreed to reassess its interpretation of the equal protection clause as applied to public school segregation.

In its landmark 1954 decision, *Brown v. Board of Education of Topeka,* the Court repudiated the "separate but equal" doctrine, declaring that racially segregated public schools are "inherently unequal."[5] Because of the significant impact of this decision, the Supreme Court delayed an implementation decree for one year, soliciting friend-of-the-court briefs regarding strategies to convert segregated, dual school districts into integrated, unitary districts. The Court's 1955 implementation decree, *Brown II,* contained the often-quoted phrase that dual school systems must be converted to unitary school systems "with all deliberate speed."[6] The Court stated that in designing and effecting desegregation remedies, the federal judiciary should be guided by equitable principles that grant courts "practical flexibility" in adjusting and reconciling public and private needs.[7]

In desegregation cases following *Brown I* and *Brown II,* federal courts have faced a two-pronged task. Initially, they must determine if the equal protection clause has been violated by official action or inaction that has created or perpetuated unlawful school segregation. Once such a violation is established, courts then must approve a remedy that is appropriate in nature and scope. Both of these undertakings have proven troublesome for the federal judiciary. The Supreme Court has recognized that there is no universal solution to the complex problems of desegregation and that state and local interests in managing their own affairs must be considered in fashioning remedies.[8]

PHASE I: SOUTHERN DESEGREGATION

The *Brown I* decision established that states may not deliberately isolate students because of race; legally sanctioned dual school systems, where school assignment is conditioned on race, violate the fourteenth amendment. During the next decade, the Supreme Court reacted to blatant violations of the *Brown* mandate, such as state officials' efforts to block desegregation in Little Rock, Arkansas[9] and an attempt to close public schools in one Virginia county while maintaining public schools in other counties in the state.[10] However, the Court offered little guidance as to what specific conditions offended the Federal Constitution. Some lower courts reasoned that as long as barriers to integration were removed (e.g., state laws and school board policies requiring segregation), the constitutional obligation was satisfied.[11]

Finally, in a trilogy of cases in 1968, the Supreme Court announced that school officials in systems that were segregated by law in 1954 were charged with an *affirmative duty* to take whatever steps were necessary to convert to unitary school systems, eliminating the effects of past discrimination.[12] The Court declared that desegregation remedies, such as free transfer plans, would be evaluated based on their *effectiveness* in dismantling dual school systems. Thus, the notion of "state neutrality" was transformed into a requirement of affirmative state action to desegregate schools; the mere removal of barriers to school integration was not sufficient. In *Green v. County School Board of New Kent County,* the Court ruled that school authorities must eliminate the racial identification of schools in terms of the composition of student bodies and "every facet of school operations—faculty, staff, transportation, extracurricular activities, and facilities."[13] Fifteen years after *Brown,* however, the extent of this affirmative duty remained far from clear.

A 1971 decision, *Swann v. Charlotte-Mecklenburg Board of Education,* often is cited as the Supreme Court's first direct attempt to identify the characteristics of an unconstitutional dual school system and the steps required to attain a unitary, nonracial system.[14] The Court reiterated that practices in the six categories identified in *Green* should be examined in determining whether there were vestiges of state-imposed segregation. Noting that the elimination of invidious racial distinctions may be sufficient in connection with transportation, support personnel, and extracurricular activities, the Court held that more is necessary in terms of constructing facilities and making faculty and student assignments. The Court endorsed assigning teachers on the basis of race until faculties are integrated and declared that new schools must be located so that the dual school system is not perpetuated or reestablished. Regarding student assignments, the Court stated that the racial balance among student bodies would be one criterion in assessing the attainment of unitary status. The Court cautioned, however, that statistical ratios are a desirable norm rather than a fixed requirement. For the vestiges of segregation to be eliminated, the school district must achieve a sufficient degree of racial balance in a sufficient number of schools, but this does not mean that every school must reflect the racial composition of the school district as a whole. Recognizing that the continued presence of a small number of predominantly one-race schools in a district does not necessarily mean that the district still practices state-imposed segregation, the Court placed the burden of proof on school officials to establish that such schools are not the result of present or past discriminatory action.

As to acceptable remedial action, the Court in *Swann* suggested pairing schools, consolidating schools, altering attendance zones, reassigning teachers, and using racial quotas as components of plans to attain unitary school districts. The Court also held that the practice of assigning students to the schools nearest their homes is not a valid basis for operating a school district if it fails to eliminate school segregation. Accordingly, the Court endorsed the use of reasonable busing as a means to integrate schools, noting that the "soundness of any transportation plan" must be evaluated based on the time involved, distance of travel, and age of students.[15]

Applying the criteria established in *Swann,* substantial desegregation was attained in southern school districts during the 1970s. Where unconstitutional segregation was found, federal courts exercised broad power in ordering remedies affecting student and staff assignments, curriculum, school construction, personnel practices, and budgetary allocations. Judicial activity was augmented by threats from the former Department of Health, Education and Welfare to terminate federal funds to school districts not complying with Title VI of the Civil Rights Act of 1964.[16] Whereas only about 1 percent of minority students in eleven southern states attended school with white children a decade after the *Brown* decision, by 1972 over half of the African-American students in the South attended schools with less than 50 percent minority enrollments.[17] Meaningful desegregation required involvement of all three branches of government, but the Supreme Court started the process and in so doing launched an era of judicial intervention in public school affairs.

PHASE II: BEYOND SOUTHERN DESEGREGATION

Since the Court in *Swann* carefully limited its decision to states with a long history of school segregation by *official policy,* questions remained regarding what type of evidence—other than explicit legislation requiring school segregation in 1954—was necessary to establish unconstitutional de jure segregation.[18] In essence, what factors would distinguish de jure segregation from permissible de facto segregation that occurs naturally through no fault of state officials?

In 1973 the Supreme Court rendered its first decision involving a school district where public schools were not segregated by law in 1954. In *Keyes v. School District No. 1, Denver,* the Court held that in "a school system like Denver's, where no statutory dual system has ever existed, plaintiffs must prove not only that segregated schooling exists but also that it was brought about or maintained by intentional state action."[19] The Court indicated that unconstitutional de jure segregation could be found in school districts other than those that maintained segregation by law in 1954 with proof that *discriminatory motive* accompanied segregated conditions. Thus, an assessment of "intent" became the key in distinguishing de jure from de facto segregation. Furthermore, the Court in *Keyes* concluded that a finding of segregative intent in a substantial part of the school system created a presumption of de jure segregation in other parts of the system. Unless the presumption was successfully rebutted, a districtwide remedy would be warranted. The *Keyes* decision essentially provided for a shifting of the burden of proof; once plaintiffs established purposeful segregation in enough schools, the defendants had to establish that other segregated schools within the system were *not* the result of intentional discrimination.

In 1974 the Supreme Court again addressed the legality of nonsouthern school segregation, striking down an interdistrict desegregation plan in *Milliken v. Bradley.*[20] The Sixth Circuit Court of Appeals had ordered a metropolitan desegregation remedy for Detroit and fifty-three suburban school districts, reasoning that intentional school segregation implicated the entire metropolitan area. Disagreeing, the Supreme Court held that the plaintiffs did not carry their burden of proof in substantiating purposeful discrimination on the part of the suburban districts. The Court emphasized that a remedy must not be broader in scope than warranted by the constitutional violations uncovered. Since intentional school segregation was substantiated only in the Detroit system, the case was remanded for the formulation of a remedy within that district.

Two years later, the Supreme Court explicitly rejected any inference drawn from its prior decisions that an equal protection violation could be established by showing that official actions had a segregatory effect, regardless of their intent.[21] The Court declared that "disproportionate impact is not irrelevant, but is not the sole touchstone of an invidious racial discrimination forbidden by the Constitution."[22] Also in 1976 the Supreme Court held that a California school district, having implemented a student reassignment plan to comply with a court order, did not have an affirmative duty to revise remedial efforts annually when demographic shifts caused some schools to become more than 50 percent minority.[23]

By 1977 most lower courts had abandoned the notion that the mere existence of segregatory conditions implied a constitutional violation in states that did not impose school segregation by law in 1954. Courts, however, were struggling to identify the requisites of unlawful intent that would trigger a duty to eliminate school segregation. Some federal courts assumed that a presumption of unlawful purpose could be established if the natural, probable, and foreseeable result of public officials' acts perpetuated segregatory conditions.[24] Yet, courts were not in agreement regarding whether intent should be determined by this objective "foreseeable consequences" test or by a subjective standard, requiring evidence that policymakers actually harbored a desire to segregate.[25]

During the latter 1970s the Supreme Court delivered several decisions that reflected a division among the justices as to the criteria to assess the legality of school segregation outside the South. In 1977 the Court found insufficient evidence of systemwide violations in Dayton, Ohio, to justify a systemwide student reassignment plan that had been ordered by the Sixth Circuit Appellate Court, and thus remanded the case for additional proceedings.[26] Two years later, however, the Supreme Court affirmed the appellate court's decision that a comprehensive systemwide remedy was justified in Dayton, based on substantial evidence of the systemwide effect of segregatory practices.[27]

In a companion case, the Supreme Court ruled that the Columbus, Ohio, school board had not fulfilled its affirmative duty to dismantle the dual school system and had instead "intentionally aggravated, rather than alleviated" racial separation in its schools, justifying the systemwide remedy imposed by the courts below.[28] In both of these 1979 cases the Court majority reasoned that if school officials were unable to refute that intentional school segregation existed when *Brown I* was rendered, their post-1954 acts must be assessed in light of their *continuing affirmative duty* to eliminate the effects of such segregation. The Court declared that a school board's conduct under an *unsatisfied duty* to eliminate school segregation must be assessed by the "effectiveness, not the purpose, of the actions in decreasing or increasing the segregation caused by the dual system."[29] Racially neutral actions cannot satisfy this duty; school officials must take affirmative steps to eradicate school segregation until all vestiges of discrimination are eliminated.

INTERDISTRICT REMEDIES

A controversial issue has involved the scope of judicial authority to order interdistrict remedies. With many cities experiencing an increasing minority population, it has been argued that meaningful school desegregation cannot be accomplished without pupil transfers between city and suburban districts. As noted previously, the Supreme Court in 1974 rejected an interdistrict remedy for the Detroit area, declaring that cross-district remedies could be ordered only with evidence of a constitutional violation in one district that produces a significant segregative effect in another.[30] Applying this principle in a subsequent case, the Fifth Circuit Court of Appeals concluded that "there must be clear proof of cause and effect and a careful delineation of the extent of the effect" for school district lines to be disturbed in a desegregation decree.[31] The Fourth Circuit Court of Appeals also recognized that if a school district has not *caused* school segregation in a neighboring district, it has no constitutional obligation to remedy such racial imbalance in the other district.[32]

Suits requesting interdistrict remedies have been rejected in a number of metropolitan areas. For example, in 1980 the Justice Department asked that the Houston Independent School District (HISD) be merged with twenty-two surrounding suburban districts, but in 1983 the Fifth Circuit Court of Appeals ruled that the HISD had eliminated vestiges of segregation in its schools.[33] Declining to order an interdistrict remedy, the appeals court determined that the remaining single-race schools were the result of uncontrollable population shifts in the city characterized by an increasing African-American and Hispanic population. An interdistrict desegregation plan also was rejected in the Cincinnati metropolitan area. In 1984 a consent decree was signed by the Cincinnati city district, the NAACP, and the state of Ohio after the federal district court removed the suburban school districts from the suit.[34] The settlement gave school officials flexibility in using various voluntary means such as magnet schools, remedial instruction, and community education programs to achieve desegregated schools, and the state agreed to provide financial assistance for these programs.

On two occasions the Eighth Circuit Court of Appeals reversed the lower court's orders calling for substantial consolidation among the Little Rock city district and two suburban school districts. In 1985 the appellate court overturned the mandated merger of the three districts to achieve countywide desegregation.[35] Finding intentional segregation on the part of each district that justified interdistrict relief, the appeals court nonetheless concluded that the lower court's remedial order was broader in scope than warranted by the constitutional violation and did not adequately consider alternative remedies or the importance of local school district autonomy. In 1989, because the three school systems had not been successful in developing their own plans to remedy the unconstitutional segregation, the federal district court appointed a metropolitan supervisor to oversee a "tridistrict" plan, including the merger of numerous functions.[36] Again reversing the lower court, the appeals court reasoned that the settlement plan proposed by the school districts should have been approved, even though some elementary schools would serve students of one race at least for a period of time. The settlement called for additional magnet schools (both intra- and interdistrict), compensatory education programs, and strategies to improve the racial balance of schools through voluntary means (e.g., establishing "incentive schools" with increased funding to attract white students to all-minority schools).

In other situations, courts have ordered interdistrict remedies with sufficient evidence of interdistrict violations. For example, the Seventh Circuit Court of Appeals ordered a one-way busing plan for the Indianapolis metropolitan area, requiring over 5,000 minority students to be bused from the city schools to six suburban districts.[37] The appeals court held that the state was responsible for school segregation in the metropolitan area because of legislation that merged municipal governments, but not school districts, within Marion County, Indiana.

The St. Louis desegregation case is somewhat unique in that the city school district and twenty-three surrounding suburban districts agreed in 1983 to implement a desegregation plan requiring each suburban district to accept inner-city minority transfers up to 15 percent of its total enrollment. The federal district court recognized its authority to order the city board of education to raise sufficient funds to support the desegregation settlement. Subsequently, the Eighth Circuit Court of Appeals held that the state could be required to pay for total capital and operating costs of magnet schools established under the settlement agreement, half of the costs of certain programs to improve the quality of education in nonintegrated schools, and half of the desegregation transportation costs.[38] However, cost-sharing arrangements between the state and school district for the St. Louis magnet school program are still being litigated, and by 1990 the goal of enrolling 14,000 students in magnet schools had not been met.[39]

A voluntary interdistrict transfer plan was part of the desegregation remedy adopted in the Kansas City metropolitan area in 1985.[40] The state was ordered to seek the participation of suburban districts in the program and to fund tuition and transportation costs for minority transferees. Minority students from the urban district brought suit in 1989, alleging that they had been denied admission into suburban school districts because of their race. Finding that *no* minority students had been admitted to suburban districts, in 1990 the Eighth Circuit Appellate Court directed the lower court to promulgate an interdistrict transfer plan and to require the state to pay transportation and tuition costs for a limited number of minority students who desired to attend suburban schools.[41]

In a few situations, court-ordered interdistrict desegregation remedies have resulted in school district mergers. For example, in the Louisville, Kentucky, metropolitan area an interdistrict student assignment plan led to merger of the city and surrounding county districts.[42] Also, an interdistrict remedy resulted in school district consolidation among the Wilmington, Delaware school district and ten suburban districts in New Castle County, Delaware.[43] However, the consolidated district subsequently was divided into four component districts. Federal courts are very hesitant to *order* mergers, but they will mandate interdistrict remedies with evidence of constitutional violations on the part of all districts involved.

FISCAL RESPONSIBILITIES

Without question, substantial costs have been incurred in desegregation litigation and in the implementation of remedial plans.[44] Yet, courts have shown little sympathy when the lack of sufficient funds has been proffered as a defense for maintaining dual school systems. In some school districts, such as Cleveland and Boston, federal courts have overseen the management of financial resources to ensure that desegregation activities are implemented.[45] In other situations, such as Buffalo[46] and St. Louis,[47] the judiciary has ordered school districts to raise sufficient funds to support desegregation plans.

In several cases school districts have argued that the state has been responsible for creating school segregation and thus should share in the costs of implementing remedial plans. In 1977 the Supreme Court ordered the state of Michigan to underwrite half of the costs of remedial programs, in-service training, guidance and counseling services, and community relations programs in the Detroit desegregation plan because the state played a role in creating the dual system.[48]

More recently, other courts have required states to share desegregation expenses based on evidence that state action has perpetuated the segregated conditions. As noted previously, the Seventh Circuit Court of Appeals assessed the cost of the one-way busing plan in Indianapolis against the state, reasoning that the state was responsible for creating the school segregation.[49] Also, Ohio was ordered to share the costs of implementing Dayton's desegregation plan,[50] and partial fiscal responsibility for school desegregation in the Little Rock metropolitan area was placed on the state.[51] Although in 1985 Tennessee was assessed 60 percent of the costs of the Nashville desegregation plan,[52] the state subsequently was relieved of any fiscal responsibility in the absence of evidence that the state had contributed to the school segregation.[53]

In a significant 1990 decision, *Missouri v. Jenkins,* the Supreme Court held that federal courts can order school districts to impose tax increases to fund desegregation remedies, but the court itself cannot impose such increases. Previously, the state had been assessed three-fourths of the costs of a magnet program and capital improvements to desegregate the Kansas City, Missouri, School District (KCMSD). Because of the KCMSD's inability to fund its portion of the plan, the lower court ordered a property tax increase in the district.[54] The Supreme Court affirmed that the federal judiciary is empowered to set aside state constitutional and statutory provisions that limit local taxing authority and to order local school boards to raise sufficient funds to support desegregation remedies.[55] The Court held, however, that the lower court abused its discretion by directly *imposing* a property tax increase rather than instructing the school board to do so.

In a somewhat unique desegregation case, the Second Circuit Court of Appeals held that education and housing officials were jointly liable for school segregation in Yonkers, New York. Although the impact of housing patterns on school segregation has been noted in several cases, in this decision the court found municipal housing authorities legally responsible for the fact that schools in a portion of the school district remained primarily segregated. The court noted that for forty years housing officials had located all low-income housing in a predominantly nonwhite section of the city. Since the court found that actions of school authorities perpetuated the segregated conditions created by the housing policies, the consent decree included joint liability.[56] In 1990, however, the Supreme Court overturned the lower court's order imposing fines on city council members who voted against the proposed public housing ordinance for Yonkers.[57] The lower court had reasoned that the council members who opposed the ordinance were in contempt of the consent decree, justifying the penalty ordered, but the Supreme Court ruled that the lower court had exceeded its authority by imposing the fines on individual council members without first seeking compliance through sanctions against the city.

Because school desegregation has national importance, the federal government has provided some financial assistance to further desegregation activities in local school districts.[58] During the 1970s, numerous school districts received federal desegregation aid under the Emergency School Aid Act (ESAA).[59] This federal aid targeted for desegregation was eliminated when the ESAA was folded into block grants to state and local education agencies under Chapter 2 of the Education Consolidation and

Improvement Act in 1981. Consequently, large urban school districts reported a substantial reduction in federal aid devoted to desegregation activities.[60] However, targeted federal funds remain available to assist school districts in establishing magnet school programs.[61]

BUSING: LIMITATIONS AND ALTERNATIVES

The reassignment of students among paired and clustered schools remains an important component of many desegregation decrees. Several courts have recognized that instructional remedies may be necessary, but are not sufficient by themselves to desegregate a school system.[62] Because pupil reassignment inevitably involves busing, this remedial tool has been the focus of substantial public attention and volatile political controversy.

Busing limitation bills that would curtail federal courts' authority to order busing of students beyond the school nearest their homes have regularly been introduced in Congress. Among provisions of the 1974 Equal Educational Opportunities Act (EEOA) were stipulations that busing be used only in situations where segregative intent was established and that the assignment of students to neighborhood schools was not a constitutional violation.[63] Although the EEOA did not place a limitation on judicial authority to order pupil reassignment where constitutional violations were found, there have been several unsuccessful attempts to secure federal legislation that would restrict the Justice Department's role in desegregation cases and curb federal judicial authority in imposing student transportation plans as part of remedial decrees.

Busing limitation measures also have generated state activity. The Supreme Court in 1971 struck down a North Carolina law forbidding the busing of students to create racially balanced schools, concluding that the provision unconstitutionally restricted local school authorities' broad discretion to formulate plans to eliminate dual school systems.[64] Nonetheless, other states have continued to consider busing limitation measures. In both Washington and California, voters in the late 1970s approved provisions restricting the use of pupil transportation to attain integrated schools. These measures were challenged under the fourteenth amendment and generated Supreme Court decisions in 1982.

In the Washington case, the Supreme Court affirmed an appellate court ruling, striking down a statewide voter initiative, which prohibited mandatory pupil assignment outside neighborhood schools for the purpose of improving racial balance.[65] Only three urban school districts with integration programs were affected by the initiative, and they joined numerous community organizations in challenging the provision under the equal protection clause. The Supreme Court agreed with the Ninth Circuit Appellate Court's conclusion that the initiative created an impermissible racial classification by treating pupil assignments for racial balance differently from assignments for other purposes. The appellate court also reasoned that the initiative was prompted by discriminatory motive and that it reallocated political power by "allowing a state-wide majority to usurp traditional local authority over local school board educational policies," which specifically burdened minority interests.[66]

In contrast, the Supreme Court upheld an amendment to California's Constitution, Proposition I, prohibiting mandatory busing except to remedy violations of the fourteenth amendment.[67] Prior to adopting Proposition I, the California Constitution prohibited de facto as well as de jure school segregation, thus requiring remedial plans to ensure racial balance in school districts where violations of the Federal Constitution had *not* been established.[68] The Supreme Court concluded that California was not legally obligated to maintain more stringent standards than required by the fourteenth amendment, which only prohibits de jure segregation. In short, once a state elects to go beyond fourteenth amendment requirements, it subsequently can repeal such action. Since Proposition I did not interfere with the authority of federal courts to order mandatory busing to remedy violations of the equal protection clause, the mere repeal of the *additional* state requirement did not abridge the Federal Constitution without evidence of discriminatory motive. The Court rejected the assertion that Proposition I reallocated the decisionmaking process for minorities, as was true with the Washington initiative.

During the past decade the federal judiciary has become less aggressive in requiring massive student reassignment plans to integrate schools. It was assumed in the early 1970s that racially balanced schools would ensure equal educational opportunities, but other approaches to attain this goal have received increasing judicial attention. Because of substantial opposition to pupil transfers for desegregation purposes and the increasing minority population in many urban school districts, there is some sentiment that remedial plans should focus on improving the *quality* of educational programs rather than on pupil reassignment *per se*. Compensatory education programs, counseling and career guidance, and bilingual/bicultural programs have been included in desegregation plans to overcome the effects of prior racial isolation.[69] In addition, most recent plans include some magnet schools that offer theme-oriented instructional programs in an effort to attract racially balanced student bodies from throughout the district. Although instructional remedies traditionally were considered supplements to student reassignment plans, magnet schools and other efforts to improve the quality of instruction have become important components of desegregation plans currently being implemented in a number of cities such as Baton Rouge, Chicago, Cleveland, Cincinnati, Detroit, Milwaukee, and Nashville.[70]

In complex litigation involving the Dallas School District, an alternative to massive pupil reassignment was approved by the Fifth Circuit Court of Appeals in 1985.[71] Previously, the federal district court had rejected a plan to give minority students the option of remaining in their neighbor-hood schools, thereby waiving their constitutional right to be transported to desegregated schools.[72] The school board then proposed a plan to return 2,300 minority students in intermediate elementary grades to neighbor-hood schools that would be remedial in nature. The appellate court held that the district court acted within its authority in approving the plan that called for partial suspension of the previous pupil reassignment program. Even though the modification established single-race remedial centers, the appeals court found it to be an appropriate remedy to attain the goal of closing the gap in reading achievement between African-American and white students.

IS AN END IN SIGHT?

In *Board of Education of Oklahoma City Public Schools v. Dowell,* the Supreme Court ruled in 1991 that the federal judiciary should terminate supervision of school districts where school boards have complied with desegregation mandates in good faith for a reasonable period of time and eliminated vestiges of past discrimination "to the extent practicable."[73] The Oklahoma City School District had been operating since 1972 under a court-ordered plan that entailed substantial student busing to achieve integration. The federal district court ruled in 1977 that the board had complied with the order in good faith for five years and was entitled to pursue its legitimate policies without further court supervision. Although judicial monitoring was removed, the 1972 decree was not dissolved. After demographic changes led to greater burdens on African-American students in continuing the student busing program, the school board in 1984 adopted a neighborhood school assignment policy for kindergar-ten through grade four. The new plan was challenged because it would re-sult in about half of the elementary schools becoming 90 percent African American or 90 percent non–African American. The lower court upheld the plan, but the Tenth Circuit Court of Appeals reversed this decision.

The appeals court focused on the application of federal law related to injunctive remedies, holding that a desegregation decree should not be lifted or modified absent "a clear showing of grievous wrong evoked by new and unforeseen conditions."[74] The court reasoned that compliance alone cannot be the basis for dissolving an injunction. Concluding that the school board failed to meet its burden of proof, the court ruled that the district's circumstances had not changed enough to justify modifying the 1972 decree.

The Supreme Court held that the appellate court's standard for dis-solving the original decree was too stringent. The Court emphasized that "federal supervision of local school systems was intended as a temporary measure to remedy past discrimination."[75] The majority reasoned that the purposes of the desegregation litigation would be fully achieved upon finding—as the district court had done—that the school system was operating in compliance with the equal protection clause and not likely to return to its former ways.[76] Noting the range in lower court interpretations of "unitary status," the Court questioned the utility of defining this term with more precision. The Court stated that in determining whether vestiges of intentional segregation have been eliminated to the extent practicable, the district court on remand should assess the six factors identified twenty-three years earlier in *Green* (student, faculty, and staff assignments; transportation; extracurricular activities; and facilities).[77] The district court also was instructed to reconsider whether current residential segregation in Oklahoma City was the "result of private decisionmaking and economics" rather than a vestige of prior school segregation.[78] Although the Supreme Court strongly suggested that the Oklahoma City system should be released from judicial oversight and the 1972 decree dissolved, this determination was left for the lower court to make.

Even before the *Dowell* decision, the end of judicial oversight of desegregation plans appeared to be in sight for a number of school districts. For example, the Norfolk, Virginia, school board's request to end court-ordered, crosstown busing and return to neighborhood-based schools and voluntary desegregation received judicial endorsement in 1986.[79] Since the school district had been declared unitary by the federal district court in 1975, the Fourth Circuit Court of Appeals reasoned that school officials had satisfied their affirmative duty to dismantle the dual school system and had no continuing obligation to bus students, even though student bodies in ten of the district's thirty-six elementary schools would be more than 90 percent African American. The court noted that once a school district has eliminated the vestiges of de jure segregation, those challenging subsequent school board actions have the burden of proving discriminatory intent. This burden was not met by plaintiffs contesting the school board's plan to eliminate busing for desegregation purposes. The court further recognized that the school board legitimately could consider the impact of "white flight" in designing a plan to stabilize school integration.

Other school districts such as Austin and Fort Worth have been declared unitary and released from judicial supervision, based on their good-faith compliance with desegregation plans and the judicial conclusion that additional efforts to eliminate single-race schools would be impractical.[80] Boston's desegregation litigation also seems to be drawing to a close after more than 400 court orders spanning two decades. The federal district court judge made national headlines in the mid-1970s when he ordered his own experts to create and monitor a desegregation plan after the Boston School Committee failed to develop an acceptable proposal. In 1987 the First Circuit Court of Appeals affirmed the district court's conclusion that judicial oversight should be withdrawn in several of the twelve areas, including student assignment practices, that had been monitored in the Boston school system.[81] The appeals court determined that a finding of "unitariness" in all areas is not required to relinquish judicial supervision over certain aspects of a remedial plan. However, the court retained jurisdiction over personnel practices to ensure desegregation of school faculties.[82]

Although school boards likely will rely on *Dowell* in their efforts to end court-supervised desegregation decrees, many school districts that have been involved in desegregation litigation for more than two decades have no immediate prospects of ending judicial oversight. Recent developments in Denver are illustrative. After operating under a desegregation plan since 1973, the school district's request to be declared unitary was rejected by a federal judge in 1985. Subsequently, school officials developed a new proposal focusing on staff and instructional remedies and maintaining substantial student reassignment.[83] In 1990 the Tenth Circuit Court of Appeals held that the Denver school district still had not achieved unitary status and thus judicial supervision would be retained.[84] The court noted that a school district does not become unitary "by simply halting its intentionally discriminatory acts and adopting a racially neutral attendance policy"; school boards must actually "*dismantle* their dual school systems."[85]

A year earlier the same court concluded that the Topeka, Kansas, school system, which had been operating under an affirmative duty to desegregate its schools since the landmark *Brown* decision, still had not achieved unitary status.[86] The court emphasized that until a school system attains this status, plaintiffs do not have to prove intentional discriminatory conduct to establish that current practices reflect vestiges of the dual system. The school district has the burden of justifying current segregatory conditions and proving that it has "eliminated all traces of past intentional segregation to the maximum feasible extent."[87]

In a 1989 decision involving school segregation in Dekalb County, Georgia, the Eleventh Circuit Court of Appeals ruled that a school district can be considered unitary only after it assures racial equality for at least three years in the six categories identified in *Green*.[88] Rejecting the First Circuit Appellate Court's position that unitary status can be achieved in some of these areas (e.g., student assignments) but not others (e.g., faculty assignments),[89] the Eleventh Circuit Appellate Court ruled that *simultaneous* compliance in *all* categories is necessary for unitary status to be attained. The court emphasized that simply closing all-black schools is insufficient to fulfill the district's obligation in terms of student assignments; the district must eliminate the racial identification of schools and "avoid reestablishment of a dual system."[90] The court stated that school officials cannot use demographic shifts as a defense to escape their affirmative duty to achieve the greatest possible degree of desegregation.

Many other school districts are still involved in litigation as courts have declined to find their systems unitary.[91] A school district's affirmative duty to desegregate schools is satisfied *only* when it eliminates the vestiges of its prior discriminatory conduct to the court's satisfaction. At that point, school boards can design policies without judicial supervision as long as they do not *purposefully* discriminate. Although the Supreme Court in *Dowell* emphasized that a school district is entitled to a precise "statement of its obligations under a desegregation decree,"[92] the constitutional requirements for terminating judicial oversight remain somewhat elusive. Because the shift in burden of proof is contingent on the judiciary's conclusion that all vestiges of segregation have been eliminated, the judicial criteria used to make this determination are indeed critical.

STAFF DESEGREGATION REMEDIES

The Supreme Court has emphasized that the integration of school staffs is an essential component of effective desegregation remedies.[93] The rationale for staff reassignments in desegregation decrees is *not* to remedy employment discrimination, but rather to vindicate the constitutional rights of minority students by assuring them the equal educational opportunities guaranteed by the fourteenth amendment.

In *Singleton v. Jackson Municipal Separate School District,* the Fifth Circuit Court of Appeals in 1970 established guidelines for merging faculties in converting from dual to unitary school systems. The court held that staff members should be assigned so that the racial ratio in each school reflects the staff racial composition systemwide. Moreover, if conversion to a unitary system requires demotions or a reduction in professional staff, (1) such demotions or layoffs must be made on the basis of "objective and reasonable nondiscriminatory standards," (2) nonracial objective criteria must be developed by the school board prior to any staff reductions, and (3) subsequent staff vacancies must be filled by individuals of the same race as those dismissed until each qualified displaced staff member has had an opportunity to fill the vacancy.[94]

During the 1970s courts often were called on to apply the *Singleton* criteria in assessing the legality of staff reduction activity in school districts dismantling dual school systems. This litigation was concentrated in the fifth federal circuit, where the bulk of court-ordered desegregation activity was taking place. Federal district courts and the Fifth Circuit Court of Appeals overturned several dismissals of African-American teachers and administrators where school boards had not applied preestablished objective criteria in making the decisions.[95] However, cases initiated under the *Singleton* criteria have subsided since major school district consolidation efforts necessitated by desegregation have been accomplished.[96]

Recent controversies have not focused on consolidation activities, but rather on efforts to give preference to minorities to attain or maintain racially balanced staffs as part of desegregation remedies. The use of racial considerations in hiring and assigning staff has generally been upheld in court-ordered as well as voluntary plans to eliminate the lingering effects of school segregation.[97] For example, the Third Circuit Court of Appeals upheld a collective bargaining agreement imposing transfers to ensure racially balanced faculties in the Philadelphia School District.[98] More recently, the Maryland federal district court held that a school district's policy of using race as a criterion to override seniority in making involuntary transfers necessitated by student enrollment shifts was an appropriate remedy since the school system had not yet achieved unitary status.[99] Rejecting both constitutional and Title VII claims of white teachers, the court reasoned that the school board had produced convincing evidence that remedial action was narrowly tailored to "serve the critical interest of reducing the racial identifiability of individual schools."[100] The First Circuit Court of Appeals in 1991 also ruled that the Boston public schools had a continuing obligation to reach the goals of 25 percent African American and 10 percent other minority faculty and staff because unitariness had not been achieved.[101]

More controversial than racial preferences in hiring and assignment practices have been efforts to protect minority employees from layoffs. Racial quotas in reducing personnel have been challenged as discriminating against nonminorities by overriding their seniority rights. In a significant 1986 decision, *Wygant v. Jackson Board of Education,* the Supreme Court struck down a school district's negotiated agreement that protected minority teachers from layoffs to maintain the percentage of minority teachers employed prior to any reduction in force.[102] The school district was not operating under a court-ordered desegregation plan, and the Court viewed *Wygant* as involving employment discrimination rather than school desegregation. As discussed in Chapter 9, the *Wygant* plurality rejected the contention that the racial composition of faculty should reflect the racial composition of the student body to ensure minority role models for students. The plurality reasoned that racial classifications in layoff policies must be justified by convincing evidence of prior discrimination, and the means employed must be narrowly designed to remedy such discrimination. Finding that the contested staff reduction policy did not satisfy either criterion, the plurality noted that school officials had other means, such as hiring goals, to increase faculty integration.

Whether the continuing impact of dual school systems would constitute the compelling justification for layoff quotas was not clarified by the Supreme Court in *Wygant,* and federal appellate courts have rendered conflicting opinions on this issue. Prior to *Wygant,* both the First and Second Circuit Courts of Appeal approved policies protecting minority teachers from layoffs where school districts had not yet eliminated the vestiges of school segregation, and the Second Circuit Appellate Court reiterated this stance in a post-*Wygant* decision.[103] These appeals courts found the principles governing employment discrimination claims to be irrelevant in school desegregation cases.

However, other courts have struck down racial preferences in layoff policies. The Sixth Circuit Court of Appeals, for example, reversed a lower court's order imposing a quota of 20 percent minority teachers in the Kalamazoo School District.[104] The order, protecting minorities from layoffs, was found to abrogate the seniority rights of nonminority teachers and to be unnecessary to protect students' constitutional rights. The appeals court declared that students "do not have a constitutional right to attend a school with a teaching staff of any particular racial composition."[105] Racial quotas in staff reduction policies are not likely to receive judicial approval unless clearly necessary to eliminate the effects of a dual system and other means of attaining this goal are not available.

CONCLUSION

Numerous school districts throughout the country remain embroiled in desegregation controversies, with many having been in litigation for well over a decade and some for nearly three decades. More than 500 school districts are under court-ordered desegregation mandates;[106] many other districts have voluntary plans in operation. Without question, voluntary or mandatory desegregation activities have had a significant impact on the operation of American public schools.

The Supreme Court's desegregation rulings reflected unanimous opinions from 1954 until 1971, but decisions rendered since 1972 have been characterized by a divided vote. From the recent and pending decisions, trends in desegregation litigation are difficult to identify. Some courts have seemed more concerned about the quality of educational opportunities afforded minority students than about pupil reassignment to achieve integrated schools, but many school districts remain under judicial supervision as they struggle to develop acceptable remedial plans. Keeping abreast of the complicated developments in a single case is extremely difficult as appeals and remands travel back and forth among the various levels of federal courts.

Although nearly forty years have elapsed since the landmark *Brown* decision, desegregation of American public schools has not been fully achieved. Segregated housing has exacerbated the problems associated with integrating public schools. Despite the complexity of desegregation litigation, some generalizations can be derived from decisions to date.

1. School segregation resulting from state laws or other intentional state action (e.g., gerrymandering school attendance zones, selecting sites for new schools to maintain racial isolation, and

assigning staff to perpetuate the racial identification of schools) violates the equal protection clause of the fourteenth amendment.

2. Segregatory effect alone does not establish unconstitutional intent; however, the consequences of official actions can be considered in substantiating discriminatory motive.

3. Where a school district has *not* achieved unitary status, school officials have an affirmative duty to eliminate the vestiges of past intentional discrimination; under such a duty, official actions or non-action are assessed in terms of their effect on reducing segregation.

4. The scope of a desegregation remedy cannot exceed the scope of the constitutional violation.

5. States can, but are not obligated to, go beyond the requirements of the fourteenth amendment in remedying school segregation, and such additional state mandates can subsequently be repealed.

6. Interdistrict desegregation remedies cannot be judicially imposed unless there is evidence of intentional discrimination with substantial effects across district lines.

7. School districts cannot plead "lack of funds" as a defense for failing to remedy unconstitutional school segregation; a state can be required to share the costs of remedial plans if found that it has played a role in creating or maintaining a school district's segregatory conditions.

8. Courts can set aside state limitations on local taxing authority and can order school boards to raise sufficient funds to support remedial plans.

9. Magnet schools and voluntary transfer policies can be central components of remedial plans as long as such remedies are effective in reducing the racial identification of schools.

10. Judicial supervision can be terminated where school districts have complied with desegregation mandates in good faith for a reasonable period of time and eliminated the vestiges of past discrimination as far as practicable.

11. In determining whether a school district has eliminated the vestiges of school segregation, courts assess racial equality in student, faculty, and staff assignments; transportation; extracurricular activities; and facilities.

12. Once a school district has eliminated the vestiges of its prior discriminatory conduct to the court's satisfaction, future acts must represent purposeful discrimination to violate the fourteenth amendment; school districts are not obligated to continue remedies *after* unitary status is attained and resegregation occurs through no fault of school officials.

13. Racial preferences can be judicially imposed in hiring and assigning personnel as part of desegregation remedies; however, racial

preferences in reducing personnel require compelling justification that they are necessary to achieve unitary status.

ENDNOTES

1. 163 U.S. 537 (1896). For a discussion of constitutional standards applied to racial classifications in employment, *see* text with note 2, Chapter 9.
2. Roberts v. City of Boston, 59 Mass. (5 Cush.) 198 (1849).
3. Gong Lum v. Rice, 275 U.S. 78, 86 (1927).
4. *See* Sweatt v. Painter, 339 U.S. 629 (1950); McLaurin v. Oklahoma State Regents for Higher Educ., 339 U.S. 637 (1950); Sipuel v. University of Oklahoma, 332 U.S. 631 (1948); Missouri *ex rel.* Gaines v. Canada, 305 U.S. 337 (1938).
5. Brown I, 347 U.S. 483, 495 (1954). For an in-depth review of litigation leading to the Supreme Court's decision, *see* Robert Kluger, *Simple Justice* (New York: Knopf, 1975). Since the equal protection clause applies only to state and not federal action, the Supreme Court relied on the due process clause of the fifth amendment in striking down segregated public schools in Washington, D.C. The Court reasoned that protected "liberties" embrace freedom from racial discrimination imposed by the federal government, Bolling v. Sharpe, 347 U.S. 497 (1954).
6. Brown v. Board of Educ. of Topeka, Kansas (Brown II), 349 U.S. 294, 301 (1955).
7. *Id.* at 300.
8. *See* Milliken v. Bradley, 433 U.S. 267 (1977).
9. Cooper v. Aaron, 358 U.S. 1 (1958).
10. Griffin v. County School Bd. of Prince Edward County, Virginia, 377 U.S. 218 (1964).
11. In Briggs v. Elliott, 132 F. Supp. 776, 777 (E.D.S.C. 1955), the federal district court declared that the Constitution "does not require integration" but "merely forbids discrimination."
12. Green v. County School Bd. of New Kent County, Virginia, 391 U.S. 430 (1968); Raney v. Board of Educ. of Gould School Dist., 391 U.S. 443 (1968); Monroe v. Board of Comm'rs of the City of Jackson, Tennessee, 391 U.S. 450 (1968).
13. Green, *id.* at 435. In 1969 the Court recognized that its "all deliberate speed" mandate had been ineffective and ordered the operation of dual school systems to be terminated "at once," Alexander v. Holmes County Bd. of Educ., 396 U.S. 19, 20 (1969) (per curiam).
14. 402 U.S. 1 (1971).
15. *Id.* at 30–31.
16. 42 U.S.C. § 2000d (1988) (prohibits discrimination on the basis of race, color, or national origin in federally assisted programs or activities).
17. *Twenty Years after Brown: Equality of Educational Opportunity* (Washington, DC: U.S. Commission on Civil Rights, 1975), pp. 46–47.

18. In the 1960s, some courts reasoned that school segregation did not warrant remedial action in school districts where segregation was not imposed by law in 1954. *See, e.g.,* Deal v. Cincinnati Bd. of Educ., 369 F.2d 55 (6th Cir. 1966), *cert. denied,* 389 U.S. 847 (1967); Bell v. School Bd. of Gary, Indiana, 324 F.2d 209 (7th Cir. 1963), *cert. denied,* 377 U.S. 924 (1964).

19. 413 U.S. 189, 198 (1973).

20. 418 U.S. 717 (1974).

21. Washington v. Davis, 426 U.S. 229, 240 (1976).

22. *Id.* at 242. *See also* Austin Indep. School Dist. v. United States, 429 U.S. 990 (1976).

23. Pasadena City Bd. of Educ. v. Spangler, 427 U.S. 424 (1976).

24. *See, e.g.,* Arthur v. Nyquist, 573 F.2d 134, 140-143 (2d Cir. 1978); NAACP v. Lansing Bd. of Educ., 559 F.2d 1042, 1046–1048 (6th Cir. 1977), *cert. denied,* 434 U.S. 997 (1977); Hart v. Community School Bd. of Educ., New York School Dist. No. 21, 512 F.2d 37, 50 (2d Cir. 1975).

25. In 1977 the Supreme Court upheld a zoning decision that tended to perpetuate racially segregated housing patterns, reasoning that plaintiffs failed to carry the burden of proving that race was a motivating factor in the decision, Village of Arlington Heights v. Metropolitan Housing Dev. Corp., 429 U.S. 252 (1977). The Court subsequently vacated appellate rulings in several desegregation cases and remanded the cases for reconsideration in light of *Arlington Heights.* *See* Metropolitan School Dist. of Lawrence Township v. Buckley, 429 U.S. 1068 (1977); School Dist. of Omaha v. United States, 433 U.S. 667 (1977); Brennan v. Armstrong, 433 U.S. 672 (1977).

26. Dayton Bd. of Educ. v. Brinkman (Dayton I), 433 U.S. 406 (1977) (on remand the lower court was instructed to ascertain how much "incremental segregatory effect" intentional discriminatory acts had on the racial composition of the district's schools and to order a remedy addressing only that effect).

27. Dayton Bd. of Educ. v. Brinkman (Dayton II), 443 U.S. 526 (1979).

28. Columbus Bd. of Educ. v. Penick, 443 U.S. 449, 461 (1979).

29. Dayton Bd. of Educ. v. Brinkman, 443 U.S. at 538.

30. Milliken v. Bradley, 418 U.S. 717 (1974).

31. Lee v. Lee County Bd. of Educ., 639 F.2d 1243, 1256 (5th Cir. 1981). *See also* United States v. Mississippi, 921 F.2d 604 (5th Cir. 1991).

32. Goldsboro City Bd. of Educ. v. Wayne County Bd. of Educ., 745 F.2d 324 (4th Cir. 1984).

33. Ross v. Houston Indep. School Dist., 699 F.2d 218 (5th Cir. 1983). In 1984 the Mexican-American Legal Defense and Educational Fund and the HISD signed a settlement designed to end twenty-eight years of desegregation litigation. *See* "Court Approves Desegregation Plan for Houston Schools," *Education Week,* November 21, 1984, p. 3.

34. Bronson v. Board of Educ. of City School Dist. of Cincinnati, 578 F. Supp. 1091 (S.D. Ohio 1984).

35. The appeals court suggested that the interdistrict violations could be remedied through strategies such as making minor district boundary adjustments, correcting segregative practices within each of the districts, improving the quality of nonintegrated schools, requiring the state to provide partial funding for compensatory and remedial programs for minority students, and establishing a limited number of countywide magnet schools. Little Rock School Dist. v.

Pulaski County Special School Dist. No. 1, 597 F. Supp. 1220 (E.D. Ark. 1984), *aff'd in part, rev'd in part,* 778 F.2d 404 (8th Cir. 1985), *cert. denied,* 476 U.S. 1188 (1986).

36. Little Rock School Dist. v. Pulaski County Special School Dist. No. 1, 716 F. Supp. 1162 (E.D. Ark. 1989), *rev'd and remanded,* 921 F.2d 1371 (8th Cir. 1990).

37. United States v. Board of School Comm'rs of City of Indianapolis, 677 F.2d 1185 (7th Cir. 1982), *cert. denied,* 459 U.S. 1086 (1982); United States v. Board of School Comm'rs of City of Indianapolis, 637 F.2d 1101 (7th Cir. 1980), *cert. denied,* 449 U.S. 838 (1980).

38. Liddell v. Board of Educ. of City of St. Louis, 567 F. Supp. 1037 (E.D. Mo. 1983), *aff'd in part, rev'd in part,* 731 F.2d 1294 (8th Cir. 1984), *cert. denied,* 469 U.S. 816 (1984). *See also* Liddell v. Board of Educ. of City of St. Louis, 758 F.2d 290 (8th Cir. 1985).

39. Liddell v. Board of Educ. of City of St. Louis, 907 F.2d 823 (8th Cir. 1990) (limiting the state's obligation for magnet school capital improvements to 50 percent of capital costs funded under a districtwide capital improvements plan was reasonable).

40. Jenkins v. Missouri, 639 F. Supp. 19 (W.D. Mo. 1985), *aff'd,* 807 F.2d 657 (8th Cir. 1986), *cert. denied,* 484 U.S. 816 (1987).

41. Jenkins by Agyei v. Missouri, 904 F.2d 415 (8th Cir. 1990), *cert. denied,* 111 S. Ct. 346 (1990).

42. Newburg Area Council Inc. v. Board of Educ. of Jefferson County, Kentucky, 510 F.2d 1358 (6th Cir. 1974), *cert. denied,* 421 U.S. 931 (1975).

43. *See* Evans v. Buchanan, 582 F.2d 750 (3d Cir. 1978), *cert. denied,* 446 U.S. 923 (1980); Coalition to Save Our Children v. Buchanan, 744 F. Supp. 582 (D. Del. 1990).

44. Court costs alone have been substantial in some cases. For example, the Cleveland school board spent over one million dollars on desegregation litigation from 1974 until 1978. *See* Nathaniel Jones, "The Desegregation of Urban Schools 30 Years after *Brown,*" *University of Colorado Law Review,* vol. 55 (1984), pp. 543–544.

45. *See* Reed v. Rhodes, 662 F.2d 1219 (6th Cir. 1981), *cert. denied,* 445 U.S. 1018 (1982); Morgan v. Kerrigan, 530 F.2d 401 (1st Cir. 1976). *See also* Lee v. Macon County Bd. of Educ., 616 F.2d 805, 811 (5th Cir. 1980) ("cost alone cannot justify continued infractions of constitutional principles").

46. *See* Arthur v. Nyquist, 712 F.2d 809 (2d Cir. 1983), *cert. denied,* 466 U.S. 936 (1984). *See also* Arthur v. Nyquist, 716 F. Supp. 1484 (W.D.N.Y. 1989) (school board's documentation was insufficient to show that additional funds it sought from the city were necessary for desegregation purposes).

47. Liddle v. Board of Educ. of St. Louis, 731 F.2d 1294 (8th Cir. 1984), *cert. denied,* 469 U.S. 816 (1984). *See also* text with note 55, *infra.*

48. Milliken v. Bradley, 433 U.S. 267 (1977).

49. United States v. Board of School Comm'rs of City of Indianapolis, 677 F.2d 1185 (7th Cir. 1982).

50. Brinkman v. Gilligan, 610 F. Supp. 1288 (S.D. Ohio 1985). *See also* Liddle v. Board of Educ. of St. Louis, 758 F.2d 290 (8th Cir. 1985); text with note 39, *supra.*

51. Little Rock School Dist. v. Pulaski County Special School Dist., 839 F.2d 1296, 1306 (8th Cir. 1988).

52. Kelley v. Metropolitan County Board of Educ. of Nashville and Davidson County, 615 F. Supp. 1139 (M.D. Tenn. 1985).

53. Kelley v. Metropolitan County Board of Educ. of Nashville and Davidson County, 836 F.2d 986 (6th Cir. 1987), *cert. denied,* 487 U.S. 1206 (1988) (the responsibility for abolishing school segregation rests with local school authorities).

54. The lower court also had ordered a state income tax surcharge to fund the program in part, but this was invalidated on appeal, 672 F. Supp. 400, 412 (W.D. Mo. 1987), *rev'd,* 855 F.2d 1295, 1315–1316 (8th Cir. 1988).

55. 855 F.2d 1295 (8th Cir. 1988), *aff'd in part, rev'd in part, and remanded,* 110 S. Ct. 1651 (1990). *See also* Jenkins v. Missouri, 931 F.2d 470 (8th Cir. 1991).

56. United States v. Yonkers Bd. of Educ., 837 F.2d 1181 (2d Cir. 1987), *cert. denied,* 486 U.S. 1055 (1988).

57. United States v. City of Yonkers, 856 F.2d 444 (2d Cir. 1988), *rev'd sub nom.* Spallone v. United States, 110 S. Ct. 625 (1990).

58. In some situations the federal government has promised aid as part of desegregation consent decrees in which federal, state, and local officials have agreed to cooperate in remedial efforts. In a widely publicized case, the Chicago school board sued the federal government for allegedly defaulting on promised desegregation aid. After a series of orders, the federal district court in 1985 held that the United States had willfully violated the 1980 consent decree and that the Chicago school district was entitled to $17 million immediately and as much as $100 million in federal funds over a five-year period. However, the Seventh Circuit Court of Appeals vacated the order, reasoning that the federal government could satisfy its fiscal obligation by giving priority to Chicago in allocating funds and searching for resources outside of desegregation programs, United States v. Board of Educ. of Chicago, 621 F. Supp. 1296 (N.D. Ill. 1985), *vacated and remanded,* 799 F.2d 281 (7th Cir. 1986).

59. The Emergency School Assistance Program, 20 U.S.C. § 4052 (1984), later became the Emergency School Aid Act, 20 U.S.C. § 3192 (1988). For a discussion of federal categorical aid programs, *see Harvard Educational Review,* vol. 52, no. 4 (1982) (entire issue).

60. In a study of twenty-eight of the nation's largest school districts, it was reported that in the 1983–1984 school year the districts were spending only one-fourth of the amount on desegregation activities that they had received under ESAA two years earlier. Richard Jung and Robert Stonehill, "Big Districts and the Block Grant: A Cross-Time Assessment of the Fiscal Impacts," *Journal of Education Finance,* vol. 10 (1985), p. 322.

61. Education for Economic Security Act, Title VII—Magnet School Assistance, 20 U.S.C. § 4052 (1984). *See also* 34 C.F.R. § 280 (1990).

62. *See* Stell v. Savannah-Chatham County Bd. of Educ., 888 F.2d 82 (11th Cir. 1989); Vaughns v. Board of Educ. of Prince George's County, 758 F.2d 983 (4th Cir. 1985); Kelley v. Metropolitan County Board of Educ. of Nashville and Davidson County, Tennessee, 687 F.2d 814 (6th Cir. 1982), *cert. denied,* 459 U.S. 1183 (1983); United States v. South Bend Community School Corp., 692 F.2d 623 (7th Cir. 1982).

63. 20 U.S.C. § 1701–1758 (1988). Title IV of the Civil Rights Act of 1964, 42

U.S.C. § 2000c-6 (1988), authorizes the Attorney General to seek redress on behalf of individuals denied equal protection of the laws, but it also stipulates that "nothing herein shall empower any official or court of the United States to issue any order seeking to achieve a racial balance in any school by requiring the transportation of pupils or students from one school to another or one school district to another in order to achieve such racial balance." Both Title IV and the EEOA have been interpreted as preserving the authority of federal courts to remedy constitutional violations; thus, they do not restrict the judiciary in ordering remedies for intentional school segregation.

64. North Carolina State Bd. of Educ. v. Swann, 402 U.S. 43 (1971).

65. Seattle School Dist. No. 1 v. Washington, 633 F.2d 1338 (9th Cir. 1980), *aff'd,* 458 U.S. 457 (1982).

66. *Id.,* 633 F.2d at 1344.

67. Crawford v. Board of Educ. of City of Los Angeles, 458 U.S. 527 (1982).

68. In 1976 the California Supreme Court interpreted the state constitution as requiring school boards "to take reasonable steps to alleviate segregation in the public schools, whether the segregation be de facto or de jure in origin." Crawford v. Board of Educ., 551 P.2d 28, 34 (Cal. 1976).

69. *See, e.g.,* Milliken v. Bradley, 433 U.S. 267 (1977); Keyes v. School Dist. No. 1, 895 F.2d 659 (10th Cir. 1990); Ross v. Houston Indep. School Dist., 699 F.2d 218 (5th Cir. 1983); Little Rock School Dist. v. Pulaski County Special Dist., 716 F. Supp. 1162 (E.D. Ark. 1989); Tracy Sivitz, "Eliminating the Continuing Effects of the Violation: Compensatory Education as a Remedy for Unlawful School Segregation," *Yale Law Journal,* vol. 97 (1988), pp. 1173–1192. A controversial strategy has focused on efforts in several urban school districts to address the special needs of male African-American students by creating separate academies for them. For a discussion of "male immersion academies," *see* Leonard Stevens, "Separate But Equal Has No Place," *Education Week,* October 31, 1990, p. 32.

70. *See* Rolf Blank and Paul R. Messier, eds., *Planning and Developing Magnet Schools* (Washington, DC: U.S. Department of Education, 1987); Jones, "Urban Desegregation"; Dennis Doyle and Marsha Levine, "Magnet Schools: Choice and Quality in Public Education," *Phi Delta Kappan,* vol. 65 (1984), pp. 265–269. In a study of 39 urban school districts with desegregation plans, it was reported in 1990 that 80 percent of the districts used magnet programs for desegregation purposes, but only about half were implementing mandatory student busing plans, "Desegregation Strategies Currently Used by Urban Districts," *Education Daily,* February 15, 1990, p. 4.

71. Tasby v. Black Coalition to Maximize Educ., 771 F.2d 849 (5th Cir. 1985). *See also* Tasby v. Wright, 630 F. Supp. 597 (N.D. Tex. 1986).

72. Tasby v. Wright, 520 F. Supp. 683 (N.D. Tex. 1981), *aff'd in part, rev'd in part,* 713 F.2d 90 (5th Cir. 1983).

73. 111 S. Ct. 630, 638 (1991). *See also* Dowell v. Board of Educ. of Oklahoma City Pub. Schools, 606 F. Supp. 1548 (W.D. Okla. 1985), *rev'd,* 795 F.2d 1516 (10th Cir. 1986), *cert. denied,* 479 U.S. 938 (1986), in which the appeals court rejected the contention that once a finding of unitariness has been entered, all judicial oversight to enforce the original decree is terminated. The court reasoned that the purpose of court-ordered school integration is to *maintain* as well as to achieve a unitary school system. The court noted that the plaintiffs

were not asserting that the school board should be legally responsible for demographic changes within the school system, but that the board intentionally abandoned a plan designed to achieve desegregated schools and substituted a plan with an apparent segregative effect.

74. 890 F.2d 1483, 1490 (10th Cir. 1989), citing United States v. Swift & Co., 286 U.S. 106, 119 (1932).

75. 111 S. Ct. at 637.

76. *Id.* at 636–637.

77. *Id.* at 638, citing Green v. County School Bd. of New Kent County, Virginia, 391 U.S. at 435. Although the Supreme Court declined to expand this list, some courts have indicated that factors in addition to the six identified in *Green,* such as dropout and graduation rates and test scores, may be appropriate to consider in certain circumstances. *See* School Bd. of City of Richmond, Virginia v. Baliles, 829 F.2d 1308 (4th Cir. 1987). *See also* Vaughns v. Board of Educ. of Prince George's County, 758 F.2d 983 (4th Cir. 1985), in which the appeals court placed the burden on school officials to refute the presumption of discrimination established by minority students' overrepresentation in special education classes and underrepresentation in programs for gifted students.

78. *Id.* at 638 n. 2.

79. Riddick v. School Bd. of City of Norfolk, 784 F.2d 521 (4th Cir. 1986), *cert. denied,* 479 U.S. 938 (1986).

80. Flax v. Potts, 915 F.2d 155 (5th Cir. 1990) (Fort Worth); United States v. Overton, 834 F.2d 1171 (5th Cir. 1987) (Austin).

81. Morgan v. Nucci, 620 F. Supp. 214 (D. Mass. 1985), *aff'd in part, vacated in part,* 831 F.2d 313 (1st Cir. 1987). For a discussion of litigation involving Boston, *see* Jones, "The Desegregation of Urban Schools," pp. 537–541.

82. *Id.,* 831 F.2d 313 (the goal of 25 percent African-American and 10 percent other minority faculty and staff had not been fully realized).

83. Keyes v. School Dist. No. 1, Denver, 609 F. Supp. 1491 (D. Colo. 1985).

84. Keyes v. School Dist. No. 1, Denver, 895 F.2d 659 (10th Cir. 1990), *cert. denied,* 111 S. Ct. 951 (1991).

85. *Id.,* 895 F.2d at 664.

86. Brown v. Board of Educ. of Topeka, 892 F.2d 851 (10th Cir. 1989), *cert. filed,* No. 89-1681, 58 U.S.L.W. 3725 (1990). The school district also was found in violation of Title VI of the Civil Rights Act of 1964, 42 U.S.C. § 2000d et seq. (1988). *See* note 16, *supra.*

87. *Id.,* 892 F.2d at 859.

88. Pitts v. Freeman, 887 F.2d 1438, 1445 (11th Cir. 1989), *cert. granted,* 111 S. Ct. 949 (1991).

89. Morgan v. Nucci, 831 F.2d 313 (1st Cir. 1987).

90. Pitts v. Freeman, 887 F.2d at 1449.

91. *See, e.g.,* Coalition to Save Our Children v. State Bd. of Educ., 757 F. Supp. 328 (D. Del. 1991); Reed v. Rhodes, 741 F. Supp. 1295 (N.D. Ohio 1990); Parents for Quality Educ. with Integration v. Indiana, 753 F. Supp. 733 (N.D. Ind. 1990); Little Rock School Dist. v. Pulaski County Special School Dist., 716 F. Supp. 1162 (E.D. Ark. 1989).

92. 111 S. Ct. 630, 636 (1991).

93. *See* Swann v. Charlotte-Mecklenburg Bd. of Educ., 402 U.S. 1, 19 (1971); United States v. Montgomery County Bd. of Educ., 395 U.S. 225, 232 (1969).

Although staff remedies have been secondary to student remedies in most desegregation plans, the Atlanta settlement was a notable exception. The terms of the 1973 Atlanta settlement led to little if any integration of students in the school district which had a predominantly minority student enrollment. Central features of the settlement were that half of the administrative positions as well as the superintendent would be African American. *See* Calhoun v. Cook, 487 F.2d 680 (5th Cir. 1973).

94. 419 F.2d 1211 (5th Cir. 1970), *cert. denied,* 396 U.S. 1032 (1970).

95. *See, e.g.,* Ward v. Kelly, 515 F.2d 908 (5th Cir. 1975); United States v. Coffeeville Consol. School Dist., 513 F.2d 244 (5th Cir. 1975).

96. Few plaintiffs in recent years have successfully challenged dismissals based on *Singleton. See, e.g.,* Lujan v. Franklin County Bd. of Educ., 766 F.2d 917 (6th Cir. 1985); Cooper v. Williamson County Bd. of Educ., 587 F. Supp. 1082 (M.D. Tenn. 1983); MacDonald v. Ferguson Reorganized School Dist. R2, 530 F. Supp. 469 (E.D. Mo. 1981). However, the *Singleton* criteria are still applied by some courts in assessing faculty and staff assignment practices. *See, e.g.,* Pitts v. Freeman, 887 F.2d 1438 (11th Cir. 1989) (school district would not satisfy *Singleton* until each school's minority staff ratio varied from the district average by no more than 15 percent).

97. *See, e.g.,* Morgan v. Burke, 926 F.2d 86 (1st Cir. 1991); Kromnick v. School Dist. of Philadelphia, 739 F.2d 894 (3d Cir. 1984), *cert. denied,* 469 U.S. 1107 (1985); Zaslawsky v. Board of Educ. of Los Angeles, 610 F.2d 661 (9th Cir. 1979).

98. Kromnick, *id.*

99. Vaughns v. Board of Educ., Prince George's County, 742 F. Supp. 1275 (D. Md. 1990). *But see* Marsh v. Flint Bd. of Educ., 708 F. Supp. 821 (E.D. Mich. 1989) (a negotiated affirmative action plan entailing racial considerations in involuntary transfers of counselors to teaching positions violated the equal protection clause).

100. Vaughns, *id.* at 1292. However, the court did instruct the school board to base its numerical ratios on the racial composition of the system's teaching force rather than the county's population.

101. Morgan v. Burke, 926 F.2d 86 (1st Cir. 1991).

102. 476 U.S. 267 (1986). *See* text with note 68, Chapter 9.

103. *See* Morgan v. Burke, 926 F.2d 86 (1st Cir. 1991); Arthur v. Nyquist, 712 F.2d 816 (2d Cir. 1983), *cert. denied,* 467 U.S. 1259 (1984); Morgan v. O'Bryant, 671 F.2d 23 (1st Cir. 1982), *cert. denied,* 459 U.S. 881 (1982).

104. Oliver v. Kalamazoo Bd. of Educ., 706 F.2d 757 (6th Cir. 1983).

105. *Id.* at 763.

106. "Integration Questions Remain in Wake of High Court Ruling," *Education Daily,* January 17, 1991, p. 1.

14
Summary of Legal Generalizations

In the preceding chapters, principles of law have been presented as they relate to specific aspects of teachers' and students' rights and responsibilities. Constitutional and statutory provisions, in conjunction with judicial decisions, have been analyzed in an effort to depict the current status of the law. Many diverse topics have been explored, some with clearly established legal precedents and others where the law is still evolving.

The most difficult situations confronting school personnel are those without specific legislative or judicial guidance. In such circumstances, educators must make judgments based on their professional training and general knowledge of the law as it applies to education. The following broad generalizations, synthesized from the preceding chapters, are presented to assist educators in making such determinations.

GENERALIZATIONS

The legal control of public education resides with the state as one of its sovereign powers. In attempting to comply with the law, school personnel must keep in mind the scope of the state's authority to regulate educational activities. Courts consistently have held that state legislatures possess plenary power in establishing and operating public schools; this power is restricted only by federal and state constitutions and civil rights laws. Of course, where the federal judiciary has interpreted the United States Constitution as prohibiting a given practice in public schools, such as racial discrimination, the state or its agents cannot enact laws or policies that conflict with the constitutional mandate unless justified by a compelling governmental interest. In contrast, if the Federal Constitution and civil rights laws have been interpreted as *permitting* a certain activity, states retain discretion in either restricting or expanding the practice.

Under such circumstances, standards vary across states, and legislation becomes more important in specifying the scope of protected rights.

For example, the Supreme Court has rejected the assertion that probationary teachers have an inherent federal right to due process prior to contract nonrenewal, but state legislatures have the authority to create such a right under state law. Similarly, the Supreme Court has declared that the use of corporal punishment in public schools does not abridge the Federal Constitution, but a number of state legislatures and school boards have prohibited this disciplinary technique or required that certain procedures accompany its use. Also, after the Supreme Court interpreted the first amendment as allowing school authorities broad discretion in censoring school-sponsored student expression for educational reasons, some legislatures responded with laws granting students editorial rights in connection with school newspapers.

Unless constitutional rights are at stake, courts defer to the will of legislative bodies in determining educational matters. State legislatures have the authority to create and redesign school districts, to collect and distribute educational funds, and to determine teacher qualifications and curricular offerings. With such pervasive control vested in the states, a thorough understanding of the operation of a specific educational system can be acquired only by examining an individual state's statutes, administrative regulations, and judicial decisions interpreting such provisions.

Certain prerequisites to public school employment are defined through statutes and state board of education regulations. For example, all states stipulate that a teacher must possess a valid teaching certificate based on satisfying specified requirements. State laws also delineate the permanency of the employment relationship, dismissal procedures for tenured and nontenured teachers, and the extent to which teachers can engage in collective bargaining.

State laws similarly govern conditions of school attendance. Every state has enacted a compulsory attendance statute to ensure an educated citizenry. These laws are applicable to all children, with only a few legally recognized exceptions. In addition to mandating school attendance, states also have the authority to prescribe courses of study and instructional materials. Courts will not invalidate such decisions unless constitutional rights are abridged. Comparable reasoning also is applied by courts in upholding the state's power to establish graduation requirements, including the use of proficiency tests as a prerequisite to receipt of a diploma. Courts have recognized that the establishment of academic standards is within the state's scope of authority.

It is a widely held perception that local school boards control public education in this nation, but local boards hold only those discretionary powers conferred by state law. Depending on the state, a local board's discretionary authority may be quite broad, narrowly defined by statutory guidelines, or somewhere in between. School board regulations enacted pursuant to statutory authority are legally binding on employees and students. For example, school boards can place conditions on employment (e.g., continuing education requirements, residency requirements) beyond state minimums, as long as they are acting within their delegated authority. Courts will not overturn a school board's decisions unless clearly arbitrary, discriminatory, or beyond the board's scope of authority.

School board discretion, however, may be limited by negotiated contracts with teachers' associations. Negotiated agreements affect terms and conditions of employment in areas such as teacher evaluation, work calendar, teaching loads, extra-duty assignments, and grievance procedures. It is imperative for educators to become familiar with all of these sources of legal rights and responsibilities.

All school policies and practices that impinge upon protected personal freedoms must be substantiated as necessary to advance the school's educational mission. The state and its agents have broad authority to regulate public schools, but policies that impair federal constitutional rights must be justified by an overriding public interest. Although courts do not enact laws as legislative bodies do, they significantly influence educational policies and practices by *interpreting* constitutional and statutory provisions. Both school attendance and public employment traditionally were considered privileges bestowed at the will of the state, but the Supreme Court has recognized that teachers and students do not shed their constitutional rights at the schoolhouse door. The state controls education, but this power must be exercised in conformance with the Federal Constitution.

In balancing public and private interests, courts weigh the importance of the protected personal right against the governmental need to restrict its exercise. For example, courts have reasoned that there is no overriding public interest to justify compelling students to salute the American flag if such an observance conflicts with religious or philosophical beliefs. In contrast, mandatory vaccination against communicable diseases has been upheld as a prerequisite to school attendance, even if opposition to immunization is based on religious grounds. Courts have reasoned that the overriding public interest in safeguarding the health of all students justifies such a requirement.

Restrictions can be placed on teachers' and students' activities if necessary to advance legitimate school objectives. To illustrate, the judiciary has recognized that students' constitutional rights must be assessed in light of the special circumstances of the school. School authorities, although considered state officials, can conduct warrantless searches of students based on reasonable suspicion that contraband posing a threat to the school environment is concealed. Similarly, vulgar expression that might be protected by the first amendment for adults can be curtailed among public school students to further the school's legitimate interest in maintaining standards of decency. Student expression that gives the appearance of representing the school also can be censored to ensure its consistency with educational objectives. And even personal student expression of ideological views that merely happens to take place at school can be restricted if linked to a disruption of the educational process.

Similarly, constraints can be placed on teachers' activities if justified by valid school objectives. Prerequisites to employment, such as examinations and residency requirements, can be imposed if necessary to advance legitimate governmental interests. Furthermore, restrictions on teachers' rights to govern their appearance and make lifestyle choices outside the classroom can be justified in some circumstances. Although teachers enjoy a first amendment right to express views on matters of public concern, expression relating to private employment grievances can be the basis for disciplinary action. Even teachers' expression on public issues can be curtailed if it impedes the management of the school, work relationships, or teaching effectiveness.

Every regulation that impairs individual rights must be based on valid educational considerations and be necessary to carry out the school's mission. Such regulations also should be clearly stated and well publicized so that all individuals understand the basis for the rules and the penalties for infractions.

School policies and practices must not disadvantage selected employees or students. The inherent personal right to remain free from governmental discrimination has been emphasized throughout this book. Strict judicial scrutiny has been applied in evaluating state action that creates a suspect classification, such as race. In school desegregation cases, courts have charged school officials with an affirmative duty to take whatever steps are necessary to overcome the lingering effects of past discrimination. Similarly, intentional racial discrimination associated with student grouping practices, testing methods, or suspension procedures, as well as with employee hiring or promotion practices, has been disallowed.

However, neutral policies, uniformly applied, are not necessarily unconstitutional even though they may have a disparate impact on minorities. For example, prerequisites to employment such as tests that disqualify a disproportionate number of minority applicants, have been upheld as long as their use is justified by legitimate employment objectives and not accompanied by discriminatory intent. Also, the placement of a disproportionate number of minority students in lower instructional tracks is permissible if such assignments are based on legitimate educational criteria that are applied in the best interests of students. Likewise, school segregation that results from natural causes rather than intentional state action does not implicate constitutional rights.

In addition to racial classifications, other bases for distinguishing among employees and students have been invalidated if they disadvantage individuals. Federal civil rights laws, in conjunction with state statutes, have reinforced constitutional protections afforded to various segments of society that traditionally have suffered discrimination. Indeed, the judiciary has recognized that legislative bodies are empowered to go beyond constitutional minimums in protecting citizens from discriminatory practices. Accordingly, laws have been enacted that place specific responsibilities on employers to ensure that employees are not disadvantaged on the basis of gender, age, religion, national origin, or disabilities. If an inference of discrimination is established, employers must produce legitimate nondiscriminatory reasons to justify their actions. School officials can be held liable for damages if substantiated that benefits have been withheld from certain individuals because of their inherent characteristics.

Federal and state mandates also stipulate that students cannot be denied school attendance or otherwise disadvantaged based on characteristics such as gender, disabilities, national origin, marriage, or pregnancy. Eligibility for school activities, such as participation on interscholastic athletic teams, cannot be denied to a certain class of students. In addition, disciplinary procedures that disproportionately disadvantage identified groups of students are vulnerable to legal challenge. Educators should ensure that all school policies are applied in a nondiscriminatory manner.

Courts will scrutinize grouping practices to ensure that they do not impede students' rights to equal educational opportunities. Nondiscrimination, however, does not require *identical* treatment. Students can be classified according to their unique needs, but any differential treatment must be justified in terms of providing more appropriate services. For example, students with learning disabilities can be provided with special services designed to address their deficiencies. In fact, judicial rulings and federal and state laws have placed an *obligation* on school districts to provide appropriate services to meet the needs of children with disabilities or English-language deficiencies.

Due process is a basic tenet of the United States system of justice—the foundation of fundamental fairness. The notion of due process, embodied in the fifth and fourteenth amendments, has been an underlying theme in the discussion of teachers' and students' rights throughout this book. The judiciary has recognized that due process guarantees protect individuals against arbitrary governmental action impairing life, liberty, or property interests and ensure that procedural safeguards accompany any governmental interference with these interests.

In the absence of greater statutory specificity, courts have held that the Federal Constitution requires, at a minimum, notice of the charges and a hearing before an impartial decisionmaker when personnel actions impair public educators' property or liberty rights. A property claim to due process can be established by tenure status, contractual agreement, or by school board action that creates a valid expectation of reemployment. A liberty claim to due process can be asserted if the employer's action implicates constitutionally protected rights (e.g., freedom of speech), damages the teacher's reputation, or forecloses the opportunity to obtain other employment. Many state legislatures have specified procedures beyond constitutional minimums that must be followed before a tenured teacher is dismissed. The provision of due process does not imply that a teacher will not be dismissed or that sanctions will not be imposed. But it does mean that the teacher must be given the opportunity to refute the charges and that the decision must be made fairly and supported by evidence.

Students, as well as teachers, have due process rights. Students have a state-created property right to attend school that cannot be denied without procedural requisites. If this right to attend school is withdrawn for disciplinary reasons, due process is required. The nature of the proceedings depends on the deprivation involved, with more serious impairments necessitating more formal proceedings. If punishments are arbitrary or excessive, students' substantive due process rights might be implicated. Children with disabilities have due process rights in placement decisions as well as in disciplinary matters. Since school authorities are never faulted for providing too much due process, at least minimum procedural safeguards are advisable when making any nonroutine change in a student's status.

Inherent in the notion of due process is the assumption that all individuals have a right to a hearing if state action impinges on personal freedoms. Such a hearing need not be elaborate in every situation; an informal conversation can suffice under many circumstances. The crucial element is for all affected parties to have an opportunity to air their views and present evidence that might alter the decision. Often, an informal hearing can serve to clarify issues and facilitate agreement, thus eliminating the need for more formal proceedings.

Educators are expected to follow the law, to act reasonably, and to anticipate potentially adverse consequences of their actions. Public school personnel are presumed to be knowledgeable of federal and state constitutional and statutory provisions as well as school board policies affecting their roles. The Supreme Court has emphasized that ignorance of the law is no defense for violating clearly established legal principles. For example, ignorance of the Supreme Court's interpretation of establishment clause restrictions would not shield educators from liability for conducting devotional activities in public schools.

Educators hold themselves out as having certain knowledge and skills by the nature of their special training and certification. Accordingly, they are expected to exercise sound professional judgment in the performance of their duties. Reasonable actions in one situation may be viewed as unreasonable under other conditions. To illustrate, in administering pupil punishments, teachers are expected to consider the student's age, mental condition, and past behavior as well as the specific circumstances surrounding the rule infraction. Failure to exercise reasonable judgment can result in dismissal or possibly financial liability for impairing students' rights.

Teachers also are expected to make reasonable decisions pertaining to the academic program. Materials and methodology should be appropriate for the students' age and educational objectives. If students are grouped for instructional purposes, teachers are expected to base such decisions on legitimate educational considerations and to anticipate negative consequences that the grouping practices might have on selected students.

In addition, educators are held accountable for reasonable actions in supervising students, providing appropriate instructions, maintaining equipment in proper repair, and warning students of any known dangers. Teachers must exercise a standard of care commensurate with their duty to protect students from unreasonable risks of harm. Personal liability can be assessed for negligence if a school employee should have foreseen that an event could result in injury to a student.

Educators also are expected to exercise sound judgment in personal activities that affect their professional roles. Teachers do not relinquish their privacy rights as a condition of public employment, but private choices that impair teaching effectiveness or disrupt the school can be the basis for adverse personnel action. As role models for students, teachers and other school personnel are held to a higher level of discretion in their private lives than expected of the general public.

CONCLUSION

One objective of this book, as noted in the introduction, has been to alleviate educators' fears that the scales of justice have been tipped against them. It is hoped that this objective has been achieved. Courts and legislatures have not imposed on school personnel any requirements that fair-minded educators would not impose on themselves. *Reasonable policies and practices based on legitimate educational objectives consistently have been upheld by courts.* If anything, legislative and judicial mandates have clarified and supported the *authority* as well as the *duty* of school personnel to make and enforce regulations that are necessary to maintain an effective and efficient educational environment. Although the federal judiciary in the latter 1960s and early 1970s expanded constitutional protection of individual liberties against governmental interference, federal courts since the 1980s have exhibited more restraint and reinforced the authority of state and local education agencies to make decisions necessary to advance the school's educational mission, even if such decisions impinge upon protected personal freedoms. Courts, however, continue to invalidate school practices and policies if they are arbitrary, unrelated to educational objectives, or impair protected individual rights without an overriding justification.

Because reform is usually easier to implement when designed from within than when externally imposed, educators should become more assertive in identifying and altering those practices that have the potential to generate legal intervention. Furthermore, school personnel should stay abreast of legal developments, since new laws are enacted each year, and courts are continually reinterpreting constitutional and statutory provisions.

In addition to understanding basic legal rights and responsibilities, educators are expected to transmit this knowledge to students. Pupils also need to understand their constitutional and statutory rights, the balancing of interests that takes place in legislative and judicial forums, and the rationale for legal enactments, including school regulations. Only with increased awareness of fundamental legal principles can all individuals involved in the educational process develop a greater respect for the law and for the responsibilities that accompany legal rights.

Glossary

Absolute privilege: protection from liability for communication made in the performance of public service or the administration of justice.

Appeal: a petition to a higher court to alter the decision of a lower court.

Appellate court: a tribunal having jurisdiction to review decisions on appeal from inferior courts.

Arbitration (binding): a process whereby an impartial third party, chosen by both parties in a dispute, makes a final determination regarding a contested issue.

Assault: the placing of another in fear of bodily harm.

Battery: the unlawful touching of another with intent to harm.

Certiorari: a writ of review whereby an action is removed from an inferior court to an appellate court for additional proceedings.

Civil action: a judicial proceeding to redress an infringement of individual civil rights, in contrast to a criminal action brought by the state to redress public wrongs.

Civil right: a personal right that accompanies citizenship.

Class action suit: a judicial proceeding brought on behalf of a number of persons similarly situated.

Common law: a body of rules and principles derived from usage or from judicial decisions enforcing such usage.

Concurring opinion: a statement by a judge or judges, separate from the majority opinion, that endorses the result of the decision but expresses some disagreement with the reasoning of the majority.

Consent decree: an agreement, sanctioned by a court, that is binding on the consenting parties.

Consideration: something of value given or promised for the purpose of forming a contract.

Contract: an agreement between two or more competent parties that creates, alters, or dissolves a legal relationship.

Criminal action: a judicial proceeding brought by the state against a person charged with a public offense.

Damages: an award made to an individual who has suffered a legal wrong.

Declaratory relief: a judicial declaration of the rights of the plaintiff without an assessment of damages against the defendant.

De facto segregation: separation of the races that exists but does not result from action of the state or its agents.

Defamation: false and intentional communication that injures a person's character or reputation.

Defendant: the party against whom a court action is brought.

De jure segregation: separation of the races by law or by action of the state or its agents.

Black's Law Dictionary (6th ed.) and various Supreme Court decisions were consulted in developing this glossary.

De minimis: something that is insignificant, not worthy of judicial review.

De novo: a new review.

Dictum: a statement made in delivering an opinion that does not relate directly to the issue being decided and does not embody the determination of the court.

Discretionary power: authority that involves the exercise of judgment.

Dissenting opinion: a statement by a judge or judges who disagree with the decision of the majority of the judges in a case.

En banc: the full bench; refers to a session where the court's full membership participates in the decision rather than the usual quorum of the court.

Fact finding: a process whereby a third party investigates an impasse in the negotiation process to determine the facts, identify the issues, and make a recommendation for settlement.

Governmental function: activity performed in discharging official duties of a federal, state, or municipal agency.

Governmental immunity: the common law doctrine that governmental agencies cannot be held liable for the negligent acts of their officers, agents, or employees.

Impasse: a deadlock in the negotiation process in which parties are unable to resolve an issue without assistance of a third party.

Injunction: a writ issued by a court prohibiting a defendant from acting in a prescribed manner.

In loco parentis: in place of parent; charged with rights and duties of a parent.

Mediation: the process by which a neutral third party serving as an intermediary attempts to persuade disagreeing parties to settle their dispute.

Ministerial duty: an act that does not involve discretion and must be carried out in a manner specified by legal authority.

Negligence: the failure to exercise the degree of care that a reasonably prudent person would exercise under similar conditions; conduct that falls below the standard established by law for the protection of others against unreasonable risk of harm.

Per curiam: a court's brief disposition of a case that is not accompanied by a written opinion.

Plaintiff: the party initiating a judicial action.

Plenary power: full, complete, absolute power.

Precedent: a judicial decision serving as authority for subsequent cases involving similar questions of law.

Prima facie: on its face presumed to be true unless disproven by contrary evidence.

Probable cause: reasonable grounds, supported by sufficient evidence, to warrant a cautious person to believe that the individual is guilty of the offense charged.

Procedural due process: the fundamental right to notice of charges and an opportunity to rebut the charges before a fair tribunal if life, liberty, or property rights are at stake.

Proprietary function: an activity (often for profit) performed by a state or municipal agency that could as easily be performed by a private corporation.

Qualified immunity: an affirmative defense that shields public officials performing discretionary functions from civil damages if their conduct does not violate clearly established statutory or constitutional rights.

Qualified privilege: protection from liability for communication made in good faith, for proper reasons, and to appropriate parties.

Reasonable suspicion: specific and articulable facts, which, taken together with rational inferences from the facts, justify a warrantless search.

Remand: to send a case back to the original court for additional proceedings.

Respondeat superior: a legal doctrine whereby the master is responsible for acts of the servant; a governmental unit is liable for acts of its employees.

Stare decisis: to abide by decided cases; to adhere to precedent.

Statute: an act by the legislative branch of government expressing its will and constituting the law within the jurisdiction.

Substantive due process: requirements embodied in the fifth and fourteenth amendments that legislation must be fair and reasonable in content as well as application; protection against arbitrary, capricious, or unreasonable governmental action.

Summary judgment: disposition of a controversy without a trial when there is no genuine dispute over factual issues.

Tenure: a statutory right that confers permanent employment on teachers, protecting them from dismissal except for adequate cause.

Tort: a civil wrong, independent of contract, for which a remedy in damages is sought.

Ultra vires: beyond the scope of authority of the corporate body.

Vacate: to set aside; to render a judgment void.

Verdict: a decision of a jury on questions submitted for trial.

Selected Supreme Court Cases

Index